Bottom Line's

Breakthroughs in
Natural
Healing
2012

Bill Gottlieb
and the Editors of Bottom Line Publications

Bottom Line
Books
www.BottomLinePublications.com

Bottom Line's Breakthroughs in Natural Healing 2012
Bill Gottlieb and the Editors of Bottom Line Publications

Copyright © 2011 by Boardroom® Inc.

10   9   8   7   6   5   4   3   2   1

Cover design by Aimee Zaleski and Gretchen Bruno

ISBN 0-88723-645-6

Bottom Line Books® publishes the advice of expert authorities in many fields. These opinions
may at times conflict as there are often different approaches to solving problems. The use
of a book is not a substitute for legal, accounting, investment, health or any other professional
services. Consult competent professionals for answers to your specific questions.

Offers, prices, rates, addresses, telephone numbers and Web sites
listed in this book are accurate at the time of publication,
but they are subject to frequent change.

Bottom Line Books® is a registered trademark of
Boardroom® Inc.
281 Tresser Boulevard, Stamford, CT 06901

www.bottomlinepublications.com

Bottom Line Books® is an imprint of Boardroom® Inc., publisher of print periodicals,
e-letters and books. We are dedicated to bringing you the best information from the most
knowledgeable sources in the world. Our goal is to help you gain greater wealth,
better health, more wisdom, extra time and increased happiness.

Printed in the United States of America

CONTENTS

Contents

Contents

Chapter 15:
SKIN CONDITIONS

Chapter 16:
STRESS, INSOMNIA & FATIGUE

Chapter 17:
WOMEN'S HEALTH

Appendix:
NATURAL HEALING MODALITIES

Contents

PREFACE

Natural Healing That Really Works

If you're in a car accident—don't ask the ambulance driver to take you to the acupuncturist. If you have a case of pneumonia—don't rely on aromatherapy. If you're having a heart attack—don't call the nutritionist.

Conventional medicine—high-tech tests, prescription medications and surgery—is your best bet for treating medical disasters. But while conventional medicine is ideal for handling a medical crisis, it's often second-rate for preventing and treating routine conditions (such as headaches or heartburn) and chronic diseases (such as arthritis and diabetes).

However, everyday and chronic health problems "respond wonderfully" to *natural* therapies, says Jacob Teitelbaum, MD, a physician in Hawaii, and author of *Pain-Free 1-2-3!* (McGraw-Hill) and several other books on natural healing.

Dr. Teitelbaum and thousands of other naturally oriented health professionals favor the modalities of natural and alternative healing—nutritional therapy, herbal therapy, acupuncture, homeopathy and many others—for several reasons.

● **Natural therapies address the *cause* of the problem rather than a symptom.** "Masking a symptom with a medication is like shooting out the blinking oil light on the dashboard of your car," says Dr. Teitelbaum.

"Yes, you're no longer *aware* of the problem—but you're not *solving* the problem, either." On the other hand, he says, natural modalities work *with* nature to help the body heal. As the underlying problem is resolved, symptoms recede and disappear.

● **Natural therapies are safe.** Medication-related problems kill nearly 200,000 people a year and put nearly 9 million in hospitals, accounting for 28% of hospital admissions, says Dr. Teitelbaum. Problems caused by natural modalities are rare.

● **Natural therapies are often more effective than conventional care.** For example, a major 10-year study shows that lifestyle methods such as diet and exercise are more effective than a prescription medication in preventing and controlling type 2 diabetes. Studies also show that regular exercise clears up mild to moderate depression more effectively than antidepressant medications. And that acupuncture relieves back pain as effectively as surgery. In fact, name almost *any* everyday or chronic problem, and natural healing handles it as well as, or *better* than, conventional medicine.

● **Compared with conventional care, natural therapies are low-cost.** "A good example is carpal tunnel syndrome, from a pinched nerve in the wrist, which causes pain and numbness in the hands," says Dr. Teitelbaum. "The usual medical approach is surgery, which costs around $3,000. But those same symptoms can be alleviated in six to 12 weeks by *inexpensive* remedies—taking vitamin B-6 and a thyroid supplement, wearing a wrist splint and reducing or stopping the activity that caused the problem."

• **Natural therapies have as much scientific evidence to support their use as conventional therapies.** This point is very much *the* point of *Bottom Line's Breakthroughs in Natural Healing, 2012.* In this new book from the editors of Bottom Line Publications, you'll find fascinating news about the latest scientific research on natural therapies, from acidophilus to zinc, and acupuncture to yoga. And you'll also find expert advice on how to *apply* that science to your own life, for health and healing.

For example, in just the first chapter of this book—"Aches & Pains from Head to Toe"—you'll discover…

• The herb ginger is *more effective* than OTC pain relievers in relieving muscle pain from overexertion. In fact, if you take ginger *before* the activity, you can even *prevent* the pain!

• How to stop weeks or months of heel pain with one, simple stretch.

• The uniquely safe and effective remedies of homeopathy can reduce the number of migraine headaches by 70%—and *cure* migraine headaches in 20% of cases! (You'll also discover the foods that commonly trigger migraines.)

• How the *words* you read, think and say can worsen or improve any type of pain—and how to use this new knowledge to reduce pain.

• A new supplement that soothes sciatica by strengthening nerve cells—and works *four times better* than other treatments.

And those are only a *few* of the scientifically proven benefits from *one* of the seventeen chapters in this remarkable new book.

How did I find them?

As a researcher and advocate for natural healing, I spend my time (and have spent my career) finding and learning about natural remedies to help you and millions of other readers achieve robust health. I relentlessly study the scientific literature on health and healing…I find the newest and most useful science-supported natural remedies…I interview hundreds of the top medical scientists and health-care practitioners about these findings…and I present to you the practical information that is proven and that *really works*. (And only *after* that information has also been reviewed and vetted by medical experts and the editors at Bottom Line Publications.)

My family and friends are always asking me about the latest breakthroughs of a natural, health-focused lifestyle, and I share with them this same research—so I've seen the benefits of my findings firsthand. I know you will find the same benefits in the pages of this book. Enjoy it in good (and better!) health.

Bill Gottlieb
September 2011

Chapter 1

ACHES & PAINS FROM HEAD TO TOE

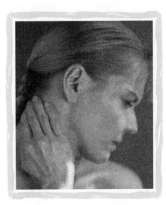

Ginger: Better Than OTC Drugs for Muscle Pain

You spent all day Saturday repainting your kitchen…woke up Sunday morning with the muscles in your arms, shoulders and back aching like crazy…and now you're reaching (ouch!) for the aspirin bottle in your medicine cabinet.

Surprising: Taking a daily ginger supplement for a couple of days before repainting your kitchen could have spared you a lot of that post-exertion muscle pain.

Researchers at the University of Georgia have discovered that ginger supplements are probably more powerful than aspirin, ibuprofen (Advil, Motrin), *naproxen* (Aleve) and other over-the-counter painkillers in easing muscle pain caused by exercise and other types of strenuous activity.

24% Less Pain

For their study, the researchers divided 74 people into two groups, with one group taking a daily capsule containing 2 grams of ginger and one group taking a placebo.

One week later, both groups were asked to repeatedly perform an exercise so intense that the researchers were certain it would trigger painful, inflamed bicep muscles.

Without holding any type of weight, they performed a bicep curl with the nondominant hand and arm. Then, with the upraised hand by the shoulder, they took hold of a super-heavy weight and lowered it very slowly. And they did that exercise over and over again—eighteen times.

Not surprisingly, the next day both the ginger and non-ginger groups had very painful arm muscles. But the ginger group had 24% less pain. Two days after the exercise, the ginger group still had a lot less muscle pain.

"The daily consumption of ginger resulted in moderate-to-large reductions in muscle pain following exercise-induced muscle injury," concluded the researchers in the *Journal of Pain*.

Why it works: "Ginger inhibits the COX-1 and COX-2 enzymes that play a role in the production of inflammation-causing compounds in the body—the same mechanism of action as over-the-counter nonsteroidal anti-inflammatory drugs (NSAIDs) such as ibuprofen and aspirin that are commonly used to relieve muscle pain," explains Chris Black, PhD, the study leader.

"But our study shows that ginger may work better than over-the-counter NSAIDs to prevent and reduce muscle pain," he adds.

Red flag: There's a good reason not to take those NSAIDs. Recent studies link over-the-counter NSAIDs to an increased risk of heart attack and stroke, with the American Heart Association recommending people take NSAIDs at the lowest possible dose for the shortest time possible.

Important: Some medical experts say that since ginger has a mechanism similar to NSAIDs, regular use may carry the same risks (which includes bleeding ulcers that kill thousands yearly). Not so, says Amanda McQuade-Crawford, a medical herbalist in Los Angeles and author of *Herbal Remedies for Women* (Three Rivers) and several other books on herbs.

"Ginger has been used as a medicinal herb and culinary spice for three to four thousand years, with almost daily use in many cultures. It may have some similar modes of action to NSAIDs, but it is not a NSAID, which can have significant negative effects from repeated use."

Bottom line: "Anything that can truly relieve muscle pain will be greatly welcomed by the many people who are experiencing it," says Dr. Black, "and our study shows that ginger can do just that."

How to Use Ginger

If you know you're in for some heavy lifting (or biking or hiking or any strenuous activity where it's likely you'll wake up the next morning with sore muscles), try taking a daily 2-gram ginger supplement for two or three days before the activity, says Dr. Black. "You'll get better results if ginger is in your system before the activity, as compared to treating symptoms afterward."

Smart idea: "People tend to be in the most muscular pain from exercise when embarking on a new exercise program and making the transition from a sedentary to an active lifestyle," says Dr. Black. "Taking ginger for a couple of days before and after exercise could help you reduce or avoid that pain."

Suggested dosage: 2 grams a day.

"But if you're generally healthy, 2 grams a day is a low dose," says McQuade-Crawford. "You might get more dramatic pain-preventing effects from a 3 or 4 gram dose." McQuade-Crawford offers the following ginger-taking regimen for a new exerciser, or for a veteran exerciser undergoing intense training or participating in an extended event, such as a marathon...

- **Start at 2 grams.**
- **After 2 or 3 days,** increase to 3 grams.
- **After 2 or 3 days,** increase to 4 grams.
- **Maintain that dose.**

And you don't have to rely on a supplement to get your ginger, says McQuade-Crawford.

Try this: Slice off a piece of ginger root about the size of the last digit of your thumb, which will supply a 2-gram dose. Juice the ginger, and add the juice to your favorite smoothie.

Also helpful: For sore muscles, you can use a ginger poultice to increase circulation to the aching area, says McQuade-Crawford.

Mix freshly grated or dried ginger with hot water into a slurry, apply it to the sore area, and cover it with a cloth. Leave the poultice on for 15 to 20 minutes. After taking it off, you'll have some redness and warmth in the area, which will dissipate in 15 to 30 minutes.

For sore muscles, she also recommends topical Arnica cream (a trauma-soothing homeopathic remedy) and icing the area for 20 minutes, twice a day. "Ginger inside and arnica and ice outside will make a big difference."

Chris Black, PhD, assistant professor of kinesiology at Georgia College and State University in Milledgeville, Georgia.

Amanda McQuade-Crawford, medical herbalist in Los Angeles, California.

Use Your Brain to Ease Your Pain Without Pills

More people are disabled by chronic pain than by diabetes, heart disease and cancer put together. An estimated 27% of US women (and 29% of men) suffer from debilitating pain, yet the problem remains vastly undertreated. Pain medications do not always bring sufficient relief—plus they can lead to side effects and/or addiction.

The good news: Like everything in your body, pain is affected by the workings of your mind. No matter what the cause of your pain, you can harness the power of your brain to reduce your suffering. Here's how…

Your limbic system, the most primitive part of your brain, controls your involuntary nervous system and emotions. Pain activates the limbic system, triggering the fight-or-flight response. As stress hormones are released, your heart beats faster, blood pressure soars, muscles tense…and various emotions are sparked, including anxiety, panic, anger and sadness. Normally, these responses are temporary—but with chronic pain, the stress of these intense reactions creates a downward spiral.

Example: The pain of chronic arthritis provokes a continuous release of stress hormones, leading to headaches and insomnia that exacerbate discomfort. As your body weakens, it produces fewer mood-boosting endorphins. Soon you're too tired and despondent to socialize, and the resulting isolation only makes you feel worse.

Helpful: If you learn to cultivate a sense of distance from your pain, you can mute the limbic system's response, reducing physical pain signals and easing the accompanying emotional suffering.

At least twice a day, go somewhere quiet and safe where you won't be disturbed…sit or lie in whatever position is most comfortable…and practice one or more of the following techniques for five to 15 minutes.

Calming Breath

Pain can take your breath away, triggering a pattern of shallow breathing that increases muscle tension and deprives cells of oxygen. Deep breathing—especially when combined with a meditative focus—helps by relaxing muscles, stimulating endorphins and reducing emotional distress.

Remember: For both of the deep-breathing techniques below, inhale slowly through your nose and then exhale slowly through your mouth. Clear your mind, and focus only on your breath. If other thoughts intrude, let them float away and refocus on your breath.

• **Flare-control breath.** This is particularly effective for pain flare-ups. As you inhale, notice your lungs filling with the vitality of your breath. Imagine your breath flowing to the area of your pain, bringing healing energy to this spot. As you exhale, imagine the pain flowing out of your body along with your breath.

• **Purifying breath.** This is especially helpful for easing troubling emotions that accompany pain. Picture your body surrounded by pure, white light. Inhaling: Imagine this light being drawn into your lungs and then spreading until your whole body glows with healing light. Exhaling: Picture a dark essence—representing fear, anger and sorrow—being expelled with your breath, leaving your body pain-free and your mind at ease.

Healing Imagery

The guided imagery method quiets the nervous system by convincing your mind that it does not feel pain. *Close your eyes and imagine either of these…*

• **A place of peace.** Picture yourself in an ideal setting of your choosing—a favorite vacation spot, a mountaintop, a lush garden, a tranquil lake. Immerse yourself in this scene by imagining what you see (majestic trees, an azure sky)…feel (a soft breeze, the warm sun)…smell (a campfire, fresh lilacs)…hear (singing birds, rustling leaves)…and taste (the salty sea, a perfect strawberry). The more details you can conjure up, the more effective the imagery is.

● **Soothing hues.** Take a few deep breaths, then focus on your pain. Note its location and intensity…describe its qualities (aching, throbbing, burning). Think of a color that represents pain (black, purple, hot pink), and imagine that your painful area is suffused with that color. Now choose a healing hue (such as white, silver or pale blue), and imagine that it has the power to dissolve your pain. Visualize the healing color pouring onto the painful area and spreading out wider and wider, until the painful color completely disappears. In your mind's eye, let that healing color continue to pour out for as long as you want—you have an unlimited supply.

Pain-Relieving Acupressure

Like acupuncture, acupressure is based on a principle of traditional Chinese medicine—that chi (energy) flows throughout the body along invisible channels called meridians, and that pain occurs when the chi becomes blocked or unbalanced. In terms of conventional Western medicine, the firm pressure applied during acupressure is thought to distract the nervous system, halting pain messages from traveling up the spinal cord to the brain.

The following techniques are particularly good for head, neck and shoulder pain, but they also ease the tension that pain elsewhere in the body can trigger in the toe neck area. Do each technique for several minutes per side.

● **Catwalk.** With your right hand, feel along the top of your left shoulder for any tender, tight or tense spot…then massage that area by "walking" your index, middle and ring fingers along it (like a cat kneading with its paws). Do this repeatedly and quickly—each finger press should last only about half a second. Repeat on the other side.

● **Thumb press.** Place your right hand behind your head, palm facing you and thumb pointing downward. With the pad of your thumb, press firmly into the base of your skull, working all the way across the right side and paying extra attention to any tight or tender spots. Repeat on the other side.

Soothing Aromatherapy

Certain scents can invigorate you when pain saps your energy…or calm you when pain leaves you tense or anxious. Aromatherapy also distracts your attention from pain and may relax muscles. Add a few drops of essential oil to a hot bath or sprinkle a few drops on a handkerchief that you hold near your nose (do not apply essential oil directly to skin).

Or: Smooth a scented lotion into your skin, especially on painful areas.

● **Invigorating scents.** Try cedar…eucalyptus…or peppermint (this one also eases the nausea that can accompany pain).

● **Calming scents.** Try bergamot…geranium…lavender…rose…or sandalwood.

James N. Dillard, MD, DC, CAc, board-certified physician, doctor of chiropractic and certified medical acupuncturist who pioneered the integrative model in pain medicine. He is author of *The Chronic Pain Solution: Your Personal Path to Pain Relief* (Bantam). Dr. Dillard now maintains private practices in New York City and East Hampton, New York. *www.drdillard.com.*

Homeopathy for Headaches

Imagine taking a super-small amount of a substance that would cause your health problem if you took a normal quantity of it—and expecting that infinitesimal dose to heal you.

Well, that's exactly what happens when you take a homeopathic remedy.

"Homeopathy represents not just a different type of drug, but a different understanding of and approach to health and medical care—one that not only makes conceptual sense, but is also safer than conventional medicine and truly works," says Dana Ullman, a homeopath in Berkeley, California, founder of Homeopathic Educational Services (*www.homeopathic.com*) and author of several books on homeopathy, including *Everybody's Guide to Homeopathic Medicines* (Tarcher/Putnam).

How Does Homeopathy Work?

Conventional medicine looks at symptoms as problems and tries to fix them with drugs or surgery, says Ullman. Homeopathy looks at symptoms as signs that the body-mind is attempting to defend and heal itself. (For example, the pain and redness of inflammation is a sign that the immune system is activating to heal the area.)

And homeopathy uses homeopathic medicines—repeatedly diluted preparations of herbs, minerals and other natural substances—to stimulate the vital force that is producing the symptom so the symptom can complete itself, leading to full recovery.

As for the minuscule dosages (often no more than a couple of molecules), Ullman compares them to nanotechnology—the use of microscopic but powerful components, such as nanoparticles in sunscreens. Homeopathy, he says, is nanopharmacology.

And nanopharmacology can help relieve headaches…

Migraine Relief

Researchers in Germany tracked 212 people who had suffered from migraine headaches for an average of 15 years—and had used homeopathy for the last two years. (Nine out of ten of the patients had used conventional medicine before turning to homeopathy.)

After two years of homeopathic treatment, the average severity of migraines had decreased by 70% (with 20% of patients "fully cured"). Overall, "migraine severity showed marked and long-standing improvement under homeopathic treatment," reported the researchers in *The Journal of Alternative and Complementary Medicine.*

But headaches weren't the only condition that improved. When the researchers investigated the severity of all the health problems of the study participants (such as insomnia, hay fever and eczema), they found those conditions decreased in severity by 49% over the two-year period of the study.

And there was also a big improvement in "quality of life"—the ability to happily and energetically participate in everyday activities.

Picking the Right Medicine

"Because homeopathic medicines are so inexpensive and so safe, you can use them either by themselves or in conjunction with other conventional and alternative treatments for headache," says Ullman.

He recommends starting with a conventional homeopathic formula for headaches that combines several remedies, such as Hyland's Headache Homeopathic Formula or Headache Soothe from Native Remedies. Follow the dosage recommendations on the label.

If a homeopathic formula doesn't work, he advises experimenting with single remedies, based on the headache symptoms described in the table on page 6.

Homeopathic remedies are widely available in stores where supplements are sold and online.

Doses: Take the single remedy every two hours, until you start to feel better, using a potency as low as 6x or 6c and as high as 30x or 30c dose. (The "x" and "c" are indications of the potency of the remedy, with higher numbers being more potent.) After that, take the medicine only if your symptoms start to worsen again. If the symptoms aren't any better after two or three doses, try another one of the remedies.

If the descriptions on the next page don't seem to match your headache, use either Belladonna, Nux Vomica or Bryonia. "One of these three medicines will help the majority of people with acute headaches that have few specific symptoms," says Ullman.

For optimal results: If self-care doesn't work, consider seeing a professional homeopath, advises Ullman. "The homeopathic physician doesn't treat one disease or one system of the body—he or she treats the whole body-mind, and that's the best way to achieve better health."

Dana Ullman, MPH, director of Homeopathic Educational Services in Berkeley, California, and author of several books on homeopathy, including *Everybody's Guide to Homeopathic Medicines* (Tarcher/Putnam). *www.homeopathic.com.*

Homeopathic Remedies for Specific Headaches

Headache Symptom	Homeopathic Solution*
Intense violent, throbbing pains that begin and pass suddenly, and the pain is aggravated by the least bit of light, noise, touch, strong smells or motion.	**Belladonna** *Who can benefit:* Anyone with headaches that are accompanied by high fever.
A steady aching pain, or a sense of heaviness with a little throbbing, aggravated by the slightest motion of your head or eyes.	**Byronia** *One distinguishing characteristic:* A person with a Byronia headache is irritable and wants to be left alone.
Pain began after too much food or alcohol… lack of sleep…or mental strain. It's accompanied by a generally sick feeling and by digestive upset.	**Nux Vomica** *Who can benefit:* A hangover headache is usually relieved by a dose or two of Nux Vomica.
Pain occurs during menstrual cycle. Or after eating ice cream. Or after eating rich or fatty food.	**Pulsatilla** *One distinguishing characteristic:* A person with a pulsatilla headache usually wants company and consolation.
Pain begins in the back of your head and extends either upwards or to the forehead—as if a band or hood were tightly bound around your head. Or vision is dimmed or disturbed, common symptoms of migraines.	**Gelsemium**
You have a migraine that comes on at regular intervals, with the pain on one side of the forehead, particularly the right.	**Iris**
Pain recurs periodically, beginning at the back of the head and extending to the right side of the head or the right eye.	**Sanguinaria** *One distinguishing characteristic:* This remedy suits headaches that recur in a consistent pattern, such as every seven days.
Pain pulsates and burns, usually on the front left part of your head, and your neck and shoulders are stiff.	**Spigelia**

*See page 5 for doses.

Surprising Foods That Trigger Migraines

Did you know that many seemingly benign foods—including citrus fruits, onions and yogurt—may make your head throb?

Neurologist Alexander Mauskop, MD, director of the New York Headache Center, says that almost any food can trigger a migraine in certain individuals, though what sets off a headache in one person may not affect another at all. Figuring out which foods to avoid can be an exercise in frustration.

Reasons: You may react to a single bite (for instance, just one almond)…or you may get a headache when you eat a full serving. Also, a certain food may set off a cascade of pain every time…or you may react to that food only when some other factor comes into play—for instance, when you're sleep-deprived or stressed.

To identify your problem foods, Dr. Mauskop recommends keeping a food diary and looking for patterns.

Simplest: Make a list of everything that you consumed in the eight hours before a migraine began…and/or use the worksheet from the American Headache Society (*www. achenet.org/tools/triggeravoidanceinformation.asp*).

More revealing: Keep a daily journal that tracks what and when you eat…exercise and sleep patterns…stress levels…menstrual cycle…weather…and anything else that you suspect might be linked to your migraines. Continue for two to three months if you typically get six or more headaches per month. For less frequent headaches, you may need to keep the journal longer to detect patterns.

High-tech help: Download the free app Headache Relief Diary (for iPhone, iPad or iPod Touch), developed by Dr. Mauskop, through the iTunes store.

Researchers do not know the exact mechanism behind all dietary migraine triggers. But foods containing naturally occurring substances called *amines*, which dilate blood vessels, often play a part—because for migraine-prone people, even tiny changes in blood vessel dilation can induce a headache. Particularly suspect are *tyramine*, *phenylethylamine* and *histamine*. Certain categories of amine-containing foods cause problems for many migraine sufferers. *Here are some of the most common culprits…*

●**Nuts.** Though Dr. Mauskop often prescribes magnesium supplements as a preventive measure for migraine patients (and nuts are chock-full of this mineral), he nonetheless cautions against nuts and nut butters because they can trigger headaches—perhaps due to their tyramine content. Almonds and peanuts are particularly problematic. Your food diary can help you determine which nuts, if any, are safe for you.

●**Fruits and fruit juices.** The most likely offenders are citrus fruits, such as grapefruits, lemons, limes, oranges and tangerines…and tropical fruits, including avocados, mangoes, papayas, passion fruits and pineapples. These all contain tyramine and phenylethylamine…citrus fruits also release histamine.

●**Dried fruits.** Raisins, prunes and dried apricots (as well as red wine) all contain amines.

Additional problem: Dried fruits also contain *sulfites*, a type of preservative known to provoke headaches in some people. Even organic versions of these foods can trigger headaches, Dr. Mauskop cautions, because some sulfites occur naturally.

●**Vegetables.** Onions, snow peas and certain beans (broad, fava, lima) all contain tyramine.

●**Fermented, aged or overripe foods.** Fermented foods, such as yogurt, beer and breads made with yeast, contain histamine. Also, tyramine levels rise when food is aged (as with certain cheeses) or no longer fresh (which is why an overripe banana or avocado, for instance, can set off a migraine).

●**Coffee and tea.** These do have amines—but that is only part of the problem. The other factor to consider is caffeine. Dr. Mauskop explains that many nonprescription and prescription headache medicines contain caffeine…and when used no more than twice weekly, caffeine often can relieve headaches.

But: For some people, caffeine—especially when consumed daily—actually can make migraines more frequent, severe and difficult to treat.

Whatever foods you end up needing to avoid, one thing to get plenty of is water. Dr. Mauskop says, "Dehydration is a known migraine inducer, so patients often get better when they drink more fluids. We call this the water cure."

Alexander Mauskop, MD, director of the New York Headache Center in New York City (*www.nyheadache.com*). He is author of *What Your Doctor May Not Tell You About Migraines* (Grand Central Publishing).

Stop Acute Low-Back Pain from Becoming Chronic

At some time or another, 80% of us develop acute low-back pain—our back hurts for a couple of days or weeks, but the problem clears up on its own.

But in an estimated 10 to 15% of people with acute low-back pain, the problem becomes chronic—the pain moves in to stay, becoming a lifetime burden…along with pain medications and their side effects…endless tests to figure out the cause…and invasive (and often unsuccessful) surgery.

Striking research finding: Two studies show that what you do during an acute attack (your behaviors) and what you think and feel about back pain (your attitudes and emotions) are crucial factors in determining whether or not you end up with a chronic condition.

Fear–Avoidance

In the first study, published in the *Journal of the American Medical Association*, Roger Chou, MD, and his colleagues at the Oregon Health and Science University in Portland analyzed 20 studies involving nearly 11,000 people with low-back pain. Those studies looked at many different factors in acute back pain to see which of them increased the risk of a person developing a chronic problem.

A standout risk factor was fear–avoidance—avoiding work, exercise and even everyday movement because you're afraid those activities will damage or worsen your back. People with high levels of fear–avoidance were 2.5 times more likely to have low-back pain one year after their acute episode.

What happens: "A person with high levels of fear–avoidance stops using his back because he think he's going to hurt it," explains Dr. Chou. "As he becomes less active, he becomes deconditioned—his muscles become weak. As his muscles weaken, his pain increases. It's a downward cycle that leads to a chronic problem."

In the second study, published in the journal *Pain*, Australian researchers also found that people with chronic low-back pain were more likely to have fear–avoidance.

People with chronic low-back pain were also more likely to catastrophize—to feel hopeless about their back pain, as if nothing would ever relieve or resolve it, and it was sure to worsen.

Those with chronic back pain also were more likely to have several other counterproductive beliefs: that anatomical factors such as a herniated disk are the main reason for low-back pain, that they had such an anatomical problem, that medications for pain relief are an effective treatment, that physical activity could harm the back and that bed rest was an effective treatment.

"All of these beliefs are exactly the opposite of what we know now is most likely to aid in the recovery from acute low-back pain," says Andrew Briggs, PhD, the study leader at Curtin University in Australia.

"The medical understanding of how acute low-back pain becomes chronic lower-back pain has changed—we now understand that most of the factors involved are not anatomical or biological, but about how people view and manage their pain," says Dr. Chou.

"In my practice, I often see two people with acute back pain who have similar x-rays and similar pain levels—but one goes on to live a life of chronic disability, and one doesn't. The difference is often in what they feel and think about the problem, and what they do about it."

Don't Rest!

Here's advice from Dr. Chou and other experts to help you stop a case of acute low-back pain from becoming chronic…

• **Stick with your usual activities.** "I tell almost everyone with acute low-back pain not to change their usual activities," says Dr. Chou. "Bed rest, for instance—resting for five to seven days—definitely makes the problem worse. Try to be as active as you can.

"Obviously, if you're in a lot of pain you don't want to run a marathon. But a low-impact activity—like walking, swimming or yoga—is usually fine."

"To help my patients figure out how much activity to do, I use the concept of 'pain real estate'—how much space in your body the pain occupies," says Lisa Morrone, PT, a physical therapist in Smithtown, New York, and author of *Overcoming Back and Neck Pain* (Harvest House). "When you begin the activity, it's okay for the size of the pain real estate to increase a little bit. But if the pain begins to take up a lot more real estate—if you had pain in your back and buttocks, and now it's also in your leg—then your activity level is too high."

• **Don't worry too much about the pain.** "Just because your back hurts doesn't mean you're hurting your back," says Dr. Chou. "You can still do activities, even if they hurt."

"Think of your acute low-back pain as a red light flashing on the dashboard of your car," says Morrone. "It's a warning light, not a panic button—and it's telling you trouble is brewing."

Caution: If your acute low-back pain is from the trauma or an accident, or you're having neurological symptoms such as weakness in the legs, see a doctor, says Dr. Chou.

• **Understand that the vast majority of people with acute low-back pain get better.** "Just knowing that can help you reframe your beliefs about back pain—preventing the depression and anxiety that can worsen the situation," says Dr. Chou.

"The way you're feeling today is not a life sentence," adds Morrone. "You're in an acute stage, but there will be recovery."

• **Understand that medical treatment is often ineffective.** "Regular exercise and a positive attitude go a long way in preventing chronic low-back pain—and are usually more effective than expensive imaging tests and surgery in correcting low-back pain," says Dr. Chou. "In fact, the vast majority of people will be better off dealing with acute back pain on their own rather than going to a doctor's office and medicalizing the problem."

• **Manage the pain with minimal drugs.** "Heat works as well as ibuprofen (Motrin, Advil) for managing an episode of acute low back pain," says Dr. Chou. He recommends a heating pad or a heated back wrap such as ThermaCare Heat Wraps (*www.thermacare.com*).

Roger Chou, MD, internist, Departments of Medicine and Medical Information and Clinical Epidemiology, Oregon Health and Science University, Portland, Oregon.

Andrew Briggs, PhD, School of Physiotherapy and Curtin Health Innovation Research Institute, Curtin University of Technology, Perth, Australia.

Lisa Morrone, PT, physical therapist, speaker and author of six books, including *Overcoming Back and Neck Pain* (Harvest House). *www.lisamorrone.com*.

Banish Back Pain with 7 Easy Yoga Poses

Low-back pain makes almost everything more difficult. But relief can be yours by practicing an age-old system of stretches and exercises.

Good news: Recent research shows that simple Iyengar-style yoga poses can gently reduce low-back pain and increase the ease of daily activities—without drugs. Additional research shows that movement is a key remedy for relieving back pain.

Props: A mat, folding chair, blanket, towel, bolster (or two blankets rolled together) and strap. Breathe slowly and deeply...never push to the point of discomfort. Practice the following poses (which have been modified for people with back pain) in the order given three to seven days per week.*

• **Savasana** (corpse pose). Place chair at end of mat, a folded blanket on seat. Lie on your back, head on folded towel. Rest calves on chair seat, knees comfortably bent and tailbone tucked under so back is not arched. Place bolster across abdomen. Let arms rest at sides, palms up. Relax completely. Hold for five minutes.

• **Supta Tadasana** (reclining mountain pose). Place short edge of mat against wall.

Lie on your back, head on folded towel, feet hip-width apart, toes pointing up, soles pressed against wall. Hold edges of mat, elbows straight, outer arms pressed down. Hold for one minute.

• **Supta Padangusthasana I** (supine big toe pose, bent knee). Start in supta tadasana pose (above). Keeping left leg pressed to floor and left sole against wall, bend right knee toward chest and clasp shin with both hands. Hold for 20 seconds, then switch legs. Do three times per side.

Straight-leg variation: Instead of clasping shin, place center of a strap across right sole and hold ends of strap. Straighten leg and flex foot, so sole faces ceiling.

*Check with a health-care professional before beginning any new exercise routine.

• **Supta Pavanmuktasana** (wind-releasing pose). Lie on your back, head on a folded towel. Bending both knees, bring knees toward chest. Grasp shins with hands, keeping knees hip-width apart. Hold for 30 seconds.

• **Adho Mukha Svanasana** (downward-facing dog). Place short edge of mat against wall. Come to hands and knees, hands shoulder-width apart, tips of thumb and first two fingers touching wall. Curl toes under and lift knees off floor, straightening legs and raising buttocks toward ceiling. Pushing down and forward with hands, stretch shoulders back and away from wall while stretching heels toward floor. Hold for 30 seconds.

• **Bharadvajasana** (seated twist on chair). Place folded blanket on chair seat, then sit backwards with hips close to front edge of seat. Spread knees and place feet on outside edges of back chair legs. Place right forearm on top of chair back and grasp front edge of seat with left hand. Keeping chest lifted, turn chest to the left, twisting gently. Hold for 20 seconds, then switch sides. Do three times per side.

• **Adho Mukha Virasana** (downward-facing hero). Place a bolster on mat. Kneel at one end of bolster, knees apart and toes together. Sit back on heels (tuck folded blanket under buttocks, if necessary). Place rolled towel in hip crease. Bending forward at hips, place hands on either side of bolster for support while lowering torso and forehead onto bolster. Rest forearms on floor. Relax completely. Hold for five minutes.

Yoga photos: Siegfried Bleher

Kimberly Williams, PhD, research assistant professor in the Department of Community Medicine at West Virginia University School of Medicine in Morgantown and leader of a recent study on yoga and low-back pain.

Top Natural Treatments For Tennis Elbow

Tennis elbow doesn't only happen to tennis players. The estimated 9 million Americans with the problem (which doctors call *lateral epicondylalgia*) include golfers, weight-lifters, housepainters, plumbers, carpenters, bricklayers, stonemasons, people who carry heavy briefcases, people who type or enter data all day and people who do a lot of sewing or knitting.

They develop the problem by repeatedly performing an activity that tightens the forearm muscles just below the elbow…which pull on the tendons that attach those muscles to the elbow…inflaming and damaging the tendons…and producing symptoms that can include shooting pain from the outside of the elbow to the forearm and wrist, a weak forearm, and a painful grip.

The typical treatment: a shot of cortisone in the tendon to calm the inflammation and ease the pain.

Recent finding: Australian researchers analyzed data from 41 studies involving 1,117 people with tennis elbow, presenting their findings in *The Lancet.* They found that while cortisone shots provided short-term pain relief, the shots didn't remedy long-term pain. In fact, one year later, people with tennis elbow who didn't get cortisone shots had less pain than people who did. The researchers also found that people who received several shots—three to six over an 18-month period—had more long-term pain than those who only got one shot.

Good news: New research shows that non-drug treatments for tennis elbow are more effective than drugs.

In a study conducted at the University of Gothenburg in Sweden, researchers found that an all-natural program of stretching and other exercises was more effective than cortisone injections and oral nonsteroidal anti-inflammatory drugs (NSAIDs) such as ibuprofen and aspirin in achieving long-term pain relief.

"For many doctors, cortisone and NSAIDs are the treatment of choice for tennis elbow," says Pia Nilsson, PhD, PT, the study leader. "But a non-drug treatment program can reduce pain and increase the function of the elbow and hand—healing tennis elbow far more effectively than drugs."

Why Drugs Don't Work

Drugs don't work because they don't address the actual problem of tennis elbow—the gradual destruction of the tendon.

New thinking: "The latest understanding of tennis elbow is that the problem is not an inflammation of the tendon," says Jonathan Mulholland, DC, assistant professor and chief of staff at the Bloomington Natural Care Center, at the Northwestern Health Sciences University in Bloomington, Minnesota. "Rather, the problem is in the collagen fibers that constitute the tendon."

Healthy collagen fibers are lined up like links in a chain, and easily relax and contract in unison. Diseased collagen fibers are mismatched and in disarray, and don't easily contract and relax. This problem is *tendinosis* (a disease of the tendon), not *tendonitis* (an inflammation of the tendon).

"NSAIDs and cortisone decrease the inflammation of tendonitis, but if that's not the main source of your pain, they're not going to have a long-term effect—and they don't," says Dr. Mulholland.

For optimal results: Repair the collagen, thereby restoring the normal structure and function of the tendon. The best way to do that: massage, stretch and strengthen.

Best Drug-Free Techniques

●**Use the "active release technique."** This uniquely effective self-massage technique was invented by James Cyriax, MD, a British orthopedic surgeon.

Using your index finger, find the spot near your elbow that is the sorest and the tightest. Apply enough pressure so that it "hurts good"—uncomfortable but not excruciating. With your index finger in place on the sore spot, simply roll back and forth across the spot (there will be enough give in the skin and muscle to do this easily) in an area about an inch wide. Do not pick up the finger and move it to other spots on the arm.

"Do this massage for five minutes while you're watching TV at night," says Dr. Mulholland.

• **Pressure the trigger points.** Another effective massage is to apply and maintain direct pressure with the thumb, straight into sore spots around your elbow and down your forearm.

"Start near the elbow and work down to the wrist," instructs Dr. Mulholland. Dig around with decent force, through the muscle. You'll find a ton of hot spots, or "trigger points," and when you find one, dig in so that it "hurts good," feeling moderately uncomfortable. Maintain the deep pressure anywhere from a few seconds to a minute or two—and the pain will start to ease off. Then move your thumb around and find another spot.

Do this pressure treatment anytime you can.

• **Stretch.** "Stretching the wrist extensor muscles that run along the top of your forearm is essential," says Dr. Mulholland.

To do that, fully extend your arm out in front of you at a 90-degree angle so that your elbow is straightened and locked with the palm facing down. Curl your wrist down toward the floor so that you feel the stretch from the back of your wrist and up your forearm. You can use your other hand to pull the hand of the affected arm down and toward you.

"Do this stretch as many times a day as you possibly can," says Dr. Mulholland. "Hold it for 20 to 30 seconds, repeating two to three times on each arm. You should see positive changes—more mobility, less pain, more strength—in one or two weeks."

• **Increase strength.** Once you've been able to reduce pain and restore normal range of motion, the next goal is to strengthen the muscles of the forearm because stronger muscles are more resistant to tennis elbow.

A good exercise to do that: Squeeze a tennis ball or rubber ball for eight to ten seconds, and repeat the squeeze five to ten times.

Do this once a day.

Pia Nilsson, physiotherapist and scientist at the Sahlgrenska Academy at the University of Gothenburg in Sweden.

Jonathan Mulholland, DC, assistant professor and chief of staff at the Bloomington Natural Care Center, Northwestern Health Sciences University, Bloomington, Minnesota.

Words That Hurt, Words That Heal

You've heard the old playground saying hundreds of time: *Sticks and stones can break my bones, but words can never hurt me.*

If recent research is right, that truism is due for an update: Sticks and stones can break my bones, but words *can activate my brain's pain matrix.*

A new study in the medical journal *Pain* shows that just reading words that describe pain can activate the pain center in your brain—perhaps worsening any pain you're already feeling!

Pain-Causing Words

Researchers at the Friedrich-Schiller University Medical School in Jena, Germany, tested 16 healthy people, asking them to read pain-related words such as "tormenting," "excruciating" and "grueling," while imagining situations that corresponded to those words.

At the same time, the researchers observed their brains, using functional magnetic resonance imaging (fMRI), a type of scan that tracks and records brain activity while it's happening.

They found that reading the pain-related words activated all the brain areas that scientists collectively call the "pain matrix" (such as the prefrontal cortex and the thalamus)—the areas that determine how you process and perceive pain.

But when the study participants read negative words that weren't directly associated with pain—such as "horrible," "terrifying" and "disgusting"—the pain matrix wasn't activated.

"These findings show that words alone are capable of activating the pain matrix—which means words have a far more important role in the experience of pain than scientists have previously thought," says Professor Thomas Weiss, the study leader.

In fact, he says, hearing your doctor say, *"This is going to hurt a little bit"* before giving you a shot…or talking a lot about your pain with family members, friends or health professionals…or thinking a lot about pain… is likely to "heighten the pain perceptions" you're about to feel or are already feeling.

Say the Words That Soothe

But you can turn this newly discovered power of words to your advantage, using positive words and imagination to reduce pain, say experts.

●**Be wise about words.** Pay attention to how you talk to yourself and others about your painful condition, says Debra Greene, PhD, an energy-health practitioner in Hawaii and author of *Endless Energy* (MetaComm Media).

Example: A doctor who is about to perform a painful procedure says to you, "This is going to hurt a little bit." Say to yourself, "This is going to help a lot."

●**Seek support instead of sympathy.** Ask those around you (loved ones, caregivers, friends) to support you in this "word wisdom" and pay careful attention to how they talk to you about your pain, says Dr. Greene. "Ask them to support you in your journey to pain relief, rather than sympathize with your current state of being in pain."

●**Imagine a best-case scenario.** If you find yourself in a "negative fantasy" about your pain—dwelling on how bad it is now, and imagining how much worse it will be in the future—do the opposite, Dr. Greene recommends. "You've been fantasizing about a worst-case scenario. Now imagine a best-

case scenario, picturing yourself strong, healthy and happy."

●**Visualize a pain-free past.** "Imagining a past state that produced pleasure and satisfaction will reduce your stress—and your pain," says Michael Ellner, a medical hypnotist in private practice in New York City and an advanced instructor for the International Medical and Dental Hypnotherapy Association. "Remember a time you felt loved and appreciated, a time when you felt safe and secure, a time when you felt strong and pain-free. Now imagine your brain is a giant sponge, soaking up those wonderful, stress-reducing feelings—so you can tap into them whenever you want, including when you're in pain."

●**Engage in positive self-talk.** "Self-talk is the internal dialogue—the continual thought-stream—that you're always generating and experiencing," explains Dr. Greene. "Speaking to yourself kindly can help ease your pain and heal your body."

However: "Try not to use negative words and concepts," says Dr. Greene, "such as 'I don't want any pain,' or 'I want my pain to go away,' or 'I want to be pain-free,' because the word 'pain' is being repeated over and over again." Instead, say:

●**I am strong and healthy.**

●**I am getting better every day.**

●**I am loved and cared for.**

Notice, says Dr. Greene, that those statements are all in present tense. (I am strong and healthy, instead of I will be strong and healthy.) "Positive self-talk is more convincing to your body-mind if it's in the present tense because the body-mind is always in the present moment." (Even a memory is a mental activity that's happening now, she points out.)

●**Follow the two-ten rule.** Set aside ten minutes in the morning and ten minutes in the evening to visualize or imagine yourself as being healthy and free of pain, says Dr. Greene. "Visualize your new pain-free self and your new life. See it…sense it…feel it… taste it…smell it. The more all your senses are involved, the more effective the visualization will be in producing positive results."

Professor Thomas Weiss, psychologist, Department of Neurology, Friedrich-Schiller University Medical School in Jena, Germany.

Debra Greene, PhD, energy-health practitioner in Maui, Hawaii, instructor at the Maui Academy of Healing Arts and author of *Endless Energy: The Essential Guide to Energy Health* (MetaComm Media). *www.yourenergymatters.com.*

Michael Ellner, medical hypnotist in private practice in New York City, advanced instructor for the International Medical and Dental Hypnotherapy Association, and faculty member and course director for "Pain Week," a leading medical conference on pain.

The New Supplement That Soothes Sciatica

The longest nerves in your body are the left and right sciatic nerves. Rooted in the lumbar (lower back) area of the spinal cord, they run through the hips and buttocks and down the back of the legs, powering muscles and providing feeling to the thighs, legs and feet.

Problem: If there's a rupture in one of the fluid-filled, cushioning disks that sit between the bones (vertebrae) of the spinal column, a gel-like substance can leak out and press on a sciatic nerve—causing painful sciatica.

The pain of sciatica ranges from mild tingling to electric agony, and parallels the path of the nerve, shooting from the low back to the buttocks and down the back of (typically) one leg. Other symptoms can include numbness and weakness in the affected leg and foot.

An estimated 3 to 5 million Americans have sciatica, and most get better in a few weeks or a few months. But in the meantime, the nerve pain is very difficult to treat.

Solution: A new study shows you can soothe sciatica—by taking a nutritional supplement of *agmatine*, a compound produced when your body breaks down the amino acid arginine, a component of protein found in small amounts in meat, fish and plants.

Four Times More Pain Relief

Sixty-one people who had suffered with sciatica from two to four months took either agmatine or a placebo for two weeks.

The agmatine group had a 28% improvement in pain levels—compared with 7% for the placebo group.

The researchers also used an extensive questionnaire to measure the participants' "general health status." The agmatine group improved by 70%, compared with 20% for the placebo group.

People suffering from sciatica "undergo significant improvement in their symptoms and in general health-related quality of life" after taking agmatine, concluded the researchers in *Pain Medicine.*

How it works: The compound may work to protect and strengthen nerve cells (neurons) in several ways, says Gad Gilad, PhD, a study researcher at Tel Aviv University in Israel. Agmatine…

• **Improves the functioning of cellular receptors for neurotransmitters,** the chemicals that send messages from neuron to neuron

• **Blocks the movement of calcium and potassium salts into neurons,** reducing pain-causing activity

• **Increases the production of polyamines,** molecules that protect nerves

• **Decreases the production of matrix metalloproteases,** enzymes that kill nerves and produce nerve pain

• **Helps regulate nitric oxide,** a "messenger molecule" that plays a key role in how neurons function

• **Limits the formation of advanced glycation end products (AGE),** a byproduct of blood sugar metabolism that damages neurons and other cells.

Suggested dosage: "There is no way to eat enough food to ingest the amount of agmatine necessary to protect nerves," says Dr. Gilad. "But taking a supplement of the compound can help a person with sciatica avoid the painful 'pins and needles,' burning and tingling sensations, and numbness and weakness that characterize the problem."

Dr. Gilad recommends Neurofencine, the agmatine supplement used in the study, which contains G-agmatine, a unique form of the compound.

"Start with two capsules twice a day, for four days," he says. "If there is no decrease in symptoms, take three capsules twice a day for as long as needed for reduction of pain and other symptoms—it may take two to three weeks before you see an effect. Once the symptoms are reduced, switch to two capsules, two times a day, for a maintenance dose."

Resource: You can order Neurofencine at *www.fornervehealth.com* or call 888-484-4523.

E-mail: *info@fornervehealth.com.*

Gad M. Gilad, PhD, Department of Physiology and Pharmacology, Sackler Faculty of Medicine, Tel Aviv University, and coauthor with Varda H. Gilad of more than 90 scientific papers on nerve function, published in the *Journal of Neuroscience Research, Brain Research, Annals of Neurology* and many other leading medical journals.

Marijuana: The Best Herb for Pain Relief?

Alaska, Arizona, California, Colorado, Hawaii, Maine, Michigan, Montana, Nevada, New Jersey, New Mexico, Oregon, Rhode Island, Vermont and Washington.

No, those aren't the states necessary to win the electoral college. They're the states where it's legal for a citizen to use medical marijuana—which means 90 million Americans have the herb *cannabis sativa* as a legitimate medical option.

And a new scientific study shows that it's an option that can relieve pain when all other medical treatments have failed…

Nothing Worked but Cannabis

The study was led by Mark Ware, MD, an assistant professor of anesthesia and family medicine at McGill University in Montreal, and reported in *CMAJ* (*Canadian Medical Association Journal*).

The researchers asked 21 people with long-term nerve pain (chronic neuropathy) caused by surgery or injury to smoke one puff of cannabis, three times a day, for five days. They didn't always smoke the same potency of cannabis, however. In one five-day period, the cannabis was a placebo: it contained no THC (*tetrahydrocannabinol*), the active ingredient. In three other five-day periods, the marijuana contained either 2.5%, 6% or 9.6% THC.

Results: When participants smoked the cannabis with 9.6% THC, they had a small but significant decrease in pain compared with smoking cannabis without THC.

But that small decrease was a huge relief to the people in the study—no other medication had worked to decrease their neuropathy, a pain problem that afflicts 15 million Americans. "We were surprised to see this degree of pain relief in this group of patients, for whom all other standard treatments had failed," says Dr. Ware.

Also important: This relatively low dose of THC did not make the participants "high"—their daytime functioning was normal while using medicinal cannabis. (And their nighttime functioning was better—they fell asleep faster and woke up less often during the night.) In fact, researchers measured the participants' blood levels of THC and found it was less than half that of blood levels typically seen in recreational users of cannabis.

"Our study showed that low doses of cannabis can relieve pain and has medical value," says Dr. Ware. "Cannabis may offer physicians and their patients another tool in treating neuropathic pain."

How it works: The body has a built-in cannabinoid system—cannabinoid molecules and cannabinoid receptors on cells that regulate a variety of functions, including movement, appetite, mood, memory and pain, explains Dr. Ware. Many of those cannabinoid receptors sit on the end of nerve cells, where they regulate messages sent from nerve to nerve. In neuropathy, there's an abnormal level of nerve activity, producing electric pain, burning and hypersensitivity. Medical cannabis can calm down that activity, decreasing pain.

Cannabis Commonsense

In 2009, the American Medical Association—noting that studies show smoked cannabis reduces pain, improves appetite in cancer patients and helps relieve spasticity and pain in people with multiple sclerosis—issued a statement urging more clinical research on marijuana and the "development of cannabinoid-based medicines." In 2008, the American College of Physicians issued a similar statement, supporting research into the medical use of marijuana.

But maybe you live in one of the 15 states that has legalized medical marijuana, and you don't want to wait for more research. Like the 15% of people with chronic pain who already use cannabis for relief (according to a survey by Dr. Ware), you may want to use medical cannabis now. What should you do?

Here are recommendations from Jean Talleyrand, MD, founder and president of Medi-Cann in California (*www.medicann.com*), the country's largest network of medical cannabis doctors…

● **First, talk to your doctor.** "If conventional medicines aren't solving your problem—as was the case in the study with patients with chronic neuropathy—consider medical cannabis as an option," says Dr. Talleyrand. "Discuss your illness with your doctor, and see if it makes sense for the treatment plan to include a recommendation for cannabis."

Who can benefit: The National Institutes of Health lists the following ways in which medical cannabis appears to have benefits…

● Managing pain in a wide variety of painful conditions

● Stimulating appetite and relieving cachexia, the extensive muscle loss and wasting away of cancer sufferers and AIDS patients

● Controlling nausea and vomiting in cancer chemotherapy

● Decreasing intraocular pressure inside the eyeball, for the relief of glaucoma

● Reducing symptoms in neurological and movement disorders, such as the spasticity of multiple sclerosis and cerebral palsy

● Temporary relief of anxiety.

The conditions most treated by medical cannabis in the MediCann clinics are…

● Low-back pain
● Anxiety
● Depression
● Migraine headaches
● Insomnia
● Neck pain
● Muscle spasms.

● **Understand the modes of delivery.** There are many different ways to use medicinal cannabis, explains Dr. Talleyrand. You can smoke it, consume edibles (such as cookies and brownies) and use an herbal tincture, a vaporizer or even a topical preparation for local pain relief.

● **Start with a small dose.** To find out what level of intake is effective, you need to dose yourself and see if the medical cannabis helps or not. If the low dose doesn't work, slowly increase the dose, via your chosen method of intake, until you find a level that's effective for your problem.

● **Be aware of the potential side effects.** Although smoking cannabis is safer than tobacco, smoking any plant material creates tars and combustion byproducts that may harm the lungs, says Dr. Talleyrand. There is also slowed reaction and loss of coordination, which is why you should never use medical cannabis at work or while driving or operating machinery. There are also possible withdrawal symptoms, such as irritability, insomnia, mood swings and mild depression.

● **Have a follow-up with your doctor.** After using medical cannabis for several months, see your doctor for a follow-up visit, to discuss the effect of the medication and its possible continued use.

Mark Ware, MD, assistant professor of anesthesia and family medicine at McGill University in Montreal, Canada.

Jean Talleyrand, MD, founder and president of Medi-Cann, the country's largest network of medical cannabis doctors, with 21 clinics in California that have treated more than 230,000 patients. *www.medicann.com*.

S-T-R-E-T-C-H to Stop Heel Pain

Sometimes your heel is, well, a heel—it hurts you. And because your feet are a primary mode of transportation, the pain is hard to ignore.

Heel pain—usually caused by plantar fasciitis—is one of the most common problems seen by podiatrists, accounting for an estimated 15 to 30% of all visits.

What happens: The long ligament on the bottom of the foot—the plantar fascia—tugs and pulls at the tissue in the heel, separating it at the bone and inflaming the area.

The main symptom is sharp pain in the heel, at the first step in the morning or after long periods of rest. The pain usually lessens after 10 to 15 minutes of walking but gets worse by the end of the day. It can also worsen when you stand for a long time or during weight-bearing exercise such as walking or running.

There are many risk factors for plantar fasciitis, including: aging; overweight; high-impact recreational activities, such as running or basketball; standing on your feet all day and frequently wearing non-supportive footwear, such as slippers.

But no matter the cause, there's an easy way to fix the problem. S-t-r-e-t-c-h...

Loosening the Ligament

A new study in the *Journal of Bone and Joint Surgery* shows that a simple stretching exercise can relieve the pain of plantar fasciitis and prevent it from recurring.

In the study, 102 people with acute plantar fasciitis (pain for less than six weeks) were divided into two groups. One group was given a stretch to perform three times a day for eight weeks. The other group received eight weeks of sonic shock-wave therapy, a non-invasive technique that delivers targeted, high-pressure radial sonic shock waves that "tenderize" and loosen the plantar fascia. (Recent research showed shock wave therapy is effective in relieving chronic plantar fasciitis—pain that lasts more than six weeks.)

After two months, 65% of the people in the stretching group said they were "totally satisfied" with the treatment, compared with 29% in the shock-wave group. After four months, the satisfied stretchers reiterated that the treatment worked.

"The earlier you learn and start performing the simple stretch used in the study, the less likely you are to develop chronic plantar fasciitis that might require extensive medical treatment," says John Furia, MD, an orthopaedic surgeon in Pennsylvania and study author.

"I have been counseling patients on the plantar fascia stretch for 15 years, and I'm a firm believer in it," adds Judy Baumhauer, MD, an orthopaedic surgeon and president of the American Orthopaedic Foot and Ankle Society (AOFAS). "Nearly 80% of my patients with plantar fasciitis have shown improvement in just eight weeks of stretching therapy."

The Pain-Relieving Stretch

Here are instructions for the pain-relieving stretch used in the study, from Dr. Furia and the American Academy of Orthopaedic Surgeons (AAOS). Perform the stretch in a seated position. (See photo on page 18.)

1. Cross your affected foot over the knee of your other leg.

2. Grasp the toes of your painful foot and bend your toes back toward your shin.

3. Place your thumb along the plantar fascia and rub it to stretch it.

4. The fascia should feel like a tight band along the bottom of your foot when stretched.

5. Hold the stretch for 10 seconds. Repeat it 10 to 20 times.

Best: Do the stretch first thing in the morning, before getting out of bed, says Dr. Furia. You can also do it after any long periods of sitting.

Important: If there's a sharp pain in your heel when you get up, repeat stretch.

Preventive Stretching

Two other stretches can help prevent plantar fasciitis, says Lowell Weil, Jr., DPM, director of the Weil Foot and Ankle Institute in Des Plaines, Illinois.

● **Seated Achilles stretch.** In a seated position, place a towel around either foot. Gently pull your foot toward you, keeping the knee straight, until you feel a stretch in your calf and Achilles tendon region. Hold 30 seconds. Repeat three times. Perform four to six times daily.

● **Standing calf stretch.** Place your hands up against a wall and stand in a staggered, lungelike position, with either foot in the rear position. Bend your front knee and keep your back knee straight and your heel firmly on the floor. Your rear big toe should point toward the front heel. Keep your head up and hips facing the wall. Lean into the wall until you feel a stretch in your calf. Hold 30 seconds, repeating three times, alternating legs. Perform four to six times a day.

More Ways to Stop the Pain

There are several other ways to help clear up an acute bout of plantar fasciitis and prevent recurrences of the problem, says Paul Langer, DPM, a podiatrist and clinical faculty member of the University of Minnesota and author of *Great Feet for Life: Footcare and Footwear for Healthy Aging* (Fairview Press). *They include...*

● **If a high-impact activity caused the problem,** stop the activity until the pain clears up.

● **Don't wear shoes that are too flexible under the arch.** If you grasp the shoe by the toe and the heel and bend it, the shoe should bend at the ball of the foot, not fold in half at the arch.

● **Don't go barefoot or in slippers around the house.**

● **Ice the affected foot with a 12- or 16-ounce frozen water bottle,** setting it on the floor and rolling the foot over it.

● **Use an over-the-counter insole to relieve tension on the plantar fascia.**

John Furia, MD, sports medicine physician with Sun Orthopaedics and Sports Medicine, in Lewisburg, Pennsylvania, author of *Collegiate Fitness: A Guide to Healthy Living* (Google Books).

Judy Baumhauer, MD, orthopaedic surgeon and president of the American Orthopaedic Foot and Ankle Society (AOFAS).

Lowell Weil, Jr., DPM, MBA, fellowship director of the Weil Foot and Ankle Institute in Des Plaines, Illinois, past president of the International Society for Medical Shockwave Treatment and a team doctor for the Chicago Bulls and Chicago White Sox. *www.weil4feet.com.*

Paul Langer, DPM, clinical faculty member of the University of Minnesota, podiatrist at Minnesota Orthopedic Specialists in Minnesota and author of *Great Feet for Life: Footcare and Footwear for Healthy Aging* (Fairview Press).

Photograph by Danita Albert.

$10 Fix for Foot Pain

Researchers recently evaluated various treatments for plantar fasciitis and discovered the best treatment—a simple, easy-to-use $10 orthotic insert that can be purchased at your local drugstore. James J. Irrgang, PT, PhD, president of the orthopedic section of the American Physical Therapy Association and coauthor of the APTA's recently issued clinical guidelines for treating plantar fasciitis, emphasizes that if you're dealing with your first bout of plantar fasciitis, it's wise to see your doctor to make sure that this is, in fact, the right diagnosis. He/she will also be able to provide advice about the various options for treating your condition.

To buy: Off-the-shelf orthotic inserts range in price from $10 to $95. There are different types for different problems—including those designed to help support arches or correct overpronation, supination, etc.—so if you have one of those issues it might affect your choice. Custom orthotics, fabricated to fit your foot exactly, might be necessary if you also have bunions, hammertoes or various ankle problems, but these are expensive, ranging from $300 to $500 or so from a doctor, and health insurance may cover only part of the cost (or sometimes none of it).

Whatever type you choose, count on using orthotics for at least three months, Dr. Irrgang says—longer if you find them more comfortable. Don't wear them just for walking or running—he says you'll get the best results with continuous wear...by wearing them in both shoes even if you experience symptoms just on one side...and by getting new ones when you see signs of wear. If you've tried the drugstore variety and they're not helpful, Dr. Irrgang suggests asking your physical therapist or doctor if another type might be better for you or if you should try a different form of treatment.

James J. Irrgang, PT, PhD, ATC (Athletic Trainer-Certified), FAPTA, researcher, Department of Orthopedic Surgery, University of Pittsburgh, Pennsylvania. Dr. Irrgang is president of the orthopedic section of the American Physical Therapy Association and was part of the APTA team that assessed treatments for plantar fasciitis.

Fibromyalgia Breakthrough: Unlearn Your Pain

Fibromyalgia affects an estimated 5 million Americans (most of them middle-aged women)—and is a very mysterious and frustrating disorder, for people with the condition and professionals who try to treat it.

"People diagnosed with fibromyalgia have pain throughout their bodies, usually in a dozen or more 'tender points' in muscles—but no one can tell them why," says Howard Schubiner, MD, director of the Mind-Body Medicine Center of the St. John Providence Health System in Warren, Minnesota, and author of *Unlearn Your Pain* (Mind-Body Publishing).

"There's no actual tissue breakdown or destruction—nothing conventionally 'wrong' in the muscles, tendons, joints or bones," he continues. "But brain imaging studies show that the pain and suffering is real, and is felt in much the same way a person feels a broken bone. And like a broken bone, the pain of fibromyalgia can be severe and even debilitating, forcing a person to spend days in bed."

And that's not the only problem. According to Dr. Schubiner, people with fibromyalgia commonly have other health problems, such as lower-back pain, migraine or tension headaches, jaw and face pain from temporomandibular joint disorder, bowel and bladder syndromes, and insomnia.

"Needless to say, it's very frustrating for a person with widespread pain to have no idea what is causing it, and to be considered crazy by some and incurable by others—and to get little or no relief from pain medications, muscle relaxants, antidepressants and mood stabilizers," Dr. Schubiner says.

But now there is relief from fibromyalgia—without drugs.

Striking research finding: A study by Dr. Schubiner and his colleagues in the *Journal of Internal Medicine* shows that a focus on the pain-triggering role of negative emotions and stress in fibromyalgia can dramatically reduce pain—and even clear up the condition!

The Stress–Pain Connection

The researchers studied 45 middle-aged women who had been suffering from fibromyalgia for an average of 13 years.

The women were divided into two groups. One group received four weeks of a therapy called Affective Self-Awareness (ASA)—learning about and accepting the connection between emotions, stress, and the pain of fibromyalgia and learning and practicing techniques for expressing and releasing emotions and reducing stress. The other group was put on a waiting list to receive ASA. Pain levels were measured at the start of the study and six months later.

After six months, pain had been eliminated or reduced to very low levels in 25% of the ASA group—in effect, their fibromyalgia had gone into remission. Overall, nearly half of the ASA group had pain reduction of 30% or more.

"These results may not seem remarkable," says Dr. Schubiner. "But consider this—these reductions in pain were measured at six months and are therefore long-lasting, and they are greater than the results found in studies of medications for fibromyalgia. In fact, the women in the wait-listed group were using medications for fibromyalgia during the six months of the study—and had no reduction in pain."

Why it works: Fibromyalgia pain is real, emphasizes Dr. Schubiner. It is processed through the central nervous system along "learned nerve pathways" that are created and then repeatedly triggered by emotional trauma and stress—in exactly the same way you create nerve pathways when you learn to ride a bicycle and then use those same pathways for the rest of your life whenever you ride again. Sometimes the origin of the trauma and stress—the "priming" event that sets you up for fibromyalgia—is in childhood (for example, physical or sexual abuse, the death of a parent). Sometimes the priming event is in adulthood (for example, marital difficulties, problems at work).

Fact: More than half of people with fibromyalgia have post-traumatic stress disorder (PTSD) or PTSD-like symptoms, such as depression and anxiety. Research shows that people victimized by workplace bullying had a four times higher risk of fibromyalgia.

Dr. Schubiner calls pain triggered by stress and emotion the Mind-Body Syndrome (MBS). "If you accept that your pain is triggered by learned nerve pathways formed during sustained negative emotional experiences and stress—by the MBS, and not by any physical illness or problem—you can then unlearn your pain, by learning to acknowledge and express your negative emotions and by reducing stress."

Good news: The understanding of MBS and the techniques of ASA may help reduce pain in many of the 50 million Americans who suffer from chronic pain problems, including low-back pain, sciatica, neck pain, whiplash, tendonitis, tension headache, migraine headaches and irritable bowel syndrome.

Affirm Health, Write Freely

Here are two techniques that can help you "unlearn" your pain, says Dr. Schubiner.

•**Affirm your essential health.** When pain or other symptoms occur, stop and take a deep breath. Then take a moment to remind yourself that there is nothing seriously wrong with your body. You are healthy, and the MBS symptoms will subside soon. Tell your mind that you realize that the symptoms are just a way of warning you about underlying feelings of fear, guilt, anger, anxiety, shame, inadequacy or other emotions. Tell your mind to stop producing the symptoms immediately. Do this with force and conviction, either out loud or silently. Take a few deep breaths, and move on with what you were doing.

For the greatest benefits: Repeat whatever positive phrases you choose every time you encounter any of your triggers, until your brain unlearns MBS pathways.

•**Write away your pain.** "Writing about stressful situations allows you to become healthier, develop perspective, and learn to let go of the emotional reactions that have imprisoned you," says Dr. Schubiner.

One such exercise is free-writing—writing faster than you normally would…writing whatever comes in your mind…allowing any thoughts and feelings to be expressed…not crossing anything out…and not worrying about spelling, punctuation and grammar.

For 10 minutes a day, free-write in response to the following sentences (use one sentence per day):

My feelings about me and _____ include:

My understandings about me and _____ include:

"The idea is to process your feelings," says Dr. Schubiner. "Expressing emotions is important, but it is also critical to understand them, gain perspective on them and begin to move past them.

"Therefore in this free-write, make sure to use phrases such as 'I see that...,' 'I realize...,' 'I hope that...,' 'I need to...,' 'I want to...,' 'I can...,' 'I will...,' 'I understand that...,' 'I appreciate...' 'I wonder if...,' 'I have learned...' and 'I have discovered...' "

Write whatever comes to your mind with a focus on understanding the topic/issue as best you can.

Once the 10 minutes is up, complete the free-write by copying the following affirmation three times: *Understanding these issues helps me feel better.*

Resource: The same techniques used in the study are in the book *Unlearn Your Pain*, which you can purchase at *www.unlearnyourpain.com*. You can also enroll in Dr. Schubiner's Mind-Body Program, read his blog and find other resources for overcoming MBS at this site.

Howard Schubiner, MD, director of the Mind-Body Medicine Center of the St. John Providence Health System in Warren, Minnesota, clinical professor at the Wayne State University School of Medicine and author of *Unlearn Your Pain* (Mind-Body Publishing).

Magic Muscle-Cramp Cures from Your Kitchen

Muscle cramps are a common problem. Medically speaking, a muscle cramp is a sudden, involuntary contraction of one or more muscles that can be very painful, sometimes leaving tenderness for up to 24 hours after the cramp subsides. Aging and overuse of the muscles are two common causes, but other triggers can include dehydration...low blood sugar...calcium, sodium and/or magnesium deficiency...underactive thyroid...kidney or liver dysfunction...peripheral vascular disease (which restricts blood flow to the legs)...nerve compression and chronic conditions such as Lou Gehrig's disease (ALS), brain tumors/cancer and multiple sclerosis.

What You Need to Know

Barry Wiese, DC, a board-certified chiropractic neurologist in private practice in Rochester, New York, cautions that there is no surefire, works-every-time solution for muscle cramps. First, you need to differentiate a run-of-the-mill (if excruciating) cramp from one that you must tell your doctor about.

Here's a list of questions to ask yourself: Are my cramps random? According to Dr. Wiese, a cramp that comes on suddenly and inexplicably is usually not a problem. Noting that the majority of random cramps are no big deal, he suggests that it's fine to try the "old standby" cures, including eating a banana (for potassium)...drinking more water to counter dehydration...light stretching of the affected area...self-massage...and heat packs to relieve pain and tenderness.

Are my cramps becoming more frequent and/or following a pattern? Cramps that begin to establish themselves in a predictable pattern—such as at a particular time of day or when you walk—may be a worrisome sign that you should discuss with your doctor.

Did I do something that might explain this cramp? If you realize that you are getting cramps often, even predictably in certain situations, start a log of when they strike including time of day...what you've eaten...how long they last...how painful they are (consider a score between one and 10)...and what you were doing before and during the episode. Share this information with your doctor.

Should I see my doctor? With persistent or worsening muscle cramps, you need to see your doctor to discuss potential causes and treatments. Though muscle cramping represents abnormal function, it's only rarely serious, Dr. Wiese says. However, he points out that "many disease processes include cramping in their list of symptoms...and for many of those, the earlier you get treated, the better the outcome—so it pays to follow a conservative, cautious route until proven otherwise."

You'll be asked about your medical history, and your doctor may suggest some tests, including blood work, to find the root cause. Treatment options could range from vitamin B supplementation…to prescription medications, such as *diltiazem* (a calcium-channel blocker) and *baclofen* (a potent muscle relaxant sometimes used to treat muscle spasms in patients with multiple sclerosis and ALS)… and possibly even quinine, the malaria treatment, though it's used only in extreme cases because of the potential adverse side effects.

Magic Kitchen Cures for Cramps

You know the scenario. You wake up in the middle of the night with searing pain in your calf or arm (a "random" muscle cramp). Hopefully, you can make it to your kitchen to open a jar of pickles—to drink the juice. Or you could just eat a pickle. Both contain acetic acid, salts and other ingredients that help neutralize the compounds or electrolyte deficiencies that may cause cramps.

Other helpful remedies you may be able to pull out of your kitchen cabinets include apple cider vinegar (mix two teaspoons with one teaspoon of honey into a glass of warm water), which works much like the pickle juice…and chamomile tea, which contains *glycine*, an amino acid that helps relieve muscle spasms.

Barry Wiese, DC, a board-certified chiropractic neurologist in private practice in Rochester, New York.

Chapter 2

AGING & LONGEVITY

Anti-Aging Hormones: Should You Take Them?

If you asked the American Medical Association (AMA) that question, the answer would be a resounding *no*.

Recent development: The AMA's Council on Science and Public Health issued a report—"The Use of Hormones for 'Anti-aging': A Review of Efficacy and Safety"—that flatly rejected the use of hGH (human growth hormone), DHEA (*dehydroepiandrosterone*), testosterone or estrogens to try to slow, stop or reverse the aging process.

The report's conclusions, hormone by hormone…

●**hGH.** "Current evidence fails to support" its efficacy as an anti-aging therapy.

●**DHEA.** No "meaningful benefit" as an anti-aging supplement.

●**Testosterone.** "Definitive evidence" of its value as an anti-aging therapy "does not exist."

●**Estrogens.** They're highly effective for the symptoms of menopause, but risks outweigh benefits.

And as for the form of those hormones favored by anti-aging doctors—the bioidentical hormones that are a molecular match for the body's own versions—the AMA said there is "no credible scientific evidence" for their value and that their "purity, potency and quality" is questionable.

The AMA's overall conclusion: "Despite the widespread promotion of hormones as anti-aging agents by for-profit Web sites, anti-aging clinics and compounding pharmacies, the scientific evidence to support these claims is lacking."

Case closed, right?

Well, not if you posed that same question to one of the thousands of doctors with years of experience treating patients with bioidentical hormones—doctors who often see age-related symptoms vanish and vibrant health return.

According to Jacob Teitelbaum, MD, a frequent presenter and lecturer at annual meetings of the American Academy of Anti-Aging Medicine, in reaching its conclusions, the AMA didn't properly review the research that reflects what most anti-aging doctors actually do: Give very low doses of bioidentical hormones, not the "massively high doses" of synthetic hormones used in studies that show potential harm from hormonal therapy.

Anti-Aging Hormonal Therapy

Here, hormone by hormone, are Dr. Teitelbaum's recommendations for working with your doctor to…

1. Find out if you might benefit from bioidentical hormone therapy.

2. Decide on the best and safest dose.

●**hGH (human growth hormone*).** Produced in the brain's pituitary gland, this hormone is used by adults for muscle-building and tissue repair.

"What the AMA said about hGH is reasonable, to a degree," says Dr. Teitelbaum. "I feel it may be premature to use hGH as an anti-aging treatment."

Better: Increase exercise, sleep and sexual activity—all of which stimulate your body's own production of hGH.

● **DHEA (*dehydroepiandrosterone*).** Manufactured by the adrenal glands, low levels of DHEA have been linked to fatigue and a general sense of not feeling well. And some studies link normal levels to longer life. "My older patients often have a dramatic boost of energy and well-being when their DHEA level is optimized to mid-range for a normal 29-year-old," says Dr. Teitelbaum.

Suggested dosage: "For patients with a suboptimal DHEA-S level, I find an optimal dose is usually 5 to 10 mg for women and 25 to 50 mg for men."

For optimal results: Although DHEA is available without a prescription, take the

---

*Human growth hormone is banned by the Food and Drug Administration as an over-the-counter drug and as a performance-enhancement substance in professional sports. It is available for prescription use only.

hormone only with the approval and guidance of a holistic physician experienced in its use. (Too-high dosages can cause acne and growth of facial hair in women.)

Resource: To find a holistic physician near you, visit the Web site of The American Holistic Medical Association at *www.holistic medicine.org* or call 216-292-6644, or visit the Web site of the American Association of Naturopathic Physicians at *www.naturo pathic.org* or call 202-237-8150.

"Your doctor can order a test for your blood level of DHEA-S, a version of DHEA, which can help guide dosage," he says.

●**Testosterone.** Production of the male hormone testosterone starts to drop around age 30—with a major decline sometimes setting in around 50. "Low levels are a common problem among my middle-aged and older patients, and can cause fatigue, a depressed outlook, low sexual desire and metabolic syndrome—a combination of high blood sugar, high cholesterol and overweight," says Dr. Teitelbaum.

Compelling scientific evidence: A recent study of men aged 51 to 90 showed that those with the lowest testosterone levels were 40% more likely to die during the study than those with the highest levels.

For optimal results: Ask a holistic physician to test you for both total (stored) and free (active) testosterone, advises Dr. Teitelbaum. "If your total testosterone is below normal—or even in the lowest 30% of the normal range—and you have symptoms suggesting low testosterone, consider a trial of bioidentical testosterone therapy. You should also consider therapy if your free testosterone is below one-third of the normal range."

Suggested dosage: A topical testosterone cream or gel (AndroGel or Testim, 1% gel), applying 25 to 50 milligrams (mg) to the skin daily. (AndroGel and Testim—standard prescription testosterone—are now bioidentical.) More is not better.

Another option: "Consider a testosterone cream from a compounding pharmacy, which creates customized medications on-site—it's much less expensive but just as effective," says Dr. Teitelbaum.

Resource: "Although there are many excellent compounding pharmacies, the company ITC makes a wide range of bioidentical hormones, and does a superb job of quality control," he says. "I recommend trying them first." Visit *www.itcpharmacy.com* or phone 888-374-0696.

"Stay in touch with your doctor after beginning treatment, working with the physician to adjust your daily dose to the level that feels best to you—the level that provides the most energy, brightest mood, clearest thinking, comfortable level of sexual desire, and the other benefits—without side effects," says Dr. Teitelbaum. "In most men, this means keeping the dose under 50 mg a day."

Surprising: "A deficiency of testosterone in perimenopausal and menopausal women can cause problems similar to low levels of testosterone in middle-aged men, such as fatigue, depression, weight gain and low libido," says Dr. Teitelbaum. "If levels are low, I treat with a testosterone cream made by a compounding pharmacy, with the usual dose ½ to 1 mg.

Red flag: But don't get your testosterone from touching a man who is using the hormone. "If a man is using a cream and a woman touches his skin where it was applied—for example, because he didn't wash his hands after application—she can end up with levels of testosterone high enough to increase her risk of diabetes."

• **Estrogen.** The decrease of the female hormone estrogen later in life can trigger a wide range of menopausal problems. "The main treatment I use in my perimenopausal and menopausal patients is the bioidentical estrogen hormone Biest, along with natural progesterone, estrogen's sister hormone," says Dr. Teitelbaum. "These hormones can be compounded into a single cream by a compounding pharmacy, with the cream applied to the skin each evening."

Suggested dosage: Very low doses are effective, and safer, says Dr. Teitelbaum. "I

currently recommend 0.1 to 0.25 mg of Biest a day—$\frac{1}{10}$ to $\frac{1}{25}$ of the old dose of 2.5 mg—along with 30 mg of progesterone," he says.

If your insurance doesn't cover the compounded estrogen, you can use a 0.1 mg (or lower) estrogen patch that contains bioidentical estradiol, along with the prescription Prometrium (100 mg at bedtime), which is equal to 30 mg of the topical cream.

Jacob Teitelbaum, MD, medical director of the Fibromyalgia and Fatigue Centers, author of the popular free iPhone application "Cures A-Z" and author of several books, including *The Real Cause, The Real Cure* (Rodale), *From Fatigued to Fantastic!* (Avery/Penguin Group), *Pain Free 1-2-3* (McGraw-Hill) and *Beat Sugar Addiction NOW!* (Fairwinds Press). *www.vitality101.com.*

Alpha-Carotene—The Live-Longer Nutrient

Meet the carotenoids, a big and colorful family of 600 health-protecting antioxidants.

The most famous member of the carotenoid clan is beta-carotene. It puts the orange in carrots. It's the carotenoid found in most multivitamin and antioxidant supplements. (It turns into vitamin A in the body.) And it's a stand-alone supplement that scientists have loved to study, testing whether beta-carotene pills could reduce the risk of heart disease, cancer and type 2 diabetes—with consistently disappointing results.

But beta-carotene has a little-known sibling: Alpha-carotene.

Surprising new finding: A new study in the *Archives of Internal Medicine* shows that alpha-carotene might be more powerful than beta-. In fact, it just might be the alpha and omega of longevity.

Ten Times More Powerful

The first phase of the study—the third National Health and Nutrition Examination Survey (NHANES III)—went from 1988 to 1994, when more than 15,000 adults had their blood levels of alpha-carotene measured.

When the researchers conducted a follow-up to NHANES III more than a decade later (an average of 14 years after the initial blood tests), they uncovered an amazing fact:

People with higher blood levels of alpha-carotene back in the 1980s and '90s were more likely to be alive in the twenty-first century!

The lowest measured blood levels of alpha-carotene were 0 to 1 micrograms per deciliter (mg/dL). Compared with that level, people at higher levels had a

- **23% lower risk of death,** at 2 to 3 mg/dL

- **27% lower risk of death,** at 4 to 5 mg/dL

- **34% lower risk of death,** at 6 to 8 mg/dL

- **39% lower risk of death,** at 9 mg/dL or higher.

And that lower risk of death was from all causes—including heart disease (number-one cause of death in the US), cancer (number two), stroke (number three), and chronic obstructive lung disease (number four).

"Alpha-carotene, rather than beta-carotene, may be directly related to reduced risk of premature death," says Chaoyang Li, MD, the study leader, from the Centers for Disease Control and Prevention in Atlanta.

Why might alpha-carotene be so protective?

Alpha- and beta-carotene are both powerful antioxidants that can protect cells from the rustlike oxidation of DNA that drives many chronic diseases. But alpha-carotene may outperform its twin, says Dr. Li.

Examples: Cancer research in the laboratory shows that alpha-carotene is 10 times more powerful than beta- in stopping the spread of *neuroblastoma* (cancer of the nerve cell). Alpha- is more effective than beta- in blocking liver cancer. Alpha- outshines beta- in stopping the growth of lung and skin cancer sparked by a cancer-promoting chemical. And a study in people links the vegetables and fruits richest in alpha-carotene—not beta-carotene—to less risk for lung cancer.

Alpha Meals

How can you make sure you're getting enough alpha-carotene?

It's unlikely you'll get it from a supplement because alpha-carotene isn't in most nutritional supplements, says Dr. Li.

Best choices: The top source of alpha-carotene is food—and it's found most abundantly in yellow-orange vegetables and fruits (carrots, pumpkin, sweet potatoes, winter squash, oranges, tangerines), in dark green vegetables (broccoli, green beans, green peas, spinach, turnip greens, collard greens, Swiss chard, and leaf lettuce) and in red peppers.

"Other vegetables and fruits contain very low or no alpha-carotene," says Dr. Li.

But 75% of the alpha-carotene in the American diet comes from just one of those vegetables—carrots.

"Based on the results of my study, I include carrots, oranges and tangerines in my daily vegetable and fruit intake of five servings a day," says Dr. Li. "In particular, I consider snacking on carrot sticks a healthy dietary habit."

Drawbacks: "Most people eat carrots raw," says Jennifer Adler, CN, a certified nutritionist, natural foods chef and founder of Passionate Nutrition in Seattle. "But the cell wall of carrots is so tough that you get only about 25% of the carotenoids. It's only when the carrots are juiced or cooked that you maximize absorption—preparation techniques that take time, which busy people don't have."

Her recommendations for quick, easy and truly nutritious cooked carrots...

- **Try roasted carrots.** "You don't have to peel them," says Adler. "Just wash them, cut them into chunks, mix them with 2 or 3 teaspoons of olive oil so that all of the carrots have a nice sheen to them. You can add some smoked paprika for a deeper flavor. Or maybe a little bit or honey or maple syrup, if you like a sweeter taste."

Put the carrots on a cookie sheet in the oven, and roast at 325° F for about 15 minutes, depending on how well done you like them.

- **Shave carrots into soup.** "If you're making a chicken, lentil or miso soup—or any soup where carrots will complement the flavor—simply shave off some carrots into the soup," says Adler. "You can do it quickly, and you aren't dirtying a cutting board that you'll have to clean later."

● **Add baby carrots to chicken or a roast.** "Any time you're baking or roasting a chicken or roasting another type of meat dish, just add a ton of baby carrots to it—pour the contents of the bag under the chicken or roast," says Adler. "The carrots will absorb the juices from the meat, making them more delicious."

● **Easy sweet potatoes.** Sweet potatoes are another delicious source of alpha-carotene. And they're surprisingly easy to prepare, says Adler.

"Any time your oven is on—say, you're roasting a chicken—also put in a baking tray full of sweet potatoes or winter squash. You hardly have to do anything to prepare these foods, and they're incredibly forgiving. Just wash them, poke some holes in them so the potato or squash separates from its skin during cooking, line them up on a baking tray, and stick them in the oven for 30 to 60 minutes.

"Once they're ready, store them in the frig and reheat one anytime you like, which takes about 10 minutes. Add a little butter or coconut oil with some salt. Or mash it to the consistency you like, adding a little milk and salt. Or make it savory with garlic—a favorite dish of many people in the nutrition and cooking classes that I teach.

"You can even grab a sweet potato for breakfast—it's not typical breakfast food, but many of my clients find it a sweet and delicious alternative."

Chaoyang Li, MD, PhD, Division of Behavioral Surveillance, Office of Surveillance, Epidemiology and Laboratory Services, Centers for Disease Control and Prevention in Atlanta, Georgia.

Jennifer Adler, CN, natural foods chef, adjunct faculty member at Bastyr University in Seattle, founder of Passionate Nutrition in Seattle and Bainbridge, Washington, and cofounder of the International Eating Disorders Institute. *www.passionatenutrition.com, www.iedinstitute.com.*

Stand Up and Stay Alive

A lot of people think there's too much violence on TV. But maybe the most violent thing about TV is simply sitting there watching it. Because new research shows your TV can kill you.

Shocking new finding: A seven-year study by Australian researchers in the journal *Circulation* found that people who watched TV for four or more hours a day were 46% more likely to die of any cause than people who watched two hours or less. And it didn't matter whether they were overweight or not—too much TV was deadly for everybody.

But sitting around watching TV isn't the only kind of sitting that's bad for you.

In a 14-year study of more than 120,000 people with an average age of 63, those who sat six or more hours a day in their leisure time were 25% more likely to die than those who sat less than three hours, reported researchers from the American Cancer Society in the *American Journal of Epidemiology*.

"Research shows that prolonged time spent sitting has important metabolic consequences," says Alpa Patel, PhD, the study leader. "It may increase total cholesterol and triglycerides, decrease good HDL cholesterol, increase blood sugar levels and increase blood pressure—all biomarkers of cardiovascular and other diseases."

The study also looked at the link between exercise and dying—and found that women who exercised the least had a 94% higher risk of dying and men a 48% higher risk.

People should reduce the time they sit and increase their physical activity, say the study researchers.

Here's how to do just that…

● **Watch Less TV**
Suggestions for cutting TV-viewing time…

● Use your TiVo or DVR. You can cut your TV viewing time up to 50% by recording your favorite shows, says Christine Louise Hohlbaum, a time management expert and author of *The Power of Slow: 101 Ways to Save Time in Our 24/7 World* (St. Martin's).

"Fast-forward through the commercials—and spend a lot less time in front of the tube."

● Use the TV guide. "Scroll through the TV guide and see what you really want to watch for the upcoming week," says Nancy Irwin, PsyD, a psychotherapist and clinical hypnotist in private practice in Los Angeles and author of *YOU-TURN: Changing Direction in Midlife* (Create Space). Then schedule it in your datebook, much like a dentist appointment.

●Use a timer. "You can purchase a timer that will automatically turn off the TV after a certain hour of the day or amount of time with the TV on," says Hohlbaum. Timers are widely available at retail stores and Web sites.

● Never use the TV as background noise. That will only tempt you to sit down and watch it, says Hohlbaum. "Use the radio instead."

● Remove all TVs from the bedroom. "There are more interesting things you can do there!" says Hohlbaum.

"Get rid of all 'excessive' TVs," agrees Dr. Irwin. "Really, how many do you need? If TV is too convenient, you watch too much of it."

●**Exercise More**

That's a relatively easy task for 95% of Americans—because they're not exercising at all.

Shocking new finding: A recent five-year study, from the Walking Behavior Laboratory at Pennington Biomedical Research Center in Baton Rouge, Louisiana, found that only 5% of Americans engage in a vigorous, leisure-time exercise.

But there's an easy way to exercise regularly, says James Hill, PhD, director of the Anschutz Health and Wellness Center at the University of Colorado and author of *The Step Diet* (Workman). Walk.

● Walking works. Anybody can start walking, he says. "There's no equipment. You can do it anytime, anywhere. And if you walk with a family member or friend, it's also a pleasurable social experience."

● Start slowly—and succeed. "The hardest part about establishing a habit of regular activity is starting," says Dr. Hill.

● Use a pedometer. A pedometer is a device that clips to your belt or waistband. It counts and displays the number of steps you take each day.

"With a pedometer, you don't have to achieve a big goal right away," says Dr. Hill. "Instead, you determine how many steps you take each day, and then you increase that number by a little bit."

Dr. Hill's Pedometer Program

1. Choose a device in the $20 to $25 price range for maximum accuracy.

2. Wear your pedometer for three days. At the end of each day, write down the number of steps your pedometer has recorded.

3. After three days, calculate the average, dividing the total number of steps by the number of days. (*Example:* 15,000 steps by three days equals 5,000 steps a day.)

4. For the next week, increase your baseline number of steps by 2,000—if your baseline was 5,000, you'd be walking 7,000 steps a day.

Examples: At work, take two, 10-minute walks during your breaks. At home, empty the wastebaskets every day.

"Once people add 2,000 steps to their daily average, they don't stop," he says. "They say to themselves, 'Oh, if I could do 2,000, maybe I could do more.' And they do."

Alpa Patel, PhD, cancer epidemiologist at the American Cancer Society.

Christine Louise Hohlbaum, time management expert, blogger and author of *The Power of Slow: 101 Ways to Save Time in Our 24/7 World* (St. Martin's) *www.powerofslow. wordpress.com.*

Nancy Irwin, PsyD, psychotherapist and clinical hypnotist in private practice in Los Angeles and author of *YOU-TURN: Changing Direction in Midlife* (Create Space). *www. drnancyirwin.com.*

James Hill, PhD, professor of pediatrics and medicine, executive director of the Anschutz Health and Wellness Center, director of the Center for Human Nutrition and director of the Colorado Nutrition Obesity Research Center at the University of Colorado, Denver. He is the author of *The Step Diet* (Workman).

Schedule Movement

Get out of your chair once every hour. Sitting for long periods increases your risk for death regardless of how physically active you are during the day, says an American Cancer Society study.

Interrupt periods of sitting with short walks, stretches or even arm windmills. Program an hourly reminder on your computer or cellphone to get up and move. Don't phone or e-mail a coworker. Walk the long way to his or her desk.

Mark A. Stengler, NMD, naturopathic medical doctor in private practice, Encinitas, California, and author of the *Bottom Line/Natural Healing* newsletter. *www.drstengler.com.*

The Supplement That Boosts Body-Repairing Stem Cells

Stem cells are like magic seeds that can turn into any kind of plant. *There are two basic types…*

- **Embryonic stem cells** (so-called "undifferentiated" cells from a three- to five-day-old human embryo) can turn into heart cells, blood cells, brain cells, bone cells—or any one of the more than 200 other types of specialized cells in the body.

- **Adult stem cells** are undifferentiated cells found in specific tissues and organs such as the heart, muscles and bones. If there is damage in that area, adult stem cells become specialized, repairing and regenerating tissue. And adult stem cells from the bone marrow generate growth factors that stop cell death and speed healing in many types of tissues.

Studies link low levels of circulating adult stem cells to a wide range of health problems, including…

- Heart attack, stroke and death from cardiovascular disease
- High blood pressure
- Prediabetes (insulin resistance) and diabetes
- Metabolic syndrome (a cluster of conditions that can include prediabetes, excess belly fat, high blood pressure and cholesterol problems)
- Alzheimer's disease
- Kidney disease
- Rheumatoid arthritis
- Sleep apnea
- Migraine headaches
- Glaucoma
- Erectile dysfunction.

The main medical technique to boost the level of circulating adult stem cells—*granulocyte colony stimulating factor* (G-CSF), a hormone that stimulates the bone marrow to pump out the stem cells—is high-tech and high-cost. And it can cause serious side effects with long-term use, such as blood clots.

Exciting development: A new study in the *Journal of Translational Medicine* shows that a nutritional supplement can boost circulating adult stem cells by up to 90%.

The Stem Cell Supplement

In the two-week study, 18 healthy people aged 20 to 72 took a nutritional supplement with these ingredients…

- **Vitamin D-3**
- **Green tea extract**
- **Astragalus** (an immune-strengthening herb used in Traditional Chinese Medicine)
- **Lactobacillus fermentum** (a "friendly" digestive bacteria)
- **Ellagic acid** (a powerful antioxidant)
- **Beta 1,3 glucan** (a unique carbohydrate shown to strengthen the immune system).

At the beginning and end of the two-week period, the researchers measured levels of two types of circulating adult stem cells…

- *Hematopoietic* **adult stem cells** (stem cells from the bone marrow)
- *Endothelial progenitor* **cells,** or EPC (stem cells that repair the endothelium, the lining of the arteries).

Results: There was an increase in hematopoietic cells up to 90%, and a 95% increase in EPC.

"I believe that aging needs to be treated as a disease—and stem cells can play a fundamental and critical role in the treatment of this disease," says Thomas E. Ichim, PhD, a study researcher. "My feeling is that daily use of this supplement might increase life span by 5 to 10 years."

"The technologies that increase circulating stem cells are very expensive to implement—but now there's a relatively inexpensive nutritional supplement that enhances the average individual's capacity to generate new stem cells and live a healthier and longer life," adds Ron Hunninghake, MD, chief medical officer at the Riordan Clinic in Wichita, Kansas, and a study researcher.

"I see a lot of patients who feel very stuck in their chronic illness, whether it's heart disease, diabetes, arthritis or another chronic ailment. This supplement—because it's potentially so broadly regenerative in its effect—could be a very useful tool to help them break out of their impasse and begin healing."

Resources: The product used in the study was Stem-Kine, with study participants taking two capsules, twice a day. It is available from many Web sites that sell supplements and at *www.stem-kine.com*, or call 800-529-0269.

Thomas E. Ichim, PhD, stem cell expert, with more than 70 published scientific papers in *Circulation, Journal of Immunotherapy, International Archives of Medicine* and many other medical journals. He is coauthor of *RNA Interference* (Humana) and the CEO of Medistem, a company specializing in cellular therapeutics.

Ron Hunninghake, MD, chief medical officer of the Olive W. Garvey Center for Healing Arts, the Riordan Clinic, Wichita, Kansas.

Reverse Immune System Aging—with Probiotics!

Scientists call it *immunosenescence,* which is a fancy way of saying your immune system is getting older.

As you age, you produce fewer B-cells, which generate antibodies, a protein that identifies invaders such as viruses as "foreign" so that other immune cells can detect and destroy them. You produce fewer T-cells, white blood cells (lymphocytes) that play many roles in sustaining and strengthening immunity. And you make fewer natural killer cells, a white blood cell that specializes in destroying viruses and cancer cells.

The likely result of these and other age-related immune changes: More and worse infections...more chronic inflammatory disorders (a sign of a weakened immune system), such as heart disease and asthma...more autoimmune disease, such as rheumatoid arthritis and lupus...and more cancer.

Some experts even equate immunosenescence with aging: As your immune defenses decline, so do you.

Surprising: A recent study from Finland shows you can help reverse that decline—by eating a slice of cheese rich in probiotics, friendly bacteria that replenish and balance the microflora, the inner ecosystem of microbes that line your colon and small intestine. (More in a moment about the link between probiotics and your immune system.)

More, Stronger Immune Cells

Fandi Ibrahim, PhD, and his colleagues at the University of Turku in Finland studied 31 seniors, ranging in age from 73 to 103. For two months, the study participants ate two different types of cheese.

For the first two weeks of the study, they ate a daily slice of cheese that didn't contain probiotics. For the next four weeks, they ate a slice of cheese enriched with two strains of probiotics—*Lactobacillus acidophilus* and *Lactobacillus rhamnosus*. Then they switched back to the non-probiotic cheese for two weeks.

The researchers measured a variety of immune parameters at the beginning of the study, right before and right after the four-week period of eating the probiotic cheese, and at the end of the study.

Key findings: After the older folks ate probiotic cheese for four weeks, their natural killer cells were better able to target cancer cells. They also had an increase in two other types of white blood cells, and those cells could kill more microbes.

Probiotic-rich cheese "may be beneficial in improving the immune response" of older people, concluded the researchers, in *FEMS Immunology & Medical Microbiology*.

Why it works: How does a friendly breed of digestive bacteria improve immunity? Well, the digestive system and the immune system are very interrelated. For example:

The digestive tract contains 70% of the antibody-producing cells in the body.

The friendly bacteria of the digestive tract activate macrophages, white blood cells that engulf and dissolve invaders.

The same bacteria also stimulate the production of cytokines, proteins that help regulate immune response.

"Normal bacteria in the digestive tract is not just involved in immune activities, it is absolutely required for developing healthy immune responses," says Kelly Karpa, PhD, author of *Bacteria for Breakfast: Probiotics for Good Health* (Trafford) and associate professor of pharmacology in the College of Medicine at Pennsylvania State University.

Probiotic Foods and Supplements

"There aren't any probiotic cheeses available in the US. Not to worry. The two strains of probiotic used in the study cheese stimulate the immune system, but many other strains of probiotics do the same," says Dr. Ibrahim.

The many probiotic-rich foods available include yogurts (such as Activia, from Dannon), milks (such as Yakult) and even bars (attune Probiotic Bar, from Attune Foods) and cereal (YogActive, from A&V 2000).

However: For daily dependability in the delivery of enough probiotics to energize your immune system, you may want to use a probiotic supplement, says Dr. Karpa.

She takes Florajen3, which includes Lactobacillus acidophilus, *Bifidobacterium lactis* and *Bifidobacterium longum*, and is widely available in retail stores and online (*www. florajen.com*).

Choosing a Supplement

Here are guidelines for choosing a probiotic supplement, from Elizabeth Lipski, PhD, CCN, a certified clinical nutritionist in Ashville, North Carolina, and author of *Digestive Wellness* (McGraw-Hill)…

● **Look for a supplement with Lactobacillus acidophilus and Bifidobacterium bifidum.**

● **Choose a refrigerated or freeze-dried product.** "Freeze-drying puts the flora into suspended animation, keeping them dormant until placed in your body," Dr. Lipski says.

● **Take at least a billion microbes, once a day.** "This is usually about ¼ to ½ teaspoon, or 1 to 3 capsules."

Fandi Ibrahim, PhD, researcher and senior scientist in the Functional Foods Forum at the University of Turku in Turku, Finland.

Kelly Karpa, PhD, associate professor in the Department of Pharmacology at Pennsylvania State University's College of Medicine and author of *Bacteria for Breakfast: Probiotics for Good Health* (Trafford).

Elizabeth Lipski, PhD, CCN, certified clinical nutritionist in private practice in Ashville, North Carolina, and author of several books, including *Digestive Wellness* (McGraw-Hill). *www.lizlipski.com.*

Fewer Calories, More Years

Seventy years of scientific research shows that restricting calories to 30% below normal intake can extend life span by up to 50% in laboratory animals. Recent research shows that calorie restriction may extend the life span of human beings as well.

Paul McGlothin and Meredith Averill are internationally recognized experts on calorie restriction and authors of *The CR Way: Using the Secrets of Calorie Restriction for a Longer, Healthier Life. Here, some of their important findings…*

Latest Research

Reporting in *Science*, researchers from the University of Wisconsin revealed the results of a study on calorie restriction in rhesus monkeys, our closest "relatives." The researchers studied 76 adult rhesus monkeys (which live an average of 27 years and a maximum of 40), dividing them into two groups. One group ate a calorie-restricted diet, and one didn't. After 20 years, 37% of the monkeys in the nonrestricted group had died, compared with only 13% in the calorie-restricted group. The calorie-restricted monkeys also had fewer incidences of heart disease, diabetes, cancer and brain disease.

Scientists at Washington University School of Medicine in St. Louis studied the biomarkers of aging of 33 people, average age 51, who ate a calorie-restricted diet for an average of six years. Compared with another group of people who ate a typical American diet, the calorie-restricted practitioners had lab results that are typical of people much younger than themselves. They had lower cholesterol, lower blood pressure, less body fat and lower glucose (blood sugar) levels.

The study participants also had lower levels of insulin (the hormone that regulates blood sugar)…C-reactive protein (a biomarker for disease-causing inflammation)…tumor necrosis factor (a biomarker for an overactive immune system)…and thyroid hormone T3 (lower levels indicate a slower, cell-preserving metabolic rate).

Why It Works

There are several theories as to why calorie restriction improves health and may increase life span. *It may…*

• **Reduce DNA damage.**

• **Reduce daily energy expenditure,** the most basic of metabolic processes, thereby reducing oxidative stress, the internal "rust" that damages cells.

• **Decrease core body temperature.** The higher your normal body temperature, the faster you age.

• **Improve how cells handle insulin,** which controls glucose. Poor glucose regulation damages cells.

• **Improve the neuroendocrine system,** the crucial link between the brain and the hormones that regulate many of the body's functions.

• **Activate a type of gene called *sirtuins*,** which protect *mitochondria*, tiny energy factories in the cells. Mitochondrial failure speeds aging.

Easy Way to Cut Back

The level of calorie restriction probably required to extend life in humans—about 20 to 30% of typical intake—is more than most people are willing to do on a regular basis, but reducing calories by even 5% can produce significant health benefits.

Estimated calorie requirements for a moderately active person age 51 or older are 2,200 to 2,400 calories a day for a man and 1,800 for a woman. Reducing calories by 5% would mean cutting between 110 and 120 daily calories for a man and 90 for a woman.

With just a few changes in your dietary routine, you easily can reduce calories by 5% or more and improve your health…

• **Favor nutrient-dense foods.** A nutrient-dense food has a high amount of nutrients per calorie. They're the healthiest foods to eat. *They include…*

Animal protein: Salmon (Alaskan wild, canned, fresh or frozen), sardines, tuna.

Good fats: Nuts…avocados…grapeseed oil, extra-virgin olive oil.

Beans: Adzuki, limas, black-eyed peas, black turtle beans, garbanzos (chickpeas), lentils (red or green), mung, pinto, soy.

Veggies: Arugula, beets, bok choy, broccoli, cabbage, carrots, chard, collard greens, garlic, kale, kohlrabi, leeks, mushrooms (maitake, portobello, shiitake), mustard greens, onions, romaine lettuce, spinach, squash (butternut, summer), sweet potatoes, tomatoes.

Grains: Barley, quinoa, wild rice, sprouted-grain breads.

Fruit: Apricots, blackberries, blueberries, cantaloupe, cranberries, kiwi, lemons, limes, oranges, peaches, raspberries, strawberries, tangerines.

Spices and herbs: Season foods with herbs and spices rather than salt, butter or sugar. Examples include basil, chives, ginger, parsley and turmeric.

• **Focus on foods with low-to-moderate Glycemic Index rankings.** High levels of glucose and insulin are linked to faster aging and disease. It's just as important to limit glucose as it is to limit calories.

The best way to regulate glucose and insulin is to choose carbohydrates with a low-to-moderate score on the Glycemic Index (GI)—carbohydrates that digest slowly so that glucose and insulin levels don't suddenly skyrocket.

The beans, veggies, grains and fruits that are nutrient-dense (listed above) have low-to-moderate GIs.

Other ways to keep glucose low…

• Start your meal with one cup of water with one tablespoon of lemon juice, which lowers glucose.

• Finish your last meal of the day as early as possible, eating complex carbohydrates and a fat source.

• After your evening meal, take a 45-minute or longer walk.

• **Keep protein intake moderate.** Excess protein can increase blood levels of the hormone *Insulin-Like Growth Factor-I* (IGF-I), which deactivates a sirtuin gene and accelerates aging.

Each day, eat 0.36 grams of protein per pound of body weight—at your healthiest, ideal body weight. That's 43 grams of protein a day for a woman whose ideal weight is 120 pounds and 55 grams of protein a day for a man whose ideal weight is 154 pounds. For comparison, typical intake for US adults is 65 grams to 90 grams. One ounce of meat or fish contains about seven grams of protein.

• **Stop eating before you're full.** Always leave the table slightly hungry. This helps you cut calories and prompts the *hypothalamus*—the emotion-generating part of the brain—to produce the hormone *orexin*, which boosts feelings of happiness. The Japanese have a concept for this healthful practice—*Hara hachi bu*—which means eat until you're 80% full.

Paul McGlothin and Meredith Averill, who have practiced calorie restriction for 17 years. They are the directors of the CR Way Longevity Center in Ossining, New York, and leaders of the CR Society International. They are the authors of *The CR Way* (HarperCollins) and the online e-book *The CR Way to Happy Dieting. www.livingthecrway.com.*

Get Your ZZZZs—and Live Longer

The consequences of chronic insomnia may be far worse than was previously known. Researchers at the University of Wisconsin, Madison, found that the risk of dying from any cause was three times higher in people who suffered from chronic insomnia than in those who slept through the night. Considering the potentially lethal consequences, seek help if you have any type of insomnia, including repeat awakenings or difficulty falling asleep.

L. Finn, et al., "Chronic Insomnia and All Cause Mortality in the Wisconsin Sleep Cohort Study," presented at the annual meeting of the Associated Professional Sleep Societies.

The Diet That Helps You Lose 20 Years in 30 Days

Patients who first try Botox often say that they want to look good for an upcoming wedding, high school reunion or other important event. Botox is very effective at treating some wrinkles, but it doesn't improve the aged look of skin. Nor can it reverse the aging effects of obesity, including lack of vitality.

The right diet can not only help you lose weight but also can make you feel and look 10 to 20 years younger…

• **Eat low-glycemic carbohydrates.** The Glycemic Index (GI) is a measure of how quickly the carbohydrates in foods turn into glucose (sugar) in the blood. A food on the GI is ranked relative to pure glucose, which is given the ranking 100.

High-GI foods cause a spike in blood sugar and a consequent dip, which causes cravings for more sugar. A consistently high-GI diet not only causes weight gain and risk for insulin resistance and diabetes compromises the radiance and suppleness of skin.

A food with a low GI causes a more even rise and fall in blood sugar than a food with a high GI. Many green vegetables, such as spinach, broccoli and asparagus, have GI rankings under 20 and are full of the antioxidants that promote beautiful skin (see next column). Slightly higher on the GI but still wholesome are whole-grain products.

Example: Oat bran bread has a 68 GI versus a French baguette with a 136 GI.

To find the GI ratings of foods, go to *www. GlycemicIndex.com.*

•**Limit refined sugar.** The trick to looking years younger just by changing your daily diet is sugar control—know how sugars work in your system and where they lurk in processed foods and avoid them.

The sugars added to many packaged foods trigger a process known as *glycosylation,* which causes the skin to become stiff and discolored.

Don't buy any product that lists sugar in the top three ingredients. Be aware that sugar goes by different names including dextrose, galactose, high-fructose corn syrup and caramel.

Fruits have a lot of fructose (sugar), but if eaten whole, they are full of fiber that slows down the sugar. Avoid drinking fruit juices. Go for the whole fruit.

•**Eat antioxidant-rich foods.** Much of the skin damage that accompanies aging is caused by free radicals, oxygen-based molecules that are produced in higher-than-normal amounts when we're exposed to sun or environmental toxins (such as cigarette smoke). Free radicals damage cells and alter genetic material, leading to skin aging, including wrinkling, and skin cancer.

Antioxidants can fight free radicals. *Here are a few of the powerful antioxidants that can help repair skin…*

•Allium—in garlic, onions and scallions.

•Anthocyanin—in berries, pomegranates, cherries, blood oranges, black beans and soybeans. *Helpful:* Blueberries are particularly good for skin. I recommend one-half cup to one cup a day. If you get tired of blueberries, switch to blackberries.

•Beta-carotene—in carrots, sweet potatoes, pumpkins and squash.

•Lutein—in spinach, kale, broccoli and brussels sprouts.

•Lycopene—in tomatoes, watermelon and pink grapefruit.

•Quercetin—in broccoli, cranberries, onions and apples.

•**Eat fish three to four times weekly.** The omega-3 fatty acids in cold-water fish, such as salmon and sardines, can help reduce acne, rosacea and other forms of skin infection and inflammation. The omega-3s also help reduce joint inflammation—important for maintaining youthful flexibility.

If you don't like fish, take a supplement of 1,000 mg of omega-3s daily.

•**Eat plain unsweetened yogurt.** It's high in protein as well as calcium—important for skin collagen as well as healthy muscles and joints. Yogurt also aids weight loss. One study found that people who ate one serving of yogurt with blueberries daily lost an average of 12 pounds in a year without doing anything else.

Look for Greek yogurt, which is strained longer and therefore is thicker—it delivers the highest amount of protein. You can add berries, nuts or a touch of honey.

•**Drink water—at least eight (and preferably more) tall glasses a day.**

Water literally plumps the skin and makes wrinkles less apparent.

Youth in a Blender

This smoothie gives you—and your skin—a good start on the day…

Breakfast Smoothie

½ cup milk (regular or skim)
½ cup plain yogurt (full-fat or low-fat)
½ cup frozen strawberries
½ cup frozen blueberries
1 teaspoon honey
4 ice cubes

Purée everything but the ice cubes in a blender. Add the ice, and purée again. Serves one.

David A. Colbert, MD, founder and head physician of New York Dermatology Group in New York City. He is co-author, with Terry Reed, of *The High School Reunion Diet: Lose 20 Years in 30 Days* (Simon & Schuster). *www.high schoolreuniondiet.com.*

Lessons from the "Super-Agers"

Want to live a long, healthy life? To learn how, just ask a "super-ager." That was the thinking of researchers at the University of California, Irvine, who recruited more than 1,000 residents from a retirement community to study what exactly caused these people to live to age 90 and beyond. Known as the "oldest-old," this group is comprised of about two million Americans and is the fastest-growing segment of the US population.

The 90-Plus Study, which is ongoing, holds important lessons for all of us who hope to reach advanced age with our mental and physical faculties intact.

What's been discovered so far…

Throw Out Your Scale

Obesity is harmful for everyone, but older adults who carry a few extra pounds are more likely to live longer than those who are lean.

Surprising result: Adults in the 90-Plus Study with a body mass index (BMI), which is weight relative to height, of 25 to 29.9—a range that is considered "overweight"—lived longer, on average, than those with BMIs of 18.5 to 24.9, the "normal" range.* (Participants'

*To learn your BMI, go to the Web site of the National Heart, Lung and Blood Institute, *www.nhlbisupport.com/bmi/.*

average age was 72 when their BMIs were measured.)

It is not clear why these extra pounds appear to be protective in older adults. It is possible that people who are somewhat overweight have better nutritional status overall than those who are lean.

In addition, people with extra fat reserves may be better able to circumvent "wasting," the age-related loss of muscle tissue and strength that can lead to frailty and an increased risk for illness.

Caution: Research shows that being obese (a BMI of 30 and higher) at any age is not associated with a longer life span. And being overweight or obese at age 21 was associated with a shorter life span.

Exercise Works

Study participants who exercised for 45 minutes or more a day, most days of the week, were 27% less likely to die within an eight-year period than those who exercised less than 15 minutes daily. Their activities included swimming, biking, tennis, vigorous walking and dancing. They also were more likely to retain more of their memory and other cognitive functions.

Striking research finding: Even participants who got very little exercise—as little as 15 minutes a day—lived significantly longer than those who were completely sedentary.

Dementia risk is quadrupled: Among the oldest-old, those who scored in the lowest 20% in physical performance—which measured such factors as balance and the ability to walk a certain distance—were four times more likely to have dementia than those who scored in the highest 20%.

Physical activity not only improves cardiovascular and cerebral blood flow but also increases circulation so that brain cells receive more nutrients. There is also strong evidence that exercise promotes *neurogenesis,* the growth of new brain cells (neurons) and the connections between these cells.

Monopoly, Anyone?

The onset of Alzheimer's disease is one of the greatest fears of older adults. The incidence of dementia from all causes, including Alzheimer's disease, doubles every five years between ages 65 and 85.

Key finding: Participants in the 21-year Bronx Aging Study who spent three hours daily engrossed in mental activities, including playing board games, reading, dancing or playing a musical instrument, were significantly less likely to develop dementia than those who spent less (or no) time doing these activities.

Examples: Participants who spent hours playing board games had a 75% lower risk of developing dementia...and those who spent a similar amount of time playing a musical instrument had a 70% lower risk.

For optimal results: Aim for three hours of such activities daily. Shorter periods of mental focus can also decrease the risk for dementia, but three hours a day seems to be optimal.

Daniel James Berlau, PhD, an adjunct assistant professor in the Department of Neurology at the University of California, Irvine, School of Medicine. He specializes in neurobiology and memory and is a principal investigator in the ongoing 90-Plus Study.

Should You Double Your Vitamin D?

Governments around the world are being advised by nutrition experts that it's time for their citizens to double their daily intake of vitamin D—particularly their older citizens.

In the US, the Institute of Medicine (IOM)—the panel of experts that advises the government on recommended daily allowances (RDA) for individual nutrients—upped the RDA for vitamin D from 400 IU daily to 600 IU for adults under 70 and 800 IU for adults over 70.

In Canada, a team of researchers from the University of Alberta and the University of Saskatchewan recommended that Canadian health-policy leaders take immediate action to increase the blood levels of Canadians by an average 36%—and thereby save up to 52,000 lives a year.

In Finland, the Finnish National Nutrition Council recommended that all Finns over 60 should have a daily intake of 800 IU—up from 400.

What's going on? Why are so many health experts waving the vitamin D flag?

New thinking: Vitamin D is a must for the absorption of calcium and therefore plays a key role in maintaining strong bones and preventing osteoporosis. But the newest understanding of vitamin D is that it's important for the health of every cell.

"We now know that every cell and tissue in the body has a vitamin D receptor," says Michael Holick, MD, PhD, professor at Boston University Medical Center and author of *The Vitamin D Solution: A 3-Step Strategy to Cure Our Most Common Health Problem*. "Which means that every cell requires vitamin D for maximum functioning and health. Increasing the amount of vitamin D in the body can prevent or help treat a remarkable number of ailments."

And "remarkable" just might be an understatement! The long list of ailments that new research shows vitamin D may prevent or treat includes...

- **Heart disease and stroke**
- **Cancer**
- **Diabetes**
- **Overweight**
- **Memory loss, mental decline, and Alzheimer's**
- **Depression**
- **Parkinson's disease**
- **Autoimmune diseases such as rheumatoid arthritis and multiple sclerosis**
- **Asthma**
- **Colds and flu**
- **Back pain**

• **Fibromyalgia**

• **Pelvic floor disorders such as urinary incontinence**

• **Infertility.**

"Essentially, all chronic diseases are linked to vitamin D deficiency," says Dr. Holick.

And since many of those chronic diseases don't show up until later in life, vitamin D is particularly important for seniors.

Newest research: A 20-year study by Australian researchers showed that people with normal blood levels of vitamin D were 36% less likely to die compared with those deficient in the nutrient.

Researchers at the Sticht Center on Aging at Wake Forest University in North Carolina studied nearly 3,000 people aged 75 and older. Those with the highest blood levels of vitamin D were the fittest—they walked faster…were able to get up out of a chair more easily…had better balance…and had more endurance and strength.

People in nursing homes who take vitamin D are less likely to fall, found researchers from the Sydney Medical School in Australia.

And in a 5-year study of more than 6,000 women aged 69 and older, researchers at the University of Minnesota found that those with higher blood vitamin D levels were less likely to become "frail"—a state of muscle weakness, exhaustion, unintentional weight loss, slow walking and inactivity.

Getting the D You Need

The IOM report said that 400 IU of vitamin D a day is plenty until you're 70, and 800 is plenty after that.

The IOM recommendations are a step in the right direction, says Dr. Holick. But, he adds, they fall far short of truly protecting your health.

Here's what you need to know about the new IOM recommendations—the accepted standard that actually falls short—and how to make sure your blood levels of vitamin D are high enough for a *lifetime* of good health.

• **Do you have a deficiency?** The IOM says that "almost all individuals get sufficient vitamin D when their blood levels are at or above 20 nanograms per milliliter (ng/ml)."

True, says Dr. Holick. Blood levels below 20 ng/ml are a sign of a severe deficiency. But that doesn't mean levels just above 20 ng/ml are sufficient for optimal health.

"There is now an abundance of evidence linking levels from 20 ng/ml and 30 ng/ml to poor health—for example, to weaker bones, a weaker immune system, and the thickening of artery walls that causes heart attacks and strokes," he says.

• **How much vitamin D should you take every day?** "With few exceptions, all North Americans are receiving…enough vitamin D," said the IOM report. Not so, says Dr. Holick.

Diet and a daily vitamin-mineral supplement (which usually contains 400 IU of vitamin D) will not maintain blood levels above 30 ng/ml.

He recommends a daily vitamin D supplement of 2,000 to 3,000 IU for adults.

• **How much vitamin D is too much?** Vitamin D is a fat-soluble vitamin, which means it's stored in the body. Levels that are too high can lead to dangerously high levels of calcium. But how much vitamin D is too much?

The IOM set an "upper tolerable limit" of daily intake at 4,000 IU. Far too cautious, says Dr. Holick.

"The scientific data show that daily intake of up to 10,000 IU a day is perfectly safe."

• **What's the best way to boost blood levels of vitamin D?** Two strategies are best, says Dr. Holick.

• Take a vitamin D supplement. Since the nutrient is found in so few foods, a supplement is the best way to ensure you're getting enough vitamin D in your diet.

• Get some summer sun—without sunscreen. Sunlight triggers the production of vitamin D in the skin—and exposing bare skin to sunlight from late spring to early fall is the best way to ensure year-long blood levels are over 30 ng/ml, says Dr. Holick. And bare means bare of sunscreen, too. Yes, always use sunscreen on your face to avoid wrinkling. But during the months of May to October, any time between 10 a.m. and 3 p.m., on two to three days a week, briefly expose your arms and legs (54% of your total skin surface) to sunlight. How much time is enough?

"It varies quite a bit from person to person, depending on skin type—from redheads with fair skin that always burns, to people of African origin who never burn," says Dr. Holick. "The easiest recommendation: Know how long it takes to get a mild sunburn on your face—and then expose your no-sunscreen arms and legs 30 to 50% of that time, following the above guidelines."

Example: If it takes half an hour of sun exposure to be pink, expose your arms and legs for no more than 15 minutes before applying sunscreen to them.

Michael Holick, MD, PhD, professor of medicine, physiology, and biophysics at Boston University Medical Center (BUMC), and author of *The Vitamin D Solution: A 3-Step Strategy to Cure Our Most Common Health Problem* (Hudson Street Press).

The Life-Extending Power of Friends

Let's start with a quiz. Of the following four factors, which is most important in increasing your odds of living longer: (a) exercising regularly, (b) not being overweight, (c) getting a yearly flu shot, (d) good social relationships with your family and friends.

Surprising: A new study has found that good relationships with family and friends are more important than regular exercise, weight control or yearly flu shots in preventing early death!

Weak Relationships=Fifteen Cigarettes a Day

The study was led by Julianne Holt-Lunstad, PhD, a professor of psychology at Brigham Young University in Utah, and published in *PLoS Medicine.* She and her colleagues analyzed data from 148 other studies on social relationships, involving more than 300,000 people. The overall result was nothing short of amazing.

Strong social relationships were linked to an increased "likelihood of survival" (living rather than dying during the study period, which averaged 7.5 years) of 50%.

To put that finding in perspective, strong social relationships may be significantly more protective of longer life than…

- **Regular exercise**
- **Maintaining normal weight**
- **Getting a flu vaccine**
- **Taking medication for high blood pressure**
- **Cardiac rehabilitation** (exercise therapy) after a heart attack.

One lifestyle change that strong social relationships didn't beat was quitting smoking—the two factors were equally protective! (Looked at another way, weak social relationships were as risky to long life as smoking 15 cigarettes a day!)

Why do strong social ties connect you to a healthier life?

"I don't think there's a single mechanism," says Dr. Holt-Lunstad. *A few ways that family and friends might improve health include…*

- **Family and friends encourage you to see a doctor when you're sick,** or to eat a healthier diet, or to take other actions that protect health.
- **Strong social relationships buffer the effects of stress**—and stress weakens the immune system, hurts the heart, and damages the body in many other ways.
- **Relationships provide a sense of meaning and purpose to life**—a factor some studies show protects health.

Friends for (More) Life

There are many effective ways to create new relationships and strengthen existing ones, says Liz Grow, MA, a licensed professional counselor specializing in relationship issues, and cofounder of Texas Professional Counseling in New Braunfels, Texas.

● **Be the friend you want to have.** "It's an old saying, but it's so true," says Grow. "Ask yourself, 'What do I need from my social relationships?' And then be the role model for providing that need to others."

Maybe it's showing interest in the other person's life, or checking in on a regular basis, or praising the other person for their accomplishments.

"You can't rely on other people changing," says Grow. "First, you have to change yourself."

Good news: Dr. Holt-Lunstad's study showed that providing support may have an even stronger effect on longer life than receiving support. "When a partner or friend perceives you as being giving and responsive, they're likely to be more responsive to you—and this can improve the quality of the relationship, contributing to well-being," she says.

● **Don't be afraid of your family and friends.** "The most important skill in maintaining strong social ties is healthy confrontation," says Grow. "Most of us are inclined to not confront challenging social situations—to ignore contact."

Better: "Sit down with the person and say, 'This is how I see the situation and this is what I feel about it. How do you see it and feel about it? I want this relationship to be stronger. What can we do to improve the situation?'"

● **Don't rely on "social networks" for true, intimate connection.** "Unless relationships transcend the cyberworld, they are not truly supportive," says Grow.

Better: To really reach out and connect, pick up the phone and talk to your family and friends. Even better, meet up for lunch, dinner or another social occasion. And establish true intimacy and connection by being honest about yourself, sharing both the good and bad about your life.

"True intimacy means opening up—letting the other person know what's going on inside you, rather than just wearing the conventional social mask that portrays only strength and happiness."

● **Find new friends.** "Although social networks may not increase intimacy, you can use the Internet constructively to find new friends that you spend time with at in-person events," says Kathleen Mojas, PhD, a clinical psychologist in private practice in Beverly Hills, California.

Her favorite site: www.meetup.com, where you can either start or find a "meetup" group of local like-minded people—from hikers, to Buddhists, to magicians, to you name it.

"It's a great place to begin expanding your network of relationships," says Dr. Mojas.

Julianne Holt-Lunstad, PhD, professor of psychology at Brigham Young University in Utah.

Liz Grow, MA, licensed professional counselor specializing in relationship issues, and cofounder of Central Texas Professional Counseling in New Braunfels, Texas. *www.texasprofessionalcounseling.com.*

Kathleen Mojas, PhD, clinical psychologist in private practice in Beverly Hills, California.

Fall-Proof Your Life

Every year in the US, about one-third of people age 65 and older fall, with 1.6 million treated in emergency rooms and 12,800 killed. But falling is not an inevitable result of aging.

Falling is associated with impairments (such as from stroke, gait or vision problems, or dementia) that are more common with age. But risk for falling is also increased by poor balance and muscle strength and by side effects of certain drugs, especially those prescribed for sleep and depression.

Training That Works

Balance training and strength training are often underutilized ways to prevent falls.

With some types of balance training, you move continuously while simultaneously "perturbing" your center of gravity—that is, you intentionally become off-balance during movement, and your body learns how to respond, building your sense of balance. Do not try this on your own. Balance training is taught by physical therapists at many rehabilitation centers.

Another type of balance training is tai chi. This meditative martial art combines gentle, flowing movements with breathing and improves balance with moves that shift weight and increase awareness of body alignment. Teachers don't have to be licensed, so look for one with at least five years' experience.

Surprising: Dancing is a form of balance training. Any type will do, including ballroom, polka or salsa. Take lessons—and go out dancing!

In strength training, you build lean muscle mass by using your body weight (in squats, push-ups and ab crunches), free weights or elastic bands, all of which provide resistance to muscular effort. Stronger muscles and good balance often make the difference between a stumble and a fall.

You can safely learn strength training at a health club with a certified instructor who can correct your form and modify moves as needed. To do these exercises at home, use a book or DVD by a certified instructor, but check with your doctor first.

Caution: If you've had two or more falls in the past year, or feel unsteady on your feet, see a doctor for a referral to a physical therapist, who can create a safe balance- and strength-training program for you.

Risky Medications

Several types of widely prescribed drugs have been linked to an increased risk for falls, including….

• **Sleep medications,** such as the new generation of drugs heavily advertised on TV, including *eszopiclone* (Lunesta) and *zolpidem* (Ambien).

• **Antidepressants,** including selective serotonin reuptake inhibitors, such as *citalopram* (Celexa)…selective serotonin-norepinephrine reuptake inhibitors, such as *duloxetine* (Cymbalta)…and tricyclic antidepressants, such as *amitriptyline* (Elavil).

• **Benzodiazepines** (antianxiety medications), such as *alprazolam* (Xanax).

• **Anticonvulsants,** such as *pregabalin* (Lyrica), a class of drugs that is prescribed not only for epilepsy but also for chronic pain problems, such as from nerve damage.

• **Atypical antipsychotics,** such as *quetiapine* (Seroquel), which are used to treat bipolar disorder…schizophrenia…and psychotic episodes (such as hallucinations) in people with dementia.

• **Blood pressure medications,** including diuretics, such as *furosamide* (Lasix)…and calcium channel blockers, such as *nifedipine* (Procardia).

Important: Taking five or more medications also is linked to an increased risk for falls.

Low Blood Pressure

Side effects of several medications (including drugs for Parkinson's disease, diuretics and heart drugs such as beta-blockers) may increase the risk of falling by causing postural hypotension (blood pressure drops when you stand up from lying down or sitting). Not enough blood flows to the heart to keep you alert and stable, and the body's normal mechanism to counteract this fails.

What to do: Ask your doctor to test you if you have symptoms, including feeling light-headed or dizzy after standing. He/she will have you lie flat for five minutes, and then check your blood pressure immediately when you stand up. You will remain standing and have your pressure checked one or two minutes later. If systolic (top number) blood pressure drops at least 20 mmHg from lying to standing, you have postural hypotension.

If this is the case, ask about reducing your dosage of hypertensive, antidepressive and/or antipsychotic medications—the three drug types most likely to cause this condition.

Also: Drink more water—at least eight eight-ounce glasses a day. Dehydration can cause postural hypotension and is common among older people, who have a decreased sense of thirst.

Helpful: When you wake up in the morning, take your time getting out of bed. Sit on the edge of the bed for a few minutes while gently kicking forward with your lower legs and pumping your arms. This will move more blood to your heart and brain. Then stand up while holding on to a nearby stable object, such as a bedside table.

Vitamin D

Vitamin D promotes good muscle strength, so people with low blood levels of vitamin D may be at increased risk for falls. If your level is below 30 ng/mL, ask your doctor about taking a daily vitamin D supplement.

Mary Tinetti, MD, director of the Program on Aging and the Claude D. Pepper Older Americans Independence Center at the Yale School of Medicine in New Haven, Connecticut. She is professor of epidemiology and investigative medicine and the Gladys Phillips Crofoot Professor of Medicine (geriatrics), also at the Yale School of Medicine.

Brain Games Help Frail Seniors' Mobility

A major push is under way in geriatric research to find new ways to reduce dangerous falls in the frail elderly, so a recent study was designed to explore whether playing electronic games might help. It came as a big surprise to researchers that what the game-playing really did was increase the ability of frail seniors to walk and talk simultaneously.

Joe Verghese, MD, professor in the Saul R. Korey Department of Neurology at Albert Einstein College of Medicine of Yeshiva University in Bronx, New York, explains that the study used a "brain fitness" computer program called MindFit (*www.Cognifit.com*). It involved 24 nonexercising elderly patients aged 70 and older, all with slower-than-average walking speed. The games challenged cognitive abilities, such as attentiveness, problem-solving, planning and organizing. For eight

Fall-Proof Your Home

To prevent falls at home…

● **Maintain bright lighting** throughout the house.

● **Eliminate throw rugs** that could cause you to trip or slip, or use strong double-sided tape to secure them.

● **Have handrails mounted on both sides of stairs** (the most common spot for falls)…and clearly mark the bottom stair with a contrasting color, such as a light-color paint on dark wood.

For more information: Go to the CDC's Web site, *www.cdc.gov*, and type "Home Fall Prevention Checklist" in the search field.

weeks, 12 seniors played these games three times a week for 45 to 60 minutes, while the control group went normally about their lives.

There was only a nominal improvement in walking speed for those who played the MindFit games. Far more notable, however, was that their ability to simultaneously walk and talk shot up by 54%.

Even more impressive: The benefit lasted. Three months later, the game-playing group was still exhibiting their improved ability to walk and talk at the same time, even though they hadn't continued to use the MindFit program. The control group experienced no short- or long-term change whatsoever.

A Promising Therapy

Dr. Verghese notes that this was a very small study and he hopes to do another, larger one to verify his results. But the preliminary findings point to a potential therapy for frail people for whom exercise seems too daunting. Engaging in electronic game play may help aging people retain an even wider range of abilities than was thought. Brain fitness training could help them to feel more confident while moving around—not only resulting in more willingness to be active but also likely reducing their vulnerability to falling as well.

Joe Verghese, MD, professor, The Saul R. Korey Department of Neurology, Murray D. Gross Memorial Faculty Scholar in Gerontology, Albert Einstein College of Medicine, Bronx, New York.

Red Alert: Iron and Copper May Be Aging You

You probably know about the nasty metals out there, such as the lead that can harm the brain and the cadmium that can cause cancer. But you probably don't think of the minerals iron and copper as metallic bad guys.

Iron helps make *hemoglobin*, the molecule that carries oxygen to every tissue and cell. Copper is part of many enzymes that spark biochemical reactions—forming the collagen in skin, the myelin that insulates nerves, and red blood cells. These two minerals are among the many nutrients included in most supplements because they're good for you, right?

Only if the diseases of aging such as Alzheimer's, heart disease and type 2 diabetes are good for you.

New thinking: The younger body needs plenty of iron and copper, says George J. Brewer, MD, of the University of Michigan Medical School, author of the report "Risks of Iron and Copper Toxicity during Aging in Humans" in the journal *Chemical Research and Toxicology*.

But in an older body—a person 50 or older—high levels of those same minerals can spark the creation of toxic free radicals. These malicious molecules—also called *reactive oxygen species* (ROS)—cause cellular oxidation, the internal rust that is behind many diseases of aging, and aging itself.

Some of the evidence…

•**Copper and mental decline.** In a six-year study from researchers at the Rush Institute for Healthy Aging in Chicago, people with the highest intake of dietary copper (mostly from taking a daily vitamin/mineral supplement with copper) had a rate of mental decline six times faster than normal. "These data are frightening!" says Dr. Brewer.

•**Copper, iron and Alzheimer's disease.** Drinking water with 0.12 parts per million of copper—a level more than 10 times lower than the EPA's allowable amount of copper in water—produced the brain plaques of Alzheimer's disease (AD) in experimental animals. "This result is a strong warning that too much copper in drinking water may be a factor causing the high rate of AD," says Dr. Brewer.

A study shows that a drug that removes excess iron from the blood slows the progression of AD.

•**Iron, copper, and heart disease.** Twelve studies link higher blood levels of iron with a higher risk for heart disease. Three studies show that people who donate blood regularly—which reduces iron levels—have less heart disease than people who don't donate.

Fifteen studies link high levels of copper in the body to a higher risk for heart disease.

•**Copper and diabetes.** Studies of animals with diabetes show they have abnormal copper metabolism.

Bottom line: "The proof linking excess copper and iron levels to the most common diseases of aging is not definitive, but I believe the risk should be taken seriously," says Dr. Brewer.

Cutting Copper and Iron

There are many ways to prevent or reverse an overload of copper and iron, says Dr. Brewer. (Follow these recommendations only with the approval and supervision of your primary care physician, he advised.)

•**Don't take supplements with copper.** "Most multivitamin/multimineral pills have inorganic copper—which becomes free copper in the body, the type that is potentially dangerous," says Dr. Brewer. (Copper in food binds to proteins in the liver and circulates in a form that's safe.) "Scan the label on your supplement bottle—and stop taking the supplement if it contains copper."

What most people don't realize: "Copper deficiency is very rare, and almost no one needs copper," says Dr. Brewer.

• **If you're a man over 50, don't take a supplement with iron.** "Men rarely need iron supplementation, unless they have chronic blood loss," says Dr. Brewer.

• **Take zinc.** Taking a zinc supplement lowers copper levels because zinc blocks copper absorption.

Recommended dosage: 40 milligrams (mg), twice daily. Use either zinc gluconate (available over-the-counter) or zinc acetate (available by prescription). Zinc sulfate can irritate the stomach.

Don't take the supplement with meals—take it one hour before or two hours after eating or drinking (anything other than water).

An optimal supplement strategy: Ask your doctor to test your blood level of free copper (the form that is toxic) and *ceruloplasmin* (bound copper). Have these tests before you start the supplements, three months later, and every month thereafter. Once free copper levels are at 7 or 8 micrograms per deciliter (ug/dL), reduce the dosage to 25 mg of zinc, twice daily. If ceruloplasmin levels drop 20% below the baseline test, it's too low—stop the zinc for about a week.

• **Eat less meat.** "The copper and iron in red meat, chicken and fish are much more 'bioavailable' than the iron and copper in vegetables—which means those minerals are much more easily absorbed from meat," explains Dr. Brewer.

Best: Reduce your intake of meat by half.

Caution: Shellfish is very high in copper. Eat it no more than once a month.

• **Install a reverse osmosis water filter.** Eighty percent of Americans have copper pipes—and copper can leach out of the pipes and into drinking water. In a nationwide sample of drinking water, 30% had levels of copper that were safe, 40% had levels that caused disease in laboratory animals, and 30% were in between.

A reverse osmosis water filter, installed at the tap used for drinking and cooking water, filters out the copper.

Resource: You can buy a "copper test card" to measure copper levels in your drinking water at *www.toxiccopper.com*.

"It is simple to use, gives the average person the ability to measure very low but toxic levels of copper in the water, and rivals equipment costing thousands of dollars," says Dr. Brewer.

• **Donate blood regularly to reduce iron.** "Men and menopausal women could donate 500 milliliters (mL) of blood every two months," says Dr. Brewer.

You may also want to ask your doctor to test iron levels every six months—the goal is to lower blood ferritin levels to 50 nanograms per milliliter (ng/mL) or below, which should take a year or two of regular blood donations.

George J. Brewer, MD, Morton S. and Henrietta K. Sellner Emeritus Professor of Human Genetics, Departments of Human Genetics and Internal Medicine at the University of Michigan Medical School in Ann Arbor, Michigan, and author of *Toxic Copper* (Raisin Publishing). *www.toxiccopper.com*.

Chapter 3

ARTHRITIS

To Your Joint Health—Alcohol Eases Arthritis

Rheumatoid arthritis (RA), a joint-destroying autoimmune disease, affects 2.5 million Americans, most of them women. For reasons scientists have yet to understand, your immune system mistakes the lining of your joints (*synovium*) for a foreign invader—and attacks it.

You end up with inflamed, red, stiff, swollen and tender joints that eventually become deformed. It's also likely that you sleep poorly…are stiff for hours every morning…feel tired a lot of the time…and have intermittent fevers, when inflammation flares.

RA could drive you to drink. And maybe it should, according to a new study.

Less Pain and Inflammation

Researchers from the University of Sheffield in England studied 1,877 people—874 had RA and 1,003 didn't.

The more alcohol imbibed by people with RA, the less severe their disease.

"We found that patients who had drunk alcohol most frequently had symptoms that were 20 to 30% less severe than patients who had never drunk alcohol or drank infrequently," says James Maxwell, MD, a study researcher. "Their x-rays showed there was less damage to joints, blood tests showed lower levels of inflammation, and there was less joint pain, swelling and disability."

Not only did alcohol ease RA, but it also may have prevented it. The researchers also found that nondrinkers were four times more likely to develop RA than people who drank alcohol more than 10 days a month.

And in a recent Dutch study, when researchers compared drinkers with teetotalers, they found a link between drinking alcohol and a lower risk for RA (73% lower)—and a lower risk for several other types of arthritis…

●**Osteoarthritis,** the wear-and-tear disease (69% lower)

• **Psoriatric arthritis,** a possible accompaniment of the skin disease psoriasis (62% lower)

• **Reactive arthritis,** triggered by an infection in another area of the body (73% lower)

• **Spondyloarthropathy,** inflammatory arthritis of the spine (66% lower).

Researchers haven't figured out why alcohol may reduce the risk of arthritis, but they have theories. Alcohol alters the activity of the immune system, says Dr. Maxwell, "and this may influence the pathways by which RA develops." As for the symptoms of RA: alcohol can ease inflammation and reduce pain, he says.

Drink Safely and Healthfully

"I tell my patients with rheumatoid arthritis that a small amount of alcohol—within the guidelines of the medications they are taking—is unlikely to harm them, and may have some benefits for their arthritis," says Dr. Maxwell.

Caution: Combined with excess alcohol, certain medications for RA such as *methotrexate* (Rheumatrex) may cause liver damage. If you have RA, talk to your doctor about alcohol intake.

You could even regard alcohol as a type of medicine, says Anthony Caporale, a professional bar instructor and bar chef in New York City, and the producer and host of *Art of the Drink TV.*

"Alcohol is in fact a drug and needs to be viewed as a drug. Just as you wouldn't open your medicine cabinet and take a bunch of pills, so you need a correct 'dose' of alcohol.

"That means you should never drink more than one drink per hour, which is 12 ounces of beer, or 5 ounces of wine, or 1½ ounces of a spirit such as vodka in a mixed drink—all of which have approximately ½ ounce of alcohol. That level of intake matches your body's ability to eliminate alcohol from your system."

And many health experts recommend a moderate daily intake of alcohol—no more than two drinks a day for men and one drink a day for women.

Particularly healthful (and popular) drinks are made with fresh fruit, such as an Old Fashioned, Piña Colada, Daquiri or Mohito, says Caporale. "Take your favorite fruit or fruits—such as pineapple, peach, oranges or cherries—mash the fruit flesh down in the bottom of the glass, add a shot of your favorite liquor and top it off with soda water to lighten the drink and add effervescence. Basically, you're making an alcohol smoothie."

Healing Drinks

Here are three "healing" drink recipes developed by Tom Potisk, DC, a chiropractor in Caledonia, Wisconsin, and author of *Whole Health Healing: The Budget-Friendly Natural Wellness Bible for All Ages* (MavenMark). "These modified drink recipes are delicious, have just a little bit of alcohol, and my patients love them," he says.

Healing "Martini"

1 shot unsweetened cranberry juice
1 shot cherry ale (Try Samuel Smith Organic Cherry Fruit Ale, available online at *www.finewinehouse.com.*)
1 shot unsweetened coconut water (*Recommended:* Naked brand.)
A small dash of stevia (a natural sweetener)
Lemon twist, for garnish

Healing ingredients: The cranberry juice is antibacterial, says Dr. Potisk. The ale is a low-alcohol alternative to the standard high-alcohol martini, and cherries are anti-inflammatory. The coconut water contains electrolytes vital for healthy blood. Stevia, a natural sweetener, doesn't elevate blood sugar.

Healing Holiday Cocktail

1 shot glass of Lambrusco
1 shot glass of unsweetened coconut water
1 shake of bitters
1 shot glass of unsweetened pomegranate juice
1 shot glass of ginger ale
1 slice of Granny Smith green apple for garnish

Healing ingredients: The Lambrusco has low levels of alcohol, says Dr. Potisk. The pomegranate juice contains antioxidants that help the cardiovascular system. The bitters contain herbs helpful to digestion. Ginger is anti-inflammatory.

Healing Eggnog

1 cup unsweetened pineapple juice

½ cup unsweetened apple juice

1 raw egg (or replace with 2 tablespoons extra-virgin olive oil)

1 frozen well-ripened banana

1 tablespoon brandy

¼ teaspoon nutmeg

Combine in a blender and blend until smooth and frothy. Serve cold with a cinnamon stick garnish.

Healing ingredients: The egg or olive oil contains essential oils, says Dr. Potisk. The juices contain vitamin C. The banana contains minerals and fiber. Brandy has a high level of antioxidants.

James Maxwell, MD, consultant rheumatologist at the Rotherham Foundation NHS Trust and an honorary senior clinical lecturer in the Academic Rheumatology Group at the University of Sheffield.

Anthony Caporale, professional bar instructor and bar chef for two decades, producer and host of Art of the Drink TV and the companion DVD *Art of the Drink*, and former beverage manager or general manager at several leading New York City restaurants, including Mesa Grill, Flip and Forty Eight. *www.artofthedrink.com, www.anthonycaporale.com.*

Tom Potisk, DC, chiropractor in Caledonia, Wisconsin, and author of *Whole Health Healing: The Budget-Friendly Natural Wellness Bible for All Ages* (MavenMark). *www.wholehealthhealing.com.*

The Best Diet for Rheumatoid Arthritis— Stop Eating!

There are lots of different diets for better health, such as the Mediterranean diet and the Zone diet.

But research shows that one of the most effective diets for rheumatoid arthritis—a diet that can dramatically reduce pain—doesn't involve any food at all.

Because the "diet" is fasting—replacing food with water for a limited period of time.

Recent finding: A new study in the *Journal of the American Dietetic Association* analyzed past studies that looked at four different diets for treating the pain of rheumatoid arthritis (RA):

- **Vegetarian or vegan diet**
- **Mediterranean-style diet**
- **Elimination diet** (eliminating specific foods thought to worsen RA in some people, such as dairy products, eggs, wheat, beef or corn)
- **Fasting,** followed by a vegetarian diet.

The most effective of the four diets for pain relief: fasting, followed by a vegetarian diet.

Little-known fact: There have been more than 30 studies on fasting in people with RA, with a study in the prestigious medical journal *The Lancet* concluding: "Fasting is an effective treatment for rheumatoid arthritis."

How Fasting Works

"The official position of the Arthritis Foundation is that there is no substantial relationship between diet and arthritis," says Alan Goldhamer, DC, a faculty member at Bastyr University in Seattle, founder of the True-North Health Center in Santa Rosa, California (where thousands of people have undergone medically supervised water-only fasts of 5 to 40 days), and coauthor of *The Pleasure Trap* (Book Publishing Company).

"But my clinical experience is completely different," he continues. "Over the past 28 years, I've seen more than 8,000 people undergo water-only fasting, and there has been a profound, consistent and predictable relationship between inflammation and pain— the hallmarks of arthritis—and the foods that people put or don't put in their mouths."

There are several possible mechanisms by which water-only fasting can influence rheumatoid arthritis and other autoimmune diseases, he says.

•**Detoxes the body.** Toxins can interfere with the health of cells and the immune system. Fasting may help remove toxins that entered from outside the body (such as pesticide residues and heavy metals) and toxic accumulations generated inside the body (such as excess cholesterol and uric acid).

•**Improves blood sugar control.** Fasting can help normalize the high blood sugar levels that can damage joints.

•**Eliminates excess water.** "During a water-only fast, the body eliminates excess sodium and excess water, a process called natriuresis," says Dr. Goldhamer. "This can reduce joint swelling in arthritis."

•**Reduces inflammation.** During water-only fasting, there is a substantial and predictable reduction of many of the biomarkers of inflammation, such as C-reactive protein, he says.

•**Reduces "leaky gut syndrome."** "Leakages in the digestive tract allow proteins that should stay in the gut to move into the bloodstream—triggering the immune system to attack them," explains Dr. Goldhamer. "In genetically sensitive individuals, this can lead the immune system to attack its own tissues, producing autoimmune diseases such as rheumatoid arthritis. Eliminating milk protein and gluten-containing grains—first by water-only fasting—can allow the gut to heal and the immune system to normalize," he says.

•**Enhances enzymes.** Enzymes are the chemical spark plugs that power the body. Fasting makes them more active and efficient.

•**Assists "neuro-adaptation."** "In the US, most people are adapted to a diet that is high in salt and fat—and a diet low in those components doesn't taste good," says Dr. Goldhamer. "But if you completely eliminated salt and fat for a month and then returned to your typical diet, the high levels of salt would produce a burning sensation in your mouth and the high levels of fat would taste repulsive."

He also says that most people are "neuro-adapted" to eating too much—the mechanisms in their brain fail to send satiety signals even when they've eaten enough calories.

"A fast dramatically alters the neuro-adaptation process, so that afterward it's easy to transition a healthy, low-fat, low-salt, low-sugar, plant-based diet—because that diet tastes good."

Medically Supervised Fasting

The safest, most effective type of fasting—the type that produces the results just described—is medically supervised, water-only fasting, says Dr. Goldhamer.

Why can't you fast on your own? Dr. Goldhamer offers this simple answer: food addiction.

"Why is there a 97% failure rate in dieting for weight loss?" he asks. "It's because people are addicted to the high levels of sugar, salt and fat in the modern diet.

"Imagine asking an alcoholic to go on a dietlike process to overcome alcoholism. Dieters are asked to limit their food choices—so the alcoholic would be asked to limit his drinks to beer and wine so that he won't overindulge. Dieters are instructed to use smaller plates so they eat less—so the alcoholic would be instructed to put his drink in a smaller cup. Dieters are instructed to put down utensils between each bite—so the alcoholic would be told to put down his glass between each sip.

"Obviously, those strategies are an absurd way to overcome alcoholism—and they're an absurd way to overcome addiction to diets high in salt, sugar and fat. The alcoholic needs to stop drinking, and you need to stop eating.

"Water-only fasting—like abstinence from alcohol in a rehabilitative setting—is a way to overcome food addiction and then re-adapt to a wholly new and healthier approach to eating."

Dr. Goldhamer says that juice fasts don't have the purifying effects of a water-only fast. "Juice fasts are a modified feeding regimen, not a fast. You don't get the same results."

Bottom line: "Truly effective fasting requires guidance and support, and the period of fasting itself can be an ordeal," says Dr. Goldhamer. "But I've seen it produce health miracle after miracle in sick people who felt helpless, were told nothing could be done for their condition—and then were healed by fasting. Fasting makes use of the innate capacity of your body that is demonstrated every time you cut your finger—the capacity to heal itself."

Resource: You can find a list of doctors trained in supervised fasting at the Web site of the Natural Health Association. *www. healthscience.org.*

Alan Goldhamer, DC, faculty member at Bastyr University, founder and director of the TrueNorth Health Center in Santa Rosa, California, and coauthor of *The Pleasure Trap: Mastering the Inner Force That Undermines Health and Happiness* (Book Publishing Company). *www.healthpromoting.com.*

Fish Oil Fights Rheumatoid Arthritis

Rheumatoid arthritis (RA) is an autoimmune condition in which the joints (usually the hands, wrists and knees) become painful, swollen, red and deformed to varying degrees. While the cause is unknown, it is believed that the immune system malfunctions and attacks its own joint tissues, causing cartilage to degenerate. One of the best natural remedies is high doses of fish oil, which has been shown in studies to reduce stiffness and the need for nonsteroidal anti-inflammatory drugs. Look for a product that includes *eicosapentaenoic acid* (EPA) and *docosahexaenoic acid* (DHA). Take 6,000 mg daily of combined EPA and DHA. If you are on a blood-thinning medication, such as *warfarin* (Coumadin), check with your doctor before taking this. It takes about 12 weeks to achieve a therapeutic benefit from fish oil.

Mark A. Stengler, NMD, naturopathic medical doctor in private practice, Encinitas, California, and author of the *Bottom Line/Natural Healing* newsletter. *www.drstengler.com.*

Imaginary Pain Relief That Really Works

If you're one of the 50 million Americans with arthritis, you might find yourself imagining the worst—joints that progressively become stiffer and more painful...limiting your ability to move around...until you're living in a disease-created cage of frustration and pain.

But a recent study shows that you can literally imagine (and create!) another, better future, a future of less pain and more mobility—with a simple technique called guided imagery.

What it involves: "Imagery is a flow of thoughts that you can see, hear, feel, smell or taste—an inner representation of your experience or fantasies," says Martin L. Rossman, MD, a physician in California specializing in mind-body healing and author of *Guided Imagery for Self-Healing* (New World Library). "Guided imagery is a flow of focused imagery in a relaxed state of mind."

The Picture of Better Health

The study—led by Carol L. Baird, DNS, of the Indiana University School of Nursing in Indianapolis—involved 30 older women with osteoarthritis who were in moderate to severe pain.

Half the women were trained in guided imagery, and then listened to a guided-imagery tape for 12 minutes, twice a day, for four months. The other women simply rested for the same periods of time.

Results: After four months, the women practicing guided imagery had less pain, more mobility and used less pain medication. There was little change in the group that rested only.

Guided imagery may help relieve the symptoms of older adults with osteoarthritis, concluded the researchers in the journal *Pain Management Nursing*. And, they said, the technique is "inexpensive and easy to learn."

How it works: "There are several well-documented reasons why imagery and relaxation are effective with osteoarthritis," says

Leslie Davenport, a psychotherapist and clinical faculty member at the Institute for Health and Healing at the California Pacific Medical Center in San Francisco, and author of *Healing and Transformation Through Self-Guided Imagery* (Celestial Arts).

"First, stress and fear amplify pain signals in the brain. With the relaxation of guided imagery, you use the same neural pathways to calm the nervous system, which eliminates or reduces the brain's amplification of pain.

"Research shows that guided imagery also influences physical functions that scientists once thought weren't under conscious control, such as the neurotransmitters that relay messages from brain cell to brain cell. With relaxing imagery, this 'natural pharmacy' of the brain is accessed, and you secrete powerful pain-relieving chemicals such as endorphins and dopamine into the bloodstream.

People often 'brace themselves' against pain, creating tense muscles that actually add to the discomfort. The relaxation that accompanies guided imagery gently unbinds the tension, bringing an experience of ease.

Recent studies using brain scans show that when you imagine something, your body reacts as if it were actually happening. In other words, when you imagine seeing bright flowers and a sunny blue sky, you actually activate the part of your brain that processes visual input. When you imagine hearing the ocean waves, you activate the hearing part of your brain. And these activated parts of the brain send signals throughout the nervous system of the body.

"This is why athletes who visualize throwing the basketball perfectly through the hoop actually perform more accurately. They use the mind to train the body to respond more precisely. A person with arthritis can use this same mind/body phenomenon for pain relief and increasing ease of movement."

A Session of Guided Imagery

"While guided imagery is a completely natural process and available to everyone, it can take a little time to learn," says Davenport.

"Give it a chance to work, committing to a month of practice before trying to measure the results. I recommend initially practicing when the pain is low or just coming on, rather than when it is intense. Practicing twice a day, for 20 minutes at a time, is ideal, although any time spent in relaxation and imagery is valuable."

What images work best for a person with arthritis?

"I believe that each person should discover the relaxing imagery that is most meaningful to him or her, rather than following a generic script," she says. "The guided imagery that is most effective is the imagery that is the best match for you, at the time your imagery sessions begins. And the images can change and evolve during the session."

Here is Davenport's recommendation for a session of guided imagery…

1. Sit or lie comfortably in a way that allows you to be both relaxed and alert— free from phone calls or other distractions.

2. Take several generous breaths. Each time you breathe in, silently say the word *peace*. Every time you exhale, silently say the word *ease*, and imagine these qualities flowing through your body. Continue for about three minutes, until you are as relaxed as possible.

3. Allow an image to form of a relaxing, peaceful place, indoors or out. It might be an open field of flowers, a quiet room, a mountaintop or even a cloud. The important thing is that the image be a place that you find personally relaxing.

4. Fully engage all of your senses as you imagine this restful spot. Notice the sounds that are part of this environment. Feel the temperature. Breathe in the aromas. Observe the quality of the light and the variety of colors.

5. Once you have fully imagined your environment, notice how you're feeling and enjoy the vitality and tranquility in your body, mind and emotions. Simply enjoy these qualities for several minutes.

6. Now imagine yourself exploring your beautiful place—walking, bending and moving freely with ease and complete comfort for several moments.

7. Now come to rest again in your peaceful environment, and imagine yourself bringing the same ease, comfort and freedom of movement into your familiar day-to-day settings—at home and wherever you go.

8. Slowly allow the images to fade for now, but keep the wonderful feelings with you, as you bring your attention back to your room and open your eyes.

Resource: You can download a free MP3 recording of a guided relaxation session that allows you to add your own, special images on the "Books, Audios, Articles" page at *www.lesliedavenport.com.*

Martin Rossman, MD, author of *Guided Imagery for Self-Healing* (New World Library). *www.healingmind.org.*

Carol Baird, DNS, CNS, associate professor in the Department of Adult Health at the Indiana University School of Nursing in Indianapolis.

Leslie Davenport, psychotherapist and clinical faculty member at the Institute for Health and Healing at the California Pacific Medical Center in San Francisco, and author of *Healing and Transformation Through Self-Guided Imagery* (Celestial Arts). *www.lesliedavenport.com.*

New Treatment for Arthritis Pain

Flavocoxid is a natural supplement that is a combination of *flavonoids* (anti-inflammatory plant chemicals). Like non-steroidal anti-inflammatory drugs (NSAIDs), flavocoxid suppresses pain-producing enzymes but is less likely to cause such side effects as gastrointestinal bleeding, so it is helpful for people who experience problems taking aspirin. It is sold at pharmacies as a capsule under the brand name Limbrel and requires a prescription. If you have osteoarthritis and can't use NSAIDs, ask your doctor about flavocoxid.

Caution: It may not be covered by insurance and can cost $4/day.

UC Berkeley Wellness Letter, 500 Fifth Ave., New York City 10110.

Glucosamine and Chondroitin— Don't Believe the Anti-Supplement Studies

Millions of Americans with osteoarthritis (OA) try to slow the progress of their painful disease with the supplements glucosamine and chondroitin sulfate, compounds that play a key role in the creation, maintenance and repair of cartilage, the cushion between joints.

And every one of them is wasting their money.

At least that was the message from Swiss scientists who recently conducted a "meta-analysis" of 10 studies on glucosamine and chondroitin, involving nearly 4,000 people with knee or hip OA.

"Glucosamine, chondroitin, and their combination do not reduce joint pain or have an impact on narrowing of joint space," concluded the researchers, in bmj.com, the online version of the *British Medical Journal.* (In OA, joint space narrows as cartilage erodes.)

And headlines in the US echoed their findings...

• **"Popular Joint Pain Remedies May Not Work,"** said United Press International.

• **"Glucosamine no better than placebo,"** reported ABC News.

• **"More Evidence that Glucosamine, Chondroitin Won't Help Ailing Joints,"** declared *Business Week.*

But those headlines would have been more accurate if they'd read something like this:

"Faulty Meta-Analysis Wrongly Discourages People with OA from Using Effective, Natural, Arthritis-Slowing Supplements."

Here's the real scientific story about glucosamine and chondroitin sulfate, including two recent positive meta-analyses that the media completely ignored (probably because bad news makes a better story).

Faulty Findings

There are several reasons why the meta-analysis conducted by the Swiss researchers was bad science, says Jason Theodosakis, MD, author of *The Arthritis Cure* and clinical associate professor at the University of Arizona College of Medicine in Tucson.

"The study looks impressive and has enough medical and scientific jargon to seem legitimate," he says. "But the study *isn't* legitimate—because the researchers made some fundamental mistakes that are not allowed in a reliable meta-analysis. The result is an improper conclusion—and improper damage to the supplements' reputation."

Meta-analyses are supposed to combine similar studies, explains Dr. Theodosakis. The studies should be of similar types of people (age, race, sex, etc)…with problems in the same area of the body (knee or hip or back, etc.)…who used the same form and dosage of a treatment…for the same period of time…with each study using the same measurements of outcome.

"The researchers failed in each of these areas," says Dr. Theodosakis. "They just seemed to pick and choose a fraction of the 58 studies that have been conducted on these supplements to create their own conclusion." (He suspects the researchers may have had a hidden agenda: to discourage the British government from covering the costs of the supplements, which are covered in other countries of the European Union, where the supplements are prescription drugs.)

Two Positive Studies

And it seems the media also pick and choose the studies they want to report. While the negative meta-analysis was featured in articles worldwide, two other recent positive meta-analyses were mostly ignored.

- **Standout scientific evidence.** In one, researchers at the University of Maryland School of Medicine analyzed three, two-year studies on chondroitin and knee OA. The results demonstrated a "significant effect of chondroitin sulfate on the reduction in the rate of decline in joint space," reported the

researchers in the journal *Osteoarthritis and Cartilage*. In other words, chondroitin slowed the progress of the disease. And they noted that their results support the recommendations of the prestigious Osteoarthritis Research Society International for use of chondroitin sulfate in patients with OA.

In another meta-analysis, published in *Rheumatology International*, a team of Korean researchers analyzed six studies involving 1,502 people with knee OA. They found that after two to three years of use, the two compounds "may retard degenerative processes affecting knee joint cartilage."

In fact, there are dozens of studies showing that glucosamine and chondroitin work, says Dr. Theodosakis. "Glucosamine and chondroitin are the oral therapies with the best risk-to-benefit ratio of any treatment for osteoarthritis." They can…

- **Slow the disease**—lessen the loss of cartilage and reduce the bone spurs that form on osteoarthritis joints

- **Provide pain relief,** compared with a placebo or FDA-approved pain relievers such as acetaminophen

- **Reduce the need for pain relievers**

- **Reduce the need for physical therapy or surgery** (One study shows that people with OA who regularly took glucosamine for a period of several years had 74% fewer joint replacements than people who didn't take it.)

- **Reduce health-care costs**

- **Cause fewer side effects than existing treatments.**

Suggested intake: Dr. Theodosakis recommends the following two products—Premier Joint, which includes 1,500 milligrams (mg) of glucosamine and 800 mg of chondroitin sulfate, and Cosamin DS, from Nutramax.

Premier Joint includes glucosamine, chondrotin sulfate and 80 mg of hyaluronic acid, a substance in synovial fluid, the movement-smoothing fluid in joints. "Synovitis—the inflammation of the membrane encapsulating synovial fluid—is a major source of pain and disability in OA," he says. "Five studies show that hyaluronic acid dramatically reduces synovitis."

Cosamin DS is widely available through online distributors and retail outlets (*www.nutramaxlabs.com*). Premier Joint is available at *www.drtheo.com* or phone 800-311-6883.

Jason Theodosakis, MD, author of *The Arthritis Cure* (St. Martin's) and *Maximizing the Arthritis Cure* (St. Martin's), clinical associate professor at the University of Arizona College of Medicine in Tucson and a member of the oversight steering committee for the National Institute of Health's GAIT study on glucosamine and chondroitin. *www.drtheo.com.*

Curcumin: Herbal Cure For Arthritis Pain

"Curcumin—the active ingredient in turmeric, the most popular spice in the cuisine of India—is a compound so powerfully rich in anti-inflammatory and antioxidant actions that it has been shown to protect and improve the health of virtually every organ of the body," says Bharat Aggarwal, PhD, director of Experimental Therapeutics at the M.D. Anderson Cancer Center in Houston, and author of *Healing Spices: How to Use 50 Everyday and Exotic Spices to Boost Health and Beat Disease* (Sterling). "To date, thousands of animal and human studies from around the world have found that curcumin can combat more than 70 maladies, such as cancer, heart disease, type 2 diabetes and Alzheimer's disease."

Good news: You can add osteoarthritis (OA) to the list. Two new studies from Italian researchers show that a curcumin-containing supplement is effective in reducing pain and increasing mobility in people with the disease.

Study Details

The first study involved 50 people with severe OA who took painkilling medication on a regular basis. They were divided into two groups. One took a curcumin supplement specially formulated for maximum absorption. The other took a placebo.

Results: After three months, the people taking curcumin had a 58% decrease in arthritis symptoms. The people taking the placebo had a 2% decrease.

The folks taking curcumin could also walk 436% farther on an inclined treadmill. The placebo group could walk 63% farther.

And among the curcumin-takers, levels of C-reactive protein (CRP)—a biomarker of inflammation—dropped by an average of 150 points in a subgroup of people with high CRP. In the placebo subgroup with high CRP, average levels dropped only 53 points.

"These results," wrote the researchers in the journal *Panminerva Medica*, show that the special type of curcumin supplement used in the study is "clinically effective in the management and treatment of osteoarthritis."

• **Less painkilling medication and fewer side effects.** The people in the curcumin group used 63% fewer painkillers, such as nonsteroidal anti-inflammatory drugs (NSAIDs) and acetaminophen. The placebo group used 8% less painkillers.

NSAIDs kill approximately 16,000 people every year and hospitalize 100,000, mostly because of sudden and severe bleeding ulcers. The curcumin group had a 67% decrease in GI complications; the placebo group had a 12% decrease.

This "marked reduction of NSAID-associated GI problems…might be related to a reduced use of these drugs, to the known GI protective effects of curcumin, or to a combination of both," noted the researchers.

• **Less money spent on arthritis treatments.** The curcumin group had a 47% decrease in other nondrug treatments for arthritis, such as physical therapy, and in costs due to complications and office visits. The placebo group had a 6% decrease.

• **Fewer hospital admissions.** The curcumin group had a 63% drop in hospital admissions and related tests, compared with a 3% decrease for the placebo group.

Curcumin "is an effective and safe agent for the complementary management of osteoarthritis, leading to better disease control, a decreased use of NSAIDs, and an overall improvement of quality of life," concluded the researchers.

How it works: Curcumin works like a master switch to reduce inflammation, affecting many pro-inflammatory enzymes, such as COX-1 and COX-2, the same enzymes targeted by NSAIDs, explains Professor Giovanni Appendino, a study researcher at the University of Piemonte in Italy.

Super Curcumin

If curcumin is such a great natural anti-inflammatory, why hasn't anybody tested it before for arthritis?

Problem: Curcumin is poorly absorbed because it's quickly destroyed by the pH of the intestines. In fact, a study shows that people who took a daily dose of 12 grams of curcumin (a huge amount) had blood levels of only 50 nanograms per milliliter (a tiny amount).

Solution: The curcumin supplement used in the study was Meriva, which increases absorption by an astonishing 20-fold over regular curcumin. (That's 2,000%.) It does so by combining curcumin with *phosphatidylcholine* (a type of fat once called lecithin), a major component of cellular membranes. This special form of curcumin—a *phytosome*—stops the compound from being destroyed and improves its uptake by cells. "The increase in bioavailability matches the use of turmeric in Indian cuisine, where the spice is often combined with fatty foods," says Professor Appendino.

And not only is Meriva absorbed better, but it seems to work better, too. "No other curcumin product on the market has the type of clinical documentation as Meriva, as well as its record of safety in long-term use," says Professor Appendino.

Suggested intake: Two 500-milligrams (mg) tablets daily, one after breakfast and one after dinner, with your doctor's approval and supervision.

"Don't expect quick action from Meriva," says Professor Appendino. "Natural medicines need time to show their efficacy, and studies show that improvement with Meriva typically occurs after several weeks of use."

Meriva is widely available in retail and on-line outlets.

Bharat Aggarwal, PhD, professor of cancer research, biochemistry, immunology and experimental therapeutics, and director of the Cytokine Research Laboratory, at the M.D. Anderson Cancer Center in Houston. He is author of *Healing Spices: How to Use 50 Everyday and Exotic Spices to Boost Health and Beat Disease* (Sterling).

Giovanni Appendino, PhD, professor of chemistry at the University of Piemonte in Italy.

How People with Arthritis Can Avoid Joint Replacement

Arthritis is easily the most common cause of physical disability in America. A recent report from the National Institutes of Health (NIH) says that nearly 50 million Americans have doctor-diagnosed arthritis (including both osteoarthritis, or OA, and rheumatoid arthritis, or RA) and predicts that that number will soar to 67 million in the next 20 years. That's a lot of stiff, painful knees, hands, shoulders and feet!

Kimberly Beauchamp, ND, a licensed naturopathic physician and health and nutrition writer in North Kingstown, Rhode Island, treats many arthritis patients. *Here she shares some supplements and natural therapies that many arthritis patients find helpful…*

Pain Soothers for Arthritis Patients

● **Zyflamend.** This proprietary blend of supplements contains 10 anti-inflammatory plant extracts that can be helpful for many people with both OA and RA. Dr. Beauchamp has patients take one capsule twice daily with meals. (Available online at *www.newchapter.com* and at many health-food stores.)

● **Red seaweed extract.** Red seaweed extract (*Lithomanion calcarea*) can help people with OA. One study reported in *Nutrition Journal* and funded by Marigot, the company that makes Aquamin (a patented red seaweed extract), found that taking the extract for one month was associated with a

20% reduction in arthritis pain. Patients also reported less stiffness and better range of motion and were able to walk farther than those taking a placebo. A typical dose would be 2,400 mg of seaweed extract in capsule form each day, Dr. Beauchamp advises. (*Note:* Seaweed contains iodine in amounts that may be dangerous to thyroid patients.)

• **Vitamin D.** Recent research indicates that vitamin D may play a key role in slowing the development and progression of both OA and RA. If you have either, it's a good idea to get your blood level of vitamin D checked, says Dr. Beauchamp. If you are deficient, she suggests taking at least 1,000 IU of vitamin D-3 (cholecalciferol) each day.

• **Peat/peloid packs (also called balneotherapy).** Commonly used in Europe, this is a form of thermal mud therapy that holds heat particularly well. Peat (or peloid packs that are sheets of peat mud on fabric) is applied to the aching area for about 20 minutes. The treatment can be done at home, but Dr. Beauchamp says it is far better to work with a physical therapist or doctor who is knowledgeable in the technique, as the packs are cumbersome and must be carefully applied to protect the skin from burning.

Oldies but Goodies

Here are some other remedies that you've likely already heard about...

• **Fish oil (omega-3 fatty acids).** Effective at reducing inflammation for both RA and OA, studies show that omega-3s can be so helpful for RA patients that they sometimes can reduce their medications. OA patients usually see results quickly. Dr. Beauchamp says two grams of fish oil daily is a common dosage, while RA patients may require higher levels to benefit. Ask your doctor about the appropriate amount for you.

• **Glucosamine sulfate/chondroitin sulfate (or chondroitin sodium sulfate).** Dr. Beauchamp often prescribes 1,500 mg of glucosamine and 1,200 mg of chondroitin daily, divided into three doses.

Caution: Glucosamine and chondroitin often are derived from crabs and other hard-shelled sea creatures, so do not take them if you are allergic to shellfish. Glucosamine and chondroitin should also be avoided by people on blood-thinning medications such as *warfarin* (Coumadin).

• **Methylsulfonylmethane (MSM)** is a sulfur derivative is beneficial for some people with OA. It may help prevent cartilage degeneration, and it's also known to decrease pain and improve physical function. It's thought that MSM works better when combined with glucosamine—take one gram of MSM twice daily with meals.

Tried-and-True Relief

• **Massage and acupuncture.** Many people, including those with RA or OA, find these treatments to be soothing—it makes sense, since both techniques increase blood flow to the muscles and ligaments around the joints (particularly the knees and hips), which are stressed by arthritis.

• **Exercise.** Acknowledging that this is usually the last thing people in pain feel like doing, Dr. Beauchamp says exercise is still essential for both OA and RA patients.

The primary benefit: Exercise delivers fresh blood cells to the affected areas, bringing in nutrients and removing waste, including acidic waste products in the muscles that may provoke inflammation. She suggests swimming, walking or perhaps working with a trainer who is knowledgeable about arthritis.

• **Weight control.** Keeping your weight down reduces the pressure on painful joints for both OA and RA patients. The NIH study mentioned earlier in the story found twice as much arthritis in obese people as in people of healthy weight. One study showed that losing just 11 pounds reduced risk for knee OA by half and significantly reduced pain in the knees of those already afflicted.

Kimberly Beauchamp, ND, licensed naturopathic doctor and health and nutrition writer based in North Kingstown, Rhode Island. Her blog, *Eat Happy*, helps take the drama out of healthy eating. *www.eathappyblog.com.*

Arthritis in The Family

The most important thing you can do to prevent or delay developing arthritis if it runs in your family is to maintain a healthy weight. If you are overweight now, don't be discouraged. It doesn't take a lot of weight loss to significantly decrease your osteoarthritis risk—dropping even 10 pounds will help.

Follow a diet that emphasizes fruits, vegetables, whole grains and healthy fats, such as monounsaturated fats (for instance, from olives, olive oil, avocados and nuts) and omega-3s (from dark oily fish, such as salmon, tuna or sardines, or from flaxseed). This not only promotes weight control but also reduces arthritis risk by providing inflammation-fighting antioxidants and essential fatty acids.

You might also consider supplementing with glucosamine and/or chondroitin sulfate. Though there is disagreement in the medical community about their usefulness, some data suggest that they may slow cartilage loss and relieve symptoms.

Regular exercise is key. Weight-bearing activities (such as walking, yoga and tai chi) help keep joints resilient. Do take care to guard against injury to your joints because the resulting inflammation, misalignment or damage to the bone or cartilage could increase your risk for arthritis. For instance, if you already have knee problems, biking and swimming are better choices.

If you're still concerned about a family history of arthritis, it's a good idea to ask your doctor for a referral to a physical therapist who can assess your gait and help you correct any misalignments that may cause excess wear on your joints. Such an evaluation is also appropriate for a person who is overweight or obese, has joint pain or has a history of injury to a joint.

Joanne M. Jordan, MD, MPH, professor and chief of the division of rheumatology, allergy and immunology at the University of North Carolina and director of UNC's Thurston Arthritis Research Center, both in Chapel Hill.

Stronger Thighs Lessen Pain in Arthritic Knees

Researchers tested strength in the quadriceps (front thigh muscles) and measured cartilage loss (using MRI scans) in people with arthritis of the knees. Participants' knees were scanned again 15 and 30 months later.

Results: Participants whose quadricep strength measured in the highest one-third had 60% less cartilage loss behind the kneecap than those in the lowest one-third. They also reported less knee pain.

Best: If you have arthritis in your knees, ask your doctor about taking swimming or water aerobics classes to safely build strength in your quadriceps.

Shreyasee Amin, MD, MPH, rheumatologist, Mayo Clinic, Rochester, Minnesota, and leader of a study of 265 people.

Body-Balancing Workout For Pain-Free Joints

When it comes to our muscles, stronger is better, right? Not necessarily. When one muscle is too strong compared with another, it creates an imbalance that leaves our joints vulnerable to inflammation, injury and pain.

According to physical therapist and certified athletic trainer Phil Page, PhD, PT, coauthor of *Assessment and Treatment of Muscle Imbalance*, as we age, certain muscles typically become overstretched, which weakens them…while certain other muscles tend to shorten, becoming strong but tight. Scientists aren't sure why this happens (though poor posture is a likely factor), but they do know that it causes abnormal wear and tear on joints.

Example: In the shoulder joint, various muscles pull from different directions on the ball at the top of the *humerus* (upper arm bone). This keeps the ball perfectly centered in the socket, as it should be. But if the muscles at the back of the shoulder become weak (as they often do) and those in front become strong and tight, the ball is pulled slightly off center...which eventually leads to joint deterioration.

Dr. Page explains that osteoarthritis often follows patterns based on muscle imbalances—for instance, weak muscles in the fronts of the thighs (quadriceps) plus tight hamstrings at the backs of the thighs (hamstrings) contribute to knee arthritis. Muscle imbalances also are associated with tendon problems, such as the painful inflammatory knee condition *patellar tendinitis*.

Fortunately, we can reduce the risk for such problems with a workout specifically designed to restore balance to joints by strengthening weak muscles (or those likely to become weak) and stretching tight ones.

Workout for Balanced Muscles

Since most people are prone to muscle imbalances, the following exercises are appropriate for just about anyone, Dr. Page says. (Of course, check with your doctor before beginning any new exercise program to make sure it is safe for you.)

Recommended: Do the moves below every other day as an addition to your usual fitness routine. The only equipment needed is a five-foot-long elastic resistance band (available at sporting-goods stores or from online vendors such as Amazon.com). Start with the stretchiest band for light resistance...work up to greater resistance by using a stronger band and/or adjusting your hand position.

To download a PDF with photos that illustrate the exercises below, visit *www. strengthbandtraining.com/2010/12/exercises-for-muscle-balance* and click on the image beneath "Exercises for Muscle Balance."

To prevent or reduce knee problems...

- **Strengthen quadriceps.**
Start: Sit in a sturdy chair, feet together. Loop center of band around right ankle. Grasp ends of band in left hand...anchor exposed portion of band firmly beneath left foot.

Move: Slowly extend right leg until knee is straight...hold for two seconds...slowly return to starting position. Do 12 to 15 repetitions ("reps"), then switch sides.

- **Stretch hamstrings.**
Start: Lie on your back, right leg straight on floor. Bend left knee in toward chest and loop center of band around sole of left foot. With hands, grasp ends of band. Straighten left leg as much as you comfortably can, sole of left foot facing ceiling.

Move: Keeping left leg straight, gently pull on ends of band to bring leg closer to you, until you feel a good stretch at the back of the leg...hold 15 to 30 seconds...return to starting position. Do three to five reps, then switch sides.

To prevent or reduce hip problems...

- **Strengthen gluteus medius (outer hip).**
Start: Stand with feet shoulder-width apart. Loop center of band around right ankle...grasp ends of band in left hand...anchor exposed portion of band firmly beneath left foot. Shift weight to left foot.

Move: Keeping knees straight and torso erect, raise right leg out to the side about 12 inches...hold for two seconds...slowly return to starting position. Do 12 to 15 reps, then switch sides.

- **Stretch piriformis (buttocks).** You do not need a band for this exercise.
Start: Sit in a sturdy chair. Bend left leg and place left ankle over right knee in a figure-four position.

Move: Without rounding your back, gently lean forward as far as you comfortably can... hold 15 to 30 seconds...return to starting position. Do three to five reps, then switch sides.

To prevent or reduce shoulder and upper-back problems...

- **Strengthen posterior rotator cuff (back of shoulder).**
Start: Tie one end of band around a fixed object (such as the doorknob of a closed door) at waist height...stand so that the object to which the band is tied is on your right side. Wrap free end of band around left

hand…bend left elbow to 90° so left hand is nearly touching belly button.

Move: Keeping left elbow tucked into your side and forearm parallel to floor, rotate the forearm outward (by rotating at left shoulder joint) so left hand moves slowly to the left (as if on a hinge) as far as you comfortably can…hold for two seconds…return to starting position. Do 12 to 15 reps, then switch sides.

● **Strengthen rhomboids and middle trapezius (upper back).**

Start: Sit in a sturdy chair, feet together, legs stretched out in front of you, knees slightly bent…wrap center of band around soles of feet. Grasping ends of band, hold arms out in front of you, angled downward and fairly straight, so hands are at hip height.

Move: Bending arms, pull hands in and up toward the sides of your waist, elbows pointing behind you. (Don't move legs.) Keeping shoulders down, squeeze shoulder blades toward each other…hold for two seconds…slowly return to starting position. Do 12 to 15 reps.

● **Stretch pectorals (chest).** You do not need a band for this exercise.

Start: Sit all the way back in a sturdy low-backed chair. Reaching arms behind you (and behind chair back), clasp hands at hip height, interlocking fingers so palms face each other and arms are fairly straight.

Move: Keeping head up and neck relaxed, slowly raise arms as high as you comfortably can…hold 15 to 30 seconds…return to starting position. Do two to four reps.

Phil Page, PhD, PT, physical therapist, certified athletic trainer and certified strength and conditioning specialist. He is director of the Thera-Band Academy, a fitness education firm, and an instructor of kinesiology at Louisiana State University, both in Baton Rouge. He is the coauthor of three books, including *Assessment and Treatment of Muscle Imbalance and Strength Band Training* (both from Human Kinetics). *www. thera-bandacademy.com.*

Arthritic Knees? Surprising Shoe Recommendation

If you have painful arthritic knees, you probably think that you should be wearing shoes that look and feel supportive—thick-soled, sturdy ones like super-structured sneakers. Not so! A recent study from Rush University Medical Center in Chicago discovered that such footwear doesn't help the problem. In fact, the research concluded that shoes offering the least amount of foot support are better for folks who suffer from osteoarthritis in their knee or knees.

Rheumatologist and study author Najia Shakoor, MD, associate professor of internal medicine at Rush, explains that when people who have knee arthritis walk around, it increases the load (or force) exerted on the inner knee, which is where arthritis most commonly occurs. This additional pressure erodes cartilage even further, eventually resulting in the hideously painful bone-on-bone contact that characterizes arthritis at its worst.

Dr. Shakoor's team evaluated the differences in load created by walking in a variety of types of shoes—heavy-soled clogs (Dansko)…walking shoes with sturdy foot support (Brooks Addiction)…lightweight, flexible sneakers with thin soles (Puma H Street)…ordinary rubber flip-flops…as well as going barefoot.

Less Is Best

To the surprise of many, researchers found that the biomechanics of the foot and knee working together created the least load when patients walked barefoot. Next best were the most minimal of shoes, such as thin-soled sneakers and even rubber flip-flops! Far better for the knees than the rigid structure of clogs and heavy-duty athletic shoes, these flexible types of shoes reduced knee load by as much as 15%.

Now, before anyone runs out to Walmart to buy flip-flops, take note. While they may have their place (the beach, for instance), Dr. Shakoor and many other experts caution against flip-flops for many folks—most particularly those with balance issues—because they may cause you to trip. Instead, look for something that has flat, flexible soles but doesn't "flip or flop" while you walk—for example, it's not hard to find sandals that strap the foot securely to the sole. Ballet flats or slip-on boat shoes (such as Docksides) are also good choices. And, when you get home, this is a great excuse to kick them off—which is what feels best of all!

Najia Shakoor, MD, associate professor of internal medicine at Rush Medical College, Chicago.

How Bad Will Your Arthritis Get?

It's not exactly a crystal ball, but doctors have a new way to predict the future health of your knees—research shows that patients who have both osteoarthritis of the knee and bone cysts are headed for severe arthritis. But don't get discouraged—if you're not there yet, you still have time to change the outcome.

Patience White, MD, chief public health officer at the National Arthritis Foundation, pediatric rheumatologist and a professor of medicine and pediatrics in the Department of Medicine at George Washington University, explains that bone cysts (abnormal pockets of synovial fluid, which is the liquid that normally lubricates joints) are present in about half of patients with osteoarthritis of the knee—most particularly if it is advanced. She says the relationship between the two is a chicken and egg dilemma—it's unclear whether people have bone cysts because of their severe arthritis or it's the other way around, that the arthritis is made more severe by the bone cysts.

To learn more about this relationship, researchers at Monash University in Melbourne, Australia, recruited and examined 109 people with knee osteoarthritis. About half of these people also had bone cysts. *The group*

was then reexamined two years later, and researchers found that...

• **Patients whose previous MRI showed both bone cysts and arthritis** at the start of the study experienced an average 9.3% loss of cartilage.

• **Those who'd had arthritis and bone marrow lesions**—less serious abnormalities that may or may not lead to bone cysts—had a 6.3% cartilage loss.

• **Individuals with arthritis only**—no cysts or bone lesions—experienced only a 2.6% cartilage loss.

With increasing bone abnormalities (i.e., lesions and cysts), the likelihood that a patient would require knee replacement also rose significantly. This research was reported in *Arthritis Research & Therapy*.

Fight Arthritis Aggressively!

Dr. White says that there's more to be learned from a larger osteoarthritis study going on now at the National Institutes of Health. In the meantime, she says there's not much you can do to treat bone cysts (they're removed surgically only in rare cases where they present specific difficulties), but their presence should be viewed as a call to action. *To that end, Dr. White urges anyone with knee osteoarthritis to...*

• **Stay active**—movement is the best medicine, Dr. White says. Physical activities such as swimming, walking, stretching and range-of-motion exercises keep your joints flexible and improve muscle strength, which helps take the strain off joints. If you are not sure about the right exercises for people with arthritis, check with your doctor and go to *www.arthritis.org* and look for the Arthritis Foundation Life Improvement Series that offers programs and DVDs on how to exercise.

• **Shed pounds if you are overweight.** The heavier you are, the more damage is done to weight-bearing joints like the knees—but the good news is, every pound lost reduces the load on each knee when you stand or walk by four pounds. That's a big result from just a bit of weight loss!

Patience White, MD, vice president of public health, National Arthritis Foundation, pediatric rheumatologist and professor of medicine and pediatrics, Department of Medicine, George Washington University School of Medicine and Health Sciences, Washington, DC.

Exercises That Cause Arthritis

If you're a middle-aged person who doesn't have osteoarthritis, but you do have one or more of the following risk factors for developing it, read the rest of this article very carefully—because a new study shows that if you regularly engage in certain types of exercises and activities, you're more likely to end up with painful knee osteoarthritis (OA).

The risk factors:

• **You're overweight.**

• **You've had a knee injury.**

• **You've had knee surgery.**

• **A close relative**—a father, mother or sibling—has had a total knee replacement.

• **You sometimes have knee pain, stiffness or swelling.**

If you're a match for one or more of the above risk factors, you need to know—and avoid—the exercises and activities that may threaten your knees…

Study Details

The study was conducted by several researchers, including Thomas M. Link, MD, professor of radiology and chief of musculoskeletal imaging at the University of California, San Francisco (UCSF), and presented at a recent meeting of the Radiological Society of North America.

The researchers examined the knees of 165 middle-aged people (45 to 55) who didn't have osteoarthritis. They used a unique type of magnetic resonance imaging (MRI) that can detect pre-arthritic damage to knee cartilage—the bone-covering, bone-cushioning tissue that erodes in osteoarthritis, causing the ends of bones to rub together. The sensitive scan detected water content (less is better)… the structure of collagen fibers (they should be neatly lined up)…the level of *glycosaminoglycans* (compounds that keeps cartilage elastic)…and other microscopic measures.

The researchers also grouped the participants by the type of exercise they did (light-intensity, moderate-intensity, high-intensity) and by how much they participated in knee-bending activities, such as climbing stairs.

Result: People with a risk factor who regularly engaged in high-intensity, high-impact, knee-stressing types of exercise—such as running, basketball, soccer or downhill skiing—had the most damage to their cartilage.

"According to the results of our study, participating in a high-impact activity, such as running, more than one hour per day, at least three times a week, is associated with more degenerated cartilage—and potentially a high risk for the development of osteoarthritis," says Dr. Link.

On the other hand (or other knee), those who engaged in light-intensity exercise such as walking had the least damage to their knee cartilage.

"Our findings indicate that light exercise, such as frequent walking—is a safer choice for maintaining healthy cartilage," says Keegan K. Hovis, RN, a study researcher.

The researchers also found that people who engaged in frequent knee-bending activities—climbing up at least 10 flights of stairs a day…regularly bending the knees to lift objects weighing more than 25 pounds… squatting…kneeling or deep-knee bending for at least 30 minutes a day—also had damaged cartilage.

And that result held up for people with and without the risk factors.

Bottom line: "Cartilage doesn't regrow, like muscle or bone," says Dr. Link. "If you have a muscle tear or a fractured bone, you're probably going to heal very nicely. But once cartilage is lost, it's lost forever.

"If you have risk factors for osteoarthritis such as overweight or a previous knee injury, you have to be very conscientious about protecting your cartilage—because you're not going to have any symptoms of cartilage loss until the loss is very advanced, and you experience the pain and stiffness of osteoarthritis.

"However, you can protect your cartilage—and reduce your risk for osteoarthritis. Maintain a healthy weight. Avoid strenuous, high-impact exercises. Avoid risky, knee-bending activities."

Exercises to avoid if you're at risk: Any exercise that is high impact, such as…

● **Running** (for more than one hour a day, more than three times a week)

● **Tennis** (and other racquet sports, such as racquetball or squash)

● **Basketball**

● **Soccer**

● **Downhill skiing.**

Exercises to favor if you're at risk: Any exercise that isn't high impact, or doesn't involve sudden, fast movements, such as…

● **Walking or hiking**

● **Swimming**

● **Using an elliptical trainer** (an exercise machine that works both the upper and lower body and is specifically designed to put less stress on joints).

Exercising with Arthritis

Dr. Link points out that once you have osteoarthritis, it's critical to continue (or start) a low-intensity exercise program such as walking.

"Once joints are damaged, inactivity is the worst thing you can do to them," he says. "Muscles around the joint atrophy, which creates more irregularity in the joint, and possibly more damage."

Several recent studies demonstrate how important regular exercise is for people with arthritis…

● **Less pain, better functioning.** In a five-year study of 150 people with knee OA, those who exercised regularly had less pain and better daily functioning, reported Dutch researchers in *Arthritis Care & Research*.

● **Works for rheumatoid arthritis (RA), too.** French scientists analyzed 14 studies on RA and exercise, involving more than 1,000 people, and found that those who exercised regularly had less joint pain and better function. "Aerobic exercise is a safe and beneficial intervention" for people with RA, concluded the researchers in *Arthritis Care & Research*.

● **Try tai chi.** The gentle, flowing, low-impact movements of tai chi reduced pain, stiffness and fatigue in people with osteoarthritis and rheumatoid arthritis, reported a team of researchers from the University of North Carolina at Chapel Hill School of Medicine, who studied 354 people with arthritis participating in the Arthritis Foundation's Tai Chi program.

Resource: To find an Arthritis Foundation tai chi class near you, go to *www.arthritis.org* and click on "Local Office Directory," or phone 800-283-7800.

Thomas M. Link, MD, professor of radiology and chief of musculoskeletal imaging at the University of California, San Francisco (UCSF).

Keegan K. Hovis, RN, research associate in the Department of Radiology at University of California, San Francisco (UCSF).

Gout-Free Life Is a Bowl of Cherries

Once upon a time, gout was called "the disease of kings"—the toe-throbbing price paid for a life of indulging in the fancy meats and drinks that only royalty could afford.

Well, scientists at the Boston University School of Medicine have news for us—the disease of kings is back. Only now it's the disease of regular folk who eat at Burger King and sleep on king-size beds. Millions of us either have gout or are at risk for getting it.

Latest finding: The rate of gout in the US has risen by 31% over the last 15 years, with 8.3 million Americans having the disease, reported the researchers at a recent annual meeting of the American College of Rheumatology.

And the rate of *hyperuricemia* (pre-gout, with blood levels of uric acid rising nearly to the point where they can congeal into the needlelike crystals of gout that painfully stab at joints) rose to 21% of American adults. That includes 31% of folks 65 and older.

"In the twenty-first century, the prevalence of gout and hyperuricemia is substantial," says Yanyan Zhu, PhD, research assistant professor at the Boston University School of Medicine and the study's lead researcher.

Anything that increases your level of uric acid can increase your risk for gout—including aging, overweight, drinking too much alcohol (particularly beer, which contains high levels of purines, a molecule that turns into uric acid) and high blood pressure.

But if you do end up with gout, two new studies show that there's a simple, natural way to help prevent agonizing gout attacks—the hot, stiff, swollen joints…the skin around the joints that turns shiny and red…the fever and chills…and the pain that's so intense even the slightest brush of a bedsheet on a gout-afflicted joint can be excruciating.

The preventive secret: Cherries.

Fruitful Treatment

The first study on cherries was reported at an annual meeting of the American College of Rheumatology by a team of researchers led by Yuqing Zhang, D.Sc, professor of medicine and epidemiology at Boston University School of Medicine.

For their study, the researchers enlisted 633 people with gout who had suffered a gout attack within the past year. Every time they had a new attack, they logged onto the Internet and filled out a lengthy questionnaire about their activities in the previous 48 hours to the attack—including their consumption of cherries, a popular home remedy for gout. They were also asked to log on and note when they were free of attacks for at least three months. After analyzing the data, the researchers found that…

● **Eating 20 cherries (one cup) in the previous two days was linked to a 50% lower risk of having a gout attack.**

● **Using cherry extract in the previous two days was linked to a 40% lower risk of a gout attack.**

Another new study on cherries and gout was conducted by researchers at the Robert Wood Johnson Medical School/University of Medicine & Dentistry of New Jersey in New Brunswick, and reported at the annual meeting of the European League Against Rheumatism.

Among 24 patients who took a tablespoon of cherry concentrate twice a day for at least four months, gout attacks were reduced by 50% or more in 9 out of 10 patients. In four patients, gout attacks stopped completely.

"Tart cherry juice concentrate should be considered an additional treatment in the control of gout," says Naomi Schlesinger, MD, the study leader.

Why it works: Both teams of researchers point to a reduction in inflammation caused by high levels of anthocyanins, antioxidants in tart cherries (and other red and purple fruits and vegetables).

The Robert Wood researchers also reported a laboratory experiment that showed a compound in tart cherries cuts the production of interleukin 1-beta, a chemical that triggers inflammation.

Cherry Therapy

Want to prevent gout attacks with cherries? Unfortunately, cherries are a seasonal fruit, explains Andrew LaPointe, owner of Traverse Bay Farms and author of the *Tart Cherry Health Report.*

To make sure you have a reliable, year-round dietary source of gout-beating cherries, he recommends one ounce a day of Montmorency tart cherry juice concentrate, which delivers 25 milligrams (mg) of anthocyanins.

Resource: You can order the concentrate (as well as cherries in season, tart cherry juice, cherry powder and cherry capsules) at *www.traversebayfarms.com.* Or call 877-746-7477.

More Ways to Control Gout

Recent research has revealed several other natural ways to help control or prevent gout…

●**More water.** Researchers linked drinking four to eight 8-ounce glasses of water daily to a 42% reduced risk of gout attacks. "This is a simple, effective lifestyle change for people with gout," says Tuhina Neogi, MD, PhD, an associate professor of medicine at Boston University Medical Center.

●**Less coffee.** Dr. Neogi and her colleagues also found that when people who typically drink two or fewer servings of caffeinated beverages a day drank three or more servings, their risk of a gout attack increased by 40 to 80%. Drinking six daily servings of caffeinated beverages was linked to three times the risk.

●**Less soda.** In a 22-year study of nearly 79,000 women, researchers at the Boston University School of Medicine found that women who drank one daily serving of soda, sweetened with a big dose of high-fructose corn syrup, also known as corn sugar, had a 74% higher risk of gout than women who drank less than one serving per month. Women who drank two or more daily servings had a 240% higher risk.

What happens: Fructose increases uric acid.

Yanyan Zhu, PhD, research assistant professor, Boston University School of Medicine.

Yuqing Zhang, D.Sc, professor of medicine and epidemiology in the Clinical Epidemiology Research and Training Unit, Boston University School of Medicine.

Naomi Schlesinger, MD, associate professor of medicine at the Robert Wood Johnson Medical School/University of Medicine & Dentistry of New Jersey in New Brunswick.

Andrew LaPointe, owner of Traverse Bay Farms and author of the *Tart Cherry Health Report. www.tartcherryhealthreport.com, www.traversebayfarms.com.*

Tuhina Neogi, MD, PhD, associate professor of medicine, Boston University Medical Center.

Got Gout? Drink Skim Milk

Elevated blood levels of uric acid increase the risk for gout, a painful and potentially disabling form of arthritis that typically affects the feet.

Recent finding: Within three hours after healthy study participants drank about 27 ounces of skim milk, their uric acid levels fell by about 10%.

Implication: Increasing the amount of skim milk in the diet may help prevent the development of gout and also assist with treatment for the disease.

More research is needed—but meanwhile, ask your doctor about drinking more skim milk.

Nicola Dalbeth, MD, senior lecturer in the Department of Clinical Medicine at the University of Auckland, New Zealand, and leader of a study of 16 people.

Chapter 4

BRAIN, MIND & MEMORY

Three B Vitamins That Protect the Brain

I f you want to slow the inevitable brain shrinkage of aging…if you want to protect your memory and other mental functions…if you want to prevent Alzheimer's disease and Parkinson's disease—then you may want to take a nutritional supplement with high levels of three B vitamins: vitamin B-12, vitamin B-6 and folic acid.

Latest development: Several new studies show that these three B vitamins can shield an aging brain from memory loss and neurological disease—and that *choline*, another B vitamin, may even help with the first stages of Alzheimer's disease.

Brain-Saving Studies

Researchers from England, Sweden, the US and Japan conducted the B-vitamin studies.

Study #1: **B vitamins slow brain shrinkage.** Researchers from Oxford University in England studied 168 people, aged 70 and older, who had mild cognitive impairment (MCI)—the stage of mental decline before Alzheimer's, with noticeable memory loss and language problems.

Troubling statistics: Ten percent of people 65 or older have MCI. Fifteen percent will develop Alzheimer's within one year, and 50% will develop it within five years.

For two years, half the study participants took a B-vitamin supplement containing 800 micrograms (mcg) of folate, 500 mcg of vitamin B-12 and 20 milligrams (mg) of vitamin B-6. The other half took a placebo.

At the beginning and end of the study, the researchers took three key measurements…

1. Blood levels of homocysteine, an amino acid derived from the breakdown of *methionine*, a component of protein.

Hidden risk: When blood levels of vitamin B-6, B-12 and folic acid are low, homocysteine levels can become abnormally high and may damage the brain.

2. Brain shrinkage.

3. Cognitive function.

Results: People who took the three B vitamins for two years had a 53% greater reduction in homocysteine levels than those who didn't take the vitamins. They also had a remarkable 30% slower rate of brain shrinkage. And those with the slowest rate of shrinkage had the highest scores in mental tests.

"This is the first study to show a potential disease-modifying effect of a treatment in people with MCI, and the first study to report a treatment that slows brain atrophy," says David Smith, MD, the study leader.

What to do: "My personal view is that people with MCI should have their homocysteine measured," says Dr. Smith. "If levels are above 10 millimoles per liter, they should talk to their doctor about starting supplementation with the three B vitamins at the dosage levels used in our study."

Study #2: Low levels of B-12, high risk for Alzheimer's. Researchers from the Aging Research Center at the Karolinska Institute in Sweden studied 271 people, aged 65 to 79, who didn't have Alzheimer's. At the start of the study, they measured two factors:

1. Blood levels of homocysteine

2. Blood levels of *holotranscobalamin*, the most biologically active component of B-12.

Seven years later, the researchers re-examined the study participants—and found that 6% of them had developed Alzheimer's. Those with Alzheimer's had average homocysteine levels 16% higher than those who didn't develop the disease. And those with Alzheimer's also had B-12 levels that were 34% lower.

"Low levels of B-12 are surprisingly common in the elderly—and may play an important role in the development of Alzheimer's disease," says Babak Hooshmand, PhD, the study leader. And not only because low B-12 is linked to high homocysteine. B-12 is also needed to maintain normal levels of *S-adenosylmethionine*, a compound that plays an important role in many brain functions.

Study #3: Improvement in early Alzheimer's. Researchers at the Massachusetts Institute of Technology studied 225 people in the early stage of Alzheimer's, dividing them into two groups.

One group drank a daily beverage containing three ingredients: 1) *choline*, a B vitamin, 2) *uridine*, a component of RNA and 3) *DHA*, an omega-3 fatty acid. The other group drank a placebo beverage.

After 12 weeks, 40% of those drinking the choline-containing beverage had an improvement in their ability to remember words, compared with 24% in the placebo group. People with the mildest cases of Alzheimer's showed the most improvement.

How it works: Animal studies show that a combination of these three compounds can help build synapses, the branchlike extensions on neurons that help relay messages from brain cell to brain cell. "If you can increase the number of synapses by enhancing their production, you might to some extent avoid the loss of cognitive ability," says Richard Wurtman, MD, the leader of the study, which appeared in *Alzheimer's and Dementia*.

If these nutrients are successful in helping Alzheimer's patients, they may also help people with Parkinson's, another disease in which there are too few synapses, says John Growdon, MD, a neurologist at Massachusetts General Hospital.

Resource: The product used in the study—Souvenaid, from Danone—is not yet available in the US. To receive an e-mail update on Souvenaid's availability, go to *www.souvenaid. com.*

Study #4: B-6 and Parkinson's disease. In Parkinson's disease (PD), cells that produce the brain chemical dopamine begin to malfunction and die, causing tremors, rigid muscles and slow movements.

Researchers in Japan studied 617 people, 249 with PD and 368 without it. Those with the lowest blood levels of B-6 had a 52% higher risk of developing PD. The study appeared in the *British Journal of Nutrition.*

Boosting B Vitamins

"The only way to get the level of B vitamins used in the study that showed a slowing of brain atrophy is to take a nutritional supplement," says Gale Maleskey, MS, RD, a nutritionist in private practice in Bethlehem, Pennsylvania.

For the best level of protection, she recommends a supplement with 500 to 1,000 mcg of B-12, 400 mcg of folic acid, and 20 mg of B-6.

"I always like to see people eat better, too," says Maleskey.

The top dietary sources of B vitamins include: dark, leafy greens and beans for folic acid and B-6, and meat, eggs and milk for B-12.

David Smith, MD, researcher, University of Oxford in England.

Babak Hooshmand, PhD, researcher, Aging Research Center at the Karolinska Institute in Sweden.

Richard Wurtman, MD, Cecil H. Green Distinguished Professor of Brain and Cognitive Sciences, Massachusetts Institute of Technology, Cambridge.

John Growdon, MD, neurologist, Massachusetts General Hospital in Boston.

Gale Maleskey, MS, RD, nutritionist in private practice in Bethlehem, Pennsylvania. *www.galemalesky.com.*

The Real Truth About Alzheimer's Prevention

We all want to do everything possible to avoid Alzheimer's disease. But experts disagree on whether anything we do to change our lifestyles will actually help.

The news media has recently reported a statement made by a panel of 15 scientists in the *Annals of Internal Medicine* that there's not enough evidence to recommend any particular lifestyle habits to prevent Alzheimer's.

How could they make such a statement?

What the headlines missed: There is, in fact, a large body of scientific evidence suggesting that certain strategies help protect against Alzheimer's disease—it's just that these interventions have yet to be definitively proven in clinical settings. Instead, the evidence we have at this time is basic scientific research, such as cellular and animal studies, as well as epidemiological research that analyzes large groups of people to discover factors that may be linked to increased or decreased risk for Alzheimer's.

Clinical research, which tests a specific agent such as medication along with a placebo, always lags behind basic and epidemiological research because it is costly and difficult to conduct.

Advice: Follow well-known Alzheimer's prevention strategies. To begin, eat healthfully—ideally a Mediterranean diet that emphasizes brain-healthy omega-3–rich fish and antioxidant-rich fruits, vegetables and nuts. And get regular aerobic exercise to stimulate blood flow to the brain. The most recent research links 45 to 60 minutes four days a week to reduced Alzheimer's risk. Pace yourself, and consult your doctor before starting any exercise program. *In addition, keep up with the latest research, and consult your doctor about incorporating simple, underrecognized strategies such as those described below...*

Avoid Copper

Current evidence: In basic research on animals and on the brain cells of people who have died of Alzheimer's, scientists at the University of Rochester Medical Center in New York recently found that copper damages a molecule that shuttles *beta-amyloid* out of the brain. Beta-amyloid is a protein that forms toxic chunks (plaque) in the brains of people with Alzheimer's, and it may play a key role in the development of the disease. This research builds on a decade of research linking excessive levels of copper in the body to Alzheimer's.

What to do: According to research published in *Chemical Research in Toxicology*, people over age 50 should avoid nutritional supplements that contain copper...take a milligram (mg) zinc supplement daily—zinc helps the body remove excess copper...limit intake of red meat, which contains a lot of copper...and use an effective filtering system to remove copper from drinking water.

My personal approach: Depending on the water source, tap water may contain significant amounts of copper even if the water isn't flowing through copper pipes. For this reason, I have stopped drinking unfiltered tap water. To remove copper from my drinking water, I use a reverse osmosis water filter to separate the water from potentially harmful substances.

Reverse osmosis filtration systems are found at home-improvement stores and online in tap or under-the-sink models (about $150) or whole-house models (up to $3,000).

Get Enough Vitamin E

Vitamin E has been studied for Alzheimer's for more than a decade, with a landmark study in the *New England Journal of Medicine* in 1997 showing that high doses of vitamin E were more effective than a placebo at delaying specific outcomes of Alzheimer's disease, such as nursing home placement. Now, a recent study links high dietary intake of vitamin E to a reduced risk for the disease.

Current evidence: In a 10-year study involving more than 5,000 people, those with the highest dietary intake of vitamin E were 25% less likely to develop Alzheimer's than those with the lowest intake, reported Dutch researchers in *Archives of Neurology.*

What to do: Eat vitamin E–rich foods, which supply the full range of vitamin E nutrients. Most vitamin E supplements do not contain the entire class of these nutrients. The data now clearly support dietary sources of vitamin E over supplements. Aim to get 15 mg of vitamin E daily.

Best sources: Wheat germ oil (20 mg per tablespoon)…almonds (7 mg per ounce)…sunflower seeds (6 mg per ounce)…and spinach (4 mg per cup, boiled).

Beware of Hospitalization And Anesthesia

Doctors have long known that some older adults develop Alzheimer's symptoms soon after being hospitalized.

Current evidence: Researchers conducted a six-year study involving nearly 3,000 people age 65 and older who didn't have dementia (cognitive decline most commonly caused by Alzheimer's). As reported in the *Journal of the American Medical Association*, those who were hospitalized for a noncritical illness, such as broken bones, had a 40% higher risk of developing dementia.

The researchers speculated that several factors might play a role in increasing dementia after hospitalization, such as hospital-acquired infections…general anesthesia, tranquilizers and painkillers taken in the hospital…and the blood pressure and blood sugar problems that frequently arise during hospitalization. Research has linked each of these factors, in varying degrees, to the development of Alzheimer's.

What to do: If you are hospitalized, try to stay in the hospital for as short a period as possible. If you need anesthesia and have a choice between general anesthesia or local or spinal anesthesia, opt for the local or spinal. As much as possible, minimize the use of optional psychoactive medications, such as tranquilizers and sleeping pills.

Have a Purpose in Life

No one knows why people who feel that they have a purpose in life tend to be less likely to develop Alzheimer's, but it does seem to help.

Current evidence: In a study published in *Archives of General Psychiatry,* researchers at the Rush University Medical Center in Chicago found that older adults with a high score on a questionnaire evaluating one's sense of purpose in life (feeling that life has meaning and having goals that guide behavior) were 2.4 times more likely to remain free of Alzheimer's than adults with a low score.

What to do: Look for ways to add meaning to your life—for example, volunteer for your neighborhood association or for local organizations that strive to improve your community. The social involvement associated with volunteering also may help guard against Alzheimer's. Research has linked social connectedness to decreased risk for the disease.

Marwan Sabbagh, MD, geriatric neurologist and founding director of the Cleo Roberts Center for Clinical Research at the Banner Sun Health Research Institute in Sun City, Arizona, one of 29 NIH-sponsored Alzheimer's Disease Centers in the US. He is author of *The Alzheimer's Answer* (Wiley).

The Best Brain Foods— What to Eat and Drink to Keep Your Mind Sharp

If you are trying to do everything possible to keep your brain in good health, chances are your diet includes well-known brain-boosting foods, such as salmon (with its beneficial fatty acids) and blueberries (with their high antioxidant and anti-inflammatory content).

Exciting development: While scientists have long relied on animal studies to support blueberries' positive effect on memory, a recent study confirms a similar effect in humans. A recent study published in the *Journal of Agricultural and Food Chemistry* reported that when nine adults in their 70s who were experiencing early memory decline drank 2 to 2½ cups of juice made from frozen wild blueberries each day for three months, they significantly improved their performance on memory and learning tests compared with seven adults who consumed a placebo drink.

Here are some less well-known options that can also confer significant brain-protecting effects (because these foods contain a wide variety of important nutrients, it's wise to consume them even if you take brain-boosting supplements, such as fish oil or vitamin B-12)…

- **Purple sweet potatoes.** Like yellow or orange sweet potatoes, the purple variety is loaded with antioxidants. But purple sweet potatoes also have special antioxidants— purple pigments called anthocyanins. These pigments help preserve the integrity of blood vessels that transport oxygen to the brain and improve signaling between nerve cells in the brain (neurons).

As we age, the integrity of the tiny blood vessels delivering nutrients and energy—in the form of blood sugar (glucose)—to the brain diminishes. But our mental sharpness is dependent on a healthy blood supply.

For the greatest benefits: Aim to eat one medium purple sweet potato (available in gourmet supermarkets and Asian grocery stores) or one yellow or orange sweet potato twice a week. Instead of topping them with butter and/or salt, try eating oven-roasted sweet potatoes with the nutrient-rich skins.

- **Sardines.** When it comes to fish that provide the most brain-boosting omega-3 fatty acids, most people think of salmon, mackerel and herring.

Even better: Sardines (along with salmon, mackerel and herring) are less likely than large fish, such as swordfish, shark and tilefish, to have high amounts of mercury and *polychlorinated biphenyls* (PCBs). Plus, sardines are budget-friendly and convenient.

For the greatest benefits: Eat three to four servings of omega-3–rich fish, including sardines—about 3.5 ounces per serving (the size of a deck of cards) weekly. When cooking fish, trim the skin—this practice significantly reduces PCB content.

- **Omega-3–enriched eggs.** As a rich source of a valuable nutrient known as choline, eggs help protect against cognitive decline by facilitating efficient communication between neurons.

For the greatest benefits: Try omega-3–enriched eggs, which have an anti-inflammatory effect that also promotes brain health. Eat four to five omega-3 eggs per week.

Important: The omega-3 content of eggs remains generally stable during scrambling and poaching, according to research. Hard-boiling may be somewhat less beneficial due to the breakdown of brain-boosting fats within eggs during boiling.

- **Ginger.** As an anti-inflammatory, ginger can preempt the manufacture of inflammatory brain chemicals and potentially can delay or slow down the progression of inflammation-related brain conditions, such as Alzheimer's.

For greatest benefits: Add one teaspoon of freshly grated ginger to your meals two or three times a week…or about one-half teaspoon of powdered ginger. If you prefer pill form, take one 500-mg ginger capsule daily.

● **Green tea.** Green tea contains *epigal-locatechin-3-gallate* (EGCG), an antioxidant that curbs brain-damaging inflammation.

Promising research: A recent study found that mice that drank water with EGCG for six months showed a 50% decrease, on average, in the amyloid plaques characteristic of Alzheimer's disease.

For the greatest benefits: Drink three to four (eight-ounce) cups daily. Decaffeinated green tea also promotes brain health but is less potent than caffeinated.

● **Coffee.** Regular consumption of caffeinated coffee can reduce risk for cognitive decline and neurodegenerative diseases, such as Alzheimer's and Parkinson's.

This brain-protective effect may be due to coffee's ability to protect the fat component of cells against oxidative stress. Since the brain is 60% fat, this could account for the positive link between coffee consumption and lower risk for neuro-degenerative diseases.

For the greatest benefits: Consider drinking two to four (eight-ounce) cups daily of home-brewed coffee, which tends to have less caffeine than coffee-shop coffee.

Helpful: If you are especially sensitive to the effects of caffeine or you suffer from insomnia, anxiety, high blood pressure or irregular heartbeat, moderate your intake of caffeine and/or try decaffeinated coffee, which still is a good, though somewhat less potent, source of antioxidants.

Alan C. Logan, ND, naturopathic physician and invited faculty member in Harvard's School of Continuing Medical Education, Boston. He is author of *The Brain Diet* (Cumberland House). *www.drlogan.com.*

The Ultimate Brain Tonic

Recently, the *Journal of Alzheimer's Disease* devoted an entire "special issue"—22 scientific papers—to a unique "therapeutic agent" that could prevent and perhaps treat brain diseases such as Alzheimer's disease and Parkinson's disease, and even slow the everyday mental decline of aging.

Scientists from the Taub Institute for Research on Alzheimer's Disease and the Aging Brain at Columbia University in New York… from the Aging Research Center at the prestigious Karolinska Institute in Sweden…and from many other US and international institutions…weighed in on the unique power of this compound to protect and energize the brain.

What is this new and effective drug?

Surprising: A very old "drug"—with a very new use. Caffeine.

First, let's take a look at what some of the studies showed, and then learn some of the best ways to ensure a healthful and effective daily intake of caffeine.

The Caffeine Cure

● **Alzheimer's disease.** In a 20-year study, people diagnosed with AD had an average daily caffeine intake of 74 milligrams (mg) (less than one cup of coffee), while those free of the disease had an average intake of 199 mg (about two cups of coffee). In all, the higher caffeine intake was linked to a 60% reduced risk of AD—a level of reduction found in many other studies on caffeine intake and AD.

Caffeine may help prevent AD by stopping the formation of two enzymes that help create *amyloid-beta*, the neuron-destroying protein found in the brains of people with AD.

Important new finding: In a recent study, researchers at the Florida Alzheimer's Disease Research Center, Tampa, found that a dose of 400 mg of caffeine reduced blood levels of amyloid-beta in about half the people tested—with levels staying lower for many hours after taking caffeine.

Suggested intake: The Florida researchers think the best daily dose of caffeine for preventing AD is 500 mg, or five 8-ounce cups of coffee.

● **Parkinson's disease.** One out of every 100 people over the age of 60 has Parkinson's disease (PD)—dopamine-producing cells in the brain die, causing tremors, rigid muscles and slow movements. The newest research shows there's also destruction in other parts of the brain, causing the memory loss and emotional problems (such as depression and apathy) that are common features of the disease.

In one 30-year study of more than 8,000 men, those who drank no coffee had a five times higher risk of PD than men who drank 28 ounces or more a day. Another study showed that people who drank one cup of coffee a day had a 50% lower risk of PD than those who didn't drink coffee.

Caffeine may prevent PD by protecting dopamine-producing cells, says a team of Brazilian researchers. For the same reason, it may even slow the progression of the disease, and help "improve the motor deficits" of PD. It may also improve the memory and emotional problems of PD.

● **Cognitive health in aging.** Everybody knows that caffeine gives you a mental jolt, making you feel more alert and focused. But recent research shows that caffeine can also inhibit mental decline in aging.

Recent research: A 10-year study shows that older people who drank three or more cups of coffee a day had a 200% slower decline in mental functions such as memory and language skills. And researchers from Columbia University found that women who regularly drank caffeine had fewer destructive lesions in the part of the brain that relays messages between brain cells.

How it works: Caffeine affects brain cells mainly by blocking cellular receptors for *adenosine*, a neurotransmitter that makes us feel tired or sleepy. Blocking adenosine also affects many other neurotransmitters (dopamine, acetylcholine, serotonin), thereby improving long-term mental abilities.

Caffeine Is Safe

Perhaps you're worried about the safety of consuming 300 to 500 mg of caffeine a day, which is a typical therapeutic dose. Relax and have another cup of coffee.

"A comprehensive review of the scientific literature found that for healthy adults, moderate daily caffeine intake poses no adverse effects on the cardiovascular system, bone status and calcium balance, or incidence of cancer," wrote the Florida researchers. "Nor does it increase the risk, frequency or severity of arrhythmias [irregular heartbeats]."

In fact, the newest research links a high intake of caffeine to lower risk of many chronic conditions, such as heart disease, stroke, type 2 diabetes, liver cirrhosis (scarring) in hepatitis C and gallbladder disease.

An Effective Dose

"I regard 100 milligrams of caffeine as a 'basic' dose of caffeine, the dose you can take when you are beginning to experiment with using caffeine to improve your mind," says Bennett Alan Weinberg, coauthor with Bonnie K. Bealer of *The Caffeine Advantage* (The Free Press). That's the amount in a six-ounce cup of instant coffee, a four-ounce cup of filter drip coffee, 12 ounces of black tea or ½ caffeine tablet.

"If you find you are comfortable taking a single 100 mg of caffeine, you may want to increase your dose to 150 to 300 mg," continues Weinberg. "Once you have found your comfortable personal pickup dose, you can experiment with repeating this dose two or even three times throughout the day.

"I recommend no more than a total daily intake of 500 to 600 mg—the amount of caffeine in three to four 6-ounce cups of filter drip coffee. This amount is probably enough to achieve significant benefits from caffeine."

Red flags: Everyone responds differently to the same dose of caffeine, says Weinberg. Consider reducing the amount of caffeine if you experience insomnia, rapid heartbeat, agitation, restlessness, bad moods or anxiety.

Caffeine Pills, Energy Drinks

For controlled and effective dosing of caffeine, Weinberg favors caffeine pills.

"In my experience, getting caffeine from a pill delivers more reliable and powerful effects—you know how much caffeine you're actually taking, whereas you never really know exactly how much coffee or tea contains."

Previously, Weinberg drank six cups of filter drip coffee throughout the day, for a total intake of 1,000 mg of caffeine. "Now, I start the day with 300 mg in pill form, sometimes taking another 100 mg or 200 mg before the day is over. I experience a more reliable and stronger boost, mentally and physically, with a drastically lowered dosage of caffeine."

Resource: Caffeine pills are widely available. Vivarin and No-Doz are two popular brands. He favors the low-cost Jet Alert, which he purchases at Amazon.com.

Weinberg does not favor caffeine-containing energy drinks as a reliable way to get caffeine. "These so-called energy drinks contain a fraction of the amount of caffeine in a cup of coffee. The manufacturers want you to think energy drinks are something special. They're not."

Gary Arendash, PhD, research professor at the University of South Florida and faculty member at The Florida Alzheimer's Disease Research Center, both in Tampa.

Bennett Alan Weinberg, coauthor with Bonnie K. Bealer of *The Caffeine Advantage* (The Free Press) and *The World of Caffeine* (The Free Press). *www.theworldofcaffeine.com.*

Keep Your Gums Healthy and Stay Smart

Researchers from New York University College of Dentistry and Copenhagen University Institute of Public Health in Denmark have found that people with periodontal inflammation were at higher risk for lower IQ and cognitive function than people who did not have gum disease. We have known about the link between gum health and cardiovascular disease—but now there is even more reason to take care of your gums.

Mark A. Stengler, NMD, naturopathic medical doctor in private practice, Encinitas, California, and author of the *Bottom Line/Natural Healing* newsletter. *www.drstengler.com.*

How Google Exercises Your Brain

Can you use the Internet to better your brain? Yes, say researchers at University of California at Los Angeles who conducted a study called "Your Brain on Google." The research team, led by Gary Small, MD, of UCLA's Center on Aging, explored whether searching the Internet stimulates areas of the brain that control decision making, complex reasoning and vision. The researchers discovered it does, but only for those who use Google or other search engines in a certain way.

Net-Net...

The study included 24 people aged 55 to 76. Half the subjects (the "Net Naïve" group) had little or no experience in searching the Internet, while the other half (the "Net Savvy" group) were skilled computer users who regularly use the Internet. This age group was chosen because researchers postulated that age-related brain changes are associated with declines in cognitive abilities, such as processing speed and working memory, and that routine computer use might have an impact—negative or positive. Both groups were asked to perform two tasks. First, to read text on a computer screen, and second, to use Google to search the Web. The reading material and research topics were interesting and similar in content (for instance, the benefits of drinking coffee, planning a trip to the Galapagos Islands, how to choose a car, etc.).

Meanwhile, as the subjects worked on their computers, researchers scanned their brains with a functional magnetic resonance imaging (fMRI) device to ascertain which parts were active. During the text-reading phase, these fMRI scans revealed similar activity for both groups in the regions that control language, reading, memory and vision. But there were very dissimilar results when the two groups performed Web searches. When the Net Naïve group searched the Internet, their brain activity was similar to what they had experienced while reading. In contrast, the Net Savvy group produced activity in areas of the brain that control decision making and complex reasoning. Previous studies have shown that this type of brain activity is important for everyday cognitive tasks.

Engaging Content

This result shows that the Internet is itself "brain stimulation," says Dr. Small. This may be especially helpful as people age because, compared with reading, Web searches require making more decisions. For instance, searchers must decide which information to pursue and which to ignore. Dr. Small says the Net Naïve group may show less brain stimulation than the Net Savvy group because of their inexperience with the Internet. When this group was given some training, their brains showed similar patterns of activity to those who were adept at Internet use.

So, if you haven't been very involved with using your computer to research topics of interest, give it a try—it's great mental exercise.

Gary Small, MD, director of the Memory and Aging Center at the Jane & Terry Semel Institute for Neuroscience & Human Behavior, University of California, Los Angeles. He is also co-author of many books, including *iBrain* (Collins Living).

The Jellyfish Cure For Dementia

Why does a species of jellyfish—the *Aequorea Victoria*—glow in the dark?

Surprisingly, the answer to that question could also be the answer to this one: How can you slow, stop or reverse memory loss and prevent dementia?

The Calcium Connection

In the 1960s, researchers discovered that when *apoaequorin*—a protein in the jellyfish—attaches itself to calcium, the jellyfish glow. Apoaequorin is a calcium-binding protein, and in 2008 the researchers were awarded a Nobel Prize in chemistry for their discovery of this unique compound.

Humans contain calcium-binding proteins very similar to apoaequorin. But they don't make us glow. They make us remember.

What happens: Electrically charged calcium ions supply the power to speed messages between brain cells (neurons). But calcium is a double-edged sword. If there's too much calcium inside the neuron, the cell is damaged and doesn't work right.

Excess calcium is held in check by—you guessed it—calcium-binding proteins, which sop up calcium outside the cell like a sponge. (And with 10,000 times more calcium outside neurons than inside, there's a lot of sopping up to do.)

But as we age, we have fewer and fewer calcium-binding proteins—and more and more calcium inside our neurons. The likely result: a decline in what scientists call "cognitive function," with memory loss, poor concentration, a harder time making decisions—and eventual dementia. (Some researchers have even proposed a "calcium hypothesis" of brain aging, in which the buildup of calcium inside neurons is seen as the cause of mental decline, in much the same way that the buildup of calcium in arteries is seen as the main cause of heart attacks and strokes.)

Important finding: Recent research shows that you can reverse cognitive decline by taking a nutritional supplement containing *aequorin*, a compound very similar to calcium-binding apoaequorin.

The Jellyfish Pill

Researchers asked 100 older people (average age, 67) with memory problems to participate in the Madison Memory Study, giving half of them 10 milligrams (mg) a day of aequorin and the other half a placebo.

Results: After three months, the aequorin group had a 29% decline in errors on tests that measured memory, decision making, concentration and mental clarity. The placebo group had a 6% increase in errors. The results were presented at a recent Alzheimer's Association International Conference.

In an earlier study on aequorin, researchers asked 56 people who said they had a poor memory to take the supplement. After three months, 63% said they were less forgetful.

The study participants also were asked to respond to the question, "Do you have trouble finding the words you want to say, finishing sentences, or naming people or things?" After three months, 74% of the study participants said they had an improvement in their ability to recall words during a conversation.

Another question posed to those in the study: "Do you need reminders to do things like chores, shopping, or taking medicines?" After three months of taking aequorin, 80% of those who needed reminders said they needed fewer of them.

Additionally, 84% of the participants had an improvement in their ability to remember driving directions, and 51% said they had an improvement in retaining any kind of information.

And a sharper mind wasn't the only benefit. They study participants slept better, too.

"I recommend that everyone take aequorin, whether they have a memory problem or not," says Dan Underwood, president and cofounder of Quincy Bioscience in Madison, Wisconsin, which was recently granted a patent for the use of aequorin to prevent and alleviate symptoms from calcium imbalance, including cognitive decline. "Although aequorin is proven to reverse memory loss in people in their 60s, why wait until you have an issue with cognition? You start losing calcium-binding proteins around the age of 40, whether your memory is immediately affected or not. If you start taking aequorin at 40 or 50, you won't have to play catch-up when you see the first signs of memory loss."

Resource: The only aequorin-containing supplement on the market is Prevagen, which is widely available in retail outlets and online.

The dosages used in studies on aequorin is the same dose in a tablet of Prevagen: 10 mg daily.

Clinicians report that people typically see results after one to three months of daily use, says Underwood.

"I recommend that my own patients who have suffered a noticeable decline in cognitive function start out with the 10 mg daily for four weeks," says Mark Stengler, NMD, a naturopathic medical doctor and director of the Stengler Center for Integrative Medicine, Encinitas, California. "If they don't notice an improvement in memory and focus, they can increase to 20 mg daily. Most of my patients benefit from taking 10 mg to 20 mg daily. Prevagen is a safe, natural memory support—and safe to take with other memory-enhancing supplements, such as omega-3 fish oils, or medications for Alzheimer's, such as *donepezil* (Aricept). And people with allergies to fish or shellfish can use it because jellyfish is neither."

Dan Underwood, president and cofounder of Quincy Bioscience, Madison, Wisconsin.

Mark A. Stengler, NMD, naturopathic medical doctor in private practice, Encinitas, California, and author of the *Bottom Line/Natural Healing* newsletter. *www.drstengler.com.*

Ginkgo—Should You Forget About It?

When older Americans turn to an herb to help protect the brain and stop memory loss, they usually turn to ginkgo biloba, one of the top-selling herbal supplements in the US. (It outsells ginseng, green tea, and valerian supplements combined.)

Latest development: If you read about a recent study on ginkgo published in the *Journal of the American Medical Association,* you might have decided that the nearly $20 million Americans spend yearly on ginkgo (with perhaps some of that cash coming from your pocket) is a big waste of money.

The study analyzed data from a previous six-year study of ginkgo, in which more than 3,000 people, aged 72 to 96, took a daily dose of either 240 milligrams (mg) of the herb daily or a placebo.

"The use of ginkgo biloba did not result in less cognitive decline in older adults with normal cognition or mild cognitive impairment," concluded the researchers. (Cognitive decline is the scientific term for the gradual erosion of mental abilities, such as memory, concentration, language skills and daily decision making. Mild cognitive impairment is the stage of cognitive decline that precedes dementia.)

In other words, ginkgo was stinko.

However: "This study had many significant limitations and may be inaccurate," says herbalist Mark Blumenthal, the founder and executive director of the American Botanical Council, a nonprofit research and education organization dedicated to providing accurate and reliable information about herbs.

Here are several reasons why Blumenthal thinks the study results may have been misleading—and why taking ginkgo is still a smart, science-proven strategy for protecting your brain.

The Flawed Study

First, says Blumenthal, the researchers did not conduct a new study—they shuffled the statistics from an earlier study to produce and publish a new set of results. (The original study did not investigate ginkgo's effect on cognitive decline. It was designed to determine if ginkgo prevented Alzheimer's disease…It didn't.)

Second, about 40% of those in the study dropped out during its six-year period—before final data were collected. The statistics reported in the new study included the dropouts.

Third, says Blumenthal, the people in the study weren't monitored for cognition until several years after the study began—making it very difficult to determine whether they experienced a decline in cognition or not.

Fourth, the average age of study participants was 79. That's a very advanced age to begin measuring the effect of ginkgo on cognitive decline. And it's not the age when

most people start taking ginkgo for its brain-protecting power, which is 50 to 60.

Ginkgo Is Still a "Go"

What this study did prove, like many studies before it, is that a daily dose of 240 mg of ginkgo biloba extract (GBE) is safe, says Blumenthal. "The safety of GBE was never called into question, and that's an important result."

How safe? A safety issue often raised about ginkgo—which works by thinning the blood and improving circulation—is that it might interact with blood-thinning drugs such as *warfarin* (Coumadin), causing internal bleeding or extending bleeding time in the case of injury or surgery. This "warranted but theoretical concern" has never been proven to be a factual risk, says Blumenthal.

However, he emphasizes that the only truly safe and effective form of ginkgo is the scientifically tested form. "When I talk about ginkgo, I am talking about the product that has been used in 90% of clinical trials, which is the standardized extract Ginkgold, manufactured by a German company and available in the US only from Nature's Way.

"Ginkgo extracts from other manufacturers do not have the same safety profile—or the same positive effects," he says. "In fact, there's a lot of adulteration and fraud in the ginkgo market right now."

But, says Blumenthal, the cognitive benefits of Ginkgold have been scientifically shown—over and over again.

Of 13 clinical trials on Ginkgold and cognition, 11 have shown benefits, including improvements in short-term memory and an increase in the speed of processing information. And Ginkgold has been shown to improve mental ability in people of any age, from seniors to college students.

Suggested intake: The dosage of Ginkgold GBE used in most research is 240 mg daily.

Blumenthal emphasizes that Ginkgold should be part of an overall brain-protecting lifestyle that includes a whole-foods diet, dietary supplements and exercise. "This comprehensive approach can positively affect your neural networks and offset the so-called 'inevitable' decline in cognition as you age."

Mark Blumenthal, founder and executive director of the American Botanical Council, and editor of HerbalGram. *www.herbalgram.org.*

Reverse Memory Loss In 12 Minutes

It wasn't so long ago that people who practiced meditation were mocked as "navel-gazers"—impractical folks who would rather close their eyes and concentrate on internal trivia than get up and do something.

But a new study shows that some people who meditate are doing something. They're reversing memory loss. And they're doing it in just 12 minutes.

Meditation vs. Mozart

Scientists from the Alzheimer's Research and Prevention Foundation in Tucson, Arizona, and the University of Pennsylvania in Philadelphia conducted the study.

They enlisted 20 people, aged 52 to 77, who had various degrees of memory loss: Ten had subjective cognitive impairment (SCI), the first stage of age-associated memory loss...seven had the more advanced stage of mild cognitive impairment (MCI)...and three were in the early stage of Alzheimer's disease.

Fifteen of the 20 participants were taught Kirtan Kriya, a simple, 12-minute meditation that they practiced daily for eight weeks. Five others were asked to listen to Mozart violin concertos for 12 minutes every day.

The researchers used a sophisticated scan to measure blood flow in the participants' brains four times: 1) before they learned to meditate, 2) during the first meditation, 3) after eight weeks of meditating and 4) during a final meditation.

The participants were also given standard tests at the beginning and end of the study that measured memory, concentration and other mental skills.

Results: After eight weeks, the brain scans of the meditators revealed a significant increase in blood flow to the parts of the brain linked to memory—the prefrontal cortex, superior frontal cortex and the superior parietal cortex. There was little change in cerebral blood flow in the music group.

The meditators also had a significant improvement in memory, concentration and cognition, while there was little change in the music group.

"A brief, simple, low-cost meditation practice called Kirtan Kriya performed for only 12 minutes daily over an 8-week period of time revealed positive results in both functional neuroimaging changes as well as an improvement in cognitive function in people with memory loss," concluded the researchers in the *Journal of Alzheimer's Disease.*

Why it works: "I use the analogy of going to the gym and becoming stronger after lifting weights for eight weeks," says Dharma Singh Khalsa, MD, the study leader, founding president and medical director of the Alzheimer's Research and Prevention Foundation in Tucson, Arizona, and author of *Meditation as Medicine* (Atria). "In the same way, Kirtan Kriya trains and strengthens the brain—it improves the blood flow, and the brain functions better.

"Anyone who does this meditation is going to have a mind that's sharper, faster, smarter and younger. They're going to be more alert, with a better memory. It's like a brain makeover."

(Dr. Khalsa has also studied Kirtan Kriya meditation on Alzheimer's caregivers—and the eight-week program improved cognition, mood and well-being.)

Dr. Khalsa thinks meditation is an excellent treatment option for people with memory loss. "The drugs that are available don't have much effect—they're definitely not the solution to this problem. Yes, some of the drugs may get rid of the plaques and tangles in the brain that are characteristic of Alzheimer's. But that's like taking the tombstones out of the cemetery—the person is still dead!

"Kirtan Kriya is a way to revitalize the brain. It has an important role in a total memory-protecting program that includes diet, nutritional supplements, regular physical exercise, mental exercises such as crossword puzzles, and stress reduction."

Simple Meditation

"Kirtan Kriya is simple, quick, practical and low-cost and doesn't require class sessions to learn it," says Dr. Khalsa.

1. The meditator says four sounds—SA, TA, NA, MA.

2. While saying the sounds, the meditator also consecutively touches the thumb to a finger of the same hand: to the index finger with SA, to the middle finger with TA, to the fourth finger with NA, and to the pinkie with MA.

3. The SA-TA-NA-MA meditation is performed: out loud for two minutes; in a whisper for two minutes; in silence (thinking the sounds) for four minutes; in a whisper for two more minutes; and out loud for two final minutes.

Important: "You can't do this meditation on the run," says Dr. Khalsa. "You need a quiet environment, without distractions such as TV, e-mail or cell phone. Do it in a comfortable position, such as sitting comfortably in a chair. If you find your mind wandering to thoughts, just say, 'Hello thought,' and return to the technique and the sound."

Resource: You can buy a CD that teaches you the meditation at *www.alzheimerspre vention.org*. On the Home Page, click on the link to the Alzheimer's Research and Prevention Foundation store or call 888-908-5766. The $12 CD is called "Audio CD of the Kirtan Kriya."

Dharma Singh Khalsa, MD, founding president and medical director of the Alzheimer's Research and Prevention Foundation in Tucson, Arizona, and author of several books, including *Meditation as Medicine* (Atria) and *The Better Memory Kit* (Hay House). *www.drdharma.com, www. alzheimersprevention.org*.

Tai Chi Could Help Balance Disorders

This Chinese martial art may help patients who suffer from dizziness and vestibular disorders, such as vertigo and balance problems, according to research from the New York Eye and Ear Institute. Researchers used individualized physical therapy or sets of physical maneuvers that doctors can perform on patients. Tai chi helps coordination, which is impaired in patients with a balance disorder.

Mark A. Stengler, NMD, naturopathic medical doctor in private practice, Encinitas, California, and author of the *Bottom Line/Natural Healing* newsletter. *www. drstengler.com*.

Physical Therapy for Vertigo and Imbalance

Trying to find an effective treatment for chronic, persistent dizziness—or vertigo—can make anyone's head spin. But instead of relying on your doctor for help with a chronic balance disorder, you may want to check in with a physical therapist.

Feeling like you are living on a merry-go-round is more common than you might think—dizziness affects more than 2.4 million Americans. While inflammation or damage to the vestibular nerve or head trauma are frequent causes, the most common by far is *benign paroxysmal positional vertigo* (BPPV). This is the medical name for a sensation of spinning that occurs when your head moves into particular positions. Here are some natural interventions from the world of physical therapy.

New Studies Show What Helps

A recent special issue of the *Journal of Neurologic Physical Therapy* (*JNPT*) focused specifically on physical therapy (PT) for chronic dizziness. Notable among the nine studies featured in this issue of *JNPT* is an intriguing new technology that may soon make life safer for people who suffer from chronic dizziness, along with some other ways that vestibular rehabilitation therapy (VRT) can help patients with a variety of balance problems.

Key finding: "Eye control" during head motion can help reduce risk for falls. One study conducted by researchers from the Atlanta Veterans Administration and Emory University in Atlanta examined how being able to keep eyes focused on a target while turning your head (this is called "gaze stability") helps reduce fall risk in older adults who complain of dizziness but have normal inner-ear function. Thirty-nine patients did balance exercises (such as trying to maintain balance while standing on soft surfaces and walking with their eyes closed), while 20 of the patients also did gaze stability exercises and the other 19 did a sham set of eye exercises.

Results: 90% of the group that did the actual gaze stability exercises showed a reduction in fall risk versus 50% of the group that did the sham gaze exercises.

Key finding: PT can improve balance even in patients with traumatic brain injury. Gaze stability and balance exercises also proved helpful to soldiers with chronic dizziness as a result of blast-induced brain injuries sustained in Iraq or Afghanistan.

Key finding: VRT can improve thinking and concentration. It appears that doing exercises for gaze stability and concentration can help improve cognitive function in people diagnosed with vestibular disorders. In a study from the University of Pittsburgh, 50% to 64% of patients who received VRT—such as using a computer to sort out images on their right and left sides (a task that helps improve visual concentration and trains the brain to "reject" confusing signals from damaged nerves or receptors)—had improved cognitive function after six weeks of PT. This may reduce risk of falling by helping to keep a person more tuned in to his/her surroundings while moving about.

Cool Tech: New Balance Belt

In another study, a specially designed balance-feedback belt was used to help patients suffering chronic dizziness relearn balance skills. The device looks like a wide, conventional belt, but it also houses small vibrators that buzz (first gently but with gathering intensity as danger of falling increases) to warn patients when they are teetering in one direction or another. Susan Whitney, PT, PhD, associate professor of physical therapy and otolaryngology at the University of Pittsburgh says she finds this device intriguing. "The study shows that people can process this information as they walk, and it helps them to stay steady," she explains, adding that it might be a benefit not only to people with balance disorders but also for anybody at risk for falls.

Note: This belt is still in the testing stages, so it's not yet available to consumers.

A Balanced Perspective

According to Michael Schubert, PT, PhD, associate professor, Department of Otolaryngology-Head and Neck surgery at Johns Hopkins School of Medicine, Baltimore, and Dr. Whitney, taken collectively these studies provide compelling evidence that PT can be extremely helpful for people with persistent vertigo or imbalance problems, regardless of the cause. If you are interested in learning more, for yourself or for someone you know who has such a problem, it is important to find a physical therapist who specializes in balance disorders. Dr. Whitney recommends two info-packed Web sites, both of which offer a list of physical therapists who specialize in balance. Take a look at NeuroPT.org and Vestibular.org…and show dizziness the door!

Susan Whitney, PT, PhD, associate professor, Departments of Physical Therapy and Otolaryngology, School of Health and Rehabilitation Services, University of Pittsburgh, and director, vestibular rehabilitation program, Centers for Rehab Services, Eye & Ear Institute, Pittsburgh.

Michael Schubert, PT, PhD, associate professor, Department of Otolaryngology-Head and Neck Surgery, Johns Hopkins School of Medicine, Baltimore.

Exercise That Can Reverse Parkinson's Symptoms

Bigger is better.... Yes, it's a cliché, but for people with Parkinson's disease, it's a valuable one. In a recent study of Parkinson's patients, every participant improved by doing exercise that involved big movements.

The research had roots in another therapeutic program for people with Parkinson's, called the Lee Silverman Voice Treatment, in which patients are urged to constantly think "loud" to counteract losing voice volume. Study leader Air Force Major Maria Alvarez, MD, and her colleagues at Wilford Hall Medical Center at the Lackland Air Force Base in San Antonio built on that concept, applying it to movement and muscle power to encourage patients to "think big" about exercise, since their movements tend to diminish as the disease progresses. The study, called ThinkBIG, included 20 randomly selected Parkinson's patients (mean age 71) who were examined at the start and again at the end, 12 weeks later. There were no medication changes for any of the participants, and each engaged in three 45-minute exercise sessions each week.

For the first eight weeks, participants engaged in "large range" movements, such as taking giant steps while swinging their arms vigorously. Then, once they had met the initial goal to improve range of motion and balance, they spent the last four weeks using the Nintendo Wii yoga and bowling systems, both of which involve arm swings and forceful movements. The program proved helpful in improving the typical ambulation of Parkinson's patients—shuffling gait, arms hanging at their sides. After 12 weeks, participants showed an average improvement of 58% in muscular function and coordination and they walked more normally. These results suggest that the exercises not only are beneficial in relieving Parkinson's symptoms but may even slow or reverse progression of the disease, says Dr. Alvarez.

3-D TVs Can Cause Seizures

The makers of 3-D televisions, such as Samsung, have warned that people with certain serious medical conditions, such as epilepsy or a family history of stroke, as well as people who are tired or under the influence of alcohol should not watch 3-D television or movies. 3-D can trigger an epileptic seizure or stroke and can lead to headaches, migraines and nausea.

Melvin Schrier, OD, retired optometrist and vision consultant, Rancho Palos Verdes, California.

Why Do Big Exercises Work?

Dr. Alvarez attributes the program's success to several factors. First, earlier studies had already demonstrated that exercise produces brain chemicals that protect against the disease's signature destruction of dopamine cells. This particular form of large-movement exercise is fun, so participants enjoyed being involved and were happy to participate—they even organized their own Nintendo Wii bowling tournament. Also, according to Dr. Alvarez, focusing on one goal—"big"—is achievable for people with neurological disorders, who often have trouble practicing and repeating complex tasks. Dr. Alvarez believes that the ThinkBIG approach would benefit patients with other neurodegenerative conditions, such as multiple sclerosis, brain injury and stroke.

If you are interested in trying this, the first step should always be to seek an evaluation by a physical therapist who can advise you on what large-movement exercises you can safely do at home. (For instance, the Nintendo Wii system uses an elevated platform that can pose a falling risk.) Where most healthy adults are urged to engage in at least 2.5 hours of exercise each week, Dr. Alvarez suggests that people with Parkinson's should do more—aiming for 30 minutes of exercise at least six days a week. If that seems overwhelming, you can try breaking it into increments of five or 10 minutes over the day.

The important thing, Dr. Alvarez says, is to keep moving—becoming sedentary makes matters much worse, exacerbating such symptoms as shaking and muscular contraction and also making it difficult to move around.

Maria Victoria Alvarez, MD, MAJ, USAF, neurologist, movement disorders specialist and Flight Commander, Wilford Hall Medical Center, Lackland Air Force Base, San Antonio.

Gripping Trick for Neurological Patients

The simple act of lifting a glass to enjoy a drink can be a challenge for elderly people and for those suffering from neurological disorders, such as multiple sclerosis (MS), Parkinson's disease, stroke or peripheral neuropathies. These conditions interfere with neuromuscular communication, and people end up overcompensating for their lack of sensitivity of touch and motor control by grasping too forcefully when trying to lift an object—so they may end up breaking the object they are trying to grasp. It's frustrating, fatiguing and can even be dangerous. But recent research offers an innovative approach to solving the problem.

A Light Touch

Recently, a team of researchers at the University of Illinois at Chicago published a study demonstrating how effectively a simple maneuver can help patients gain better control over their grip. All it takes is a light touch on the wrist with the other hand (see opposite column). An earlier study had used this technique with stroke patients. The Illinois team tried it with MS patients, and it worked. The patients were able to soften and better manipulate their grips to perform the task at hand (which, in the study, was to lift a cup that was outfitted with sensors to measure grip strength).

Alexander Aruin, PhD, DSc, lead author of the study, explains that various sensors in the joints, muscles and other parts of the body feed *proprioceptive* information (having to do with your ability to sense the position and location of the body and its parts) into the brain. Age and certain neurological conditions can cause these sensors to break down, resulting in the common problem of overgripping. Researchers found that involving the other hand gives your brain information from more sensory receptors, thus improving the likelihood that the nervous system will respond efficiently.

This technique is easy, safe and costs nothing to try...but Dr. Aruin cautions that the research involved only those with moderate—not severe—impairment. *Here's how to do it...*

• **Before lifting an object,** reach over with your other arm, lightly placing the index finger of that hand on the inner wrist of the arm with which you will be lifting the object.

• **Now, to lift an object, wrap your hand around it** but without trying to move it yet.

• **Keeping the index finger on the wrist at all times,** lift the object and use it (if that's the plan—for instance, to sip from a cup) and then, with your index finger remaining on your wrist, put the object down.

• **Once the task is fully completed,** remove your gripping hand from the object and then remove the finger from your wrist.

It may take a few attempts to get this to work for you, but keep practicing. When you start to feel that your arms are working together in a sort of gentle ballet and your grip is softer than before but controls the object successfully, you've got the hang of it!

Alexander Aruin, PhD, DSc, professor of physical therapy and bioengineering, University of Illinois at Chicago, associate professor of physical medicine and rehabilitation, Rush Medical College, and director, Knecht Movement Science Laboratory, Chicago.

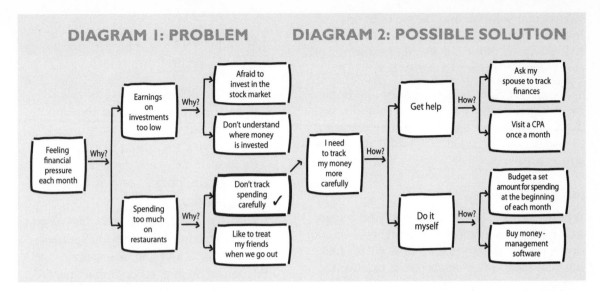

DIAGRAM I: PROBLEM   DIAGRAM 2: POSSIBLE SOLUTION

Solve Any Problem in 3 Simple Steps

Five years ago, Ken Watanabe, a Harvard MBA who worked at one of the world's leading consulting firms, walked away from a lucrative career to write a children's book. He was alarmed that school-age kids in his native Japan were good at memorizing large amounts of information but not very effective at applying it to real-life situations. He wanted to teach them in a fun way to broaden and organize their approach to problem-solving and become more proactive in shaping the world.

But something unexpected happened. Watanabe's 110-page book became a phenomenon among adults in Japan...and the country's best-selling business book of the year. Since then, it's been published in a half-dozen countries around the world, including, most recently, the US.

Here Ken Watanabe describes his secrets to problem-solving...

The Three Steps

Good problem-solving isn't an innate talent. It comes from a way of thinking using a set of techniques that you can practice and improve upon. Most people rely too much on their instincts when they try to solve a problem, especially when they feel flustered or overwhelmed. They tend to grasp at the first or second solution that pops into their heads, even if it doesn't seem completely adequate.

The following steps outline a simple, structured approach that works for addressing almost any kind of problem, big or small.

•**Step 1.** Identify your problem and the root difficulties causing it. People tend to think about their situations in such vague, universal terms that they get overwhelmed.

Example: You feel stressed and unhappy because you never have enough money each month. Stress and unhappiness are symptoms, not underlying problems that you can take action to remedy. You have to analyze more deeply. Is the actual problem that you're not earning enough money? Or is it that you're spending too much each month? To identify problems, you may find it helpful to think of yourself as a doctor trying to cure a patient. List potential causes for a problem, arrive at a hypothesis for the most likely cause and focus on addressing that cause.

•**Step 2.** Come up with multiple solutions. List as many as you can, no matter how improbable. This often leads you to creative and unexpected solutions. Even if you think a particular solution may be the right one, get into the habit of challenging this conclusion. Ask yourself, *What are the shortcomings of this solution? Is there a better way?*

•**Step 3.** Prioritize your actions and implement a plan. After you select a solution, you need to follow through on it and be prepared to modify it—or replace it—until the problem is resolved.

Helpful Tools

When you jot down thoughts and create graphic representations of them, you break down problems into manageable parts, making sure every possible avenue is explored…

• **The Logic Tree.** This is useful for clarifying your problem and its root causes.

How it works: Write your problem in a box on the left side of a piece of paper. (See Diagram 1 on page 79.) Ask "Why?" you have that problem. For each answer, draw an arrow to the right, and put it in a box. Now ask "Why?" for each of the answers in the boxes. Keep repeating the process until you have identified all of the possible root causes of the problem.

The Logic Tree also can help you brainstorm a variety of solutions to a problem after you've identified the root cause.

Example: Say that you have determined from the first Logic Tree that the root cause of your money problems is that you don't track your spending well enough. Start a new Logic Tree for possible solutions. (See Diagram 2 on page 79) In a new box on the left side of a piece of paper, write "I need to track my money more carefully." Then ask "How?" Follow the same format as Diagram 1, answering every "How" until applicable solutions are determined.

•**Pros and cons box.** This is useful for evaluating which competing solutions are the best ones. The box allows you to line up and compare the benefits and drawbacks of possible solutions at a glance.

To Perform Better, Say "–ing"

Volunteers doing a word puzzle described their experience in the imperfective ("I was solving a word puzzle") or perfective ("I solved a word puzzle") verb form. Next, they took a memory test about the puzzle…and did another similar puzzle.

Results: Participants who had used the imperfective ("was solving") remembered more about the first puzzle and did better on the second than participants who used the perfective.

Implication: Thinking of a past experience as ongoing and not yet completed facilitates recall and improves future performance.

Try it: Instead of saying "I exercised yesterday," say, "I was exercising yesterday." This might increase your odds of making it to the gym again tomorrow!

Will Hart, PhD, survey methodologist, National Opinion Research Center, University of Chicago.

How it works: Draw three columns. Label the first "Possible Solutions," the second "Pros" and the third "Cons." List each solution, and fill in its corresponding pros and cons. You can further refine the process by marking each pro and con entry using a star system. Three stars is very attractive or very unattractive depending on whether it's in your pro or con list, two stars is moderately attractive/unattractive, and one star is marginally attractive/unattractive.

•**Count the stars.** If they are in the pro column, more stars is good. If they are in the con column, more stars is bad.

Ken Watanabe, author of the best-selling *Problem Solving 101: A Simple Book for Smart People* (Portfolio). He is founder and CEO of Delta Studio, an education, entertainment and media company in Tokyo. *www.problemsolvingtoolbox.com.*

Wake Up Smarter

When you think about ways to boost your brainpower, you probably think about learning a second language or doing crossword puzzles—things that activate and challenge your mind.

But there's an easier way to improve your memory and learning skills. Go to sleep.

Surprising: Recent studies show that a good night's sleep—or a nap or a short non-sleeping break from mental activity—are some of the best ways to retain information you just learned or memorized. Sleep can even help you remember to call your mom on her birthday!

Sleep Builds Memory

"There are four basic theories about how sleep improves memory," says Mark A. Mc-Daniel, PhD, a professor in the Department of Psychology at Washington University in St. Louis, Missouri. *Sleep might…*

1. Reduce mental interference, so memories are more likely to be "consolidated"—to stick in your brain

2. Refresh and strengthen the mental connections you already have

3. Create new connections from recent learning or experiences

4. Help you create mental summaries of new knowledge and concepts, improving learning.

But however the Sandman works to build memory and learning, several new studies show that he does a good job…

•To remember a task for tomorrow, think about it at bedtime. Dr. McDaniel and a colleague recently conducted a study that found that a good night's sleep helps you remember prospective goals—actions you want to do tomorrow (but tend to forget because you're doing other things).

Examples: Taking your medication with breakfast. Calling your mother on her birthday. Turning off your cell phone at the movies. Going to the gym after work. Delivering a message to a friend.

For the greatest benefits: "Form your goal for the next day right before sleeping," says Dr. McDaniel. "Then link it to something you know you're going to do the next day. For example, if tomorrow is my mother's birthday and I want to be certain to call her, I should think to myself right before falling asleep, 'When I open the refrigerator in the morning to get the milk for my cereal, I should remember to call my mother.' Also, picture the refrigerator in your mind—even five refrigerators, floating above your head!

"Forming that intention right before falling asleep is likely to be more effective in remembering to do it the next day, as compared to trying to remember your intention during your busy day."

•Nappers are smarter. Napping at midday may help tidy the brain's "memory storage area," making room for new information, says Matthew Walker, PhD, an assistant professor at the University of California, Berkeley, who reported the results of his study at the annual meeting of the American Association for the Advancement of Science.

In the study, 39 people tried to memorize the pairing of 100 faces and names, during a noon session. At 2:00 p.m., half the group napped and half didn't. At 6:00 p.m., both groups performed the memorization task again. Those who napped performed 10% better than the first time. Those who didn't nap performed 10% worse.

In another study, people performed 40% better on a memory test after napping—particularly if they were dreaming while they napped (REM sleep), reported Sara C. Mednick, PhD, author of *Take a Nap! Change Your Life* (Workman) and assistant professor of psychiatry at the University of California, San Diego, at the annual convention of the American Psychological Association.

"REM sleep is important for pulling together all the information we process on a daily basis and turning it into memories we can use later," says Dr. Mednick.

"Dreams are the brain's way of processing, integrating, and really understanding new information," adds Robert Stickgold, PhD, associate professor of psychiatry at Harvard Medical School, who also conducted a recent study on REM-napping and memory.

Healthful strategy: "Without a midday rest, we are not able to perform at optimal levels throughout the day," says Dr. Mednick. "In fact, our performance falls apart. Napping maintains and even boosts our skills."

Give yourself permission to nap, adds Debra Greene, PhD, an energy-health specialist in Hawaii, and author of *Endless Energy* (MetaComm Media). "A lot of us have negative mental programming around naps, as if taking a nap means we're lazy or unproductive. But it's just the opposite. Napping is a normal part of our daily rhythms and makes us more productive."

● **Take a break, strengthen a memory.** You don't even have to sleep or take a nap to consolidate new information—just take a mental break, reported scientists from New York University, who compared mental powers in people who took a break and people who didn't.

"Taking a coffee break after a session of learning or memorizing can actually help you retain the information you just learned," says Lila Davachi, PhD, an assistant professor in the Department of Psychology and Center for Neural Science at New York University. "Your brain wants you to tune out other tasks so you can tune in to what you just learned.

"Your brain is working for you when you're resting, so rest is important for memory and cognitive function," she continues. "This is something we don't appreciate much, especially when today's information technologies keep us working round-the-clock."

Best: "After an encounter with new information, make yourself take a five-minute break," says Dr. McDaniel.

Recommendations for Rest

Here are recommendations for a better naptime or bedtime, from Dr. Greene. Try one and see if it works for you. *If it doesn't, try another…*

● **Use an eye mask.** "Light activates the pineal gland and signals us to wake up. A comfortable eye mask can help you nap or sleep more deeply.

● **Scan your body and let go of tension.** Tension stored in the body is a common reason why many people can't easily fall asleep, says Dr. Greene. To let go of the tension, close your eyes and "scan" your body for tense areas, starting at the top of the head and moving down to your toes.

"When you find a tight area, you can release it in several different ways, depending on your primary personal style," she says. "If you're primarily a verbal person, give yourself a verbal command, such as 'Let go' or 'Relax.' If you're primarily a visual person, picture the area as relaxed, perhaps by visualizing a fluffy cloud where the tension is. If you're primarily kinesthetic—if you feel things—than just sense the tense area and feel it letting go."

● **Reposition your tongue.** "Many people hold a tremendous amount of tension in the jaw that prevents them from falling asleep," says Dr. Greene. To help release that tension, put the tip of your tongue on the roof of your mouth, just behind your front teeth.

● **Focus on your breathing.** "This helps get you out of 'noisy head thought-land' into a state of deep relaxation," says Dr. Greene. "Just feel the air coming in through your nostrils, filling your lungs, and then feel the air as it exits through your nostrils.

"If a thought comes, don't interact with it. It's like a bus—you may be standing by the road, but you don't have to get on every bus that comes along!" If the thought is particularly persistent or worrisome, write it down, and promise yourself that you'll deal with it later, she says.

Mark A. McDaniel, PhD, professor, Department of Psychology at Washington University, St. Louis, Missouri.

Matthew Walker, PhD, assistant professor and principal investigator at the Sleep and Neuroimaging Laboratory, Department of Psychology, University of California, Berkeley.

Sara C. Mednick, PhD, author of *Take a Nap! Change Your Life* (Workman) and assistant professor of psychiatry at the University of California, San Diego.

Robert Stickgold, PhD, director of the Center for Sleep and Cognition at Beth Israel Deaconess Medical Center and associate professor of psychiatry at Harvard Medical School, both in Boston.

Debra Greene, PhD, an energy-health specialist in Maui, Hawaii, instructor at the Maui Academy of Healing Arts and author of *Endless Energy: The Essential Guide to Energy Health* (MetaComm Media). *www.yourenergymatters.com.*

Lila Davachi, PhD, assistant professor, Department of Psychology and Center for Neural Science at New York University

Sleep Late to Restore Brain Power

Evidence demonstrates that sleeping in on the weekend is a smart idea after a tough week at work (or anywhere else). Americans have a sleep debt that makes the national budget deficit look minor, warns Matthew Edlund, MD, MOH, an expert on rest, biological clocks, performance and sleep based in Sarasota, Florida, and author of *The Power of Rest*. Sleep is as important to health as food and water, and we should stop feeling guilty for allotting time for our bodies to rest, recharge and regenerate, he says.

Here's Proof...

At the University of Pennsylvania School of Medicine, researchers conducted a study of the effect of sleep deprivation on the brain power of 159 healthy adults aged 22 to 45. A control group of 17 spent 12 consecutive days in the sleep lab—10 hours in bed each night for seven nights—while the others spent 10 hours in bed for the first two nights, then were in bed only from 4 a.m. to 8 a.m. for five consecutive nights. Next, this group was assigned randomized amounts of recovery sleep, up to 10 hours per night.

All participants completed 30-minute computerized tests to assess their levels of alertness and neurobehavior performance every two hours while awake—and no one will be surprised to learn that in comparison with those who had adequate sleep, people with restricted sleep experienced...

- **Impaired alertness**
- **Shortened attention span**
- **Reduced reaction time.**

Why You Need a Vacation

Normal function (alertness and performance) was restored in sleep-deprived participants after just one solid night of recovery sleep— 10 hours, or the equivalent of squeezing in extra shut-eye on Saturday morning after a long week. (The more recovery sleep, the higher the scores.) In contrast, participants whose sleep continued to be restricted to an average of four to six hours per night performed poorly on tests and continued to get worse as their restricted sleep continued. Researchers warned that even 10 hours of sleep in one night is not enough to bounce back if you continually push yourself too hard and burn the candle at both ends.

Dr. Edlund explains that many studies have shown that even a few weeks of normal sleep won't make up for a longtime habit of sleep deprivation—and he adds that nowadays people rarely know what it's like to feel fully rested. In that case, it is likely to take more than a day—think many weeks, and that's only if you don't go back to your old ways—to get back to par...which is why we need to take vacations.

Study results were published in the journal *Sleep*.

Indulge in Some Extra Shut-Eye

The best scenario, of course, is to not allow yourself to become sleep-deprived in the first place—but this is not always possible. Most people require seven or eight hours a night to be at their best the next day. But when that doesn't happen, we now know that you can get tremendous benefit from snoozing a little longer even for just one morning. It gives your brain time to recover and reboot—you'll be more focused, productive and energetic as a result.

Matthew Edlund, MD, MOH (masters in occupational health), Center for Circadian Medicine, Sarasota, Florida. Dr. Edlund is author of *The Power of Rest: A 30-Day Plan to Reset Your Body* (HarperOne). Visit his Web site at *www. therestdoctor.com.*

The Memory-Making Nutrient Vegetarians Might Be Missing

Most people become vegetarians because they want to be healthier.

Problem: There might be a side effect of meatless cuisine—faulty memory.

Solution: If you're a vegetarian, a single supplement may restore your memory to normal levels—creatine.

Muscling Up Memory

Creatine is an amino-acid–like compound found mostly in red meat and fish. More than 70 clinical studies show that regularly taking a creatine supplement can help build muscle and strength. Now researchers are discovering that creatine can also buff up your memory.

In one study, UK researchers gave creatine or a placebo to people 65 and older. They found the supplement improved both short- and long-term memory. "Creatine supplementation aids cognition in the elderly," concluded the researchers in the journal *Neuropsychology, Development, and Cognition.*

Vegetarians have lower levels of creatine because they get less of the nutrient in their diets. That fact led researchers at the University of Swansea in England to see if a creatine supplement might boost memory in vegetarians. They studied 121 people (some vegetarians, some meat-eating omnivores), dividing them into two groups. One group took 20 grams of creatine for five days; the other group took a placebo. Before they began taking creatine and after five days, the study participants took a variety of tests to measure their memory, concentration and language skills.

Results: Memory improved by 40% in the vegetarians taking creatine—but didn't improve at all in the omnivores.

Why it works: Creatine plays a key role in the formation of ATP, the fundamental fuel of the body, thereby providing more energy to the brain.

Taking Creatine

There are two effective ways to take a creatine supplement, says Adrian Velarde, a certified personal trainer at Total Body Health Solutions, in Huntington Beach, California, who frequently counsels athletes on using creatine for bigger, stronger muscles.

The first way is creatine loading—starting with a high dose.

Suggested intake: 20 to 30 grams per day for one week, in three divided doses, with meals. Five to 15 grams per day for two to six weeks, in three divided doses, with meals.

Maintenance dose: five to 15 grams per day. Take the maintenance dose for six weeks, then stop taking it for six weeks, in alternating on-off cycles.

If you don't want to creatine load, says Velarde, start with a total daily dose of two to 15 grams, following the previous instructions (in divided doses, three times a day, with meals, in six-week on-off cycles).

Velarde prefers creatine powder to pills because he thinks it's better absorbed. Mix it with water.

Resource: Creatine is widely available. Velarde says that new forms of so-called concentrated creatine—creatine ethyl ester (CEE) and Krealkalyn Creatine—aren't any better than the standard and proven form, creatine monohydrate.

Caution: Although numerous studies with humans show that creatine is very safe, use it only with your doctor's approval and supervision. You could experience side effects with the nutrient if you have kidney or liver problems, or type 2 diabetes.

Adrian Velarde, NASM certified personal trainer at Total Body Health Solutions in Huntington Beach, California.

Why Your Neurons Hate High Blood Sugar (and How to Protect Them)

Sugar isn't sweet to your brain. That's the conclusion of several recent studies, which show that people with chronically high levels of blood sugar (glucose) and insulin (the glucose-controlling hormone that shoots up when blood sugar levels are high) are more likely to have memory problems and other types of cognitive decline.

•**"Greater cognitive decline."** Dutch researchers measured memory and other mental abilities at the beginning and end of a five-year study of 2,613 people who were 43 to 70 years old. People with type 2 diabetes—a disease of chronically high blood sugar and insulin—had a rate of cognitive decline that was 2.6 times higher than people who didn't have diabetes. Among those 60 and older, the five-year decline was 3.6 times greater among those with diabetes. "Middle-aged individuals with type 2 diabetes showed a greater decline in cognitive function than middle-aged individuals without diabetes," concluded the researchers in *Diabetes Care.*

•**From mild cognitive impairment to dementia—via diabetes.** Mild cognitive impairment (MCI) is the stage of memory loss and mental decline before dementia. A study by British researchers found that people with MCI and diabetes are three times more likely to develop dementia than people with MCI who don't have diabetes.

•**Higher glucose and insulin, more Alzheimer's.** In a 15-year study, Japanese researchers performed autopsies on people who had been tested for glucose and insulin levels during their lifetime. Those with the highest levels of glucose were 71% more likely to have the brain plaques that are the hallmark of Alzheimer's disease. Those with the highest levels of insulin were 203% more likely to have the plaques. "Adequate control of diabetes might contribute to a strategy for the prevention of Alzheimer's disease," concluded the researchers in *Neurology.*

Surprising new risk factor: "High brain levels of insulin are neurodegenerative," says Robert Krikorian, PhD, director of the Cognitive Disorders Center and associate professor of clinical psychiatry at the University of Cincinnati College of Medicine. "Excess insulin produces higher levels of brain-harming inflammation and higher levels of beta-amyloid, the neuron-destroying plaques that are a feature of Alzheimer's."

But a recent study by Dr. Krikorian and his colleagues shows that *chromium*—a glucose-balancing, insulin-controlling nutritional supplement—may help stop cognitive decline.

Chromium for Your Cranium

Dr. Krikorian studied 26 people with MCI, dividing them into two groups. One group took a daily supplement of 1,000 micrograms (mcg) of chromium, which dozens of studies show can balance blood levels of glucose and regulate the body's production and use of insulin. The other group took a placebo.

Results: After three months, those taking the chromium had an improved ability to remember and learn. There was little change in the placebo group.

These findings suggest that supplementation with chromium can enhance cognition and brain function in older adults at risk for neurodegeneration, concluded Dr. Krikorian and his colleagues in the journal *Nutritional Neuroscience.*

How it works: Chromium controls blood sugar by improving the functioning of insulin receptors, the structures on cells that allow insulin to move glucose out of the bloodstream. (If your insulin receptors don't work, you have insulin resistance.) *Specifically, chromium…*

•**Helps cells make more insulin receptors**

•**Boosts an enzyme that helps those receptors work**

•**Blocks an enzyme that turns those receptors off.**

"If chromium were a drug for diabetes, everyone would have touted it as a wonder drug," says Richard Anderson, PhD, a researcher at the Beltsville Human Nutrition Center and author of more than 70 studies on chromium.

MCI and Insulin Resistance

Dr. Krikorian thinks that just about everyone with MCI has blood sugar and insulin problems—and therefore needs more chromium.

"We've enrolled more than 150 people with mild cognitive impairment in studies I've conducted," he says. "Their average waist circumference is 40 inches—a very reliable indicator of insulin resistance.

"We've also found that the average fasting glucose level of people with MCI is 98 milligrams per deciliter (mg/dL), just a couple of points below the standard measurement for borderline diabetes." (Levels above 83 mg/dL harm the brain, he adds.)

Recommendation: Dr. Krikorian routinely recommends that all his patients with MCI take a daily dose of 400 mcg of chromium picolinate, the best-absorbed form of the supplement. The chromium picolinate supplement used in the study was Chromax, from Nutrition 21.

"I think everyone with MCI—and even people who don't have MCI—should be supplementing their diet with chromium. That's because everyone eats some sugary, starchy junk food, which routinely raises glucose and insulin levels."

Robert Krikorian, PhD, director of the Cognitive Disorders Center and associate professor of clinical psychiatry at the University of Cincinnati College of Medicine.

Richard Anderson, PhD, researcher at the USDA's Beltsville Human Nutrition Center in Maryland.

Does Cholesterol Cause Dementia?

It's beginning to seem that there's no end to the possible number of pathways leading to dementia—the latest, according to new research, is elevated cholesterol. It's not only bad for your heart but also for your brain. So, what does this mean for those of us who haven't taken action to lower our cholesterol?

How High Is Too High?

At Kaiser Permanente of Northern California, Rachel Whitmer, PhD, and her colleagues analyzed the records of 9,844 patients who completed health evaluations as part of a preventive screening program in the 1960s and 1970s, when they were 40 to 45 years old. Decades later (when the participants were 61 to 88 years old), 596 of them had been diagnosed with dementia—either Alzheimer's disease or vascular dementia, the second most common type of dementia.

Dr. Whitmer looked back at all participants' cholesterol levels—and found that those who had had high total cholesterol (240 milligrams per deciliter [mg/dL] or higher) when screened in their 40s now had a 57% higher risk for Alzheimer's and a 26% higher risk for vascular dementia. Participants whose cholesterol had been borderline high (200 mg/dL to 239 mg/dL) when screened now had a 23% higher risk for Alzheimer's and a 50% higher risk for vascular dementia than those with cholesterol under 200 mg/dL.

The study had some limitations, including a lack of information about whether participants had cholesterol-lowering therapy and no differentiation among types of cholesterol, which we now know is an important health factor. Additional research also is needed to answer some key questions, including why high cholesterol raises dementia risk. Findings were published in *Dementia & Geriatric Cognitive Disorders*.

For a Long, Happy, Healthy Life...

These results suggest that you have a higher risk of dementia if you had even moderately high cholesterol earlier in life. But study coauthor Alina Solomon, MD, PhD, of the Department of Neurology at the University of Kuopio in Finland, says that this doesn't mean that people with elevated cholesterol should automatically begin taking statin

Eat Your Way to a Better Memory

Oranges are a great source of folate, which boosts recall and information processing. Aim for one medium-sized orange per day. Black beans are rich in fiber and vitamin B-1, which helps memory by synthesizing acetylcholine, a neurotransmitter that is crucial for memory. Aim for one-half cup a day. Sage improves recall for up to four hours after consumption. Add one teaspoon of sage-infused olive oil to canned or homemade soup, or use it in a meat marinade.

Natural Health, One Park Avenue, New York City 10016, *www.naturalhealthmag.com.*

drugs—which can have potentially serious side effects. Consult with your doctor, suggests Dr. Solomon, and, if appropriate, look first at making lifestyle changes, which will definitely have a positive effect on your cholesterol and your brain. Though you may not be able to control such risk factors as age and genetics, you can help prevent age-related diseases by eating well, exercising, maintaining a healthy weight and controlling stress. Not only are these measures key to living a good, long life but also, it seems, to being able to enjoy it.

Rachel Whitmer, PhD, research scientist, Division of Research, Kaiser Permanente of Northern California, Oakland, California.

Alina Solomon, MD, PhD, Department of Neurology, University of Kuopio, Kuopio, Finland.

CANCER

Antioxidants Are Anticancer

Many new studies show that antioxidants are in fact anticancer. "Antioxidant nutrients such as vitamin C and vitamin E help neutralize free radicals, unstable molecules that can damage cellular DNA, increasing the risk of cancer," says Susan Silberstein, PhD, founder of the Center for Advancement in Cancer Education, and creator of the Beat Cancer Kit series and other educational materials on cancer prevention and treatment.

●**Vitamins A, C and E against colon cancer.** Higher intakes of the antioxidant vitamins A, C and E are linked to a 24 to 30% lower risk of developing colon cancer, reported researchers from the Harvard School of Public Health. The vitamins may work because they break "free radical chain reactions," said the researchers in the journal *Cancer Causes and Control*.

●**Selenium against bladder, esophageal and stomach cancers.** "Selenium is considered to be an antioxidant, and high blood levels have been linked to a lower risk of cancer," wrote a team of Spanish scientists in the journal *Cancer Epidemiology, Biomarkers and Prevention*. In their study, people with the most selenium in their diets had a 39% lower risk of bladder cancer compared with people with the least. "The lower the levels of selenium, the higher the risk of developing bladder cancer," says Nuria Malats, MD, PhD, the study leader.

In another study, people with the highest dietary intake of selenium had a significantly lower risk of esophageal and stomach cancer.

How it works: In the body, selenium forms 25 different compounds called selenoproteins, most of which are powerful antioxidants, says Dr. Malats.

●**Vitamin E against bladder cancer.** People with the highest intake of the antioxidant vitamin E were 34% less likely to develop bladder cancer compared with people with the lowest intake, reported Australian researchers.

"Bladder cancer is a disease that typically affects older people," wrote the researchers in *Cancer Causes and Control*. "Vitamin E acts as an antioxidant and could be more beneficial under conditions of the greatest oxidative stress, such as aging."

●**Carotenoids against breast cancer.** Smokers with the highest dietary intake of the antioxidants beta- and alpha-carotene had a 60% lower risk of breast cancer compared with smokers with the lowest dietary intake, reported Swedish researchers.

"A protective effect of carotenoids may be more pronounced among smokers because tobacco smoke induces oxidative stress," they wrote in the *European Journal of Cancer*.

Another important development: Researchers from Vanderbilt University School of Medicine in Nashville conducted a study of nearly 5,000 women newly diagnosed with breast cancer. Those who took an antioxidant supplement (vitamin E, vitamin C or a multivitamin supplement) had a 22% lower risk of a recurrence of breast cancer and an 18% lower risk of dying from any cause in the six months after diagnosis.

"Our results do not support the current recommendation that breast cancer patients should avoid use of vitamin supplements," they concluded in *Cancer Epidemiology, Biomarkers and Prevention*.

●**Green tea against breast, prostate, lung and endometrial cancer.** Green tea contains the powerful antioxidant EGCG (*epigallocatechin gallate*).

In a study of nearly 75,000 women conducted by researchers from the Vanderbilt School of Medicine, those who started to regularly drink green tea at age 25 or younger had a 31% lower risk of developing premenopausal breast cancer. "Regularly drinking green tea may delay the onset of breast cancer," wrote the researchers in the journal *Annals of Epidemiology*.

In another study, smokers who didn't drink green tea had a 13 times higher risk of lung cancer than smokers who drank

at least one cup a day, reported Taiwanese researchers.

And a study by researchers from the Mayo Clinic showed that supplements of EGCG triggered an average 20% drop in leukemia cell count among 42 people with chronic lymphocytic leukemia (CLL).

"The profound effect that antioxidants in green tea and other antioxidant-rich foods have on our bodies is more than anyone would have dreamt just 25 years ago," says Gerald Weissmann, MD, editor-in-chief of *The FASEB Journal*, commenting on a study in the journal showing that EGCG dramatically limited cancer growth in laboratory animals genetically altered to develop human prostate cancer.

Adding Antioxidants

How do you make sure the "profound effect" of antioxidants are taking effect in your body? *Here are some of Dr. Silberstein's recommendations…*

●**Eat more antioxidant-rich foods.** The antioxidant activity of foods is calculated by a measurement called "Oxygen Reactive Absorbent Capacity" (ORAC), says Dr. Silberstein. *The most recent analysis by the US Department of Agriculture shows the top ORAC foods include…*

●**Apples** (Red Delicious, Granny Smith, Gala)

●**Artichoke hearts**

●**Beans** (red, red kidney, pinto, black)

●**Berries** (blueberry, cranberry, blackberry, raspberry, strawberry)

●**Cherries**

●**Dark chocolate**

●**Garlic**

●**Green leafy vegetables and cruciferous vegetables** (spinach, kale, broccoli, cauliflower, etc.)

●**Nuts** (almonds, pecans, hazelnuts, filberts, pistachio)

●**Peaches**

●**Pears**

- **Plums and prunes**
- **Pomegranate juice**
- **Red wine.**

"Keep the oncologist away—eat a red apple every day," says Dr. Silberstein.

She also recommends a daily berry smoothie, containing any of the berries on the high-ORAC list, as well as a banana, almond milk (for its extra dose of antioxidants), and a tablespoon of freshly ground flaxseed oil (for its anticancer omega-3 fatty acids).

Additional antioxidant-adding ideas: Mix kidney beans into salads that emphasize dark leafy greens such as spinach. Eat vegetable bean soups. Cook greens with fresh cut garlic. Eat a little bit of dark chocolate a couple of times a week.

Bottom line: Make sure you eat lots of antioxidant-rich fruits and vegetables with dark, vibrant colors, including them in every meal.

- **Take an antioxidant supplement derived from fruits and vegetables.** As a nutritional insurance policy, Dr. Silberstein advises her clients to take a powdered antioxidant supplement derived from fruits and vegetables. She favors the product Juice Plus+.

"It's dehydrated from 17 different vegetable and fruit juices, encapsulated without loss of nutritional integrity," she says.

Compelling scientific evidence: In a study by researchers from the University of Texas Health Science Center, people who took Juice Plus+ for two weeks had the following increases in blood levels of antioxidants: beta-carotene, 510%; alpha-carotene, 119%; lutein/zeaxanthin, 44%; lycopene, 2,046% and vitamin E, 58%. At the same time, their blood levels of peroxides—a sign of oxidation—decreased fourfold, dropping from 16.85 to 4.22 nmol/ml.

These changes "reflect functionally improved oxidative defense mechanisms," wrote the researchers in *Current Therapeutic Research.*

Other studies show Juice Plus+ can reduce three risk factors for cancer—chronic inflammation, damaged DNA and an age-related weakening of the immune system.

Resource: You can find more information about Juice Plus+ and purchase the product at *www.juiceplus.com.*

- **Drink a high-antioxidant green tea.** Dr. Silberstein recommends 710EGCG green tea, an organic, high-antioxidant EGCG-rich green tea developed by Sin Hang Lee, MD, a doctor in private practice in New Haven, Connecticut, in conjunction with a green tea institute in China.

"You're not going to have anticancer activity from green tea unless the tea contains a sufficiently high concentration of EGCG—and this tea does," she says.

Resource: You can find more information about the tea and purchase it (along with brewing instructions to maximize its EGCG content) at *www.teaforhealth.com.*

Susan Silberstein, PhD, founder of the Center for Advancement in Cancer Education, an international lecturer on nutrition and cancer prevention, author of *Hungry for Health* (Infinity), creator of the Beat Cancer Kit series and many other educational materials on cancer prevention and treatment. *www.susansilberstein.com, www.beatcancer.org, www.hungerforhealth.net.*

Nuria Malats, MD, PhD, leader of the Genetic and Molecular Epidemiology Group, Human Cancer Genetics Program, Spanish National Research Center, Madrid.

Double the Cancer-Beating Power of Broccoli

Broccoli contains *sulforaphane*, a powerful anticancer compound, and recent research offers several explanations for exactly how it battles cancer. *Sulforaphane...*

- **Targets and kills cancer stem cells,** preventing new tumors from growing, reported scientists at the University of Michigan Comprehensive Cancer Center in Clinical Cancer Research.

- **Supports the "tumor suppressor" gene p53,** keeping it normal and active, reported scientists at the Lombardi Comprehensive

Cancer Center at Georgetown University in the *Journal of Medicinal Chemistry.*

• **Switches on hundreds of anticancer genes and switches off hundreds of pro-cancer genes,** reported researchers at the Institute of Food Research in England, who studied 24 men with precancerous prostate lesions, feeding them four servings of broccoli a week for one year and periodically testing the genetic activity of their prostate tissue.

Another important development: Researchers at the University of Illinois have discovered an easy way to double the amount of sulforaphane you absorb from broccoli—just add some broccoli sprouts to the meal!

Broccoli, Turbocharged

The sulforaphane in broccoli is linked to a carbohydrate, and that link has to be broken for sulforaphane to go to work in your body. Fortunately, broccoli is equipped for the task—it also contains *myrosinase*, the enzyme that breaks the link.

Problems: If you overcook broccoli, you destroy myrosinase.

And the heating process used to create the broccoli powder found in broccoli supplements also destroys myrosinase. In both cases, you're consuming broccoli thinking it will help prevent cancer—but you're probably not doing yourself much good!

Solutions: Add myrosinase-rich broccoli sprouts to a broccoli meal. Or eat a handful when you take a broccoli supplement.

In their study, the researchers from the University of Illinois fed people meals that contained: 1) broccoli powder, 2) broccoli sprouts, or 3) broccoli powder and broccoli sprouts. Twenty-four hours after each meal the researchers measured how much sulforaphane was absorbed.

Adding the sprouts to the powder more than doubled the absorption of sulforaphane—from 19 to 49%.

The results were reported in *Nutrition and Cancer.*

"To increase broccoli's benefits, you could sprinkle broccoli sprouts on your broccoli," says Elizabeth Jeffery, PhD, a professor of nutritional sciences at the University of Illinois and a study researcher.

Some other suggestions from Dr. Jeffery for maximizing broccoli's cancer-fighting power…

• **Steam it.** "Steaming broccoli for two to four minutes is the perfect way to protect both the enzyme and the vegetable's nutrients," she says.

• **Don't microwave or boil it.** In other research, Dr. Jeffery found that microwaving broccoli (for as little as 30 seconds) or boiling it destroys the enzyme.

• **Add uncooked radish or arugula to the broccoli-containing dish.** They also contain high levels of myrosinase.

• **Eat three to five servings of broccoli a week.** That's the level that's protective, she says.

• **Substitute a similar cancer-fighting food.** Sulforaphane belongs to a family of cancer-fighting compounds called *isothiocyanates* (ITCs)—and Brussels sprouts, cabbage, cauliflower, arugula and mustard are also rich in ITCs. You could replace one or two servings of broccoli a week with one of those foods, says Dr. Jeffrey.

Smart idea: Put mustard sauce on the broccoli.

• **Eat the broccoli, skip the powder.** Although supplements of broccoli powder are available, Dr. Jeffery doesn't favor them—and not just because you don't absorb the sulforaphane. You might also miss out on all the other health-protecting factors in broccoli.

"A whole food such as broccoli is very different from one compound such as sulforaphane," she says. "The broccoli has many different nutritional factors in it. And even if those factors aren't anticancer, they might support the body's utilization of the active, anticancer compounds. Emphasize the broccoli, not the broccoli pills."

Grow Broccoli Sprouts at Home

You can purchase broccoli sprouts in most supermarkets. Fresh sprouts are crisp and brightly colored. Old sprouts are limp, slimy and yellowed.

You can also grow broccoli sprouts at home. *Here's how...*

1. Use three tablespoons of broccoli seeds.

2. Soak in water in a covered glass jar for 12 hours.

3. Put an absorbent paper towel on the bottom of a flat plastic container with a clear, ventilated lid.

4. Drain the water from the jar and spread the moist seeds on the surface of the towel.

5. Cover the container with the lid.

6. Put the container on a kitchen counter or in other sunny indoor location (but not in direct sunlight). The area should have a constant temperature of no less than 70°F.

7. The seeds will sprout in five days and be ready to eat in six or seven days.

8. Before eating, rinse the sprouts and, if you like, remove the seed hulls.

9. Store the container with the unused portion in the refrigerator, eating the rest of the sprouts as soon as possible.

Elizabeth Jeffery, PhD, professor of nutritional toxicology and professor of nutritional sciences in the Department of Food Sciences and Human Nutrition at the University of Illinois at Urbana.

Vanishing Cancers

A common belief about cancer is that it is an irreversible process. Normal cells become malignant and grow uncontrollably. The only way to stop the process is to remove or kill the cancer through surgery, chemotherapy and/or radiation. Cancer cannot just disappear.

That belief is proving to be untrue. In a recent study in *Archives of Internal Medicine*, researchers from Norway and the US analyzed the six-year incidence of invasive breast cancer in two very similar groups of Norwegian women.

About 119,000 of the women had mammograms every two years. Another 110,000 women in the study had not had mammograms and then had one mammogram.

To the surprise of the researchers, the six-year incidence of breast cancer in the two groups was quite different. The more frequently screened group had a 22% higher incidence of breast cancer.

So, what caused less cancer to be found in the second group? The intriguing theory is that cancer did indeed start in this group at an equal rate...and then spontaneously disappeared without ever being noticed (because the women were not being screened).

Other research has shown that spontaneous regression of cancer occurs in cases of advanced melanoma, advanced kidney cancer and neuroblastoma (a childhood cancer of nerve tissue). Regression also occurs in colonic adenomas (precancerous growths of the colon) and in precancerous lesions of the cervix.

Keith I. Block, MD, one of America's top integrative cancer therapy experts, explains that the number of documented cases of spontaneous cancer remission is quite low. He estimates that only one in 500 cancer tumors regress without surgery, chemotherapy or radiation.

However, he suggests that the unalterable, one-way trajectory of cancer is an outdated paradigm.

Cancer is not only mutagenic—propelled by damage to DNA—it also is mitogenic and the growth (mitogenesis) of cancer cells may be stopped by inhibiting molecular signaling and correcting disruption in the body's internal biochemical environment. This can be influenced by lifestyle factors that are alterable through personal choices.

Why Cancers Vanish

There are three main factors that can cause a cancer to regress...

• **Innate biology.** Some people are born with a naturally stronger constitution that is capable of stopping a cancer before it takes firm hold.

●**Transformation of the body's biochemical and molecular environment.** Many lifestyle factors influence the body's inner biochemical and molecular environment, including what you eat, how much you exercise and how much stress you're under.

The latest research shows that positive lifestyle factors can influence genes by turning on the tumor-suppressor genes and turning off the tumor-promoting genes.

●**Better communication.** This includes two types of communication—biochemical communication between cells and emotional communication with yourself and others.

What happens: In a normal biochemical environment, one cell sends a message to another, *Don't grow, I'm using this space.* One reason tumor cells can divide and grow is that they don't receive this message.

The breakdown in communication is fundamental in the biology of cancer in other ways. Studies show that meditation—one way to communicate with your inner spirit—reduces cancer-causing inflammation.

Close personal relationships also are relevant. A preclinical study from researchers at The University of Chicago suggested that social isolation and its impact on stress resulted in a greater than threefold increase in the onset of breast cancer.

Steps You Can Take

Various lifestyle factors can strengthen you against cancer…

●**Exercise and fitness.** Numerous studies link increased physical activity to lower incidence of cancers of the colon, lung, prostate, testicles, breast, ovaries and uterus.

Exercise counters many cancer-causing biological factors, including cancer-fueling molecules called growth factors…oxidative stress (a kind of internal rust)…a weakened immune system…and poor response to inflammation. Aim for a minimum of 30 minutes of aerobic exercise daily, which can be divided into multiple sessions.

●**Whole-foods diet.** The right diet deprives a tumor of the compounds it most likes to feed on and supplies you with nutrients that help your body keep malignant cells in check.

Example: The Japanese have long had a diet rich in land and sea vegetables and fish—and low in meat, refined sugars and high-fat foods. Japan also has lower cancer rates than the US and better survival rates. For instance, men in Japan and the US are equally likely to have very early prostate cancer—the kind that never causes clinical problems—but American men have much higher rates of the clinical type that can lead to advanced prostate cancer.

Bottom line: If you eat too much dietary fat and refined carbohydrates, you run the risk of increasing body fat and weight while weakening your immune system and increasing oxidative stress, inflammation and blood levels of substances that promote tumors.

●**Power foods.** There are "power foods" rich in phytochemicals that are uniquely anticancer. These include turmeric…grapes (with the phytochemical resveratrol)…green tea…milk thistle…ginger…and pomegranate.

But to get enough turmeric, resveratrol and all the rest, you would have to eat curry and guzzle grape juice until you exploded.

Best: Supplements and concentrates, such as "green drinks," often sold in health-food stores. Talk to your doctor about the best supplements for you.

●**Stress reduction.** Chronic anxiety and stress contribute to cancer's ability to thrive in your body.

What happens: Stress triggers biochemistry that is procancer—high levels of certain growth factors…an excess of oxidation-causing free radicals…high blood sugar…and raging inflammation.

Techniques such as relaxed abdominal breathing, progressive muscle relaxation and calming imagery can help you create emotional ease.

If You Have Cancer

The fact that a cancer can vanish without conventional treatments is important knowledge for a person diagnosed with cancer and for his/her doctor. However, a patient should never simply wait for a cancer to disappear. Getting started quickly on a plan of care can be essential for one's survival—losing time can be detrimental, even life-threatening.

Keith I. Block, MD, director of integrative medical education at University of Illinois College of Medicine and medical director of Block Center for Integrative Cancer Treatment in Evanston, Illinois. He is author of *Life Over Cancer* (Bantam). *www.blockmd.com.*

Do Medical Tests Give You Cancer?

Sophisticated imaging technologies (such as MRIs, CTs and ultrasounds) have advanced medicine to unimaginable levels by enabling doctors to look inside our bodies. But it is important to be aware that everything has its price. *Among the downsides to all this testing...*

●**Cumulative exposure to radiation from imaging tests** over your lifetime increases your risk for cancer.

●**Imaging equipment is expensive,** and doctors and hospitals may need to recoup the investment as quickly as possible. Some experts believe that overuse has been a significant contributor to our exorbitant healthcare costs.

●**The images are not as precise as we'd like to think...**in fact, in many cases, they're actually interpretations (based on calculations performed by computer software) and not pictures at all.

●**All this information adds up to many instances of "false positive" results,** which in turn can lead to unnecessary anxiety and stress for patients and unnecessary (and often risky) medical procedures.

To Save Yourself from Unnecessary Tests

Patients need to advocate for themselves. First and foremost, do not make the assumption that every imaging test suggested by your doctors is necessary and important. Knowing something about the risks and benefits of the different types will help you discuss intelligently with your doctor what's right for you. Having this knowledge will also help you understand and keep track of your imaging-test history so that you don't have radiation-based exams that are redundant or for problems that could be diagnosed with a different technique.

E. Stephen Amis, Jr., MD, chair of radiology at both the Albert Einstein College of Medicine and Montefiore Medical Center in Bronx, New York, explains what we should know about the five most common diagnostic imaging tests.

Ultrasound (Also Called Sonography)

Ultrasound uses high-frequency sound waves to create real-time images of organs and blood as it flows through vessels. Commonly used to monitor fetal development, ultrasound can also be used to diagnose abdominal organ abnormalities, gallbladder or kidney stones or an aneurysm in the aorta.

Pros: Ultrasound requires no ionizing radiation and, Dr. Amis says, "presents no known dangers." The scans can be done quickly. Ultrasound is among the least expensive imaging procedures, and the machines it uses are small and portable.

Cons: Ultrasound scans show less detail than CT and MRI scans, and not all structures can be visualized with this technology.

Best used for: Ultrasound is best for evaluating abdominal and reproductive organs, the developing fetus, vascular structures (such as the abdominal aorta) and joints.

Magnetic Resonance Imaging (MRI)

This procedure uses a powerful magnet and radio frequency pulses to "view" most internal body structures. It utilizes a large scanner that transmits the data to a computer, providing a detailed interpretive image of the structures in the body. Sometimes a contrast dye is used to heighten image quality. MRI is especially useful in neurological, cardiovascular, musculoskeletal and oncological imaging.

Pros: MRI uses no ionizing radiation and produces sharp, high-contrast images of different tissues, especially valuable in visualizing the brain and its blood vessels.

Cons: Some people find having an MRI scan quite uncomfortable (two common complaints—obese people don't fit easily into the machines, and being inside can create claustrophobic feelings, for which some people require mild sedation). Scans take a long time—often 30 minutes to an hour—and patients must remain perfectly still and may be required to hold their breath for short periods. A small percentage of people are allergic to the contrast dye, and it's not known whether MRI is safe for pregnant women. A particularly dangerous problem is that the magnets exert powerful force on anything and everything metallic that is on or in the body, and as a result, MRI scanners have been known to cause pacemakers to malfunction.

Best used for: MRI is the best choice for soft tissue imaging, including to diagnose cardiovascular disease, as well as for oncological and musculoskeletal imaging.

X-Ray

These are created by sending beams of radiation through the area of concern to capture an image on photographic film—or these days, more typically on a digital image recording plate. To obtain real-time images of functioning organs or blood vessels, X-ray technology is sometimes combined with contrast dyes injected into the body (called fluoroscopy).

Pros: X-ray technology is relatively inexpensive, is easy to use and produces high-resolution images of bone with less radiation than CT scan.

Cons: The type of radiation used, called ionizing radiation, is carcinogenic, albeit weakly. The radiation accumulates over the course of a lifetime, and excessive doses are believed to increase risk for cancer.

Best used for: X-ray is typically the first choice for diagnosing or monitoring calcium-dense tissue (broken bones, dental cavities) and pneumonia and other chest diseases.

Computed Tomography (CT or CAT Scan)

A CT scan is like an X-ray taken to the next level. The patient lies on a table that moves through a machine as numerous X-ray beams and electronic detectors rotate, following a spiral path, around the body. Computers use the resulting data to create two-dimensional cross-sectional views of parts of the body—these can be further manipulated to create multidimensional views as well. CT scans are most widely used for diagnosing causes of abdominal pain, diseases of internal organs and injuries to the liver, spleen, etc.

Pros: Scans can be completed in a matter of seconds, making CT scans indispensable in emergencies. CT scans produce very detailed images of bone, soft tissue and blood vessels, and can be used in patients with pacemakers and other metallic implants.

Cons: CT scans deliver higher doses of ionizing radiation than X-rays, so with multiple scans, in particular, cancer risk is increased. X-rays, including CT scans, are not recommended for pregnant women—in emergencies, however, they may be required.

Best used for: A CT scan is the imaging test doctors use for diagnosing severe headache, chest pain, abdominal pain and trauma and generally in emergency-room settings. This technology is also often used for diagnostic "work-ups" for cancer, stroke and brain problems, among other illnesses and injuries.

Nuclear Imaging

In nuclear imaging, patients are injected with (or, alternately, ingest or inhale) a minute amount of radioactive material. A scanner or camera is then used to gather images from specific organs in the body. The process is similar to an X-ray, but the radiation beams emanate from the inside out, which enables doctors to see clearly what's deep inside the body. This technique is often used to diagnose or measure the progression of specific diseases, such as cancer or cardiovascular disease.

Pros: Nuclear images provide a view that no other technique can obtain.

Cons: It can take hours or days for the radioactive tracer to accumulate in the body and then additional hours to perform the imaging test. Image resolution may not be as clear as those taken with other forms of imaging. Though the radioactive contrast material is designed to exit the body via the urine or stool within a day or two, the radioactive waste then remains in leaching fields and septic systems and is unaffected by sewage treatment methods, so there are concerns about the cumulative environmental impact of this particular form of imaging. Also, it's quite rare, but some patients have reactions to injected materials—typically these are mild, though severe reactions have been reported.

Informed Decision Making

Patients aren't the ones who should demand one type of imaging test over another. Even doctors, when they are patients, take counsel from their physicians. But, as a patient, you absolutely should feel comfortable questioning your doctors about the risks and benefits—and necessity—of any imaging study.

Important: Always bring up the scans you've had before—the type, how many and what they were for—so that your doctor can make an informed recommendation about what you need next. If you're interested in learning more about imaging techniques, Dr. Amis recommends visiting RadiologyInfo. org, which is cosponsored by the American College of Radiology and the Radiological Society of North America.

E. Stephen Amis, Jr., MD, FACR, professor and university chair, Department of Radiology, The Albert Einstein College of Medicine and Montefiore Medical Center, Bronx, New York.

Shocking Connection— Nighttime Light and Breast Cancer

When you think of carcinogens—cancer-causing substances—you probably think of cigarette smoke, radiation or asbestos.

What you probably don't think of is the light bulb in your bedroom.

Surprising new risk factor: Researchers at the University of Haifa in Israel looked at the rates of five common cancers in 164 countries—and matched them to the level of "light-at-night" (LAN).

The countries with the most LAN had a 30 to 50% higher rate of breast cancer, concluded the researchers in the journal *Cancer Causes and Control*.

And·in a recent study of 1,679 women, the same researchers linked "exposure to LAN in the sleeping habitat" (the bedroom) to a 22% higher risk of breast cancer.

This "is the first study to have identified an unequivocal positive association between bedroom-light intensity and breast cancer risk," wrote the researchers in the journal *Chronobiology International*.

LAN and Cancer

There are several ways that nighttime light might increase the risk of breast and other types of cancer, says Erhard Haus, MD, a professor in the Department of Laboratory Medicine and Pathology at the University of Minnesota.

•**Less melatonin.** LAN decreases the production of melatonin, the hormone that aligns your sleep-wake cycle (circadian rhythm) to nature's light-dark cycle.

What happens: Less melatonin may boost estrogen—and higher levels of estrogen are linked to breast cancer. Melatonin is also a powerful antioxidant—less of it means there's more of the oxidizing, DNA-damaging free radicals that may trigger cancer. And melatonin stimulates the immune system, which protects against cancer.

Recent research: The researchers at the University of Haifa injected animals with cancer cells and then divided them into several groups…

1. Animals exposed to a daily cycle of 16 hours of light and 8 hours of darkness (long days)

2. Animals exposed to 8 hours of light and 16 hours of darkness (short days)

3. Animals exposed to the 16/8 cycle but also given melatonin.

The animals in the "long days" group had the largest tumors (an average of 5.9 cubic centimeters). The animals in the "short days" group had the smallest tumors (0.85 cubic centimeters). But the animals in the long days group who were given melatonin had tumors that were almost as small as the short days group (1.8462 cubic centimeters).

"LAN harms production of melatonin, a hormone that is released from the pineal gland during the dark part of the 24-hour cycle and which is linked to the body's cyclical night-day activity," says Abraham Haim, PhD, of the Israeli Center for Interdisciplinary Research in Chronobiology at the University of Haifi. "When this hormone is suppressed, the occurrence of cancer rises."

● **Broken body clock.** Every cell in the body is controlled by nine "clock genes" that regulate their movements and life cycle, says Dr. Haus. LAN affects the brain area (*suprachiasmatic nucleus*) that regulates clock genes, perhaps triggering the development and growth of cancer cells.

Let There Be Dark

Experts in chronobiology recommend several ways to reduce LAN or its impact…

● **Take a melatonin supplement.** Taking the same daily level produced by your body may help normalize your circadian rhythms and protect you from LAN-caused cancer, says Dr. Haus.

Suggested intake: 0.5 to 1 mg melatonin, 30 minutes before bedtime.

● **Dim your lights during the evening,** says Matthew Edlund, MD, medical director of the Gulf Coast Sleep Institute and Center for Circadian Medicine and author of *The Body Clock Advantage* (Circadian Press). "Try to create evening lighting that is the same type human bodies were evolved to experience—less and less illumination as the night goes forward, and at least an hour of dim light and restful activity right before bedtime."

Healthful strategy: "Take a hot bath with dim lighting before you sleep," he says.

Turn off your electronic devices at least one hour before bedtime, says Dr. Edlund. "There is an extraordinary amount of light being transmitted from computer monitors, TVs, iPads, cell phones and the like."

● **Reserve your bedroom and bed for sleep and sex,** says Michael Smolensky, PhD, adjunct professor of biomedical engineering at The University of Texas in Austin, and author of *The Body Clock Guide to Better Health* (Henry Holt). "Don't watch TV, snack, chat on the phone, use the Internet, or do other types of work in bed."

Turn your bedroom into a sanctuary, adds Dr. Edlund. "Make your bedroom soundproof and lightproof, particularly by putting up blackout drapes."

"Install window blinds in the bedroom," agrees Dr. Haim.

"Avoid LAN—dim the lights in your bedroom or turn them off," adds Dr. Haus.

Wear sleep masks (eye covers) while sleeping, recommends Dr. Haim.

Resource: Sleep masks are available in retail stores and online. For an excellent selection, try *www.dreamessentials.com*.

Erhard Haus, MD, professor, Department of Laboratory Medicine and Pathology at the University of Minnesota and editor of *Biological Rhythms in Clinical and Laboratory Medicine* (Springer).

Abraham Haim, PhD, Israeli Center for Interdisciplinary Research in Chronobiology, University of Haifi.

Matthew Edlund, MD, medical director of the Gulf Coast Sleep Institute and Center for Circadian Medicine and author of *The Body Clock Advantage* (Circadian Press) and *The Power of Rest* (HarperOne). *www.therestdoctor.com*.

Michael Smolensky, PhD, adjunct professor of biomedical engineering at The University of Texas in Austin, and author of *The Body Clock Guide to Better Health* (Henry Holt).

Grill Safe to Reduce Cancer Risk

Grilling can be among the healthiest types of cooking because it gives foods a delicious flavor while using little or no added fat. But grilling also can produce toxic compounds.

Recent study: Researchers at University of Minnesota analyzed data on the cooking methods, amount of meat eaten and the doneness of meat for nearly 63,000 participants. They found that those who preferred their steaks well-done and who used grilling and other high-heat cooking methods were about 60% more likely to develop pancreatic cancer than those who cooked their meat at a lower temperature and/or for less time.

Other studies have confirmed that the high heats used in grilling increase the risk for a variety of cancers, including cancers of the colon and rectum.

Example: A recent study based on data from the Ontario Cancer Registry found that people who ate well-done red meat more than twice a week had a 57% higher risk of developing colon cancer than those who ate their meat medium or rare.

To reduce cancer risk, it's always wise to limit your intake of red meat to no more than 18 ounces (cooked) a week and minimize consumption of processed meats, such as hot dogs, bacon and sausage. *There also are simple steps to take to reduce grilling dangers...*

Too Hot, Too Long

Grills that burn gas, briquettes or hardwood charcoal easily can achieve temperatures of 500°F or more...covered ceramic grills can exceed 1,000°F. High heats are ideal for searing meats and sealing in the juices, but prolonged cooking at high temperatures produces dangerous chemical by-products. These include...

•**Heterocyclic amines (HCAs),** which form when animal proteins, including the proteins in meat, chicken and fish, are cooked at high temperatures for extended periods.

•**Polycyclic aromatic hydrocarbons (PAHs),** which are formed when the fat from cooking meat drips onto a heat source (such as hot coals or metal or ceramic "smoke bars") and produces a smoky flare-up. Like HCAs, PAHs are thought to be potent carcinogens.

•**Advanced glycation end products,** potentially cancerous chemical compounds, that, also like HCAs, are produced at increased levels when foods are cooked at hot temperatures for prolonged periods.

Safer Grilling

Take the following steps to reduce risk...

•**Marinate.** Meat that is marinated for as little as 15 to 20 minutes prior to grilling produces up to 90% less HCAs than unmarinated meat. It might be because the acidic ingredients used in marinades, such as lemon juice and vinegar, change the molecular structure of meat protein and inhibit HCA production.

•**Season with spices.** Meats that are coated with antioxidant herbs and spices, such as rosemary, turmeric, ginger and cumin, as well as garlic, produce fewer HCAs during grilling than unseasoned meats.

•**Cook cooler.** For cancer prevention, the temperature of the grill is more important than the time on the grill. One study found that meats cooked at a lower-than-usual temperature but for two minutes longer had only about one-third of the HCAs as meat that was cooked at a higher temperature for a shorter time and to the same doneness.

After searing the meat, move it to a cooler part of the grill...or raise the grill rack a few inches so that the meat is farther from the heat. With gas grills, you can use the high-heat setting to quickly sear the meat, then lower the flames for slower cooking.

•**Shorten the cooking time.** Meat that is cooked rare, medium-rare or medium will produce significantly lower levels of HCAs than meat that's well-done. When grilling a medium-rare steak, the internal temperature should be 145°F—that's hot enough to kill disease-causing microorganisms but cool enough to limit the production of HCAs.

A steak cooked to medium doneness will be 160°F inside.

Important: Always cook poultry to an internal temperature of 165°F to kill salmonella and other organisms.

You also can shorten cooking time by precooking in a microwave or an oven. Do this with foods such as chicken and ribs. Do not precook burgers or steak, though, because precooking removes some of the juices that make these foods flavorful.

• **Cut meat into small pieces before grilling.** Chunks of beef or pork (when making kebabs, for example) will cook more quickly than a whole steak or roast, which will reduce the level of HCAs.

• **Cook lean to avoid flare-ups.** Slicing off the visible fat from meats before grilling reduces fatty flare-ups and the production of PAHs. Also, avoid fatty cuts of meat (such as rib-eye steak), and choose lean beef for hamburgers.

• **Avoid smoking foods.** People often use mesquite or other types of wood chips when grilling and smoking meats. The smoke produced by these chips may increase cancer risks.

• **Use more vegetables.** HCAs are produced only when animal proteins are subjected to high-heat cooking...and PAHs are produced by fat drippings.

You can avoid both risks by grilling vegetables, such as onions, broccoli, mushrooms, zucchini, eggplant and peppers. A little olive oil brushed on veggies before grilling is fine.

By shifting the balance in a meal to a smaller portion of meat, fish or poultry and adding more vegetables, there are two benefits—less meat automatically means less of meat's cell-damaging compounds, and more plant foods means more of the protective phytochemicals that inactivate those compounds.

Karen Collins, RD, a registered dietitian, syndicated columnist and nutrition adviser to the American Institute for Cancer Research, Washington, DC. She was the expert reviewer for the Institute's international report, "Diet, Nutrition, Physical Activity and the Prevention of Cancer: A Global Perspective." www.karencollinsnutrition.com.

The Dangerous Plastic Epidemic—How a Leading Scientist Protects Her Family

You probably know that plastics can release toxic chemicals. But you may not know quite what to do about it because plastics are everywhere.

The problem: A chemical commonly used in plastics, *bisphenol-A* (BPA), has powerful, hormonelike effects. It is an endocrine disruptor that has been linked to increased risk for a variety of cancers, including breast and prostate cancers. A government task force issued a report suggesting that BPA also might be an *obesogen,* a chemical that causes obesity. In addition, there's some evidence that BPA is linked to low sperm quality in men.

A study that looked at 2,517 Americans ages six and older found that 93% had traces of BPA in their bodies.

You may not be able to avoid plastics altogether, but you can minimize your exposure. *Patricia Hunt, PhD, a leading BPA researcher, describes what she does to keep herself and her family safe...*

• **Don't take the receipt.** The thermal paper that's used for many receipts—from ATMs, supermarkets, etc.—often is coated with BPA. (It keeps the ink from running.) BPA is readily absorbed by the skin. Studies have shown that people who handle a lot of receipts tend to have higher-than-expected levels of BPA.

Caution: The *transdermal* (through the skin) delivery of BPA is enhanced if you have cream or oil on your hands when you handle a receipt. And you certainly shouldn't hold a receipt in your mouth while you're fumbling for the car keys. If you must take a receipt, wash your hands afterward.

• **Be wary of "BPA-free" plastics.** Some companies have phased out products made of plastics that contain BPA and have developed a new kind of plastic that doesn't contain BPA. More and more companies are introducing these BPA-free plastics.

It's a step in the right direction—but unfortunately, other chemicals in plastics may be just as risky.

Example: Some companies advertising BPA-free containers are using plastics made from structurally related compounds, such as *bisphenol-AF* or *bisphenol-S*. Does this make them safer? We don't know for certain, but recent studies suggest that *bisphenol-AF* actually may be more dangerous.

Until we know more, try to use reusable food and drink containers that are made from glass or stainless steel.

● **Don't let plastic wrap touch food.** Even at room temperature or in the refrigerator, Saran-type wraps can potentially release some of their chemicals into the foods that they touch.

Seek alternatives to clear plastic wraps (such as tinfoil or glass storage containers) or use plastic wraps only to cover containers. Or wrap food in a paper towel or waxed paper before putting it into a plastic bag. Also, be aware that a "dry" product is less likely to absorb toxic chemicals than a "wet" product.

● **Don't heat plastics.** Don't put plastics in the dishwasher or microwave. We're all familiar with the plastic-y smell that wafts from a freshly washed plastic container or a microwave-hot container. In reality, that is the smell of chemicals escaping.

High heat accelerates the migration of chemicals out of household plastics such as containers and spatulas.

Caution: Don't assume that all products labeled "microwave safe" are truly safe. It means only that the plastic won't melt in the microwave. It doesn't mean that it's chemical-free.

● **Discard damaged containers.** We all have our favorite storage containers that are the perfect size and shape. We tend to hang on to them even when the lids don't fit right and the sides are warped.

If you're not ready to get rid of all your plastic, at least discard the damaged items. A damaged plastic container is breaking down. When this happens, chemicals are being released.

● **Freeze safely.** Cold is less likely than heat to accelerate the migration of chemicals from containers into food. However, we know that even very low levels of BPA can produce profound changes in the body. The longer food is in contact with any BPA-containing plastic, the greater the risk of exposure. I recommend using glass canning jars for freezing.

● **Choose waxed paper sandwich bags.** We're so used to plastic bags—for sandwiches, cut vegetables, leftover fruit, etc.—that we forget that these are fairly recent inventions.

● **Buy from the butcher.** This is difficult because supermarkets are convenient and usually have the best prices on meats. Unfortunately, most of the meats in supermarkets are bedded on trays of Styrofoam-like material, a polystyrene. Then they're wrapped in plastic, which also releases chemicals, so the meats get it from above and below.

Better: Meats from a traditional butcher shop usually are wrapped in brown or white paper. Ask your butcher to use old-fashioned butcher paper—some of the new papers may be coated with plastic.

● **Replace the plastic you use most often.** Once you realize how much plastic you have in the kitchen, it's tempting to throw up your hands and give up. If this is how you're feeling, a good first step is to find safer alternatives for the plastic things that you use regularly.

Examples: I replaced my plastic ice cube trays with metal trays—the old-fashioned kind that have a lever to loosen the cubes. I use wood cutting boards instead of plastic. When I pack my lunch, I include a reusable bamboo spork, which has a spoon on one end and a fork on the other—you can find them online.

● **Opt for opaque.** The food industry prefers clear or translucent packaging because it looks "cleaner." But in many cases, clear items, plastics are more likely to contain BPA and/or other harmful compounds.

Better: If you're going to use plastic items, choose ones made from polypropylenes. These often are the opaque plastics.

Some plastic containers are stamped with recycling codes that indicate the types of plastic used. For example, containers marked with a "1" are made from polyethylene terephthalate. Products stamped with a "2" are made from high-density polyethylene. Unfortunately, these codes don't tell very much about how safe a particular plastic is.

Helpful: Use the mnemonic "5, 4, 1, 2—all the rest are bad for you." The "good" recycling codes may or may not contain harmful chemicals—but the "bad" ones almost certainly do.

•**Watch out for cans.** The vast majority of canned foods and beverages come in containers that are lined with a BPA-containing resin. Oily foods, such as tomato sauce, are particularly bad, so I buy that only in bottles.

Eden Foods really works to ensure that its canned goods are safe (*www.edenfoods. com*). Other companies such as H.J. Heinz, ConAgra and Hain Celestial have begun using BPA-free linings in some of their cans and have set timelines for eliminating the chemical from all products.

Patricia Hunt, PhD, a leading BPA researcher, reproductive biologist and geneticist and the Edward R. Meyer Distinguished Professor in the School of Molecular Biosciences at Washington State University in Pullman.

The Antiperspirant-Cancer Connection

For many people, the thought of getting dressed without applying an antiperspirant seems downright unhygienic, not to mention antisocial. But a recent review of research suggesting a link between antiperspirants and two deadly forms of cancer—breast cancer and prostate cancer—presents a theory that may change some minds.

"Both of these cancers are hormone-dependent," explains Kris G. McGrath, MD, associate professor of medicine at Northwestern University Feinberg School of Medicine and author of the review, which was published in *Medical Hypotheses*. Dr. McGrath believes that the hormone problem may be located in the underarms and that antiperspirant use may be driving it.

Two Similar Cancers

According to statistics from the US National Cancer Institute's Surveillance Epidemiology and End Results Program, the number of cases of breast cancer and prostate cancer in the US has been eerily similar throughout the 20th century, and for 2009 the figures are nearly identical—about 192,000 new cases of each. Dr. McGrath doesn't think this is just a coincidence.

Breast and prostate cancers share many characteristics. Both have hormone-dependent growth, in both cases primarily by sexual steroids. Both cancers are treated with hormonal manipulation, and breast cancer is additionally treated with aromatase inhibitors to block the conversion of male hormones (androgens) to female hormones (estrogens).

A Possible Cause

Hormone-replacement therapy using synthetic forms of estrogen plus progesterone has been associated with breast cancer—but according to Dr. McGrath, rates of both breast cancer and prostate cancer started rising many years ago, well before the introduction of oral contraceptives and hormone replacement. "So," Dr. McGrath asked, "where are the hormones coming from? My hypothesis is that the problem started in the underarm after the introduction of aluminum salt-based antiperspirants in 1902.

"When antiperspirants block the sweat glands located under the arm," Dr. McGrath explains, "the hormones they contain can't leave the body." Instead, these hormones have the potential to be reabsorbed by the body—posing a potential excessive exposure to breast and prostate tissue. Even worse, antiperspirant use during puberty could be exposing breast and prostate tissue to unwanted hormones at a time of critical growth and development.

Look at the label on your antiperspirant and you'll probably see that it contains some form of an aluminum salt. These chemicals are used because they plug sweat ducts. The apocrine glands are considered an organ—by blocking them you are essentially blocking an organ and its function, according to Dr. McGrath. He added that antiperspirants are considered drugs by the FDA.

Choose a Better Alternative

So what can we do about underarm sweating and odor without blocking the glands? Deodorants (as opposed to antiperspirants), which mask odors without blocking the sweat glands, can be a good option, but avoid products that contain petroleum-based *propylene glycol*, which is thought to be carcinogenic. (Propylene glycol derived from a vegetable source is fine.) Two deodorant brands he likes are the widely sold Tom's of Maine (*www.tomsofmaine.com*) and Terra Naturals (*www.terranaturals.com*). (*Note:* Dr. McGrath is a spokesperson for Terra Naturals.)

Andrew L. Rubman, ND, medical director of the Southbury Clinic for Traditional Medicines, offered another suggestion for safely reducing the bacteria that cause underarm odor—good old baking soda. To use, mix about one teaspoonful of baking soda into enough warm water to make a thin, milky paste, which you then rub into your armpit.

Or, he suggests, you can easily make your own totally natural, safe deodorant at home with just three ingredients: coconut oil, tea tree oil and lavender oil. First, warm up about one tablespoon of food-grade coconut oil...add a few drops of both tea tree oil and lavender oil. Stir and refrigerate until it solidifies, about an hour. Then you can apply a bit (use sparingly so it won't get onto your clothing) of the mixture to your armpits just as you would with a commercial deodorant. "It feels good and you'll smell great," says

Dr. Rubman. "And you won't have to worry about blocking your apocrine glands."

Kris G. McGrath, MD, associate professor of medicine, Northwestern University, Feinberg School of Medicine, Chicago.

Andrew L. Rubman, ND, medical director, Southbury Clinic for Traditional Medicines, Southbury, Connecticut.

Cancer Cells Love Fructose—Don't Feed Them!

The white crystals that we know as table sugar consist of two simple sugars—glucose (the same substance as blood sugar) and fructose (which gives fruit its sweet taste).

Troubling statistics: In the last 35 years, Americans increased their daily sugar intake by 19%, to an average of 22.2 teaspoons (335 calories) a day.

And a lot of that sugar was high-fructose corn syrup (HFCS). This corn-based sweetener is, like table sugar, a combination of fructose and glucose—but with a much higher percentage of fructose. HFCS use by food manufacturers has increased 10-fold since 1970, with Americans consuming an average of nearly 60 grams per day, or 10% total calories.

All that fructose might be increasing our risk for cancer.

Carcinogenic Sugar

A recent study in the *International Journal of Oncology* shows that adding fructose to a culture of breast cancer cells changes them into the type of cancer cell more likely to spread throughout the body.

In another new study, in the journal *Cancer Research*, scientists at UCLA found that adding fructose to pancreatic cancer cells speeded their growth.

"The modern diet contains a lot of refined sugar, including fructose, and it's a hidden danger implicated in a lot of modern diseases, such as obesity and diabetes," says Anthony

Heaney, MD, the study leader and associate professor of medicine and neurosurgery at UCLA's Jonsson Comprehensive Cancer Center. "In this study, we show that cancers can use fructose to fuel their growth. This has major significance for cancer patients, given the high level of fructose consumption in the typical diet."

And recent epidemiological studies on fructose—comparing large groups of people with high fructose intake to similar groups with low intake—link fructose to…

• **32% increased risk of breast cancer**

• **37% increased risk of colon cancer in men**

• **200% increased risk of pancreatic cancer** (with 300% increased risk of pancreatic cancer in overweight, sedentary women).

Fructose-Free

You can (and should) systematically reduce the fructose in your diet, says Richard J. Johnson, MD, professor and chief of the Division of Renal Diseases and Hypertension at the University of Colorado, Denver, and author of *The Sugar Fix: The High-Fructose Fallout That Is Making You Fat and Sick* (Pocket Books).

Best: He recommends starting with a two-week fructose-free phase that eliminates as much fructose from your daily menu as possible. "After that, you can resume eating small servings of foods that contain fructose."

For the Two-Week Phase…

On the menu—foods to choose. All the foods that you are allowed to eat during this two-week period contain less than 1 gram of fructose in a standard serving—and the majority have less than 0.5 grams.

• **Vegetables.** There are almost no limitations on vegetables, from artichokes to zucchini. However, some vegetables do have appreciable amounts of fructose. Stick to green cabbage (not red or purple), dill pickles (no other variety, such as sweet bread and butter), russet potatoes (no other potatoes allowed), yellow squash (no other colors) and no more than one-half tomato per day.

• **Breakfast cereals.** Cheerios (toasted whole-grain oat variety only), Cream of Wheat, Grape-Nuts, grits, oatmeal, Shredded Wheat (unfrosted).

• **Breads and pasta.** Biscuits (plain or buttermilk), English muffin (sourdough), matzo (plain), Melba toast, pasta (all varieties), pita (white), pumpernickel bread, rye bread, sourdough bread, tortillas (corn or flour).

• **Grains.** Barley, bulgur, rice (white or brown), wild rice.

• **Legumes.** Adzuki beans, black beans, chickpeas or garbanzo beans, cowpeas or black-eyed peas, lentils, soybeans (tofu).

• **Meat and poultry.** Beef, chicken, lamb, pork, turkey.

• **Fish.** Albacore tuna, halibut, lake trout, salmon, sole (and other white or lighter-fleshed varieties).

• **Dairy.** Cheese (low-fat varieties are preferable), milk (low-fat or fat-free is preferable), yogurt (low-fat or fat-free, plain, unflavored).

• **Nuts and seeds.** Almonds, brazil nuts, hazelnuts or filberts, macadamia nuts, peanuts, pecans, pumpkin seeds, sesame seeds, sunflower seeds, walnuts.

• **Dessert and snack foods.** Club crackers, popcorn, pretzels, Ritz crackers, Saltines, Triscuits, sugar-free cookies, cakes, and frozen treats.

• **Beverages.** Coffee (unsweetened), diet soda and other sugar-free beverages, seltzer, teas (unsweetened).

• **Fats and oils.** No specific limitations—olive oil and canola oils are the best choices.

• **Condiments.** Garlic, lemon juice, mustard (except honey mustard), salsa, sugar-free salad dressing, Tabasco sauce, vinegar.

Off-the-menu—foods to avoid. The following foods are high in fructose. Don't consume any of these foods during the first two weeks.

●**Sweet foods.** Candy; cookies, cakes, pies, and other baked goods; fruit; fruit juice and other beverages that contain fruit (such as fruit punch; honey; soda and other soft drinks (other than diet varieties); sports drinks.

●**Foods with "hidden" sugar.** Beware when purchasing processed foods—many contain added sugar and HFCS. Don't eat any products that include one or more of these "hidden" sources of fructose on the label: corn sugar, beet sugar, brown sugar, cane sugar, corn sweetener, corn syrup (which may be a blend of fructose and glucose), demerara sugar, fruit juice concentrate, granulated sugar, high-fructose corn syrup, honey, invert sugar, maple syrup, molasses, muscovado sugar, raw sugar, sucrose, syrup, table sugar, tagatose, turbinado sugar.

Avoid any processed food that does not provide an ingredient list.

Other actions that can help you during the fructose-free phase…

●**Take a nutritional supplement.** Eliminating fruit from your diet for two weeks may also eliminate some important nutrients. To replace them, take a daily vitamin-mineral nutritional supplement and 250 milligrams (mg) of vitamin C.

●**Use an artificial sweetener.** If you want to sweeten a food, use an artificial sweetener such as aspartame (NutraSweet and Equal), saccharin (Sweet'N Low and others) or sucralose (Splenda).

●**Resist restaurants.** Consider avoiding restaurants and takeout food while on the fructose-free phase—unless you know for certain the meals you want to order don't contain sugar or HFCS.

●**Be prepared for fructose withdrawal.** In rare cases, you may develop "withdrawal" symptoms from sugar and fructose, such as headaches and fatigue, and intense craving for sweets. (It's not clear why this phenomenon happens.) These symptoms fade quickly. *There are two ways to ease withdrawal…*

●Drink plenty of water. Five to eight cups a day is a good goal.

●Eat a small serving of sugar-free chocolate. This may ease the cravings.

The Low-Fructose Lifestyle

Once you have successfully completely the two-week fructose-free phase, you can resume a healthy (but limited) relationship with fructose, says Dr. Johnson.

●**Limit fructose intake to 25 to 35 grams per day.** If you ate a typical American diet, that's approximately one-third to one-half of the fructose you were consuming every day. If you exceed 35 grams, you risk triggering the biological mechanisms that may promote cancer and other diseases.

●**Pay close attention to the amount of fructose.** In his book *The Sugar Fix*, Dr. Johnson includes an extensive list of the fructose content of foods. This list can help you estimate how much fructose you're getting from most of the foods that make up a typical diet. You can also access a list of foods high in fructose at *www.nutritiondata.com*. (Click on "Tools" and select "fructose" in the drop-down menu.)

Consult the fructose table when selecting foods in the following categories: Breads and grains, bread toppings and condiments, salad dressings, breakfast cereals, beverages, alcoholic beverages, sweeteners, desserts and dessert toppings, and fast foods. Learn which processed foods are best to avoid completely, such as fast-food frozen desserts. (Dairy Queen's Reese's Peanut Butter Cup Blizzard contains 60 grams of fructose.)

Anthony Heaney, MD, the study leader and associate professor of medicine and neurosurgery at UCLA's Jonsson Comprehensive Cancer Center in Los Angeles.

Richard J. Johnson, MD, professor and chief of the Division of Renal Diseases and Hypertension at the University of Colorado, Denver, adjunct professor of the Division of Nephrology, Hypertension, and Renal Transplantation at the University of Florida and author of *The Sugar Fix* (Pocket Books).

The Secrets of Beating Recurrence

Are you a cancer survivor? If so, you have a lot of company. Every year, hundreds of thousands of Americans diagnosed with cancer continue to live, says a new report from the Centers for Disease Control and Prevention (CDC). And that has added up to millions of people.

Currently, one in 20 of us—approximately 11.7 million American adults—are cancer survivors. (Forty years ago, there were only three million cancer survivors in America.)

The CDC also found that 60% of survivors are 65 or older…22% were diagnosed with breast cancer…and 19% were diagnosed with prostate cancer.

Obviously, 100% of cancer survivors don't want their cancer to recur. But whether or not you have a recurrence isn't just a matter of chance. "There are steps you can take to reduce your risk of recurrence," says Keith Block, MD, medical director of The Block Center for Integrative Cancer Treatment in Skokie, Illinois, and author of *Life Over Cancer* (Bantam). It depends on what you do.

"If you return to the same diet and lifestyle as when you were diagnosed—a diet and lifestyle that may have contributed to your developing cancer in the first place—it's more likely your cancer will recur," he says. "You need to work as hard as possible to change the internal environment of the body so that it is less hospitable to cancer cells—and that effort includes a comprehensive revision of what you eat, how often you exercise, how well you manage stress and other lifestyle factors."

Preventing Recurrence

Several recent studies highlight specific diet and lifestyle changes that may help stop cancer from recurring…

● **Soy and breast cancer.** In a seven-year study of more than 5,000 women with breast cancer, researchers at the Vanderbilt University Medical Center found that women with the highest intake of soy had a 32% lower rate of recurrence and a 29% lower rate of dying from the disease.

And the link between soy foods, recurrence and death rates followed a "linear dose-response pattern," say the researchers—the more soy the women ate, the lower their risk of recurrence and death from breast cancer, with benefits peaking at 11 grams a day of soy protein. (Amounts over 11 grams weren't more protective.) The results were published in the *Journal of the American Medical Association*.

"Soy foods are rich in *isoflavones*, a major group of phytoestrogens [an estrogen-like compound in plant foods] that has been hypothesized to reduce the risk of breast cancer," says Xiao Ou Shu, MD, PhD, the study leader. "However, the estrogen-like effect of isoflavones and the potential interaction between isoflavones and tamoxifen [an anti-estrogen cancer drug] have led to concern about soy food consumption among breast cancer patients.

"We found that soy food intake was associated with lower recurrence and mortality among breast cancer patients, is safe, and is potentially beneficial for women with breast cancer," she says.

What to do: To ensure an intake of 11 grams of soy protein a day, eat a selection of foods from the following list, courtesy of the Soy Foods Association of North America…

●Soy bar, 14 grams

●Soy burger (1 patty), 13 to 14 grams

●Tofu (4 ounces), 13 grams

●Soy pasta (½ cup, cooked), 13 grams

●Edamame (edible raw soybeans in the pod, ½ cup), 11 grams

●Soy nuts (roasted, unsalted, ¼ cup), 11 grams

●Soy breakfast patty (2 patties), 11 grams

●Meatless soy ground (⅓ cup), 10 grams

●Soy milk (1 cup), 7 grams

●Soy cereal (1¼ cup), 7 grams

- Soy chips (1 bag), 7 grams
- Soy nut butter (2 tbsp), 7 grams
- Soy yogurt (vanilla), 6 grams
- Soy pudding (½ cup), 6 grams.

• **Stress reduction and breast cancer.** In an 11-year study of 227 women with breast cancer, researchers at Ohio State's Comprehensive Cancer Center found that women who were enrolled in a "psychological intervention program"—which taught patients how to cope with their disease—were 45% less likely to have a recurrence and 56% less likely to die from the disease compared with women not in the program. And even women who did have a recurrence were 59% less likely to die from the disease if they were in the program.

The program included many stress-reduction techniques, such as progressive muscle relaxation…problem solving for common difficulties of cancer such as fatigue…education on finding support from family and friends…as well as diet and exercise recommendations.

"Stress declined for those in the intervention group," says William E. Carson, III, MD, surgical oncologist and study researcher. "They learned how to cope, and they put those lessons into practice. We're finding that reducing stress may be another powerful therapy to fight the disease."

What to do: There are many stress-reduction techniques that work, such as progressive muscle relaxation, mindfulness-based stress reduction or cognitive behavioral therapy, says Dr. Block. "Choose one that is practical and meaningful for you."

However: He points out that the women in the study were part of a comprehensive program that included a stress-reduction technique, problem solving, support from family and friends, nutrition and fitness recommendations, and encouragement to keep up with medical follow-ups. "In fighting recurrence, a comprehensive approach is preferable to a single strategy," says Dr. Block.

• **Green tea and breast cancer.** In an analysis of data from nearly 6,000 women with breast cancer, those who drank three or more cups of green tea daily had a 27% lower risk of recurrence, reported researchers from the Harvard School of Public Health in the journal *Breast Cancer Research and Treatment.*

What to do: Drinking even more green tea daily might produce better results, says Dr. Block.

Trap: "The potential benefits of green tea may not be realized if you don't make comprehensive dietary changes, emphasizing anticancer foods that include vegetables (particularly crucifers such as broccoli), fruits, whole grains, legumes and fish rich in omega-3 fatty acids such as salmon and sardines," says Dr. Block.

• **Weight control and prostate cancer.** In a 13-year study of more than 1,300 men with prostate cancer, those who gained five or more pounds in the five years before or one year after their surgery for the disease were two times more likely to have a recurrence compared with men whose weight was stable, reported researchers from Johns Hopkins Bloomberg School of Public Health in the *Journal of Clinical Oncology.*

"By avoiding weight gain, men with prostate cancer may both prevent recurrence and improve overall well-being," says Elizabeth Platz, ScD, MPH, a study researcher.

What to do: "The good news is that being physically active—exercising regularly—reduced the risk of recurrence associated with obesity," says Dr. Platz.

• **Quitting smoking and lung cancer.** People with early-stage lung cancer who don't quit smoking at the time of diagnosis have a five-year survival rate of 29 to 33%—while those who do quit smoking have a survival rate of 63 to 70%, reported UK researchers in the *BMJ-British Medical Journal.*

These findings support the theory that continued smoking affects the behavior of a lung tumor, say the researchers, and provides a strong case for offering smoking cessation treatment to patients with early-stage lung cancer.

What to do: "It's never too late to stop," says Dr. Block.

"It's also important to eat an antioxidant-rich diet low in saturated fat and high in fiber, plant-based sources of protein and omega-3 fatty acids. An individualized antioxidant supplement regimen may also improve lung function."

Keith Block, MD, medical director of the Block Center for Integrative Cancer Treatment in Skokie, Illinois, director of integrative medicine education, College of Medicine, University of Illinois at Chicago, editor-in-chief, Integrative Cancer Therapies, and author *Life Over Cancer* (Bantam). *www.block md.com, www.lifeovercancer.com.*

Xiao Ou Shu, MD, PhD, of Vanderbilt University Medical Center in Nashville, Tennessee.

William E. Carson III, MD, professor of surgery and associate director for clinical research at Ohio State's Comprehensive Cancer Center, Columbus.

Elizabeth Platz, ScD, MPH, associate professor at the Johns Hopkins Bloomberg School of Public Health and co-director of cancer prevention and control at the Johns Hopkins Sidney Kimmel Comprehensive Cancer Center, both in Baltimore.

Pills That Prevent Cancer

A pill that can prevent cancer? Not long ago it would have seemed far-fetched, but now we actually do have drugs that hold back cancer risk…. But at what cost? For example, while the drug *finasteride* can reduce the risk for prostate cancer, its potential side effects include impotence and loss of libido. Tamoxifen can lower certain breast cancer risks—but it, too, comes with serious potential problems, including an increased likelihood of developing uterine cancer, blood clots, cataracts and stroke. Deciding whether or not to take such drugs is difficult, to say the least, and the issues are not the same for everyone.

Based on your individual and family health history, the risk/benefit equation for anticancer drugs may work out differently—this is something you can discuss with your doctor. The good news is that there are safe, natural substances that help prevent cancer. Not 100% for everyone, but not even the drugs can claim that. Mark Stengler, NMD, author of *The Natural Physician's Healing*

Therapies, describes what he suggests to his patients for cancer prevention, or to slow cancer's progress.

Anticancer Supplements

●**Vitamin D.** Dr. Stengler says that if he had to choose just one supplement to fight cancer, it would be vitamin D-3. Not only is it a potent immunity booster and inflammation fighter, but it's also critical for the support of normal cell division. Vitamin D is most notably helpful for breast, colorectal and prostate cancers.

What to do: Get your blood level of vitamin D tested and aim to achieve at least a mid-range level. For many patients, Dr. Stengler prescribes 2,000 IU daily to be taken with a meal.

●**Fish oil.** Dr. Stengler often prescribes fish oil for patients who are fighting cancer. Two omega-3 fatty acids in fish oil—EPA (*eicosapentaenoic acid*) and DHA (*docosahexaenoic acid*)—support the immune system and block the production of cancer-promoting hormones. Studies also demonstrate that fish oil helps fight wasting symptoms, including weight and muscle loss, in cancer patients.

What Dr. Stengler does: Dr. Stengler typically prescribes one gram per day in total of EPA and DHA…or directs patients to eat two to three weekly servings of cold-water fish such as salmon, herring or sardines.

●**Glucosinolate.** Dr. Stengler pointed to research from Johns Hopkins identifying *glucosinolate*, an extract from broccoli and broccoli sprouts, as a powerful detoxifier and antioxidant. It works by blocking the action of free radicals, which are activated oxygen molecules that damage cells and precipitate cancer. While eating cruciferous vegetables of all kinds, including broccoli, bok choy, cabbage, kale, cauliflower and Brussels sprouts, is a smart dietary strategy, taking glucosinolate as a supplement adds further protection.

Dr. Stengler's approach: He often prescribes BroccoMax, made by Jarrow (800-726-0886, *www.jarrow.com*). A typical dose is one or two 250-milligram (mg) capsules per day.

Kitchen Cures: Foods That Fight Cancer

●**Tomatoes.** Research demonstrates that men who follow a diet high in the antioxidant compound *lycopene* have lower rates of prostate cancer—and it is an important cancer fighter for women, too. Tomatoes are the most concentrated food source of lycopene, and cooked tomato products, such as tomato sauce and paste, are even better ways to get lycopene than raw tomatoes. Other good food sources include apricots, guava, watermelon, papaya and pink grapefruit.

Dr. Stengler says: A daily dose of 5 mg to 10 mg of a lycopene supplement can help protect against prostate cancer—and for women, against breast and cervical cancers. If you are eating lycopene-rich vegetables and fruits, you'll get better nutrient absorption by combining them with a small amount of oil or fat (such as olive oil in pasta sauce or on salad).

●**Mushrooms.** Author of *The Health Benefits of Medicinal Mushrooms*, Dr. Stengler is a strong believer in mushrooms for cancer prevention. He recommends mushroom extracts such as *Grifola frondosa* (Maitake), *Lentinula edodes* (Shiitake) and *Coriolus versicolor* (Yun zhi, or "Turkey Tail"). Published research says that these mushrooms have the potential to improve the concentration and activity of immune markers that are implicated in cancer, including natural killer cells, tumor necrosis factor (which causes the death of cancer cells), T-helper cells and a variety of interleukins.

What Dr. Stengler does for his patients: For prevention, he suggests taking 25 mg to 50 mg of maitake gold extract (available from various companies) daily. He often directs patients with cancer to eat one-quarter cup of mushrooms two or three times per week, using the varieties named above.

●**Turmeric.** Evidence suggests that this bright yellow antioxidant, which can be used on its own as a spice and is also an ingredient of Asian curry powder, helps suppress breast, colon and skin cancer. Curcumin, an active compound of turmeric, is anti-inflammatory and helps prevent new blood vessel growth (angiogenesis) associated with cancer tumors. Up to 3 grams per day of turmeric is considered safe.

How Dr. Stengler uses it: Dr. Stengler typically directs cancer patients to take turmeric in capsule form up to three times daily. He adds that for prevention purposes, it's great to use turmeric frequently in your cooking.

●**Green tea.** In a meta-analysis of studies examining tea and lung cancer risk, investigators found that increasing green tea consumption by just two cups a day was associated with an 18% decreased risk for lung cancer. Green tea contains powerful antioxidant polyphenols that appear to kill off cancer cells. Other research suggests that green tea may stave off cancers of the skin, esophagus, stomach, colon, pancreas, bladder, prostate and breast.

Dr. Stengler advises: Drink two cups of green tea daily (or more, if you are a smoker).

The list goes on…

Other potentially beneficial supplements include vitamin C, vitamin K, panax ginseng and folate. Dr. Stengler says that all these remedies have a long track record for safety and effectiveness and can improve your resistance to cancer…enhance your natural defense mechanisms if you already have cancer…and help minimize side effects of conventional cancer therapies.

Of course, before deciding on any anticancer strategy—whether screening, prevention or treatment, and including natural ones—carefully discuss the risks and benefits with your physician so that you can make an informed decision about whether or not it is right for you and to be certain that there are no negative interactions with other medications.

Mark A. Stengler, NMD, naturopathic medical doctor in private practice, Encinitas, California, and author of the *Bottom Line/Natural Healing* newsletter. *www.drstengler.com.*

Shark Cartilage Is A Fish Story (But Fish Oil Is Fantastic)

Sharks Don't Get Cancer.

That was the provocative title of a book published nearly 20 years ago, claiming that supplements of shark cartilage could stop *angiogenesis* (the growth of new blood vessels that shunt nutrients and oxygen to a tumor), thereby stopping cancer in its tracks. A year after its publication, the book's author appeared on the popular news program *60 Minutes*—spurring many cancer patients to buy over-the-counter shark cartilage supplements. Today, OTC shark cartilage is still going strong, with more than 40 brand-name products on the market.

Latest development: It's likely that none of them work.

Can Sharks Attack Cancer?

In a six-year clinical trial sponsored by the National Cancer Institute, researchers at 53 universities and hospitals in the US and Canada studied nearly 400 people newly diagnosed with lung cancer, dividing them into two groups. Along with chemotherapy and radiation, one group also received a twice-daily dose of liquid shark cartilage, formulated by a pharmaceutical company. The other group received chemotherapy, radiation and a placebo.

Results: Those taking the placebo survived an average of 14.4 months after diagnosis, while those taking shark cartilage survived an average of 15.6 months—a result that wasn't statistically significant. In other words, there was no difference between taking shark cartilage and taking a placebo.

"Clearly, these results demonstrate that shark cartilage is not an effective therapeutic agent for lung cancer," says Charles Lu, MD, an associate professor in the Department of Thoracic Head and Neck Medical Oncology at the University of Texas MD Anderson Cancer Center, which enrolled 60 patients in the study.

"These findings also have to cast major skepticism on the shark cartilage products that are being sold over-the-counter," he adds. "There is absolutely no data showing the efficacy of shark cartilage as a cancer-fighting agent—no data showing improvements in survival time, in tumor shrinkage or in clinical benefits to cancer patients."

The Fish Story That's True

But there is plenty of new data showing that other types of fish can fight cancer—particularly fatty fish such as salmon, tuna, mackerel and sardines, all of which deliver high levels of the anti-inflammatory omega-3 fatty acids DHA (*docosahexaenoic acid*) and EPA (*eicosapentaenoic acid*).

• **Lower risk of colon cancer.** In a five-year study of more than 1,500 people, researchers at the National Institutes of Health found that those with the most omega-3 fatty acids in their diets had a 51% lower risk of developing colon cancer than those with the least. These results support the theory that omega-3s are beneficial in preventing colon cancer, concluded the researchers in the *American Journal of Epidemiology*.

• **EPA as anticancer medicine.** In a six-month study, British researchers treated 55 people at high risk for colon cancer with either two grams daily of EPA or a placebo. Those taking the EPA had an average 12% reduction in the number of precancerous colon growths (polyps) and an average 12% reduction in their size. Those taking the placebo had a 10% increase in the number of polyps and a 17% increase in their size. The results were reported in the journal *Gut*.

• **Lower risk of breast cancer.** In a six-year study of more than 35,000 postmenopausal women, researchers at the Fred Hutchinson Cancer Center in Seattle found that those who regularly took fish oil supplements had a 32% lower risk of breast cancer.

• **Surviving prostate cancer.** Canadian researchers analyzed the results from four studies involving nearly 50,000 men with prostate cancer. Those who ate the most fish had a 63% lower risk of dying from the disease.

How it works: There are several ways omega-3s may work to battle cancer, says Artemis P. Simopoulos, MD, a doctor in Washington, DC, and author of *The Omega Diet* (HarperPerennial).

"Tumors feed on linoleic acid, a pro-inflammatory omega-6 fatty acid, and omega-3s limit the amount of linoleic acid that tumors can withdraw from the bloodstream," she says. "Omega-3s also decrease the number of enzymes that are needed for the creation of cancer-promoting compounds. Additionally, omega-3s make cancer cells more vulnerable to damage by free radicals, increasing the likelihood of cell death. And omega-3s may turn off genes in cancer cells, promoting their self-destruction and slowing tumor growth."

Maximizing Omega-3s

The healthiest, most protective dietary intake of omega-3s is 1,000 milligrams (mg) or more of EPA and DHA daily, says Floyd H. Chilton, PhD, a professor in the Department of Physiology and Pharmacology at Wake Forest University in North Carolina who has studied omega-3s for more than 30 years. *His recommendations to reach that level…*

•**As often as possible, eat fish high in omega-3.** Analyses in his laboratory show that the following fish contain more than 500 mg of omega-3s per 3.5-ounce serving—mackerel, Coho salmon, Sockeye salmon, Copper River salmon, canned wild Alaskan salmon, canned gourmet salmon (prime fillet), canned skinless pink salmon, trout and canned albacore tuna.

•**Occasionally, eat fish with moderate levels of omega-3.** These fish contain between 150 and 500 mg of omega-3 per 3.5-ounce serving: haddock, cod, hake, halibut, shrimp, sole, flounder, perch, black bass, swordfish, oysters, Alaska king crab and farmed Atlantic salmon.

•**Take a fish oil supplement daily.** "Unless you eat fish at every meal, it's difficult to get enough omega-3 fatty acids from your diet," says Dr. Chilton. He suggests supplementing the diet with a fish oil supplement.

"Buy fish oil supplements that contain at least 500 mg of combined EPA and DHA per capsule—typically in a 1,000- to 1,200-mg capsule of total oil, which allows you to achieve your targeted omega-3 intake with just one or two capsules a day," says Dr. Chilton.

Charles Lu, MD, associate professor, Department of Thoracic Head and Neck Medical Oncology, University of Texas MD Anderson Cancer Center, Houston.

Artemis P. Simopoulos, MD, author of *The Omega Diet* (HarperPerennial).

Floyd H. Chilton, PhD, professor, Department of Physiology and Pharmacology, Wake Forest University, Winston-Salem North Carolina, and author of *The Gene Smart Diet* (Rodale).

Pistachios vs. Lung Cancer…Ex-Smokers Take Note

N uts, nuts, nuts—researchers seem to find more healthful benefits almost every time they study them. Recent nut news involves one of the worst diagnoses anyone can get—lung cancer.

The recent study, from Texas Woman's University-Houston Center, found that eating pistachio nuts daily may help to reduce the risk for lung cancer. The heroic nutrient is *gamma-tocopherol*, a form of vitamin E that has been shown to be protective against lung cancer and that epidemiologists believe may also lower the risk for other types of cancer, including prostate cancer. It is abundant in pistachio nuts.

In this particular study, researchers asked 36 healthy individuals—men and women—to consume their normal diets for two weeks. Then, for four weeks, 18 of the study participants added about 68 grams (about 2.4 ounces) of pistachios to their diets, while the other 18 participants continued eating normally. At the end of the study, individuals on the pistachio diet had indeed accumulated higher levels of gamma-tocopherol in their blood. Because it is an antioxidant that may protect cells from damage caused by free radicals, it's thought this may help prevent lung cancer from developing.

Pistachio Power

Pistachio nuts provide other important nutrients as well, including fiber, vitamin B-6, phosphorus, thiamine (vitamin B-1), iron, magnesium and potassium. And they can also benefit the cardiovascular system by improving lipid profiles, says study author Ladia Hernandez, PhD, RD, LD, a senior research dietitian in the Department of Epidemiology at MD Anderson Cancer Center.

According to Dr. Hernandez, the one downside to eating pistachios (assuming that you aren't allergic to them) is that they have a high calorie content. But she notes that "the results of this study showed that consumption of 68 grams [roughly two small handfuls] per day of pistachios did not lead to significant weight gain." (*Note:* When the nuts were weighed, they were unshelled and roasted, and participants were given the choice of salted or unsalted pistachios.)

Pistachios are very delicious, and they can be used in many healthful ways, raw or roasted…in salads, meatloaf and stuffing for chicken and other fowl…ground and used as a crust for fish…combined with fresh fruit in desserts. If you need a healthful snack idea, you might want to add pistachios to your shopping list.

Ladia M. Hernandez, PhD, RD, LD, senior research dietitian, department of epidemiology, University of Texas MD Anderson Cancer Center, Houston.

The Symptom-Relieving Power of Acupuncture

For practitioners of the ancient science of Traditional Chinese Medicine (TCM), health is the natural expression of a balanced, strong flow of *chi*, the life-energy that streams throughout the body via invisible channels called meridians. In acupuncture, a modality of TCM, blockages and imbalances in chi are eased and corrected by inserting tiny, painless needles into key points on meridians.

Most oncologists probably don't believe in chi and meridians, which they can't detect on X-rays or spot on MRIs. But that's not stopping them from sending their cancer patients to acupuncturists.

There's more and more "new research data…to support the use of acupuncture for symptom management in cancer patients," wrote doctors from the Dana-Farber Cancer Institute in Boston in a recent article about "oncology acupuncture" in the journal *Current Treatments in Oncology*.

The newest studies show acupuncture can…

• **Relieve joint pain and stiffness.** Postmenopausal women with breast cancer are often prescribed an aromatase inhibitor—a drug such as *anastrozole* (Arimidex) that blocks the production of cancer-fueling estrogen. But 50% of women who take the drug end up with a burdensome side effect: joint pain and stiffness.

In a study of acupuncture as a remedy for joint pain caused by aromatase inhibitors, 43 women taking the drug received either real or fake acupuncture treatments, twice a week for six weeks. (In fake, or sham acupuncture, needles are barely inserted and they're not placed at real acupuncture points.)

Compared with the sham acupuncture group, the women receiving real acupuncture had significant decreases in joint pain and stiffness, with 20% no longer needing to take pain medication. Overall physical well-being also improved. The results were reported in the *Journal of Clinical Oncology*.

"This study suggests that acupuncture may help women manage the joint pain and stiffness that can accompany aromatase inhibitor treatment," says study leader Katherine D. Crew, MD, an assistant professor of medicine at Columbia University Medical Center in New York.

• **Cool hot flashes.** Aromatase inhibitors also can cause hot flashes in women with breast cancer.

In a study by oncologists at the Henry Ford Health System in Detroit, 50 women with aromatase-induced hot flashes were treated for 12 weeks with either acupuncture or the medical "therapy of choice," the antidepressant *venlafaxine* (Effexor)—which, the researchers noted, has "numerous adverse effects."

Both treatments worked to reduce hot flashes—but the women receiving acupuncture didn't have any side effects.

And when acupuncture treatments and Effexor were discontinued after three months, the women on the drug started having lots of hot flashes again—"whereas hot flashes in the acupuncture group remained at low levels," wrote the researchers in the *Journal of Clinical Oncology*.

"Acupuncture had the additional benefit of increased sex drive in some women, and most reported an improvement in their energy, clarity of thought and sense of well-being," they added.

Also: A study in the journal *Urology* showed that acupuncture can help men receiving hormone treatments for prostate cancer, reducing hot flashes up to 76%.

● **Reduce nausea and vomiting.** Nausea and vomiting are a common side effect of chemotherapy.

Researchers at the James P. Wilmot Cancer Center at the University of Rochester tested acupressure for the problem—wearing a special wristband that presses on an acupoint thought to reduce nausea.

The people who wore the bands had a 24% reduction in nausea compared with a 5% reduction in people who didn't wear the bands.

"Acupressure bands are an effective, low-cost, nonintrusive, well-accepted and safe" addition to therapy with anti-nausea drugs, concluded the researchers in the *Journal of Pain Symptom Management*.

● **Relieve dry mouth and difficulty swallowing.** In people with head and neck cancer, radiation can damage the saliva glands, causing dry mouth (*xerostomia*).

Irish researchers analyzed data from 18 studies that used acupuncture to treat the problem. The evidence "suggests that acupuncture is beneficial for irradiation-induced xerostomia," they concluded.

In another study on people with head and neck cancer treated with chemotherapy and radiation, acupuncture helped ease not only dry mouth but also swallowing problems, overall pain and fatigue, reported researchers at the Dana-Farber Cancer Institute.

And when doctors from Memorial Sloan-Kettering Cancer Center in New York treated patients who had undergone surgery for head and neck cancer with acupuncture, they found "significant reductions in pain, dysfunction and xerostomia" compared with patients receiving "usual care."

● **Stop persistent hiccups.** Cancer patients sometimes develop persistent hiccups. In a study of 16 people with the problem, 13 had "complete remission" of their hiccups with acupuncture, and 3 "experienced decreased hiccups severity," with less discomfort, distress and fatigue.

"Acupuncture may be a clinically useful, safe, and low-cost therapy for persistent hiccups in patients with cancer," concluded the team of researchers from the National Institutes of Health in the *Journal of Alternative and Complementary Medicine*.

● **Ease advanced cancer.** In a study of 26 people with advanced cancer (4th Stage, or metastatic cancer, which has spread beyond the site of the original tumor, often to the bones, brain and other organs), eight weeks of acupuncture treatments reduced anxiety, fatigue, pain and depression, and improved "life satisfaction," reported researchers from Dana-Farber Cancer Institute in the journal *Integrative Cancer Therapies*.

Bottom line: "Acupuncture is safe, tolerable and effective for a range of side effects resulting from conventional cancer treatments," concluded a researcher from Columbia University College of Physicians and Surgeons in the medical journal *Current Treatment Options in Oncology*.

Maximizing Acupuncture

"For a person with cancer, acupuncture can offer help in many ways," says David Sollars, LAc, an acupuncturist, founder of FirstHealth of Andover, Massachusetts, and author of *The Complete Idiot's Guide to Acupuncture and Acupressure* (Alpha).

"It can relieve pain, stabilize difficult emotional states, boost the strength of the cancer-fighting immune system, and reduce the impact of side effects from chemotherapy, radiation, and surgery.

"Not only that, it is empowering for a patient undergoing cancer care to take a safe action such as acupuncture that they know will have a positive effect—just that added intentionality has healing benefits in and of itself," says Sollars.

Here are his recommendations for maximizing your experience of acupuncture if you're a cancer patient…

●**Three ways to find a good acupuncturist.** "Personal recommendations are the best way to find an effective doctor, lawyer, accountant or mechanic—and they're the best way to find an effective acupuncturist who treats cancer patients," says Sollars.

You can also ask your primary care doctor or oncologist, since many doctors now refer cancer patients to acupuncturists. "This also opens up communication between the doctor and the acupuncturist, ensuring better care from each," he says.

Or you can also use the Web site of a national acupuncture organization to find a licensed acupuncturist near you.

Resource: www.aaaomonline.org, Web site of the American Association of Acupuncture and Oriental Medicine. Under "Patients" on the home page, click "Find Practitioner."

●**Know when not to go to the acupuncturist.** If you've just had chemotherapy and your white or red blood cell count is very low…if you're feeling too fatigued or sick to leave the house…it's not the time for acupuncture.

Best: An acupuncture treatment *before* you undergo another round of chemotherapy or radiation, to strengthen your body.

Safety guidelines: Experts in oncological acupuncture at the Leonard P. Zakim Center for Integrative Therapies at the Dana-Farber Institute have created these guidelines to identify cancer patients who should not receive acupuncture…

●Absolute neutrophil (white blood cell) count less than 500/microliter

●Platelet (a component of blood that facilitates clotting) count less than 25,000/microliter

●Altered mental state

●Clinically significant cardiac arrhythmias

●Any unstable medical conditions.

Even after remission, acupuncture can help. Acupuncture is often an excellent treatment for side effects that linger after cancer treatment, such as joint pain and hot flashes from aromatase inhibitors, difficulty swallowing and persistent hiccups, says Sollars.

Katherine D. Crew, MD, assistant professor of medicine, Columbia University Medical Center, New York City.

David Sollars, LAc, founder of FirstHealth of Andover, an integrative medical group practice in Massachusetts, and author of *The Complete Idiot's Guide to Acupuncture and Acupressure* (Alpha). *www.firsthealthofandover.com, www.acuapp.com.*

If Your Loved One Has Cancer, Offer Your Touch

Research sponsored by the National Cancer Institute has discovered a powerful treatment for people with cancer that can decrease stress, anxiety and depression…reduce fatigue…relieve pain…and ease nausea.

The Loving Touch of a Caregiver's Hands

Striking research finding: The study looked at 97 cancer patients and their caregivers (spouse or family member), dividing them into two groups.

Half the caregivers watched a DVD called *Touch, Caring and Cancer* and read the accompanying manual—and then gave three massages a week for four weeks to the cancer patients. The other half read to the cancer patients three times a week from a book the patients said they would enjoy.

Those receiving the massages had less…

•**Stress/anxiety** (44% less compared with 28% less for the reading group)

•**Pain** (34% less compared with 18%)

•**Fatigue** (32% less compared with 20%)

•**Depression** (31% less compared with 22%)

•**Nausea** (29% less compared with 12%).

The results were published in the *Journal of the Society for Integrative Oncology.*

"It appears that caregivers receiving video instruction can achieve some of the same results as professional massage therapists," says William Collinge, PhD, the study leader and author of *Partners in Healing: Simple Ways to Offer Support, Comfort, and Care to a Loved One Facing Illness* (Shambhala).

"This has important implications for the quality of life of cancer patients, helping them feel better," says Dr. Collinge. "But it's also important for caregiver satisfaction. Cancer caregivers are at risk of distress themselves—they can feel helpless and frustrated at not being able to help. This gives them a way to help the patient feel better and increase their own effectiveness and satisfaction as a caregiver. It also appears to strengthen the relationship bond, which is important to both caregiver and patient."

The New Caregiver

"About one-third of adults have been in a caregiving role in the past year for a loved one with cancer or another chronic illness," says Dr. Collinge. "Caregiving is becoming a universal dynamic in relationships. And there are very simple complementary therapies—such as touch—that can make a big impact on both the person with the illness and the caregiver."

If you're a caregiver, here is what Dr. Collinge says you need to understand and do to help your loved one (and yourself) with the caring power of touch…

•**Know the benefits.** "A caring touch introduces so many dimensions of healing," says Dr. Collinge. "Skin to skin contact is so comforting by itself. It improves emotional intimacy between the person with cancer and the caregiver—it reassures the person with cancer of the presence and caring of the other person."

And then there are all the physiological benefits of touch—the relaxation from touch triggers the release of mood-boosting endorphins that can counter stress, anxiety and depression, and reduce pain, nausea and fatigue.

"Touch is unique. You won't find a single drug or other treatment that can yield all of its simultaneous benefits."

•**Be reassured about safety.** "The brief training of the *Touch, Caring and Cancer* video and manual can overcome some of the historical fears and misunderstandings about touch and cancer," says Dr. Collinge.

"It reassures the caregiver that touch and massage can't spread the cancer, or that cancer is somehow contagious.

"The manual also provides a precaution checklist to discuss with the cancer patient's doctors, so that the caregiver can simply and easily avoid any type of touch or area of touch that would cause pain or discomfort."

•**Understand that even simple touch works.** "For example, you can relax a person's whole body just by massaging their hand," says Dr. Collinge, "and you can do that while sitting in a waiting room or watching TV at home. Just lightly resting your hand on a loved one can provide comfort and relaxation."

Cell Phones Double the Risk of Brain Cancer

That's the shocking results from the INTERPHONE study, a 10-year, 13-country investigation by the World Health Organization into a possible link between cell phone use and brain cancer.

The study involved 5,117 people ages 30 to 59 with brain cancer, and the same number of similar people without the disease. Both groups answered questionnaires about the past level of cell phone use. Those with the highest level of use had more brain cancer.

"The study confirms previous reports showing what many experts have warned— that long-term use of cell phones increases the risk of brain cancer," says David Carpenter, MD, director of the Institute for Health and the Environment at the University of Albany in Rensselaer, New York.

Specifically, says Dr. Carpenter, the study showed…

• **Using a cell phone for 30 minutes a day for 10 years** was linked to a 95% increased risk of *glioma* (a type of brain tumor)—nearly twice the risk of those who seldom or never used cell phones.

• **Two to four years of heavy cell phone use** was linked to a 68% increased risk of glioma.

• **The tumors were more likely to occur on the side of the head** most used for calling.

Bottom line: "The INTERPHONE study strongly indicates that extensive use of a cell phone on one side of the head increases risk of glioma on that side of the head— and the risk increases the more hours you use the phone," says Dr. Carpenter.

Theory: From cellular and animal studies, scientists think cell phones may trigger cancer by affecting genes, altering the process of cell division, he says.

Another important development: A few months after the publication of the study, the International Agency for Research on Cancer, a division of the World Health Organization, issued a statement saying cell phones are "possibly carcinogenic."

Protecting Your Brain

"The risks documented in this study must be taken seriously as a warning to limit cell phone use," says Dr. Carpenter. *His recommendations…*

• **Use a landline whenever possible.** "Never using a cell phone is my best recommendation, but that's impractical in this wireless world."

• **When you use a cell phone, use a wired earpiece.** "A wired earpiece is better than Bluetooth, and Bluetooth is better than holding the cell phone to your head," he says.

• **Don't wear the cell phone on your body.** "Recent research shows men who wear cell phones on their hips have lower sperm counts," says Dr. Carpenter, "and I wouldn't be surprised if future research shows that wearing a cell phone on the hip elevates the risk of prostate cancer and colon cancer."

He also urges parents to limit their children's use of cell phones—because a child's growing body may be particularly vulnerable to the effects of electromagnetic frequencies from cell phones.

"One scientific study shows that if an individual begins using a cell phone under the age of 20, their risk of brain cancer is five-fold higher when they are older than 20," says Dr. Carpenter. "The big question is whether we're going to see a striking elevation in rates of brain cancer from cell phone use in children and teenagers who have been using the devices all their lives."

David Carpenter, MD, director, Institute for Health and Environment, University of Albany, Rensselaer, New York.

• **Realize that you might offer more benefits than a massage professional.** "Some of the people in this study—such as older caregivers who were at home all day—would give short massages six or seven times a day," says Dr. Collinge. "When we asked them why, they'd say, 'We just enjoy it so much that we do five minutes here and five minutes there several times a day.' That means some people were giving 50 mini-massages a week—for enduring impact, that's so much greater than could be achieved by the patient seeing a massage therapist once a week."

• **Attitude matters more than technique.** "The bottom line is not how you touch, but receiving the permission and encouragement to touch," says Dr. Collinge. "The technique is really of minimal importance. What's important is the actual touching, and the compassionate presence of the caregiver."

• **Expand your concept of caregiving.** "We have the notion in our culture that caregiving is about changing the linens, monitoring medications, bringing good food, bathing, taking the patient to appointments and other similar tasks," says Dr. Collinge. "But we can expand the notion of home caregiving to include some simple complementary therapies such as touch that are deeply satisfying both to the person being cared for and the person doing the caring."

• **Watch the video and read the manual.** The DVD and manual used in the study—*Touch, Care and Cancer*—is available at *www.partnersinhealing.net*.

William Collinge, PhD, director of Collinge Associates, Kittery, Maine, which provides consultation and research in integrative health care. He is author of several books, including *Partners in Healing* (Shambhala) and executive producer of the *Touch, Caring, and Cancer* DVD program. *www.collinge.org, www.partnersinhealing.net*.

Chapter 6

DEPRESSION, ANXIETY & THE "BLAHS"

Six Supplements That Can Make You Happier

If you're feeling low, you may have low blood levels of various nutrients. Recent studies show that B vitamins...the omega-3 fatty acids in fish oil...vitamin D...zinc...vitamin C...and the amino acid-derived compound SAMe (*S-adenosyl methionine*)...can help lift the burden of depression.

Why they work: "Optimal brain chemistry is dependent on optimal nutrition," says Hyla Cass, MD, a psychiatrist in private practice in Pacific Palisades, California, and author of *Natural Highs: Feel Good All the Time* (Avery). "If various vitamins, minerals and amino acids aren't available in sufficient quantities, you can't make enough neurotransmitters, the chemical messengers in your brain that control mood, memory and many other emotional and mental functions.

"The psychiatric profession has largely ignored this reality. But nutrients should be the first line of defense against depression. They

often work better than antidepressants. And they don't have side effects. In fact, they usually have side *benefits*, such as a healthier heart and immune system."

Antidepressant Nutrients

Here is the latest research on nutrients that can prevent or treat depression...

•**Vitamins B-6 and B-12.** In a 12-year study of more than 3,500 people aged 65 and older, researchers at the Rush University Medical Center in Chicago found that those who took vitamin B-6 and/or vitamin B-12 in nutritional supplements had a lower risk of becoming depressed. (A diet high in foods rich in the two B vitamins wasn't linked to lower risk.)

Key findings: Each additional 10 milligram (mg) intake of vitamins B-6 and B-12 was linked to a 2% lower risk of depression—for example, a person taking 50 mg of B-6 had a 10% lower risk of depression than a person not taking the nutrient.

"Our results support the hypotheses that high total intakes of vitamins B-6 and B-12 are protective of depressive symptoms in older adults," concluded the researchers in the *American Journal of Clinical Nutrition*.

In another study, in the *European Journal of Clinical Nutrition*, Japanese researchers linked higher blood levels of the B vitamin folate to a 50% lower risk of becoming depressed.

Suggested intake: "Older people often have very poor absorption of vitamin B-12, and may benefit from higher amounts, such as 1,000 micrograms (mcg) daily," says Dr. Cass.

She suggests 20 to 100 mg a day of vitamin B-6.

"You also need about 400 mcg of folate daily," she says.

●**Omega-3 fatty acids (fish oil).** In a study by Canadian researchers of 432 people with depression, 50% improved when they took a daily fish oil supplement containing 1,050 mg of *eicosapentaenoic acid* (EPA) and 150 mg of *docosahexaenoic acid* (DHA). The results were published in the *Journal of Clinical Psychiatry*.

And when researchers at the University of Illinois analyzed the results of 15 studies on omega-3 supplements and depression, they found that high-EPA supplements (but not high-DHA supplements) improved symptoms.

Suggested intake: A fish oil supplement containing at least 1,000 mg of EPA. Examples: OmegaBrite (*www.omegabrite.com*), o3mega+ joy (*www.genuinehealth.com*).

●**Vitamin D.** Older people with low blood levels of vitamin D have twice the risk of becoming depressed, reported researchers from the National Institute on Aging, who conducted a six-year study on nearly 1,000 people aged 65 and older. The results were published in the *Journal of Clinical Endocrinology & Metabolism*.

And in a study in the *International Archives of Medicine* of nearly 8,000 Americans aged 15 to 39, people with low blood levels of vitamin D were 85% more likely to become depressed. The researchers theorized that vitamin D works to prevent depression by protecting brain cells from "oxidative degenerative processes."

Suggested intake: Dr. Cass recommends a vitamin D blood test. If your levels are lower than 50 nanograms per deciliter (ng/dL), she suggests supplementing at 5,000 IU daily, and taking another test six months later. Once you've reached the 50 ng/dL level, continue to supplement at 2,000 IU daily.

You can ask your doctor for vitamin D blood tests, or you can order a relatively inexpensive twice-yearly home test at *www.grassrootshealth.net*, the Web site of an organization that specializes in awareness and treatment of vitamin D deficiency. The total cost for the twice-yearly home tests is $60.

●**Zinc.** In a study of 30 people by Japanese researchers, those who took a daily zinc supplement for 10 weeks had a significant reduction in depression and feelings of dejection, and also felt less angry and hostile.

"Zinc supplementation may be effective in reducing anger and depression," concluded the researchers in the *European Journal of Clinical Nutrition*.

Suggested intake: 15 mg daily. Try zinc citrate, a highly absorbable form, says Dr. Cass. She favors zinc citrate from Natural Factors.

●**Vitamin C.** Researchers in Canada gave a twice-daily supplement of 500 mg of vitamin C (1,000 mg a day) to hospital patients. After one week, the patients had a rise in blood levels of vitamin C—and a 34% drop in "mood disturbance," wrote the researchers in the journal *Nutrition*.

"Earlier studies, both in our hospital and in other centers, demonstrated that the majority of acutely hospitalized patients have subnormal levels of vitamin C in their blood—and deficiencies of vitamin C have been linked to psychological abnormalities," says L. John Hoffer, MD, PhD, a study researcher. "Most physicians are unaware of the problem, and patients are rarely given vitamin supplements.

But treating the problem with a vitamin C supplement is safe, simple and cheap."

The researchers theorize that low levels of vitamin C in the cerebrospinal fluid may adversely affect brain functions and mood.

Suggested intake: 1,000 mg of vitamin C daily, as used in the study.

●**SAMe.** The body produces SAMe by combining the amino acid *methionine* and ATP (*adenosine triphosphate*), a fundamental fuel. SAMe helps in the process of *methylation*, a crucial biochemical reaction that regulates genes, hormones, cellular membranes—and neurotransmitters.

Researchers at the Center for Treatment-Resistant Depression at Harvard Medical School studied 73 depressed people who hadn't been helped by standard antidepressant drugs (selective serotonin reuptake inhibitors, or SSRIs). For six weeks, they took an antidepressant and a daily dose of 1,600 mg SAMe (or a placebo).

Twenty-eight percent more people taking SAMe had a reduction in their depression symptoms. And 34% more people taking SAMe had a complete remission of depression.

"SAMe can be an effective, well-tolerated and safe adjunctive treatment strategy" for people who aren't responding to their antidepressants, concluded the researchers in the *American Journal of Psychiatry*.

"This new finding…suggests significant, clinically meaningful differences in outcome among patients who had SAMe added to their antidepressant medication treatment compared with those taking a placebo with their medication," says George Papakostas, MD, the study's lead researcher and associate professor of psychiatry at Harvard Medical School.

Suggested intake: "Start with 200 mg of SAMe once or twice daily," advises Dr. Cass. "If you don't see results in a few days, you can gradually increase the dose by 200 mg every three days, up to a maximum of 400 mg four times daily, or 1,600 mg. Once your mood feels stable, you can gradually reduce your intake to a lower maintenance dose. In general, the longer SAMe is used, the better the results."

Product: The brand of SAMe used in the Harvard study was SAM-e Complete from Nature Made (*www.naturemade.com*).

Hyla Cass, MD, psychiatrist in private practice in Pacific Palisades, California, and author of several books, including *Natural Highs: Feel Good All the Time* (Avery). *www.cassmd.com.*

L. John Hoffer, MD, PhD, Lady David Institute for Medical Research, Montreal, Canada.

George Papakostas, MD, associate professor of psychiatry at Harvard Medical School and director of treatment-resistant depression studies in the Department of Psychiatry at Massachusetts General Hospital, both in Boston.

Antidepressants Don't Work—Here's What Does

About three-quarters of patients who are treated for depression take one or more antidepressant medications. In fact, about 10% of all Americans are taking these drugs.

Antidepressants, including Prozac and other selective serotonin reuptake inhibitors (SSRIs), can help patients with severe depression, but they are not effective for most patients with mild-to-moderate depression. A recent report in the *Journal of the American Medical Association* concluded that some of the most widely prescribed antidepressants are no more effective than placebos for these patients.

Also, these drugs commonly cause sexual problems, weight gain and other side effects, including an inability to feel empathy for others. These side effects might be acceptable for someone who is incapacitated with depression, but the risk-benefit ratio isn't acceptable for the types of depression that can be treated with other methods. Here's how to relieve depression without taking medications.

Important: Never stop taking an antidepressant without your doctor's approval, and be sure to taper off slowly.

119

Grow a Happy Brain

We have learned in recent years that chronic depression causes significant brain damage. Patients produce less *dopamine*, one of the neurotransmitters that affects the ability to feel pleasure. The *hippocampus*, one part of the brain associated with emotions, can shrink by up to 20%. Cells lose *endorphin* (the pleasure hormone) receptor sites, which further inhibits pleasurable feelings.

Good news: Much of this damage can be reversed with positive emotions—by trying the strategies in this article and continuing to use the ones that work for you. Just as the areas of the brain associated with hand coordination get larger when a musician practices his/her instrument, people with depression can increase the areas of the brain associated with positive emotions.

Keep Track

Sudden mood changes can be a hallmark of depression. The dramatic ups and downs that some patients experience are triggered by unfelt feelings. Because of their past experiences (such as childhood trauma), they have learned to mute their feelings—experiencing them is too painful.

Example: You might go to bed feeling fine, then wake up in the throes of depression. You are reacting to something, but because you don't know what that something is, you feel buffeted by forces beyond your control.

Solution: A mood journal. Every day, keep track of what's happening when you experience any type of mood change. Write down what you're feeling, what you were doing when you first noticed the feeling and what you were thinking about or remembering at the time.

This is a powerful tool to help you circumvent your defense mechanisms. You will start to recognize more of your feelings and understand why you're having them. This won't make the emotional pain disappear (you might even feel more upset when you first start doing this), but you will start to recognize emotional causes and effects. This knowledge will lead to solutions as well as a greater sense of control.

Do Something

Patients with severe depression can be almost catatonic—just getting out of bed or taking a shower can seem impossible. With milder forms of depression, procrastination is one of the biggest hurdles. Starting something is risky. There might be failure. There will be frustrations and setbacks. Self-esteem may be threatened. Doing nothing can feel like a safer alternative, even though the lack of accomplishment will make the depression worse.

People don't accomplish things because they are naturally productive and energetic. They become productive and energetic by doing things.

Solution: Every day, make yourself do something that gives you a sense of accomplishment. You might make a commitment to work in the yard or fix a garden fence. You might decide to write a few lines of a poem.

It doesn't matter what the activity is, as long as you do something. People who set goals and deadlines (I'm going to write for 10 minutes tomorrow at 10 a.m.) and follow through almost always notice an improvement in mood. Once they experience that uplift, they are more likely to keep trying new things.

Get Off the Mental Roller Coaster

Depression is accompanied by thought patterns that are rife with distorted perceptions and faulty logic.

Example: A healthy individual who gets a flat tire will focus on the immediate problem—Darn, I have a flat tire. I'll have to get it fixed.

Someone with depression will imagine the worst possible scenario. All of my tires must be going bad. I don't have the money to replace them all. *I might have to get another job...*

They get so worked up that they forget they are dealing with a simple problem. Instead, the imaginary scenario dominates their thinking.

Solution: Take yourself off the mental roller coaster. When you start imagining the worst, think *Stop*. Ask yourself how likely any of these dire outcomes really is. Once people understand that they're prone to making exaggerated—and erroneous—generalizations, they find it easier to mentally step back and focus on the real problem. Oh, it's just a flat tire. It feels like a huge problem, but it's not.

Watch Your Mind

Recent studies have found that people who practice mindful meditation—noting the thoughts that run through their minds without letting those thoughts upset them—have increased activity in the prefrontal part of the brain. This is where positive emotions are processed and negative emotions are controlled.

Mindfulness means watching your mind at work. You are aware of yourself and your thoughts, but you are detached from the emotional components. People who practice mindfulness become more thoughtful about their emotions and are less likely to react to them.

This is critical for people with depression. They tend to ruminate too much. They worry about things that haven't happened and attach too much importance to things that don't matter.

Solution: Daily meditation. Find a quiet place where you won't be interrupted for 20 or 30 minutes. Get comfortable, close your eyes and start to breathe slowly and deeply. Focus only on your breathing. As thoughts or feelings drift in and out of your mind, acknowledge them, then let them float off, like bubbles in a pool of water. Whenever you get distracted, return your mind to your breathing.

Don't expect to experience bliss—that's not the purpose. It's more like exercise for the brain. People who do this daily find that they're generally calmer and more resilient against stress. They learn to detach from their emotions long enough to think about what those feelings really mean and how important (or unimportant) they are.

Walk It Off

Studies of depressed adults show that those who exercise three times a week improve just as much in the short-term as those who take antidepressants. People who continue to exercise are more likely to avoid future depressive episodes than those who rely solely on medication.

Exercise appears to stimulate the growth of new brain cells, the opposite of what happens with depression. It stimulates the production of endorphins. It also promotes feelings of accomplishment and physical well-being.

Solution: Walk briskly three or more times a week. You will probably notice significant improvement in mood within the first week. Those who exercise harder or more often tend to report the greatest improvement.

Richard O'Connor, PhD, psychotherapist in private practice with offices in Canaan, Connecticut, and New York City. He is former executive director of the Northwest Center for Family Service and Mental Health and author of *Undoing Depression: What Therapy Doesn't Teach You and Medication Can't Give You* (Little, Brown). *www.undoingdepression.com.*

Herbs for Your Nerves

Twenty-five million Americans have chronic anxiety—what psychologists called an "anxiety disorder." *Signs of anxiety disorder can include...*

● **You have intense feelings of worry that most other people don't experience.** These feelings wake you up at night or come unexpectedly at any time of day. (Generalized Anxiety Disorder)

● **You experience panicky feelings (even a full-scale panic attack, with breathlessness, sweating and a racing heart) when you leave home, drive on a highway, go to a shopping mall or get on an elevator.** And you spend hours every day thinking about, fearing and expecting these anxious, panicky feelings. (Panic Disorder)

● **You give up important activities in your life because of anxiety.** (Social Anxiety Disorder)

Other types of anxiety disorders include post-traumatic stress syndrome, obsessive-compulsive disorder, and specific phobias (such as fear of flying that is so intense you never travel by airplane).

The most common treatment for an anxiety disorder is an anxiety-reducing drug—either a *benzodiazepine*, such as Xanax, Valium or Ativan; or an antidepressant, such as Paxil, Lexapro or Zoloft.

Red flags: Benzodiazepines are potentially addictive, with anxiety possibly worsening when you stop the drug. Antidepressants can have disruptive side effects such as weight gain, a stalled sex drive or even suicidal tendencies you didn't have before taking the medication.

One option: You might want to try an anti-anxiety herb instead.

"With the rising cost of prescription medications and their unwanted side effects…it is not surprising that there is a universal interest in finding effective, natural anti-anxiety treatments with a lower risk of adverse effects or withdrawal," wrote a team of researchers in a recent issue of *Nutrition Journal*.

The researchers analyzed the results of 21 studies on anti-anxiety herbs, involving more than 2,600 people. Their conclusion:

"Herbal supplementation is an effective method for treating anxiety and anxiety-related conditions without the risk of serious side effects."

Another recent review of anti-anxiety herbs appeared in the journal *Medical Science Monitor*, concluding that scientific studies "support a role for these preparations as useful alternatives in the management of the stress and anxiety of everyday life."

The Best Anti-Anxiety Herbs

Here are the herbs that work best for easing anxiety, say experts.

● **Kava.** Several scientific studies show that this herb from the South Pacific can reduce anxiety and promote relaxation, says Benjamin Weeks, PhD, of Adelphi University, author of the article on anti-anxiety herbs in *Medical Science Monitor*.

How it works: Kavalactones—the active ingredients in kava—increase levels of GABA (*g-aminobutyric acid*), a neurotransmitter that calms the activity of brain cells.

Caution: There are several cases linking the intake of kava to liver damage. In 2002 the FDA issued a warning about the herb, causing many supplement companies to stop selling it.

However, none of the more than 400 people who participated in scientific studies on kava developed liver damage from taking the herb, notes Shaheen Lakhan, MD, PhD, co-author of the article on anti-anxiety herbs in *Nutrition Journal*. "Kava was considered to be well-tolerated until 1998, when the first reported case of liver damage occurred," he continues. "These rare but serious side effects may have occurred due to poor-quality kava, as well as other factors, such as taking too much of the herb."

Recommended: The company Herb Pharm produces a high-quality kava extract, says Mark Blumenthal, founder and executive director of the American Botanical Council and editor of HerbalGram. Follow the dosage recommendations on the label (*www.herbpharm.com*).

● **L-theanine.** This unique amino acid (a building block of protein) is found in green tea, and studies show it can calm anxiety and ease feelings of stress, says Dr. Weeks.

How it works: L-theanine increases alpha waves, the type of brain wave linked to a calm yet alert state of mind, such as in meditation. L-theanine may also increase GABA.

Recommended: 200 milligrams (mg), two to three times daily, say the Japanese researchers who studied L-theanine.

Best: Suntheanine, the patented form of L-theanine used in the studies showing the amino acid can calm anxiety and increase alpha waves. It is the ingredient in most (but not all) L-theanine products.

● **Chamomile.** A recent study from researchers at the University of Pennsylvania showed that an extract of chamomile reduced anxiety in people with Generalized Anxiety Disorder.

How it works: Chamomile may modulate several compounds that play a role in anxiety, including noradrenaline (a stress hormone), and dopamine and serotonin (neurotransmitters).

Recommended: The herb is well-known for its safety, posing virtually no risk, says Amanda McQuade-Crawford, a medical herbalist in Los Angeles. If you have anxiety, drink a cup of chamomile tea when you feel anxious, anywhere from one to three cups a day, she says. "You should feel calmer 15 to 20 minutes after drinking the tea."

Best: Use high-quality chamomile. "Look for tea from whole, dried flowers rather than broken bits of petal and powder," says McQuade-Crawford. "To test for quality, crush the whole dried chamomile between your fingers—it should release an applelike scent."

Anti-Anxiety Formulas

Other effective anti-anxiety herbs include gotu kola, hops, lemon balm, passionflower, magnolia bark, valerian root and 5-HTP (an amino acid derived from the seeds of the African shrub *Griffonia simplicifolia*).

For optimal results: Taking a combination of several anti-anxiety herbs is a better strategy than taking one at a time, say experts. *Recommended anti-anxiety formulas include...*

●**Relarian.** This combination of L-theanine, 5-HTP, valerian and GABA is found in the "relaxation drink" Mini Chill, from Stevenson Products (*www.minichill.com*).

"If you're anxious about flying, or taking a test or going on a first date, drinking a Mini Chill will relieve feelings of anxiety and help you relax, without causing drowsiness," says Dr. Weeks. "I have used it, and I have given it to people at times of anxiety and stress, and it definitely helps you calm down."

● **Calming Balance.** Along with high doses of stress-reducing B vitamins, this product also contains L-theanine, passionflower, and magnolia bark, says Jacob Teitelbaum, MD, a physician in private practice in Hawaii who formulated the product, from Enzymatic Therapy.

"Calming Balance produces an anti-anxiety effect within 30 minutes, but the effects continue to increase over two weeks of continued use," he says. "At that point, your anxiety should be under control. Once anxiety is normalized, you can lower the dose (from three capsules a day to two or one) or take it only as needed.

Resource: The product is available at *www.endfatigue.com* and through other retailers.

●**AnxioFit-1.** "This herbal formulation from Hungarian scientists is a big surprise because it doesn't contain an herb classically used for anxiety," says Blumenthal. "It contains a special extract of *Echinacea angustifolia* root at only 20% of the level people would take for prevention of colds and flu. But an unpublished clinical trial shows that it has a significant anti-anxiety effect."

Resource: The product is available in the US through EuroPharma, at *www.europharmausa.com*.

Follow the dosage recommendation on the label: A higher dose is not more effective.

Benjamin Weeks, PhD, professor of biology, Adelphi University, Garden City, New York.

Shaheen Lakhan, MD, PhD, executive director of the Global Neuroscience Initiative Foundation, an international public-benefit charity organization to advance neurological and mental health patient welfare, research and education.

Mark Blumenthal, founder and executive director of the American Botanical Council and editor of herbalgram. *www.herbalgram.org*.

Amanda McQuade Crawford, medical herbalist in Los Angeles. *www.mcquadecrawford.com*.

Jacob Teitelbaum, MD, physician in private practice in Hawaii and author of *Real Cause, Real Cure* (Rodale). *www.endfatigue.com*.

For Emotional Upset— Flower Remedies To the Rescue

Bach Original Flower Remedies are unique homeopathic formulas for when you feel anxious, despondent or generally out of sorts. They are a system of treatments based on the idea that plant remedies, specifically dilutions of flower materials, can

Emotional Symptoms	Remedy
Hiding your troubles behind a smile	Agrimony
Unidentified anxiety	Aspen
Critical and intolerant	Beech
Weak-willed and seeking praise	Centaury
Doubting your judgment	Cerato
Fear of losing control	Cherry Plum
Repeating old patterns and making the same mistakes	Chestnut Bud
Controlling others	Chicory
Lack of motivation and concentration	Clematis
Embarrassed about yourself	Crab Apple
Feeling overwhelmed by your responsibilities	Elm
Self-doubt and discouragement	Gentian
Hopelessness	Gorse
Loneliness	Heather
Jealousy, envy, revenge, suspicion	Holly
Dwelling in the past	Honeysuckle
Fatigue of mind and body	Hornbeam
Frustrated by the slow pace of people and things	Impatiens
Lack of self-confidence	Larch
Shyness, anxiety	Mimulus
Unexplained sadness that comes and goes	Mustard
Struggling against the odds and not giving up (when you should)	Oak
Mental and physical exhaustion	Olive
Dissatisfied	Pine
Fear for a loved one	Red Chestnut
Extreme terror	Rock Rose
Driving yourself hard to set an example	Rock Water
Indecisive	Scleranthus
Emotional trauma	Star of Bethlehem
Despair	Sweet Chestnut
Argumentative	Vervain
Strong-willed to the point of dictatorial	Vine
Too influenced by others	Walnut
Feeling disconnected from family, friends and people in general	Water Violet
Persistent worry	White Chestnut
Unfulfilled ambitions	Wild Oat
Indifferent and apathetic	Wild Rose
Bitterness	Willow

help ease specific mental states or emotions. Flowers are connected to our emotions in all sorts of ways—think of how a fresh bouquet is an instant uplifter.

Mark Stengler, NMD, has been using these remedies for more than 15 years with his patients who are dealing with emotional problems. They are not designed to be a substitute for therapy, but are often successful in complementing counseling. The flower remedies also can help patients who want to reduce physical ailments that are worsened by stress, such as ulcers or digestive problems. *Here's how Bach Flower Remedies might help you...*

How to Benefit

One of the most popular flower remedies is Bach Rescue Remedy. This formula of five different flower-derived preparations helps people feel calmer and more focused during acute bouts of anxiety or crisis. But the Bach Flower Remedy treatment system is much more far-reaching than that.

Developed by Dr. Edward Bach, an English bacteriologist, surgeon and pathologist working in the 1930s, the system includes 38 different flower remedies, each one associated with relieving a different negative emotion or emotional state. Dr. Bach believed that flower remedies help the body achieve a healthy emotional state that in turn restores physical health. The pursuit of this type of mind-body synergy is known as psychoneuroimmunology, which is based on the interaction between psychological states and the nervous and immune systems.

Even today, Bach Flower Remedies are created according to Dr. Bach's specifications. Using only plants grown in the wild, the remedies are prepared by allowing the flowers to steep in water and direct sunlight, and the branches and leaves are boiled in water. The plant matter is then removed, and the remaining water is believed to retain the "energy," or frequency, of the plant—this is the kind of theory that underlies homeopathy.

In a University of Miami study, researchers found that Bach Rescue Remedy helped study participants reduce high levels of situational anxiety. Among the few other studies conducted on Bach Flower Remedies, results have been unconvincing, except that all agree the preparations are safe. Dr. Stengler's experience with patients has been much more positive.

The Remedies

To get the most out of these preparations, choose the remedy that best matches your emotional state now (see the table on page 124). Dr. Stengler generally recommends using no more than three remedies at a time.

Getting Results

Use four drops of each remedy at a time. Put them directly in your mouth, or dilute them in six ounces of water. Take them at least 10 minutes after eating...

•**For acute problems, take the remedy every one to two hours daily.** Change remedies if you are not feeling better in two days.

•**For chronic problems, take the remedy two or three times daily.** Change remedies if you are not feeling better after two weeks.

•**For less serious problems, sip the diluted mixture throughout the day.** Change remedies if you are not feeling better after two weeks.

Make a new diluted solution every day. Some people feel better immediately. For others, it may take days to a few weeks. Then use as needed. If your symptoms change, choose other remedies. They are nontoxic and safe to take with other medications.

Bach Flower Remedies are available at health-food stores and online. One bottle costs about $12 to $16. For more details, visit the Web site of the Bach Centre in England (*www.bachcentre.com*) or Nelsons, the company that distributes the remedies (800-319-9151, *www.bachremedies.com*).

Caution: Flower remedies are not a substitute for medical attention for serious symptoms of depression or anxiety.

Mark A. Stengler, NMD, naturopathic medical doctor in private practice, Encinitas, California, and author of the *Bottom Line/Natural Healing* newsletter. *www.drstengler.com.*

Virtual Reality Treats Phobias

One of the latest technological intrigues is therapists using virtual reality (VR) technology to help people overcome crippling phobias—such as the fear of heights, storms, public speaking, even spiders!

Imaginative Approach, Real Benefits

A study from Emory University in Atlanta, published in *Behavior Therapy*, found that VR helped about 76% of patients overcome their fears, making it as effective as traditional exposure therapy (where the therapist helps the patient confront the anxiety-provoking experience directly). Cynthia D. Jones, MS, LPC, a counselor at Duke University Faculty Practice in Psychiatry, runs the VR Therapy program there. She describes VR as being like "exposure therapy with a kick." And it works fast. "Most patients need only three or four sessions," she says. "I had one patient overcome fear of flying and be ready to fly after one session!"

Jones believes that the unique method of delivery is a key reason that the therapy is so successful, explaining that it seems to help break down the stigma around a phobia and turns it into "an interesting project." Patients get to learn about themselves and their bodies' reactions in a safe, private environment, avoiding the stress and potential embarrassment of having a panic attack in public. She likens it to using training wheels to learn to ride a bike, noting that "eventually the training wheels come off, but not until the rider feels ready."

Another advantage: The phobia-causing activity can be repeated as often as needed, even during a single session. In contrast, a plane can only take off and land once each flight—plus, flying is expensive!

Still, Not Always Easy...

But this treatment is not all fun and games. According to Jones, the virtual exposure still brings on physiological symptoms such as rapid heartbeat and sweating. Patients are taught new skills that help them bring their bodies and minds back down from the anxiety, learning to create a new behavioral response to the situation that gradually replaces the fear.

An important benefit: The VR experience lets the therapist watch how the patient reacts at specific points during the simulation, which is helpful in identifying the "root" issue.

VR therapy is not appropriate for everyone. For instance, if you have a seizure disorder, the VR screen can be overstimulating. If you typically suffer from motion sickness, the simulation of movement in VR therapy can bring on nausea.

However, if you suffer from a phobia, this treatment is certainly worth checking out. One good resource to start with is *www.virtuallybetter.com*, a site that lists clinics that offer VR therapy for phobias and allows visitors to preview what the therapy is like.

Cynthia D. Jones, MS, LPC, mood disorder counselor, Duke University Faculty Practice in Psychiatry, Durham, North Carolina.

Feeling Blue? Try Five Minutes of Green!

Going "green" isn't only good for the environment. It's also good for your mood.

Newest Research

Study after study shows that "activity in the presence of nature"—such as a walk in a park or gardening in the backyard—decreases your risk of mental illness and improves well-being, says Jules Pretty, PhD, of the University of Essex in England.

Examples: Dr. Pretty and his colleagues measured psychological and physical well-being after an outdoor walk in a natural environment and after an indoor walk in a

mall. *Comparing the two walks, when people walked outdoors they were...*

- **92% less depressed**
- **86% less tense**
- **81% less angry**
- **80% less fatigued**
- **79% less confused**
- **56% more vigorous.**

But is Mother Nature's feel-better medicine fast or slow acting? Exactly how much time do you have to spend in a natural setting to improve your outlook and energy levels?

To find out, Dr. Pretty and his colleagues analyzed the results of 10 studies that investigated the health-giving power of "green exercise"—walking, gardening, cycling, fishing, boating or horseback riding in natural environments, including city parks.

Results: Five minutes of green exercise was all it took to improve mood by 54% and self-esteem by 46% (two key indicators of mental health), concluded the researchers in the journal *Environmental Science and Technology*.

"This suggests that there is a health benefit from any short engagement in green exercise," says Dr. Pretty.

"Exposure to nature via green exercise is a readily available therapy with no obvious side effects," he continues. "I believe there would be a large benefit to individuals and to society if more people were to 'self-medicate' with green exercise."

For the greatest benefits: Green areas near water (an ocean, river or lake) had the biggest positive effect.

Also helpful: If you have to stay indoors, simply looking at a natural scene—or even just imagining one—can change your brain and mood for the better, according to two recent studies.

In the first study, European researchers took brain scans of people while they looked at either images of natural, tranquil scenes or images of a busy highway. Looking at the natural images connected various areas of the brain; looking at the highway disrupted those same brain connections. The results were published in the journal *NeuroImage*.

In the second study, researchers from the University of Rochester in New York found that just imagining a natural setting caused people to feel more energetic and alive. "Nature is fuel for the soul," says Richard Ryan, PhD, the study leader. "Often when we feel depleted we reach for a cup of coffee, but research suggests that a better way to get energized is to connect with nature."

The Earth Connection

Shaman and healer Brant Secunda agrees: Nature nourishes the soul.

"We are an extension of the body of Mother Earth, just like a tree or a flower," says Secunda, coauthor with triathlete Mark Allen of *Fit Soul, Fit Body* (BenBella Books). "You probably experienced this feeling of connecting to the earth the first time you saw a tall mountain peak, a vast forest or an open hillside with the grasses swaying in the wind. Whether you knew it or not, your soul and your heart were feeling love for that place and from that place. And in that moment, all the problems, worries and stresses of life disappeared."

Secunda recommends three ways to connect to nature...

●**Go for a "connecting" walk.** "Walking outdoors in a natural setting is one of the best ways to get away from modern life and connect with the power of nature," says Secunda.

"As you walk, visualize an umbilical cord coming from the end of your spine and going down into the earth. This is a very real energy cord that always anchors and connects you to the earth. Then, from your heart, imagine or feel another cord extending out from your soul, a cord that connects you with everything that you see in front of you. By doing this, you are connected to the earth from the front and from the back. It is a very simple yet powerful technique."

●**Feel the love of Mother Earth.** "Once again, start by walking outside, preferably in a natural area, whether it's in the city, country or wilderness," says Secunda. "With each step you take, visualize Mother Earth's love coming into your body through your feet and traveling up to your heart. Fill your heart with her love. Let the love of Mother Earth dissolve any problems you have. Do this for 15 to 20 minutes."

●**Center yourself between earth and sky.** "Our proper place in the universe is directly between earth and sky," says Secunda.

"Being in the middle, between these two great forces of nature, balances your soul. Try the following exercise anytime you feel your life needs balance, perhaps because of excessive demands on your time or another type of emotional strain. It is perfect to do while you are outside in nature."

1. Sit or lie down on the ground. Feel your connection to the sun and the earth.

2. Visualize the light of the sun coming down through the top of your head. Feel it throughout your body and in your heart. Concentrate on this image.

3. Now, imagine the light going down into Mother Earth. Feel connected to both the light and the earth.

4. Feel your connection to the earth. Draw the love of Mother Earth up into your heart and throughout your body. Imagine this as a natural happening in the process of feeling connected to the love of Mother Earth.

5. Send that love to Father Sun. Feel your connection to all life.

Jules Pretty, PhD, professor and director of the Interdisciplinary Centre for Environment and Society, Department of Biological Sciences, University of Essex, UK.

Richard Ryan, PhD, professor of psychology, psychiatry and education, Department of Clinical and Social Psychology, University of Rochester, New York.

Brant Secunda, shaman-healer in the Huichol tradition of Mexico, director of the Dance of the Deer Foundation Center for Shamanic Studies and coauthor of *Fit Soul, Fit Body* (BenBella Books). *www.shaminism.com.*

Mark Allen, six-time Ironman Triathlon World Champion, and coauthor of *Fit Soul, Fit Body* (BenBella Books). *www.markallenonline.com, www.fitsoul-fitbody.com.*

Bounce Back from a Bad Mood

B ad breaks and difficult days often darken our disposition—but we don't have to let those low spirits linger. We actually have more control over our moods than we realize.

How to quickly bounce back from the blues…

"Travel" to a Happier Time

Make a list of five of the happiest moments from your past. Now close your eyes, and imagine one of those moments in as much detail as possible. Visualizing happy times encourages the brain to release endorphins. This helps lower blood pressure and makes us feel happy, almost as if the pleasant experience were occurring at this very moment.

Helpful: The more sensory details you include in your visualization, the greater the odds that you will experience this mood-boosting endorphin rush. Where are you standing in the vision? Can you feel the breeze on your face? Are you holding something in your hands? What do you hear, see and smell?

Imagine That Others Are Conspiring to Help You

Bad moods often feed paranoia—the sense that others are working against you. To feel better, imagine that other people are plotting to your benefit instead.

If you have trouble imagining such things, that might be a sign that you should be spending more time with helpful, positive-minded people. Then good thoughts on your behalf won't be so hard to imagine.

Count Your Complaints

When you air any particular complaint for the third time (to yourself or others), imagine it turning to vapor and floating away. Voicing our problems or writing about them in a journal can help us get them out of our system. But when we vent about the same problems over and over, the retellings don't help us move on—they keep us in a rut.

After the third airing, raise the problem again only if the additional mention is part of a genuine effort to fix the problem…reposition your goals and plans in response to the problem…make light of the problem…or cast the problem in a new and more positive light.

Example: It's OK to mention a health problem again to say that it was a wake-up call to start a healthy diet.

Assign Yourself a Task

Achieving a task helps you feel more in control. Researchers at the University of Michigan found that nothing matters more to people's sense of well-being than whether they have a strong feeling of control over their lives. To exercise your sense of control—and boost your mood—assign yourself an achievable task related to a personal goal, large or modest. Set a deadline so that you can measure the accomplishment.

Examples: Clean a room…get 30 minutes of exercise…or speak with one professional contact about a career transition that you might like to make.

Retell the Incident

Retell the incident that's making you feel bad in a less painful way. Martin Seligman, PhD, director of the University of Pennsylvania's Positive Psychology Center, has discovered that the way we tell ourselves the stories of our setbacks can mean more to our moods than the severity of those setbacks.

If you tell yourself a problem or misstep is temporary, limited to a single occurrence or mainly someone else's fault, you are likely to rebound quickly…but if your "self-talk" says that the error is permanent or a reflection of who you are, your ill mood is likely to linger.

Example: If you've been laid off, replace the thought *I wasn't good enough to keep my job* with *This economy is costing a lot of good people their jobs, but it will turn around.*

More Mood Boosters

● **Repeat the word "forward."** Saying "forward" silently to ourselves when we feel bad reminds us that our bad mood likely is related to a past event—but the past is less important than where our lives are headed in the future.

● **Cuddle a loved one.** Experiencing tender, caring physical contact can improve your mood and even lower your blood pressure. If there's no one you can turn to for a hug, visit a pet store and hold a few puppies. Some animal shelters even will let you take a dog home for a week without a long-term commitment.

● **Let yourself feel bad—later.** If you cannot reverse your bad mood, postpone it. Select a time later in the day or week to feel bad. Pencil it in on your calendar. Your mind might be willing to go along with this because you're not denying the right to feel bad—only delaying when this happens. Better yet, you might not feel like feeling bad anymore once the bad-mood time arrives.

Karen Salmansohn, host of the show "Be Happy Dammit" on Sirius satellite radio. Based in New York City, she is author of *The Bounce Back Book: How to Thrive in the Face of Adversity, Setbacks, and Losses* (Workman). Her research into bouncing back from problems began after she was the victim of an assault. *www.notsalmon.com.*

How to Create A New You

Anything is possible—but we reject certain alternatives without a second thought. We've convinced ourselves—or social conditioning has convinced us—that rejecting these options is necessary or proper.

Examples: An unemployed office worker might automatically reject a blue-collar job… a retiree might automatically decide he's too old to go on a backpacking trip in the mountains.

We need to dislodge our negative beliefs if we wish to weigh all of our options, overcome the power of "no" and elevate our lives to a higher level. *Here, the negative beliefs that are holding us back and what to do…*

● **Negative belief—We're stuck with our habits.** A habit is simply a shortcut imprinted on the brain. We cook our eggs the same way every morning or sit in front of the television every evening because we have done this so many times that we now do it without making a conscious choice.

A habit is just a choice that is ingrained for practical purposes, but the fact that our habits have become ingrained does not mean that we cannot pursue alternatives.

What keeps us trapped is the "spell of no." We voluntarily renounce the power to change, while at the same time blaming our bad habits as if they have an independent will. The spell that our habits hold over us is one that we have created and thus one that we can break.

What to do: Examine your unwanted habits objectively, as if they belonged to someone else. Ask yourself why you have chosen a bad habit. Search for a hidden benefit that it provides. Does this habit make you feel like a victim, a convenient way to avoid taking responsibility for your problems?

Spend six weeks doing what you want to do, rather than what your habit encourages you to. After six weeks, the new way of doing things will be imprinted on your brain in place of the old habit.

● **Negative belief—Our obsessions are not really obsessions.** People tend to believe the term "obsessive" applies only to those with mental disorders. We certainly don't consider ourselves obsessive. In truth, many of us are obsessive—we simply choose to overlook our obsessions because we believe that the things we obsess about are things that deserve this much time and energy.

Examples: Obsessions that people tend to view as positive include obsessions with health and safety…career or income…religion…their children's success…or a political or charitable cause.

There might be positive aspects to these obsessions, but having any obsession robs us of our ability to make objective choices—automatically saying *yes* to spending our time and resources on an obsession means automatically saying *no* to alternatives. This blunts our ability to evolve and get the most from our lives.

What to do: Stop taking pride in your consistency or single-mindedness even in pursuit of a good cause. Engage in activities that reduce your stress levels, such as meditation or hobbies. Relaxed minds are more open to new alternatives.

•**Negative belief—Our fears are valid because they seem valid to us.** External threats aren't what make the world seem unsafe—it's the concerns and beliefs that we project onto every situation that create our fears. If we worry about crime, then everyone we pass on the street becomes a potential mugger. If we're afraid of heights, then even a small stepladder may seem too dangerous to climb.

Our fears deny us our most basic freedom, the freedom to feel safe in the world. They encourage us to reject possibilities that deserve our consideration by making them seem too risky. Some threats are real, but our fears don't help us identify these. Our fears deprive us of our ability to rationally evaluate dangers.

What to do: Don't try to fight your fears at times when you feel afraid—that's when fears are most powerful. At these times, just remind yourself that fear is a passing emotion that soon will be released. Later, when you are calm, recall the fear for objective examination. With long-standing fears, remind yourself that the fact that you have worried about something for years does not mean that this thing is especially dangerous—it just means that your mind has had a lot of time to blow it out of proportion.

Show yourself compassion about your fears. Fear is not a sign of weakness. It affects everyone.

•**Negative belief—People don't change.** Most of us think this from time to time when those close to us chronically repeat mistakes or misbehavior. Yet paradoxically, most of us believe that we, personally, are capable of change and growth. We cannot have it both ways—if we are capable of change, then other people must be, too.

In fact, not only are people capable of change, we all change all the time. When we think, *People don't change*, we're just giving in to resignation and defeatism. Thinking in this way could dissuade us—and those around us—from attempting positive growth in the future.

What to do: View yourself as in a perpetual state of change. Search for options for anything in your life that seems fixed and unchangeable. Don't listen to naysayers when you attempt change—their warnings and criticisms are rooted in defeatism, not reality. Encourage attempts to change by others, particularly when these changes are new and fragile.

Example: If a seemingly stingy friend finally offers to pick up a small check, don't make a joke or belittle the effort. Choose to view this person as generous and offer a heartfelt thanks. Your positive reaction could reinforce your friend's attempt to change and encourage greater generosity in the future.

•**Negative belief—"Bad" thoughts are forbidden and dangerous.** Many of us waste energy repressing thoughts that we wish we didn't have. These "bad" thoughts might be feelings of jealousy, rage, lust or a desire for vengeance. Trouble is, repressing thoughts doesn't make them go away—it allows them to grow.

Viewing some of our own thoughts as bad also encourages us to divide ourselves into a good side and a bad side, creating an inner struggle that we can never win.

The truth is, we all have thoughts that we wish we didn't have. That doesn't mean we're bad people, as long as we don't act on these thoughts.

What to do: Understand that it is not in our power to stop "bad" thoughts. It is in our power to let these thoughts pass rather than repress them or act on them. Don't believe that the thoughts drifting through your mind define who you are—these thoughts are not you.

Never condemn yourself for your thoughts. Give up the impossible goal of totally controlling your mind.

Deepak Chopra, MD, member of the American Association of Clinical Endocrinologists and senior scientist with The Gallup Organization. He is the author of many books, including *Reinventing the Body, Resurrecting the Soul: How to Create a New You* (Harmony).

New Scientific Discovery: A Rabbit's Foot Really Works

You stroke a rabbit's foot for good luck. Or wear your lucky shirt or blouse on a day when you want to be at your best.

These are superstitious behaviors. Even though you may do them, deep down you know they're nonsense, right?

No, superstitions are *practical*, say a team of scientists—because they can improve your self-confidence and skill.

The Superstition Experiment

Psychologists at the University of Cologne in Germany conducted an experiment to test the power of superstition to improve performance.

First, they asked 72 volunteers to show up at the laboratory with a "personal lucky charm"—and the volunteers obliged, bringing old stuffed animals, lucky stones and other objects.

When each volunteer arrived, the researchers took away the charm, supposedly to take a photograph of it. But they gave the charm back to only half the volunteers, telling the other half that there was a problem with the camera equipment and they'd return the charm later.

Next, all the volunteers played either a memory game or a word game—and those who still had their lucky charms with them performed much better!

Querying the participants after the two games, the researchers found that the superior performance was probably caused by greater self-confidence—produced by belief in the power of the lucky charm.

In two similar experiments, the researchers found that the ability to sink golf putts improved when people thought they were using a "lucky ball"…and the ability to perform an intricate physical task (quickly putting little balls into little holes) improved when people thought that those watching them had their "fingers crossed" for good luck.

"Activating a good-luck superstition leads to improved performance by boosting people's belief in their ability to master a task," concluded the researchers in the journal *Psychological Science*.

Superstition, Super Results

Superstition can enhance performance in several ways, says Srinivasan S. Pillay, MD, assistant clinical professor of psychiatry at Harvard Medical School and author of *Life Unlocked: 7 Revolutionary Lessons to Overcome Fear* (Rodale). *Superstition can…*

● **Improve your confidence**—the belief that you'll succeed

● **Increase what psychologists call self-efficacy**—the belief you have the abilities to succeed

● **Make you more persistent**—more willing to stick with a task until it's completed

● **Decrease your anxiety,** allowing you to focus more fully on the task at hand

● **Help you feel supported**—you don't think you're taking on the task alone

● **Relieve you of some responsibility for the outcome**—responsibility that can be a mental burden, interfering with ease of performance and success.

In short, superstition improves what Dr. Pillay calls "possibility thinking"—if the lucky charm worked before, it can work again, even if the task seems impossible to achieve. (*Example:* Soon after the long-distance runner Roger Bannister broke the 4-minute mile—a speed thought to be impossible—several other athletes ran 4-minute miles.)

And you can improve the power of superstition to help you achieve your goals, says Nancy Mramor, PhD, a psychologist in private practice in Pittsburgh and author of *Spiritual Fitness* (Llewellyn). "A lucky charm works because of the associations it has with past successes," says Dr. Mramor. *To strengthen those associations…*

1. Hold or rub the object in the same way, every time.

"This convinces the body that the object will work in the way you want it to," she says.

2. Repeat a special word or phrase when holding the object.

"This adds positive associations," she says.

Example: Say the word "Success" or the phrase "I will succeed."

3. Remember past successes. "When you use the object, think deeply and clearly about past successes associated with that object— how you felt, what you heard and what you saw. Recalling at least three specifics is very important," she says. "The first convinces your mind, the second convinces your emotions and the third convinces your body."

Srinivasan S. Pillay, MD, assistant clinical professor of psychiatry at Harvard Medical School and author of *Life Unlocked: 7 Revolutionary Lessons to Overcome Fear* (Rodale).

Nancy Mramor, PhD, psychologist in private practice in Pittsburgh, Pennsylvania, and author of *Spiritual Fitness* (Llewellyn). *www.drnancyonline.com.*

Mindfulness=Happiness

What were you thinking about in the past minute or two? Were you completely focused on whatever you were doing—maybe settling down with this book and starting to read this article? Or were you thinking about things you weren't doing—perhaps ruminating about the past, or worrying about the future, or imagining an event that never happened at all?

Well, if your mind was wandering from the present, your heart was probably feeling a little lost.

Surprising: A recent study from psychologists at Harvard University shows that if you spend a lot of time thinking outside the present, you're more likely to feel unhappy.

The Harvard Study

The researchers studied 2,250 people, aged 18 to 88, using an iPhone Web app that they developed for the experiment.

At random moments during the day, the Web app contacted the study participants through their iPhone, asking three questions…

1. How are you feeling right now? (The participants selected a number from 0 to 100, with 0 being "very bad" and 100 being "very good.")

2. What are you doing right now? (Participants chose from 22 activities, such as walking, eating, shopping or watching television.)

3. Are you thinking about something other than what you're currently doing? (Participants could answer the question in one of four ways: 1. no; 2. yes, something pleasant; 3. yes, something neutral; 4. yes, something unpleasant.)

The answers were recorded in a database, with researchers eventually collecting more than 250,000 "data points" from the study participants.

Results: "People's minds wandered frequently, regardless of what they were doing," reported the Harvard researchers in the journal *Science*.

On average, the participants' minds were wandering 47% of the time. (At least 30% of the time during every one of the 22 activities—except making love.)

And people were much less happy when their minds were wandering than when they were not.

"What people were thinking was a better predictor of their happiness than what they were actually doing," says Matthew Killingsworth, PhD, a study researcher.

When the data were analyzed for each person, an individual's level of moment-to-moment mind wandering was two times more predictive of his or her happiness than the activity the person was doing.

When the data were analyzed for all 2,250 participants, mind wandering was five times more predictive of happiness than activity.

"Mind wandering in our study was generally the cause and not merely the consequence of unhappiness," says Dr. Killingsworth. (Even "pleasant" mind wandering didn't improve happiness. And "neutral" or "unpleasant" mind wandering worsened it.)

Bottom line: "This study shows that our mental lives are pervaded, to a remarkable degree, by mind wandering—by the non-present," says Dr. Killingsworth.

"Many philosophical and religious traditions teach that happiness is to be found by living in the moment, and practitioners are trained to resist mind wandering and to 'be here now.' The traditions suggest that a wandering mind is an unhappy mind—and the traditions are right."

Keep Attention in the Present

Proven: A wandering mind is an unhappy mind. But why?

"People feel bad when they're helpless and good when they're in control, with influence over their surroundings," says Christopher Willard, PsyD, a psychologist in private practice in Boston and author of *Child's Mind: Mindfulness Practices to Help Our Children Be More Focused, Calm, and Relaxed* (Parallax Press).

"When your mind is wandering in the future, thinking about things that haven't happened but could go wrong, you feel helpless—and anxious. When your mind is wandering in the past, thinking regretfully about something you did or didn't do, you feel helpless—and depressed. But when you're

in the present, you feel empowered and in control—you feel your best."

Good news: You can reduce the emotional toll of mind wandering by teaching your mind to stay focused in the present—with a technique called mindfulness, says Donald Altman, a psychotherapist in Portland, Oregon, and author of *The Mindfulness Code* (New World Library). *Here are some of his and Dr. Willard's suggestions to become more mindful…*

●**Accept the moment.** "How often have you rejected this moment with the idea that being elsewhere was far better and more fulfilling?" says Altman. "The next time you feel impatient or ill at ease, pause right where you are and don't be so quick to run off to something else. Instead, see if you can accept the moment for what it is. Notice your frustration, impatience or boredom—and nurture a willingness to accept what is present in your life."

●**Wake up from fantasy.** "Fantasies distract us from the actual here and now," says Altman. "When you notice a fantasy, turn your attention to the present moment by turning toward your surroundings—to colors, shapes, sounds, smells and sensations."

Example: If you're driving, feel your hands on the steering wheel and listen to the sound of the tires on the pavement.

●**Focus on the breath.** Turn your attention to your breathing for a few moments, says Dr. Willard. "Sit or stand up straight. Put one hand on your belly and one hand on your chest. Feel your chest and belly move as you breathe in and out. This calms your nervous system and helps bring you into the present moment."

●**Scan your body.** "Take one minute and scan your body," says Dr. Willard. "Ask yourself, for example, 'Do I have an itch? A stomachache? Does my arm feel relaxed? Is my foot sweaty? Is my jaw tense or relaxed?' This exercise narrows your focus and helps you get out of your head."

●**Notice sounds.** Pay attention to the sounds in your environment, says Dr. Willard. "Take 30 seconds to a minute and count five sounds—for example, an airplane overhead, low voices in the distance, the air conditioner in your room, birds chirping and the sound of the TV upstairs. This is very effective at bringing you into the present."

Matthew Killingsworth, PhD, creator of *www.track yourhappiness.com*, Department of Psychology, Harvard University, Boston.

Christopher Willard, PsyD, psychologist in private practice, Boston, and author of *Child's Mind: Mindfulness Practices to Help Our Children Be More Focused, Calm, and Relaxed* (Parallax Press).

Donald Altman, psychotherapist in Portland, Oregon, and author of *The Mindfulness Code: Keys for Overcoming Stress, Anxiety, Fear, and Unhappiness* (New World Library). *www.mindfulpractices.com, www.mindfulnesscode.com.*

Protect Yourself from "Toxic" People

Communication is challenging enough with the "normal" people in your life—the ones who want to cooperate and make life better for everyone. When you are forced to deal with jerks—people who don't care about social give-and-take—communication can seem next to impossible, leaving you drained and upset.

Jerks tend to trigger powerful negative emotional reactions that take a long time to recover from and that interfere with clear thinking.

As a psychiatrist, I refer to jerks as "toxic people."

If being around a toxic person is having a destructive effect on your physical or emotional health, you may need to get that person out of your life completely. But in many cases, you can "neutralize" the negative effect that a toxic person has on you. *Here, simple ways to do it...*

●**Recognize when a person is toxic.** Everyone can be uncooperative and selfish some of the time—and the techniques in this article can work during those times. But a toxic person is different from a person who is just having a bad day.

Toxic people have a distinctive view of life. They perceive the world as having cheated them out of something or as owing them

something. Nothing good that happens to them changes that perception for long.

In contrast to healthy people, who feel entitled to what they deserve...and neurotics, who do not feel entitled to what they deserve...toxic people feel entitled to what they don't deserve. They do not play by the usual rules of getting along with others. They feel justified in taking, with no compulsion to give.

This belief system reveals itself in different ways for different types of toxic people. A toxic bully may aggressively push others around to get his/her way, whereas a toxically needy person may feel entitled to have his hand held constantly or insist that other people fight his battles. Bullies scream and demand. Toxically needy people whine and complain.

●**Adjust your expectations.** We expect people to behave reasonably, and the shock that we feel when toxic people do not do so can be quite painful.

Toxic people sometimes may appear to be caring and cooperative. This behavior will last only until they get what they want. Don't be fooled into thinking that they have changed.

In addition, the strategies that usually work with nontoxic people—such as empathizing or appealing to fairness—do not work with toxic people.

Once you have identified a person as toxic, your smartest move is to protect yourself from being blindsided. Expect the person to act solely in his own interests even when he appears to be kind and caring.

●**Hold part of yourself back.** Toxic people get what they want by pushing others off balance. They do so by acting in ways that trigger rage, fear, guilt and other strong emotions in others. Remind yourself not to get emotionally engaged. This is their issue, not yours.

Helpful: Pause before responding. No matter what the toxic person says or does, make a practice of waiting several seconds or more before you reply. Stay calm.

The longer you wait before responding, the more the toxic person may escalate his behavior. For example, he may get even angrier or whine even more. But the behavior is less likely to upset you because you are keeping your emotional distance.

What to Say to a Jerk

Three good responses to nearly every type of toxic person...

• **"Huh?" This one word can stop a jerk in his tracks.** Use a mild, neutral tone of voice. Do this when the toxic person says something utterly ridiculous but acts as if he is being perfectly reasonable. This response conveys that what the toxic person is saying doesn't make sense. It works because it signals that you are not engaging with the content of what he said.

• **"Do you really believe what you just said?"** Use a calm, straightforward tone, not a confrontational one. This question works because toxic people often resort to hyperbole to throw others off balance. They are prone to using the words "always" and "never" to drive home their points. However, don't expect the toxic person to admit that he is wrong. He is more likely to walk away in a huff—which is fine because then you won't have to waste more energy dealing with him.

• **"I can see how this is good for you. Tell me how it's good for me."** This response is a useful way to deal with a toxic person's demands. If he stalls or changes the subject, you can say, "Since it's not clear how this is good for me, I'm going to have to say no."

Here are other responses to specific types of toxic people...

Bye to Bullies

A bully gets what he wants by scaring other people. Even when he is behaving himself, his presence triggers fear because you never know when he will explode.

What to do...

Disengage: Most bullies use words and tone of voice as their weapons. Say silently to yourself, *This person is not going to physically harm me.* Picture his words as rubber bullets that, instead of hitting you between the eyes, zoom over your shoulder.

8 Signs of a Toxic Person...

1. Interrupts.
2. Doesn't take turns.
3. Takes advantage of people who are down.
4. Gloats in victory.
5. Is sullen in defeat.
6. Is not fair.
7. Lacks integrity.
8. Is the kind of person you'll avoid if you possibly can.

Caution: If there is any possibility that the person may be physically violent, leave at once.

Respond: Take a deep breath, and say out loud, "Ah, geez, this is going to be a long conversation" or "You gotta be kidding" (said mockingly to show that the bully hasn't scared or offended you).

Whatever the bully's reaction—whether he demands an explanation or continues to attack—you can calmly say, "You're upset, I'm starting to shut down, and before we get to anything constructive, the sun is going to set, and then we're going to have to start all over again tomorrow because I don't see us reaching any conclusion."

If he keeps pushing and says, "I am not upset—you're just not listening," you say, "Nah, forget it, it's gone, gone...the opportunity even to get into a conversation is gone, finito, flew the coop." The bully eventually will give up.

You can repeat this approach the next time. If the bully says, "Don't try that with me again," you just say, "Sorry, I find this exhausting, and I need to preserve my energy. If you can figure out a way to talk with me instead of at me, I'm willing. Until then, count me out." Then walk away—which will be easy once you let go of the expectation that you will ever reach a win-win solution with this person.

Neutralize Needy People

Unlike people who have a healthy need for others, toxically needy people expect constant help and attention and often use guilt to get it. No matter how much you do for them, it is never enough. They act like victims, suck you dry and leave you feeling depressed and incompetent because nothing ever gets better for them.

What to do…

Disengage: Imagine that the needy person has a hook that he is trying to snag you with, but the hook has missed you.

Respond: A needy person might say in a nails-on-a-chalkboard voice, "It's not fair." Pause and calmly but firmly say, "It is completely fair to everyone that it affects."

Give It to Takers

The taker constantly asks you for favors but never seems to have the time or energy to pitch in when you need help. Whereas needy people make you feel as if they are sucking you dry, takers make you feel as if they are grabbing at you.

What to do…

Disengage: Picture the taker as a child grabbing at you to get your attention. Imagine yourself calmly tapping him on the wrist and saying, "Now, now, wait your turn."

Respond: Make a mental list of ways the taker could help you. The next time he asks for a favor say, "Sure! And you can help me out by…" If he balks, say, "I assume you don't mind doing a favor for me in return, right?"

Insist on a quid pro quo each time, and the taker will soon move on to an easier target.

Mark Goulston, MD, psychiatrist, business consultant, executive coach, and FBI and police hostage negotiation trainer, Santa Monica, California. His books include *Just Listen: Discover the Secret to Getting Through to Absolutely Anyone* (Amacom). *www.markgoulston.com.*

Chapter 7

DIABETES

The Surprising Secret To Living Longer with Diabetes

Diabetes is a deadly disease. High levels of glucose in the bloodstream damage the circulatory system, doubling the risk of heart attack and stroke. Extra glucose also corrodes the kidneys—and a person diagnosed with advanced kidney disease has the same odds of dying as a person diagnosed with lung cancer.

Troubling statistics: A 50-year-old with diabetes has an average life span 8.5 years shorter than a 50-year-old without the illness. And anyone with diabetes is twice as likely to die as someone without the disease.

It's no surprise, then, that each year, diabetes causes or contributes to the death of more than 230,000 Americans.

But a new study shows that there's a surprising way to decrease your odds of dying from diabetes—ask your family, friends and doctor to help you out!

Trust and Health

Researchers at the University of Washington in Seattle conducted a five-year study, involving 3,535 adults with diabetes.

They divided the study participants into two "relationship styles." (The styles are part of a psychological perspective called attachment theory, which sees early-life experiences as shaping the way you act in relationships, including your ability to trust others.)

1. An "interactive" style—you find it easy to get close to and rely on other people. The statement that describes an interactive: "I am comfortable depending on other people." (About 60% of us are interactive.)

2. An "independent" style—you tend to be either dismissive of the importance of close relationships or you're afraid of them. The statement that describes an independent: "It is very important for me to feel independent—I prefer not to depend on others." (About 40% of us are independent.)

Surprising research finding: After five years, those with an independent style had a death rate that was 33% higher than those with an interactive style.

Why is independence deadly in diabetes? Probably because the independents are less likely to seek support from family, friends and health-care providers—and diabetes is a disease where you need a lot of support to help you survive, says Paul Ciechanowski, MD, the study leader and associate professor of psychiatry and behavioral sciences at the University of Washington in Seattle.

"On the other hand," says Dr. Ciechanowski, "if you have a more interactive and collaborative style you're likely to figure out how to get the help you need."

An independent style may produce the following behaviors and results seen more frequently among the independents…

- **Missed doctor appointments**

- **Poorer home treatment of diabetes,** in such areas as foot care, exercise, diet, oral and injectable medication use, blood sugar monitoring and smoking cessation

- **Higher glucose (blood sugar).**

"Many behaviors related to diabetes are optimally carried out in collaboration with others—family, peers and health-care providers," says Dr. Ciechanowski. In fact, he adds, the key elements of diabetes control—such as cooking diabetes-friendly meals, exercising and quitting smoking—are usually accomplished only with support. "Like it or not, self-care for diabetes is a complex regimen, and you can't do it alone," he says.

And if diabetes becomes severe and there are complications—such as pain, poor eyesight or walking problems—the self-reliant attitude that may have propelled you to personal and professional success has now become a deadly liability.

Finding Help

If you've had an independent style all your life, it's unlikely you'll change, says Dr. Ciechanowski. But you can learn specific behaviors that make it less likely your style will increase your risk of death. *His recommendations…*

- **Acknowledge the downside of the independent style.** "If you're independent, you have to recognize that the self-reliant style that has served you well for most of your life—allowing you to be a self-starter and go-getter, and perhaps advance more rapidly in your career—isn't necessarily going to help you manage a chronic illness such as diabetes," says Dr. Ciechanowski.

- **Change the way you do things—one thing at a time.** You don't have to suddenly start reaching out to everyone, he says. You only have to develop an interactive style in certain areas—starting with one area of diabetes care that you choose. (That way, you'll feel like you're in the driver's seat.)

For example, maybe you decide to check in with your doctor regularly. Or maybe you ask someone for help in monitoring your blood glucose levels.

"Try one area of interaction—while still being the self-reliant person that is such a fundamental part of your identity," says Dr. Ciechanowski. "You don't need to change your whole personality—you just want a task to accomplish relative to one area of diabetes care—and to interact with others to accomplish that task. Once you've succeeded in being interactive in one area, try another."

Helpful: Even if you're for the most part independent, you've probably had the experience of collaborating with people in various circumstances, such as work—and it led to greater success. "Imagine yourself in a situation where you worked with a team or were helped by others—and apply it to diabetes," says Dr. Ciechanowski.

- **Talk to your health-care provider about trust.** "If you have an independent style, you don't trust others because you may have been hurt, ignored, abandoned or not paid attention to in earlier periods of your life—and you put up a defense or armor so that it won't happen again," explains Dr.

Ciechanowski. "The creation of the style is in large part from failed promises.

"And now you're in a health-care system where promises are regularly broken—where you show up and have to wait a long time...and then the doctor flies in and out in a few minutes...and it seems that nobody answers your questions or asks how you really feel. In such a situation—where you're getting the implicit message that you're not worthy of anyone's attention—you need to be an empowered, proactive patient, and tell the doctor that this style of care doesn't work for you.

"You might ask, 'What would work for me to be an engaged patient and to trust you...for you to take the time to answer my questions?'

"And if a provider or system isn't working for you—look for another system and another provider, and set the rules of the game right from the start," Dr. Ciechanowski continues. "After all, if you went to an attorney or an accountant and they didn't understand and respond to your needs, you'd find another professional. Do the same with your health-care provider."

Paul Ciechanowski, MD, associate professor of psychiatry and behavioral sciences at the University of Washington in Seattle.

9 out of 10 Don't Know They Have Prediabetes

Thirty percent of American adults have prediabetes—blood sugar levels that are above normal but not high enough to be diagnosed as diabetes.

Shocking new finding: Ninety-three percent of people with prediabetes don't know they have the condition, say researchers from the Centers for Disease Control and Prevention in a new study in the *American Journal of Preventive Medicine*.

And that's a shame, say experts, because simple lifestyle measures can control prediabetes, stopping it from becoming diabetes—

and even reverse the condition, returning high blood sugar levels to normal. Here's how to find out if you have prediabetes—and how to get blood sugar levels back under control...

Do You Have Prediabetes?

The same medical tests used to detect diabetes also detect prediabetes, says Steve Parker, MD, a physician in Phoenix, Arizona, and author of *Conquer Diabetes & Prediabetes* (px-Health). *The two most common tests are...*

• **The fasting plasma glucose (FPG) test,** which measures blood glucose (blood sugar) in a person who has not eaten anything for at least eight hours. Normal is 99 mg/dL and below. Prediabetes is 100 to 125. Diabetes is 126 and above (on at least two separate occasions).

• **The hemoglobin A1c test (hbA1C),** which measures the percentage of red blood cells saturated with glucose (glycated). It's a good indicator of blood sugar levels over the previous few months. Normal is 5.6% or lower. Prediabetes is 5.7% to 6.4%. Diabetes is 7% and above.

You should ask your doctor for a blood sugar test if you have several risk factors for prediabetes (the more risk factors, the more likely it is you have the condition). *They include...*

• **Aged 45 or older**

• **Obesity (body mass index 30 and up)**

• **Waist size more than 40 inches in men and more than 35 inches in women**

• **Parent or sibling with diabetes**

• **Diabetes during pregnancy**

• **Physically inactive**

• **High blood pressure (140/90 mm/HG or above)**

• **Low HDL cholesterol (below 35 mg/dl)**

• **High triglycerides (above 250 mg/dl)**

• **Polycystic ovary syndrome (PCOS).**

If a test shows that you have prediabetes (or diabetes), you should have a second test to confirm the diagnosis.

What should you do if you have prediabetes?

"I tell my patients that they don't have diabetes, but they do have a one in four chance of developing diabetes in the next three to five years—with its increased probability of heart attack, stroke, nerve damage and pain, blindness, kidney failure, and foot and leg amputations," says Dr. Parker. "And then I tell them there are simple ways to put their condition in reverse."

Reversing Prediabetes

"There are three key goals to beat prediabetes—stabilize blood sugar, lose weight and exercise regularly," says Dr. Parker.

●**Stabilize blood sugar and lose weight— with a modified Mediterranean diet.** "Ninety percent of people with prediabetes are overweight—but losing just 5 to 10% of that weight can significantly lower the risk of developing diabetes," says Dr. Parker. To jumpstart weight-loss in his prediabetic patients, he recommends a modified Mediterranean diet.

"The standard Mediterranean diet is relatively high in carbohydrate-rich breads, pasta, fruits, legumes and certain high-carb vegetables," he explains. "But people with prediabetes aren't able to digest and process carbohydrates normally. That's why it makes sense to cut their carbohydrate intake in order to balance their blood sugar. A low-carb Mediterranean diet is an excellent way to do that— and an excellent way to lose weight, too."

The foods in the diet…

●**Protein.** Unlimited fish, meat, chicken, turkey, eggs, shrimp and lobster. "Whenever you're hungry, eat a can of tuna, or a chicken breast or a hard-boiled egg or an ounce of cheese," says Dr. Parker. "Protein balances blood sugar and satisfies the appetite. Many of my prediabetic patients love this diet, because even though they're cutting calories, they're never hungry."

●**Olive oil, virgin or extra-virgin.** At least 2 to 3 tablespoons (tbsp) daily.

●**Nuts and seeds.** One ounce daily, or about a handful.

●**Vegetables.** Two, seven-ounce salads daily of low-carbohydrate vegetables. (A cup of vegetables is eight ounces.)

Those vegetables include: alfalfa sprouts, asparagus, arugula, avocado, broccoli, Brussels sprouts, cauliflower, chard, cucumber, eggplant, endive, green beans, lettuce, mushrooms, okra, olives (pickled green or ripe black), parsley, pickles (dill or sour, not sweet or "bread and butter"), radicchio, radishes, sauerkraut (canned), scallions, snow peas, spinach, summer squash, sweet peppers.

●**Cheese.** Up to three ounces daily of mozzarella, provolone, swiss, cheddar, blue, Monterey Jack, Colby, Brie, Parmesan, feta, Gouda, goat's milk, ricotta, cottage. "Other types of cheese have too many carbs," says Dr. Parker.

●**Wine.** Six to 12 ounces daily, preferring antioxidant-rich red to white. Instead of wine, you can substitute with another 7 ounces of vegetables, or 0.7 ounces of dark chocolate (65 to 85% cacao), or 12 ounces of beer (a brand under 10 grams of carb) or 1.5 ounces of distilled spirits (whiskey, rum, vodka, gin).

●**Oils, spices and condiments.**

Unlimited of the following, unless otherwise noted: butter, plant oils (with olive oil strongly favored), vinegar (cider, red wine or distilled), salt, pepper, mayonnaise (not low-fat), yellow mustard (1 tablespoon daily), salad dressing (with three or fewer grams of carbohydrates per 2 tbsp), Worcestershire sauce (1 tbsp), A1 Steak Sauce (1 tbsp), paprika, cumin, turmeric, cinnamon, ginger, coriander, anise, Spanish saffron, lemon or lime juice (2 tbsp daily), mint, parsley, garlic (3 cloves daily), dill pepper, sumac.

"This diet starts to lower blood sugar levels from day one," says Dr. Parker.

After three months on the diet, ask your doctor for another A1c test. If your blood sugar is under control, you can add more carbohydrates, including one daily serving each of: vegetables, fruit (such as ½ cup of blueberries or ½ cup of cantaloupe), legumes (such as ¼ cup of black beans or kidney beans), yogurt and other dairy products (such as ½ cup of whole milk yogurt) and whole grains (such as ½ slice of whole wheat bread).

Dr. Parker isn't the only health professional who thinks a modified Mediterranean diet is a good long-term strategy for people with prediabetes.

"For most people with prediabetes and overweight, I recommend a moderate-carbohydrate, Mediterranean-style diet that is 45 percent carbohydrate, and includes plenty of healthy fats such as olive oil, and lots of high-fiber foods such as vegetables, legumes and whole grains," says Sandra Woodruff, MS, RD, a nutrition consultant in Tallahassee, Florida, and coauthor of *The Complete Diabetes Prevention Plan* (Avery).

• **Exercise five days a week.** "Exercise is an excellent way to resolve a prediabetic condition and avoid developing diabetes," says Dr. Parker.

"Exercise sensitizes your muscles to insulin, the hormone that moves glucose out of the bloodstream and into muscles and other cells—and a person with prediabetes needs regular exercise," adds Woodruff.

Dr. Parker recommends 30 to 40 minutes of exercise, at least 5 days a week, alternating days of aerobic exercise (such as brisk walking) with days of strength training (using weights, exercise bands or other resistance methods).

Best: "Start slow and go slow," says Dr. Parker. For example, walk five minutes a day for two weeks…increase to 10 minutes a day for the next two weeks…20 minutes a day the fifth and sixth week…and 30 minutes a day the seventh and eighth week.

"The body requires two weeks to adjust to a new level of conditioning—and then you can add more activity," he says.

"After two months, you'll have comfortably adjusted to the habit of exercising—and that habit is a must to control blood sugar levels and stop the advance of prediabetes."

Steve Parker, MD, internist in private practice, Scottsdale, Arizona, and author of *Conquer Diabetes & Prediabetes* (pxHealth) and *The Advanced Mediterranean Diet* (pxHealth). *www.diabeticmediterraneandiet.com.*

Sandra Woodruff, MS, RD, nutrition consultant in Tallahassee, Florida, and coauthor of *The Complete Diabetes Prevention Plan* (Avery). *www.eatsmarttoday.com.*

What You Must Do At Noon to Prevent Diabetes

Move over red wine, green tea and blueberry juice—black coffee may be the healthiest beverage of all…particularly if you want to prevent diabetes.

Standout scientific evidence: An international team of researchers from Australia, France, Holland, Scotland and the US analyzed data from 18 studies involving more than 500,000 people—and found a strong link between coffee consumption and the risk of diabetes. *Compared with people who didn't drink any coffee…*

• **Each daily cup of coffee consumed** (caffeinated or decaffeinated) was linked to a 5 to 10% reduced risk

• **Drinking 3 to 4 cups daily,** to a 25% reduced risk

• **Drinking 6 cups daily,** to a 40% reduced risk.

"It could be envisioned that we will advise our patients most at risk for diabetes to increase their consumption of coffee in addition to increasing their levels of physical activity and weight loss," wrote the researchers in the *Archives of Internal Medicine.*

But is it safe? "There are sometimes claims that coffee may do harm by increasing the risk for cardiovascular disease, but there is no evidence for this," says Lars Rydén, MD, a cardiologist and diabetes specialist at the Karolinska Institute in Sweden. "People may drink coffee safely."

Why it works: There are many ways that the compounds in coffee might protect against diabetes, says Rob M. Van Dam, PhD, assistant professor in the Department of Nutrition at the Harvard School of Public Health…

• **Caffeine triggers the release of hormones** such as epinephrine that lower glucose (blood sugar) levels.

- **Magnesium** works with enzymes that are a must for glucose metabolism and insulin sensitivity.

- **Lignans** (a plant compound) are anti-inflammatory antioxidants.

- **Chlorogenic acids** (antioxidants) reduce chronic inflammation (linked to the development of diabetes)…help produce enzymes that cut glucose output by the liver…reduce the intestinal absorption of glucose and improve insulin sensitivity.

Recent finding: In a three-month study, 47 habitual coffee drinkers stopped drinking coffee for one month, consumed four cups a day for the second month, and eight cups a day for the third month.

Higher coffee intake increased blood levels of chlorogenic acid and decreased two biomarkers of chronic inflammation. "Coffee consumption appears to have beneficial effects on subclinical inflammation," concluded researchers from the German Diabetes Center in the *American Journal of Clinical Nutrition*.

Is Timing Everything?

In another recent study on coffee and diabetes, Brazilian researchers analyzed 11 years of health data from nearly 70,000 women.

Results: Those who drank more than one cup of coffee a day had a 34% lower risk of developing diabetes compared with those who didn't drink any.

Surprising finding: But the link between coffee consumption and diabetes was true only in women who drank coffee at lunchtime!

"Our findings strongly suggest that only coffee taken with lunch may reduce diabetes risk," wrote the researchers in the *American Journal of Clinical Nutrition*.

A Good-for-You Cup of Coffee

Research links every kind of coffee to a reduced risk of diabetes—caffeinated or decaffeinated, filtered or instant, taken black or with cream and sugar. But it's healthier for a

person who wants to prevent or control diabetes to avoid regular intake of the high-calorie, high-sugar, high-fat coffee concoctions so commonly served at today's coffee shops, says Lori Barr, MD, a physician and self-described "vibrant living expert" in Austin, Texas.

Maybe you don't like unsweetened coffee. What should you do if you want to enjoy its protective effect?

Unsweetened coffee may be more flavorful than you imagine—if you drink the right kind of coffee, says Kenneth Davids, editor and principal writer of the Web publication *www.coffeereview.com* and author of *Coffee: A Guide to Buying, Brewing, and Enjoying* (St. Martin's).

"The reason more people don't drink more black coffee is because they're not drinking good coffee," says Davids. "If you buy a good coffee, it has a natural balance of bitterness and sweetness that doesn't require sugar." *When Davids says good coffee, he means…*

- **Fully ripened beans.** "The coffee bean is a fruit," he says. "If the bean is picked when it's ripe, sweet and juicy, and the green and overripe beans are separated out, the coffee will have natural sweetness to it, regardless of the variety or where it's grown."

- **Medium roast.** "Many people are into dark roasts, and dark roasts are typically served in coffee shops such as Starbucks," he says. "But a dark roast is bitter."

Bottom line: "I always encourage people to try a coffee with ripe beans, at medium roast, and discover whether they really need sugar—because a lot of people have never tasted coffee like that."

Finding Good Coffee

Davids provided this list of coffee companies that sell coffees that meet his criteria of ripeness and medium roast.

Large national roaster: Green Mountain Coffee Roasters (*www.greenmountaincoffee. com*; 888-879-4627)

Medium-sized roasters with some national presence: Intelligentsia Coffee Roasters, Chicago (*www.intelligentsiacoffee.com*;

888-945-9786); Stumptown Coffee Roasters, Portland (*www.stumptowncoffee.com*, Portland: 503-230-7797; Seattle: 206-860-2937; New York: 347-294-4295)

Small, elite roasters with the best possible coffees and good wholesale coffees on the Internet: Terroir Coffee, New England (*www.terroircoffee.com*, 866-444-5282); Café Grumpy, New York City (*www.cafegrumpy.com*, 212-255-5511, 718-499-4404, 718-349-7623); PT's Coffee, Topeka, Kansas (*www.ptscoffee.com*, 888-678-5282); Klatch Coffee, southern California (*www.klatchroasting.com*, 877-455-2824); Barefoot Coffee, northern California (*www.barefootcoffee.com*, 408-293-7200); Paradise Roasters, Minnesota (*www.paradiseroasters.com*, 763-433-0626); Temple Coffee, Sacramento (*www.templecoffee.com*, 916-454-1282).

Lars Rydén, MD, cardiologist and diabetes specialist at the Karolinska Institute in Sweden.

Rob M. Van Dam, PhD, assistant professor in the Department of Nutrition at the Harvard School of Public Health, Boston.

Lori Barr, MD, physician in Austin, Texas, and author of *Tame Your Mind, Save Your Life. www.loribarr.com.*

Kenneth Davids, editor and principal writer of the Web publication *www.coffeereview.com* and author of three books on coffee, including the bestselling *Coffee: A Guide to Buying, Brewing, and Enjoying* (St. Martin's).

Flatten Your Belly, Prevent Diabetes

Research links obesity to type 2 diabetes, with overweight folks having a 2- to 6-fold higher risk of developing the disease. Some health experts even call the two problems by one name: *diabesity*.

A new study shows a better name might be *diabelly*.

Surprising finding: Researchers from the University College London and other UK institutions set out to discover why the rate of type 2 diabetes is nearly two times higher in Americans than in the UK. Type 2 diabetes usually develops in middle-aged or older people, so the researchers analyzed health data from thousands of Americans and Brits aged 52 to 85.

To their surprise, they found that slightly higher levels of overweight among Americans did not explain their higher rates of diabetes. More belly fat did.

American woman had waists there were on average two inches bigger than their UK counterparts. American men had waists that were 1.2 inches bigger. Even Americans who weren't overweight had bigger bellies than UK folks of similar weight.

"Americans carry more fat around their middle sections than the English, and that was the single factor that explained most of the higher rate of diabetes in the US," says James P. Smith, PhD, the study leader.

And in a recently completed 10-year study of people aged 65 to 75, those who had a four-inch increase in waist size during the study had a 70% higher risk of developing diabetes, reported researchers from the University of Washington at Seattle in the *Journal of the American Medical Association.*

What happens: Belly fat is also called visceral fat because it wraps around your viscera, the internal organs in your abdomen such as your liver (which stores glucose, or blood sugar) and your pancreas (which manufactures insulin, the hormone that guides glucose out of the bloodstream into cells). But visceral fat isn't very neighborly to the nearby viscera. Fat cells in belly fat are different from fat cells anywhere else in the body, say the UK researchers.

They pump out hormones and inflammatory compounds that directly interfere with the ability of insulin and the liver to store blood sugar, a condition called insulin resistance. Glucose levels in the bloodstream stay elevated—and you're more likely to develop diabetes.

And belly fat isn't only bad for blood sugar.

A recently completed 14-year study of more than 100,000 people aged 50 and older linked a "large waist circumference" with a doubled risk of dying from any cause. Older studies link excess belly fat to high blood pressure, stroke, heart disease, breast cancer and dementia.

Belly-Reducing Foods

The UK researchers specified the exact waist sizes that put people in the study at low-, medium- and high-risk for diabetes...

- **Low-risk.** Under 37 inches for men...under 31 inches for women

- **Moderate-risk.** 37 to 40 inches for men...31 to 35 inches for women

- **High-risk.** Above 40 inches for men...above 35 inches for women.

How can you reduce your waist size—and your risk for diabetes?

Reduce chronic, low-grade inflammation, which helps reduce the accumulation of visceral fat, says Cynthia Sass, RD, a nutritional consultant in private practice in New York City and coauthor of *Flat Belly Diet!* (Rodale).

And one of the best ways to do that, she says, is to increase your intake of anti-inflammatory monounsaturated fatty acids (MUFA), found in abundance in foods such as oils (canola, safflower, sesame, soybean, walnut, flaxseed, sunflower, olive, and peanut), olives, nuts and seeds, avocados, and dark chocolate.

Standout scientific evidence: A study in the journal *Diabetes Care* showed that eating a MUFA-rich diet prevented the accumulation of belly fat, compared with diets with the same level of calories but higher levels of carbohydrates or saturated fats.

Sass offers these dietary recommendations for "eating a MUFA at every meal," a key strategy in reducing belly fat:

- **Oils.** Brush sliced vegetables such as tomatoes, peppers and eggplant with garlic-infused extra-virgin olive oil and roast in the oven. Whisk sunflower oil with balsamic vinegar to dress a garden salad.

- **Olives.** Toss steamed vegetables in olive tapanade or enjoy whole Mediterranean olives as part of a snack with whole-grain crackers, fruit and Brie.

- **Nuts and seeds.** Whip natural nut butter into fruit smoothies. Use crushed or chopped nuts to encrust baked chicken, fish or tofu.

- **Avocados.** Mash them for guacamole and serve with crudités. Spread on whole-grain toast in place of butter at breakfast.

- **Dark chocolate.** Melt and drizzle over fresh fruit. Stir into your morning oatmeal, adding berries or pitted cherries.

More Fat-Busters

Other recommendations for decreasing belly fat include...

- **Stress less, sleep more.** "Too much stress and too little sleep is a recipe for belly fat," says Sass. "Stress has been shown to increase cortisol, a hormone linked to increased belly fat. Too little sleep has been shown to boost cravings for fatty, sugary foods."

(For recommendations on reducing stress and improving sleep, please see the chapter "Stress, Insomnia & Fatigue," page 289.)

- **Exercise often.** "Physical activity, such as brisk walking for about 30 minutes a day, is a tremendous aid in overcoming insulin resistance and reducing belly fat—because when you move for 30 minutes or more, your muscles are more receptive to insulin for the next 24 hours," says Dale Peterson, MD, a physician in private practice in Sapulpa, Oklahoma, and author of *Building Health by Design* (Third Chapter).

James P. Smith, PhD, Distinguished Chair in Labor Markets and Demographic Studies, RAND Corporation.

Cynthia Sass, MPH, RD, nutritional consultant in private practice in New York City, contributing editor at *Shape* magazine, author of several books, including *Cinch! Conquer Cravings, Drop Pounds and Lose Inches* (HarperCollins) and *Flat Belly Diet!* (Rodale). www.cynthiasass.com.

Dale Peterson, MD, physician in private practice, Sapulpa, Oklahoma, and author of *Building Health by Design* (Third Chapter). www.drdalepeterson.com.

Exercise Less, Lower Blood Sugar More

Study after study shows that regular exercise can help prevent and control type 2 diabetes—mainly because it makes your muscles more sensitive to insulin, the hormone that guides glucose out of the bloodstream and into muscle, fat and liver cells.

To balance blood sugar, experts recommend a minimum of either 150 minutes a week of moderate-intensity exercise (such as brisk walking) or 60 minutes a week of vigorous-intensity exercise (such as jogging).

"Unfortunately, most people fail to meet even those minimum physical activity guidelines, citing 'lack of time' as their major reason for not exercising regularly," says Martin J. Gibala, PhD, in the Department of Kinesiology at McMaster University in Canada.

Could there be a way to spend a whole lot less time exercising but still get the same glucose-balancing benefits?

Yes, says Dr. Gibala—high-intensity interval training (HIIT). You exercise vigorously in a burst of 60 seconds, rest for 60 seconds (or engage in low-intensity exercise or "active rest"), repeat the burst, rest, repeat the burst, etc.

"A growing body of scientific evidence suggests that HIIT triggers the same types of physical changes as traditional exercise—with a lot less exercise, and therefore a lot less time."

Problem: HIIT is usually so intense that it can only be done by fit, healthy young people.

Not any more.

Exciting development: Dr. Gibala conducted a study in which older people with type 2 diabetes used a modified, slightly less rigorous form of HIIT—and it worked.

Their muscles responded better to insulin. Their blood sugar levels were lowered.

"We have shown that interval training does not have to be 'all-out' in order to be effective," he says. "Doing 10, one-minute sprints on a standard stationary bike, with about one minute of rest in between, three times a week, works as well as many hours of conventional long-term biking that is done less strenuously."

The intensity of the sprints equals 95% of maximum heart rate.

Example: The formula used to estimate maximum heart rate is 220 minus your age.

So if you're 60, your maximum heart rate would be around 160 (220 minus 60). And 95% of 160 is a heart rate of 152 beats per minute.

This less extreme HIIT method may work well for the older, slightly overweight and less fit among us, says Dr. Gabala—a description that matches the situation of many people with type 2 diabetes, who tend to be middle-aged, overweight and sedentary.

"Lack of time is no longer an excuse for not exercising, now that high-intensity interval training can be tailored for the average adult," he continues. "While still a demanding form of training, the exercise protocol we used in the study is possible for just about anyone—and you don't need more than an average exercise bike to do it."

HIIT for Beginners

The first step in beginning HIIT is getting your physician's permission to start an exercise program, says Warren Potash, a specialist in exercise therapy and sports nutrition in Moorpark, California.

The second step is to buy a heart monitor, so you can know your exact level of exertion. (You can purchase a decent monitor at sporting good stores or online for as little as $25, says Potash.)

If you have diabetes and you're overweight, Potash suggests starting with a "safe and age-appropriate" approach to HIIT.

"We're not trying to cure your diabetes in two weeks with super-intense exercise," he says. "We're trying to develop a lifelong habit of regular activity that leads you to greater health."

Session 1 of HIIT might consist of exercising on a stationary bike or treadmill until you reach 65% of your maximal heart rate. *Then…*

● **First interval**—70% HIIT for one minute, 68% "active rest" for one minute

● **Second interval**—73% HIIT one minute, 70% active rest one minute

● **Third interval**—73% HIIT one minute, 70% active rest one minute

● **Fourth interval**—73% HIIT one minute, 70% active rest one minute.

"Less is more early on," says Potash. "Once you know what you're capable of, then you can gradually adapt to more intervals, at higher levels of HIIT."

A few recommendations from Potash…

● **Don't start the next interval until your breathing has returned to a normal level during active rest.**

● **A trick to get your heart rate lower and your breathing under control:** "Breathe in deeply through your nose for two to three seconds and then blow out as hard as you can through your mouth, doing this once or twice—it lowers the heart rate instantly," says Potash.

● **Ideally, work with an exercise therapist or trainer** who can design an HIIT program that works best for you.

Martin J. Gibala, PhD, associate professor, Department of Kinesiology at McMaster University in Canada.

Warren Potash, specialist in exercise therapy and sports nutrition in Moorpark, California. *www.learn2trainsafely.com.*

Control Diabetes with Qigong

Wouldn't it be great if you could just wave your arms to get better control over your blood sugar? A research scientist at Bastyr University in Washington has adapted the ancient Chinese practice of movement called qigong (pronounced *chee-gong*) to help people with type 2 diabetes achieve better blood sugar control…feel better…and even reduce their reliance on drugs.

Study author Guan-Chen Sun, PhD, assistant research scientist at Bastyr, qigong teacher and executive director and founder of the Institute of Qigong & Internal Alternative Medicine in Seattle, says there are many types of qigong. What makes his version unique is the way it explicitly incorporates an energy component.

Dr. Sun named his new system Yi Ren Qigong (Yi means "change" and Ren means "human") and says it works by teaching diabetic patients to calm the chi, or "life energy" of the liver (to slow production of glucose) and to enhance the chi of the pancreas (exhausted by overproducing insulin). The goal of this practice is to "improve the harmony between these organs and increase energy overall," he says, noting that his patients have achieved significant results—reduced blood glucose levels, lower stress and less insulin resistance. Some were even able to cut back the dosages of their medications.

How Do They Know It Worked?

Dr. Sun's research team studied 32 patients, all on medication for their diabetes.

The patients were divided into three groups. One group practiced qigong on their own at home twice a week for 30 minutes and also attended a one-hour weekly session led by an instructor. The second group engaged in a prescribed program of gentle exercise that included movements similar to the qigong practice but without the energy component for an equivalent period of time. And the third group continued their regular medication and medical care but did not engage in structured exercise.

The results: After 12 weeks, the qigong patients had lowered their fasting blood glucose, their levels of self-reported stress and improved their insulin resistance. The gentle exercise group also brought down blood glucose levels, though somewhat less…and lowered stress. It was worse yet for the third group—blood glucose levels climbed and so did insulin resistance, while there was no reported change in their stress levels. The study was published in *Diabetes Care.*

You can learn more details on the Bastyr University Web site at *www.bastyr.edu/continuinged.*

Guan-Cheng Sun, PhD, assistant research scientist at Bastyr University, Kenmore, Washington, qigong teacher, executive director and founder of the Institute of Qigong & Internal Alternative Medicine, Seattle.

Strong Muscles Help Ward Off Diabetes

Maintaining a healthy weight helps to fend off diabetes. But now researchers at the University of California, Los Angeles, have found that having strong muscles can prevent diabetes. *Sarcopenia* (low muscle mass and strength) was associated with insulin resistance, a precursor to diabetes. To maintain muscle mass, consume low-fat protein, such as chicken or tofu, and participate in strength-training exercises. Men and women should have their testosterone levels checked and, if necessary, treated, since low levels can affect muscle mass.

Mark A. Stengler, NMD, naturopathic medical doctor in private practice, Encinitas, California, and author of the *Bottom Line/Natural Healing* newsletter. *www.drstengler.com.*

After Exercise, Low-Carb Meals Are Best

If you have diabetes—or even insulin resistance, which is a sign that you are on the way to having diabetes—you've probably been told to exercise to improve your health. And, of course, you know that what you eat is important, too. But what may come as news to you is that what you eat after exercise matters—a lot. That was the intriguing conclusion of investigators at the University of Michigan at Ann Arbor.

Eat to Improve Insulin Sensitivity

In this study measuring the effect of exercise and post-exercise meals on insulin sensitivity, Jeffrey F. Horowitz, PhD, and his team asked nine healthy, sedentary, non-obese men to each participate in four separate experimental trials on different days. During three of these trials, the subjects exercised on a treadmill and stationary bicycle for 90 minutes, then ate different types of meals throughout that day.

The morning after each session (22 hours after the last meal), researchers tested each subject's metabolic activities, including a blood test for insulin sensitivity. They found that all three exercise sessions improved insulin sensitivity, but the effect was most pronounced when the men had eaten lower-carbohydrate meals after exercise. These results were published in the *Journal of Applied Physiology*.

Fewer Carbs = Better Metabolism

Eating different types of food after exercise produces different effects on the body's metabolism, Dr. Horowitz explains, noting that even modest cutbacks in carbohydrates helps.

To apply these findings, there's no need to go to extremes. This is only part of the story—for fitness and weight loss, regular, consistent exercise is, of course, also a must. Dr. Horowitz and his team are now working with obese individuals to identify the minimum level of exercise that will improve insulin sensitivity that extends into the next day.

Jeffrey F. Horowitz, PhD, associate professor, department of movement science, School of Kinesiology, University of Michigan, Ann Arbor.

The All-Day, All-Night Guide to Controlling Your Diabetes

From the time you wake up until you go to bed, it is essential to keep your blood sugar as stable as possible if you have diabetes.

Reasons: Over time, uncontrolled elevated blood sugar harms the blood vessels, kidneys, eyes and nerves, increasing the risk for heart attack, stroke, kidney failure, blindness and tissue damage that can require limb amputation. Diabetes also is linked to dementia.

Despite these dangers, scarcely half of the 23 million Americans who have been diagnosed with diabetes have their disease under control. If you're struggling, you can significantly improve your blood sugar control by eating the right foods and doing the right things at the right times of day.

Throughout the Day

It is key to eat foods that digest slowly, so blood sugar remains relatively stable...and avoid foods that are digested quickly, triggering rapid blood sugar spikes. This also helps control weight—an important factor because excess weight contributes to diabetes complications. *Guidelines*...

•**Have 40 grams (g) to 50 g of carbohydrates at each meal.** Stick with mostly complex carbs (whole grains, vegetables, nuts)...limit refined carbs (cakes, white pasta). Check labels!

•**Avoid foods with more than 10 g of sugar per serving.**

•**Have some lean protein every day—** chicken, fish, lean beef, low-fat dairy, eggs, tofu. Most people get enough protein, so you do not need protein with each meal unless your doctor recommends this.

•**Limit starches** (corn, peas, potatoes, sweet potatoes) to one serving per meal.

•**Limit fruit to two servings per day.** A serving equals one small handheld fruit (peach, plum)...half an apple or half a banana...12 grapes...one cup of strawberries... or one-half cup of blueberries, raspberries or diced fruit (such as melon). Avoid pineapples and dried fruits, which are high in sugar.

•**At Wake-up Time.** Test your blood sugar before breakfast. If it is high, you may have eaten too many carbohydrates too close to bedtime the night before. Or your levels may have fallen too low during the night, so your liver released more glucose (sugar), causing a blood sugar "rebound." Talk to your doctor—you may need to adjust your medication dosage and/or timing.

•**At Breakfast.** The morning meal helps get your metabolism running efficiently, so don't skip it.

Ideal: One or two slices of whole-grain bread with a soft spread that contains cholesterol-lowering plant sterols, such as Smart Balance or Promise Activ...plus a two-egg vegetable omelet. It is fine to use whole eggs—but if you have high cholesterol, make your omelet with egg whites instead and limit egg yolks to two per week.

Another good choice: One cup of unsweetened or lightly sweetened whole-grain cereal that contains no more than 25 g of carbohydrates per cup, such as Cheerios or Product 19...plus one-half cup of blueberries and one cup of low-fat milk. Don't be fooled into thinking that high-fiber necessarily equals healthful—you still must check labels to see if the food is too high in carbs.

Your doctor may advise you to take a dose of diabetes medication right before breakfast.

Also: If you have diabetic nerve damage, take 100 micrograms of vitamin B-1 daily. If you take blood pressure medication, morning is the best time because blood pressure typically is higher during the day than at night. If you plan to drive, test your blood sugar before leaving home.

•**In Midmorning.** A midmorning snack generally is not necessary unless your doctor advises you to have one (for instance, due to the type of insulin you are on). However, if you start to feel weak or dizzy, have a snack that provides no more than 10 g of carbohydrates—for instance, a small tangerine, half a banana or two graham cracker squares.

•**At Lunch.** Good choices include a sandwich, such as turkey, lettuce and tomato on whole-wheat bread...or sushi with rice (preferably brown).

Common mistakes: Eating too much (especially at restaurants)...choosing a fruit plate (too much sugar and no protein)...overdoing it on chips or condiments (which can be high in fat or sugar).

•**In Midafternoon.** Again, have a snack only if you feel weak or your doctor recommends it, and limit yourself to no more than 10 g of carbs.

Good choices: About 15 pistachios...10 almonds...or one-third of an ounce of whole-grain crackers.

●**At Dinner.** Check your blood sugar before dinner. If you are on oral diabetes medication, take it just before your meal.

Dinner should include four ounces of lean protein...several generous servings of vegetables...and one serving of a starch. Have a green salad, but skip the high-carb, high-fat dressings. Instead, drizzle greens with lemon juice, balsamic vinegar, safflower oil and/or olive oil.

Limit: One alcoholic drink daily, consumed with a meal. Opt for five ounces of wine...12 ounces of a low-carb beer, such as Miller Lite...or one ounce of distilled liquor (Scotch, vodka). Avoid mixed drinks, which often are high in carbs.

Dessert options: A scoop of low-carb, no-sugar-added ice cream...berries...two Lorna Doone cookies...or three Social Tea Biscuits.

●**In the evening.** This is the best time to exercise to maximize muscle cells' absorption of glucose. Strength training and stretching are good, but aerobic exercise is most important because it increases insulin sensitivity (cells' ability to respond to insulin) for up to 14 hours. Each week, aim for two-and-a-half hours of moderate-intensity aerobic exercise, such as walking...or one-and-a-half hours of strenuous activity. For blood sugar control, 30-minute workouts generally are most effective. As part of your exercise regimen, consider tai chi. In one study, diabetes patients who did this martial art significantly lowered their blood sugar levels.

Caution: Ask your doctor before starting an exercise program. Test blood sugar before each workout. If it is below 100 milligrams per deciliter (mg/dL), have a snack before exercising. Do not work out when your blood sugar is higher than 250 mg/dL—when blood sugar is this high, exercise may elevate it even further. If you have retinopathy (damaged blood vessels in the retina), to protect vision, do not lift weights above eye level.

●**At Bedtime.** If you are on long-acting insulin, a bedtime injection controls nighttime glucose levels. If you take cholesterol-lowering medication, do so now—it is most effective at night. Test your blood sugar at bedtime. If it is somewhat elevated (but not above 250 mg/dL), lower it with 10 minutes of moderate exercise.

Insomnia doesn't raise blood sugar, but the stress it creates can.

To promote sleep: Turn off the cell phone, TV and computer at least 30 minutes before bedtime so your mind can quiet down. Take a warm bath (checking your feet for wounds or signs of infection, because diabetes often damages nerves in the feet).

Have you been told that you snore? Diabetes patients are prone to sleep apnea (repeated halts in breathing during sleep), which contributes to poor blood sugar control. Do you frequently get up at night to urinate? It could be a sign that your medication needs adjusting. If you have either symptom, tell your doctor.

Stanley Mirsky, MD, associate clinical professor at Mount Sinai School of Medicine and founder of the Stanley Mirsky MD Diabetes Education Unit at the Mount Sinai Metabolism Institute, both in New York City. He is coauthor of *Diabetes Survival Guide* (Ballantine).

Beans Lower Blood Sugar as Well as Meds

In a recent study, diabetics who ate one-half cup of beans a day—garbanzo, black, white, pinto or kidney beans—had significantly lower fasting glucose, insulin and hemoglobin A1C, a marker of long-term glucose control. When eaten as a regular part of a high-fiber, low-glycemic-index diet, beans lower hemoglobin A1C by an average of 0.48%, which lies at the lower level of effectiveness for medications such as *metformin* (Glucophage).

Cyril Kendall, PhD, research scientists, Department of Nutritional Sciences, University of Toronto, and the Clinical Nutrition and Risk Factor Modification Centre, St. Michael's Hospital, Toronto, and leader of research analyzing 41 trials regarding the effects of beans on blood sugar levels, published in *Diabetologia*.

Drink Blueberry Smoothies, Improve Blood Sugar Control

Researchers from Louisiana State University have found that drinking two blueberry smoothies daily helped obese, prediabetic adults improve their blood sugar control. The blueberry smoothie contained 22.5 grams of freeze-dried blueberry powder. Everyone can benefit from eating blueberries year-round. You can buy them frozen in the off-season...and freeze-dried blueberry powder is available online and at health-food stores. Sprinkle a teaspoon of the powder on toast (instead of jam), or stir a half cup of fresh blueberries into yogurt.

Mark A. Stengler, NMD, naturopathic medical doctor in private practice, Encinitas, California, and author of the Bottom Line/Natural Healing newsletter. www.drstengler.com.

Diabetes and Fruit

Some fruits do, indeed, have a high sugar content, but that doesn't mean you should give up this healthy habit. Fruits are low in fat and rich in phytonutrients, vitamins, minerals and fiber—and in moderation (two or three servings daily), they can be safely consumed by those with diabetes. One general way to choose fruits is using the Glycemic Index, which measures how slowly a food increases blood sugar (the lower the number, the more healthful). Choose low-to-mid-GI fruits such as cherries (22), plums (24), grapefruit (25) and bananas (47). A high-GI fruit is anything over 70.

Eating fruit with other foods also can prevent a spike in insulin. Combining fruit with low-GI foods, such as a slice of whole-grain bread, can prevent the insulin spike that comes with eating a high-GI fruit. To find the GI of specific fruits and other foods, go to *www.glycemicindex.com*.

Also helpful: Watch your serving size. One-half cup to one cup of most fruits counts as one serving. Some individuals have food sensitivities to certain fruits—and regardless of their GIs, these fruits (one example is grapefruit) can spike an individual's glucose level. Only by monitoring your diet and glucose levels closely will you truly know which fruits work best for you.

Mark A. Stengler, NMD, naturopathic medical doctor in private practice, Encinitas, California, and author of the Bottom Line/Natural Healing newsletter. www.drstengler.com.

Supercharged Cinnamon For Superior Blood Sugar Control

There are now so many cellular, animal and human studies on the ability of the spice cinnamon to control high blood sugar that a leading expert on the subject decided to review and sum up all the research, publishing his findings in the *Journal of Diabetes Science and Technology*.

Compelling scientific evidence: 11 studies on people show that eating more cinnamon or taking a daily cinnamon supplement can help...

• **Improve long-term blood sugar** (glucose) control in people with type 2 diabetes. (Type 1 diabetes is an autoimmune disease. As many as three million Americans may have this form. Type 2 diabetes is mostly a lifestyle disease, caused by overweight and lack of exercise, affecting 25.5 million Americans.)

• **Decrease fasting glucose**—a measurement of glucose levels taken eight hours after eating. (If two fasting glucose tests on two different days detect levels higher than 126 mg/dL, you're diagnosed with diabetes.)

• **Improve insulin sensitivity**—the ability of muscle, fat and liver cells to respond to insulin, the hormone that guides glucose out of the bloodstream and into those cells. (Chronically high blood levels of insulin—caused by a condition called insulin resistance—indicate poor blood sugar control, which is a risk factor for type 2 diabetes. An estimated 80 million Americans have this problem.)

• **Improve metabolic syndrome,** a condition in which you have at least three of several risk factors for type 2 diabetes and heart disease, including insulin resistance, high blood pressure, low HDL, overweight and high triglycerides.

• **Decrease spikes in glucose levels after eating.** (High, post-meal levels of glucose are a sign of advancing diabetes and—because they damage the arteries—a risk factor for heart disease.)

• **Improve risk factors for heart disease** (high bad LDL cholesterol, low good HDL cholesterol, high total cholesterol, high triglycerides) in people with diabetes, a disease that doubles the risk of heart attack and stroke.

"Components of cinnamon may be important in the alleviation and prevention of the signs and symptoms of metabolic syndrome, type 2 diabetes, and cardiovascular and related disease," concluded Dr. Anderson and his colleagues.

Twenty Times More Powerful

Of the 11 studies on people reviewed by Dr. Anderson, five tested a unique cinnamon supplement—a water extract of the spice. That includes the most recently conducted study discussed in his review, reported by an international team of researchers at the annual meeting of the Federation of American Societies for Experimental Biology.

Latest finding: In the study, 137 people with type 2 diabetes were divided into two groups. Half took a 500 milligram (mg) supplement of water extract of cinnamon, while the other half took a placebo.

After two months, the cinnamon group had a 7.5% drop in fasting blood sugar, compared with a 1.6% drop in the placebo group.

Cinnamon was also four times more powerful than the placebo in controlling post-meal blood sugar levels.

This study "adds to the growing evidence that aqueous [water] cinnamon extract may be beneficial for insulin-resistant populations," says Barbara Stoecker of Oklahoma State University, a study researcher.

In fact, the water extract of cinnamon used in the study is 20 times more powerful at sparking insulin activity than any other tested herb, spice or medicinal extract, says Dr. Anderson. "The effects of adding more of the aqueous extract of cinnamon appear similar to adding more insulin," he continues. "This results in increased insulin sensitivity."

Why is the extract so powerful? Because the insulin-activating parts of cinnamon—*catechin, epicatechin, procyanidin,* and other plant compounds known as polyphenols—are found mostly in the watery part of the spice, not in the oil, explains Dr. Anderson. A water extract concentrates these compounds—giving the cinnamon added glucose-controlling power.

Why it works: Dr. Anderson's laboratory research on animals shows the cinnamon extract probably works by...

• **Improving insulin signaling** (the ability of insulin receptors on the outside of cells to communicate with the hormone)

• **Boosting nitrous oxide,** a glucose-regulating compound in muscle

• **Regulating genes involved in blood sugar control**

• **Blocking immune factors that play a role in insulin resistance.**

The extract is also a powerful antioxidant, protecting cells from damaging oxidation and inflammation, both of which play a role not only in diabetes but also in heart disease, stroke, Alzheimer's and cancer. (Laboratory research shows the water extract of cinnamon can protect experimental animals from those diseases.)

Suggested intake: In the most recent study and in many others, participants took 500 mg a day of CinSulin, a water extract of cinnamon.

It is available online and in many stores where supplements are sold.

Web site: *www.cinsulin.com*

Phone: 303-333-8361
E-mail: info@cinsulin.com

Cinnamon as Food

But several of the 11 studies used the spice itself—either in a capsule or sprinkled liberally on food—to achieve more balanced blood sugar levels. The amounts used in the study ranged from ¼ to 1½ teaspoons a day (with low and high levels usually showing the same results).

You can purchase the spice either as cinnamon sticks (harvested dried bark that has been rolled into quills) or cinnamon powder (ground quills). Look for quills that are tightly rolled, evenly colored and blemish free, says Bharat Aggarwal, PhD, author of *Healing Spices* (Sterling), who prefers the quills to powder for richer taste. "Once ground, cinnamon begins to lose the fragrance that comes from its volatile oils, so it's best to buy whole quills and grind them as needed," he says. "The quills are somewhat tough, so you'll need a sturdy spice grinder.

"If you buy ground cinnamon, you'll get the most fragrance from the finest quality, which is smooth rather than gritty," he continues. "Whole quills keep for three years, as long as they aren't in extreme heat. Ground cinnamon begins to fade in flavor after a few months."

Perhaps the most popular way to add cinnamon to the diet is to sprinkle it on a hot cereal such as oatmeal or on buttered toast.

Also try: Other ideas from Dr. Aggarwal on eating more cinnamon…

●**Sprinkle on apples, bananas, melons and oranges.**

●**Mix with mint and parsley in ground beef for burgers and meatloaf.**

●**Mix into rice pilaf.**

●**Put a cinnamon quill** in beef or vegetarian stews, or in lentil soup.

●**Combine equal parts of cinnamon, cardamom and black pepper** and rub it into pork tenderloin or lamb before baking.

●**Add to hot cocoa** to enhance the flavor of the chocolate.

●**Sprinkle into pastry dough** for pies and quiches.

●**Make spiced tea.** Put a quart of brewed tea in a pot, add two cups of apple juice, a lemon slice and two cinnamon sticks. Simmer gently for 10 minutes.

Richard Anderson, PhD, researcher in the Diet, Genomics, and Immunology Laboratory of the Beltsville Human Nutrition Research Center, a division of the United States Department of Agriculture.

Barbara Stoecker, PhD, professor in the Department of Nutritional Sciences at Oklahoma State University.

Bharat Aggarwal, PhD, professor of cancer research, biochemistry, immunology and experimental therapeutics at the MD Anderson Cancer Center in Houston, Texas, and author of *Healing Spices: How to Use 50 Everyday and Exotic Spices to Boost Health and Beat Disease* (Sterling).

Cashew Nut Extract Helps Diabetes

The cashew plant is recognized around the world for its medicinal properties, including an ability to stimulate blood sugar absorption. So researchers from the University of Montreal, the Université de Yaoundé in Cameroon and Lava University, Quebec, investigated which part of the plant contains the highest amounts of the compounds responsible for improving blood sugar absorption. They found that the nut extract, which contains concentrated amount of *anacardic acid*, simulated blood sugar absorption better than extracts from the leaves or bark.

Easiest way to get anacardic acid: Eat a handful of raw cashew nuts, which contain the beneficial compound.

Mark A. Stengler, NMD, naturopathic medical doctor in private practice, Encinitas, California, and author of the *Bottom Line/Natural Healing* newsletter. *www.drstengler.com*.

Wild Kudzu Root May Help Metabolic Syndrome

The kudzu root, a nuisance of a vine that grows wild in the southern portion of the US, may soon be put to good use to help people who have metabolic syndrome, a constellation of symptoms, including hypertension, high cholesterol and abdominal obesity that increases risk for diabetes, heart disease and stroke. A recent study shows that kudzu root, an ancient Chinese herb historically used to treat menopausal symptoms, neck and eye pain, anginal pain and even the common cold, may actually help to remedy this modern-day epidemic.

Scientists have long suspected that controlling blood glucose levels might be the key to managing metabolic syndrome. To that end, researchers at the University of Alabama at Birmingham tested the effects of kudzu root on blood glucose, blood pressure and blood lipids (fats) in rats with high blood pressure and at risk for type 2 diabetes. For two months, half were fed a diet that contained a small (0.2%) amount of kudzu root extract. The others (the control group) were fed the same diet without the kudzu extract. At the end of the study, the kudzu-treated rats had lower blood pressure, blood lipids and blood glucose. Moreover, the kudzu-treated rats showed improved control of blood glucose. The study was published in the *Journal of Agricultural and Food Chemistry*.

How Does It Help?

According to J. Michael Wyss, PhD, professor of cell biology and medicine at the University of Alabama at Birmingham, an isoflavone (an antioxidant found in plants) called *puerarin* might be the effective agent that reduces the symptoms of metabolic syndrome. "It appears that puerarin works by limiting the ability of glucose to cross from the gut into the blood, thereby buffering blood sugar so that it does not rise rapidly after a meal," he explains. "This causes glucose in the blood to be taken up by muscle tissue. High levels would allow more to go into fat cells for storage."

Kudzu is available in health-food stores in pill and powder form. Dr. Wyss cautions, however, that more testing is needed to determine safety and efficacy for metabolic syndrome, especially since it has the potential for drug interactions. He also warns that people with estrogen-sensitive cancers (such as breast, ovarian or prostate cancers) and those taking the drug *tamoxifen* should not take kudzu because the herb contains phytoestrogens, substances that mimic estrogen, and have the potential to interact with estrogen receptors. In fact, any use of kudzu should be considered only in consultation with a physician.

In the future, Dr. Wyss believes that kudzu most likely will be used as a complement to other treatment approaches to metabolic syndrome, which include lifestyle modifications (healthy eating habits, exercise and weight loss) and drugs to bring glucose, blood lipids and blood pressure to the recommended levels.

J. Michael Wyss, PhD, professor of cell biology, medicine, neurobiology and psychology at the University of Alabama at Birmingham.

Pycnogenol Helps Diabetic Retinopathy

Pycnogenol (pronounced *pic-noj-en-all*), an extract from the bark of the French maritime pine, is known to improve circulation, reduce swelling and ease asthma. Now Italian researchers have found another use for it—it helps patients with diabetes who are in the early stages of diabetic retinopathy, a complication of diabetes in which the retina becomes damaged, resulting in vision impairment, including blurred vision, seeing dark spots, impaired night vision and reduced color perception.

According to Mark Stengler, NMD, all people with diabetes are at risk for diabetic retinopathy—and it's estimated that as many as 80% of people with diabetes for 10 years or more will have this complication.

Participants in the Italian study had been diagnosed with diabetes (the researchers did not specify whether the patients had type 1 or 2 diabetes) for four years, and their diabetes was well-controlled by diet and oral medication. Study participants had early stage retinopathy and moderately impaired vision. After two months of treatment, the patients given Pycnogenol had less retinal swelling as measured by ultrasound testing. Most important, their vision was significantly improved. The vision of those in the control group did not improve.

Dr. Stengler's view: If you have type 1 or 2 diabetes, undergo a comprehensive eye exam at least once a year. If retinopathy is detected, it would be wise to supplement with Pycnogenol (150 milligrams daily). Pycnogenol has a blood-thinning effect, so people who take blood-thinning medication, such as *warfarin*, should use it only while being monitored by a doctor.

Mark A. Stengler, NMD, naturopathic medical doctor in private practice, Encinitas, California, and author of the *Bottom Line/Natural Healing* newsletter. *www.drstengler.com*.

PGX—The New Miracle Fiber That Beats Diabetes

Fiber is the indigestible portion of food, and there are two kinds...insoluble and soluble.

• **Insoluble fiber** (found in foods such as wheat bran, nuts and potato skins) absorbs water in the intestinal tract, forming the large, moist stools that keep you regular.

• **Soluble fiber** (found in foods such as beans, oats, apples, carrots and psyllium seeds) creates a thick, slow-moving slurry in the stomach and small intestine.

What it does: The slurry slows the rate at which carbohydrates turn into blood sugar (glucose). This rate is called the Glycemic Index (GI)—the faster the absorption, the higher the GI. (White bread has a GI of 100; broccoli of 15.) A high-GI diet has been linked to type 2 diabetes—and to heart disease, gallbladder disease and breast cancer.

The thicker or more viscous the soluble fiber, the better it is at slowing the digestion of carbohydrates and aiding blood sugar control.

Problem: Highly viscous fibers aren't palatable when added to the diet in amounts needed for blood sugar control.

Examples: psyllium (from psyllium seeds), glucomannan (from the roots of the Asian konjac plant) and guar gum (from guar beans, grown in India and Pakistan).

Discovering PGX

A highly viscous but palatable fiber has been the quest of many food scientists—including scientists in the laboratory of Michael Lyon, MD, medical director of the Canadian Centre for Functional Medicine in British Columbia and coauthor of *How to Prevent and Treat Diabetes with Natural Medicine* (Riverhead).

"We tested many fiber blends and they became thick very quickly," he says. "They glued up the teeth and mouth, and tasted awful.

"Also, they didn't have stability," he continues. "They were thick in the glass, but they didn't stay thick in the intestinal tract."

Dr. Lyon and his colleagues experimented with different soluble fibers...in different amounts...preheating them...applying pressure to them...and doing everything else they could think of to produce a fiber that was highly viscous and pleasant to consume and stayed viscous in the gut.

They eventually produced PolyGlycoplex (PGX), a specially processed combination of three viscous fibers—konjac powder, sodium alginate and xanthan gum. They were amazed by its unique properties...

• **PGX had 3 to 5 times more viscosity than any other soluble fiber.**

• **Its viscosity was delayed**—sprinkled on food or added to juice, it didn't immediately thicken, so it was palatable.

• **It stayed viscous in the small intestine.**

• **It lowered the GI of high GI foods by up to 60%**—an effect never seen before with any other fiber. (White bread baked with PGX has a lower GI than whole-wheat bread, and white rice with PGX sprinkled on it has a lower GI than brown rice.)

• **And best of all, new studies show that PGX effectively controls blood sugar**—in preliminary research, it is even more effective than a top-selling diabetes drug.

Newest Research

Scientists call spikes of blood sugar levels after a meal *postprandial hyperglycemia. Studies show that preventing these spikes can help...*

• **Prevent diabetes**

• **Manage prediabetes so it doesn't become diabetes** (Prediabetes is a fasting blood sugar level from 100 mg/dL to 125; above that level is diabetes.)

• **Manage diabetes so it doesn't advance**

• **Prevent cardiovascular disease,** which kills most people with diabetes (post-meal glucose spikes damage arteries).

• **PGX lowers post-meal blood sugar.** Dr. Lyon and colleagues in Canada and Australia conducted three studies on PGX and postprandial glycemia, reporting their results in the *European Journal of Clinical Nutrition.*

In the studies, they gave people PGX as either a nutritional supplement or a granulated powder dissolved in water. The participants took PGX before, with, and/or after meals.

Results: PGX reduced postprandial hyperglycemia by up to 50%—a very sizeable decrease. And the more PGX the participants took, the lower their post-meal blood sugar levels.

The powder form of PGX was effective at maintaining reduced glucose levels. The supplement form, when given at dinner, lowered glucose levels after the next morning's breakfast.

"PGX in granular form has biologically important, dose-related effects on acute postprandial glycemia," concluded the researchers. "As little as 7.5 grams of the granules reduces blood glucose responses over 120 minutes by 50%. PGX in capsule form… had a biologically important effect when consumed with the evening meal whereby it improved glucose tolerance at breakfast."

• **PGX works with many foods.** In another study by Dr. Lyon and his colleagues, PGX reduced postprandial hyperglycemia after meals when it was sprinkled on or mixed with any one of several different foods—cornflakes, rice, strawberry yogurt, granola, white bread or a frozen turkey dinner. The addition of PGX also changed several of those foods from high to medium to low GI.

"Sprinkling or incorporation of PGX into a variety of different foods is highly effective in reducing postprandial glycemia and lowering the GI of a food," concluded the researchers in *Nutrition Journal.*

Using PGX

PGX is available as a nutritional supplement and as granules that you either sprinkle on food or mix with water.

It's widely sold in retail stores in the US and Canada, and online. To find a store near you that sells PGX products, visit the Web site *www.pgx.com* (in the dropdown menu under "About PGX" go to "Where to Buy" and enter your address).

Here are Dr. Lyon's recommendations for using the product…

• **With a meal.** Sprinkle 5 grams (a level teaspoon) of the granular form onto a moist food, such as rice or pasta…into a soup…into a sauce that you're adding to a food…into yogurt…or into a smoothie before you blend it.

"The granules are the most effective form for controlling blood sugar, and they're the most cost-effective, too," says Dr. Lyon.

And don't worry about the taste. "PGX really doesn't have any taste—it takes up the flavors of whatever it's put into."

The granules are sold either in bulk (a large container with a 5-gram scoop) or in individual, per-meal 5-gram packets.

Red flag: If you add PGX to a food and let it sit for 20 minutes, it will congeal into an unpalatable gel. Eat the meal within a few minutes after adding PGX.

●**As a beverage.** Sprinkle the granules into water before the meal and drink the water. "Put PGX in a bottle of water, shake it and drink it," says Dr. Lyon.

●**As a supplement.** Take a soft gel capsule, following the dosage instructions on the label.

Michael Lyon, MD, medical director of the Canadian Centre for Function Medicine in British Columbia, adjunct professor in the Food, Nutrition, and Health Program at the University of British Columbia in Vancouver, and coauthor of *How to Prevent and Treat Diabetes with Natural Medicine* (Riverhead) and *Hunger-Free Forever* (Atria).

Magnesium: Mineral Shield Against Diabetes

Diabetes—the disease of chronically high levels of blood sugar—is an epidemic.

Ten percent of American adults have it, including 40% of people 65 and older. In fact, the rate of diabetes is rising so fast, the Centers for Disease Control predicts the number of Americans with the disease will triple by 2050.

Key fact not widely reported: One reason so many of us get diabetes may be that so few of us get enough of the mineral magnesium in our diets.

In a recently completed 20-year study of nearly 4,500 Americans, researchers from the University of North Carolina at Chapel Hill found that those with the biggest intake of magnesium (200 milligrams [mg] per every 1,000 calories consumed) had a 47% lower risk of diabetes than those with the smallest intake (100 mg per every 1,000 calories consumed). The study also linked lower magnesium intake to higher levels of a biomarker of insulin resistance and three biomarkers of chronic inflammation (C-reactive protein, interleukin-6, fibrinogen).

What happens: Insulin is the hormone that ushers blood sugar (glucose) out of the bloodstream and into cells. In insulin resistance, cells don't respond to the hormone, and blood glucose levels stay high—often leading to diabetes. And inflammatory biochemicals trigger the manufacture of proteins that increase insulin resistance.

"Magnesium has an anti-inflammatory effect, and inflammation is one of the risk factors for diabetes," says Ka He, MD, the study leader. "Magnesium is also a co-factor in the production of many enzymes that are a must for balanced blood sugar levels."

Compelling Scientific Evidence

Other recent studies also link magnesium intake and diabetes…

●**10 times more magnesium deficiency—in people with diabetes.** Compared with healthy people, people with newly diagnosed diabetes were 10 times more likely to have low blood levels of magnesium, and people with "known diabetes" were 8 times more likely to have low levels, reported researchers from Cambridge University in the journal *Diabetes Research and Clinical Practice.*

●**Low magnesium, high blood sugar.** People with diabetes and low intake of magnesium had poorer blood sugar control than people with a higher intake of magnesium, reported Brazilian scientists. "Magnesium plays an important role in blood glucose control," they concluded in the journal *Clinical Nutrition.*

●**More nerve damage.** Nerve damage—diabetic neuropathy, with pain and burning in the feet and hands—is a common complication of diabetes. Indian researchers found that people with diabetic neuropathy had magnesium levels 23% lower than people without the problem.

●**Magnesium protects diabetic hearts.** High blood sugar damages the circulatory system, with diabetes doubling the risk of heart attack or stroke. In a study from Italian researchers, taking a magnesium supplement strengthened the arteries and veins of older people with diabetes. The results were in the journal *Magnesium Research*.

Bottom line: "Based on evidence from the study I led and other studies, increasing the intake of magnesium may be beneficial in diabetes," says Dr. He.

More Magnesium

The recommended dietary allowance (RDA) for magnesium is 420 mg a day for men and 320 mg a day for women.

However: In a study conducted by the Centers for Disease Control, no group of US citizens tested—including Caucasian, African-American, Hispanic-American, men or women—consumed the RDA for magnesium. "Substantial numbers of US adults fail to consume adequate magnesium in their diets," concluded researchers in the journal *Nutrition*.

They also found that magnesium intake decreased as age increased—a troublesome finding, since diabetes is usually diagnosed in middle-aged and older people.

Healthful strategy: "I recommend increasing the intake of foods rich in magnesium, such as whole grains, nuts, legumes, vegetables and fruits," says Dr. He.

Best food sources of magnesium include…

●**Nuts and seeds** (almonds, cashews, pumpkin seeds, sunflower seeds, sesame seeds)

●**Leafy green and other vegetables** (spinach, Swiss chard, kale, collard greens, mustard greens, turnip greens, cabbage, broccoli, cauliflower, Brussels sprouts, green beans, asparagus, cucumber, celery, avocado, beets)

●**Whole grains** (whole-grain breakfast cereals, wheat bran, wheat germ, oats, brown rice, buckwheat)

●**Beans and legumes** (soybeans and soy products, lentils, black-eyed peas, kidney beans, black beans, navy beans)

●**Fruit** (banana, kiwi fruit, watermelon, raspberries)

●**Fish** (salmon, halibut).

Consider a magnesium supplement. But magnesium-rich food may not be sufficient to protect you from diabetes, says Michael Wald, MD, director of nutritional services at the Integrated Medicine and Nutrition clinic in Mt. Kisco, New York. That's because many factors can deplete the body of magnesium or block its absorption. *They include…*

●**Overcooking greens and other magnesium-rich foods**

●**Eating too much sugar**

●**Emotional and mental stress**

●**Taking magnesium-draining medications,** such as diuretics for high blood pressure

●**Exposure to environmental toxins** such as pesticides

●**Bowel diseases and bowel surgery.**

"Low blood levels of magnesium are very common," says Dr. Wald. And conventional doctors rarely test magnesium levels.

Recommended: To help guarantee an adequate blood level of magnesium, Dr. Wald recommends taking Perque Magnesium Plus Guard. For maximum absorption and effectiveness, this doctor-developed supplement contains four different forms of the mineral (magnesium glycinate, magnesium ascorbate, magnesium citrate, magnesium stearate). It also contains nutritional cofactors that help the mineral work in the body.

The supplement is available at *www.perque.com* and through many other retail outlets, both online and in stores where supplements are sold. Follow the dosage recommendations on the label.

Ka He, MD, MPH, ScD, associate professor of nutrition and epidemiology at the Gillings School of Global Public Health and the School of Medicine at The University of North Carolina at Chapel Hill.

Michael Wald, MD, physician and director of nutritional services at the Integrated Medicine and Nutrition clinic in Mt. Kisco, New York. *www.intmedny.com.*

Can Bread Cause Diabetes?

We know that food—specifically too much of it and the resulting weight gain—causes type 2 diabetes. But could *what* we eat cause type 1 diabetes? Perhaps, says a recent study that has linked wheat consumption to the development of type 1 diabetes in young people (generally age 40 and younger).

Unlike the more common type 2, type 1 diabetes is a progressive autoimmune disorder that people develop early in life. Some cases have clear genetic roots, but scientists have believed that environmental factors could also play a role—including, possibly, something in the diet. This small study from the University of Ottawa demonstrates that one factor may be wheat consumption.

Wheat and Diabetes Link

The study included 42 men and women, mostly young adults, with type 1 diabetes and a control group of 22 similar young people who did not have diabetes or any other known autoimmune disease. Researchers wanted to see how the immune systems in those with diabetes would respond to wheat.

What they learned: Twenty of the 42 diabetes patients were "high responders" to wheat, which was demonstrated by heightened immune system activity. According to the researchers, this response was found at a "significantly higher" rate than in the control group. Also, nearly all patients in this group carried a gene known to increase risk of diabetes.

Wheat and What Else?

Wheat cannot be said to actually have caused the onset of diabetes in these patients, says Andrew Rubman, ND, medical director of the Southbury Clinic for Traditional Medicines in Southbury, Connecticut, but the study does make a case that wheat consumption (specifically gluten found in wheat, rye and barley)

could play a role in turning the genetic diabetes switch to "on" for those who carry the risk gene. Other factors may be involved too, he notes, while affirming that this study provides an early seed of knowledge that may someday help people avoid diabetes onset, or at the very least reduce the distress it causes. While there is more to learn, it is a healthy habit for all, especially children, to limit wheat consumption, rotating it with assorted other grains in order to minimize its impact on the body.

Dr. Rubman says that gluten avoidance might prove useful for people who already have type 1 diabetes because it may reduce the impact of the disease. If you have this type of diabetes, try a gluten-free diet for four to six months to see if symptom severity and blood sugar control improve. If the answer is yes, Dr. Rubman advises staying gluten-free for life.

Andrew L. Rubman, ND, medical director, Southbury Clinic for Traditional Medicines, Southbury, Connecticut. *www.southburyclinic.com.*

More Diabetes with Your Steak?

Many health-conscious consumers adopt low-carb eating habits to lose weight and ward off heart disease and diabetes. But be careful—it can backfire. A recent study warns that a low-carbohydrate, Atkins-style diet with lots of animal protein actually may increase your risk for type 2 diabetes.

At the Harvard School of Public Health in Boston, postdoctoral research fellow Lawrence de Koning, PhD, and his colleagues analyzed the medical records of 41,140 men (all free of heart disease, cancer and diabetes at the start) in the Health Professionals Follow-Up study. The participants completed questionnaires about their eating habits once every four years for more than 20 years, during which time 2,761 of the men developed type 2 diabetes.

After taking into account risk factors such as body mass index, physical activity, family history of diabetes, smoking, coffee and alcohol consumption and total caloric intake, Dr. de Koning and his team found that the men whose diets were lowest in carbohydrates (averaging 37% of calories) but high in animal protein (18% of calories) and animal fat (26% of calories) had a 41% higher risk for type 2 diabetes than men consuming a higher carbohydrate (57% of calories) diet where animal protein (10% of calories) and animal fat (12% of calories) were lower.

Dr. de Koning presented these results at the June 2010 meeting of the American Diabetes Association. It's important to note that the findings are preliminary, based on an observational study, and further research is necessary.

What to Eat?

Dr. de Koning said it isn't that low-carbohydrate, high-protein and high-fat diets are inherently harmful…it's the *type* of protein and fat you consume. The problem with animal sources of protein, especially red and processed meat, relates to their fat and iron content. Taking in lots of saturated fats (as found in these meats) can reduce insulin sensitivity. Additionally, iron can accumulate in body tissue, generating oxidative stress, insulin resistance and (if the iron accumulates in the pancreas) problems in secreting insulin.

Note: Iron is an important nutrient, and deficiency brings its own set of problems, so people who are anemic may be advised to eat meat. Red meat (beef, of course, but also lamb, pork and veal) is rich in heme iron, which is the most effective at reversing iron deficiency, since it is absorbed better than nonheme. Moderation and balance are key.

A better way: The Nurses' Health Study (also from Harvard) found that eating greater quantities of vegetable proteins and vegetable fats as part of a low-carbohydrate diet was inversely associated with diabetes risk, said Dr. de Koning.

For most folks, the best high-protein, low-carb diet includes very little red or processed meat, a smattering of chicken and fish, and lots of vegetable proteins (including legumes and nuts) and vegetable fats. Good protein sources include tofu (10.3 grams of protein per one-half cup)…black beans (15.2 grams of protein per cup…roasted beets (3.9 grams of protein per one-half cup)…and almonds (6 grams of protein per quarter cup).

Eating a low-carb diet can be all-around healthy. It helps control your weight and, said Dr. de Koning, "may actually reduce your risk for chronic diseases if your sources of fat and protein (what you replace the carbs with) are chosen carefully." That means that red meat should be ordered *rarely*…rather than rare, medium or well-done.

Lawrence de Koning, PhD, research fellow, Department of Nutrition, Harvard School of Public Health, Boston.

Five Beverages That Can Cause Diabetes

To prevent diabetes, we're often told by health experts what not to eat, such as too many refined carbohydrates from breads, pasta and ice cream.

What not to *drink* may be just as important.

Latest finding: Researchers at the Harvard School of Public Health analyzed health data from 310,000 people who participated in 11 studies that explored the connection between sugar-sweetened beverages (SSBs) and diabetes.

Fact: SSBs include soda, fruit drinks (not 100% fruit juice), sweetened ice teas, energy drinks and vitamin water drinks. And in the last few decades, the average daily intake of calories from SSBs in the US has more than doubled, from 64 to 141. The beverages are now "the primary source of added sugars in the US diet," wrote the Harvard researchers in *Diabetes Care*.

The researchers found...

Drinking one to two 12-ounce servings of SSBs per day was linked to a 26% increased risk of type 2 diabetes, compared with people who drink one or less SSB per month.

The increased risk for diabetes among those drinking SSBs was true even for people who weren't overweight, a common risk factor for diabetes. The researchers concluded that while SSBs are a risk factor for overweight, they're also a risk factor for diabetes whether you gain weight or not.

"The association that we observed between sodas and risk of diabetes is likely a cause-and-effect relationship," says Frank Hu, PhD, professor of nutrition and epidemiology at the Harvard School of Public Health.

Theory: A typical 12-ounce serving of soda delivers 10 teaspoons of sugar. That big dose of quickly absorbed sugar drives up blood sugar (glucose) levels...in turn driving up blood levels of insulin, the hormone that moves glucose out of the bloodstream and into cells...leading to insulin resistance, with cells no longer responding to the hormone and blood sugar levels staying high...eventually leading to diabetes.

SSBs also increase C-reactive protein, a biomarker of chronic, low-grade inflammation, which is also linked to a higher risk for diabetes.

"Cola-type beverages" also contain high levels of advanced glycation end products, a type of compound linked to diabetes, say the researchers.

And many SSBs are loaded with fructose, a type of sugar that can cause extra abdominal fat, another risk factor for diabetes.

Bottom line: "People should limit how much sugar-sweetened beverages they drink and replace them with healthy alternatives, such as water, to reduce the risk of diabetes, as well as obesity, gout, tooth decay and cardiovascular disease," says Vasanti Malik, PhD, a study researcher.

Good-for-You Beverages

"I help many of my clients break the habit of regularly drinking soda, sweetened ice tea

If You Have Gum Disease, Look for Diabetes

Researchers at New York University College of Nursing found that 93% of Americans with periodontal disease were at high risk for diabetes, while a far smaller proportion of people without gum disease—about 63%—were at risk for diabetes. If you have periodontal disease, get it treated—and be sure that you are tested for diabetes.

Mark A. Stengler, NMD, naturopathic medical doctor in private practice, Encinitas, California, and author of the *Bottom Line/Natural Healing* newsletter. *www.drstengler.com.*

and other sugary beverages," says Lora Krulak, a healthy foods chef and self-described "nutritional muse" in Miami, Florida. "I show them how to make other beverages that have natural sugar or are naturally sweetened, so they don't miss the sugary drinks."

One of her favorite thirst-quenching combinations...

2 to 3 liters of water (sparkling or non)
Juice of 2 lemons
Juice of 2 limes
Small bunch of mint
Pinch of salt
1 tablespoon of maple syrup, honey, or coconut sugar or stevia to taste (stevia is a natural, low-calorie sweetener)

Let the mixture steep for 30 minutes before drinking.

"It's good to make a lot of this drink, so it's in your refrigerator and you can grab it any time," says Krulak. When leaving home, put some in a water bottle and carry it with you.

Cut Sugar Cravings

"If one of my patients is craving sugary drinks, it means his or her blood sugar levels aren't under control," says Ann Lee, ND, LAc, a naturopathic doctor and licensed acupuncturist in Lancaster, Pennsylvania.

To balance blood sugar levels and control sugar cravings, she recommends eating every three to four hours, emphasizing high-protein foods (lean meats, chicken, fish, eggs, nuts and seeds), good fats (such as the mono-unsaturated fats found in avocados and olive oil) and high-fiber foods (such as beans, whole grains and vegetables).

She also advises her clients to take nutritional supplements that strengthen the adrenal glands, which play a key role in regulating blood sugar levels.

Recommended: Daily B-complex supplement (B-50 or B-100) and vitamin C (2,000 to 5,000 milligrams daily, in three divided doses, with meals).

For healthy drinks, she recommends green tea sweetened with honey or stevia, or a combination of three parts seltzer and one part fruit juice.

Frank Hu, MD, PhD, professor of nutrition and epidemiology at the Harvard School of Public Health, Boston.

Vasanti Malik, research fellow in the Harvard School of Public Health, Boston.

Lora Krulak, healthy foods chef and "nutritional muse" in Miami, Florida. *www.lorakrulak.com*.

Ann Lee, ND, LAc, naturopathic doctor and licensed acupuncturist in Lancaster, Pennsylvania. *www.doctornaturalmedicine.com*.

Chapter 8

DIGESTIVE DISORDERS

Constipation: What Your Doctor May Not Tell You

Constipation is one of those ailments that most people think they know how to treat—the majority believe that simply eating more fiber is the answer. But this often doesn't work.

What few people realize: Chronic constipation can have some very surprising causes…and dietary changes alone help only about one-third of those with the condition. What's more, if overused, some of the same laxatives that relieve constipation initially can exacerbate it in the long run, so most people need additional help to really get rid of their constipation.

What's Normal?

Most people have one to three bowel movements daily, while others have as few as three a week. This variability is normal.

What's more important are changes in bowel habits, particularly if you're having fewer bowel movements than usual and also are experiencing other symptoms that could indicate a more serious problem—such as blood in stool (colon cancer)…unexplained weight loss (diabetes or colon cancer)…or weight gain (low thyroid function).

The first step: Even though not all people with constipation will improve by eating a fiber-rich diet, it's still wise to start by eating more fruits, vegetables, legumes and whole grains that are high in fiber. In general, people who consume 20 g to 35 g of dietary fiber daily—and who exercise regularly—are less likely to suffer from constipation than those who mainly eat a meat-and-potatoes diet.

Examples of fiber sources: One cup of oatmeal or a bran muffin provides 4 g to 5 g of fiber.

Helpful: Be sure to eat the vegetables and fruits that are most likely to draw water into the stool to facilitate soft, bulky bowel movements.

Best vegetables to ease constipation: Those in the Brassica family, such as broccoli, asparagus, Brussels sprouts, cauliflower and cabbage.

Best fruits to ease constipation: Peaches, pears, cherries and apples (or apple juice).

If your constipation doesn't improve within a few weeks, then…

1. Check your medications. Many prescription and over-the-counter medications slow intestinal movements and cause constipation. Narcotic painkillers, such as *oxycodone* (OxyContin) and the combination of *acetaminophen* and *oxycodone* (Percocet), are among the worst offenders. Tricyclican-tidepressants, such as amitriptyline, also can cause it. So can medications that treat high blood pressure (calcium channel blockers) and Parkinson's disease.

Helpful: Constipation also can be triggered by the antihistamines used in allergy medications, such as *cetirizine* (Zyrtec) and *diphenhydramine* (Benadryl), if used daily. Lowering the dose of an antihistamine drug or taking it less often may reduce bouts of constipation.

2. Get your magnesium and potassium levels tested. Most people get sufficient amounts of both minerals in their diets. But if you take a daily diuretic or laxative or have an intolerance to gluten (a protein found in wheat, barley and rye), you may be deficient. Low magnesium or potassium decreases the strength of intestinal contractions—this may contribute to diarrhea or constipation.

Important: If constipation doesn't improve within a month of boosting your fiber intake, see your doctor. The problem could be due to a deficiency of either or both minerals. If a blood test shows that you have low magnesium and/or potassium, supplements can restore normal levels within a week or two (ask your doctor for the appropriate dosage).

3. Be cautious with calcium. High-dose calcium often causes constipation, particularly in people who take antihistamines or other drugs that slow intestinal transit time (how long it takes food to pass through the bowel).

Advice: Get most of your calcium from calcium-rich foods. If your constipation is related to high-dose calcium supplements, talk to your doctor about limiting the supplement dose to 500 mg to 1,000 mg daily—and be sure to eat plenty of high-fiber foods and drink lots of fluids.

4. Drink at least two quarts of fluids daily—more if you exercise or engage in activities that cause you to perspire heavily. Drinking this much fluid increases lubrication and makes stools larger, which helps them pass more easily (and frequently). Water is best—it has no calories and usually is the most readily available fluid.

5. Avoid laxatives. Some of the most popular products actually can increase constipation. So-called stimulant laxatives, such as Dulcolax and castor oil, cause the intestinal muscles to stretch and weaken with continued use. People who use these products frequently may become dependent—they can't have a bowel movement without them.

Important: It's fine to use these products occasionally—when, for example, you haven't had a bowel movement for several days and are feeling uncomfortable. But if you use them more than once or twice a week, it's too much. Talk to your doctor about healthier methods such as those described in this article.

6. Relax and reregulate. If you get enough fiber and drink enough fluids but still are constipated, see your doctor. You may have a type of constipation known as dyssynergic defecation (different parts of the anorectal area—pertaining to the anus and rectum—contract and relax at the wrong time).

This type of constipation can be diagnosed by giving patients oral radiopaque markers that allow the doctor to view intestinal movements on an abdominal X-ray. Normally, people initiate a bowel movement by instinctively contracting the upper part of the rectum while relaxing the lower part. People with dyssynergic defecation constipation often do the opposite. Stools aren't propelled through the colon, or they get "hung up" due to inappropriate muscle movements.

People with this type of constipation usually are referred to a gastroenterologist, who often uses biofeedback, along with exercises such as Kegels (a type of pelvic-muscle exercise), to help them learn to relax and contract different parts of the anorectal area. They're also taught not to strain during bowel movements—this decreases the force of intestinal contractions and impairs one's ability to have a bowel movement.

Norton J. Greenberger, MD, clinical professor of medicine at Harvard Medical School and senior physician at Brigham and Women's Hospital, both in Boston. He is a former president of the American Gastroenterological Association and coauthor of Four Weeks to Healthy Digestion *(McGraw-Hill).*

Prebiotics and Probiotics: Tiny Entities That Can Heal Your Gut

If you don't know much (or anything) about prebiotics—with an "e"—you are far from alone. Many people don't know the difference between prebiotics and their better known cousins, probiotics. Both can be used to optimize digestive health and boost immunity. According to Leo M. Galland, MD, a specialist in digestive health, they have beneficial similarities.

Prebiotics—What Probiotics Eat

Your high school Latin provides an easy and obvious way to differentiate prebiotics from probiotics—focus on the "pre." Prebiotics are the predecessor. Their primary purpose is to provide nourishment to probiotics, thus helping to sustain a healthy level of these good bacteria in the gut.

Unlike probiotics, prebiotics are not bacteria—they're a form of soluble fiber that can be found in a few complex carbohydrates. What makes them unique is their ability to pass unabsorbed through the small intestine, which makes them available to feed tissue and probiotics in the large intestine. One of the most common prebiotics is a kind of complex fructose polymer found in some plant foods called *inulin* (which, in spite of the similarity in names, has nothing to do with insulin). There are other kinds, including non-inulin prebiotics and a type called *fructo-oligosaccharides* (or FOS).

Research has shown prebiotics to be beneficial for people with Crohn's disease and ulcerative colitis. Prebiotics can serve as a natural remedy to ease constipation, and they can be helpful for a number of other digestive complaints, including constipation-associated irritable bowel syndrome (IBS) and some cases of inflammatory bowel disease. Prebiotics also help absorption of calcium and magnesium in people who have low mineral levels in their diets, and there's some evidence that they might help prevent colon cancer as well.

Are Dietary Sources Sufficient?

Some foods are rich sources of prebiotics. For instance, *inulin* can be found in generous amounts in Jerusalem artichokes (a potato-like tuber)…chicory…jicama…and dandelion. And many common foods contain lesser amounts of inulin and/or FOS, such as onions, garlic, leeks, bananas, tomatoes, spinach and whole wheat.

Since prebiotics aren't abundant in these foods, it can be useful to take prebiotic supplements if you have certain types of digestive problems.

Dr. Galland prescribes prebiotic supplements for many of his patients, noting that a typical dose can range from 4 grams to 8 grams. They come in various forms, including powders and capsules. *He often prescribes…*

• **Extracts of Jerusalem artichokes or extracts of chicory,** best for chronic constipation.

• **FOS extracted from fruits and grains,** which can be helpful for constipation and colitis.

• **Non-inulin prebiotics,** which include oat beta-glucan—a soluble fiber that is separated from oats to make supplements. These have the additional benefit of lowering cholesterol. Oat beta-glucan is less likely to cause gas or bloating than inulin and can be excellent for boosting immune function, Dr. Galland says.

Start Slowly and Discuss With Your Doctor

Since this is all fairly complex, it is important to consult with a physician who has expertise in treating patients with prebiotic supplements. If you and your doctor agree that prebiotics may be helpful to you, plan to start slowly and increase the dosage gradually, or your body may overrespond, Dr. Galland cautions. "Let your GI tract get used to the prebiotics and shift the bacteria slowly," he says. Stop taking them if you notice an upset stomach, gas, diarrhea, bloating and other uncomfortable digestive symptoms that don't dissipate within a few days.

A group that is especially likely to experience such difficulties, Dr. Galland says, is people with inflammatory bowel disease—as well as some folks with other types of digestive problems. Why? While the prebiotics are not themselves irritating, they may increase production of irritants by stimulating the growth of beneficial intestinal bacteria, Dr. Galland explains.

Note: Unpleasant as it may be, this actually may be a sign that the prebiotics are beginning to do their job.

Some people should avoid prebiotics altogether, including people who have fructose malabsorption, a limited ability to absorb fructose (including that found in inulin-based prebiotic supplements and inulin-containing foods such as Jerusalem artichokes). If you have this problem, you may experience gastrointestinal problems (gassiness, bloating, diarrhea) that get worse if you take prebiotics. Don't know whether this might apply to you? Here's a clue. People with fructose malabsorption are very likely to get gassy and/or bloated or have diarrhea if they consume the sweeteners sorbitol or xylitol, because these are fermented by the same bacteria that ferment inulin.

Are You Using Probiotics Correctly?

Known to help increase bowel regularity while decreasing gas and bloating, *probiotics* are making their way onto many top-10 health lists, so it's not surprising to find them tucked into all manner of foods and beverages, with labels touting their health benefits.

However, the formula for using probiotics to optimize your health is somewhat more nuanced than merely spooning up a daily serving of yogurt!

Probiotics Go Mainstream

Probiotics are definitely getting more respect. Doctors are beginning to promote probiotic supplements to replenish the valuable intestinal bacteria that antibiotics would suppress. Probiotics have made their way into the hospital world, too—they're given to patients to help prevent deadly intestinal diseases that have resulted from antibiotic-resistant superbugs…researchers are studying their use for premature babies…and a few doctors are urging consideration of a new hand-hygiene protocol that involves dipping caregivers' hands into probiotic solutions after scrubbing to recolonize the skin with good bacteria.

Maybe those doctors are also telling patients to buy probiotic-fortified foods at the supermarket—and there's nothing wrong with doing so. But Dr. Galland says that we won't achieve any meaningful benefits by relying on these probiotic-fortified food sources alone.

Why We Need Supplements

Dr. Galland explains that the acid naturally present in most probiotic-containing foods actually suppresses the probiotics at least partially. It's impossible to know how many cultures survive and prove beneficial. He believes that supplements are a better route since they reliably deliver a beneficial number of probiotic organisms.

Dr. Galland prescribes specific types of probiotics in certain situations. He suggests people work with their own doctor or naturopath to address individual needs. *For example…*

• **For people with no particular health concerns,** Dr. Galland might suggest 20 billion Colony Forming Units (CFUs) of combined *lactobacillus* and *bifidobacterium* "as a good general preventative for intestinal and respiratory tract infections."

• **For people taking antibiotics,** *Saccharomyces boulardii* (S. boulardii, brand name Florastor) usually is the best choice (this particular probiotic is not a bacteria but a yeast). It's also helpful in boosting effectiveness of Flagyl (*metronidazole*) and is used to treat *Clostridium difficile* colitis and antibiotic-associated colitis, as well as other bacterial and nonbacterial intestinal infections.

Note: Dr. Galland says that S. boulardii should be taken only for the duration of antibiotic or Flagyl treatment, after which he switches his patients to a bacteria-based probiotic.

• **For patients having abdominal surgery,** Dr. Galland prescribes *Lactobacillus plantarum* for a few weeks before and after surgery, since research shows that it helps reduce postoperative infections. Other studies demonstrate that *lactobacillus probiotics* can help to reduce frequency of diarrhea and abdominal pain in cancer patients as well.

• **For gas and bloating,** Dr. Galland says that certain soil-based organisms (called "SBOs"—for instance, one kind is *Bacillus laterosporus*) can be helpful. These probiotics aren't normally found in the human digestive system and they won't take up permanent residence, so patients who find them beneficial may want to continue taking them daily even after their symptoms have subsided, he adds.

What's Best for You?

As with prebiotics, Dr. Galland says that it may take some trial and error to identify which probiotics are helpful in achieving the desired results without upsetting your system. He has found Lactobacillus plantarum beneficial for many of his patients, but it isn't always the right choice. Experienced doctors often use sophisticated stool test results to identify the types of bacteria already in a patient's system, since this information can help determine the best course of pre- and probiotic therapy, along with other natural supplements that will yield good results.

If you want to try adding probiotics to your personal health regimen, talk to a doctor with expertise in this area and expect to start slowly and watch closely to see what works best. (You'll know it's working if it helps diminish digestive difficulties, such as gas, indigestion and irregular bowel movements.) This may mean that you end up trying several different types of probiotics before you find what helps your system function best. Stick with it though, since these beneficial bacteria have the potential to transform your health for the better.

Leo Galland, MD, founder and director of the Foundation for Integrated Medicine in New York City. He is the author of *Power Healing* (Random House) and *The Heartburn and Indigestion Solution*, an e-book available online at *www.fatresistancediet.com*.

The Placebo That Soothes Your Gut— Even When You Know It's Fake!

When medical researchers want to conduct the most rigorous type of scientific study that really proves whether or not a drug works, the study is always "placebo-controlled." The researchers divide the study participants into two groups—one group takes the drug, while the other group takes a placebo, a fake, lookalike pill. To be proven effective, the drug has to outperform the placebo by a "statistically significant" margin—and that's not easy!

What you may not know: Placebos work. By a mysterious process that scientists are just starting to analyze and understand, believing a fake drug is real can trigger the healing powers of the body, sometimes producing the same results as the drug.

Placebos are so routinely effective that a recent survey of nearly 700 US doctors found that half of them regularly prescribe pills they think won't have any real effect on a patient's illness (such as a vitamin), usually telling the patient the pill is a powerful or new drug not typically prescribed for the problem. The doctors do this because they (and everyone else) think that the only way a placebo can work is if you don't know it's a placebo—if you're somehow deceived or fooled into thinking it's the real thing.

Important new development: Researchers from Harvard Medical School found that a placebo can relieve the symptoms of irritable bowel syndrome even when the people taking it know it's a placebo!

The Real Placebo

Irritable bowel syndrome (IBS) affects 36 million Americans, causing abdominal bloating and cramping, excess gas and either diarrhea or constipation. This difficult-to-treat condition is called a functional disorder—doctors know what is happening (a problem with GI function) but not why.

In the study, 80 people with IBS were divided into two groups. One group received a placebo they knew was a placebo. They were told they were being given "placebo pills made of an inert substance, like sugar pills, that have been shown in clinical studies to produce significant improvement in IBS symptoms through mind-body self-healing processes," explains Ted J. Kaptchuk, the study leader and associate professor of medicine at Beth Israel Deaconess Medical Center of Harvard Medical School.

(In two previous studies on IBS, Kaptchuk and his colleagues showed that placebos given the usual way—without the patient knowing they were placebos—can effectively control symptoms. "It's not because the symptoms of IBS aren't real," he says. "It's because IBS is a type of illness that is more susceptible to mind-body healing.")

"Not only did we make it absolutely clear that these pills had no active ingredient and were made from inert substances, but we actually had 'placebo' printed on the bottle," says Kaptchuk.

The placebo group also received a 15-minute educational presentation about placebos. They were told…

1. The placebo effect is powerful.

2. The body can automatically respond to placebo pills like Pavlov's dogs who salivated when they heard a bell.

3. A positive attitude helps but isn't necessary.

4. Taking the pills faithfully is critical.

The other group didn't receive a placebo or any other type of new treatment. In fact, the researchers were very careful to make sure that for the duration of the three-week study no one changed their self-care regimen for IBS, and that both groups received the same type of medical treatment—except for the placebo.

Results: After three weeks, the researchers compared the placebo and the non-placebo groups. *Those taking the placebo had…*

● **50% greater reduction in the severity of IBS symptoms** (severity of abdominal pain, frequency of abdominal pain, severity of abdominal distention, dissatisfaction with bowel habits)

● **53% greater improvement in quality of life** (the degree to which IBS interferes with everyday life)

● **32% greater adequate relief of IBS** (measured by a "yes" or no" answer to the question, "Over the past week have you had adequate relief of your IBS symptoms?").

These positive results compare favorably to results from studies on drugs currently used to treat IBS, noted the researchers.

"Our results challenge 'the conventional wisdom' that placebo effects require 'intentional ignorance,'" wrote the researchers in the medical journal *PLoS One*.

Your Body's "Inner Pharmacy"

How does a placebo produce real healing when it's nothing more than a non-active substance such as sugar?

"The placebo effect follows the same chemical pathways in the body as 'real' medicine," says Howard Brody, MD, PhD, a family physician, director of the Institute for Medical Humanities at the University of Texas Medical Branch at Galveston and author of *The Placebo Response: How You Can Release the Body's Inner Pharmacy for Better Health* (Cliff Street).

"If a medicine works by turning on certain brain pathways—such as a drug that increases the neurotransmitter dopamine in Parkinson's disease—then the placebo does that. If a medicine works by decreasing inflammation—such as anti-inflammatory drugs for arthritis—then the placebo does that.

"That's because as part of its biological apparatus the body has an 'inner pharmacy' of self-healing chemistry—and when you use the placebo you 'phone in' a prescription to your own inner pharmacy."

To activate your inner pharmacy with a placebo, Dr. Brody recommends a strategy somewhat similar to that used in the Harvard study…

Endow the placebo with positive meaning. "If you attribute meaning to the placebo pill—if you think and believe it will work—then the following sequence is set in motion," says Dr. Brody.

1. You think and feel differently, and the chemistry of the brain changes.

2. Because the brain is linked to the rest of the body, your changed brain chemistry changes biochemical pathways.

3. When the brain-body pathways change, the tissues of the body can change.

4. If those tissues change, healing can occur.

Create a ritual of medicine-taking. "Medicine relies largely on rituals—which are a way of triggering positive responses from your repertoire of stored experiences," says Dr. Brody. "If you take your placebo at a certain time of day with a glass of orange juice, make sure you always take it that way, at that time. Be conscious of rituals, and use them to help you heal."

Find a doctor who supports the placebo response. A doctor who listens to you…who feels and expresses concern and care for you…and who helps you feel a sense of mastery and control over your symptoms…is the type of doctor who is most likely to reinforce the placebo response, says Dr. Brody.

Ted J. Kaptchuk, associate professor of medicine at Beth Israel Deaconess Medical Center of Harvard Medical School, Boston.

Howard Brody, MD, PhD, family physician, director of the Institute for Medical Humanities at the University of Texas medical branch in Galveston and author of *The Placebo Response: How You Can Release the Body's Inner Pharmacy for Better Health* (Cliff Street).

Beware of Heartburn Drugs

The popular heartburn medications known as proton-pump inhibitors (PPIs) are the third-highest-selling class of drugs in the US with an estimated one of every 20 Americans taking them. However, recent research shows that PPIs can be harmful—and frequently are overprescribed.

FDA warns of danger: Based on a review of several studies, the FDA has recently issued a warning about a possible increased risk for fractures of the hip, wrist and spine in people who take high doses of prescription PPIs or use them for more than a year.

Other important findings: A recent study of hospital patients treated for infection caused by the bacterium *Clostridium difficile* (which leads to severe diarrhea) found that those who took a PPI were 42% more likely to have a recurrence of the infection than those not taking the drug. A number of studies have also linked PPIs to possible increased pneumonia risk—the drugs make it more likely that pneumonia-causing microbes will survive in the stomach and migrate into the lungs.

The irony is that PPIs, such as *esomeprazole* (Nexium), *omeprazole* (Prilosec) and *lansoprazole* (Prevacid), don't actually address the underlying cause of heartburn. Instead, these drugs work by shutting down production of stomach acid—but this acid is essential for absorbing nutrients as well as controlling harmful stomach bacteria. Reduced stomach acid can increase susceptibility to foodborne illness, such as salmonella, and can increase risk for small intestine overgrowth (which causes faulty digestion and absorption).

According to Leo Galland, MD, a number of natural remedies attack the root cause of heartburn very effectively—without harming your health.

The Problem with PPIs

Heartburn occurs when the contents of the stomach back up into the esophagus (acid reflux), causing a sensation of burning and discomfort. Contrary to popular belief, heartburn is not caused by excess stomach acid. In fact, most people with heartburn have normal levels of stomach acid.

Instead, acid reflux occurs because the valve that is supposed to keep the stomach's contents in the stomach—called the lower esophageal sphincter (LES)—relaxes at the wrong time.

Taking medications that neutralize stomach acid (as antacids do) or reduce production of stomach acid (as PPIs and similar drugs known as H2 antagonists do) makes the reflux from your stomach less acidic, but it does nothing to make the faulty valve work better.

What's more, since acid reflux contains digestive enzymes—which can be just as irritating to the esophagus as stomach acid—your reflux may still cause you problems, such as heartburn, belching or sore throat, even after taking these acid-fighting medications.

Addressing the Root Cause

If you use a PPI drug and want to stop, taper off gradually.

Here's how: Talk to your doctor about switching to a 20-milligram (mg) dose of *omeprazole*, the mildest PPI, for several weeks. From there, switch to an H2 antagonist, such as *cimetidine* (Tagamet) or *ranitidine* (Zantac), for a week or two. These drugs are less potent acid inhibitors.

At that point, ask your doctor about stopping acid-suppressing medication altogether. *While tapering off the drug, begin working on correcting the underlying problem of your leaky LES valve...*

•**Eat more frequent, smaller meals.** Aim for five small meals daily. A distended stomach is the biggest stimulus for the LES to open.

•**Chew your food well.** The act of chewing signals the LES to stay closed. Chew each mouthful of food 10 to 20 times.

•**Don't eat within three hours of bedtime.** This allows your stomach to empty into the small intestine before you go to sleep.

•**Switch to a reduced-fat diet (no fried, fatty or greasy foods)**—and minimize your intake of chocolate, coffee and alcohol. All of these foods can impair the function of the LES. These dietary changes help reduce symptoms in 70 to 80% of Dr. Galland's heartburn patients. Try it for one week to see if it helps you. If the reduced-fat diet doesn't improve your symptoms, try cutting back on carbohydrates instead. In about 10% of people with heartburn, the reflux is triggered by high-carbohydrate foods, such as bread, pasta and potatoes.

Follow these dietary changes until you have been totally off acid-suppressing drugs for at least six weeks. Then experiment to see if changing the diet provokes symptoms such as heartburn.

The Natural Approach

If the lifestyle changes described above don't adequately ease your heartburn symptoms, a number of natural products can be very effective at improving LES function. After checking with your doctor, you can try the following supplements (available at most health-food stores or online) one at a time. If a supplement doesn't improve symptoms after one week, discontinue it. If it does help but you need more relief, continue taking it while adding the next supplement on the list.

Continue taking these supplements for at least six weeks. Then try stopping the supplements to see if you still need them. They are safe to use indefinitely if necessary.

●**Calcium citrate powder.** This is the most important supplement you can take for acid reflux. Calcium in your body's cells stimulates the LES to close, but studies have shown that when the esophagus becomes inflamed from chronic reflux, the LES no longer responds to these cellular signals. This leads to even more inflammation, creating a vicious cycle.

To be effective in these cases, the calcium needs to have direct contact with the esophagus. That's why Dr. Galland recommends a solution of calcium powder in water rather than pills.

Typical dose: 250 mg mixed in two to four ounces of water after dinner and after other meals as needed (up to four doses per day).

Good brands: NOW Foods (888-669-3663, *www.nowfoods.com*)...ProThera, Inc. (888-488-2488, *www.protherainc.com*).

Caution: People with kidney stones or chronic constipation should consult with their doctors before taking calcium citrate powder.

●**Digestive enzymes.** While these products help acid reflux in many people, it's not completely clear why. One possible reason is that they help the stomach empty faster.

Typical dose: One to two capsules or one-half teaspoon powder mixed with two to four ounces of water after each meal.

Good brands: AbsorbAid (866-328-1171, *www.iherb.com*)...NOW Foods Optimal Digestive System 90.

●**Betaine hydrochloride.** This digestive aid is typically used by people who do not produce adequate levels of stomach acid. In people with heartburn, betaine hydrochloride helps the stomach empty, thus reducing the possibility of reflux.

Typical dose: One to two capsules (typically 360 mg each) after meals.

Good brands: Country Life (800-645-5768, *www.country-life.com*)...NOW Foods.

●**Deglycyrrhizinated licorice.** This supplement appears to have a direct soothing effect on the esophagus, reducing inflammation—which, in turn, helps improve LES function.

Typical dose: 150 mg to 300 mg, just before or after meals.

Good brands: Integrative Therapeutics, Inc. (800-931-1709, *www.integrativeinc.com*)...NOW Foods.

●**Aloe liquid.** Derived from the aloe vera plant, this supplement reduces heartburn by soothing the esophagus.

Typical dose: Four ounces, just before or after meals.

Good brands: George's Aloe (254-580-9990, *www.warrenlabsaloe.com*)...Lily of the Desert (800-229-5459, *www.lilyofthedesert.com*).

●**Sustained-release melatonin.** Most people think of the hormone melatonin as a sleep aid, but it also affects a number of gastrointestinal functions, including tightening the LES.

Typical dose: 3 mg to 6 mg, taken shortly before bedtime.

Good brands: NutriCology (800-545-9960, *www.nutricology.com*)...Jarrow Formulas (310-204-6936, *www.jarrow.com*).

Caution: People with certain autoimmune diseases (including rheumatoid arthritis) should avoid melatonin.

Leo Galland, MD, founder and director of the Foundation for Integrated Medicine in New York City. He is the author of *Power Healing* (Random House) and *The Heartburn and Indigestion Solution*, an e-book available online at *www.fatresistancediet.com*.

A Natural Alternative to Gallbladder Surgery

Cholecystectomy, the surgical removal of the gallbladder, is commonly recommended for people suffering from abdominal pain and other symptoms associated with gallstones. In fact, cholecystectomy is among the top 10 hospital procedures performed in the US. According to naturopathic physician Jamison Starbuck, gallbladder surgery should be a last resort, not an initial treatment.

Here's why: The gallbladder acts as a storage container for bile, a digestive compound made in the liver. Bile helps the intestines break down fats, stimulates *peristalsis* (the movement of your intestine that pushes your food along) and assists in the elimination of stool. When you eat, the gallbladder contracts, secreting bile into your small intestine. If you don't have a gallbladder, bile goes directly from the liver into the digestive tract, constantly dripping into the small intestine. This inhibits good digestion and can lead to diarrhea, constipation, inflammation of the stomach lining (gastritis) or a small intestine ulcer (due to irritation caused by bile). Gallstones don't always cause pain. But if they do, you may experience cramping in your upper right abdomen or under your right shoulder blade.

As an alternative to gallbladder surgery, anyone who has been diagnosed with gallstones or gallbladder pain can usually experience a reduction in pain and the size of stones by following these steps…

• **Go easy on meat and dairy.** Consumption of the saturated fats and proteins found in animal-based foods, including dairy products, increases the formation of gallstones (fish does not have this effect). On the other hand, boosting one's intake of fiber, legumes, fruits, vegetables and plant oils can decrease the size and number of gallstones.

• **Take lipotrophic factors.** These nutrients, including certain vitamins and amino acids, help move fat out of the liver and gallbladder.

Recommendations for lipotrophic factors: Choline and methionine (both available at natural-food stores)—900 milligrams (mg) of each daily, divided and taken with meals… folic acid—800 micrograms (mcg daily)…and

vitamin B-12—800 mcg daily. This regimen is typically taken for three months.

• **Try botanical medicines.** The herbs greater celandine, fringe tree and dandelion promote bile production in the liver and stimulate bile flow from the gallbladder. Dr. Starbuck typically prescribes a tincture made of equal parts of these three herbs, which can be found at stores that sell botanical medicines. A typical adult dose is 30 drops in two ounces of water, twice daily, taken 30 minutes away from food, typically for three months.

Important: Discontinue these herbs if they cause any symptoms, such as diarrhea. If you've been diagnosed with serious liver or gallbladder disease, discuss this protocol with your physician before trying it—your liver may be sensitive to dietary changes or botanical medicines.

Jamison Starbuck, ND, naturopathic physician in family practice and a guest lecturer at the University of Montana, both in Missoula. She is a contributing editor to *The Alternative Advisor: The Complete Guide to Natural Therapies and Alternative Treatments* (Time Life).

Is Wheat Making You Sick?

These days, most people have heard of celiac disease. Affecting about one in every 100 Americans, it's a digestive disease in which the body reacts adversely to gluten (a protein found in wheat, barley and rye). But there's a similar condition, known as wheat intolerance, that few people know about—this food sensitivity can cause just as many problems for sufferers as celiac disease.

Wheat-intolerant people have no symptoms when they eat barley or rye, but ingesting wheat often leads to such complaints as indigestion, bloating, canker sores, constipation, headache, sinusitis, respiratory problems, insomnia, joint pain and fatigue.

Researchers don't yet know just how many people have wheat intolerance, but from what Jamison Starbuck, ND, can see in her practice, the sufferers of wheat intolerance outnumber those with celiac disease. Because people with either celiac disease or wheat intolerance experience similar symptoms after ingesting wheat, distinguishing the two conditions can be tricky. But a simple diagnostic clue helps—people with undiagnosed celiac disease are chronically unwell. Because celiac disease stresses the immune system, it drains a person's energy. People with wheat intolerance, on the other hand, are generally well but suffer episodic ailments, usually related to the amount of wheat consumed.

If you suspect that you may have celiac disease, see your doctor for an exam and blood tests. If you think wheat intolerance may be your problem, try a simple home test. Avoid wheat in any form for seven to 10 days, paying close attention to how you feel each day, then reintroduce it at each meal for two days (or less often if you get symptoms).

Read labels! Wheat is hidden in many unexpected products, such as candy bars, soy sauce, cream soups, pudding and luncheon meats. Since wheat is obviously a main component of bread, pasta, pizza and baked goods, wheat avoidance also can be a good way to shed a few pounds.

If you feel better when you avoid wheat than when you eat it, you have wheat intolerance. You can determine the degree of your wheat intolerance through trial and error. Some people can tolerate one serving of wheat per day without experiencing symptoms, while others can eat wheat only once a week. Still others feel best if their diet is completely wheat free.

How to Eat Without Wheat

"What will I eat?" is a common response when Dr. Starbuck suggests a trial period—or a lifetime—of wheat avoidance. Fortunately, there are numerous wheat-free products, including wheat-free breads, pastas, pizzas and crackers, available at many supermarkets, health-food stores and online stores. For cooking, you can purchase flour made from rice, chickpeas, quinoa, millet or tapioca. Wheat-free recipes and cookbooks can be found at local libraries, bookstores and online. Interestingly, many people with "hay fever"—a seasonal grass allergy—are wheat-intolerant. When they avoid wheat during the peak grass-growing seasons of spring and early summer, their hay fever symptoms are often reduced.

*Jamison Starbuck, ND, naturopathic physician in family practice and a guest lecturer at the University of Montana, both in Missoula. She is a contributing editor to *The Alternative Advisor: The Complete Guide to Natural Therapies and Alternative Treatments* (Time Life).*

Vitamin E: The Best Treatment for Fatty Liver Disease

The liver is the biggest organ in the body—because it has a lot to do! Among other activities, it pumps out the bile acid that digests fats…processes protein…stores glucose, vitamin B12, iron and copper…generates blood-clotting factors…metabolizes medications and breaks down toxins…and removes waste products from the blood.

But as Americans get fatter—with nearly 7 out of 10 of us overweight—our livers are getting fatter. And sicker.

Key fact not widely reported: An estimated one-third of Americans have *nonalcoholic fatty liver disease* (NAFLD), with at least 20% of liver cells filled with fat globules. (Another 10 million have alcoholic fatty liver disease caused by heavy drinking—more than 2 drinks a day for a woman and more than 3 drinks a day for a man.)

For millions with NAFLD, the condition advances to nonalcoholic *steatohepatitis* (NASH), where many liver cells are not only fat-filled but also inflamed and possibly scarred.

"There is an increasing prevalence of NASH in this country, something that is directly related to the obesity epidemic," says Joel Lavine, MD, chief of gastroenterology, hepatology and nutrition at New York-Presbyterian/Morgan Stanley Children's Hospital in New York City.

And NASH is often a precursor of liver problems that are a whole lot worse.

One out of 7 people with NASH eventually develop cirrhosis—irreversible scarring of the liver, with symptoms that can include indigestion, fatigue, fluid retention and confusion. Cirrhosis can lead to liver cancer or liver failure.

NASH is also linked to an increased risk for heart attack and stroke.

Problem: There aren't any medications that control or reverse NASH.

Solution: A recent study in the *New England Journal of Medicine* shows that a vitamin can effectively treat the disease.

Vitamin E Beats the Drug

The study involved 247 people with NASH, which is diagnosed with a liver biopsy. They were divided into three groups.

One group took 800 milligrams (mg) daily of vitamin E, a powerful antioxidant that can protect liver cells. A second group took the diabetes drug *pioglitazone* (Actos), which earlier studies showed might help the liver. A third group took a placebo.

Results: After two years, 43% of those taking vitamin E had dramatic improvements— less fat in the liver, less inflammation, and less liver degeneration.

Although Actos outperformed the placebo, it didn't produce "statistically significant" improvements in NASH—which vitamin E did. (And those taking Actos gained an average of 10 pounds, a known side effect of the drug.)

"This study is an important landmark in the search for effective treatments for NASH," says Patricia Robuck, PhD, senior advisor at the National Institute of Diabetes and Digestive and Kidney Diseases.

"The good news is that cheap and readily available vitamin E can help many of those with NASH," adds Dr. Lavine.

In a similar study, presented at the annual meeting of the American Association for the Study of Liver Disease, vitamin E controlled NASH in overweight children with the disease. "This study reinforces the earlier finding that vitamin E improves NASH in adults," says Dr. Lavine.

And a study by Malaysian researchers showed that taking 400 milligrams daily of vitamin E for one year can help NAFLD, completely curing the condition in 15 of 30 people taking the nutrient and improving it in five.

Important: When people in the NASH study who were taking vitamin E stopped taking the nutrient, their level of liver enzymes started to rise, an indication of returning liver problems. People with NASH need to stay on vitamin E for the treatment to work, says Dr. Lavine.

Natural Therapy for NASH

Anyone who is overweight or has a family history of liver disease should ask their doctor to be tested for NASH with a liver biopsy, says Dr. Lavine.

If the disease is present, he recommends medically supervised treatment with vitamin E, at the same dosage used in the study.

Joel Lavine, MD, chief of gastroenterology, hepatology and nutrition at New York-Presbyterian/Morgan Stanley Children's Hospital in New York City, and a faculty member in the Department of Pediatrics at Columbia University College of Physicians and Surgeons.

Pat Robuck, PhD, senior advisor, National Institute of Diabetes and Digestive and Kidney Diseases, Bethesda, Maryland.

New, Drug-Free Treatments for Inflammatory Bowel Disease

An estimated 1.4 Americans have inflammatory bowel disease (IBD)—and they know it's not called inflammatory for nothing.

Their bowels have fiery flare-ups of disease, with urgent, frequent and bloody diarrhea, and severe abdominal cramps. During flare-ups they're exhausted, with little appetite.

There are two main types of IBD. If the inflammation occurs in a single, continuous section of the surface of the colon and rectum, it's called ulcerative colitis. If the inflammation occurs, for example, in patches at the border of the small and large intestine and burrows into intestinal walls or mucus membranes, it's called Crohn's disease. In both types, an overactive immune system may be to blame.

What happens: The immune system mistakes food, bacteria and other materials in the gut for foreign invaders and attacks them, sparking intestinal inflammation.

Gastroenterologists don't know the cause of the abnormal immune response of IBD, although genes play a role. (If you have a parent or sibling with IBD, you're more likely to get it.) And most gastrointestinal specialists think the only way to treat IBD is with powerful anti-inflammatory and immunosuppressant drugs, or with bowel-removing surgery if drugs can't control the disease. (About 75% of people with Crohn's and 33% with ulcerative colitis end up having the surgery.)

Alternative: "Drugs only mask the symptoms of IBD and provide no true relief or cure," says David Dahlman, DC, a chiropractic physician, director of the Hyde Park Holistic Center in Cincinnati, Ohio, and author of *Why Doesn't My Doctor Know This?—Conquering Irritable Bowel Syndrome, Inflammatory Bowel Disease, Crohn's Disease and Colitis* (Morgan James).

Dr. Dahlman has treated thousands of people with IBD, and thinks the condition has three main causes…

1. An imbalance of bacteria in the digestive tract, caused mainly by taking antibiotics and other gut-damaging medications

2. An imbalance of the biochemistry of the digestive tract, caused by an unnatural diet and nutritional deficiencies

3. Food allergies that complicate the problem—with each IBD-sufferer allergic to a unique set of foods.

By rebalancing the bacteria using probiotics (supplements of gut-friendly bacteria)… rebalancing the biochemistry of the digestive tract with a whole-foods diet and nutritional supplements…and detecting and eliminating food allergies…you can effectively treat IBD, he says.

Natural Healing for IBD

Several recent studies support Dr. Dahlman's ideas about the cause and treatment of IBD…

● **The power of probiotics.** "Large therapeutic doses of normal bowel bacteria are a must to begin restoration of health in your gastrointestinal system," says Dr. Dahlman.

New study: Italian doctors treated 131 IBD patients with either a "high-potency probiotic mixture" (VSL#3) or a placebo for two months. Those taking the probiotics had a 32% greater decrease in disease activity during flare-ups. VSL#3 supplementation is able to reduce disease activity in patients affected by ulcerative colitis, concluded the doctors in the *American Journal of Gastroenterology.*

Resource: You can order VSL#3 at *www. vsl3.com* or call (866) 438-8753.

Dr. Dahlman favors the high-potency probiotics Lactoviden and Bifoviden, from Metagenics. They are available at his Web site (*www.drdahlman.com*) and through many other online retailers of supplements.

● **Dietary therapy.** "Many people have had poor nutritional habits for a long time—eating a lot of processed food and fast food—and those choices can play a role in the development of IBD," says Dr. Dahlman. Whole foods can help heal the bowel.

New study: Japanese doctors treated 16 patients with Crohn's disease using a vegetarian diet and found that it was "highly effective" in preventing flare-ups in 15 patients.

And in a 10-year study of more than 67,000 middle-aged women, French researchers found that those who ate the most meat were 45% more likely to develop IBD than those who ate the least. The results were in the *American Journal of Gastroenterology.*

"Eliminate simple sugars, bowel-irritating alcohol and fast foods," recommends Elizabeth Lipski, PhD, CCN, a certified clinical nutritionist in Asheville, North Carolina, and author of *Digestive Wellness* (McGraw-Hill). "One study of people with ulcerative colitis showed that flare-ups occurred almost four times as frequently when fast foods were eaten twice a week."

● **Detecting food allergies.** "If you have food allergies, each time you eat the offending food your immune system will react to it, triggering gastrointestinal symptoms," says Dr. Dahlman. "That's why the most important test for a person with IBD is a food allergy test—because everyone with the condition has specific food allergies that need to be identified and eliminated before they can ever get well."

New finding: In a study by Swiss researchers of 79 people with Crohn's disease, eliminating food allergens reduced abdominal pain and stool frequency and improved well-being.

"Immune responses" to food "may be a reason for the perpetuation of inflammation in Crohn's disease," wrote the researchers in the journal *Digestion*.

"Food allergies and sensitivities play a significant role in ulcerative colitis and Crohn's disease, occurring in approximately half of all cases," says Dr. Lipski. "The most common offenders are dairy products, grains and yeast."

To detect food allergies, Dr. Dahlman recommends asking your doctor for the ELISA blood test, which measures your immune system's level of allergic response to 88 foods.

● **Anti-inflammatory nutrition.** The anti-inflammatory omega-3 fatty acids are important "pharmaconutrients" for patients with IBD, according to a team of Japanese researchers. They compared blood levels of omega-3s in two groups of IBD patients—those in remission and those with frequent flare-ups. Those in remission had levels that were 57% higher.

And in a four-year study of more than 25,000 people conducted by UK researchers, those with the highest dietary intake of omega-3s were 44% less likely to develop ulcerative colitis compared with those with the lowest intake. Increasing the intake of omega-3s may help prevent ulcerative colitis, concluded the researchers in the *European Journal of Gastroenterology & Hepatology*.

"Salmon, mackerel, herring, tuna, sardines and halibut are excellent dietary sources of omega-3s," says Dr. Lipski. "You can also take fish oil capsules daily—many studies show benefits of fish oil in IBD with daily dosages between 3.5 and 5.5 grams."

David Dahlman, DC, chiropractic physician, director of the Hyde Park Holistic Center in Cincinnati, Ohio, author of *Why Doesn't My Doctor Know This?—Conquering Irritable Bowel Syndrome, Inflammatory Bowel Disease, Crohn's Disease and Colitis* (Morgan James). *www.drdahlman.com.*

Elizabeth Lipski, PhD, CCN, certified clinical nutritionist in Asheville, North Carolina, and author of *Digestive Wellness* (McGraw-Hill). *www.lizlipski.com.*

For a Comfier Colonoscopy—Drink Warm Water

Every year, 141,000 people are diagnosed with colorectal cancer, and more than 51,000 die of the disease.

Obviously, you want to prevent colon cancer. And one way to do that is with a colonoscopy, a diagnostic procedure that reduces the risk of dying from colorectal cancer by about 70%.

What happens: As you lie on your left side, a thin, long, flexible tube with a light and camera at the end is inserted into the anus and then moved into the rectum and colon. As it is slowly snaked up and then back down the length of your large bowel, images of the bowel wall appear on a screen. If a doctor sees a polyp (*adenoma*)—a growth that's usually benign but can develop into a tumor—he inserts an instrument into the tube and removes the polyp, preserving some tissue for a biopsy to see if it contains cancer cells.

Cancer experts recommend that everyone have a colonoscopy at age 50. If results are negative—if there are no polyps or cancer—

the procedure is typically repeated a decade later. If you had one or more polyps, the procedure is repeated sooner.

Problem: Even though a sedative and pain killer are prescribed for the 30-minute procedure, it's still uncomfortable. That's because the bowel is inflated with pumped-in air for better viewing of the bowel wall; you can feel pressure and pain, and develop cramps.

Because it's potentially painful, many people skip the test—even though they might be risking their lives.

Better: New studies show there are several natural ways to reduce discomfort and anxiety during a colonoscopy—and produce more accurate results.

The Peaceful Colonoscopy

• **Drink warm water.** Korean researchers studied 64 people about to undergo a colonoscopy, dividing them into three groups.

Right before the procedure, one group drank about 2 quarts of warm water. A second group drank the same amount of cold water.

A third group didn't drink any water.

Results: The doctors had an easier time inserting the tube into those who drank the warm water.

The people who drank the warm water also reported the least pain during the colonoscopy and two hours later.

And the doctors found they also were able to perform a more complete test in those who drank the warm water, seeing 6 to 8% more of the colon wall than in those who drank cold or no water.

The results were in the *American Journal of Gastroenterology.*

• **Listen to relaxing music.** Gastroenterologists at the University of Missouri analyzed the results of eight studies that investigated using music to ease the pain and anxiety of a colonoscopy.

"Music improves patients' overall experience with colonoscopy," concluded the doctors in the journal *Digestive Diseases and Sciences.*

"Listening to relaxing music during colonoscopy helps reduce anxiety, pain, and dissatisfaction during the procedure—it's a simple, inexpensive, natural way to improve your comfort, and I highly recommend it," says Murat Gulsen, MD, a gastroenterologist who conducted a study on music and colonoscopy.

Resource: A wide variety of music designed for relaxation and stress relief is available at *www.soundings.com.*

• **Take probiotics for two weeks.** Korean doctors studied 104 people scheduled for a colonoscopy, giving half a daily supplement of gut-friendly bacteria (probiotics) and half a placebo in the two weeks before the procedure.

Results: Probiotics improved the doctor's ability to see the colon wall during the test, and decreased the number of unpleasant GI symptoms after the colonoscopy, reported the researchers in *Digestive Diseases and Sciences.*

• **Schedule your procedure for the morning.** Gastroenterologists at the Cleveland Clinic analyzed results from nearly 4,000 colonoscopies and found that doctors detected more polyps in the morning, and that detection rates declined with each hour of the passing day and were at their lowest late in the afternoon. All in all, polyp detection rates were 20% higher before noon than after 12:00 p.m.

Reason: "Physician fatigue, which usually increases as the day progresses," concluded the doctors in the *American Journal of Gastroenterology.*

• **Wait a decade before your second test.** Researchers at the University of Texas Medical Branch at Galveston studied 24,000 Medicare patients who had had negative colonoscopies. They found that 46% had a second colonoscopy within 7 years. "A large proportion of Medicare patients who undergo screening colonoscopy do so more frequently than recommended," concluded the researchers in the *Annals of Internal Medicine.*

Murat Gulsen, MD, the School of Medicine, Gaziantep University, Turkey.

Chapter 9

EYES, EARS & TEETH

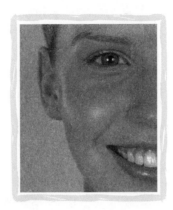

The Cataract Prevention Diet

Tucked behind the cornea and pupil of the eye is the light-focusing lens, which is made of protein and water. As years pass, its precise array of protein fibers are oxidized, like rusting metal. The fibers collapse into light-blocking clumps—and vision clouds, blurs and dims.

You have a cataract. And you're not alone.

More than 50% of Americans over 65 and 70% over 75 have cataracts—and every year 400,000 of them opt for cataract surgery. The cornea is cut, the lens is sucked out and an artificial lens is inserted.

Cataract surgery has a 90% success rate in improving eyesight. But surgery means scalpels, anesthesia, discomfort, risk and bills. You want to stay cataract-free for as long as possible.

Now: A recent study shows that one of the best ways to do that is by eating a healthy diet.

More Veggies, Less Cataracts

Researchers at the University of Wisconsin, Madison, studied nearly 2,000 women aged 55 to 86 who had filled out a questionnaire about their daily diet. Seven years later, the researchers found out who had developed a cataract and who hadn't.

Results: Women eating a healthy diet had a 37% lower risk of developing cataracts compared with women who ate an unhealthy diet.

The healthy diet was rich in vegetables, fruits, beans, whole grains, lean meat, fish and eggs, and lower than average in fat, saturated fat, cholesterol and salt.

"Healthy diets are associated with lower risk for cataract," concluded the authors in the *Archives of Ophthalmology.* "Eating foods rich in a variety of vitamins and minerals may contribute to postponing the occurrence of cataract," they added.

Eye-Protecting Produce

"Any time you increase your intake of nutrient-rich vegetables and fruits, you're going to

177

decrease your risk of developing a cataract," says Marc Grossman, OD, LAc, an optometrist and acupuncturist at Integral Health Associates in New Paltz, New York, and coauthor of *Natural Eye Care* (Keats).

That's because, he says, vegetables and fruits deliver high levels of nutrients the body uses to produce *glutathione*, an eye-protecting super-antioxidant; *lutein* and *zeaxanthin*, pigment-containing compounds that protect the eye from lens-damaging ultraviolet light; and vitamin C, which nourishes the lens.

● **Glutathione.** "Glutathione is the most important antioxidant in the body and is essential for maintaining good vision," says Dr. Grossman. "The oxidized protein in cataracts is always low in glutathione."

Best choices: The top glutathione-building foods are garlic, onions and cruciferous vegetables such as broccoli, cauliflower, kale, collard greens, cabbage and Brussels sprouts.

● **Lutein and zeaxanthin.** These two pigment-containing nutrients are like "nature's sunglasses," protecting the eyes from cataracts, says Dr. Grossman.

Best choices: Eggs, kale, spinach, turnip greens, collard greens, romaine lettuce, broccoli, zucchini, corn, peas and Brussels sprouts.

● **Vitamin C.** "The concentration of vitamin C in healthy eyes is higher than almost anywhere in the body, and the antioxidant plays an important role in preventing cataracts," says Dr. Grossman.

Best choices: Citrus fruits, papaya, strawberries, bell peppers, broccoli, cauliflower, kale, mustard greens, Brussels sprouts and parsley.

● **Juice.** Dr. Grossman encourages his patients to drink at least one pint a day of an antioxidant-rich vegetable and fruit juice. "Juicing is a highly effective and efficient way for the body to absorb essential nutrients into the blood and cells," says Dr. Grossman. "It can take as little as a few minutes for the body to start utilizing nutrients from freshly made juice."

Try this: A mixture consisting of 75% of any combination of kale, spinach, carrot, celery, endive, and parsley, and 25% of any combination of apple and blueberry.

Other Ways to Prevent Cataracts

These other dietary and lifestyle recommendations can also help prevent cataracts, says Dr. Grossman:

● **Take a lens-nourishing supplement.** Dr. Grossman recommends the supplement Advanced Vision Support or Vit-Eyes Complete, both of which deliver cataract-preventing dosages of lutein, zeaxanthin and vitamin C, along with other cataract-preventing agents such as the antioxidant alpha-lipoic acid and the herb bilberry. They are both available at his Web site, *www.naturaleyecare.com.*

● **Cut back or eliminate sugar.** "High levels of sugar in the blood contribute to cataract formation," says Dr. Grossman. "People with diabetes, for example, have a three to four times higher risk of developing cataracts. That's because blood sugar interferes with the ability of the lens to pump out excess sugar from the eye and maintain its clarity."

● **Drink lots of water.** "A lot of cataracts occur because people become dehydrated," he says. "I recommend eight to ten 8-ounce glasses a day, which maintains the flow of nutrients to the lens and the release of waste and toxins from the tissues."

● **Limit alcohol consumption to one glass of red wine at night.** "Alcohol interferes with liver functions, which reduce glutathione levels," he says.

● **Exercise regularly.** In one study, the fittest men had a 50% lower risk of cataract. "It's quite likely that moderate exercise decreases the risk of developing cataract," says Paul Williams, PhD, the study leader.

● **Wear a hat and UV-blocking sunglasses outdoors.** "Ultraviolet light from the sun can cause cumulative damage to the lens," says Dr. Grossman. "Wraparound sunglasses with an amber or brown tint are best at blocking out UV rays."

•**Stop smoking.** "Cigarette smoking causes about 20% of all cataracts," says Dr. Grossman.

•**Avoid microwaves.** "Radiation leakage from microwaves are a direct cause of cataracts," he says. "Avoid peeking into the oven door window while you cook."

Marc Grossman, OD, LAc, optometrist and acupuncturist, Integral Health Associates, New Paltz, New York, and coauthor of *Natural Eye Care* (Keats). *www.drgrossman2020.com, www.naturaleyecare.com.*

Paul Williams, PhD, principal investigator, Life Science Division, Lawrence Berkeley Lab, US Department of Energy.

Revolutionary Nutrient Therapy for Macular Degeneration

Imagine sitting back in a comfortable chair in your holistic physician's office and providing your body with such a boost of nutrients that you are able to see more clearly after the one-and-a-half-hour treatment session than you could before it. That's what happened to Lou, an 83-year-old patient who had age-related macular degeneration (AMD), a disease in which the macula (part of the retina) degenerates, causing vision loss. Lou had "wet" AMD, the more severe form of the disease in which abnormal blood vessels form, leaking fluid into the macula.

The treatment that helped Lou was intravenous (IV) nutrient therapy, a technique in which vitamins and other nutrients are delivered directly into the bloodstream in an IV solution, flooding the body's cells with higher levels of the nutrients than they would get from ingesting them. IV nutrient therapy can help both wet and "dry" AMD, a less severe form of the disease.

IV nutrient therapy is also used to treat patients with chronic fatigue and heavy metal poisoning. It has been found to help viral hepatitis C…heart arrhythmias caused by nutritional imbalances…and neurological diseases, such as Parkinson's. AMD responds particularly well to IV nutrient therapy.

One of the leading practitioners of IV nutrient therapy in the country is Paul Anderson, ND, a professor of naturopathic medicine at Bastyr University near Seattle. He created the IV nutrient therapy for AMD. *Here Dr. Anderson reveals more about this treatment…*

How It Works

The eyes' tissues are extremely responsive to nutrients—which is why holistic physicians tell their patients to take antioxidants such as lutein, which has been found to slow the progression of AMD. IV nutrient therapy delivers up to 100 times the concentration of antioxidants taken orally. While there have been no studies yet on IV nutrient therapy for AMD, patients who have had the treatment report extremely positive results that include restoration of most—but not all—of the vision that had been lost. The therapy can be effective at stopping the disease from progressing further.

First, a patient is cleared for IV nutrient therapy based on a medical exam and blood tests to ensure that the liver and kidneys can handle the treatment. (Patients also are monitored throughout the treatment.) The infusion for AMD includes vitamin C (for its antioxidant properties) and selenium and zinc (minerals that help the body absorb antioxidants), chromium (an element that strengthens blood vessels) and l-carnitine (for its neuroprotective benefits). Dr. Anderson gives patients at least six infusions, usually two a week for the first three weeks. If the patient is age 75 or older or has advanced AMD, he may recommend as many as 12 infusions. Each infusion takes about one-and-a-half to two hours and typically costs $150 to $200. Check to see if your insurance plan covers this type of treatment.

After a patient's nutrient levels have gotten this boost, the patient can maintain any improvement in vision by following a therapeutic regimen of oral supplements combined with a diet high in *flavonoids*, plant nutrients that have antioxidant properties. This regimen also can be used to help prevent AMD.

Flavonoids are important to eye health because they can neutralize inflammation in the eye. Foods high in flavonoids include beans (red kidney beans, pinto beans), dark-colored fruits (blueberries, cranberries, blackberries) and vegetables (cabbage, onions, parsley, tomatoes). Make these foods a regular part of your diet. *Recommended maintenance supplements include...*

•**A multivitamin** to ensure that patients get many vitamins and minerals that are in the IV treatment.

•**Fish oil** that contains the omega-3 fatty acids DHA and EPA. These help to maintain the healthy structure and function of ocular tissue and keep eye cell membranes fluid and flexible.

Dose: At least 1,000 milligrams (mg) to 2,000 mg daily. Some patients need even more.

•**Eye-health supplement.** These supplements contain nutrients that support eye health.

Brand to try: Eye-Vite (made by KAL and available at health-food stores and online), which contains zinc, beta-carotene, vitamin E and bilberry fruit extract (a rich antioxidant) and other nutrients.

•**Lutein and zeaxanthin,** two carotenoids that benefit macular tissue. The best way to ensure that you get the appropriate amounts of carotenoids is to take them in supplement form.

Dose: 15 mg daily of lutein and 3 mg daily of zeaxanthin with a meal.

•**Taurine and l-carnitine.** These amino acids are beneficial to eye health because they help nerve tissue in the brain conduct impulses needed for vision.

Dose: 500 mg daily of taurine and 1,500 mg daily of l-carnitine.

•**A high-density bioflavonoid supplement.** To ensure that you get enough flavonoids, it is recommended that you take a supplement such as Cruciferous Complete (made by Standard Process, 800-558-8740, *www.standardprocess.com*), which contains phytochemicals from plants in the Brassica family (vegetables such as kale and Brussels sprouts). These vegetables protect against free radicals (disease-causing molecules), help eye function and stimulate the body's cleansing systems. Follow label instructions.

When patients are properly screened for IV nutrient therapy by a physician trained in this treatment, IV therapy is safe. To locate a physician who administers IV nutrient therapy, contact International IV Nutritional Therapy for Physicians (503-805-3438, *www.ivnutritionaltherapy.com*). This organization helps people find IV nutrient therapists in their areas.

Mark A. Stengler, NMD, naturopathic medical doctor in private practice, Encinitas, California, and author of the *Bottom Line/Natural Healing* newsletter. *www.drstengler.com*.

Herbal Help for Dry Eyes

The most common reasons Americans visit eye doctors aren't cataracts, glaucoma or nearsightedness.

It's dry eyes.

"Three out of ten Americans are afflicted with dry eye, a disorder of the tear film, the essential coating that protects the surface of the eyes, washes away debris and irritants and creates a crystal-clear window through which we see," says Robert Latkany, MD, founder and director of the Dry Eye Clinic at the New York Eye & Ear Infirmary and author of *The Dry Eye Remedy* (Hatherleigh).

There are many possible causes of dry eyes, says Dr. Latkany, including wearing contact lenses, working at the computer for long hours, allergies, the skin condition rosacea, menopause, eye surgery (such as laser surgery for vision improvement) and the autoimmune disease Sjögren's Syndrome.

And there are many treatments that can help relieve symptoms such as burning, itching and redness, including drinking more water, taking frequent breaks from the computer, eye drops and artificial tears.

Exciting development: A new study shows that taking an herbal supplement of sea buckthorn oil can help relieve dry eye.

See Better with Sea Buckthorn

"Usually, dry eyes are treated with eye drops and artificial tears, but these treatments only temporarily improve symptoms and don't address the real cause of the disease," says Riikka Järvinen, PhD, of the Department of Biochemistry and Food Chemistry at the University of Turku in Finland and a study researcher.

"Berries from the sea buckthorn shrub have been used in Asian traditional medicine for centuries, and there is evidence that sea buckthorn seed and oil can improve dry eye and dry mouth in people with Sjögren's Syndrome," says Dr. Järvinen. "There is also evidence that oils containing the right proportion of omega-3 and omega-6 fatty acids can improve dry eye, as can antioxidants—and sea buckthorn oil provides all these factors."

The study: Dr. Järvinen and her colleagues studied 86 people with dry eyes, dividing them into two groups.

For three months during the fall and winter (a time when dry eye is often at its worst because of low humidity in heated houses), one group took sea buckthorn oil and the other took a placebo.

The researchers found that the herbal supplement protected the quality of the tear film and reduced burning and redness.

They also found 20% fewer symptoms of dry eye in the contact lens wearers who took sea buckthorn oil. They could wear their lenses longer without discomfort and used eye drops less.

Why it works: Sea buckthorn oil may work by decreasing eye-irritating inflammation and oxidation, says Dr. Järvinen.

Suggested intake: "Supplementation with 2 grams a day of sea buckthorn oil may help with the symptoms of dry eyes," she says. "My dry eye symptoms have been relieved by using the supplement."

Sea buckthorn supplements are widely available online and in stores where nutritional supplements are sold.

Other benefits: Scientific research shows the supplement may also help…

- **Balance blood sugar**

- **Reduce platelet aggregation,** a blood-thickening risk factor for heart attack and stroke

- **Speed skin healing after burns** (used topically)

- **Reduce eczema symptoms,** such as redness and itchiness.

Robert Latkany, MD, founder and director of the Dry Eye Clinic at the New York Eye & Ear Infirmary and author of *The Dry Eye Remedy: The Complete Guide to Restoring the Health and Beauty of Your Eyes* (Hatherleigh).

Riikka Järvinen, PhD, the Department of Biochemistry and Food Chemistry at the University of Turku, Finland.

Eye Fatigue—Is It Your Computer or Something More Serious?

By the end of each day, vision tends to get a little fuzzy, and sometimes eyes actually ache. This could be due to many hours spent staring at the computer screen or other close-up work.

Recent research calls this eye strain *computer vision syndrome* (CVS), which produces such symptoms as tired eyes, headaches, an uncomfortable burning sensation and blurry vision, after as few as four hours a day in front of the screen. According to Kent M. Daum, OD, MS, PhD, a professor of optometry and vice president and dean for academic affairs at Illinois College of Optometry, CVS is a real condition, but he stresses the importance of being sure the cause is fatigue, not something else. Other possible causes include problems with the body's system for moving the eyes and changing or coordinating focus…inappropriate prescription eyewear…uncorrected astigmatism…or, says Dr. Daum, "it might mean that the patient is asking the eyes to do something that they shouldn't—like the classic example of a law student who spends 15 hours a day studying." There are many things that can cause eye fatigue, so it is very important to get your eyes checked and have a trained clinician tell you what the real problem is.

One Glaringly Obvious Cause

After you've confirmed that CVS is the likely culprit, the first corrective step you can take is to evaluate the lighting in the area where you do your computer work. "You should not see any glare off your computer screen," Dr. Daum says. Being able to see any reflection—of a window, a desk lamp or overhead lighting—means your eyes have to work harder to bring the resulting blurred image into focus, which can lead to eye strain.

Try this: To make sure your computer screen is free of glare, hold a folder or magazine above and then on each side of your monitor so that it sticks out four to five inches. The screen should look exactly the same with or without the magazine. If the screen darkens or shows a shadow or a reflection, there is glare. Fixes can include moving the light source…moving and/or re-angling the monitor to block the light (you might have to move your work station to another part of the room to accomplish this)…closing your blinds…or turning off any lights that reflect on your screen. The American Optometric Association cautions against facing an unshaded window or having one at your back while working on a computer due to the impact of glare. Along the same lines, Dr. Daum advises against using a laptop computer outdoors, as the light against the screen will strain your vision.

Keep Your Distance

Dr. Daum says the best distance to sit from your computer screen typically falls somewhere between 20 and 28 inches but that a variety of factors, including height, age and vision issues, need to be considered in determining what's most comfortable for your eyes.

"People put their computers in all sorts of odd places, like on a counter or side table, where there's not enough room to get close enough or far enough away from the screen to be comfortable," he comments. Another helpful measure is to enlarge the text on your computer screen to a size that you don't have to squint to see. Eyes that have to work extra hard tire more easily.

Personal Training for Your Eyes

When it comes to soothing and restoring tired eyes or relieving strain from the workday, Dr. Daum informs that there are eye exercises that may help you feel better…

• **Look away.** Lift your eyes from the computer screen at least once an hour, but preferably more often, to give them a break. Try gazing into the distance for a few minutes to reduce your focusing effort—looking outdoors can be refreshing, too, if you have a window nearby.

• **Compresses.** If your eyes feel tired at the end of the day, a cold compress is wonderfully soothing. Soak a washcloth in cool water, wring it out a bit and then fold it and use it to cover your eyes while you lie down or rest your head against the back of a chair. Do this for a couple of minutes to refresh the eyes. Some people like to use tea bags that have been soaked (and allowed to cool to a comfortable temperature if you made tea!), then squeezed to eliminate excess liquid. Caffeine in the tea may help shrink puffiness, and antioxidants can soothe redness…cucumber or raw potato slices work well too.

If you have specific concerns, such as focusing or eye movement problems, it is important to get advice from your doctor concerning eye exercises that are tailored to your specific problem.

Kent M. Daum, OD, MS, PhD, professor of optometry and vice president and dean for academic affairs at the Illinois College of Optometry in Chicago. He is a Fellow of the American Academy of Optometry.

Extended-Wear Hearing Aid Can Make Life Easier

The Lyric hearing aid is professionally inserted deep into the ear canal. It is placed four millimeters from the eardrum and is worn continuously for three to four months, then removed and replaced with a new one. The Lyric eliminates common problems people have with hearing aids, such as losing them, battery insertion and poor hearing at night when hearing aids are removed, including not hearing the phone or an alarm while sleeping. Some people find that the Lyric provides better sound than conventional hearing aids. It is invisible and can be worn while showering or bathing, but it cannot be worn when swimming under water and must be removed for MRI testing or ear exams—and it must be reinserted only by a professional. It comes in a number of sizes but does not fit everyone comfortably. A subscription for two ears costs about $3,300 to $3,400 a year, which includes a year's worth of devices—new ones are provided at each follow-up visit, every three to four months. (Conventional hearing aids cost from $600 to more than $2,000.) For information, go to *www.lyrichearing.com*.

Lynn Sirow, PhD, audiologist and adjunct assistant professor, City University of New York, and director, Port Washington Hearing Center, Port Washington, New York.

Turn the Sound Down

Ringing. Buzzing. Roaring. That's what tinnitus sufferers hear when others hear silence. About half of those with tinnitus hear the sounds all the time—for others, the sounds are intermittent, without a predictable pattern.

Tinnitus can make it difficult to concentrate, sleep and hear what other people are saying. *But there are strategies that can help...*

Many Causes

The most common cause of tinnitus is exposure to loud noise. It also can occur as part of the normal aging process. In addition, tinnitus can be a symptom of other health conditions, including vascular problems such as high blood pressure...nervous system disorders (including multiple sclerosis)...middle-ear infections...and sometimes depression. Treating the health condition may lessen the severity of the tinnitus.

It's estimated that 10 to 15% of adults worldwide experience some degree of tinnitus. Men tend to have problems with tinnitus more often than women, especially as they get older. (They're more likely than women to be exposed to excessive noise.) There are no drugs that can cure tinnitus, and the approaches that do work are unpredictable. What's effective for one patient might not work for someone else, so you may need to try several of the following strategies.

Music Masking

Low-volume background music causes partial masking, in which the sounds of tinnitus become less noticeable. Music masking "distracts" the brain's neural circuits. Even when you're not consciously aware of the background music, it draws your attention away from the tinnitus sounds.

The music should be soft and something that you can easily ignore. Quiet instrumental music often is a good choice. Set the volume so that you can barely hear it. If the tinnitus sounds still are prominent, increase the volume just a little. Keep doing this until the sounds of tinnitus start to fade.

Hearing Aid

The majority of people with tinnitus have some degree of hearing loss and must strain to hear normal sounds. When they do this, the severity of tinnitus also can increase.

Using a hearing aid often helps. It allows you to hear normal sounds more clearly, which diverts attention from the tinnitus sounds. The amplification of sounds also may make the brain's sound-processing regions less likely to produce tinnitus sounds. In addition, hearing aids produce their own low-level sounds, which can mask tinnitus.

In patients with both hearing loss and tinnitus, about 50% notice an improvement in the tinnitus when they start using a hearing aid.

Counseling

Many patients with persistent severe tinnitus experience emotional problems, such as anxiety, depression and feelings of helplessness. They also may have trouble concentrating and sleeping. Between 70% and 80% of patients who work with a professional report a significant reduction in tinnitus-related stress. The best way to get treatment is to contact an audiologist or the American Tinnitus Association (*www.ata.org*). Some psychologists, otologists and psychiatrists also can be helpful. *A professional might recommend the following...*

● **Progressive muscle relaxation.** This is a relaxation technique in which patients are taught to first contract and then relax the muscles in the legs, abdomen, chest, arms and face. Each muscle is contracted for about 10 seconds and relaxed for 20 seconds. Patients who do this daily experience less emotional stress. This usually doesn't eliminate tinnitus, but it does lessen its effects.

● **Improving concentration skills.** Most patients with tinnitus report that the noise makes it difficult to focus on daily tasks, such as reading and listening to others. I recommend that they take frequent breaks and find ways to reward themselves when they have completed tasks. Taking notes or asking questions also can help a tinnitus patient stay actively engaged in a task.

Better Sleep

About half of the patients who attend tinnitus clinics report that they sleep poorly. Persistent insomnia invariably causes daytime fatigue, which may increase awareness of tinnitus sounds.

Thirty minutes before bedtime, relax with progressive muscle relaxation (described above) or other soothing activities, such as deep breathing or listening to music. You'll sleep better, and the tinnitus probably will be less intrusive.

Other sleep strategies...

● **Don't bathe immediately before bedtime.** It raises body temperature, which can amplify tinnitus sounds.

If you go to bed and don't fall asleep in 20 minutes, get up and do something else. Try again when you feel sleepy.

If you feel anxious at night, set aside 20 minutes earlier in the evening to write down your concerns. People who set aside a specific "worry time" tend to fall asleep more quickly when they go to bed.

● **Use sound enrichment.** Tinnitus patients usually sleep better when they have some kind of low-level sound enrichment in the bedroom. This could be produced by a "white noise" or "sound relaxation" machine, a radio set between stations or a fan or air purifier.

Change in Medications

Dozens of prescription and over-the-counter drugs are ototoxic—they can affect inner-ear hair cells and cause both tinnitus and hearing loss. Aspirin is one of the most common culprits. Others include antibiotics (such as *gentamicin* and *vancomycin*), drugs used in chemotherapy (such as *vincristine*) and diuretics used to lower blood pressure.

Most drugs cause tinnitus only when they're taken in high doses and for extended periods of time. Aspirin, for example, is unlikely to cause problems when patients follow the label directions or are on daily low-dose aspirin therapy.

If you start experiencing tinnitus after starting a new medication, talk to your doctor. In most cases, the tinnitus will go away when you stop taking the drug, lower the dose or switch to a different medication.

Ear Protection

Loud noise is not only the main cause of tinnitus. It also can increase the risk that existing tinnitus will get worse.

Use some form of ear protection, such as earmuffs or earplugs, when you are in any very noisy environment. This includes any time you are around noisy outdoor equipment, such as lawn mowers, leaf blowers and snowblowers, as well as household appliances, such as vacuum cleaners and blenders.

Richard S. Tyler, PhD, professor in the departments of otolaryngology–head & neck surgery and speech pathology and audiology at University of Iowa, Iowa City. He is editor of *The Consumer Handbook on Tinnitus* (Auricle Ink).

Popular Drugs Linked to Hearing Loss

Among 27,000 men who were tracked for 18 years, those age 60 and older who used *acetaminophen* (Tylenol) or nonsteroidal anti-inflammatory drugs (NSAIDs), such as *ibuprofen* (Advil) or *naproxen* (Aleve), two or more times weekly were 16% more likely to develop hearing loss than those who did not. Regular aspirin users had no increased risk.

Theory: Acetaminophen depletes glutathione, an antioxidant that protects the ears, and NSAIDs reduce blood flow to them.

Sharon Ellen Curhan, MD, clinical researcher, department of medicine, Harvard Medical School, Boston.

A New, Easier Way to Ease Dry Mouth

Thirty million Americans have dry mouth (xerostomia), including 30% of people 65 or older. It sounds like little more than a nuisance. But it can desiccate your life.

As salivary glands stop working properly (producing less than half the normal amount of saliva), symptoms can include trouble swallowing…trouble speaking…bad breath…indigestion (from a lack of *amylase*, an enzyme in saliva that triggers starch digestion)…chronically dry lips, with cracks in the corners that

are targets for yeast infections…and rampant tooth decay (as teeth-destroying bacteria are no longer flushed out of the mouth by *lysozyme*, another saliva enzyme).

"The decrease in the quality of life for someone with severe dry mouth can be devastating," says Ross Kerr, DDS, clinical associate professor at the New York University College of Dentistry.

There are many causes of dry mouth, including medications (the most common cause), menopause, diabetes, Parkinson's disease, depression, autoimmune diseases such as Sjögren's Syndrome, rheumatoid arthritis and cancer treatments such as radiation and chemotherapy.

Problem: "The mouth rinses, gels and sprays for easing dry mouth don't last very long, so the patient is dosing all the time," says Dr. Kerr.

Recent breakthrough: A new "mucoadhesive" patch for dry mouth sticks to the roof of the mouth for several hours, stimulating lubrication and providing long-term relief. And a recent study shows that it works.

Patching Up Dry Mouth

Researchers in the Department of Oral Medicine at Hebrew University treated 20 people with dry mouth with either the patches (OraMoist) or the leading over-the-counter treatment for dry mouth (Biotene mouthwash).

The patches stimulated five times more saliva production than the mouthwash. Twice as many people using the patches said they felt more moisture in their mouths and reductions in the sensations of dry mouth. And 70% of those using the patches said they would use them again, compared with 30% of those using the mouthwash.

"OraMoist was superior to Biotene in improving xerostomia symptoms and in overall patient satisfaction," reported the researchers in the journal *Quintessence International*.

"Oral disorders such as dry mouth require sustained residence of the active remedy in the mouth for effective treatment," says Abraham J. Domb, PhD, a study researcher.

"Mucoadhesive patches are made of safe ingredients that adhere to the oral mucosal tissue and slowly erode, while releasing active remedies for two to six hours, providing the desired residence time for effective therapy."

What kind: The mucoadhesive patch used in the study was OraMoist, from Quantum Health. *It includes several ingredients that help increase saliva flow…*

- **Tricaprin,** a patented fatty acid compound that makes the mouth feel lubricated

- **Xylitol,** a naturally occurring sugar substitute that reduces the amount of decay-causing bacteria and also stimulates saliva production

- **Citrus oil and natural lemon flavor,** both of which stimulate saliva production

- **Sea salt,** which helps maintain the normal pH of the saliva

- **Oral enzymes naturally found in saliva**

- **The patch itself,** which also stimulates saliva.

"People with dry mouth find the patches very easy to use and very effective," says Jonathan Bregman, DDS, a dental consultant and expert on the early detection of oral cancer. "I am also a believer in natural ways to heal, and this patch very much fits that model. I have recommended it to thousands of dentists and other health-care providers."

"Some of my patients now swear by the patches," adds Dr. Kerr. "They use them every single day."

OraMoist is widely available in drugstores and online. You can order it at *www.oramoist.com* or call 800-448-1448.

Ross Kerr, DDS, clinical associate professor in the Department of Oral and Maxillofacial Pathology, Radiology and Medicine at the New York University College of Dentistry in New York City.

Abraham J. Domb, PhD, Institute of Drug Research, School of Pharmacy, Faculty of Medicine, Hebrew University, Jerusalem.

Jonathan Bregman, DDS, a dental consultant and expert on the early detection of oral cancer. *www.bregmanconsulting.com.*

The Good Fat That Prevents Gum Disease

When you have gum disease—the infected, inflamed, swollen and bleeding gums that dentists call *gingivitis*—a lot of other diseases might tag along.

What you may not realize: The bacterial overload and inflammation of gum disease may spark disease-causing inflammation all over the body. *Gum disease has been linked to a higher risk of…*

- **Heart disease**
- **Stroke**
- **Diabetes**
- **Metabolic syndrome**
- **Alzheimer's disease**
- **Pancreatic cancer**
- **Osteoporosis**
- **Rheumatoid arthritis**
- **Kidney disease**
- **Pneumonia**
- **Pregnancy problems.**

"Given what we know about the relationship between gum diseases and other diseases, taking care of your oral health isn't just about a pretty smile," says Samuel Low, DDS, associate dean and professor of periodontology at the University of Florida College of Dentistry and president of the American Academy of Periodontology.

Unfortunately, a lot of us don't take care of our oral health. Forty-eight percent of American adults have gingivitis, including 85% over 65.

And a new study from researchers in the Division of Oral Health at the government's Centers for Disease Control and Prevention shows that 50% more Americans than previously estimated have periodontitis—advanced erosion of gum tissue and the surrounding bone.

"This study is a call to action for anyone who cares about his or her oral health—and overall health," says Dr. Low.

"You should take good care of your oral health with daily tooth brushing and flossing, and a cleaning every three to six months," adds Steven Roth, DMD, a dentist in New York City.

Recent development: Three new studies show that increasing your dietary intake of anti-inflammatory omega-3 fatty acids might improve your oral health.

Omega-3 Protects Your Gums

In a five-year study of more than 9,000 adults, those with the highest intake of the omega-3 fatty acid DHA (docosahexaenoic acid) had a 22% lower risk of periodontitis, reported researchers from Harvard Medical School in the *Journal of the American Dietetic Association.*

And in a five-year study of 55 people with periodontal disease, those with the highest dietary intake of DHA had 49% less gum and bone loss than those with the lowest intake, reported Japanese researchers in the journal *Nutrition.*

And researchers at the College of Dentistry at the University of Kentucky in Lexington discovered that omega-3 fatty acids not only reduce inflammation—they also directly fight five types of oral bacteria that cause gum disease and tooth decay.

"This study suggested that omega-3 fatty acids could have a positive therapeutic effect for improving oral health via their antibacterial activities, besides their anti-inflammatory activities," concluded the researchers in the journal *Molecular Oral Microbiology.*

"To date, the treatment of periodontitis has primarily involved mechanical cleaning and a local antibiotic application," says Asghar Naqvi, MD, who led the study from Harvard Medical School. "A dietary therapy might be a less expensive and safer method for the prevention and treatment of periodontitis."

What to do: The main dietary source of omega-3 fatty acids is fish oil, either from eating fatty fish such as salmon, tuna, sardines or mackerel, or taking a fish oil supplement.

"I am a big fish oil user," says Dr. Roth, "and I recommend that all my patients eat at least two servings of fatty fish a week and take a fish oil supplement."

"I recommend a diet rich in omega-3 fatty acids, including salmon, flaxseed and walnuts," adds Oloph Granath, DDS, a dentist in Santa Rosa, California.

Probiotics Work, Too

Dr. Granath also recommends sucking on a probiotic-containing lozenge before bedtime to increase the amount of good oral bacteria in your mouth and decrease the amount of disease-causing bad bacteria.

"Oral probiotics can really help people who have been battling gum disease for a long time," he says…and a recent study agrees.

The study: Researchers at the College of Dental Sciences in Karnataka, India, studied 30 people with gingivitis, dividing them into two groups. One group sucked on probiotic-containing lozenges twice a day. After three weeks, the probiotic group had big reductions in the oral bacteria that cause the disease—and significant reductions in the severity of periodontitis. The results were in the *Journal of Oral Microbiology.*

Recommended: Dr. Granath uses EvoraPlus probiotic mints, from Oragenics. You can order them at *www.oragenics.com.*

Samuel Low, DDS, associate dean and professor of periodontology at the University of Florida College of Dentistry and president of the American Academy of Periodontology.

Steven Roth, DMD, dentist in private practice, New York City. *www.smilesny.com.*

Asghar Naqvi, MD, clinical investigator at the Beth Deaconess Medical Center at Harvard Medical School.

Oloph Granath, DDS, dentist in private practice, Santa Rosa, California, and a member of the Holistic Dental Association. *www.stunningsmiles.com.*

Tooth Knocked Out? What to Do

Do you know what to do if you knock out a tooth? Michael Apa, DDS, a restorative and aesthetic dentist and instructor at NYU College of Dentistry, says you can save that missing molar...if you follow the right steps.

First Aid for Teeth

First of all, be aware that a knocked-out tooth is a dental emergency and that it's important to act fast. The longer a tooth is out of the socket, the less likely it can be "re-established." In that case, you'd need an implant.

Here's what to do if you get a tooth knocked out: If the tooth is loose but hasn't left the socket...

• **Gently try to move the loose tooth back into place beside the tooth next to it,** placing it very close so the edges touch one another smoothly. This doesn't usually hurt.

• **Do not put anything other than your clean fingers in your mouth...**it's important to avoid introducing additional nonresident bacteria.

• **See your dentist immediately.** If it's after office hours, call the emergency number...or, if that's not an option, go to the nearest urgent-care clinic or hospital emergency department.

If the tooth is out of the socket...

The goal is to try to put the tooth back into place in the gum, if it can be done. Time is of the essence—you'll have the best chance of saving the tooth if you get to the dentist (or an urgent-care clinic or the hospital emergency room) within 30 minutes. *Meanwhile...*

• **If the tooth fell onto the ground,** pick it up and clean it in your own saliva, saline solution, milk (any kind), baby formula or water (in this order of preference). Do not scrape off dirt or clean the tooth with alcohol.

• **Take care to handle the tooth by the crown (the biting end),** avoiding contact with the roots and nerve endings so you don't injure or contaminate them.

• **Try to insert the tooth back into place in your gum.** Push it in by gently biting or using your fingers to approximate its normal position. Hold a wet (warm or cool, not hot) tea bag in your mouth, biting down softly on it to keep the tooth in place.

• **If you can't put the tooth in place yourself (or if it makes you too nervous),** tuck the tooth in your mouth firmly against your cheek, your lower lip or under your tongue and keep it there until you can get to the dentist. Saliva protects it and keeps it from drying out. Though it may sound bizarre, another adult (if willing) can hold the tooth for you in this way as well.

• **Another option is to put the tooth in milk (whole is best, but low-fat and skim are fine, too).** If that is not available, use any sugarless, soft dairy product, such as yogurt or cottage cheese—the milk proteins will help keep the nerves and blood vessels alive. Do not put the tooth in a plastic bag or tissue even to transport it, as the nerves and blood vessels will dry out and die.

• **If you need to clean your mouth, rinse gently with water**—your dentist will clean it more thoroughly.

• **Do not eat or drink anything.**

Your dentist will clean your gum and stop the bleeding before trying to permanently re-implant your tooth. This is typically done by inserting and then splinting the tooth (with wires, a metal arch bar or plastic bond) for 10 to 14 days, which is how long it takes to fully reattach. Most people will not need stitches nor antibiotics, though a tetanus booster may be necessary if the tooth fell on the ground.

You'll need to continue to monitor the tooth for some time afterward, with regular follow-up visits. Sometimes root canal becomes necessary down the road, as the nerves may have suffered irreparable damage.

Resource: The American Dental Association has endorsed an FDA-approved emergency kit, Save-A-Tooth ($16), containing a storage case and special saline solution for one tooth. It is available from Amazon.com. One final note—this advice is meant for coherent adults, not children or adults who are groggy from injury and likely to swallow or inhale a loose tooth.

Michael Apa, DDS, partner in The Rosenthal-Apa Group, a private aesthetic dentistry practice in New York City, and instructor at New York University College of Dentistry.

Chapter 10

HEART DISEASE & STROKE

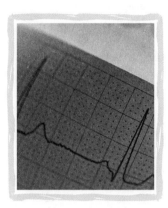

Find a Red Yeast Rice You Can Trust

Red yeast rice is a traditional food and medicine from China, made by fermenting rice with the yeast *Monascus purpureus*. It contains more than a dozen different *monacolins*, compounds that block the activity of an enzyme key to the production of cholesterol. (Cholesterol-lowering statin drugs also provide monacolins—typically a high dose of one synthetic monacolin.)

Millions of Americans take a red yeast rice supplement to lower bad LDL cholesterol and total cholesterol, spending a total of $20 million yearly on the products.

And many recent studies show that red yeast supplements can work—sometimes even better than a statin.

•**Red yeast rice outperforms a statin.** Doctors at the University of Pennsylvania Perelman School of Medicine studied 43 people with high LDL cholesterol who had stopped taking statin medication because of muscle pain and fatigue (myalgia), a side effect estimated to affect 20 to 30% people who take a statin. (The side effect is probably caused by monacolin blocking the production of coenzyme Q10, a compound that helps supply muscles with energy.)

Half the people in the study took 2,400 milligrams (mg) of red yeast rice, twice a day. The other half took 20 mg of *pravastatin* (Pravachol) twice a day, a statin that delivers a natural rather than synthetic form of monacolin.

Results: After 12 weeks, those taking red yeast rice had a 30% drop in "bad" LDL cholesterol, while those taking Pravachol had a 27% drop. (Two people taking statins and one person taking red yeast rice developed myalgia.)

Red yeast rice "achieved a comparable reduction of low-density lipoprotein cholesterol" as Pravachol, concluded the researchers in the *American Journal of Cardiology*.

•**Red yeast rice—an "acceptable" alternative to statins.** A team of doctors analyzed cholesterol-lowering results in 25 patients with high cholesterol who couldn't tolerate a statin (mainly because of myalgia) and switched on their own to red yeast rice.

The average drop was 21% in LDL cholesterol and 15% in total cholesterol after starting red yeast rice, and "many patients achieved their LDL cholesterol goal," wrote the doctors in the *American Journal of Cardiology*.

Red yeast rice "was an acceptable alternative in patients intolerant" of statins, concluded the doctors.

• **Lower LDL and total cholesterol.** Norwegian doctors studied 42 patients, giving half of them red yeast rice and the other half a placebo. After four months, those taking red yeast rice had a 23% drop in LDL and a 15.5% drop in total cholesterol.

Red yeast rice "demonstrated a significant cholesterol-lowering effect," concluded the doctors in the *Scandinavian Cardiovascular Journal*.

Is Your Red Yeast Reliable?

But there might be a problem with your supplement—it may not contain much red yeast rice! And it might be contaminated with a toxin linked to kidney cancer.

Recent study: A team of doctors from the University of Pennsylvania Health System and ConsumerLab.com tested the ingredients of 12 red yeast rice products.

They tested for monacolins in two ways: 1) amount of total monacolins and 2) quantity of monacolin K, the monacolin that is purified into *lovastatin*, the statin in the drugs Mevacor, Altocor and Altoprev, and the monacolin in red yeast rice considered to have the biggest effect in lowering cholesterol.

They also tested for a contaminant that has shown up in some red yeast rice products—citrinin, a toxin from fungus that is linked to kidney cancer.

• **Total monacolins.** There was a huge difference (36-fold) in the amount of total monacolins among the products—from a minuscule 0.31 mg to a whopping 11.15 mg per capsule.

• **Monacolin K (lovastatin).** There was also a big difference in levels of monacolin K from product to product, ranging from 0.10 mg per capsule to 10.09 mg per capsule. (The usual pharmaceutical dose of lovastatin is 10 to 80 mg a day.)

Key fact not widely reported: Red yeast rice manufacturers can't list the level of monacolin K—because to do so would violate FDA guidelines, making the over-the-counter product into an illegal drug, explains Tod Cooperman, MD, president of ConsumerLab.com and a study author.

In other words, there's no standardization among the products for total monacolins or monacolin K—so how do you know the product that you're taking is effective? You probably don't.

• **Citrinin.** Four of the products had elevated levels of citrinin. Ironically, the product that had the most citrinin also had the least monacolin K and other monacolins. "The people taking this product are getting a supplement that provides absolutely no benefit and that is toxic to the kidneys," says Doug Hansen, MD, an assistant professor of medicine at the University of Colorado and medical director of Altitude Family Medicine in Denver.

In other words, there was no guarantee of purity in the products—so how do you know the product you're taking is safe? You probably don't.

Good news: Fortunately, say experts, you can find red yeast rice supplements that do contain the amount of monacolin K and total monacolins that can lower cholesterol, and that don't contain citrinin.

Real Red Yeast Rice

Here are several red yeast rice products shown to contain reliable levels of monacolins and no citrinin, say experts.

• **Red Yeast Rice from Traditional Supplements.** This product contains a red yeast rice from Sylvan Bioproducts, which is grown and processed in the United States and is citrinin-free, says Dr. Hansen.

The Sylvan formulation of red yeast rice was the one used by doctors from the University of Pennsylvania in several studies in which red yeast rice (along with fish oil and lifestyle counseling) successfully lowered LDL cholesterol.

Red Yeast Rice from Traditional Supplements is available at GNC and online.

For optimal results: "If you're seeking an alternative to statins, and a modest reduction in LDL, red yeast rice works really well," says Dr. Hansen. "You can expect a reduction of 20 to 25%. If you add fish oil and lifestyle modification, such as a Mediterranean diet and regular exercise, you can expect a 35 to 40% reduction."

Recommended intake: 1,200 to 2,400 mg daily, taken before bedtime. "Monacolin has a short duration of action, and works best when the body is producing the most cholesterol, which is during sleep," says Dr. Hansen.

Also vital: He recommends you only take red yeast rice with the approval and supervision of a physician. "There is the same potential for muscle and liver damage with red yeast rice as there is with statins, plus the potential for a subtherapeutic response, where the supplement is not working to lower LDL and total cholesterol," he says.

He also recommends taking 100 mg of co-enzyme Q10 with the supplement, to prevent myalgia and other side effects.

Trap: "A lot of people don't understand that red yeast rice is a statin—and they take a statin prescribed by their doctor and they take red yeast rice," says Dr. Hansen. "That creates a huge risk for side effects."

●**Organic Red Yeast Rice, from Naturals.** This product also contains the citrinin-free Sylvan formulation. It is available at *www.naturals-supplements.com*, or call 866-352-7520.

●**Red Yeast Rice, from NOW Foods.** "This is a high-quality product that is contamination-free," says Dr. Hansen. It is widely available in retail stores and online. *www.nowfoods.com*, 888-669-3663.

●**Choleast, from Thorne Research.** "This product contains red yeast rice and COQ10,

which helps protect against myalgia," says Joshua Levitt, ND, a naturopathic physician in private practice in Hamden, Connecticut. The testing by ConsumerLab.com verified the product is free of citrinin. *www.thorne.com*, 800-228-1966.

●**BioCor Red Yeast Rice, from Real Natural Products.** This product is used by cardiologist M. Hafeez Chaudhry, at the Heart Center in Takoma Park, Maryland.

"We prescribe and encourage patients to use this brand of red yeast rice," he says. "It contains a consistent amount of monacolin K and no citrinin."

The product is widely available online at retail Web sites, including *www.realnatural remedies.com*, 888-825-5612.

Also helpful: You can find the results of the ConsumerLab.com testing of red yeast rice supplements—including the four products contaminated with citrinin—at *www.consumerlab.com*. Access to reports at the site requires a subscription.

Tod Cooperman, MD, president of ConsumerLab.com, a company that identifies the best-quality health and nutritional products through independent testing. *www.consumerlab.com*.

Doug Hansen, MD, assistant professor of medicine at the University of Colorado and medical director of Altitude Family Medicine, Denver, Colorado. *www.altitudemedicine.com*.

Joshua Levitt, ND, naturopathic physician in private practice, Hamden, Connecticut.

M. Hafeez Chaudhry, MD, cardiologist at the Heart Center, Takoma Park, Maryland.

Are Statin Drugs Destroying Your Muscles?

Recent research has uncovered disturbing information that muscle damage is much more common among statin users than was previously known. If you take a statin, such as *simvastatin* (Zocor) or *atorvastatin* (Lipitor), you risk the breakdown of the muscles in your arms and legs and suffering *myalgia* (muscle aches and pain) or *myopathy* (a disease in which muscle fibers cease to function).

It is estimated that myalgia develops in 10% of statin users. (*Rhabdomyolysis*, a condition in which muscles actually dissolve, is another potential consequence of statins, although this side effect is not as common as myalgia and myopathy.)

Researchers at University of Bern, Switzerland, and Tufts-New England Medical Center, Boston, reported in *Canadian Medical Association Journal* that 57% of study participants suffered statin-induced muscle damage. Some even had muscle damage after they had stopped taking the drugs. Remember, too, that the heart is your body's most active muscle. It's no surprise that there is a strong relationship between the use of statins and the development of cardiomyopathy, a life-threatening disease of the heart muscle.

Nutrients That Protect Your Muscles

Several dietary supplement regimens can help protect muscles.

If you take a statin, then take the first two nutrients for as long as you are on the statin…

• **Coenzyme Q10 (CoQ10).** While reducing the body's production of cholesterol, statins also interfere with the body's manufacture of CoQ10, a vitamin-like nutrient. CoQ10 supplements can significantly reduce statin-induced muscle myopathy. Take 100 milligrams (mg) to 200 mg of CoQ10 daily.

• **Vitamin D.** Vitamin D is needed for the normal synthesis of muscle tissue. Statins disrupt the biochemical process that makes vitamin D in your body, and it's likely that statins will significantly increase the incidence of sarcopenia and fractures. Take at least 2,000 international units (IU) of vitamin D daily. Have your vitamin D level checked by a physician and take a higher dose if necessary.

If you have stopped taking a statin because of muscle pain, try either of the following (in addition to the two nutrients above)…

• If the muscle pain is bearable, try one or two of the supplements below for one month and then evaluate how you feel. If you still feel pain, try different supplements from the group below.

• For severe pain, take a more aggressive approach and use all the supplements below until your muscle pain subsides.

• **Magnesium.** Your body uses this essential mineral to help break down food and make *adenosine triphosphate* (ATP), the chemical form of energy in the body. Take 300 mg to 400 mg daily of magnesium citrate, aspartate or amino acid chelate.

• **Amino acids.** You need these protein building blocks to make muscle.

Best: Take an amino acid supplement that contains eight to 10 amino acids.

Most important amino acids to supplement: The three branched-chain amino acids (BCAA), which are L-leucine, L-isoleucine and L-valine. Studies have shown that these supplements increase muscle synthesis in seniors. They are made by many companies. Take 5 grams (g) to 10 g daily of a multi–amino acid blend or 3 g daily of BCAAs.

• **Methylsulfonylmethane (MSM).** MSM supplements are rich in the sulfur and chemical methyl groups, both important building blocks of tissue and biochemicals. MSM supplements are a safe, natural anti-inflammatory that can help muscles recover from statin-related damage. Take 3,000 mg to 4,000 mg daily.

• **Turmeric extract.** Rich in curcumin, turmeric is an anti-inflammatory that aids muscle healing. Curcumin blocks dozens of different inflammatory processes in the body.

Brand to try: Terry Naturally's CuraMed (866-598-5487, *www.europharmausa.com*). Take 750 mg one to two times daily.

If you have muscle pain and continue to take a statin…

Anyone taking a statin who experiences muscle pain should stop taking the statin (under a doctor's supervision). If you do continue to take the statin, you can take all of the remedies described above indefinitely.

Mark A. Stengler, NMD, naturopathic medical doctor in private practice, Encinitas, California, and author of the *Bottom Line/Natural Healing* newsletter. *www.drstengler.com*.

Heart Supplements That Can Save Your Life

One of the most common reasons that people take nutritional supplements is to improve their heart health.

Problem: Very few cardiologists are aware of the ways in which heart supplements work synergistically—that is, by taking carefully selected supplements in combinations, you will heighten the effectiveness of each one. Over the past 22 years, internist and cardiologist Dennis Goodman, MD, has treated thousands of heart patients with this approach.

What you need to know to make the most of your nondrug regimen for better heart health...*

The Essential Three

Dr. Goodman recommends three daily supplements to anyone who is concerned about heart health...

• **Fish oil capsules** primarily lower harmful blood fats known as triglycerides but also have a mild blood pressure–lowering effect.

Typical dose: 1 gram (g) total of the omega-3 fatty acids *eicosapentaenoic acid* (EPA) and *docosahexaenoic acid* (DHA) for blood pressure benefits. To reduce triglyceride levels, the typical daily dose is 2 g to 4 g total of EPA and DHA.

Caution: Fish oil can increase bleeding risk, so talk to your doctor if you take a blood thinner, such as *warfarin* (Coumadin).

• **CoQ10** helps enhance energy production in cells and inhibits blood clot formation.

Typical dose: 50 milligrams (mg) to 100 mg per day. CoQ10, which is commonly taken with the classic HDL-boosting treatment niacin (vitamin B-3), also helps minimize side effects, such as muscle weakness, in people taking cholesterol-lowering statin drugs.

• **Red yeast rice** is an extract of red yeast that is fermented on rice and is available in tablet, capsule, powder and liquid form. Long

*To find a doctor to oversee your heart-health supplement regimen, consult the American Board of Integrative Holistic Medicine, *www.holisticboard.org*.

used by the Chinese, it mimics the action of cholesterol-lowering statin drugs.

Typical dose: 600 mg twice daily.

Red yeast rice is often used in combination with plant sterols, naturally occurring chemical compounds found in small amounts in fruits, vegetables and nuts...and added to food products, including butter substitutes, such as Promise Activ and Benecol spreads.

Typical dose: About 400 mg daily of plant sterols.

Also important: Low levels of vitamin D (below 15 nanograms per deciliter [ng/mL]) have been linked to a 62% increase, on average, in heart attack risk.

Typical dose: 5,000 international units (IU) of vitamin D-3 per day for those who are deficient in the vitamin...at least 1,000 IU daily for all other adults.

Better Blood Pressure Control

The heart-friendly properties of fish oil are so well-documented that the American Heart Association endorses its use (by eating fatty fish at least twice weekly and/or taking fish oil capsules).

To enhance fish oil's blood pressure–lowering effect, ask your doctor about adding...

• **L-arginine.** This amino acid boosts the body's production of the chemical compound nitric oxide, which causes the blood vessels to dilate, thereby lowering blood pressure.

Typical dose: 150 mg daily.

L-arginine is also used to treat erectile dysfunction and claudication (impeded blood flow in the extremities) and has a mild and beneficial HDL-boosting effect.

Caution: L-arginine should not be taken by children or pregnant or nursing women, or by anyone with genital herpes—it can stimulate activity of the herpes virus. Possible side effects include indigestion, nausea and headache.

• **Lycopene.** This phytochemical is found in tomatoes—especially processed tomato sauce—watermelon, pink grapefruit, red bell peppers and papaya. Dr. Goodman usually recommends that patients try L-arginine first, then add lycopene, if necessary, for blood pressure reduction.

Research conducted at Ben-Gurion University in Israel has shown that lycopene lowers *systolic* (top number) blood pressure by up to 10 points and *diastolic* (bottom number) by up to four points.

A potent antioxidant, lycopene is also thought to have potential cancer-preventive effects, but this has not been proven.

Typical dose: 10 mg daily.

In rare cases, lycopene supplements can cause diarrhea and/or nausea. Because tomatoes and other acidic foods can aggravate ulcer pain, people with stomach ulcers should consult their doctors before consuming tomatoes and tomato-based products regularly.

Boost HDL Cholesterol

In addition to taking CoQ10 and niacin, ask your doctor about trying…

●**Policosanol.** This plant-wax derivative has been found to boost HDL levels by more than 7%. The research on policosanol is considered controversial by some, but Dr. Goodman has found it to be an effective HDL booster in his practice.

Typical dose: 10 mg daily.

There is also some evidence that policosanol may have LDL- and triglyceride-lowering benefits. There are no known side effects associated with policosanol.

Bonus: Used together, CoQ10, niacin and policosanol will allow you to raise your HDL levels while taking much lower doses of niacin (about 20 mg daily). A lower niacin dose reduces the risk for facial flushing, a common side effect in people who take the vitamin.

Reduce LDL Cholesterol

Red yeast rice extract and plant sterols (both described earlier) are well-known natural methods of lowering LDL cholesterol levels.

To lower your LDL cholesterol further, ask your doctor about adding policosanol (described earlier), along with…

●**Pantethine.** This is a more biologically active form of pantothenic acid (vitamin B-5).

Typical dose: 600 mg daily.

Numerous small studies have found that pantethine significantly lowers LDL cholesterol and triglycerides.

●**Grape seed extract.** This antioxidant-rich substance reduces the blood's tendency to clot and helps lower blood pressure by boosting levels of the chemical compound nitric oxide found in the body. Some research shows that grape seed extract also reduces LDL cholesterol.

Typical dose: 200 mg daily.

Best Nutrients For Heart Health

Food is our best source of nutrients. That's because food sources offer a variety of minerals, vitamins and antioxidants that work synergistically to boost the nutritional value of each. Dr. Goodman urges all of his patients to get ample amounts of the following heart-healthy nutrients from food…

●**Antioxidants,** which help prevent plaque formation on the walls of your arteries.

Good sources: Pomegranate, blueberries, and fruits and vegetables in general.

●**Magnesium,** which helps regulate blood pressure and stabilize heart rhythm.

Good sources: Dark green, leafy vegetables…soybeans…almonds…cashews…black-eyed peas…and peanut butter.

●**Potassium,** which helps regulate blood pressure and heart function.

Good sources: Apricots, cantaloupe, melons, kiwi, oranges (and orange juice), bananas, lima beans, tomatoes, prunes, avocados…as well as meat, fish and poultry.

Caution: If you have kidney disease, consult your doctor before consuming potassium-rich foods.

In addition, studies suggest that grape seed extract helps protect against Alzheimer's disease.

Caution: Because grape seed extract has a blood-thinning effect, it should not be taken by anyone who uses warfarin or other blood-thinning medications or supplements.

Dennis Goodman, MD, clinical associate professor of medicine at New York University School of Medicine in New York City and at the University of California in San Diego and director of integrative medicine at New York Medical Associates, a group private practice in New York City. He is board certified in internal medicine, cardiology, interventional cardiology, critical care, clinical lipidology and holistic (integrative) medicine. *www.dennisgoodmanmd.com.*

Should You Take "Mega-Doses" of Omega-3?

Hardly anybody seriously questions whether or not the omega-3 fatty acids found in fish oil—EPA (*eicosapentaenoic acid*) and DHA (*docosahexaenoic acid*)—can help the heart. *Decades of studies link a higher intake of omega-3s to…*

• **Less chronic inflammation,** which fuels heart disease

• **Lower triglycerides,** a heart-hurting blood fat

• **Lower levels of the small, dense LDL particles** that experts say are the true bad guys in "bad" LDL cholesterol

• **Higher levels of good HDL cholesterol**

• **Less platelet aggregation,** which helps stop blood from clumping into artery-clogging clots

• **Lower blood pressure**

• **A steadier heartbeat.**

But what's still very much debated is *how much* omega-3 you need to protect your heart.

The American Heart Association recommends people without heart disease eat two servings of fish a week, emphasizing fatty fish such as salmon. (Two servings of salmon supply 2 to 4 grams of omega-3s, or about 400 milligrams [mg] daily.) They also recommend that people with heart disease take 1 gram a day of EPA/DHA. But is that really enough?

Now: A new study points to the amount that might be optimal. And it's a lot more than you're probably getting.

20 Times Higher, A Whole Lot Healthier

Pointing out that most studies on omega-3 and health have looked at people with low intakes of the nutrient, a team of researchers from the Fred Hutchinson Cancer Research Center in Seattle studied 330 people (average age 45) among Yup'ik Eskimos in Alaska—many of whom consume 20 times more omega-3s than the average American.

Yup'ik men get an average of 3.7 grams EPA/DHA daily; the average American male gets 140 mg. Yup'ik women get an average of 2.4 grams; the average American woman gets 90 mg.

But one thing that wasn't different about the Yup'iks and the average American was weight—70% of the Yup'iks were overweight or obese, the same percentage as the rest of the US population.

But perhaps because of all that "extra" omega-3 in their diet, the overweight Yup'iks had uniquely healthy levels of several risk factors for heart disease—levels you wouldn't typically find in an overweight person. *Their high blood levels of EPA and/or DHA were linked to…*

• **Lower triglycerides**

• **Higher HDL cholesterol**

• **Lower LDL cholesterol**

• **Lower total cholesterol**

• **Lower C-reactive protein, a biomarker of inflammation.**

"Increasing EPA and DHA intakes to amounts well above those consumed by the general US population may have strong beneficial effects on chronic disease risk," concluded the researchers in the *American Journal of Clinical Nutrition.*

More Research

Other recent research links omega-3s to a healthier heart…

●**More stable plaque.** Many heart attacks and strokes happen when a chunk of plaque breaks off and plugs an artery. Plaques with higher levels of EPA are more stable, reported UK researchers in the journal *Atherosclerosis*.

●**Omega-3 and statins better than statins alone.** Adding omega-3 supplements to statin therapy tripled the reduction of triglycerides compared with taking just statins, reported Korean researchers in the *European Journal of Clinical Nutrition*.

●**More flexible arteries.** People who ate a meal supplemented with 4.7 grams of omega-3s had more flexible arteries after the meal than people who ate a meal without the supplement, reported UK researchers in the journal *Clinical Nutrition*.

Optimal Levels of Omega-3

Omega-3 is good for your heart. But should you try to get the 3 to 4 grams daily consumed by the Yup'iks? Maybe, says one doctor. Definitely, says another.

"Even though the American Heart Association recommends 1 gram of fish oil daily as a heart-protecting dose, going over that level doesn't seem to have any downside," says Doug Hansen, MD, an assistant professor of medicine at the University of Colorado and medical director of Altitude Family Medicine in Denver, Colorado.

Dr. Hansen points to a recent study showing that a dosage from 3 to 6 grams daily was the level that reduced the risk of sudden cardiac death—a type of lethal heart stoppage that strikes more than 250,000 Americans yearly. "Clearly, there is a risk that the 1 gram daily recommendation is underestimating," he says.

Recommended intake: For patients without heart disease, he recommends 1 to 1.5 grams a day and eating two to three servings of fatty fish a week.

For people with high triglycerides or heart failure, he often increases the dose to 3 to 4 grams.

Dr. Hansen favors several over-the-counter brands for a safe, pure fish oil, including fish oils from Carlson, Nordic Naturals and NOW Foods. For the "least expensive omega-3 on the market" that is also high quality, he recommends Kirkland Omega 3 One Per Day Fish Oil, the Costco house brand.

Trap: Many people who think they're getting 1 gram a day of omega-3s from a supplement probably aren't, he says. "Three out of four of my patients who take fish oil are misreading the label. They look at the total grams of fish oil, which is larger than the total dosage of EPA and DHA—and they end up not taking 1 gram a day of the omega-3s."

●**The 6-gram solution.** A dose of 6 grams daily is recommended by Dave Woynarowski, MD, a physician in private practice in Lancaster, Pennsylvania, and coauthor of *The Immortality Edge: Realize the Secrets of Your Telomeres for a Longer, Healthier Life* (Wiley).

"I think fish oil is the missing link to human health," he says. "I conducted a meta-analysis of more than 500 studies on fish oil for heart disease, rheumatoid arthritis and many other conditions—and found that 5.8 grams daily was the level that was most protective and curative. An intake of about 6 grams daily is also the level that creates a ratio of 4-to-1 omega-3s to omega-6 fatty acids in the bloodstream—and that's the ratio shown to be most effective in preventing heart disease.

"People might say this is an inordinately high level of omega-3 to be recommending. In response, I say that the conventional recommendations are inordinately low."

And like Dr. Hansen, he says safety is not an issue. "Unless a patient is in the midst of a stroke, there is no risk of increased bleeding with omega-3s, even when taking a blood-thinning medication. The idea that usage of high doses of fish oil would create spontaneous bleeding is nonsense."

Doug Hansen, MD, assistant professor of medicine at the University of Colorado and medical director of Altitude Family Medicine in Denver, Colorado. *www.altitudemedicine.com.*

Dave Woynarowski, MD, physician in private practice in Lancaster, Pennsylvania, and coauthor of *The Immortality Edge: Realize the Secrets of Your Telomeres for a Longer, Healthier Life* (Wiley). *www.drdavesbest.com.*

The Best Level of Vitamin D for Your Heart

The first thing to understand about vitamin D is that it's not a vitamin. "It's a pre-hormone produced in your skin by sun exposure, and it helps repair and maintain every organ and system in your body—including your arteries and your heart," says John Cannell, MD, president of the Vitamin D Council, a non profit educational group.

Vitamin D, he explains, regulates about 5% of the human genome—about 1,000 genes. And those genes (among their many functions)...help produce the powerful antioxidant *glutathione*, which protects your arteries from disease-causing oxidation... prevent calcium from being deposited in the wrong places, such as your arteries...maintain the youthful elasticity of your arteries... and help heart cells (*cardiomyocytes*) keep your heart beating strongly.

Studies have linked low blood levels of vitamin D to two- and three-fold higher risk of dying from heart disease, says Dr. Cannell—making a deficiency a risk factor on par with high blood pressure and high cholesterol.

Recent Breakthrough

Two of the newest studies on vitamin D confirm the link between vitamin D and heart health—and also show the optimal blood level of vitamin D for protecting the heart. (It's a lot higher than most experts recommend.)

"Vitamin D replacement therapy has long been associated with reducing the risk of fractures and diseases of the bone," says J. Brent Muhlestein, MD, director of cardiovascular research at the Intermountain Medical Center and Heart Institute, and leader of two new studies on vitamin D and heart disease.

"But our findings show that vitamin D could have far greater implications in the treatment and reduction of cardiovascular disease and other chronic conditions than we previously thought."

In the first of the two studies, Dr. Muhlestein and his colleagues examined the patient records of more than 41,000 people. They found 64% with a vitamin D deficiency—a blood level below 30 nanograms per milliliter (ng/mL). *And those who were deficient also had "highly significant increases in the prevalence of"*...

- **Coronary artery disease**
- **Heart attack**
- **Heart failure**
- **Stroke**
- **High blood pressure (a leading risk factor for heart attack and stroke)**
- **High cholesterol (another risk factor)**
- **Peripheral vascular disease (clogged arteries in the legs)**
- **Diabetes (which doubles the risk of heart attack and stroke).**

"We have confirmed a high prevalence of vitamin D deficiency in the general healthcare population, and an association between vitamin D levels and cardiovascular risk factors and diseases," concluded the researchers in the *American Journal of Cardiology*.

In a second study, Dr. Muhlestein and his colleagues supplemented the diets of people with low blood levels of vitamin D with the nutrient. *After one year, those who achieved blood levels of 43 ng/mL had*...

- **33% fewer heart attacks**
- **20% less heart failure**
- **30% fewer deaths.**

They also had less diabetes, kidney failure and lower blood pressure.

Their analysis showed that 43 ng/mL was the optimal level for protection—higher blood levels did not confer more benefit.

"It was very important to discover that so-called 'normal' levels are too low for heart health," says Heidi May, PhD, a cardiovascular clinical epidemiologist with the Intermountain Medical Center Heart Institute, and a study author. "Giving physicians a higher level to look for gives them one more tool in identifying patients at risk for heart disease—and offering them better treatment."

Dr. Muhlestein agrees—and says the results of these studies have changed the way he treats his patients.

"Randomized trials on vitamin D and heart disease—in which one group of study participants receives vitamin D and another group receives a placebo—are in process," he says. "But based on these findings, I feel there is enough information to start a new approach to treatment.

"Treatment options are simple," he continues. "Start with a blood test of the patient's vitamin D level. If low levels are detected, prescribe supplements."

Recommended intake: "Increasing vitamin D intake by 1,000 to 5,000 international units (IU) a day may be appropriate," he says. "Supplements are the best source of vitamin D, because they are relatively inexpensive and can be found at almost any supermarket or drugstore."

"Although everyone is different, I typically recommend supplementing the diet with 1,000 IU of vitamin D a day," says Doug Hansen, MD, an assistant professor of medicine at the University of Colorado and medical director of Altitude Family Medicine in Denver.

"If a vitamin D blood test shows levels are between 20 to 30 ng/mL, I recommend 2,000 IU daily. If they are less than 20 ng/mL, I recommend 4,000 IU.

"The Institute of Medicine, which sets the recommended daily allowances, recently said that up to 4,000 IU a day is safe, and I feel confident about the safety of these higher doses."

John Cannell, MD, president of the Vitamin D Council. *www.vitamindcouncil.com.*

J. Brent Muhlestein, MD, director of cardiovascular research at the Intermountain Medical Center Heart Institute, Murry, Utah.

Heidi May, PhD, cardiovascular clinical epidemiologist with the Intermountain Medical Center Heart Institute, Murry, Utah.

Doug Hansen, MD, assistant professor of medicine at the University of Colorado and medical director of Altitude Family Medicine in Denver, Colorado. *www.altitudemedicine.com.*

Does Calcium Hurt Your Heart?

A study published in the *British Medical Journal* is raising questions about the safety of one of the most popular supplements—calcium.

Controversial new finding: In a University of Auckland analysis of 11 studies that tracked nearly 12,000 older adults—half of whom received 1,000 milligrams (mg) in calcium supplements daily while the other half took a placebo—the group that took calcium was up to 30% more likely to have a heart attack than the placebo group.

The researchers theorize that calcium supplements may increase heart attack risk by promoting calcification in blood vessels, but they intend to investigate further.

Other experts point out that the researchers did not analyze what happens when calcium is taken with vitamin D (necessary for calcium absorption) and that the majority of existing studies have shown no link between calcium supplements and heart attack risk. As a result, they encourage those who take calcium to keep taking it. If you are concerned about using calcium supplements, discuss it with your doctor.

What we know now: Despite the questions about calcium supplements, there's widespread agreement that eating calcium-rich foods is a safe way for most people to boost their intake of this vital mineral.

The recommended daily intake from all sources is 1,200 mg for men and women age 50 and older…and 1,000 mg for adults under age 50.

Dairy products are among the most widely consumed sources of calcium, but there are plenty of little-known dietary sources that provide significant amounts of the mineral. Each of these tasty, calcium-rich foods will not only help protect your bones but also liven up your diet in unexpected ways. *Dawn Jackson Blatner, RD, LDN, lists her favorite calcium-rich foods…**

*Whenever possible, check food labels for exact calcium levels.

Vegetables and Fruit

Some people know that broccoli is a good source of calcium (one cup cooked offers 62 mg). *Even better sources...*

●**Collard greens.** One-half cup cooked has 178 mg of calcium.

●**Okra.** One-half cup cooked contains about 90 mg.

●**Kale.** One cup raw delivers about 90 mg.

Delicious simple snack: Kale chips.

To prepare: Wash one bunch of kale thoroughly. Remove stems, rip up the leaves into chip-sized pieces and place them on a baking sheet that has been spritzed with an olive oil–based cooking spray. Spray the kale, too, sprinkle with a little salt or cayenne (you can skip black pepper—kale is naturally peppery) and bake at 400°F for eight to 10 minutes. Makes about four cups of chips.

●**Bok choy.** One-half cup cooked contains 79 mg of calcium.

Smart idea: The next time you go to an Asian restaurant, ask for some bok choy to be added to your stir-fry (go easy on the soy sauce or ask for the low-sodium variety—excess sodium weakens bones).

Looking for a sweet afternoon snack? *Great calcium-rich options...*

●**Dried figs.** Five figs (about one-quarter cup) provide 68 mg.

●**Orange.** One medium orange has 52 mg.

●**Blackberries.** One cup has 42 mg of calcium.

Protein-Rich Calcium Sources

Many foods that we rely on as protein sources also provide good amounts of calcium. *Examples...*

●**Sardines and canned salmon** are excellent calcium sources thanks to their edible bones—three ounces contain 325 mg and 212 mg, respectively.

●**Tofu** (a soy-based food commonly used in Asian cooking) has a reputation for being tasteless, but its spongy texture actually soaks up any flavor you add, from pasta sauce to chocolate. Most people don't realize that tofu is a good source of protein and calcium—three ounces (the size of a deck of cards) provides 171 mg of calcium.

Some people have avoided tofu because of a possible link between soy and breast cancer. But a 2009 study of 5,042 female Chinese breast cancer survivors published in the *Journal of the American Medical Association* found that dietary soy was associated with decreased mortality and cancer recurrence.

For the most health benefits, choose whole soy foods, such as tofu and edamame (green soybeans—one-half cup shelled has 49 mg of calcium), instead of more processed versions that use only parts of the soybean (soy "isolates"), such as soy protein powders and soy burgers. If you're concerned, talk to your doctor before adding soy-based foods to your diet.

●**Beans are another rich source of calcium.**

Good choices: White beans—one-half cup has 81 mg...garbanzo beans—one-half cup has 40 mg. Toss a few handfuls into your soups, stews and pastas.

●**Nuts also can help boost your calcium intake.**

Good choices: Almonds—one-quarter cup offers 92 mg...and almond butter—two tablespoons provide a total of 86 mg.

●**Seeds, such as in tahini** (sesame seed paste), which often is used when making hummus or salad dressing. It boasts a surprising amount of calcium—two tablespoons have 128 mg.

Tasty calcium-rich dressing: Combine two tablespoons of tahini, the juice of one-half lemon, one medium garlic clove (minced or crushed), two teaspoons of grated, fresh ginger, one teaspoon of honey, four tablespoons of water and salt and pepper to taste in a bottle with a lid and shake vigorously for 30 seconds. Makes six tablespoons.

Surprising Calcium Sources

There also are a few totally unexpected calcium sources...

●**Corn tortillas.** Two six-inch tortillas have a total of 91 mg.

●**Blackstrap molasses.** Two tablespoons have a total of 82 mg.

Remember: Calcium is not the only key to keeping your bones strong. Your bones also need weight-bearing exercise...a diet low in sodium, caffeine and meat (all of which degrade bone)...and adequate vitamin D to promote calcium absorption. To keep your bones healthy, be sure to focus on all of these approaches.

Dawn Jackson Blatner, RD, LDN, registered and licensed dietitian in Chicago. Blatner is a national media spokesperson for the American Dietetic Association and the nutrition consultant for the Chicago Cubs. She is also the author of *The Flexitarian Diet* (McGraw-Hill) and teaches classes at Chicago's Chopping Block Cooking School.

Why Your Heart Adores Chocolate

Now there's a reason other than romance for putting chocolates in heart-shaped boxes—recent studies confirm that eating a little bit of the confection every day is one of the best gifts you can give your heart, your arteries and your entire cardiovascular system.

Here's a sampler of recent research...

High Blood Pressure

High blood pressure—a reading of 140/90 to 159/99—damages arteries, and is a major risk factor for heart attack and stroke. Chocolate can help keep high blood pressure under control.

●**Safer exercise for people with high blood pressure.** If you're overweight, your blood pressure can shoot up during exercise because your arteries don't widen as well as they should.

Cocoa flavanols—potent plant compounds found mainly in dark chocolate—improve the health of the *endothelium*, the arterial lining that generates the chemical nitric oxide, which signals arteries to expand.

Researchers from the University of South Australia studied 24 overweight people, with an average age of 55 and an average blood pressure of 134/87 (an unhealthy level just below high blood pressure, called prehypertension). They divided them into two groups. One group drank a daily high-flavanol cocoa beverage and the other drank a low-flavanol beverage. A week later the groups switched, with the group drinking the high-flavanol cocoa now drinking the low, and vice versa.

Two hours after downing the beverage, the participants exercised at moderate intensity for 10 minutes on a stationary bike, while their blood pressure was continuously monitored.

The researchers also measured *flow-mediated dilation* (FMD)—the amount of blood flowing in an artery, an indicator of endothelial health. (The more flow, the better.)

Results: The people who drank the high-flavanol cocoa had a 14% lower increase in blood pressure during exercise, and a 68% lower increase in the *diastolic* (lower) reading. (Higher diastolic pressure is, by itself, a risk factor for heart attack and stroke.)

The high-flavanol group also had a 44% greater FMD.

"The consumption of cocoa flavanols could allow for safer and more efficient exercise performance in a population" at risk for heart attack and stroke, "thus placing less stress on the cardiovascular system," wrote the researchers in the *British Journal of Nutrition*. The study, they continued, "adds to the growing evidence that high flavanol cocoa consumption may benefit individuals with cardiovascular risk factors."

●**Lowering high blood pressure.** Researchers at the University of Adelaide in Australia analyzed 15 studies on dark chocolate and high blood pressure—and found an average drop of 5 points systolic and 3 points diastolic in people with hypertension and prehypertension.

Benefit: That's the same drop in blood pressure you're likely to achieve with 30 minutes a day of physical activity, say the researchers—

and it can reduce the risk of a heart attack or stroke by 20%.

Reversing Heart Disease

Chocolate may help strengthen the weakened arteries of people with heart disease.

● **Repairing damaged arteries.** Researchers from the University of California-San Francisco studied 16 people (average age 64) under medical treatment for coronary artery disease. The study participants drank a high-flavanol cocoa beverage twice a day for 30 days, and then switched to a low-flavanol cocoa beverage for 30 days.

Their FMD was 47% better when they were drinking the high-flavanol cocoa.

They also had twice as many endothelial progenitor cells, a type of cell that helps repair and maintain the endothelium.

"This benefit is similar to that achieved by statins and with lifestyle changes such as exercise and smoking cessation," says Yerem Yeghiazarians, MD, the leader of the study, which appeared in the *Journal of the American College of Cardiology*.

The participants also had a drop in high blood pressure.

"It's not often that we're able to identify a natural food compound that can demonstrate a benefit on top of traditional medical treatment," says Carl Keen, PhD, professor of nutrition and internal medicine at the University of California-Davis, and a study author. "And perhaps most importantly, for the first time, we found that cocoa flavanols might even directly mobilize important cells that could repair damaged blood vessels."

Product: The study participants drank cocoa made from CocoaVia from Mars, a high-flavanol cocoa powder that delivers 350 mg of cocoa flavanols and 50 calories per serving.

● **Lowering LDL cholesterol.** Chinese scientists analyzed eight studies on dark chocolate and cholesterol, involving 215 people. They found that "cocoa consumption significantly lowered" bad LDL cholesterol by 6 mg/dL in people with risk factors for heart disease, such as diabetes.

How it works: Flavanols inhibit the production and absorption of cholesterol…help cells process LDL so it doesn't stick to arteries…and cocoa butter contains a type of monounsaturated fatty acid that studies link to an "ideal profile" of cholesterol levels, explained the researchers in the *American Journal of Clinical Nutrition*.

Preventing Heart Attack and Stroke

But chocolate does more than help people who already have risk factors for cardiovascular disease or the disease itself. It can also help prevent the problem.

Less than an ounce does it. In an 8-year study by German researchers involving nearly 20,000 people, those who ate the most chocolate (an average 7.5 grams daily, about ¼ ounce, or one square of a 100-gram chocolate bar) had a 39% lower risk of a heart attack or stroke than those who ate the least (1.7 grams daily, about 1⁄16 of an ounce).

"Chocolate consumption appears to lower cardiovascular disease risk," concluded the researchers in the *European Heart Journal*.

● **Five times a week for protection.** Researchers from Harvard Medical School analyzed health data from nearly 5,000 people with an average age of 52. Those who ate chocolate at least five times a week were 57% less likely to develop heart disease than those who didn't eat chocolate. The results were in the journal *Clinical Nutrition*.

● **Staying out of the hospital—and the cemetery.** In a 10-year study of more than 1,200 women aged 70 and older, German researchers found that those who ate chocolate at least once a week were 35% less likely to be hospitalized or die from heart disease compared with those who rarely ate chocolate. The findings were in the *Archives of Internal Medicine*.

● **Less heart failure.** In a study of more than 31,000 women aged 48 to 83, those who ate one to two servings of dark chocolate a week had a 32% lower risk of developing heart failure compared with women who ate less chocolate, reported researchers from

Harvard Medical School in the journal *Circulation: Heart Failure.*

• **Fewer strokes—and fewer deaths from stroke.** Researchers from the University of Toronto in Canada investigated the link between chocolate consumption and the risk of stroke—and found one serving of chocolate a week was linked to a 22% lower risk of stroke, and eating 50 grams of chocolate a week (just under 2 ounces) was linked to a 46% lower risk of dying after a stroke.

The Chocolate Cure

"Dark chocolate is now the new, guilt-free superfood—isn't this the best nutrition news to come along in decades!" says Janet Brill, PhD, RD, a diet and nutrition expert, and author of *Prevent a Second Heart Attack* (Three Rivers).

Her recommendations for healthfully increasing your intake of dark chocolate:

• **"It's the cocoa component of chocolate that contains the flavanols,** and dark chocolate has the higher percentage of cocoa," she says. "Sample several dark chocolate products until you find one that appeals to you."

Trap: "Watch out for impostors such as white chocolate, hot chocolate mixes, chocolate syrups and milk chocolate bars—all of which are low in flavanols."

Suggested intake: "I recommend you eat no more than an ounce [28 grams] of dark chocolate a day, choosing a product with 70% cocoa," says Dr. Brill. "Keep in mind that chocolate is a treat and certainly not a low-calorie food. Most of the mammoth premium chocolate bars sold in the supermarket are 100 grams, with a serving described as three or four squares. That's about 40 grams—and that's much more than you should eat."

Cocoa powder: Low-calorie, low-sugar, high-flavanol. Perhaps the healthiest way to increase cocoa flavanols in your diet is cocoa powder, says Dr. Brill. "Natural cocoa powders have the highest level of flavanols, followed by unsweetened baking chocolates, dark chocolates, and semisweet baking chips." *When choosing a cocoa powder look for…*

• **The words natural cocoa powder unsweetened on the label.**

Example: Scharffen Berger unsweetened natural cocoa powder.

• **Cocoa powder produced using the Broma process**—not using Dutch processing with alkali, which strips cocoa of flavanols. (Look out for the word alkali on the label.)

Try this: "The best way to get your chocolate is with unsweetened cocoa powder," agrees Deborah Klein, RD, a registered dietitian in California and author of *The 200 Superfoods That Will Save Your Life* (McGraw-Hill).

Her suggestion: "For a delicious daily drink, mix one tablespoon of unsweetened cocoa powder with a teaspoon of agave nectar, in a mug of hot water, with a dash of cinnamon."

Yerem Yeghiazarians, MD, associate professor of medicine and researcher in the Eli and Edythe Broad Center of Regeneration at the University of California-San Francisco.

Carl Keen, PhD, professor of nutrition and internal medicine at the University of California-Davis.

Janet Brill, PhD, RD, diet, nutrition and fitness expert, director of nutrition for Fitness Together, the world's largest organization of personal trainers, and author of *Prevent a Second Heart Attack* and *Cholesterol Down* (both from Three Rivers Press). *www.drjanet.com, www.preventasecondheartattack. com, www.cholesteroldownbook.com.*

Deborah Klein, RD, registered dietician in California, author of *The 200 Superfoods That Will Save Your Life* (McGraw-Hill). *www.livitician.com.*

Eat Your Way to Low Cholesterol

If you have high cholesterol, your primary objective should be to find a way to lower it without drugs and their side effects…the good news according to Kenneth H. Cooper, MD, MPH, is that just eating the right foods often can reduce cholesterol by 50 points or more.

Most people know to eat a low-fat diet, but there are certain foods that can help lower cholesterol that may surprise you…

Macadamia Nuts

Macadamia nuts are among the fattiest plant foods on the planet, about 76% total fat by weight. However, nearly all of the fat is monounsaturated. This type of fat is ideal because it lowers LDL (bad) cholesterol without depressing HDL (good) cholesterol.

A team at Hawaii University found that study participants who added macadamia nuts to their diets for just one month had total cholesterol levels of 191 milligrams/deciliter (mg/dL), compared with those eating the typical American diet (201 mg/dL). The greatest effect was on LDL cholesterol.

Macadamia nuts are higher than other nuts in monounsaturated fat, but all nuts are high in vitamin E, omega-3 fatty acids and other antioxidants. Data from the Harvard Nurses' Health Study found that people who ate at least five ounces of any kind of nut weekly were 35% less likely to suffer heart attacks than those who ate less than one ounce per month.

Caution: Moderation is important because nuts—macadamia nuts, in particular—are high in calories. Limit servings to between one and two ounces daily—about a small handful a day.

Rhubarb

Rhubarb is ideal for both digestive health and lowering cholesterol because it contains a mix of soluble (see "Oats" later in this article) and insoluble fibers.

A study reported in *Journal of the American College of Nutrition* found that participants who ate a little less than three ounces of rhubarb daily for four weeks had an average drop in LDL cholesterol of 9%.

This tart-tasting vegetable isn't only an ingredient in pies. You can cut and simmer the stalks and serve rhubarb as a nutritious side dish (add some low-calorie strawberry jam for a touch of sweetness).

Rice Bran

It's not as well-known for lowering cholesterol as oats and oat bran, but rice bran is just about as effective and some people enjoy it more. A six-week study at University of California, Davis Medical Center found that people who ate three ounces daily of a product with rice bran had drops in total cholesterol of 8.3% and a reduction in LDL of 13.7%.

You can buy rice bran in most supermarkets—it's prepared like oatmeal. Or you can try prepared rice-bran breakfast cereals, such as Quaker Rice Bran Cereal and Kenmei Rice Bran.

Red Yeast Rice

Made from a yeast that grows on rice, red yeast rice contains monacolins, compounds that inhibit the body's production of cholesterol.

One study found that people who took red yeast rice supplements and did nothing else had drops in LDL of 23%. When the supplements were combined with healthy lifestyle changes, their LDL dropped by about 42%.

Red yeast rice may be less likely than statins to cause the side effect *myopathy* (a painful muscle disease).

Recommended dose: 600 milligrams (mg), twice daily. It is available online and at health-food stores.

Green Tea

Green tea is a concentrated source of polyphenols, which are among the most potent antioxidants. It can lower LDL cholesterol and prevent it from turning into plaque deposits in blood vessels. In one study, men who drank five cups of green tea daily had total cholesterol levels that were nine points lower than men who didn't drink green tea.

Three to five cups daily are probably optimal. Black tea also contains polyphenols but in lower concentrations than green tea.

Vitamins C and E

These vitamins help prevent cholesterol in the blood from oxidizing. Oxidized cholesterol is more likely to cling to artery walls and promote the development of atherosclerosis, the cause of most heart attacks.

Dr. Cooper advises patients with high cholesterol to take at least 400 international units (IU) of *d-alpha-tocopherol*, the natural form of vitamin E, daily. You might need more if you engage in activities that increase oxidation, such as smoking.

For vitamin C, take 1,000 mg daily. People who get the most vitamin C are from 25 to 50% less likely to die from cardiovascular disease than those who get smaller amounts.

The Big Three

In addition to the above, some foods have long been known to reduce cholesterol, but they are so helpful that they bear repeating again...

• **Cholesterol-lowering margarines.** Benecol is a margarine that contains *stanol esters*, cholesterol-lowering compounds that are extracted from plants such as soy and pine trees. About 30 grams (g) of Benecol (the equivalent of about three to four pats of butter) daily will lower LDL by about 14%.

Similar products, such as Promise Buttery Spread, contain sterol esters. Like stanols, they help block the passage of cholesterol from the digestive tract into the bloodstream. We used to think that sterols weren't as effective as stanols for lowering cholesterol, but they appear to have comparable benefits.

• **Oats.** They are among the most potent nutraceuticals, natural foods with medicine-like properties. Both oat bran and oatmeal are high in soluble fiber. This type of fiber dissolves and forms a gel-like material in the intestine. The gel binds to cholesterol molecules, which prevents them from entering the bloodstream. A Harvard study that analyzed the results of 67 scientific trials found that even a small amount of soluble fiber daily lowered total cholesterol by five points. People who eat a total of 7 g to 8 g of soluble fiber daily typically see drops of up to 10%. One and a half cups of cooked oatmeal provides 6 g of fiber. If you don't like oatmeal, try homemade oat bran muffins. Soluble fiber also is found in such foods as kidney beans, apples, pears, barley and prunes.

Also helpful: Psyllium, a grain that's used in some breakfast cereals, such as Kellogg's All-Bran Bran Buds, and in products such as Metamucil. As little as 3 g to 4 g of psyllium daily can lower LDL by up to 20%.

• **Fish.** People who eat two to three servings of fish a week will have significant drops in both LDL and triglycerides, another marker for cardiac risk. One large study found that people who ate fish as little as once a week reduced their risk for a sudden, fatal heart attack by 52%.

Heart-healthy fish includes salmon, tuna, herring and sardines. Other good sources of omega-3 fatty acids include walnuts, ground flaxseed, tofu and canola oil.

Fish-oil supplements may provide similar protection, but they are not as effective as the natural food, which contains other beneficial nutrients as well.

Kenneth H. Cooper, MD, MPH, founder of the Cooper Clinic and The Cooper Institute for Aerobics Research, both in Dallas. A leading expert on preventive medicine and the health benefits of exercise, he is author of *Controlling Cholesterol the Natural Way* (Bantam). *www.cooperaerobics.com.*

Are You Cooking The Health Out of Your Food?

Inflammation is the body's natural, temporary, healing response to infection or injury. But if the process fails to shut down when it should, inflammation becomes chronic—and tissues are injured by excess white blood cells and DNA-damaging free radicals.

Result: Elevated risk for heart disease, cancer, diabetes, osteoporosis, arthritis and other diseases.

Richard E. Collins, MD, "the cooking cardiologist," offers his advice on how to prevent chronic inflammation: Follow a diet that is rich in immune-strengthening nutrients...and use cooking techniques that neither destroy food's disease-fighting nutrients nor add inflammatory properties to it.

Smart Ways with Vegetables

Deeply colored plant foods generally are rich in antioxidants that help combat inflammation by neutralizing free radicals.

Examples: Healthful flavonoids are prevalent in deep yellow to purple produce…carotenoids are found in yellow, orange, red and green vegetables.

Exceptions: Despite their light hue, garlic and onions are powerful antioxidants.

Unfortunately, these nutrients are easily lost.

For instance: Boiling or poaching vegetables causes nutrients to leach into the cooking water—and get tossed out when that potful of water is discarded. The high heat of frying causes a reaction between carbohydrates and amino acids, creating carcinogenic chemicals called *acrylamides*. And even when healthful food-preparation techniques are used, overcooking destroys nutrients. *Better…*

• **Microwave.** This uses minimal water and preserves flavor (so you won't be tempted to add butter or salt). Slightly moisten vegetables with water, cover and microwave just until crisp-tender.

• **Stir-fry.** In a preheated wok or sauté pan, cook vegetables over medium-high heat for a minute or two in a bit of low-sodium soy sauce.

• **Steam.** This beats boiling, but because steam envelops the food, some nutrients leach out. To "recycle" them, pour that bit of water from the steamer into any soup or sauce.

• **Stew.** Nutrients that leach from the vegetables aren't lost because they stay in the stew sauce.

• **Roast.** Set your oven to 350°F or lower to protect vegetables' nutrients and minimize acrylamides.

The Right Cooking Oils

Do you cringe when the Food Network chefs sauté in unrefined extra-virgin olive oil? You should. This oil has a very low smoke point (the temperature at which a particular oil turns to smoke) of about 325°F—and when oil smokes, nutrients degrade and free radicals form.

Best: Sauté or stir-fry with refined canola oil, which has a high smoke point. Or use tea seed cooking oil (not tea tree oil)—its smoke point is about 485°F.

Try: Emerald Harvest (*www.emerald-harvest.com*) or Republic of Tea (800-298-4832, *www.republicoftea.com*).

Rule of thumb: If cooking oil starts to smoke, throw it out. Use a laser thermometer (sold at kitchenware stores) to instantly see oil temperature—so you'll know when to turn down the heat.

Richard E. Collins, MD, director of wellness at South Denver Cardiology Associates in Littleton, Colorado, and author of *The Cooking Cardiologist* (Advanced Research) and *Cooking with Heart* (South Denver Cardiology Associates). *www.thecookingcardiologist.com.*

Garlic—Strong Herb for A Stronger Heart

"Back in 3,000 BC, Charak, the father of India's Ayurvedic Medicine, claimed that garlic 'strengthens the heart and keeps blood fluid,'" says Bharat Aggarwal, PhD, director of Experimental Therapeutics at the MD Anderson Cancer Center in Houston and author of *Healing Spices* (Sterling).

Five thousand years later, medical experts are still proclaiming the power of garlic to fortify the heart—but with a difference. They're saying the most effective form of garlic is found in garlic supplements.

"Many studies show that dried or powdered garlic is more therapeutic than fresh," says Dr. Aggarwal.

Newest Research

Here are the most recent studies…

• **Slowing atherosclerosis.** Noting the "previous studies demonstrated that aged garlic extract reduces multiple cardiovascular risk factors," researchers in the Division of Cardiology at the Los Angeles Biomedical Researcher

Institute at Harbor-UCLA studied 65 people (average age 60) with heart disease. Half took an aged garlic extract and half didn't.

Results: After one year, those taking the garlic had significantly slower progression of arterial clogging, as measured by coronary artery calcium scanning. They also had lower total cholesterol, lower bad LDL cholesterol, higher good HDL cholesterol, lower levels of immune factors linked to heart disease, and lower levels of biomarkers for oxidation.

Aged garlic extract is "associated with… reduced progression of atherosclerosis," concluded the researchers in the journal *Preventive Medicine*.

Brand: The supplement used in the study was Kyolic Aged Garlic Extract Total Heart Health Formula 108, from Wakunaga Nutritional Supplements.

● **Lowering uncontrolled high blood pressure.** Australian researchers studied 50 people who were being treated for high blood pressure with medications but without success. Half the study participants took 960 milligrams (mg) a day of an aged garlic extract supplement, standardized for 2.4 mg of *S-allylcysteine*, an active ingredient. The other half took a placebo.

Results: After three months, the systolic blood pressure of the garlic group was 10 points lower than the placebo group—a drop comparable to that achieved by blood pressure medication.

Aged garlic extract can lower systolic blood pressure, at a level similar to current first-line medications, in patients with treated but uncontrolled hypertension, concluded the researchers in the medical journal *Maturitas*.

Brand: The supplement used in the study was Kyolic Garlic High Potency Everyday Formula 112, from Nutralife.

● **Lowering the risk of a heart attack.** Russian researchers from the Moscow Municipal Cardiology Health Center studied 51 people (aged 40 to 65) with high cholesterol and other risk factors for heart disease, dividing them into two groups. One group took 300 mg a day of time-released garlic powder

(Allicor). The other group took a placebo. At the beginning of the study and after one year, the researchers estimated the participants' risk of having a heart attack, based on a standard scoring system that takes into account age, blood pressure, cholesterol, triglycerides, smoking, diabetes and family history of heart disease.

Results: Those taking garlic had a 40% drop in risk of heart attack—along with a big average drop in bad LDL cholesterol of 30 mg/dl.

"A 12-month treatment with Allicor results in the significant decrease of cardiovascular risk," concluded the researchers in the journal *Lipids in Health and Disease*.

● **Boosting antioxidants.** Heart disease advances when bad LDL cholesterol is oxidized and becomes incorporated into white blood cells called foam cells, which are the building blocks of artery-clogging plaque, explains Stephen Sinatra, MD, a cardiologist at the New England Heart Center in Manchester, Connecticut, and author of *Reverse Heart Disease Now* (Wiley).

In a study by Turkish researchers, 17 people took garlic supplements for one month—and had a significant increase in total antioxidant capacity, a measure of the body's ability to fight oxidation.

● **Preventing cardiomyopathy in diabetes.** "People with diabetes have at least twice the risk of death from heart disease, with heart disease accounting for 80% of all diabetes-related deaths," says Wei-Wen Kuo, PhD, in the Department of Biological Science and Technology at China Medical University in Taiwan.

"They are especially vulnerable to a form of heart disease called diabetic cardiomyopathy, which inflames and weakens the muscle tissue of the heart."

In an animal study, Dr. Kuo and his colleagues fed either garlic oil or corn oil to animals with experimentally induced diabetes—and the animals fed garlic oil had much less damage to the heart muscle.

"Garlic oil possesses significant potential for protecting hearts from diabetes-induced cardiomyopathy," concluded the researchers in the *Journal of Agricultural and Food Chemistry*.

Why it works: "Garlic's most active ingredient is allicin, which transforms into organosulfurs—which minimize the oxidation, inflammation and other processes that advance heart disease," says Dr. Aggarwal. "In addition, garlic is brimming with vitamins, minerals and other powerful nutrients that guard against heart disease."

Taking a Garlic Supplement

"Studies show statistically significant changes in cholesterol levels and other parameters of heart health when the daily dosage is between 600 and 900 mg of standardized garlic extract per day," says David Heber, MD, PhD, director of the UCLA Center for Human Nutrition and author of *Natural Remedies for a Healthy Heart* (Avery).

"Start off with 500-mg tablet every day and then boost the dosage to between two to four tablets per day after a week or two."

Red flag: "Avoid garlic supplementation if you take Coumadin," says Dr. Sinatra. "The blood-thinning properties of both can make the blood too thin."

"If you do take a garlic supplement, don't feel you have to stop cooking with this wonderful herb," adds Seth Baum, MD, a cardiologist in Boca Raton, Florida, and author of *The Total Guide to a Healthy Heart* (Kensington).

Bharat Aggarwal, PhD, professor of cancer research, biochemistry, immunology and experimental therapeutics at the MD Anderson Cancer Center in Houston, Texas, and author of *Healing Spices: How to Use 50 Everyday and Exotic Spices to Boost Health and Beat Disease* (Sterling).

Stephen Sinatra, MD, cardiologist at the New England Heart Center in Manchester, Connecticut, and author of *Reverse Heart Disease Now* (Wiley). *www.drsinatra.com*.

Wei-Wen Kuo, PhD, Department of Biological Science and Technology at China Medical University in Taiwan.

David Heber, MD, PhD, director of the UCLA Center for Human Nutrition and author of *Natural Remedies for a Healthy Heart* (Avery).

Seth Baum, MD, cardiologist in Boca Raton, Florida, and author of *The Total Guide to a Healthy Heart* (Kensington).

Salt by the Numbers: Startling Findings from The Latest Studies

You probably know that the higher a person's intake of salt (which is 40% sodium), the higher his or her blood pressure is likely to be—which in turn increases the risk for stroke, heart attack, heart failure, chronic kidney disease and dementia.

What many people have not heard: New studies are very specific about the health impact of excess salt. *The results are startling…*

● **If US residents cut their daily sodium intake by 1,200 milligrams** (mg) on average—that's only about half a teaspoon of salt per day—each year, there would be 32,000 to 66,000 fewer strokes…54,000 to 99,000 fewer heart attacks…and 44,000 to 92,000 fewer deaths from any cause.

Also: National health-care costs would decrease by $10 billion to $24 billion.

●**An analysis of 13 studies involved 177,025 participants** from around the world who were followed for 3.5 to 19 years.

Conclusion: Compared to people with an average daily salt intake of about two teaspoons, those who consumed only about half that much salt had a 23% lower risk for stroke and a 17% lower risk for cardiovascular disease.

●**A multicenter clinical trial involved more than 3,000 participants** who followed a fairly typical American diet or a reduced-sodium diet for 18 to 48 months. Those in the reduced-sodium group made only modest changes—decreasing their intake on average by less than half a teaspoon of salt per day. Yet this was enough to lower their risk for stroke, heart attack or other major cardiovascular event by 30% over the next 10 to 15 years.

How Salt Wreaks Havoc

To function properly, the body does need some sodium—but only about 500 mg per day. When sodium consumption is excessive, the kidneys cannot eliminate all of it. Fluid is retained in the blood vessels, which increases blood pressure. This damages blood vessel walls, accelerating the progression of atherosclerosis (thickening and hardening of the arteries). Salt also appears to thicken the muscle in the heart's left ventricle, the chamber that pumps blood throughout the body. In addition, a high-salt diet may contribute to a decline in kidney function and an increased risk for kidney stones.

The right number for you: Some people are more sensitive to salt than others. *As a general guideline, the American Heart Association recommends…*

• If you are age 40 or older, are African-American or have high blood pressure, limit yourself to 1,500 mg of sodium (about two-thirds of a teaspoon of salt) per day.

Note: About 70% of the US population falls into this group.

• If you do not meet any of the conditions in the preceding paragraph, limit yourself to 2,300 mg of sodium (just under one teaspoon of salt) per day.

Troubling comparison: Among US women, the average daily intake of sodium jumped nearly 70% from 1971 to 2000. The typical American woman now consumes about 3,000 mg per day—twice the amount that's recommended for most people.

What Should You Do?

About 80% of the sodium in the average American's diet comes from canned and processed foods and restaurant meals. Vigilance is required to avoid sodium overload.

When you shop…

• Buy whole foods whenever possible, rather than processed foods.

• If you must buy frozen entrées, choose ones with no more than 600 mg to 800 mg of sodium per serving.

• Select snack foods with no more than 200 mg of sodium per serving (and limit your portion to a single serving).

• Notoriously salty processed foods include canned goods (soups, vegetables, beans)…deli meats and sausage…condiments (ketchup, pickle relish, soy sauce)…bottled salad dressings…and snack foods (popcorn, chips). Avoid these or look for low-sodium or unsalted versions.

When you dine out, remember…

• Some fast-food meals contain nearly triple the salt limit recommended for an entire day! If you visit a fast-food restaurant, forgo the fries in favor of a salad (going light on the dressing)…choose a hamburger instead of a cheeseburger (one slice of American cheese adds almost 400 mg of sodium)…skip the pickles and mayonnaise.

• Check to see if the menu includes a section of low-sodium dishes. If not, request that your meal be prepared with little or no added salt.

At home…

• Put away the saltshaker. When cooking or at the table, use other seasonings—spices, herbs, vinegar, lemon juice—to bring out food's flavor.

JoAnn E. Manson, MD, DrPH, professor of medicine and women's health at Harvard Medical School and chief of the division of preventive medicine at Brigham and Women's Hospital, both in Boston. Dr. Manson is author, with Shari Bassuk, ScD, of *Hot Flashes, Hormones & Your Health* (McGraw-Hill).

Blood Pressure Drugs Increase Cancer Risk

In a recent study, people who used an *angiotensin-receptor blocker* (ARB), such as *losartan* (Cozaar) or *telmisartan* (Micardis), for an average of four years had a 25% higher incidence of lung cancers—and 8% to 11% more cancers overall—than people who did not use the drugs. ARBs can trigger the development of new blood vessels, which speeds tumor growth.

Self-defense: Talk to your doctor about possibly switching to an alternative drug.

Ilke Sipahi, MD, assistant professor of medicine, Case Western Reserve University, Cleveland, and lead researcher of a meta-analysis published in *The Lancet Oncology*.

Chant Your Way to a Healthy Heart and Mind

When sports fans cheer in unison for their teams, they are chanting… when protesters shout, "What do we want? Justice! When do we want it? Now!" they are chanting…and when tough-as-nails Marines intone, "I don't know but I've been told…" while marching, they are chanting. And it's highly likely that most of these folks don't realize that this chanting is good for their health. Modern medical researchers are demonstrating that even the simplest forms of chanting are remarkably good for your heart health…and you don't need to be part of a stadium full of fans to reap the benefits.

Chanting Improves Mind, Body and Spirit

Studies show that chanting triggers the well-known "relaxation response," slowing the heartbeat, brain waves and respiration while also producing stress-lowering endorphins. Several studies from the University of Pennsylvania School of Medicine and the Alzheimer's Research and Prevention Foundation have found that daily practice of a 12-minute Hindu chant (saa-taa-naa-maa accompanied by specific finger movements) may help slow development of Alzheimer's disease. Just eight weeks of this chanting practice improved memory and brain function in patients with mild cognitive impairment, a benefit supported by before and after brain scans showing evidence of physical changes in their brains, including improved blood flow.

Robert Gass, EdD, coauthor of the book *Chanting: Discovering Spirit in Sound*, has taught and led group chanting around the world. He believes that the primary benefit of a chanting practice is the peace of mind it induces. "It takes you out of your daily life and to-do list and reminds you of your deeper nature and your existence beyond the outer pulse of life," says Gass. He adds that vocalizing through chant—really belting it out if you like—can also energize you and create a sense of real joy. *But Gass says that chanting has other very specific benefits as well, including…*

- **Deep breathing.** Chanting has a strong impact on breathing patterns. When you chant, you begin with a quick deep inhalation followed by a slow exhalation. This changes your ratio of blood gases—in fact, researchers have found that chanting boosts levels of nitric acid, which relaxes smooth muscles in arteries and aids in blood flow, including to the brain. This helps bring mental clarity and focus.

- **Good vibrations.** At the core of chanting is a technique called toning, which involves intentionally elongating a vowel sound (such as eeeeeeee) in a monotone that becomes sort of an "internal massage" that helps induce relaxation in your bones and other tissues. To experience it, try this: Loudly tone the sound ahhhhhh and sense the vibration it makes in your chest…now switch it to eee and notice how the vibration moves up into your throat. Studies have found that toning can improve lung function for people with Parkinson's disease. It has also been shown to enhance the flow of cerebrospinal fluid, therefore stimulating the organs and bones as well as the frontal lobes of the brain.

- **Sharper focus.** Chanting can provide cognitive benefits of meditation without the stillness required—in fact, some people who find it difficult to quiet their minds enough to do standard meditation do quite well with chanting instead. It can also be an effective way to begin a meditation, says Gass, especially at the end of a busy day.

- **Affirmation practice.** Chanting can serve as an opportunity to repeat and reinforce affirmations such as "I am at peace" or "Life is good" or whatever has personal meaning to you at the moment. In fact, Gass used this chanting technique when he was battling a life-threatening melanoma a number of years ago. Several times each day, every day, he chanted the words "I choose life," an affirmation that he says helped him endure the rigors of treatment and strengthen his courage.

209

Chanting 101

Though it sounds mystical, the truth is that chanting is totally practical—not least because it requires no equipment or preparation and doesn't cost a penny. You can chant in the car to calm yourself and pass the time...in the shower to start your day on a cheerful note...whenever you need it to eclipse a bad mood...or as a distraction from temptations (food, smoking...what's yours?).

• **You can chant anything you want.** You don't have to say anything meaningful, though many people do—you can choose words or a phrase from your own religious tradition, perhaps the word "amen" or "aleinu." Individuals trying to lower blood pressure can try a classic and popular Buddhist chant, "Nam-myoho-renge-kyo" (it means, roughly, "I dedicate my life to the mystic law of the Lotus [karma] and the teachings of Buddha"). Or you can simply open your mouth and intone "ohmmmmmmm." Gass says that his grandmother, healthy and spry well into her 80s, told him that she had heard it was good to chant an Indian word every day. And so she did, and the word she chose...Cheyenne.

Other ways to explore chanting: You can buy chanting CDs (or download chants to your iPod or MP3 player). You also may want to try group chanting, which Gass says is both powerful and exhilarating. Search "chanting" (or "kirtan," which is a call-and-response version often practiced with yoga) on the Internet to find programs in your area.

Practice, Practice...

Whatever sounds you select to chant, you will gain the greatest benefits if you do it at least once or twice a day.

Here is how...

• **Choose a quiet place where you will be undisturbed,** and sit in a comfortable position with your eyes closed.

• **Chanting for even a few minutes will be of benefit,** but, as Gass points out, longer regular sessions will strengthen your chanting vocal cords (making the chanting less tiring) and also deepen the experience for you.

• **Take a quick deep breath, then exhale slowly as you chant.** The more you practice, the more you'll be able to chant on a single breath.

• **Try different sounds and chants** till you find a style that feels right for you.

• **When you finish, sit quietly for a few minutes** and "listen" to the calmness...and feel the vibrating energy the chanting produced within you.

Eventually you will begin to think of your chant as an old friend. It is always there to relax and comfort you no matter what situation you may be in.

Robert Gass, EdD, coauthor of Chanting: Discovering Spirit in Sound *(Broadway Books), has a background in psychology, music and spiritual studies, among other disciplines, and has taught and led group chanting around the world. He is based in Boulder, Colorado. He is also a composer and has recorded more than 20 CDs with his singing group, On Wings of Song.* www.sacredunion.com.

The Four Best Ways to Prevent a Stroke

Nearly 800,000 times a year—every 40 seconds—the brain of an American comes under attack. From a stroke.

What happens: A clot blocks the flow of blood to the brain—an ischemic stroke, accounting for 83% of all strokes. Or a blood vessel in the brain ruptures—a hemorrhagic stroke, accounting for 17%.

Those "brain attacks" are often deadly or disabling.

Stroke is the third leading cause of death (after heart disease and cancer), killing 143,000 yearly. It's also the leading cause of disability—the paralysis, spasticity, pain, speech problems, memory loss and other harrowing symptoms that make stroke one of the most dreaded of diseases.

Good news: A new study from Canadian researchers shows that there are 10 risk factors for stroke that account for 90% of the cases—and you can take control over many of them.

Study Details

The study looked at risk factors for stroke in 6,000 people—3,000 who had a stroke and 3,000 similar people who didn't.

The researchers found that 10 risk factors accounted for 90% of all strokes...

- **More than 30 drinks per month or binge drinking (380% higher risk)**
- **History of high blood pressure (264%)**
- **Heart disease (238%)**
- **Current smoking (209%)**
- **Ratio of blood fats known as apolipoprotein B (apo B) to apolipoprotein AI (apo AI) (89%)**
- **Lack of physical activity (69%)**
- **Abdominal obesity (65%)**
- **Diabetes (36%)**
- **Poor diet (35%)**
- **Psychosocial stress/depression (35%).**

"Targeted interventions that reduce blood pressure and smoking, and promote physical activity and a healthy diet, could substantially reduce the burden of stroke," concluded the researchers in the medical journal *The Lancet*.

Here's what you need to know about controlling those four risk factors...

High Blood Pressure, Poor Diet

You can handle two risk factors at once—high blood pressure and poor diet—by eating a healthy, pressure-lowering diet, says J. David Spence, MD, PhD, director of the Stroke Prevention and Atherosclerosis Research Center at the Robarts Research Institute in Ontario.

- **The anti-stroke diet.** Scientific evidence from the DASH study (Dietary Approaches to Stop Hypertension) shows that a diet high in fruits, vegetables and nonfat dairy products and low in the saturated fats and cholesterol found in full-fat animal products can reduce blood pressure as much as pressure-lowering medication, says Dr. Spence.

He also cites the Lyon Heart Study, which found the Mediterranean diet was linked to a 60% reduction in stroke.

"Many studies also indicate that salt restriction is important for lowering blood pressure, particularly for people over 65 and for African-Americans, populations that are more sensitive to the pressure-raising effects of salt," he says. His recommendations...

- **More fruits and vegetables** (five to nine servings daily)
- **More grains and beans**
- **More fish**
- **Less beef, lamb and pork** (replaced with poultry). Eat no more than two ounces of red meat a day, he says. "To feel satisfied, eat a four-ounce serving every other day. Learn to make pastas, stir fries, chilies, curries and other dishes without meat. Make them tasty using spices such as vinegar, lemon or lime juice, hot peppers, garlic, onion, paprika or ginger."
- **Replace butter with nonhydrogenated margarine made with canola oil.**
- **Reduce salt,** watching out for high-salt foods like pickles, chips, salami and ham. "Adding salt to your food actually makes your taste buds shrivel," says Dr. Spence. "If you use spices other than salt to make your foods tasty, your buds will grow back in three weeks. You'll taste the natural salt that's already in food and you won't miss the added salt."

Smoking

"Smoking is the only risk factor for stroke that you can eliminate rather than reduce," says Dr. Spence.

His advice: Just quit.

The key to quitting: Understand the difference between trying to quit and really quitting.

"If a child is drowning in a cold lake, you don't try to convince yourself to jump in and save the child," he says. "You just do it. If you know that smoking is increasing your risk of stroke, and you want to live, you don't try to quit—you just do it.

"Once you've made up your mind to quit, the hard part is over. Then it takes about three weeks—using a nicotine patch or anti-smoking medication such as Zyban [*bupropion*]—until the cravings and physical discomfort are over."

Physical Activity

"Among the actions you can take to prevent stroke, physical activity is near the top of the list," says David Chiu, MD, director of the stroke center at the Methodist Hospital in Houston, Texas.

He recommends a simple solution: 30 minutes of brisk walking, three to four times a week. "Every stroke expert would tell you that is one of the easiest ways to prevent stroke," he says.

Bottom Line

"You may be able to reduce your risk of stroke without drugs by trying nondrug methods first," says Larry B. Goldstein, MD, director of the Duke Center for Cerebrovascular Disease and the Duke Stroke Center in Durham, North Carolina. "That means eating a diet low in saturated fats, with plenty of fruits and vegetables, walking briskly 20 to 30 minutes several days a week, and stopping smoking."

J. David Spence, MD, PhD, director of the Stroke Prevention and Atherosclerosis Research Center at the Robarts Research Institute in London, Ontario, and professor of neurology, internal medicine, physiology and pharmacology at the University of Western Ontario.

David Chiu, MD, director of the Eddy Scurlock Stroke Center at the Methodist Hospital in Houston, Texas.

Larry B. Goldstein, MD, director of the Duke Center for Cerebrovascular Disease and the Duke Stroke Center, and professor of medicine (neurology) at Duke University and the Durham VA Medical Center, all in Durham, North Carolina.

A Doctor's Own Cardiac Comeback Plan

In 2002, Marc Wallack, a surgeon, started having chest pains while jogging. Though heart disease runs in his family—his father and paternal grandfather died of heart attacks—he thought he had heartburn and took antacids. After four days of "heartburn," he finally saw a doctor and learned that all of his coronary arteries were 95% blocked. He needed bypass surgery to survive.

The operation was a success, but Dr. Wallack, then in his 50s, found that his life had changed dramatically. He was afraid to fall asleep at night because he was worried that he wouldn't wake up again. He wondered if his heart could withstand exercise or sex.

What Dr. Wallack realized is that while surgery and cardiac rehabilitation keep patients alive, they don't necessarily help them live. *Here, he shares his eight steps to a complete recovery, physically and mentally…*

Step 1: **Get sleep.** The majority of patients who undergo heart-related procedures sleep poorly following their procedures. Nearly half experience some degree of insomnia for eight weeks or more. Even when patients think they sleep soundly, they often have little or no rapid-eye movement (REM) or slow-wave sleep, both of which are critical for recovery.

Nighttime fears—particularly of death and disability—are extremely common in heart patients. The resulting sleep disturbances increase the risk for subsequent heart disease.

I used prescription sleep medications for about three months before I was able to sleep most nights without them. New generations of medications, such as *eszopiclone* (Lunesta) and *zolpidem* (Ambien), are extremely safe (though carry some risk for dependency).

I also discovered that I felt calmer and slept better when there was static noise in the background. I used a white noise machine. Or you can use a fan, and there are Internet sites that play white noise through the computer.

Example: www.simplynoise.com.

In addition, I slept with the blinds open so that I could see the lights outside (I live in New York City)—it made me feel alive.

Step 2: **Overcome depression.** Nearly one in three heart attack survivors experiences postsurgical depression, in part because microclots can travel to the brain and cause mood changes. According to researchers at University of Maryland and Columbia University Medical Center, patients who were depressed after cardiac surgery were twice as likely to die from heart problems within seven years, compared with those who were not depressed.

Talk therapy, sometimes combined with antidepressants, can help patients get past their depression and regain a sense of balance. One study found that patients who attended group therapy after heart surgery and/or a heart attack had a 60% lower rate of rehospitalization than those who didn't get therapy.

Step 3: Get back into the world. It can take months or longer to recover from major surgery. Patients are weak and disoriented. They often are reluctant to leave home, even after their doctors say it's OK to do so, because they're afraid of falling or that they'll somehow damage their hearts.

Getting out of the house is a major step in recovery. Everyone needs sunlight, fresh air and a change of scenery. Even gentle exercise, such as walking to a corner store, can alleviate depression and improve your motivation to recover. Bring a friend or family member if you're not sure of your ability to get around on your own. Eventually work up to driving and going out by yourself to build your confidence.

Step 4: Optimize doctor visits. Patients who have had heart surgery initially have numerous postsurgical doctor visits. These often are stressful because patients fear that they might hear bad news. The anxiety surrounding these visits can undermine the patient's confidence and make him feel more like a patient than a person. To counteract that, my wife and I turned a doctor visit into an outing. We would go out to breakfast or lunch first. (I tried to make my appointments for first thing in the morning or the first appointment after lunch so that I wouldn't have to wait long for the doctor.)

Helpful: Bring someone with you when you see a doctor or undergo tests. Your mind can go blank when you're the patient, so you need someone who can listen carefully, take notes and ask questions.

For further peace of mind, ask your cardiologist what's the best way to contact him/ her. Get the names and contact information for key people in the office, such as the nurse practitioner. You need to know who to call or e-mail if, for example, you notice that your heart is beating faster than usual.

Step 5: Make love again. After the first few months of recovery, ask your doctor if it's OK for you to have sex. Heart patients often worry that the exertion of sex will strain their hearts. Not true. The odds of having a heart attack during sex, even if you already have had a heart attack, are typically about 20 in one million. Less than 1% of patients who die of a heart attack do so during sex.

Step 6: Eat for recovery. I advise most postsurgical patients to eat small meals frequently. The lingering effects of anesthesia can make people feel nauseous and reluctant to eat. Pain medications often inhibit appetite. So does prolonged bed rest and postsurgical fatigue.

My story: Every time I ate, I worried that the food would instantly clog my arteries or cause a clot to form. This wasn't rational, and it made it difficult for me to gain weight and recover my strength after surgery.

I found that smoothies were ideal.

I made them with low-fat yogurt, skim milk, fruit and ice. They didn't upset my stomach, and the more I ate, the more I wanted to eat.

Step 7: Prepare for career issues. After my surgery, I was surprised to discover that some of my colleagues were vying for my job. When you go back to work, don't talk much about your health history, and don't let people see you taking your medicine.

But ask your boss or human resources representative for accommodations, such as time off for rehab three times a week or the OK to take a 15-minute nap every day. Chronic work stress doubles the odds of experiencing a second heart attack within six years. Give yourself time to get back into the groove.

Step 8: Set an exercise goal. Regular exercise improves cholesterol, lowers blood pressure and reduces stress. Just as important, it gives you a goal. People need strong goals to get through the grueling months of rehabilitation.

My goal was to run another marathon after I recovered. This gave me the internal strength to try to get better even when I was so weak that I could only take a few steps. I did run a marathon in November 2005, a little more than three years after my surgery.

Develop an exercise program with a rehabilitation expert who can work with you for the first few months (this typically is covered by insurance). Your first exercise goal might be to build up enough strength so that you can comfortably walk up and down stairs or to work in the yard without fatigue. No matter what you hope to achieve, the best way to get there is to move your body again.

Marc Wallack, MD, chief of surgery at Metropolitan Hospital in New York City and vice-chair of the department of surgery at New York Medical College, Valhalla. He is author, with his wife, Jamie Colby, of *Back to Life After a Heart Crisis: A Doctor and His Wife Share Their 8-Step Cardiac Comeback Plan* (Avery). *www.backtolifethebook.com.*

Is Air Travel Bad for Your Heart?

It's become such a hassle to fly that it makes perfect sense to hear that air travel is bad for your heart—but this particular warning has nothing to do with the stresses of late flights and airport security or even the likelihood that you'll get exposed to illness from a fellow flier. A recent study from the Harvard School of Public Health found that some people may unexpectedly experience cardiac arrhythmia—extra heartbeats—while flying.

The study brought together 39 men and women (average age was 63), one-third of whom had been diagnosed with heart disease. Over the two-day study period, they each spent two five-hour sessions in a hypobaric chamber—one session simulated atmospheric conditions at sea level, while the other session created the air pressure conditions you would experience in the cabin of a jetliner flying at 20,000 to 40,000 feet. The participants' heart rates were monitored during both tests. Those without heart disease were unaffected, but among those with heart disease, six people experienced arrhythmias...though, interestingly, none were aware of the extra beats.

Calling these findings "statistically significant," the study's lead author, Eileen McNeely, PhD, an instructor in the department of environmental and occupational medicine and epidemiology research at the Harvard School of Public Health, says researchers are now trying to determine the extent to which they are "clinically significant." "It's obvious that there are some physiological changes associated with flying," she says, "but we're not sure about the magnitude of the risk." She explains that sustained arrhythmia brings an increased risk for stroke or cardiac arrest. In the study, the extra beats were not sustained, she says, "but we don't know if this is always the case."

Dr. McNeely points out that the available data document very few in-flight medical emergencies, so the overall risk that this will happen is quite low. However, it's worth noting that there's no research available that follows the health of air travelers after they've landed, so we don't know whether passengers have medical issues later that are connected to arrythmias that occurred in the air. Dr. McNeely thinks that it is important to learn more about physiological changes people experience while flying to ascertain whether there are specific dangers that warrant taking precautions—or even, for vulnerable people, not flying.

In the meantime, she says it makes sense for airline passengers to follow the health advice currently given to people traveling to high-altitude locations in the mountains. To prepare for flying, Dr. McNeely advises that otherwise healthy men over age 45 and women over 55 or who are postmenopausal (categories that put people at greater risk of arrhythmia) should...

●**Drink plenty of fluids the day before you fly and during your flight.** Dehydration can make you more vulnerable to cardiac problems. Avoid alcohol for the same reason.

● **Get plenty of rest.** Try to get as much rest in the few days before your flight as you can. In other words, don't run yourself ragged getting ready with the idea that you'll get to catch up on sleep once onboard.

● **Avoid excess stress.** Pack early and leave plenty of time to get to the airport and through security.

Interesting note: Noise can be a central nervous system stressor—noise-canceling headphones in flight can help you stay relaxed.

The risk of in-flight emergency is higher for people with heart disease or who have a lung condition that inhibits oxygen uptake (such as emphysema). *For these people, Dr. McNeely advises doing all of the above, plus…*

● **Avoid long walks through the airport.** Take the in-airport shuttle so you don't wear yourself out before your flight.

● **Ask your cardiologist whether you should bring supplemental oxygen or a portable oxygen concentrator on board.**

● **Under a doctor's supervision, consider regular supplementation with L-carnitine and coenzyme Q10.** Both of these can limit the ill effects of decreased oxygen delivery to the heart.

Eileen McNeely, PhD, instructor, Harvard School of Public Health, Environmental and Occupational Medicine and Epidemiology Research, Boston.

Is Sex Good For The Heart?

In a recent finding, men who had sex once a month or less were approximately 50% more likely to suffer cardiovascular events, such as heart attack, stroke or heart failure, than men who had sex at least twice a week. Further research is needed. The frequency of sex may simply indicate a man's overall health. In the meantime, men should discuss with their doctors any sexual problems.

Susan A. Hall, PhD, research scientist, Department of Epidemiology, New England Research Institutes, Watertown, Massachusetts, and lead author of a study of 1,165 men, published in *The American Journal of Cardiology*.

Protect Yourself From Heart-Hurting Air Pollution

Here's the dirty little truth about tiny particles of air pollution—they can and do cause deadly cardiovascular disease (CVD), such as heart attack and stroke.

And it's not a whistle blower at a power plant making that claim.

It's a new scientific statement from the American Heart Association, which reviewed the last six years of research on the link between air pollution and CVD—and found a very strong link.

The Polluted Heart

"It looks like the cardiovascular system is uniquely sensitive to air pollution levels," says Robert D. Brook, MD, associate professor of internal medicine in the Division of Cardiovascular Medicine at the University of Michigan and an author of the statement.

The type of pollution that does the dirtiest work is fine particulate matter—the congealed specks of floating carbon, metals and other compounds that spew from exhaust pipes, industrial smokestacks and coal-fired power plants.

The risk from fine particulate matter is both short-term and long-term, says Dr. Brook.

In "susceptible individuals," just a few hours or days of exposure to air pollution can increase the risk of irregular heartbeats (arrhythmias), heart attack, stroke, heart failure and death, he says.

And susceptible doesn't mean you're on your last legs. *You're susceptible if…*

● **You're 60 or over** (aging is a risk factor for heart disease).

● **You have diabetes,** which can damage arteries.

● **You're overweight or obese,** which studies link to susceptibility.

● **You're at high risk for CVD,** which means you have two or more risk factors, such as high blood pressure and high LDL cholesterol.

●**You have CVD,** which means you have angina…or you've already had a heart attack or stroke…or you've had a cardiovascular procedure such as angioplasty or bypass surgery…or you have heart failure (a weak heart muscle).

Several years or more of exposure to air pollution may increase anyone's risk for CVD, says Dr. Brook.

Air pollution can also increase the risk for premature death from any cause, shortening life from a few months to several years.

And there's no "safe" level of exposure to fine particulate matter, just as there's no "safe" level of exposure to secondary smoke—even a little air pollution can do a lot of damage, he says.

What happens: There are "multiple pathways" by which fine particulate matter affects the cardiovascular system, says Dr. Brook.

●**It can spark artery-damaging inflammation**—just as smoking and excess saturated fat (to cite two examples) can inflame and damage your arteries.

●**It can weaken the cells of the endothelium,** which line the artery and generate artery-relaxing nitric oxide.

●**It irritates the sympathetic nervous system,** which regulates heart rate.

And any one, or several, or all of these pathways can lead to high blood pressure, blood clots, clogged and weakened arteries and irregular heartbeats, which in turn can lead to heart attack, stroke and death, says Dr. Brook.

Bottom line: The fine particulate matter of air pollution should be recognized as a "modifiable risk factor" for CVD and for premature death, concluded the American Heart Association in their scientific statement.

Protecting Yourself

Fortunately, there are several ways you can modify this risk factor.

●**Modify your other CVD risk factors.** "The main message for susceptible people

is to use medical care and lifestyle changes to control their other modifiable risk factors, such as high blood pressure, high cholesterol, diabetes and smoking," says Dr. Brook.

●**Know when the air is unhealthy—and stay indoors.** You can find a map that displays daily air-quality levels across America at the Web site *www.airnow.gov.* It shows where air quality is good…moderate…unhealthy for sensitive groups…very unhealthy…and hazardous.

"Limit your exposure as much as possible by decreasing time outside when particle levels are high and the air is unhealthy," says Dr. Brook.

That's particularly important if you're susceptible (or "sensitive," as the Web site calls it)—one of the many people with an older or weaker cardiovascular system that is more vulnerable to air pollution.

●**Reduce your time in traffic.** "In today's world, traffic is a common source of exposure to particulate matter," says Dr. Brook.

Healthful strategy: Don't exercise next to highly trafficked roads or outside during rush hour.

●**Use a HEPA filter.** Researchers studied 45 healthy people in a small town in Canada where wood-burning stoves—which generate fine particulate matter—were the main source of air pollution. For one week, the participants used high-efficiency particle air (HEPA) filters in their homes. For another week, they used the same filters—but with the filters removed.

Results: The HEPA filters reduced the amount of indoor fine particulate matter by 60%.

When people used the working HEPA filters, they had 9% better endothelial function (as indicated by a test for blood flow) and 33% lower levels of C-reactive protein (a biomarker of inflammation).

"This simple intervention can improve air quality indoors—where the majority of time is spent—and reduce cardiovascular-related health risks," concluded Ryan Allen, PhD, assistant professor at Simon Fraser University in Burnaby, British Columbia, and the study

Brushing Your Teeth Keeps the Cardiologist Away

Now there is additional proof that dental problems don't end in your mouth. Researchers from University College London found that people who reported brushing their teeth less than twice daily, on average, had a 70% increased risk for heart disease compared with those who brushed at least twice daily. That's even more reason to get your toothbrush busy twice a day.

Mark A. Stengler, NMD, naturopathic medical doctor in private practice, Encinitas, California, and author of the *Bottom Line/Natural Healing* newsletter, *www.drstengler.com*.

leader, in the *American Journal of Respiratory and Critical Care Medicine.*

"We were surprised to see the magnitude of effects from air pollution in the people we studied—people who didn't have many of the underlying problems that make you more susceptible to air pollution, such as aging and diabetes," says Dr. Allen.

"You wouldn't expect those young and relatively healthy people to be susceptible to the cardiovascular effects of air pollution—but they were."

For the greatest benefit: "There's enough evidence to recommend HEPA filters—which are relatively inexpensive to purchase and operate—as a possible intervention against air pollution, particularly for susceptible groups, such as those with cardiovascular disease," says Dr. Allen.

He points out that a previous study showed the ability of HEPA filters to reduce fine particulate matter in homes in a heavily trafficked area of a big city—and also to reduce endothelial damage in those who used them.

The researchers used two HEPA filters in the study: the Honeywell model 50300 in the main activity room, and the quieter Honeywell 18150 in the bedroom.

Robert D. Brook, MD, associate professor of medicine, Division of Cardiovascular Medicine, University of Michigan, Ann Arbor.

Ryan W. Allen, PhD, assistant professor, faculty of health sciences, Simon Fraser University, Burnaby, British Columbia, Canada.

After Heart Surgery, Have a Drink

More than 80 scientific studies link moderate alcohol intake—an average of one to two drinks a day for men and one drink a day for women—to a healthier cardiovascular system. *The benefits of imbibing may include...*

- **Lower risk of heart disease and heart attack**
- **Lower risk of stroke**
- **Lower risk of congestive heart failure**
- **Lower risk of death in people with atrial fibrillation (irregular heartbeat)**
- **Lower risk of heart disease with diabetes.**

Latest findings: Several new studies show that moderate drinking may also help after you've had coronary bypass surgery...after you've had a heart attack...or after you've had a stroke.

More Drinks, Fewer Deaths

Italian researchers studied more than 1,000 men who had bypass surgery, following their habits and health for 3½ years after the operation.

Those who drank moderately had 25% fewer heart attacks, strokes, additional bypass surgeries and deaths, compared with nondrinkers, reported the researchers at a meeting of the American Heart Association.

However: Bypass patients with heart failure who drank four or more drinks a day were twice as likely to die of heart disease, compared with nondrinkers.

"The benefits of moderate amounts of alcohol have been documented in healthy individuals, but our analysis showed a benefit from moderate alcohol intake in postcoronary bypass patients," says Umberto Benedetto, MD, PhD, a study researcher from the University of Rome La Sapienza in Italy.

In another study of more than 16,000 people who had a heart attack or stroke, those who drank moderately after the event had a 20% lower risk of dying from any cause, reported Italian researchers in the *Journal of the American College of Cardiology*.

"We observed that regular and moderate consumption of alcohol has beneficial effects even for people already affected by a heart attack or stroke," says Simona Costanzo, MD, the study leader.

And in a study of 325 people who had a heart attack, those who drank moderately before the attack and continued to drink afterward were: 35% less likely to have angina, 21% less likely to be hospitalized again for heart disease, and 25% less likely to die within three years of the heart attack, compared with moderate drinkers who quit drinking after the heart attack.

"There are no adverse effects for moderate drinkers to continue consuming alcohol after an acute myocardial infarction [heart attack], and they may have better physical functioning compared to those who quit," concluded the researchers in the *American Journal of Cardiology*.

Gin Is Tonic

How does alcohol help the heart?

To answer that question, Harvard scientists examined 13 well-known biomarkers for heart disease in more than 50,000 men and women, says Eric Rimm, ScD, an associate professor at the Harvard School of Public Health. *Among moderate drinkers, three biomarkers were common in 100% of the men and 80% of the women...*

- **High HDL,** the "good" cholesterol that carries fat away from arteries.

- **Low fibrinogen,** a protein that increases the risk of artery-clogging clots.

- **Low hemoglobin A1c,** a biomarker for long-term control of blood sugar. (Diabetes doubles the risk of heart disease.)

Important: Many studies show that these three biomarkers are improved not by any particular element in wine, beer or spirits, says Dr. Rimm, but by ethanol—the alcohol in alcoholic drinks.

In other words, one or two drinks a day of any alcoholic drink—not just red wine or imported beer or double-malt Scotch—protects the heart.

Example: A drink is 5 ounces of wine, 12 ounces of beer, or 1½ ounces of 80% distilled spirits or liquor, such as whiskey or vodka.

And the study found the greatest degree of protection among those who drank regularly. One or two drinks a day, three to seven days a week, was the healthiest pattern, says Dr. Rimm.

But one or two drinks a day does not mean seven to 14 drinks on Saturday night, he adds. "Immoderate drinking—binge-drinking, or consistently drinking three or more drinks a day—puts you at higher risk for heart disease and many other chronic health problems."

"When we talk about moderate alcohol consumption, we mean drinking regularly, at low doses, within a healthy lifestyle, such as the Mediterranean diet," agrees Licia Iacoviello, MD, PhD, a research associate professor at the University of Buffalo who has studied the alcohol and health. "A glass of wine or beer during meals has always been an integral part of the Mediterranean way of eating.

"And the heart-healthy research shows drinking has to be not only moderate but also regular. A moderate consumption throughout the week is positive. The same amount of weekly alcohol, concentrated in a couple of days, is definitely harmful."

Who Shouldn't Drink

Immoderate or unsafe alcohol intake is a serious public health problem, says Dr. Rimm, with 16,000 people dying every year in alcohol-related car accidents. Needless to say, there are many people who shouldn't drink. *Don't drink if...*

- **You're pregnant**
- **Your father or mother suffered from alcoholism**
- **You're on a blood-thinning medication like *warfarin***
- **You have breast cancer or a family history of the disease**
- **You're about to drive, operate heavy machinery or do anything that requires normal reaction time.**

"Those are only a few examples of the many scenarios where drinking is inappropriate, moderate or otherwise," says Dr. Rimm. "Discuss your alcohol intake with your doctor."

Umberto Benedetto, MD, PhD, the University of Rome La Sapienza, Italy.

Simona Costanzo, MD, Catholic University of Campobasso, Italy.

Eric Rimm, ScD, associate professor at the Harvard School of Public Health and the Channing Laboratory at the Harvard Medical School.

Licia Iacoviello, MD, PhD, research associate professor in the Department of Social and Preventive Medicine at the School of Public Health and Health Professions at the University of Buffalo.

Emotions That Can Poison Your Heart—and The Relaxing Antidote

"Taking something to heart" means you're deeply affected. And recent research shows you *literally* take negative emotions to heart (and to the rest of your cardiovascular system)—with anxiety, anger and depression linked to more heart attacks, more heart failure and even more heart transplants...

●**Anxiety.** In a seven-year study of nearly 97,000 veterans, those with anxiety disorders had an up to 43% higher risk of suffering a heart attack than vets without the problem, reported researchers in the *American Heart Journal*.

And in a six-year study of more than 1,000 people with coronary heart disease, Dutch researchers found that those with generalized anxiety disorder (GAD) had a 74% higher risk of heart attack, heart failure, stroke or death.

●**Anger.** People who are angry and aggressive are 40% more likely to have thickened carotid arteries of the neck, raising their risk of heart attack or stroke, reported researchers from the National Institutes of Health in *Hypertension: Journal of the American Heart Association*.

●**Type D personality.** Dutch researchers studied 6,000 people with heart disease and Type D personality, which is characterized by chronic anxiety, irritation, depression, keeping emotions bottled up out of fear of disapproval and pessimism. They found the Type Ds had nearly a four times higher risk of heart attack, heart failure, angioplasty or bypass procedures, heart transplantation or death than non-Ds.

●**Stress hormones.** People with the highest blood levels of cortisol—a hormone generated during stress—have a five times higher risk of dying from cardiovascular disease than those with the lowest levels, according to a six-year study of 861 people aged 65 and older, reported by Dutch researchers in the *Journal of Clinical Endocrinology & Metabolism*.

Bottom line: Stress—in this case, emotional stress—is the key to understanding the effect of negative emotions on the cardiovascular system, says cardiologist John M. Kennedy, MD, medical director of preventive cardiology and wellness at Marina Del Rey Hospital in California and author of *The 15 Minute Heart Cure: The Natural Way to Release Stress and Heal Your Heart in Just Minutes a Day* (Wiley).

"Constant stress—including the stress of negative emotions—exposes our delicate cardiac tissues to toxic levels of stress hormones, which make our cardiovascular system vulnerable to heart attacks, arrhythmias and congestive heart failure—the three most common cardiac conditions in the United States," he says.

There are many mechanisms by which stress and stress hormones increase the risk for heart disease, he explains. *They include…*

- **Increased vascular resistance** (higher pressure in the arteries)
- **Enhanced platelet activity** (thick, clot-prone blood)
- **Hypertension** (high blood pressure)
- **Coronary vasospasm** (constriction that limits blood flow)
- **Inflammation**
- **Electrical instability** (erratic heartbeat)
- **Enhanced atherosclerosis** (plaque build-up in the arteries).

But there's an antidote for negative emotions and emotional stress, says Dr. Kennedy—positive emotions and emotional vitality.

"Emotional vitality is a positive state associated with interest, enthusiasm, excitement and energetic living—and a recent study has proved the importance of emotional vitality in maintaining optimal cardiovascular health," says Dr. Kennedy.

The study: 6,000 men and women were followed for 15 years; during this time, 1,200 developed coronary artery disease. Even after allowing for traditional cardiac risk factors, the study demonstrated that patients with positive attitudes and higher emotional vitality were less likely to develop heart disease.

"The researchers speculated that the patients with a more positive coping attitude and higher emotional vitality had better coping mechanisms for dealing with unexpected life stress," says Dr. Kennedy. "And as a cardiologist, I can tell you that the most important factor in preventing and treating heart disease is learning an effective, self-directed way to deal with stress."

To help his patients (and you) resist stress and increase emotional vitality, Dr. Kennedy has created the B-R-E-A-T-H-E technique…

The B-R-E-A-T-H-E Technique

"You can defuse stressful situations with the B-R-E-A-T-H-E technique, and protect your heart," says Dr. Kennedy.

Here are his abridged instructions, adapted from the book *The 15 Minute Heart Cure*, where you can find the technique presented in full…

- **B: Begin.** You can choose a quiet place in your home and practice soon after waking, which can help you focus and achieve your daily goals. Some people use the B-R-E-A-T-H-E technique just before climbing into bed, which helps them to relieve racing thoughts and to achieve more quality sleep. Wherever and whenever you decide to B-R-E-A-T-H-E, be sure to practice the same way each time. When you begin, pick a quiet and cozy place, where you won't be interrupted for 15 minutes. Begin your exercise with a positive attitude, knowing that this 15 minutes is a well-deserved gift.

- **R: Relax.** To elicit the relaxation response requires focused and conscious breathing. *To breathe consciously…*

1. **Sit in a comfortable chair with arm rests, and let the gravity of your body sink into it, with your body as relaxed as possible.** Feel the weight of your arms and legs supported by the chair. Feel your feet comfortably in contact with the ground.

2. **Pay attention to your breathing.** To help focus on your breathing, place one hand on part of your chest or abdomen and watch your hand rise and fall with each breath.

3. **Inhale through your nose, if possible.** If not, breathing in through your mouth will suffice.

4. **Inhale deeply and slowly (through your nose) and feel it in your abdomen.** You'll see and feel your abdomen rise with each inhalation. Your chest should move only slightly.

5. **Exhale through your mouth, keeping your lips, tongue and jaw relaxed.** Extend your exhalation, if you can, to a count of seven.

6. Relax and focus on the sound and feeling of long, slow, deep breaths.

7. Listen to the conversation between your heart and your brain. As you inhale, notice your pulse slightly increasing; as you exhale, your heart rate will decrease.

8. Repeat for seven breaths. You'll know it's time to go on to the next step in B-R-E-A-T-H-E when you feel all your muscles relaxed and your entire weight supported by your chair.

● **E: Envision.** Envision your heart parts—the arteries, the muscle, the valves and the electrical system—as healthy and strong. Envision your heart as strong and powerful, with all the parts working synergistically and efficiently.

● **A: Apply.** Apply this technique in times of heavy stress, as an effective coping mechanism.

● **T: Treat.** The B-R-E-A-T-H-E technique is a pleasurable and therapeutic exercise—that treats stress and your heart. These 15 minutes will make you feel revitalized and energized, like a spa treatment.

● **H: Heal.** By practicing 15 minutes daily, you will train the neural networks that connect your heart and your brain—and constantly elicit the relaxation response, so that you can use B-R-E-A-T-H-E anytime and virtually anywhere.

● **E: End.** When you have successfully completed your exercise, you will feel deeply relaxed and ready to face the rest of the day. Before you end, imagine how you might use this technique throughout your day to help defuse a stressful situation. In order to reap the many health benefits of the B-R-E-A-T-H-E technique, concentrate on staying positive, being relaxed, and flowing with everything.

John M. Kennedy, MD, medical director of preventive cardiology and wellness at Marina Del Rey Hospital in California and author of The 15 Minute Heart Cure: The Natural Way to Release Stress and Heal Your Heart in Just Minutes a Day *(Wiley). www.the15minuteheartcure.com.*

Quick Self-Test Signals For Stiff Arteries

Physical fitness has been shown to delay age-related arterial stiffness, a risk factor for cardiovascular disease.

Recent study: Participants sat on the floor, legs straight, then bent forward at the waist to see how far they could reach toward or past their toes. Among middle-aged and older adults, the least flexible people generally had the stiffest arteries, as measured by a test called pulse-wave velocity. Researchers theorize that stretching exercises may prompt physiological reactions that slow age-related arterial stiffening.

Best: Incorporate flexibility exercises, such as stretching, yoga and Pilates, into your regular workouts.

Kenta Yamamoto, PhD, research fellow, department of integrative physiology, University of North Texas Health Science Center, Fort Worth, and leader of a study of 526 people.

The "Secret" Organ That Prevents Plaque-Filled Arteries

There's a little secret about controlling the prevention of deadly plaque and clots. It's all about the *endothelium* (pronounced en-doe-THEE-lee-um), the thin layer of cells that lines the inside of blood vessels. The endothelium is so vast and involves so many physiological functions that researchers now consider it to be an organ.

To protect yourself from cardiovascular disease, focus on the lining of your blood vessels. The endothelium plays a crucial role in the cardiovascular system—producing chemicals that open blood vessels…influencing the formation and breakdown of dangerous blood clots…and helping to maintain blood flow throughout the body.

Fact: The health of your endothelium is within your control. *Here's what you need to know…*

The Endothelium Is Everywhere

There are long miles of blood vessels in your body—and endothelial cells are active participants in keeping them healthy.

Healthy blood vessels flex and stretch as they accommodate blood flow throughout your body. Their lining is slick, allowing blood to flow freely and preventing plaque and blood clots from sticking.

Unhealthy arteries are rigid, and their endothelium is sticky, attracting plaque and blood clots and causing diseases such as atherosclerosis and peripheral artery disease (hardening of the arteries of the legs and the arms).

How Well Does Your Endothelium Work?

Your chances of having endothelial dysfunction are high if you have any risk factors for cardiovascular disease, such as elevated cholesterol or homocysteine...are overweight, sedentary or smoke...or have diabetes. Everyone over age 40 should have a screening test for endothelial function.

One common test: Pulse-wave velocity. During this noninvasive test, a sensor placed on the wrist detects electric pulses that pass through the artery in advance of blood flow. The stiffer the artery wall, the faster the wave moves. This test can be provided by any type of physician and costs about $50 to $125.

How to Help Your Endothelium

You may be surprised to find out how easy it is to help your endothelium—and how easy it is to harm it.

In a landmark study published more than a decade ago, researchers from the State University of New York at Buffalo found that two or three hours after study participants ate a fast-food meal high in saturated fats and trans fats, their endothelial function (measured by blood flow) was reduced by half. This was a stunning finding—your body does know what you eat and knows it fast.

To improve blood vessel tone...

• **Eat a Mediterranean-style diet.** Consume a diet that emphasizes fish, poultry, legumes, whole grains, olive oil, fruits and vegetables—and minimizes intake of saturated fats and trans fats. The Mediterranean diet is high in antioxidants, omega-3 fatty acids and other healthful fats that can keep the endothelium pliant.

• **Exercise.** There is evidence that a sedentary lifestyle increases the risk for endothelial dysfunction. When people with heart disease begin a supervised exercise regimen, their endothelial function and blood flow improve significantly.

Lesson: If you're sedentary, get moving. Start by going for short walks. People who are already active should make sure that they participate in aerobic exercise (walking, jogging, swimming) for at least 20 to 30 minutes most days of the week.

Supplements for Your Blood Vessels

To prevent or treat endothelial dysfunction, consider taking all of the supplements listed below...

• **L-arginine.** This amino acid is the most important supplement for endothelial dysfunction. It helps the body produce nitric oxide, which relaxes and opens blood vessels. Nuts, soy and legumes contain L-arginine, although not enough to provide the same benefit as a supplement. To prevent endothelial dysfunction, take 500 milligrams (mg) to 1,000 mg of L-arginine daily. Those with atherosclerosis, peripheral arterial disease, high blood pressure or congestive heart failure can take 1,000 mg to 2,000 mg daily.

Brand to try: Perfusia-SR by Thorne Research (800-228-1966, *www.thorne.com*), a time-released supplement that ensures that your body maintains optimum levels of L-arginine throughout the day.

Caution: Don't take L-arginine if you have herpes (either herpes simplex virus-1 or herpes simplex virus-2), since it may trigger outbreaks...are pregnant or nursing...or immediately following a heart attack because it may lower blood pressure too much.

•**Garlic.** The body converts *allicin*, one of the compounds in garlic, to the compound hydrogen sulfide, which has a blood vessel–relaxing effect similar to that of nitric oxide.

Dose: 2.4 grams daily of aged garlic extract.

•**Fish oil.** Omega-3 fish oil has a mild blood-thinning effect and has been shown to improve endothelial function.

Dose: One fish oil supplement daily with 2,000 mg of EPA and DHA combined.

•**Vitamins E and C.** Studies have found that vitamins E and C, individually or in combination, prevented endothelial dysfunction after participants ate a fast-food meal. If you're not already taking them, try 400 international units (IU) daily of vitamin E and 1,000 mg of vitamin C.

•**Niacin.** Niacin, also known as vitamin B-3, increases HDL (good) cholesterol and enhances its ability to protect the endothelium. Look for nonflushing forms of niacin.

Dose: 500 mg twice daily. Niacin may elevate liver enzymes—so have your doctor monitor your levels.

Mark A. Stengler, NMD, naturopathic medical doctor in private practice, Encinitas, California, and author of the *Bottom Line/Natural Healing* newsletter. *www.drstengler.com.*

Chapter 11

MEN'S HEALTH

Urinary Incontinence: Not Just a Woman's Problem

An estimated 16% of women (including one-third of women 65 and older) have urinary incontinence (UI)—accidentally leaking a little bit of urine, often after coughing, sneezing, laughing or lifting something.

Men are notorious for holding things in—they're just too macho for UI, right? Wrong, says a new scientific study.

Latest finding: Millions of American men have either moderate or severe UI, reports a team of doctors in a recent issue of the *Journal of Urology.*

Here's what this finding means—and what other new research shows is the best way to control UI...

The Problem Men Don't Discuss

The study was conducted by Alayne D. Markland, DO, and her colleagues in the Department of Veterans Affairs Medical Center in Birmingham, Alabama, and the University of Alabama.

They analyzed health data from more than 5,000 men—and found that nearly 5% had moderate or severe UI, including 16% of men over 75. Moderate UI is leaking more than just a few drops at least monthly. Severe UI is leaking more than just a few drops every week or even every day.

Forty-nine percent of the men had urge urinary incontinence—having a strong urgency to urinate but not getting to the bathroom in time. Thirteen percent had stress urinary incontinence—coughing, sneezing, laughing or bending over, and leaking a small amount of urine. The others had both types of UI.

The study found risk factors for moderate and severe UI included...

•Aging (an 80% increased risk for every 10-year increase in age)

•Major depression (260% increased risk)

- **High blood pressure (30%)**

- **Prostate problems (20%).**

Aging might cause UI in several different ways, says Dr. Markland. The bladder—the storage tank for urine—can't hold the same amount of urine. The muscles that help retain urine become weaker. The body becomes less responsive to stimuli—including signals from the bladder that it's time to urinate. Or maybe a disease or injury, such as arthritis or a broken hip, slows you down on the way to the bathroom.

Experts don't know why major depression and high blood pressure are linked to a higher risk of UI, but it might be the drugs used to treat those problems.

Example: A diuretic for high blood pressure increases the amount of urine, increasing the likelihood of UI.

As for prostate problems—an enlarged prostate (benign prostatic hypertrophy, or BPH) can irritate the bladder. And 65% of men who have radical prostatectomy (the removal of the prostate to treat prostate cancer) experience incontinence up to five years after the surgery.

But whatever the cause, UI can be very distressing.

"I treat a lot of men with this problem—and they're often disturbed or even devastated by it," says Dr. Markland. Some men hate wearing diapers or pads, and won't go out in public, she says. Some take early retirement because they can't do their job without leakage. Some stop exercising because they don't want to leak. Some don't travel because they're afraid to get on a plane.

But if so many men have UI…and it's so disturbing to so many of them…why is it commonly thought of as only a woman's problem?

Example: One book on the topic, titled *The Incontinence Solution,* is subtitled *Answers for Women of All Ages.*

"This is an underreported problem among men," says Dr. Markland. "It's not a 'manly' topic—men usually don't tell doctors about it, and doctors usually don't ask about it.

"On the other hand, I find that men are less likely to put up with the problem than women. They want to do something about it now—they want to fix it."

And another recent study shows men can do just that—without drugs or other complicated medical treatments.

Self-Care Therapy That Works

In a study in the *Journal of the American Medical Association,* Dr. Markland and her colleagues treated 208 men with incontinence one year after radical prostatectomy. The men were divided into three groups.

One group received behavioral therapy—training the muscles used to stop the flow of urine (pelvic floor muscles), along with everyday strategies to decrease leakage. A second group received not only behavioral therapy but also two other treatments—in-office biofeedback (to help correctly contract pelvic floor muscles) and mild, daily, at-home electrical stimulation to the pelvic floor. A third group didn't receive any treatment.

Results: After two months, the group receiving behavioral therapy had a 55% average reduction in "incontinence episodes"—from 28 to 13 per week.

The group receiving behavioral therapy as well as biofeedback and electrical stimulation had almost the same level of improvement (51%, from 26 to 12 episodes per week).

The no-treatment group had a small 24% reduction, from 25 to 21 weekly episodes.

Good news: Behavioral therapy worked—and additional medical treatments didn't improve it, which means you don't have to use drugs for optimal care.

Here are Dr. Markland's recommendations for at-home behavioral therapy…

- **Train your muscles.** Strengthening the pelvic floor muscles—the muscles you tighten automatically when you stop the flow of urine—helps control UI. *To do it…*

1. Locate the muscles. You can locate them by stopping or slowing the stream of urine the next time you go to the bathroom. The muscles you use to do that are the pelvic floor muscles. Another way to identify them is to tighten the same muscles that you use to stop yourself from passing gas in public. Or stand naked in front of a full-length mirror and tighten the muscles—if your penis is moving up and down, you're using the right muscles.

2. Tighten the muscles. Several times a day, squeeze the muscles and hold the contraction for ten seconds. At first, you may not be able to hold for very long, but don't worry. Start by holding for a count of three—one Mississippi, two Mississippi, three Mississippi—then let go. Over time, build up to a count of ten.

3. Don't tighten the wrong muscles. You may have a tendency to contract your abdominal or buttocks muscles by mistake. Breathing normally and regularly while tightening the pelvic floor muscles will help you keep those other muscles relaxed. You can also put one hand over your abdomen to double-check that you're not tightening the muscles there.

4. Do the exercise 45 times a day—fifteen in a row, three times a day, holding each contraction for 10 seconds.

Smart idea: The best way to remember to do your exercises is to pick a few activities you do every day—such as taking a shower, brushing your teeth, watching TV or driving—and do the exercises during those activities.

• **Squeeze before you sneeze.** You can also use your pelvic floor muscles to help stop an incident of UI that's just about to happen.

With urge urinary incontinence: Instead of running to the bathroom, use those muscles to control the urge.

With stress urinary incontinence: If you squeeze those muscles right before you cough or sneeze, you can help prevent leakage.

• **Drink enough water.** You might think drinking less water is the way to prevent UI, but that's not the case. Overly concentrated urine irritates the bladder, increasing the risk of leakage.

Recommended: Drink eight, eight-ounce glasses of water a day. "Most people are not drinking that much," says Dr. Markland.

• **Drink less caffeine-containing beverages.** Caffeine is a diuretic—it causes the bladder to fill more quickly, which means you'll have to urinate more frequently. It also irritates the bladder directly.

Recommended: Limit your caffeine to 150 milligrams (mg) daily.

An eight-ounce cup of brewed coffee contains 100 to 165 mg. An eight-ounce glass of iced tea contains 70 mg, and eight ounces of cola has 46.

For optimal results: "Cut caffeine intake gradually," says Dr. Markland.

Example: If you're drinking three, four or more cups of coffee daily, switch those cups to half-caffeine, half-decaf. Gradually switch to decaf for all but one cup a day.

• **Keep a bladder diary.** "Keep a record of when you go to the bathroom and when you have leakage," says Dr. Markland. "Any time you write something down, you pay more attention to it. Maybe you'll say to yourself, 'Wow, I'm going 10 times a day. Maybe if I had stronger pelvic floor muscles I could postpone things a bit.'"

• **Expect results—but not immediately.** "Behavioral therapy isn't a quick fix," says Dr. Markland. "It takes anywhere from six to eight weeks to see an effect. Just stick with it and you'll see results."

Bottom line: "Nobody needs to suffer with urinary incontinence—it's not a 'normal' part of aging," she says. "But doctors aren't going to bring it up. You have to bring it up—and then you can start doing things to fix it."

Alayne D. Markland, DO, geriatric medicine, Department of Veterans Affairs Medical Center in Birmingham, Alabama, and associate professor in the Department of Medicine at the University of Alabama, Birmingham.

Erectile Dysfunction: New Findings You Need to Know

There are four new and crucial facts you need to know about erectile dysfunction (ED)…

1. If you have ED, you're more likely to die of heart disease than somebody who doesn't.

2. The leading drug used to treat ED might make you deaf.

3. A popular over-the-counter treatment for ED poses a risk to your heart.

4. There's an easy, drug-free way to prevent ED.

The CVD/ED Connection

CVD is an abbreviation for cardiovascular disease—the weakened or clogged arteries that can trigger a heart attack or stroke.

Like CVD, ED is also a problem of damaged blood vessels and poor blood flow—not to the heart, and not to the brain, but to the penis.

Now: A growing body of new research shows ED may be an early warning sign of CVD.

Researchers from Germany studied 1,519 men, comparing those with ED to those without the problem. *Over five years, those with ED were…*

- **1.9 times more likely to die of CVD**

- **2 times more likely to have a heart attack**

- **1.2 times more likely to be hospitalized for heart failure**

- **1.1 times more likely to have a stroke**

- **2 times more likely to die of any cause.**

"ED is an early predictor of cardiovascular disease," says Michael Bohm, MD, the lead author of the study and chairman of internal medicine in the Department of Cardiology and Intensive Care at the University of Saarland, Germany.

And Dr. Bohm's study isn't the only recent research to find a connection between CVD and ED.

- **Heart problems follow ED.** Men with ED will often develop heart problems within two to three years of being diagnosed—and experience a "cardiovascular event" such as a heart attack within five years, reported researchers in the *International Journal of Clinical Practice*. In a similar study, Chinese researchers found that 70% of men admitted to a hospital for a heart attack had ED in the six months prior to the admission.

- **Diabetes and ED lead to heart disease.** Men with diabetes and ED (compared with men with diabetes who didn't have ED) were 35% more likely to develop heart disease…19% more likely to have a heart attack…and 36% more likely to have a stroke, reported Scottish researchers in the *Journal of American Cardiology.*

- **More clogged arteries.** Men with ED had a 54% higher risk of having arterial blockage than men without ED—making ED a risk factor similar to high blood pressure and smoking, reported researchers from the Mt. Sinai School of Medicine in New York, at the annual meeting of the American Urological Association.

What to do: "Men with ED going to a general practitioner or a urologist need to be referred for a cardiology workup to determine existing cardiovascular disease and proper treatment," advises Dr. Bohm.

He points out that many men who see their general practitioner or urologist for ED are prescribed an ED medication…and it works…and they never show up at the doctor's again. And that's a big mistake.

"You are being treated for ED but not the underlying cardiovascular disease," he says. "You are being placed at risk. You need to ask your doctor to check for other risk factors of cardiovascular disease."

And if you take Viagra, Levitra or Cialis for ED, you may also want to ask your doctor to check your hearing.

Erection Gained, Hearing Lost

In a study of more than 11,000 men aged 40 and older, a scientist in the School of Public Health at the University of Alabama at Birmingham found that those taking Viagra (*sildenafil*) were twice as likely to have hearing impairment than those not taking the drug. There was no link between Cialis (*tadalafil*) or Levitra (*vardenafil*) and hearing problems.

No one knows exactly how Viagra might cause hearing loss, says Gerald McGwin, Jr, PhD, the study author. It might increase pressure in the middle ear...the biochemical changes that spark the erection might also damage structures in the inner ear...and it might activate genes that damage some of the cells that transmit sound.

"It is prudent that patients using these medications, specifically sildenafil, be warned about the signs and symptoms of hearing impairment and, if they have hearing problems, be encouraged to immediately seek medical attention to potentially forestall permanent damage," wrote Dr. McGwin in the *Archives of Otolaryngology Head and Neck Surgery*.

Caution: If you decide to stop taking Viagra, don't replace it with the natural supplement Enzyte.

A Shock to the Heart

Researchers from Loyola University gave the "male enhancement" herbal supplement Enzyte to healthy young men and then performed several EKG (electrocardiogram) tests in the hours after they took the pill.

They found a significant increase in the men's *QT intervals*, an electrical sign of a type of arrhythmia (irregular heart beat) that can cause sudden cardiac death. It's a side effect that caused the FDA to pull two drugs off the market: *cisapride* (brand-name Propulsid for ulcers) and *terfenadine* (the antihistamine Seldane).

"Clinicians should advise their patients to avoid this dietary supplement until more evidence is available," conclude the authors in the *Archives of Internal Medicine*.

Prevent ED—Take a Walk

You might prevent ED...and the risk of ED drugs...and potentially dangerous "male enhancement" products...by going for a daily walk, according to a recent study.

Men who were "moderately active"—for example, walking briskly 30 minutes a day, four times a week—were 65% less likely to have erectile difficulties than men who weren't, reported Erin McNamara, MD, of the Duke University Medical Center, at the annual meeting of the American Urological Association.

"We now know that erectile dysfunction can be a kind of marker for heart disease, because it's all the same concept—small blood vessels that are supplying the penis with blood, just like in heart disease," she says. "With exercise, you have increased blood flow, and increased blood flow to the penis is going to help with erections. That's the physiologic part of how exercise improves sexual function.

"Then there's the psychological part of it—I think people who exercise more feel better about themselves and have a better outlook, and that transfers into better sex."

Recommendation: "Brisk walking, four times a week, 30 minutes a day—it's really not that much!" she says.

Michael Bohm, MD, chairman of internal medicine in the Department of Cardiology and Intensive Care at the University of Saarland, Germany.

Gerald McGwin, Jr, PhD, Department of Epidemiology, School of Public Health, University of Alabama at Birmingham.

Erin McNamara, MD, urologist and study author, Duke University Medical Center.

How to Make More Sperm

Ten to 15% of couples who are trying to have a baby are infertile—they haven't been able to conceive after several months of unprotected intercourse.

What most people don't realize: When we think of infertility, we usually think of it as a woman's problem—a problem with ovulation or with the fallopian tubes, for example. But in an estimated 40 to 50% of cases, it's the man who has the fertility problem. And 9 times out of 10, the problem is a low sperm count—too few sperm to successfully conceive.

It's a problem most men would rather not think about.

"Men are certainly interested in potency and impotency, but are generally reluctant to consider their fertility status," says John Herr, PhD, director of the Center for Research in Contraceptive and Reproductive Health at the University of Virginia in Charlottesville. "They think a lot about the organ of semen delivery, but much less about its cargo."

But a test to determine sperm count can and often should be the first step for a couple who has been trying to conceive for several months without success, says Dr. Herr. "It reduces unnecessary testing for the women by first determining if the problem is most likely the man's."

Problem: A lot of guys are reluctant to present a semen sample at the doctor's office.

And that reluctance can be a real problem for couples in their mid-thirties or older who are trying to conceive…who need to have an answer about infertility fairly quickly…but the man hesitates to be tested…and months pass. (This is a very common scenario, says Dr. Herr.)

Solution: A new over-the-counter testing device allows you and your partner to accurately access sperm count in the privacy of your own home.

An Accurate At-Home Sperm Test

The product SpermCheck Fertility uses cutting-edge genomic technology to determine sperm count—and a recent study by Dr. Herr and his colleagues in the journal *Human Reproduction* shows that it was 97 to 98% accurate, compared with another home test on the market with 72% accuracy (which is not very accurate for an infertile couple). In fact, the new sperm test is just as accurate as the standard test used in fertility clinics.

The small, plastic device contains two "wells" for the sperm sample, and two windows where results are read, seven minutes after you insert the samples.

The color-coded results show when the sperm count is 20 million or higher (normal), below 20 million (low), or lower than 5 million (very low).

There are various types of people who might want to use the test, says Dr. Herr…

●**A couple that has infertility—in order for the woman to avoid unnecessary testing, by testing the man at home first.**

●**An older man who is contemplating a second marriage and wants to know if he's still fertile.**

●**A man who suspects he may be infertile because of one or more risk factors, such as testicular cancer or previous use of anabolic steroids.**

●**A man of any age who simply wants to know his sperm count.**

What to do: Take two home tests, says Dr. Herr.

If your first test is below 20 million, it might reflect a temporary situation—because sperm count varies with the time of day…the last time you ejaculated…your level of stress…your diet…and other possible factors.

"Wait a week and take a second test," says Dr. Herr.

If the test was below 5 million both times, see a fertility specialist immediately, and start sorting out your options, says Dr. Herr. Counts below 5 million are what fertility experts call severe *oligozoospermia*—a very low sperm count that signals a fertility specialist it's time to consider an assisted reproduction technique, such as in vitro fertilization (IVF).

Resource: As of this writing, SpermCheck Fertility is not yet available in drugstores, but is scheduled for a nationwide retail rollout. It is widely available online at many Web sites, including *www.spermcheckfertility.com, www.fairhavenhealth.com, www.amazon.com* and others. The price of the test is $34.95.

Improving Sperm Count

If you have a low sperm count and see an infertility specialist, he'll probably look for hormonal defects and other problems with medical solutions.

But there are natural ways to improve sperm count—and prevent a low sperm count in the first place.

"The effect of nutrition, stress and other lifestyle issues on male infertility is very much underappreciated," says Dr. Herr. For example, adequate levels of many vitamins and minerals are absolutely necessary for spermatogenesis, he points out.

If your sperm count is below 5 million, seek the counsel of a male infertility specialist, says Dr. Herr. But if your sperm count is borderline—hovering around 20 million—he suggests spending six months "tweaking your lifestyle" to see if the count can be improved.

- **Don't use tobacco.**

- **Eliminate alcohol.**

- **Don't use recreational drugs.**

- **Don't use the oral or injectable anabolic steroids** that some athletes have taken to enhance sports performance, particularly various forms of testosterone.

- **Keep your cell phone out of your pocket or off your hip.** Studies link this habit to decreased sperm count. It's best not to carry your cell phone on your body, says Dr. Herr.

- **Exercise regularly.**

- **Spend enough time in the sun to produce sufficient vitamin D,** a nutrient that boosts calcium absorption, a mineral that supports healthy sperm. (See pages 37–38 for guidelines on sun exposure and vitamin D.)

- **Avoid beverages with stimulants, such as coffee and energy drinks.**

- **Minimize your intake of refined sugar and carbohydrates.**

- **Maximize your intake of fruits and vegetables.**

- **Take a multivitamin-mineral supplement,** to ensure adequate intake of nutrients that play a role in spermatogenesis, such as vitamin A, zinc, magnesium and selenium.

- **Eat soy** (a phytoestrogen that affects sperm production) only in moderation.

- **If you're overweight, lose weight.**

- **Approach your fears and anxieties with strategies that promote self-mastery,** such as meditation, mindfulness, relaxation, and spending time in nature.

Many new studies support Dr. Herr's advice—and offer other options for creating plenty of healthy sperm.

- **Eat more antioxidant-rich fruits and vegetables.** Men with a low intake of antioxidants such as vitamin C (in citrus fruits and leafy green vegetables) and lycopene (in tomatoes, watermelon and pink grapefruit) had "poor semen quality," say Spanish researchers in the journal *Fertility and Sterility*.

- **Can the cola.** In a study of more than 2,500 men, those who drank more than a quart of cola every day had sperm counts that were 30% lower than those who drank less than a quart, reported Danish researchers in the *American Journal of Epidemiology*. The cola drinkers also ate more fast food and fewer fruits and vegetables, noted the researchers.

- **Lose weight.** Obesity is associated with fewer motile sperm (sperm that swim forward in a straight line) and fewer rapidly moving sperm, reported Argentinean scientists in *Fertility and Sterility*. The study also found that the semen of obese men had lower amounts of *neutral alphaglucosidase* (NAG), an enzyme involved with sperm maturation. Obese men may be able to improve sperm quality by losing weight, concluded the researchers.

- **Take your laptop out of your lap.** Ten to 15 minutes of working with a laptop in your lap overheats the scrotum to levels that can damage sperm, reported researchers from the State University of New York at Stony Brook in the medical journal *Fertility and Sterility*. Frequent use of laptops might contribute to reproductive problems, said Yefim Sheynkin, MD, a study researcher.

Important: A pad under the laptop didn't reduce scrotal temperature, but sitting with legs spread wide rather than together slowed scrotal heating.

Best: Place the laptop on a desk.

Also dangerous: Other factors can overheat the scrotum, such as tight underwear or tight pants, and saunas or hot tubs.

● **Avoid BPA.** Higher urinary levels of the plastic additive bisphenol-A (BPA) were linked to 23% lower levels of sperm, reported researchers from the University of Michigan in the journal *Reproductive Toxicology*. For more information on ways to reduce your exposure to BPA, see "The Dangerous Plastic Epidemic" on page 99.

● **Ejaculate daily.** Men whose sperm had a higher-than-normal level of DNA damage improved their sperm quality by ejaculating every day for one week before their partners' peak fertility, reported researchers at the European Society of Human Reproduction and Embryology. Prior to the daily ejaculation, 32% of the group's sperm was rated as damaged, on average. After the daily ejaculation, damaged sperm fell to 24% overall—with 80% of men dropping to 12% damaged sperm.

Why it works: The longer sperm stays in the testicular ducts, the greater its exposure to free radicals, which damage sperm.

John Herr, PhD, director of the Center for Research in Contraceptive and Reproductive Health at the University of Virginia in Charlottesville.

Yefim R. Sheynkin, MD, assistant professor and director of male infertility and microsurgery at Stony Brook University Hospital, New York.

Does Sugar Make You Less of a Man?

An updated version of "real men don't eat quiche" might turn out to be "real men don't eat sugar"...based on a recent study in which testosterone levels were found to plunge after men consumed sugar.

Researchers at the Harvard Reproductive Endocrine Sciences Center and Massachusetts General Hospital in Boston gave a glucose tolerance test to 74 men, average age 51. This is a standard test in which subjects drink a 50-gram, 75-gram or 100-gram dose of pure glucose (in this case, 75 grams), after which their blood levels of sugar and insulin are measured at 30, 60, 90 and 120 minutes. Researchers also measured testosterone levels and found that for 73 of the 74 subjects, testosterone was significantly reduced after drinking the glucose.

Aside from the fact that few men feel comfortable messing with their testosterone levels, another reason this is important is that it demonstrates how eating sugar could have a profound effect on the results of medical tests for hormones. Where men had previously been told that they didn't need to fast prior to having blood drawn for such a test, it appears that the results are skewed by blood sugar levels—so fasting may be necessary.

Testosterone, the major male sex hormone, affects energy, well-being and libido and helps maintain bone density, muscle mass and even red blood cell production. Testosterone production peaks in adolescence for males, and though there are considerable individual variations, it generally begins to wane around age 40 as men experience andropause. So it is no wonder that testosterone replacement therapy has become big business and is frequently prescribed by doctors who advertise themselves as specialists in "antiaging medicine."

Andrew L. Rubman, ND, thinks these findings make perfect sense. "Men are becoming aware of the fact that stressful lives, poor diet and poor lifestyle can depress testosterone levels," he says, "so it's wise to now look at yet another factor—sugar—that influences this important hormone." He notes that not only is this a significant finding that will likely impact how testing is done going forward, it also raises questions about how reliable results are for men whose testosterone levels were checked with a nonfasting test. Men may be doing themselves harm by taking testosterone that they don't need or by taking the wrong dosage.

Interestingly, the men who were the most "normal" in their response to the glucose test had the greatest drop in their testosterone levels, though Dr. Rubman says this isn't as surprising as it might seem. He points out that people who focus on eating pure and organic foods and who don't take many medications often can feel the effect of a single aspirin, whereas a drug abuser could take several codeine tablets and hardly notice. The effect with sugar is similar—a little bit has a greater impact in people who don't eat much of it.

His advice is to consider sugar a "recreational substance, to be enjoyed as a condiment and in close proximity to meals." Men taking testosterone replacement should ask their doctor for a retest of their levels after three days of simple sugar avoidance with a 24-hour urine catch and an overnight fast. (Your last meal before fasting should be light protein, such as chicken or fish and a salad.) "The results will be much more clinically significant and will help keep your doctor from giving you an unintentional overdose of testosterone," says Dr. Rubman, adding that "sugar is like cheap wine—the pleasurable effect is short-lived and the payback may not be worth it."

Andrew L. Rubman, ND, medical director, Southbury Clinic for Traditional Medicines, Southbury, Connecticut. *www.naturopath.org.*

Still Sexy at 75

Why stop at 75 years old—how about being sexy at 85, or even 95? Seventy-five to 95 was the age range of 2,783 men studied by Australian researchers, in a scientific paper on sex and aging in a recent issue of the *Annals of Internal Medicine*, one of the world's leading medical journals.

The researchers asked the men several questions: Is sex important to you? How many sexual encounters have you had in the last 12 months? Are you satisfied with the frequency of your sexual activity? *The answers...*

• **Yes, I like sex.** Forty-nine percent of the men considered sex at least "somewhat important."

• **Yes, I'm having sex.** Thirty-one percent of the men had had a sexual encounter within the past 12 months.

• **Yes, I want more sex.** Fifty-seven percent were satisfied with the frequency of their sexual activity—meaning 43% were having less sex than they wanted.

If so many older men still like and are having sex—and want more sex than they're having—why is it so commonly believed that a sexy older guy is a contradiction in terms... or, even worse, a "dirty old man"?

"We wrongly denounce old men as lovers," says Katherine Anne Forsythe, MSW, a sexuality educator in northern California, with a specialty in intimacy and aging.

"Men in the second half of life—men over fifty—have taken a heavy hit in our society regarding their sexuality," she continues. "That's because there are a pack of mistruths about men, age and sexuality perpetuated by advertising and cultural mindsets." *They include...*

• Sustained intercourse is for the younger man—older men just can't stay hard enough to "do it" for any length of time.

• Men in midlife-plus have to struggle to get and maintain erections.

• Men (and women) become asexual and lose interest in sex as they age.

All of these ideas are false, says Forsythe. "Men over 50, 60, 75, even 90 can be great lovers for three basic reasons. First, they are not in a hurry. Second, they put their partner's needs first. Third, they have learned that great sex doesn't have to include intercourse at all—it's only one option."

Sexy at Any Age

"Sexuality is a basic human need," emphasizes Forsythe. "We are born sexual beings and we die sexual beings—and that never changes, even in a youth-centric culture that refuses to acknowledge and support mature sexuality."

To keep in touch with your natural, life-long sexuality, Forsythe suggests...

●**Don't depend on pills.** "What man wants to chance not getting hard when the passion begins?" says Forsythe. "When the suggestion of failure looms, enter the he-roes—Viagra, Cialis and Levitra. But these are not magic pills.

"When dependence on the drug rather than your natural libido becomes the source of confidence, performance anxiety is height-ened—and the seed of worry grows. You might think, 'What if I forget the pill next time?' You might believe that you have lost your ability to get hard without the drug."

Better approach: "Yes, some physical changes happen as you age—it may take lon-ger to get hard, and you may not be as hard as you were when you were 25," says For-sythe. "But these physical changes can lead to creative thinking.

"What if you took the emphasis off erec-tions and off intercourse and off orgasm? What if intercourse became just one option on a menu of lots of options? What if you decided that great sex happened over hours, not minutes? What if playing and teasing and opening up to new erotic ideas became part of your regular repertoire?

"This type of creative thinking invites slow touch, and spending time to caress and tease."

And, she adds, it also invites talking to your partner...

●**Turn foreplay into foretalk.** Ask your partner what pleases her and what doesn't—and act on it, says Forsythe.

"Find out what really feels good—to both of you. Talk about ways the total experience can work better for the two of you—who likes what and when. That's far superior to two individuals trying to perform and get what they can out of it for themselves."

●**Celebrate the fact that you've gotten older—and better.** "Older men have quiet confidence and patience that allows for enjoy-ment of the entire sexual experience, his own and his partner's," says Forsythe.

"The mellowness of having been 'around the block' with age—and, most likely, a high number of partners—permits him to let go of having to rush and prove and perform.

"Plus, the physical aging process slows down the urgency that leads to the 'wham-bam-thank you ma'am' needs of his younger male counterpart. The necessity to ejaculate takes a backseat to touch and connection.

"Without those pressures, older men—and women—can see themselves as equal part-ners in a titillating, creative escapade.

"Creativity and curiosity allow variety in new erotic adventures—expanding play with oral sex, sampling new sex toys, play acting, even an evening of cuddling, fondling and holding.

"Everything can slow down or speed up, according to the needs of the partners. What could be sexier?"

Katherine Anne Forsythe, MSW, sexuality educator in northern California, with a specialty in intimacy and ag-ing, and author of *Sexperienced: Guide for the Seasoned Woman Seeking New Possibilities* (CreateSpace). *www.geta secondwind.com.*

Want to Attract Women? Wear This Color

What physical attributes make a man attractive to a woman?

Scientists have studied the ques-tion—and generated some answers...

●**Symmetrical facial features, with a prominent chin and cheekbones**

●**Symmetrical, muscular body—but not muscle bound**

●**Shoulders somewhat wider than the hips**

●**Slightly taller than average**

●**A relatively deep voice.**

But what if your features aren't symmetri-cal? What if you're a little bit flabby...your shoulders are slight...you're 5 foot 6...and when you sing in the shower you sound more like Barry Gibb from the Bee Gees than crooner Barry White?

You might want to wear a red shirt. Or at least a red tie.

Eye-opening finding: Women are more attracted to a man when he wears red, reports an international team of psychologists in the *Journal of Experimental Psychology.*

Seeing Red—And Loving It

The researchers conducted a series of seven experiments, involving 288 women and 25 men from the US, England, Germany and China.

In the first, 32 women and 25 men briefly viewed a black-and-white photo of a man in a polo shirt—but the photo was surrounded by a border of either red or white. *The participants were asked to answer three questions...*

1. How attractive do you think this person is?

2. How pleasant is this person to look at?

3. If I were to meet the person in this picture face to face, I would think he is attractive.

The researchers rated the participants' answers on an attractiveness scale. For the men, the red surroundings bumped up attractiveness ratings by more than 10%, a statistically significant result. But the men were color-blind—their ratings were the same whether the background was red or white.

In a second experiment, 55 women looked at photos of a man in a shirt that was digitally colored either red or green. Once again, the women rated the man in red as significantly more attractive. They also found the man in red more desirable—as in, they would be more likely to date, kiss and engage in sexual activity with him. (Don't head out to the Men's Store just yet, guys—read on....)

In a subsequent study, the researchers found that women perceived a man wearing a red T-shirt as probably higher in status (more powerful) compared with a man in a blue T-shirt. And once again, they found a man in red more generally attractive and more sexually attractive.

"Red is typically thought of as a sexy color for women to wear," says Andrew Elliot, PhD, of the University of Rochester, the study leader. "Our findings suggest that the link between red and sex also applies to men."

But Why Is Red Sexy on a Man?

"We found that women view men in red as higher in status, more likely to make money, and more likely to climb the social ladder," says Dr. Elliot. "And it's this high-status judgment that leads to the attraction."

Okay. But why does red signal a higher rank?

Two factors, says Dr. Elliot: culture and biology.

"In human societies across the globe, red has traditionally been a part of the regalia of the rich and powerful," he explains. "People in ancient China, Japan and sub-Saharan Africa all used vibrant red tints to convey prosperity and elevated status, and ancient Rome's most powerful citizens were literally called 'the ones who wear red.' Even today, businessmen wear a red tie to indicate confidence, and celebrities and dignitaries are feted by 'rolling out the red carpet.'

"Along with this learned association between red and status, there is a biological role for red," he continues. "In non-human primates, such as mandrills and gelada baboons, red is an indicator of male dominance and is expressed most intensely in alpha males."

Females of these species mate more often with alpha males, who in turn provide protection and resources.

"When women see red it triggers something deep and probably biologically engrained," Dr. Elliot concludes. "We say in our culture that men 'act like animals' in the sexual realm. It looks like women may act like animals, too, in the same sort of way."

The Gentleman in Red

What's the best way for a man to use red to increase his attractiveness to women?

Just a little red goes a long way, says Catherine Poole, CH, a color consultant and a clinical hypnotist in Abingdon, Virginia.

"Red is powerful and should be used carefully—seductively rather than aggressively," she advises. "Accents with red are better than a lot of it—wear a red tie, not a red suit.

"And hue is important, too—women favor cool reds such as brick-red and maroon over blazing, fire-engine red."

Her other recommendations...

• **Wear maroon for a romantic evening.** "Use a darker red if you want to create a romantic moment, with a feeling of warmth."

• **Wear bright red for active fun.** "If you're planning a day outdoors or an evening of dancing with the woman of your dreams, choose a bright red accent."

• **Wear a red tie.** "Presidents and businessmen communicate their power and status by wearing a red tie—and you can do the same," says Poole.

• **Or a red belt.** "Even just a strip of red can work," she says.

• **Wear red underwear.** "Even if the woman doesn't see it, you'll feel sexier and more confident."

• **Put a red pillow on your couch.** "This is a good example of using red as an accent," she says. "It's a nice touch, without overdoing it."

• **Take red to bed.** If you're trying to fire up a marital relationship, a red pillowcase can help, she says. "Or wear a pair of pajamas with some red in it."

Also helpful: Because red is so stimulating, you can use it for purposes other than attracting women, says Poole.

Exercising in the morning? Put on red socks. If you need extra energy to help you exercise in the morning, put on a pair of red socks, she counsels.

Working late? Change into red. If you're really tired but still have work to do, change into a red shirt.

Andrew Elliot, PhD, professor of psychology, Department of Clinical and Social Sciences in Psychology, University of Rochester, New York.

Catherine Poole, CH, color consultant to Reebok, Rubbermaid, Fresh Air Choice and other companies and brands, and a clinical hypnotist in Abingdon, Virginia. *www.catherine poole.com.*

Can Baldness Be Cured?

There's never been a better time for a man to be bald. A shaved head is considered a cool look, so much so that plenty of men who *have* hair are choosing to go without. That said, going bald doesn't work for everyone. Some scalps are more attractive than others and some men (women too) experience thinning hair as a blow to their self-esteem.

This is exactly the kind of vulnerability that marketers love to exploit. Products and services to fix hair loss abound. For example, the FDA has recently approved a laser device (the HairMax LaserComb) that can be used by men at home to help hair grow. The laser encourages hair growth by stimulating circulation in the capillary bed and hair follicle. All the user has to do is sweep the device over the scalp for 10 to 15 minutes at a time, three times a week. In the FDA application, the study authors admit they're unclear exactly how their device works, but they say that there is a possibility that it improves hair tensile strength and rate of growth (and even reduces graying) due to "improvement in micro-circulation."

The price for a seemingly easy fix for baldness? $495.

Some doctors are skeptical. Amy McMichael, MD, associate professor of dermatology and director of the Hair Disorders Clinic at Wake Forest University Baptist Medical Center, explains that while there is research showing that the device helps to stimulate hair growth, the results are "modest." In her opinion, the hair growth isn't significant enough to justify the price of the device.

So Now What?

Acknowledging that "hair loss can be very devastating," Dr. McMichael urges people who are upset about it to see a dermatologist, as there are some drugs that can safely be used off-label that may be effective. Also, Rogaine (a trace dose of the antihypertensive drug *minoxidil* in a solution or foam base) is now available over the counter.

Dr. McMichael stresses that if your thinning hair is bothering you, it is important to act quickly. "Most hair loss is progressive. It can get worse over time," she notes. "Early intervention is important. It's much easier to keep what you've got than to replace it."

Amy J. McMichael, MD, associate professor of dermatology/director, Hair Disorders Clinic, Wake Forest University Baptist Medical Center, Winston-Salem, North Carolina.

Self-defense: Learn about the symptoms at the Web site of the National Institute of Mental Health (*www.nimb.nih.gov*) and/or by speaking with your primary care physician or a specialty mental health professional.

James Paulson, PhD, associate professor of pediatrics, Eastern Virginia Medical School, Norfolk, and leader of a study of 28,004 men, published in The Journal of the American Medical Association.

New Fathers and Pospartum Depression

About 10.4% of American men become depressed either during their mate's pregnancy or within the year following the baby's birth.

Reason: Pregnancy and new parenthood are times of immense change and stress for both parents—including an overall rethinking of life roles, from being independent adults to parents who are responsible for an infant. Symptoms include persistent sadness and/or irritability…low energy…changes in sleep and appetite…persistent negative thinking…feelings of hopelessness…and loss of interest in hobbies.

Walk Your Way to Better Sex

Men who walked briskly for 30 minutes a day, four times a week—or did equivalent exercise—were two-thirds less likely to report sexual dysfunction than men who were sedentary. Exercise may increase blood flow in all parts of the body—including the penis—making it easier to get an erection. And men who work out tend to feel better about themselves, which may improve their sexual performance.

Erin McNamara, MD, urology resident, Duke University Medical Center, Durham, North Carolina, and leader of a study of 178 healthy men, average age 62, presented at a recent meeting of the American Urological Association.

Chapter 12

OSTEOPOROSIS

Tomato Juice—The New Super Drink for Bones

Leticia G. Rao, PhD, director of the Calcium Research Laboratory at the University of Toronto, had been studying bone health for decades.

For many years, her focus was on medications to treat the bone-eroding disease of osteoporosis—conducting cellular experiments on their ability to encourage *osteoblasts* (the cells that build up bone) and discourage *osteoclasts* (the cells that break down bone).

Meanwhile, over in the Department of Nutritional Sciences at the University of Toronto, her husband, A. Venket Rao, PhD, was studying the antioxidant *lycopene*, a type of plant pigment (*carotenoid*) found mainly in tomatoes that had been linked to the prevention of prostate cancer.

Dr. Rao (Mr.) asked Dr. Rao (Mrs.) to mix some lycopene in with those osteoblasts and osteoclasts to see what effect the antioxidant might have on bone cells. And she said yes to the proposed experiment, for better or worse results.

Surprising finding: "Lycopene stimulated osteoblasts to increase in number and differentiate into cells capable of making bone," she says. "And lycopene prevented osteoclasts from eating bone." These findings, she wrote in the *Journal of Medicinal Food*, may be important in the "treatment and prevention of osteoporosis."

That was back in 2003.

Now: In a recent study in the journal *Osteoporosis International*, Dr. Rao and her colleagues tested lycopene not in petri dishes but in people—and found that it has the power to protect their bones.

The Lycopene Effect

The researchers studied 60 postmenopausal women, aged 50 to 60. They divided them into groups, each with different levels of daily lycopene intake—from 30 to 70 milligrams (mg)—from both tomato juice and lycopene supplements. One group took placebo supplements.

Results: After four months, the groups drinking tomato juice or taking lycopene had a big increase in their blood levels of the nutrient. No surprise there.

But they also had significant decreases in levels of N-telopeptide (NTx). This compound is a biomarker for "bone resorption"—the higher your level of NTx, the more active your bone-destroying osteoclasts, and the more bone you're losing. In fact, NTx is such an accurate measure of bone loss, that it's used as a standard medical test for osteoporosis. If your NTx is high, your doctor will probably prescribe a bone-protecting drug, and tell you to take bone-protecting, bone-building calcium and vitamin D, says Dr. Rao.

Good news: The drop in levels of NTx among the lycopene groups was the same as that seen in studies of postmenopausal women taking bone-building calcium and vitamin D supplements. In other words, says Dr. Rao, lycopene may be just as effective as calcium and vitamin D in preventing and treating osteoporosis.

Needless to say, those taking the placebo didn't have a decrease in NTx. Just the opposite. They had an increase, indicating an accelerating destruction of bone.

And Dr. Rao isn't the only scientist who has found a link between lycopene and bone health.

Researchers at Tufts University conducted a 17-year study of nearly 1,000 people with an average age of 75 at the start of the study—and found that those with the most lycopene in their diets had a 47% lower risk of hip fracture than those with the least.

Why Lycopene Works

In the study by Dr. Rao published in *Osteoporosis International*, the women who increased their intake of lycopene also had a big increase in antioxidant activity and a big decrease in oxidative stress, the destruction of cells by molecules called reactive oxygen species (ROS), or free radicals.

ROS have been linked to the destruction of cellular DNA (in cancer)…arterial cells (in heart disease and stroke)…brain cells (in Alzheimer's and Parkinson's)…bronchial cells (in asthma)… retinal cells (in blindness-causing age-related macular degeneration)… and many other types of cells (and many other chronic diseases).

ROS also injures bone cells—and lycopene protects them.

"Lycopene has the highest antioxidant activity among all carotenoids, and ten times more antioxidant activity than vitamin E," says Dr. Rao. (It's no wonder that higher lycopene intake also has been linked to a lower risk of various cancers, heart disease, diabetes, rheumatoid arthritis, lupus, obesity and even death from any cause.)

Suggested intake: "Our findings are the first to show that lycopene intervention, given in capsule or juice form, supplying at least 30 mg/day, may decrease the risk of osteoporosis by decreasing oxidative stress and bone resorption," concluded Dr. Rao in *Osteoporosis International*.

"Therefore, our study suggests that lycopene may be used as a natural or complementary supplement" to "reduce the risk of osteoporosis."

And Dr. Rao—a woman in her sixties who has been diagnosed with osteoporosis—is taking her own findings very seriously. "I have increased my daily intake of lycopene to 30 mg based on the study results," she says.

You can get that amount from two eight-ounce glasses of tomato juice, or a lycopene supplement. Lycopene is also found in watermelon, pink grapefruit, papaya, guava and rose hips, but tomato juice or lycopene supplements are the most reliable way to get lycopene on a daily basis, says Dr. Rao.

If you decide to take a lycopene supplement, look for a product with Lyc-O-Mato, a highly absorbable formulation of lycopene used in many lycopene supplements—and the type used in the study.

Important: Her study found that increasing daily lycopene intake from 30 mg daily to

60 mg did not provide additional protection against bone loss. Two daily doses totaling 30 mg is "just right."

Leticia G. Rao, PhD, director, Calcium Research Laboratory, St. Michael's Hospital, University of Toronto.

The Real Secret to Strong Bones Is Not What You Think

Contrary to popular belief, the degenerative bone disease osteoporosis is not an inevitable result of aging.

Recent research: An important but overlooked cause of osteoporosis is an acid-forming diet.

Susan E. Brown, PhD, author of *Better Bones, Better Body*, discusses her insights…

The Acid/Alkali Balance

For survival, the body must maintain a balance between acids and alkalis, with good health depending on slight alkalinity. If the body's alkali reserves run low—a condition called chronic low-grade metabolic acidosis—alkaline mineral compounds are drawn from bones to buffer excess acids in the blood. The immediate benefit is that the body's pH (a measure of acidity or alkalinity) is balanced. But over time, if bone mineral compounds are not replenished, osteoporosis develops.

Bone-depleting metabolic acidosis is easily reversible through diet. Yet the average American diet is woefully deficient in many of the nutrients needed to balance pH.

To protect bones: Follow the dietary suggestions at right. It's generally best to get nutrients from food. However, to help ensure adequate intake, take a daily multivitamin/mineral plus the other supplements noted… and consider additional supplements as well.

Before you start: Gauge your pH with a urine test kit, such as those sold in some pharmacies…or use the Better Bones Alkaline for Life pH Test Kit.

Cost: $29.95 (*www.betterbones.com*, click on "Visit Our Store," or call 877-207-0232). An ideal first morning urine pH is 6.5 to 7.5. The lower your pH is, the more helpful supplements may be. As with any supplement regimen, talk to your doctor before beginning.

Bone-Supportive Diet

For a diet that builds bones…

• **Emphasize vegetables** (particularly dark, leafy greens and root vegetables), fruits, nuts, seeds and spices—these are alkalizing.

Daily targets: Eight servings of vegetables…three to four servings of fruit…two servings of nuts or seeds…and plentiful spices.

• **Consume meat, poultry, fish, dairy, eggs, legumes and whole grains in moderation**—they are acidifying.

Daily targets: One serving of meat, poultry or fish…one serving of eggs or legumes… one to two servings each of dairy and whole grains.

• **Minimize sugar,** refined grains and processed foods…limit coffee to two servings daily…limit alcohol to one serving daily. All these are very acidifying.

• **Fats neither increase nor decrease blood acidity**—but for overall health, keep fat intake moderate and opt for those that protect the heart, such as olive oil.

Important: It's not the acidity of a food itself that matters, but rather its metabolic effects. For instance, citrus fruits taste acidic, yet once metabolized, they are alkalizing.

Minerals That Bones Need Most

Bone is composed of a living protein matrix of collagen upon which mineral crystals are deposited in a process called mineralization. Key minerals, in order of importance…

• **Potassium** neutralizes metabolic acids and reduces calcium loss.

Daily goal: 4,000 milligrams (mg) to 6,000 mg.

Sources: Avocados, baked potatoes, bananas, beet greens, cantaloupe, lima beans, sweet potatoes.

●**Magnesium** boosts absorption of calcium and production of the bone-preserving hormone calcitonin.

Daily goal: 400 mg to 800 mg.

Sources: Almonds, Brazil nuts, kelp, lentils, pumpkin seeds, soy, split peas, whole wheat, wild rice.

●**Calcium** gives bones strength.

Daily goal: 1,000 mg to 1,500 mg.

Sources: Amaranth flour, broccoli, canned sardines with bones, collards, dairy, kale, mustard greens, sesame seeds, spinach.

Also: Supplement daily, at a two-to-one ratio, with calcium citrate or calcium citrate malate plus magnesium—increasing calcium intake without also increasing magnesium can exacerbate asthma, arthritis and kidney stones.

●**Zinc** aids collagen production and calcium absorption.

Daily goal: 20 mg to 30 mg.

Sources: Alaskan king crab, cashews, kidney beans, meat, oysters, sesame seeds, wheat germ.

●**Manganese** helps form bone cartilage and collagen.

Daily goal: 10 mg to 15 mg.

Sources: Beets, blackberries, brown rice, loganberries, oats, peanuts, pineapple, rye, soy.

●**Copper** blocks bone breakdown and increases collagen formation.

Daily goal: 1 mg to 3 mg.

Sources: Barley, beans, chickpeas, eggplant, liver, molasses, summer squash.

●**Silica** increases collagen strength and bone calcification.

Daily goal: 30 mg to 50 mg.

Sources: Bananas, carrots, green beans, whole grains.

●**Boron** helps the body use calcium, magnesium and vitamin D.

Daily goal: 3 mg to 5 mg.

Sources: Almonds, avocados, black-eyed peas, cherries, grapes, tomatoes.

●**Strontium** promotes mineralization.

Daily goal: 3 mg to 20 mg.

Sources: Brazil nuts, legumes, root vegetables, whole grains.

●**Vital vitamins**

The following vitamins enhance bones' self-repair abilities…

●**Vitamin D** is essential because, without adequate amounts, you cannot absorb enough calcium. Many people do not get adequate vitamin D from sunlight. Vitamin D deficiency accounts for up to 50% of osteoporotic fractures.

Daily goal: 1,000 international units (IU) to 2,000 IU.

Best source: A daily supplement of cholecalciferol (vitamin D3)—foods that contain vitamin D (fatty fish, fortified milk) do not provide enough and are acidifying.

●**Vitamins K-1 and K-2** boost bone matrix synthesis and bind calcium and phosphorous to bone.

Daily goal: 1,000 micrograms (mcg) of K-1…and 90 mg to 180 mg of K-2.

Sources: Aged cheese, broccoli, Brussels sprouts, collard greens, kale, spinach, green tea.

If you supplement: For vitamin K-2, choose the MK-7 form.

Caution: Vitamin K can interfere with blood thinners, such as *warfarin* (Coumadin)—so talk to your doctor before altering vitamin K intake.

●**Vitamin C** aids collagen formation, stimulates bone-building cells and helps synthesize the adrenal hormones vital to post-menopausal bone health.

Daily goal: 500 mg to 2,000 mg.

Sources: Cantaloupe, kiwifruit, oranges, papaya, pink grapefruit, red peppers, strawberries.

●**Vitamins B-6, B-12 and folate** help eliminate homocysteine, an amino acid linked to fracture risk.

Daily goal: 25 mg to 50 mg of B-6...200 mcg to 800 mcg of B-12...800 mcg to 1,000 mcg of folate.

Sources: For B-6—avocados, bananas, brown rice, oats, turkey, walnuts. For B-12—beef, salmon, trout. For folate—asparagus, okra, peanuts, pinto beans.

●*Vitamin A* helps develop bone-building osteoblast cells.

Daily goal: 5,000 IU.

Sources: Carrots, collard greens, pumpkin, sweet potatoes.

If you supplement: Choose the beta-carotene form.

Susan E. Brown, PhD, medical anthropologist, certified nutritionist and director, The Center for Better Bones and Better Bones Foundation, both in Syracuse, New York. She is author of *Better Bones, Better Body* (McGraw-Hill) and *The Acid-Alkaline Food Guide* (Square One). *www.betterbones.com.*

Watch Out for Osteopenia Overtreatment

You probably know someone who has been diagnosed with osteopenia—or you have received this common diagnosis yourself. To many women, the word sounds scary...but all it really means is that your bones are somewhat less dense than those of a normal young woman. It does not indicate that you have the level of bone loss associated with osteoporosis, nor that you are prone to having fractures in the near future.

Problem: Too often, osteopenia is treated as if it were a serious disease. This has led millions of women who are only in their 50s or 60s to take medication to prevent further bone loss—even though hip fractures do not occur until age 81, on average...and even though certain bone-building drugs appear to be linked to an increased risk for blood clots, heart-rhythm irregularities and, ironically, thighbone fractures and jawbone degeneration.

Such overtreatment is even more disturbing considering that the majority of women in their 50s have osteopenia—meaning that their bone density is 10% to 20% lower than that of an average 25-year-old. Endocrinologist Bruce Ettinger, MD, of the University of California Medical Center, San Francisco, says, "An X-ray test called a DEXA (dual-energy X-ray absorptiometry) is used to measure a person's bone density and compare it to that of an average 25-year-old—but of course a woman in midlife or beyond isn't going to have the bones of a 25-year-old."

Reason: A woman's bone density typically peaks between the ages of 25 and 30, and after that it slowly decreases for the remainder of her life. So bone-density scores that are slightly off are totally normal in your 50s.

The DEXA result is called a T-score. The average T-score of a 25- to 30-year-old woman is 0.0. Having a T-score of -2.5 indicates 25% lower bone density and is the beginning of the range at which osteoporosis is diagnosed. At this level, treatment is indeed often warranted. The controversy arises when the T-score is -1 to -2.4, which is the osteopenia range.

Breakthrough: Two new online risk-assessment questionnaires are helping counteract the assumption that osteopenia automatically requires treatment beyond the usual bone-building strategies of doing regular weight-bearing exercise and getting enough calcium.

How: By giving a more accurate sense of an individual's risk of experiencing a fracture of the hip or other bone within the next 10 years. Instead of relying solely on a woman's DEXA T-score to determine the need for medication, these tools help doctors and patients gauge the relative importance of various other factors that affect bone health, including age, height and weight...lifestyle (alcohol use, smoking)...ethnicity...personal health history and medication use...and family history.

Bottom line: The National Osteoporosis Foundation concluded that medication is appropriate only if risk assessment reveals that a woman has a hip fracture risk of at least 3%

or an overall fracture risk of at least 20% over the next 10 years.

What to do: Take either or both of these online risk-assessment tests yourself—they are free and simple to use and generally provide similar feedback. (Where the questionnaires ask for your "femoral neck BMD," fill in your DEXA T-score if you know it—otherwise, leave it blank.) *Then discuss your results with your doctor...*

• **For the World Health Organization "FRAX" fracture risk-assessment tool,** go to *www.shef.ac.uk/frax* and click on "Calculation Tool."

• **For the Foundation for Osteoporosis Research and Education fracture risk calculator,** go to *www.riskcalculator.fore.org.*

Bruce Ettinger, MD, emeritus clinical professor of medicine at the University of California Medical Center, San Francisco, and adjunct investigator, division of research, Kaiser Permanente Medical Care Program for Northern California.

Depression Raises Osteoporosis Risk

Researchers analyzed data on depression and bone density from 23 research projects in eight countries.

Findings: On average, people with depression had substantially lower bone density than people who were not depressed. The association was stronger in women—including young women—than men.

Theory: Depression elevates activity of *osteoclasts*, cells that break down bone.

Self-defense: If you have depression, see a mental health professional for help...and get periodic bone scans to screen for osteoporosis. Also, increase your physical activity—exercise helps guard against both depression and osteoporosis.

Raz Yirmiya, PhD, professor of psychobiology, Department of Psychology, Hebrew University of Jerusalem, Israel, and leader of a meta-analysis involving 23,468 people.

Go Ahead and Pound (On) Your Aging Bones

You can't turn back the clock, but according to some very interesting recent research, you can—and perhaps should—act as young as you feel when you play sports. The conventional wisdom has been that older folks should avoid high-impact sports like running due to the risk for fracture or other debilitating injury. But this research demonstrates that older individuals would benefit from more challenging exercise...and those who do work out hard build up their bone mineral density, resulting in stronger bones that are less likely to break.

Researchers at the University of Pittsburgh Medical Center used ultrasound scans to examine the bones of 560 male and female athletes, ages 50 to 93, who were in town to participate in the 2005 National Senior Games. Scans revealed that the athletes competing in high-impact sports had substantially higher bone mineral density than those who were there for low-impact events such as swimming and shuffleboard.

Pound the Pavement

Vonda Wright, MD, an orthopedic surgeon and the study's lead researcher, says these findings can be put to use by the rest of us. "We want you to pound your bones!" exclaims Dr. Wright.

Though conventional wisdom says older folks should accept that they can't do all that they used to do, she says that it's fine—even smart—to participate in the types of activities, including track-and-field and sports like volleyball, squash and basketball, where you bang your hands and feet fast and hard against balls or the ground. Jogging, running and jumping rope fit into this category, while walking or playing golf (even though the ball gets hit with some force) do not, because they involve a softer surface and/or a more leisurely pace.

Dr. Wright agrees that low-impact sports—such as swimming or pedaling a stationary bicycle—are beneficial for building strong muscles and a healthy cardiovascular system, but she notes that high-impact sports confer these same benefits and the advantage of increasing bone density.

Why Is This Good?

Our bones are made of organic and inorganic matter—the latter being *crystalline*, which literally sparks upon compression. Decades-old research has established that hard, quick impact creates a type of electrical current (called *piezoelectric*) that helps preserve bone density and, surprisingly, actually speeds the healing of fractures.

Dr. Wright offers this advice to people who want to maintain strong bones...

● **Give high-impact exercise a try**...but check with your doctor first, especially if you already know that you have low bone density. Those who can't or don't want to do high-impact exercise should still engage in brisk walking, which is also of benefit.

● **Don't become discouraged if it hurts a bit** (though be aware that severe pain is—as always—to be paid attention to). Generally speaking, it's okay to work through an ache such as the burned-out feeling of muscle you've worked hard...but if you experience sharp or acute pain, it's better to stop. Dr. Wright says that enduring a bit of soreness is a "relatively small price to pay for avoiding a fractured bone in the future."

● **Don't be a hero.** Start slow and easy and assess how your body is taking to your new regimen. A good way to get started is with short bursts of activity—a day on and a day off.

● **Don't let age deter you from participating in high-impact sports** even if your performance isn't as good as you'd wish. As Dr. Wright says, "Even at age 85, there's no evidence that our bodies are not capable of jogging—even if at that age it might look more like shuffling!"

Vonda Wright, MD, assistant professor, Department of Orthopaedic Surgery, University of Pittsburgh School of Medicine, and orthopedic surgeon at the University of Pittsburgh Medical Center. She is author of *Fitness After 40: How to Stay Strong at Any Age* (Amacom).

Calcium and Vitamin D: You Need Both for Healthy Bones

I f you want to keep your bones healthy as you age, it's important to be sure that you are getting vitamin D and calcium in adequate amounts—both, not one or the other.

Each has important health benefits on its own, while together these two are like "team health" for older adults. The US Department of Agriculture has recently published research highlighting how important it is to get sufficient calcium and vitamin D...so it's worth revisiting your daily regimen of these two vital nutrients.

Calcium + D = Strong Bones

More than 25 million adults (men and women) in the US either already have or are at risk for osteoporosis. It's common to equate osteoporosis with inadequate calcium, but according to Andrew L. Rubman, ND, inadequate vitamin D is a far more pervasive threat.

Here's why: When calcium levels fall, the body activates vitamin D. It gets sent to the gut to encourage better calcium absorption and to the kidneys to limit calcium loss in urine. Without enough of it, bones grow thin and brittle.

What You Can Do

This is why getting calcium alone isn't the answer to bone health—you must also get enough vitamin D. You can get it from foods (salmon, tuna, mackerel, fish liver oils, D-fortified foods such as milk, orange juice and breakfast cereals), and your body can synthesize it from 10 to 15 minutes of daily sun exposure. But the body's ability to manufacture vitamin D diminishes with age, and most Americans are short on it, so Dr. Rubman prescribes up to 2,000 IU daily of vitamin D3 (cholecalciferol) to many patients.

Note: The government-recommended intake was recently increased to 600 IU daily for adults ages 51 to 70—but some experts agree that this is still too low. In the meantime,

Dr. Rubman suggests asking your doctor to test your D3 level to see if you are deficient—especially important for seniors, he notes, as well as all people who may not be spending much time in the sun.

To get enough calcium: The official recommended calcium intake for American adults age 50 and older is 1,200 mg daily, and this is generally sufficient if your body is absorbing it properly. However, insufficient stomach acid due to aging or stress or, worse, the persistent use of acid-blocking medications can impede this process. A supplement is one option but perhaps not necessary—most people can get sufficient calcium from dietary sources. Cow's milk, even though it contains 300 mg of calcium per cup, is not necessarily the best choice since it is tough for many people to digest fully.

Here are some good dietary sources: One cup of goat's milk contains 325 mg of calcium…a cup of collard greens 350 mg… three ounces of canned salmon 180 mg… and a cup of boiled black-eyed peas 210 mg. That's practically a day's worth of calcium right there!

Getting sufficient amounts of these vital nutrients isn't hard—and it is vitally important. Remember—when it comes to bone health, calcium and vitamin D need each other to deliver the benefit.

Andrew L. Rubman, ND, founder and director, Southbury Clinic for Traditional Medicines, Southbury, Connecticut. *www.southburyclinic.com.*

Thyroid Problems—the Secret Risk Factor for Weak Bones

The thyroid gland is located in the neck, and it pumps out a hormone that is like the body's gas pedal—it controls the metabolic speed of just about every cell in the body. Including bone cells…

Surprising finding: Researchers in the Department of Internal Medicine at the Uni-

Vitamin D Testing

The best way to check if you have insufficient levels of vitamin D is to get the 25-hydroxy vitamin D blood test. Your score should be at least 30 nanograms per milliliter (ng/mL). This test is not routinely included in checkups, so you have to ask your doctor for it—and ask your insurance company whether it is covered.

Vitamin D deficiency is linked to osteoporosis, muscle pain, decreased immunity, and increased risk for respiratory infection, heart attack and some cancers. More than half of Americans are deficient in vitamin D—so whether or not you opt to get tested, it is wise to supplement year-round with 1,400 international units (IU) to 2,000 IU of vitamin D daily. Do not take high doses without your doctor's okay—exceeding 10,000 IU daily could lead to dangerously high blood levels of calcium.

Michael F. Holick, PhD, MD, director, Bone Healthcare Clinic and Vitamin D, Skin and Bone Research Lab, Boston University School of Medicine.

versity of California, Davis, analyzed health data from 3,567 people aged 65 or older.

They found 13% of the men in the study had subclinical hypothyroidism—their thyroid function was lower than normal but not low enough to produce symptoms.

They also found 2% of the men in the study had subclinical hyperthyroidism—their thyroid function was higher than normal but not high enough to produce symptoms.

But a closer analysis of the data showed that many of the men with hypo- and hyperthyroidism had a symptom after all—their bones were breaking two to three times more often than the bones of men without thyroid problems!

•**Men with hypothyroidism had a 231% higher risk of a fracture.**

•**Men with hyperthyroidism had a 327% higher risk of fracture.**

"Older men with subclinical hypothyroidism or hyperthyroidism are at increased risk for hip fracture," concluded the researchers in the *Archives of Internal Medicine*.

"Subtle changes in thyroid function could affect the bone over many years, perhaps causing fragility in the 'architecture' of the bone, the protein matrix that forms its underlying structure," says Jennifer Lee, MD, the study leader.

The Thyroid-Bone Connection

"The results of this study aren't surprising to me at all," says Richard Shames, MD, a physician in private practice in Cotati and San Rafael, California, and coauthor of several books on the thyroid, including *Thyroid Mind Power* (Rodale).

"Bone is constantly being broken down and rebuilt," he says.

"That process is controlled by the calcitonin hormone produced by the thyroid gland, and by the parathyroid hormone produced by the parathyroid glands, four rice-sized structures nestled right next to the thyroid.

"There is a skyrocketing epidemic of thyroid problems and of osteoporosis—and I believe these two epidemics are very closely related. Hypothyroidism causes gradual but long-term destruction of the bone. Hyperthyroidism destroys bone more quickly."

His recommendations…

• **Test your thyroid function.** Dr. Shames favors a home thyroid test that he says is far more accurate than the standard test offered by most laboratories, which often fails to detect hypothyroidism.

You can order the test (Basic Thyroid Profile) at *www.canaryclub.org*.

If your results indicate hypo- or hyperthyroidism, he recommends the following steps for self-care…

• **Take vitamin D.** Vitamin D helps thyroid hormone do its job, he says. He recommends at least 2,000 international units daily.

• **Take selenium.** This mineral helps convert the stored form of the thyroid hormone

(T4) into the active form (T3), Dr. Shames says. He recommends 200 micrograms extra daily.

• **Take carnosic acid.** This antioxidant—found abundantly in the herb rosemary—is crucial to thyroid function, he says. He recommends 80 to 90 milligrams daily.

For optimum results: A multi-ingredient supplement that provides vitamin D, selenium and rosemary leaf extract (and other nutritional factors for thyroid support) is Thyrosol Thyroid Support from Metagenics, says Dr. Shames. It is widely available online.

After using thyroid-supporting over-the-counter products for three to six months, retest your thyroid levels, he advises.

"If a self-care approach using over-the-counter products does not improve your hypo- or hyperthyroidism, you may need prescription medication."

Jennifer Lee, MD, assistant professor in the Division of Endocrinology, Diabetes and Metabolism, in the Department of Medicine, at University of California, Davis, associate physician in endocrinology and adjunct investigator in the Division of Research at the Kaiser-Permanente Oakland Medical Center.

Richard Shames, MD, physician in private practice in Cotati and San Rafael, California, and coauthor of several books on the thyroid, including *Thyroid Mind Power* (Rodale). *www.thyroidmindpower.com*.

The Best Beer for Your Bones (Yes, Beer)

You know calcium-rich, vitamin D-fortified milk is good for bones. But *beer*? It's famous for building bellies but certainly not bones.

Key fact not widely reported: Beer is the richest dietary source of the mineral *silicon*—and silicon is a must for healthy bones.

The Silicon Story

Nutritional scientists have dubbed iron and zinc essential minerals—but the typical dietary intake of silicon (which is not yet recognized as essential) is twice that of iron and zinc, points out Ravin Jugdaohsingh, PhD, a senior research scientist in the Department of Nutrition at King's College, London.

Kids get most of their daily silicon (68%) from grains.

Men get most of their silicon from beer, which (along with drinking water) supplies the most absorbable or "bioavailable" form of silicon—*orthosilicic acid*, or OSA. (Beer is rich in bioavailable silicon because it's made from silicon-rich grains such as barley or wheat that are processed in a way that liberates their OSA.)

Women get most of their silicon from bananas and string beans. But although there's a lot of silicon in those two foods, it's not always bioavailable. (For example, only 4% of the silicon in bananas is absorbed.)

But whatever the dietary source of silicon, a recent study shows that people who have more of it in their diet have stronger bones…

●**Denser hip bones.** Dr. Jugdaohsingh and his colleagues studied nearly 3,000 people and found that those with the most silicon in their diet had hip bones with the highest bone mineral density (BMD), a biomarker for stronger bones.

"Higher dietary silicon intake…may have salutary effects on skeletal health…that has not been previously recognized," he concluded in the *Journal of Bone Mineral Research*.

●**Supplementing with silicon.** New research also shows that adding silicon to the diets of women with osteoporosis (eroded, fracture-prone bones) and osteopenia (pre-osteoporosis) can strengthen bone.

Noting that "mounting evidence supports a role for silicon in bone formation," Dr. Jugdaohsingh and his colleagues studied 134 women with weak bones, giving them supplements of calcium and vitamin D or those two supplements and a silicon supplement. After 12 months, those taking silicon had the biggest boost in bone collagen, a protein in bones. (Calcium makes bones denser. Collagen makes bones more flexible and therefore more fracture-resistant—the bone bends but doesn't break.)

The results suggest that combining silicon with calcium and vitamin D "is of potential use in osteoporosis," concluded the researchers in *BMC Musculoskeletal Disorders*.

Pale Ale, Strong Bones

But as pointed out earlier, the most bioavailable form of silicon—OSA—is found in beer and water. In fact, a recent study in the *British Journal of Nutrition* showed that 64% of the silicon in beer was absorbed, much more than any other silicon-rich food, and as much as a silicon supplement. *And that well-absorbed silicon is building bone…*

●**More beer, more bone.** In a study of more than 2,400 people, men who drank 1 or 2 bottles of beer a day had hip BMD that was 4% higher than men who didn't drink beer, reported researchers from Tufts University in the *American Journal of Clinical Nutrition*. (However, men who drank more than 2 drinks per day had lower BMD—showing, as have many other studies on alcohol and health, that moderate alcohol intake can be good for you, but heavy intake is almost always bad for you.)

Because beer is such an important source of silicon in the diet, Charles Bamforth, PhD—professor of food science in the Department of Food Science & Technology at the University of California, Davis, and author of *Beer: Health and Nutrition* (Wiley-Blackwell) and many other books about beer and brewing—decided to conduct a study to find out exactly which beers supply the most silicon.

His findings were recently reported in the *Journal of the Science of Food and Agriculture*…

●**Malted barley beer is tops.** Beers with high levels of malted barley and hops are the richest in silicon.

●**Pale ales are best.** Among malted beers, pale-colored malts—so-called "pale ales"—have the most silicon (probably because they're heated less than darker malts).

●**Lagers are good.** "Lagers were quite high in silicon as well," says Dr. Bamforth.

• **Wheat beers are worst.** Wheat beers, along with stouts, porters and low-alcohol beers, contain the least silicon.

Bottom line: "First and foremost, drink the beer you enjoy," says Dr. Bamforth. "Trying to force down a beer you don't like for the sake of your bones isn't going to work. After all, even wheat-based beers still have significant levels of silicon in them, compared to other dietary sources. So choose the beer you like the best.

"Beer often gets a bad rap, but it is not empty calories," he continues. "It has nutritive value—and even one, 12-ounce bottle of beer a day can help you make sure you're getting enough silicon for stronger bones."

A Bottle of Water Works Too

Bottled water from natural sources can also contain high levels of OSA that might help prevent osteoporosis, says Dr. Jugdaohsingh.

Examples: Fiji Water (from Fiji) and Spritzer Water (from Malaysia).

New finding: In a recent study by researchers at the Center for Human Nutrition at the University of California, Los Angeles (UCLA), drinking Fiji Water for three months increased urinary silicon levels.

"Artesian aquifer bottled water is a safe and effective way of providing easily absorbed dietary silicon to the body," concluded the researchers in *Nutrition Journal*. And they recommended future studies to investigate "the mineral's potential as an alternative prevention or treatment to drug therapy for osteoporosis."

Also try: You could also take a silicon supplement—but most of them have low bioavailability, says Dr. Jugdaohsingh.

Best: Biosil, from BioMineral, according to a team of Belgian researchers at the University of Antwerp.

It is widely available online and in retail stores where supplements are sold. Follow the dosage recommendation on the label.

Ravin Jugdaohsingh, PhD, senior research scientist in the Department of Nutrition at King's College, London.

Charles Bamforth, PhD, professor of food science in the Department of Food Science & Technology at the University of California, Davis, and author of *Beer: Health and Nutrition* (Wiley-Blackwell) and many other books about beer and brewing.

Chapter 13

OVERWEIGHT

Natural Alternatives to Dangerous Obesity Drugs

There are lots of drugs aimed at helping you lose weight. They work by muting your appetite…or by blocking your absorption of calories…or by speeding up your metabolism. But all those weight-loss drugs have one thing in common.

They don't do you much good in the long run.

"Anti-obesity drugs fail to provide lasting benefits for health and well-being," writes Jason Halford, MD, at the University of Liverpool in England, in a review of current weight-loss drugs in the medical journal *Nature Reviews Endocrinology*.

Latest development: A study in the *New England Journal of Medicine* showed that the widely used weight-loss drug *sibutramine* (Meridia) increased the risk of heart attacks and strokes—after which the manufacturer pulled it off the market.

And Meridia isn't the only diet drug with recently revealed problems. There are now 12 cases linking liver failure to the fat-blocking drug *orlistat* (Xenical, Alli), with two people dead and three needing liver transplants. At the request of the FDA, the manufacturer has added warnings to the drug's label.

Natural Alternatives

But even though weight-loss drugs don't work very well and are sometimes dangerous, a weight-loss aid is not necessarily a bad idea, says Harry Preuss, MD, CNS, a professor in the Department of Medicine and Pathology at Georgetown University Medical Center and author of *The Natural Fat-Loss Pharmacy: Drug-Free Remedies to Help You Safely Lose Weight, Shed Fat, Firm Up, and Feel Great* (Broadway).

If you're overweight—and 7 out of 10 of us are—a safe and effective weight-loss aid can lend a helping hand in the daunting task of shedding pounds and keeping them off with diet and activity, says Dr. Preuss. "Natural weight-loss supplements can safely and effectively help you control your cravings, burn more body fat, and even stop the formation of new fat cells."

Here are several supplements that recent research shows can help you shed pounds and keep them off…

●**Multivitamin-mineral supplement.** Chinese researchers studied 87 overweight women aged 18 to 55, with one group taking a multivitamin-mineral supplement and another group taking a placebo. After seven months, those taking the supplement had lost 7.5 more pounds than the placebo group. (As an added benefit, the supplement takers also had lower levels of total cholesterol and bad LDL cholesterol.)

"In obese individuals, multivitamin and mineral supplementation could reduce body weight and fatness," concluded the researchers in the *International Journal of Obesity.*

● **Conjugated linoleic acid (CLA).** Researchers from Thomas Jefferson University in Philadelphia reviewed dozens of recently published studies on "dietary supplements commonly used for weight loss." One supplement they found particularly effective was conjugated linoleic acid (CLA), a component of the saturated fat in meat and dairy products.

CLA changes the way the body metabolizes fat, and studies show it can…

● Promote fat loss and muscle gain—without dieting or exercise, according to Swedish researchers in the *American Journal of Clinical Nutrition.* In their three-month study, participants lost five pounds of fat and gained two pounds of muscle.

● Stop weight-gain over the November-to-January holidays, according to researchers from the University of Wisconsin-Madison. "CLA prevented weight gain during the holiday season among overweight adults," wrote the researchers in the *International Journal of Obesity.*

● Target and decrease body fat in overweight postmenopausal women, according to researchers from Ohio State University.

Suggested intake: 3 grams a day, the amount used in most weight-loss studies, says Dr. Preuss.

●**Calcium.** People in a two-year weight-loss program who had the highest dietary intake of calcium and the highest blood levels of vitamin D (which aids in the absorption of calcium) lost an average of 11.7 more pounds than those with lower levels of calcium and vitamin D, reported Israeli researchers in the *American Journal of Clinical Nutrition.*

In a four-year study from researchers at the Creighton University Medical Center in Nebraska, postmenopausal women who took 1,400 milligrams (mg) of supplemental calcium gained 56% less abdominal fat. "Increasing calcium intake can prevent gain of fat mass," concluded the researchers in the journal *Nutrition & Metabolism.*

And in a study of 63 overweight women with low dietary calcium intake (below 800 mg daily), supplementing the diet with 1,200 mg of calcium and 400 IU of vitamin D sparked weight loss of 13.2 pounds over 15 weeks—while women who didn't receive the supplement lost only 2.2 pounds.

"Our hypothesis is that the brain can detect the lack of calcium and seeks to compensate by spurring caloric intake, which obviously works against the goals of any weight-loss program," says Angelo Tremblay, PhD, of Laval University in Canada, the study leader. "Sufficient calcium intake seems to stifle the desire to eat more and is important to ensure the success of any weight-loss program."

Red flag: More than half of all overweight women don't get 800 mg of calcium a day.

●**Green tea and green tea extract.** In a study of 10 overweight men, taking a green tea extract of *epigallocatechin gallate* (EGCG) boosted fat burning after a meal by 33%, reported Swiss researchers in the *European Journal of Clinical Nutrition.*

And in a recent study by Italian researchers, fifty overweight people took either a green tea extract or a placebo for three months while following a low-calorie diet. Those taking the extract lost an average of 31 pounds; those taking the placebo lost 11 pounds. Green tea extract "appears to be a safe and effective tool for weight loss," concluded the researchers in *Alternative Medicine Review.*

EGCG works by boosting the activity of the sympathetic nervous system—but without boosting heart rate or high blood pressure, says Dr. Preuss.

Suggested intake: 325 mg EGCG daily, says Dr. Preuss—the amount used in many studies that show a green tea extract can aid weight loss and help prevent weight regain.

Harry Preuss, MD, CNS, professor in the Department of Medicine and Pathology at Georgetown University Medical Center, Washington DC, and author of *The Natural Fat-Loss Pharmacy* (Broadway).

Angelo Tremblay, PhD, professor, Department of Social and Preventive Medicine, Laval University, Quebec, Canada.

Melt Away Abdominal Fat

The size of your waist is believed to be a better indicator of health problems than the number on the scale or your body mass index (BMI), a measure of weight relative to height.

It is far more healthful to have a "pear" body shape (fat stored around the hips, buttocks and thighs) than an "apple" shape (fat stored around the middle). Both men and women with apple shapes (men with waists of 40 inches or more and women with waists of 35 inches or more) are more likely to be insulin resistant—a condition in which the cells do not receive insulin properly and which often leads to diabetes—than those with smaller waists. In fact, research shows that having just an extra four inches around your waist increases your risk for heart failure by 15%. Belly fat is associated with a greater risk for stroke, and every additional two inches around the waist in men increases the risk for deep-vein thrombosis and pulmonary embolism (blockage of the main artery of the lungs) by 18%.

Why abdominal fat is so bad: This fat, also known as visceral fat, produces hormones that work against you in the following ways…

- **Releasing free fatty acids** (the breakdown product of fat cells that circulate in the bloodstream)

- **Decreasing insulin sensitivity** (the degree to which your cells recognize insulin and use it properly)

- **Increasing *cytokines,*** compounds that contribute to inflammation and insulin resistance, including *resistin,* another chemical that reduces insulin sensitivity

- **Decreasing hormones** such as *leptin* that help regulate metabolism and appetite.

Help Is on the Way

Abdominal fat often is associated with hormonal imbalances, such as high insulin (yes, even insulin is a hormone)…high cortisol… and high estrogen. Once the vicious cycle of abdominal weight gain and hormonal imbalance begins, it is hard to stop—especially because each one causes the other.

A hormone-balancing protocol may help those who are caught in this cycle. The protocol is followed for at least two months and up to six months. The results can be impressive.

The Protocols

If you are a man with a waist measurement of 40 inches or more or a woman with a waist of 35 inches or more, ask your doctor to test your levels of cortisol, insulin and estrogen.

Note: Excess estrogen is not just a female problem. While high levels most often occur in women younger than 45 and in postmenopausal women, they can appear in men as well, especially when made worse by the presence of environmental estrogens, compounds found in many plastic household products.

If you have excess estrogen…

High levels of estrogen, particularly combined with low levels of progesterone, can cause abdominal fat. Either a male or female patient with excess estrogen, especially in conjunction with low levels of progesterone (a condition called estrogen dominance), can benefit from an estrogen detox program. This includes eating two to three daily servings of cruciferous vegetables (such as broccoli, cabbage, Brussels sprouts, cauliflower and kale), which contain plant compounds called *indoles* that help regulate estrogen metabolism and can make estrogen less toxic.

Supplements that help include *indole-3-carbinol* and *diindolylmethane* (DIM). These phytochemicals in supplement form are similar to those found in cruciferous vegetables. Patients take 300 milligrams (mg) to 400 mg daily of indole-3-carbinol and 200 mg to 400 mg of DIM daily. Both the food (for the fiber) and the supplements are recommended because it's difficult to get enough of these phytochemicals through food only.

For women who are perimenopausal or menopausal (and some men with prostate problems) with this type of hormonal imbalance, I also may prescribe a bioidentical progesterone cream.

If you have insulin resistance…

Abdominal fat and insulin resistance often go together like the proverbial chicken and egg, and it isn't always easy to know which one was there first. Insulin resistance increases the chances of developing type 2 diabetes and cardiovascular disease. It can be effectively treated by eating a diet with high-fiber foods, including vegetables, legumes and grains. Regular exercise also helps keep insulin resistance under control. Insulin-resistant patients can try PGX, a form of glucomannan fiber.

Brand to try: Natural Factors PGX Daily (800-322-8704, *www.naturalfactors.com* for a store locator).

Also helpful: Chromium picolinate, a trace mineral (start with 500 micrograms [mcg] daily and increase to 1,000 mcg daily, if needed), which can help balance blood sugar levels… and resveratrol (50 mg to 100 mg daily), which improves insulin resistance.

If you have high levels of cortisol…

Cortisol, the major stress hormone produced by the adrenal glands, can signal the body to store fat around the middle. For patients whose blood tests reveal high cortisol levels, a basic program of aerobic exercise (30 minutes daily of swimming, jogging, bicycling or walking)…strength training… stress reduction…and deep breathing have all been found to lower cortisol levels. The herb ashwagandha also can help normalize blood cortisol levels.

Brand to try: Sensoril Ashwagandha made by Jarrow Formulas (310-204-6936, *www.jarrow.com* for a store locator). Take one 225-mg capsule daily. Women who are pregnant or breast-feeding should not take this herb.

Mark A. Stengler, NMD, naturopathic medical doctor in private practice, Encinitas, California, and author of the *Bottom Line/Natural Healing* newsletter. *www.drstengler.com.*

Do Antibiotics Make You Fat?

Everyone has a theory about why Americans are so fat. Here's one you may not have heard: Homeopathy expert Dana Ullman, MPH, suggests that our country's collective weight gain may be directly related to our overuse of antibiotics.

One of the ways Ullman validates his reasoning is by pointing out that antibiotics are already known to make animals fat. Farmers regularly dose livestock with antibiotics—the ostensible purpose is to ward off disease, but these drugs also disrupt metabolism of fat by altering the balance of microbes in the animals' guts. The result is fatter cows—not to mention fatter profits for the food industry. Ullman suspects the same processes are at work when humans take antibiotics that end up disrupting digestion.

Too Much of a Good Thing?

We already know that when it comes to antibiotics, we're taking the bad with the good. There's no question that these drugs can bring about miraculous recovery from illnesses that once claimed many lives. They play an important role in modern medicine. But scientists have long voiced concern that antibiotics are also destructive—especially when used indiscriminately, which they often are. Patients "demand" antibiotics whenever they have a sore throat or a cough, for example, and doctors too often comply—research verifies that doctors write untold thousands of antibiotic prescriptions annually for people with colds, the vast majority of which are caused by viruses that antibiotics can't fight! Remember that antibiotics are poisons, albeit useful ones.

While it was once controversial, no one today disputes that the excessive use of antibiotics has fueled antibiotic resistance and the evolution of superbugs such as antibiotic-resistant *Staphylococcus aureus* and tuberculosis. Antibiotics also disrupt intestinal function, and, as you'll see, this is the crux of the antibiotics-obesity connection.

Making the Case: Antibiotics and Obesity

While they suppress bad disease-causing microbes, antibiotics simultaneously decrease beneficial flora, leading to unintended consequences. Women know, for instance, that taking antibiotics for an infection often brings on a vaginal yeast infection, the result of diminishing the organisms that normally control the body's yeast population. That's not the only example, however.

Antibiotics are substantially eradicating *Helicobacter pylori* bacteria here in the US and in other developed countries. This was huge news when it was discovered in the 1980s that certain strains of H. pylori are linked with ulcers and gastric cancer. Yet eradicating H. pylori has some surprise consequences, since these bacteria are also involved in mediating *ghrelin*, an important hormone involved in hunger and fat regulation.

Also, it's known that in the gut—most particularly the colon—many species of healthful bacteria are involved in metabolizing and storing fat and other nutrients. Digestion is disturbed when the normal bacteria balance gets changed, leading to problems such as constipation and malabsorption of nutrients higher up in the system. It's not much of a leap to wonder whether all this is contributing to rising obesity rates.

Scientists Agree

Ullman is in excellent company with his questions concerning antibiotics and obesity. Research from diverse places, including Cornell University, Emory University, the University of Colorado and Stanford University School of Medicine conclude that antibiotics are related to inflammatory processes that eventually result in metabolic syndrome and diabetes, both related to excess weight. At the Marseille School of Medicine in France, investigators using data from the food industry concluded that antibiotics act as growth promoters in animals—the researchers speculate that the drugs might likewise be contributing to the obesity epidemic in humans.

One cycle of antibiotics will not make you fat, Ullman concedes. Yet physicians commonly prescribe repeated rounds of these drugs for recurrent infections, acne and more. By disturbing broad swaths of microbes, frequent use of antibiotics will eventually render your inner ecosystem far more vulnerable.

If you must have antibiotics, talk to your medical doctor or a naturopathic physician about how to restore the proper balance of bacteria to your body. If you are obese, you may also want to consider having your gut bacteria levels checked as well.

Ullman emphasizes that antibiotics must be handled with great care and used sparingly. "Antibiotic" literally means "anti-life," he notes. Should it come as a surprise that they could be dangerous in more ways than we know?

Dana Ullman, MPH, founder and president of the Foundation for Homeopathic Education and Research and coauthor of *The Homeopathic Revolution: Why Famous People and Cultural Heroes Choose Homeopathy* (North Atlantic Books). He is director of Homeopathic Educational Services, Berkeley, California. *www.homeopathic.com.*

Common Medical Problems That Cause Obesity

Many obese people suffer for years trying and failing at diet after diet, but what they don't know is that there may be an underlying medical condition that is thwarting their efforts. If they address that challenge, weight loss can be achieved.

Jared Zeff, ND, LAc, a naturopathic doctor and adjunct professor of naturopathic clinical theory at Bastyr University in Seattle, says that he sees four common medical problems over and over that lead, directly or indirectly, to uncontrollable weight gain. In fact, he says, he sees these problems not only in people who are obese but also in many who are simply overweight. *Here's what they are...*

● **Food intolerances mess up digestion.** Dr. Zeff says that just about all the obese patients he has treated have malfunctioning digestive systems, most often associated with an intolerance to one or more common foods, such as milk protein (casein)...eggs...potatoes...certain fruits...soy...wheat...and meat. When you eat foods that your body doesn't tolerate well, it ends up affecting your ability to digest other foods that wouldn't normally be troublesome and interferes with nutrient absorption—the resulting undernourishment leaves people so hungry that they remain ever on the prowl for more food.

Dr. Zeff's advice: You can identify your intolerances by temporarily following this strict diet—it's tough but worth it.

What you can eat: Fish (only the kind that has fins, not shellfish or other types)... most vegetables (but no potatoes, corn or soy—or products made from them)...brown rice...and the grains quinoa and millet. Walnut oil and other nut oils are okay (assuming that you aren't allergic to nuts), but avoid olive oil since it's from fruit. Avoid everything else including wheat...eggs...dairy products...animal meats...all fruit...alcohol...and all added sugars aside from a bit of pure maple syrup, which you can use as a sweetener.

You can expect some digestive discomfort, such as bloating and bowel changes, for the first few days, but within 10 days or so, you'll feel better. In fact, you are likely to feel quite wonderful!

At about two weeks, you should start to add back the foods you eliminated, one at a time—a new one every three to four days. Foods that bring digestive distress are the ones you are intolerant of, and you'll need to give them up permanently.

● **Sluggish thyroid slows metabolism.** Another biological problem that leads to obesity is a sluggish thyroid gland, which may be your problem if you have such symptoms as excess weight, tiredness, feeling cold, depression, and coarsening hair or having your hair fall out. This often goes undetected even after thyroid testing, since doctors may not factor in the subtleties of hormone test results.

Dr. Zeff's advice: Noting first that treatment must be individualized, Dr. Zeff says that a typical strategy might be to start by enhancing iodine nutrition with a daily dose of seaweed powder (one-half to one teaspoonful mixed in water or juice or sprinkled on foods as a seasoning).

Caution: Do not do this if you are allergic to iodine. Then Dr. Zeff might prescribe weekly acupuncture and/or a variety of approaches to stimulate thyroid function.

● **Adrenal fatigue affects blood sugar.** Often the result of too much stress for too long, adrenal fatigue is characterized by exhaustion (especially in mid-afternoon), low blood pressure and a tendency toward low blood sugar—leading to overeating and sugar craving. Adrenal fatigue is diagnosed through a variety of blood tests.

A tip-off: Dr. Zeff says people with adrenal fatigue often feel more comfortable wearing sunglasses much of the time because their pupils dilate too easily.

Dr. Zeff's advice: Again, treatment varies, but Dr. Zeff says that he commonly treats adrenal fatigue with different products that help rebuild and strengthen the adrenal glands. Specifically, he often recommends a blend of licorice root, ginseng, *Eluthrococcus* (also known as Siberian ginseng) or other similar adrenal support...or he may give adrenal gland substance in pill form, either a pure adrenal tissue extract or one combined with nutrients that the adrenals need to function well (vitamin C, certain B vitamins and zinc). It may take six weeks to three months to normalize adrenal function, says Dr. Zeff, adding that it is important to correct life stress factors as well so that you don't start the same cycle again.

• **Overeating as self-medication.** It's no surprise that there often are psychological issues behind obesity, leading people to "self-medicate" with food—perhaps trying to dull emotional angst from a difficult childhood or an unsatisfactory marriage. Dr. Zeff says that the big reason people do this is that it not only fills an emotional void, but it also works physiologically. Having food in your gut encourages production of serotonin (much of which is manufactured in the intestine), the brain chemical that increases a sense of well-being. But of course, it eventually backfires as weight—and health problems—pile on.

Dr. Zeff's advice: Happily, there is a way to get the feel-good effect without overeating. Tryptophan, an amino acid, also increases serotonin and enhances satiety. For some people, the 5-HTP version of this amino acid works better—your doctor will determine which is right for you. Dr. Zeff cautions that these supplements should be taken only under the supervision of a knowledgeable health-care professional and should not be taken with Prozac or other selective serotonin reuptake inhibitor (SSRI) antidepressants.

...And Then What?

While there are other, less common biological problems behind obesity, these are the principal ones, says Dr. Zeff. He says that patients are encouraged when they see weight beginning to come off as these problems are addressed and treated and, of course, they continue to lose even more when he puts them on a diet of mostly proteins, vegetables and a bit of fruit. He advises avoiding grains, particularly wheat, potatoes, sugars and other simple carbs that produce a lot of insulin. As for exercise, patients start with whatever they can tolerate, adding longer and more intense workouts as they lose weight and gain more energy.

Obesity is a complex issue, to be sure, says Dr. Zeff, but he has seen time and again that it can be effectively addressed with strategies such as these. You can find a naturopathic physician at *www.naturopathic.org*, the Web site for the American Association of Naturopathic Physicians.

Jared Zeff, ND, LAc, naturopathic doctor in private practice and adjunct professor of naturopathic clinical theory at Bastyr University, Seattle.

Graze Your Way to Weight Loss

Somewhere between the rigidity of eating three meals a day with nothing in between and the self-indulgence of mindless snacking is a middle ground called grazing. Now research from the University of Texas at Austin says that grazing is a good thing—in fact, the more frequently people eat, the more likely they are to be healthy.

Using data from the American Time Use Survey, conducted by the US Bureau of Labor Statistics, the report found that those who spread the amount they eat over more time have a body mass index (BMI) that is 0.2 lower, on average, than those who spend less time eating...and they also have better self-reported health. While the difference in BMI is not huge, for a person of average height it results in a few pounds less weight.

Good Grazing...Bad Grazing

You might think that this study's findings go against the grain...after all, isn't too much eating the cause, in part, of weight gain and many health problems? But science supports grazing, says David Grotto, RD, LDN, a former spokesperson for the American Dietetic

Association and author of *101 Foods That Could Save Your Life*. "When there are large gaps of time between meals, the body goes into a self-preservation mode, reserving calories and storing fat," he explains. "If you eat more frequently, your body ratchets up metabolism and burns calories. Also, when you graze, you're less apt to overeat at the next meal." Note the really important part of what Grotto said—eating more frequently…not eating more.

Grotto has some suggestions on how to keep grazing healthful. First and foremost, he says, it is important to stay aware of what and how often you eat. "Don't think you can simply graze to your heart's content," he says. "Research clearly shows that calories consumed shouldn't be greater than energy spent if you are to avoid gaining weight."

The best grazing foods, he says, contain protein, fiber, monounsaturated fats and/or slow-digesting, complex carbohydrates. These will make you feel fuller than other foods, and you'll be inclined to consume fewer calories. Nuts are a good choice as they contain monounsaturated fats, which take a long time to digest. One study showed that women who ate one to two ounces of nuts a day lost more weight and kept it off longer than women who did not eat nuts. To avoid monotony, mix a variety of nuts (almonds, walnuts and pistachios, for example) with oat cereal, dried fruit and dark chocolate. Keep some handy in a resealable bag and eat a few at a time. Also healthy are snacks like apple slices, cheese and whole-grain crackers, and peanut or almond butter.

Andrew L. Rubman, ND, has a dissenting opinion on the greatness of grazing: "It isn't necessary to eat all day to keep the body supplied with a steady stream of healthful nutrients. If you don't skip breakfast, lunch or dinner…consistently make smart dietary choices…and take the time to chew thoroughly during meals, you'll digest your food more completely, have a steady stream of nutrients coming into your body from the gastrointestinal tract, and not feel the need to graze." However, he adds, if you can't seem to fit in three

healthful meals a day, a certain amount of grazing may be a good short-term solution.

David Grotto, RD, LDN, nutrition counseling consultant and former spokesperson for the American Dietetic Association and author of *101 Optimal Life Foods* (Bantam).

Andrew L. Rubman, ND, medical director, Southbury Clinic for Traditional Medicines, Southbury, Connecticut. *www.southburyclinic.com*.

Want to Resist That Extra Helping? Tighten a Muscle! (It Really Works)

Weight gain—the relentless, year after year accumulation of extra pounds—consists of many small moments of weak willpower, of knowing better but eating worse.

Two scoops of ice cream instead of one…a butter-laden muffin instead of an apple…a bagful of chips instead of a handful.

Of course, you wish you had more willpower…more ability to resist fatty, sugary, salty temptation. But the flesh is weak.

Striking research finding: No, the flesh is *strong*.

New and surprising scientific research shows that you can put the power back in willpower simply by tightening your muscles—enabling you to make healthier food choices.

Here's all you need to know about the scientific secret of boosting your inner strength by tensing a muscle…

Tense Your Muscles, Change Your Mind

"For most people, self-control poses a dilemma," says Aparna Labroo, PhD, a psychologist who specializes in the power of feelings to influence decisions, and professor of marketing at Rotman School of Management, University of Toronto.

"For instance, dieters face a self-control dilemma whenever they have to say no to a pleasurable, indulgent food in favor of a less

255

tasty but healthy food, in order to achieve long-term weight loss."

To overcome such self-control dilemmas, we try to increase our willpower, and we do that in various ways, she says. For example, you might try to banish thoughts of temptation and think instead about the long-term benefits of restraint.

And as you try to think your way to greater resolve, says Dr. Labroo, you might also clench your fist or grit your teeth or otherwise scrunch your muscles—reflecting the inner turmoil of your "self-resolve dilemma."

"But," she asks, "rather than reflecting the turmoil that results from inner combat, could such actions also help a person keep turmoil at bay? Might clenching your fists, gritting your teeth or scrunching your muscles also firm willpower and improve self-control?"

She's asking those questions because she's an expert in a new area of psychology called "embodied cognition"—the recognition that the body can influence the mind, rather than the other way around.

Example: When you're happy, you smile. By intentionally smiling—even when you're not in a good mood—you can feel yourself become happier.

"Firmed muscles that usually result from trying to recruit willpower—for example, clenched fists—could be used to prime willpower, enabling you to engage more effectively in self-control," says Dr. Labroo.

To find out if that inspired idea could be an everyday reality, Dr. Labroo and her colleagues conducted five unusual experiments on muscle-tensing and willpower—two of which involved choosing a healthy food over a fattening alternative.

Apple or Chocolate Bar?

In one experiment, the scientists waylaid 66 people who were on their way to a snack bar on campus, and asked them about their health goals. Then the scientists gave them a task to do while they shopped for food at the snack bar—instructing half the participants to make their food selection while stretching

their fingers, and the other half to make the selection without stretching them.

Among those with strong health goals, those who stretched their fingers were more likely to spend their money on a healthy snack (fresh fruit, green tea or yogurt) than an unhealthy snack (ice cream, butter croissant, candy, chocolate), compared with those who didn't stretch their fingers.

Another experiment involved 98 people on a diet. Those who contracted a bicep while reading about a healthy or unhealthy food choice were more likely to later choose a healthy snack (an apple) over an indulgent snack (a chocolate bar), compared with people who didn't contract their bicep.

Other versions of muscle-tightening experiments showed that people were…

• **More willing to donate money to charity while firmly grasping a pen,** compared with people who held a pen lightly.

• **More willing to keep their right hand in a bucket of ice water** while firmly grasping a pen in the other hand, compared with people who held the pen lightly.

• **More willing to drink a disgusting-tasting concoction for their health** when contracting calf muscles by lifting a heel off the floor, compared with people who kept their foot flat on the floor.

"These five studies provide remarkable evidence that simply tightening one's muscles can firm one's resolve and facilitate self-control," says Dr. Labroo. "Put simply, steely muscles can lead to a steely resolve."

Important: Tensing your muscles probably works better than trying to suppress thoughts of temptation, she says. "Research shows that when you try to suppress a thought, it tends to reappear even more strongly."

Building Willpower

Based on her findings, Dr. Labroo has these recommendations for tensing muscles to help you resist dietary temptation…

• **Tense any muscle you like.** "In our studies, we used multiple ways to tense muscles—clenching your fist, stretching your fingers, tightening your calf muscles and firming your biceps. They all worked."

● **Tense your muscle at the exact time you need more willpower.** If you use the technique repeatedly before the time when you actually need the willpower, you'll likely deplete your willpower rather than strengthen it.

"Yes, tightening a muscle while engaging in self-control facilitates self-control—but this effect occurs only when you're engaged in the act of willpower," says Dr. Labroo.

● **Use muscle-tightening only when you really mean it.** "In our experiments, the effects occurred only among people who want to recruit their willpower, whether in a specific situation or for long-term goals," says Dr. Labroo.

Bottom line: "This technique provides an easy but effective way to increase the probability of your success at self-regulation," says Dr. Labroo. "When people tighten their muscles while exerting self-control, they can also strengthen willpower—and thus further enhance their self-control."

And muscle-tightening can work for situations other than resisting tempting food choices—it's a technique you can use in any situation where you want to summon more willpower, she says.

Aparna Labroo, PhD, psychologist specializing in the power of feelings to influence decisions, and professor of marketing at Rotman School of Management, University of Toronto.

Evaporate Extra Weight—with Two Glasses of Water

W hy do so many people gain weight as they get older? That's the question Brenda Davy, PhD, RD—an associate professor in the Department of Human Nutrition, Foods and Exercise at Virginia Tech—was conducting studies to find out.

In one experiment, she compared the appetites of young people and older people by feeding them both a 500-calorie appetizer of two cups of yogurt and then seeing if the young folks and old folks differed in the amount of calories they would later consume at an all-you-can-eat meal. To refine the results, she also gave some of the participants an alternative appetizer of two cups of water. She wasn't studying water. She didn't care about the water. The water was, in scientific terms, a "control condition" so she could better analyze the effects of the yogurt.

Eye-opening finding: Much to her surprise, the older folks who drank the two cups of water consumed fewer calories at the all-you-can-eat meal!

Dr. Davy had a new question—Could water help control appetite? Since then, she and her colleagues have conducted several studies on water and calorie intake.

● **58 fewer calories per meal—with two glasses of water.** In a 2007 study involving 50 people who weren't overweight, Dr. Davy found that older people (aged 60 to 80) who drank 16 ounces of water before an all-you-can-eat meal consumed an average of 58 fewer calories at the meal than older people who didn't drink water. (The water didn't reduce calorie intake in young people. More about that in a moment.)

● **74 fewer calories per meal—with two glasses of water.** In a 2008 study with 24 overweight older adults (average age 61), those who drank 16 ounces of water before an all-you-can-eat meal consumed an average of 74 fewer calories.

Now: Dr. Davy recently conducted another study—on people drinking water not only before one meal, but before three meals a day, day after day, week after week, for a couple of months.

44% More Weight Loss

Dr. Davy and her colleagues studied 48 overweight people aged 55 to 75, dividing them into two groups. For 12 weeks, both groups ate a low-calorie diet—1,200 daily calories for women and 1,500 for men. But one group also drank two cups of water before every meal—before breakfast, before lunch and before dinner.

The water group lost 15.5 pounds.

The no-water group lost 11 pounds.

That means the water group lost 44% more weight—in scientific terms, a very "significant" difference.

When combined with a low-calorie diet, drinking 16 ounces of water before each main meal leads to greater weight loss than a low-calorie diet alone, concluded Dr. Davy in *Obesity*.

And Dr. Davy has also conducted a new, year-long study—and found that the study participants who continued to drink two glasses of water before every meal maintained their weight loss.

Why Water Works

There are several reasons why water might help older people consume fewer calories and lose weight, says Dr. Davy.

• **Less hunger.** Drinking water fills you up, so you eat less. "Drinking water before a meal or with a meal reduces sensations of hunger and increases satiety, the sensation of feeling full," she says.

That's particularly important for older people, because they're less sensitive to their own sensations of hunger and satiety—and therefore less able to regulate their intake of calories.

Water might also work better in older than in younger people because older people have slower "gastric emptying"—food moves out of the stomach into the intestines more slowly, so water produces a longer-lasting feeling of fullness.

• **More water, less soda.** Drinking more water also leads to drinking less soda and other high-calorie beverages, says Dr. Davy. In her 12-week study, the people drinking water before meals drank 100 calories a day less of other beverages.

• **More self-monitoring.** Because you're paying closer attention to water intake, you might play closer attention to other aspects of weight control (a process weight-loss experts call "self-monitoring"), improving your ability to keep calories in check. "Any kind of self-monitoring—whether making sure you drink water before every meal, or weighing yourself every day, or keeping a food diary—improves a person's ability to lose weight," says Dr. Davy.

More Research

Dr. Davy isn't the only scientist who has shown that water can play a key role in weight loss.

• **More water, more weight loss.** Researchers at the Children's Hospital Oakland Research Institute analyzed data from a previous weight loss study of 173 overweight women (aged 25 to 50). The more water the women drank, the more weight they lost. "Drinking water may promote weight loss in overweight dieting women," concluded the researchers in the journal *Obesity*.

• **More water, less soda—and 194 fewer daily calories.** Researchers analyzed health data from 4,755 people and found that water drinkers drank fewer soft drinks and fruit drinks—and consumed 194 fewer calories a day than people who didn't drink water.

• **"Important role to play."** Researchers from the Department of Nutrition in the School of Public Health at the University of North Carolina in Chapel Hill reviewed all the studies to date on water and "weight status" in a recent issue of *Nutrition Reviews*. The studies "suggest water has a potentially important role to play in reducing" calorie intake and in "obesity prevention," they concluded.

For optimal results: It's simple, says Dr. Davy—just drink 16 ounces of water 15 to 20 minutes before every main meal.

And she says water might help young people prevent weight gain. "For young people, replacing other beverages with water might be a very feasible and low-cost way to maintain their current weight."

Brenda Davy, PhD, RD, associate professor in the Department of Human Nutrition, Foods and Exercise at Virginia Tech, Blacksburg, Virginia.

If You Regain the Weight, You Can Still Keep the Health... With Exercise

You cut calories. You walked 30 minutes a day. And you lost the weight. But if you're like 90% of people who lose weight, you found it very difficult to maintain the habits that helped you shed the pounds, and you slowly but surely (or quickly but surely) regained the weight you lost.

Well, that's the bad news. But it's not all the news.

Good news: A new study shows that if you continue to exercise after weight loss, you can keep many of the health benefits you gained while losing weight—even if you gain the weight back!

The Exercise Advantage

Researchers at the University of Missouri studied 77 overweight people, putting them on a weight-loss program for four to six months that included five days a week of moderate-intensity activity (either brisk walking or very slow jogging). On average, the participants lost 9.7% of their body weight.

But then the researchers did something very unusual. They put the study participants on a weight-regain program for the next four to six months—and, on average, the participants regained 54% of their lost weight.

But those 77 people were divided into two groups during the weight-regain program—one group continued to exercise and the other didn't.

After losing weight during the first phase of the study, just about all the participants had big improvements in what scientists call "metabolic" markers of health.

Their blood pressure went down. Their bad LDL cholesterol went down. Their good HDL cholesterol went up. Their total cholesterol went down. Their triglycerides went down. Their too-high blood sugar levels went down. They trimmed not only their overall body fat but also their abdominal fat,

a risk factor for heart disease and diabetes. In short, they were a whole lot healthier.

Compelling scientific evidence: And most of those metabolic parameters stayed healthier—in the people who continued to exercise.

But in those who stopped exercising, most of the metabolic parameters deteriorated—their blood pressure went up, their blood sugar went up, their bad LDL cholesterol went up, and their good HDL cholesterol went down.

"Aerobic exercise can counter the detrimental effects of partial weight regain on many markers of disease risk," concluded the researchers in the *Journal of Applied Physiology.*

"Although many people are successful at losing weight through diet and exercise, the majority of them will relapse and regain the weight," says Tom R. Thomas, PhD, professor in the College of Human Environmental Sciences at the University of Missouri and the study leader.

"The findings of this study indicate that regaining weight is very detrimental. However, exercise can counter those negative effects. The findings support the recommendation to continue exercising after weight loss—even if the weight is regained.

"It's clear that the message to lose weight isn't working because so many people regain weight. A new message is to keep exercising—to reduce disease risk and improve overall health.

"Don't worry so much about losing and maintaining weight," says Dr. Thomas. "Focus on exercise."

The Best Exercise

Most of the people in the study exercised by brisk walking.

"Walking is the most popular form of physical activity in the United States—and it is considered the best exercise for fighting off disease," says Janet Brill, PhD, a fitness expert and author of *Prevent a Second Heart Attack* (Three Rivers). *Her recommendations for making walking a daily habit...*

● **Make walking a priority in your life.** "If you cast a positive light on exercise, and acknowledge that it is the best 'medicine' for health and healing, then you will be more likely to embrace this lifetime 'prescription,'" she says.

• **Set a target.** "Choose a set distance—and plan to walk that distance and back, every day."

Best: "For good health and disease prevention, the intensity or speed of walking is not as important as the frequency and distance —so walk a long distance comfortably," says Dr. Brill.

• **Walk with a buddy or a dog.** "This may make walking more enjoyable for you," she says.

New finding: People who have dogs but don't regularly walk them are 58% more likely to be overweight than dog owners who regularly walk their pets, reported research-ers from the George Washington University School of Public Health and Health Services in Washington, DC. The non-walkers were also twice as likely to have high blood pressure and had a higher risk of diabetes.

• **Try a treadmill.** If outdoor walks aren't for you, walk indoors on a treadmill, says Dr. Brill. "Place it in front of the television and walk during your favorite show."

Tom R. Thomas, PhD, professor in the Department of Nutrition and Exercise Physiology in the College of Human Environmental Sciences at the University of Missouri, Columbia.

Janet Brill, PhD, RD, diet, nutrition and fitness expert, director of Nutrition for Fitness Together, the world's largest organization of personal trainers, and author of *Prevent a Second Heart Attack* and *Cholesterol Down* (both from Three Rivers Press). *www.drjanet.com, www.preventasecondheartattack.com, www.cholesteroldownbook.com.*

Chapter 14

RESPIRATORY & IMMUNE PROBLEMS

Cure Allergies the Natural Way

Seasonal allergies are most commonly associated with springtime. But the flare-ups that occur in the summer can be just as bad—if not worse—due to the added discomfort caused by unpleasant climate conditions, such as heat and humidity.

Interesting new fact: Allergy symptoms may be lasting even longer due to extended pollen seasons brought on by climate change, according to a recent analysis.

That's why it's more important than ever for the 40 million Americans who suffer from seasonal allergies to use the most effective therapies—with the fewest side effects.

Good news: You don't have to fill your medicine cabinet with powerful drugs that simply temporarily relieve your allergy symptoms and potentially lead to side effects ranging from headache and drowsiness to difficulty breathing. Instead, you can get relief from the natural remedies described in this article.

The Root of the Problem

Most doctors treat allergies with a regimen that includes oral antihistamines, such as *loratadine* (Claritin) or *cetirizine* (Zyrtec), to block the release of histamine so that runny noses and itchy eyes will be reduced...and/or inhaled steroids, such as *triamcinolone acetonide* (Nasacort) or *flunisolide*, to reduce inflammation, mucus production and nasal congestion.

Problem: Aside from the side effects these drugs can cause, many allergy sufferers experience a "rebound effect"—that is, when the drug wears off, the histamine that has been suppressed by the medication explodes, causing an even bigger allergic reaction.

Important: To transition from medication to the natural regimen described here, first take the natural remedy with the medication, then slowly wean yourself off the medication over a few weeks.

Try these three simple natural approaches...

Step 1—Supplements

Mother Nature has tools that work with your body to stop allergy symptoms. The following naturally occurring substances* have few side effects and often are just as effective as over-the-counter and prescription allergy medications.

Advice: Try quercetin, then add others in severe cases.

• **Quercetin** is a bioflavonoid, a type of plant pigment that inhibits histamine-producing cells. It's found in citrus fruits, apples and onions but not in amounts that are sufficient to relieve allergy symptoms. For optimal relief, try quercetin tablets.

Typical dose: Up to 600 milligrams (mg) daily depending on the severity of your symptoms. Quercetin also can be taken as a preventive during allergy season. Discuss the dose with your doctor. Quercetin is generally safe. Rare side effects may include headache and upset stomach. People with kidney disease should not take quercetin—it may worsen the condition.

Good brands: Quercetin 300, order at *www.allergyresearchgroup.com* or call 800-545-9960...or Quercetone, 800-228-1966, *www.thorne.com.*

• **Stinging nettle** is a flowering plant that, when ingested, reduces the amount of histamine that the body produces in response to an allergen. Look for a product that contains 1% silicic acid (the key ingredient).

Typical dose: 500 mg to 1,000 mg once or twice a day depending on the severity of symptoms.

Caution: Some people are allergic to stinging nettle. In rare cases, oral stinging nettle may cause mild gastrointestinal upset.

Good brands: Nature's Way Nettle Herb, 800-962-8873, *www.natauresway.com*...or Solgar Stinging Nettle Leaf Extract, 877-765-4274, *www.solgar.com.*

• **Fish oil.** The same potent source of omega-3 fatty acids that is so popular for preventing the inflammation that leads to heart disease also helps with allergies. Look for the words "pharmaceutical grade" and "purified" or "mercury-free" on the label. This ensures that the product is potent enough to have a therapeutic effect and has undergone a manufacturing process that removes potential toxins. Choose a brand that provides at least 500 mg of *eicosapentaenoic acid* (EPA) and 250 mg of *docosahexaenoic acid* (DHA) per capsule.

Typical dose: Take 2,000 mg of fish oil per day. Consult your doctor if you take a blood thinner.

Good brands: Nordic Naturals Arctic Omega, 800-662-2544, *www.nordicnaturals. com*...or Vital-Choice fish oils, 800-608-4825, *www.vitalchoice.com.*

Step 2—Nasal Cleansing

Inflammation in the nasal passages due to allergies prevents the sinuses from draining and can lead to sinus infection.

Self-defense: Nasal cleansing once daily during allergy season reduces the amount of pollen exposure and can prevent the allergic reaction in the first place.**

One option: Flush your nasal passages with a neti pot. A neti pot looks like a miniature teapot with an elongated spout (available at drugstores for $8 to $30). Add one tablespoon of aloe vera gel and a pinch of salt to the warm distilled water you place in the pot.

What to do: While standing over a sink, tilt your head horizontally, left ear to ceiling, and gently insert the spout into your left nostril. As you slowly pour the mixture into the nostril, it will circulate through the nasal passages and out the right nostril. Continue for 10 seconds, breathing through your mouth, then let the excess water drain. Repeat on the other nostril. Be sure to run your neti pot through the dishwasher or clean with soap and hot water to disinfect it after every use.

Alternative: If using a neti pot feels uncomfortable, try using a syringe bulb...or

---

*Consult a doctor before trying this regimen if you are pregnant or have a medical condition.

**Nasal cleansing may be irritating for some people. If you experience any irritation, discontinue it immediately.

cup warm water (mixed with salt and aloe) in your hand and breathe it in slowly.

Even better: Use a nasal irrigator, which is more thorough and takes less effort than a neti pot. This instrument forcibly expels water—and uses the same aloe/salt/water mixture as you would in a neti pot.

Recommended: The Grossan Nasal Irrigator, developed by ENT doctor Murray Grossan, 800-560-9007, *www.hydromedonline.com*, $97...or SinuPulse Elite Advanced Nasal Irrigation System, 800-305-4095, *www.sinupulse.com*, $97.

Step 3—Acupressure or Acupuncture

Acupuncture and acupressure can relieve allergies by stimulating certain pressure points to encourage blood flow, reduce inflammation and release natural painkilling chemical compounds known as endorphins.

●**Acupressure.** For 30 to 60 seconds, push (with enough pressure to hold your head on your thumbs) each thumb into the area where each brow meets the nose. Then, press your thumbs just below your eyebrows and slide along the ridges. Finally, press beneath both cheekbones, moving outward with both thumbs toward the ears. Do this sequence three times daily.

●**Acupuncture.** While acupressure helps relieve allergy symptoms, acupuncture is generally more effective. Six to 10 sessions with a licensed acupuncturist during allergy season usually work best.

Other Remedies

●**Allergy shots and drops.** These traditional approaches are in many ways quite natural. Small amounts of an allergen extract are injected. After a number of treatments, you build up a natural resistance to the allergen. Allergy drops (placed under the tongue) are an alternative to allergy shots and work in much the same way.

●**Speleotherapy and halotherapy.** Used for centuries in Europe, these treatments are gaining popularity in the US. With speleotherapy, patients spend time in salt caves. Halotherapy uses man-made salt rooms that simulate caves. The salt ions combined with unpolluted air seem to improve lung function in those with respiratory and sinus ailments as well as allergies.

Salt mines and salt rooms are not always easy to find. Try searching online under "salt therapy."

Recommended: During allergy season, four to 12 speleotherapy or halotherapy sessions may be helpful. A 45- to 60-minute session typically costs $10 to $15.

Richard Firshein, DO, director of the New York City–based Firshein Center for Comprehensive Medicine. He is author of *Reversing Asthma* (Grand Central) and *The Vitamin Prescription* (Xlibris). *www.drfirshein.com*.

Have Hay Fever? Take Tree Bark!

Yes, you might think ingesting part of a tree is the last way to treat hay fever—an allergy to the pollen from trees (or grasses, weeds or fungus) that can cause a stuffy, red nose...sneezing...coughing...itchy eyes and an itchy and scratchy throat.

Hay fever is a seasonal illness, though some people have the problem in the spring and the summer and the fall...as they react to more than one type of pollen.

But whether you have the condition for a couple of weeks or a couple of months—and an estimated 60 million Americans have it at one time of the year or another—you're probably miserable while it's happening.

A recent study showed that 85% of folks with hay fever (which doctors call allergic *rhinitis*) felt their activities were either moderately or severely impaired—their ability to concentrate at work or school...relax at home...enjoy outdoor activities or sleep at night.

You can take an antihistamine to control the symptoms, of course. But wouldn't it be great if there was a natural remedy that could prevent the symptoms before they started? Now there is.

New finding: A study shows that taking a supplement derived from pine tree bark—starting several weeks before hay fever season—can reduce symptoms during the season.

Pine for Relief

The study was conducted by Canadian scientists and published in the journal *Phytotherapy Research*. The researchers studied 39 people with allergy to birch pollen.

Three to eight weeks before the onset of birch pollen season in Ontario, Canada (mid-April to the end of May), half the study participants started taking a daily dose of 100 milligrams (mg) of Pycnogenol, a powerful antioxidant derived from the bark of the Maritime Pine, which grows near the ocean in southwest France. The other half took a placebo.

Results: When pollen season hit, those taking Pycnogenol had 35% fewer eye symptoms (red, burning, itchy, tearing eyes) and 21% fewer nasal symptoms (stuffy, runny or itchy nose) than the placebo group.

Those taking Pycnogenol also had a much lower increase in levels of antibodies to birch pollen (it's the antibodies that spark the allergic reaction)—a 19% increase, compared with 32% for the placebo group.

And the longer the participants took Pycnogenol before the allergy season, the better they did. "The best results were found with people who took Pycnogenol seven to eight weeks ahead of allergy season," wrote the researchers. In fact, only 13% of those who took the supplement starting eight weeks before the season had to take antihistamines, compared with 50% in the placebo group.

"This study confirmed that taking Pycnogenol naturally relieves eye and nasal symptoms of hay fever patients owing to lower pollen-specific antibodies," concluded the researchers.

"For the many people seeking alternatives to conventional treatment for allergic rhinitis, Pycnogenol may represent an effective

and completely natural solution, void of any side effects," says Malkanthi Evans, PhD, the study's lead researcher.

How it works: "Pycnogenol is anti-inflammatory, and can help decrease the many immune factors that spark an allergic reaction," says Fred Pescatore, MD, author of *The Allergy & Asthma Cure* (Wiley).

Suggested intake: He recommends starting Pycnogenol eight weeks before your hayfever season, taking 100 mg twice a day, and continuing to take it throughout the season, stopping at the end.

Fred Pescatore, MD, author of *The Allergy & Asthma Cure* (Wiley). *www.drpescatore.com.*

Malkanthi Evans, PhD, scientific director at KGK Synergize, London, Ontario, Canada.

Natural Infection Fighters

Antibiotics enable millions of people to survive infections that used to be fatal. However, the widespread use of these drugs has increasingly led to antibiotic resistance—some harmful organisms can keep making people sick even when treated with the newest, most powerful antibiotics.

We tend to hear a lot about the overuse of antibiotics, but medications used to treat viruses and fungi also can be harmful.

For example, over-the-counter and prescription drugs used to treat yeast infections have the potential to cause side effects ranging from headache to seizures, while antiviral medications can lead to gastrointestinal problems, dizziness and difficulty breathing in those with lung disease. Overuse of prescription drugs to treat viruses or fungi, such as *oseltamivir* (Tamiflu) and *acyclovir* (Zovirax), also can lead to resistance to these medications.

Little-known fact: Because the immune system of a healthy adult is quite effective at eliminating many types of bacteria, viruses and fungi, many infections can be successfully treated with natural products that strengthen immunity and fight microorganisms.

Important: Always see a doctor if the affected area is becoming more inflamed… seems to be spreading…is accompanied by a fever…or is not improving.

Conditions that typically improve within 24 to 48 hours when treated with natural antimicrobial agents (unless indicated otherwise, all can be found in health-food stores)…*

Bronchitis

Bronchitis is inflammation of the lining of the bronchial tubes, which carry air to the lungs. Acute bronchitis is usually due to a virus and often develops in conjunction with a cold or some other upper-respiratory tract ailment.

Natural treatment: Add 10 drops of liquid *allicin* (an active antibacterial and antiviral compound in garlic) to the reservoir of a portable nebulizer (a device that converts liquid into a fine mist that can be inhaled). Breathe the mist until all of the extract is gone. Repeat the treatment once or twice a day until the infection is gone.

Also helpful: Take eight (180 mg) capsules daily of Allimax, fresh-garlic supplements that can shorten the duration of the illness.

Sore Throat

Most sore throats are caused by viruses, such as those that cause the common cold or flu.

Natural treatment: Perform a yoga exercise known as the Lion Pose to increase blood and lymph circulation at the back of the tongue. This movement promotes the migration of immune cells to the area to help fight the infection.

What to do: Stick out your tongue as far as it will go, and hold it there for three to four seconds. Repeat the movement five or six times daily until your sore throat is gone.

*Caution: If you have an allergy to a particular natural substance (such as garlic), do not use a remedy that contains the substance.

Also helpful: Gargling with saltwater helps ease sore throat pain.

For better results: Add a few drops of bitter orange oil to a mixture of one-quarter teaspoon salt and one-half cup warm water to help kill bacteria, including some organisms that cause strep throat.

Important: Use a "bass voice" when you gargle the mixture (every few waking hours). The lower-pitched gargling sound causes more of the solution to get into the throat.

Sinusitis

Infections of the sinus cavities typically cause headache, facial pain or pressure and a loss of smell and taste. Antibiotics can help in some cases, but most sinus infections are caused by organisms, such as viruses or fungi, that aren't killed by antibiotics.

Natural treatment: N-acetyl-cysteine (NAC), an amino acid that promotes the drainage of mucus and mobilizes infection-fighting white blood cells.

Typical dose: 600 mg, three times daily.

Bladder Infection

Virtually every woman gets an occasional urinary tract infection (UTI), either in the urethra (the tube that allows urine to leave the body) and/or the bladder. Though relatively rare in men, UTIs become more common in those over age 50—a time when prostate enlargement tends to occur and can lead to an infection when urine fails to drain properly from the bladder. Antibiotics work for both women and men but often lead to yeast infections and other side effects.

Natural treatment: Unsweetened cranberry juice (one eight-ounce glass daily)** is widely used to help prevent UTIs. Cranberry contains *anthocyanidins*, compounds that are thought to help prevent *Escherichia coli* (E. coli), the cause of most UTIs, from adhering to tissues in the urinary tract.

For better results: Also take an herb called *uva ursi* (500 mg three to five times

**If you take *warfarin* (Coumadin), consult your doctor before drinking this amount of cranberry juice—the juice may increase the effects of blood-thinning medication.

daily). If symptoms do not significantly improve within 24 hours, consult a physician before continuing this treatment.

Important: Drink a minimum of six glasses of water daily (in addition to the juice) until the infection is gone. It dilutes the concentration of bacteria in the bladder...reduces irritation...and helps flush out harmful organisms.

Ear Infection

Several studies in children show that most ear infections don't require antibiotics. It's likely that the same is true for adults, particularly for infections affecting the ear canal (swimmer's ear).

Natural treatment for swimmer's ear: Use a clean bulb syringe or eyedropper to administer three to five drops daily of a 50-50 mixture of distilled water and hydrogen peroxide, followed by three to five drops of a 50-50 solution of white vinegar and distilled water.

Also helpful: A combination supplement that includes echinacea, goldenseal and berberis (such as Source Naturals' Wellness Formula), along with a multisupplement containing bioflavonoids, zinc and vitamins C and A. Follow dosage instructions.

Important: Patients who get frequent ear infections should try eliminating dairy and bananas from their diet. These foods are believed to lead to the production of thicker-than-normal mucus that inhibits normal ear drainage.

Steven Sandberg-Lewis, ND, naturopathic physician and clinical professor of naturopathic medicine at the National College of Natural Medicine in Portland, Oregon. He is author of *Functional Gastroenterology* (National College of Natural Medicine).

Restore Natural Immunity—with Zinc

If your immune system isn't supplied with enough of the mineral zinc, it won't work right.

That's because even a mild deficiency of zinc can interfere with the activity of T-cells, a type of white blood cell in the army of the immune system.

T-cells help fight bacterial, viral and fungal infections...protect the body from dust and other potential allergens...stimulate other cells to produce antibodies...and keep specialized, immune-signaling proteins on high alert. (The HIV virus is so deadly because it destroys T-cells.)

That explanation about zinc and immunity is courtesy of Ananda Prasad, MD, PhD, of Wayne State University School of Medicine in Detroit, the scientist who discovered that zinc is an essential mineral in human nutrition, and the author of a recently published scientific paper titled "Zinc in Human Health: Effect of Zinc on Immune Cells."

Dr. Prasad and his colleagues recently put his ideas about zinc deficiency and immunity to the test. And they chose older people to be test subjects because the immune system inevitably weakens with age, a process called immunosenescence. Results of their research were published in the *American Journal of Clinical Nutrition*.

They studied fifty people aged 55 to 87, giving half a daily zinc supplement of 45 milligrams (mg) and half a placebo. After one year, the zinc group had 67% fewer everyday infections. Fewer colds. Less flu. Fewer cold sores.

Now: Several additional studies show that zinc can power up immunity, helping to prevent and treat many different types of infections.

Newest Research

• **Pneumonia.** Older people with adequate zinc levels were 50% less likely to develop pneumonia, reported researchers from Tufts University in Boston in the *American Journal of Clinical Nutrition*. They recommend a daily dosage of 30 mg to improve immune function.

• **Hepatitis C.** Researchers in Germany found that combining interferon (the standard drug treatment) with zinc for hepatitis C is more effective than using interferon alone. And for those not cured of the disease, zinc reduces digestive problems, helps stop uncontrolled weight loss, and improves the health of hair and fingernails. "Zinc is recommended as a complementary therapy for chronic hepatitis C," concluded the researchers in *Molecular Medicine Reports*.

●**HIV/AIDS.** Noting that zinc deficiency "occurs in 50% of HIV-infected adults," researchers at Florida International University in Miami gave 231 people with HIV either zinc or a placebo for 18 months.

Those taking the placebo were four times more likely to have "immunological failure," concluded the researchers in the journal *Clinical and Infectious Diseases*. Those taking zinc also had 50% less diarrhea than those not taking the mineral.

●**Tuberculosis.** Tuberculosis patients who took zinc had more rapid curing of their disease with medications than patients who didn't take zinc, reported researchers at the University of Texas in El Paso.

●**Inner ear infections.** Researchers at the University of Milan in Italy studied 122 children with chronic ear infections, treating them with either a zinc-containing supplement or a placebo. After three months, those taking zinc had 32% fewer new infections.

●**Heart disease.** We don't ordinarily think of clogged arteries (atherosclerosis) as an immune problem. But arteries become clogged when the immune system responds to initial damage to the arterial wall, further inflaming blood vessels and advancing the disease.

In a study conducted by Dr. Prasad and his colleagues, 40 healthy people aged 56 to 83 took either 45 mg of zinc or a placebo. After six months, those taking zinc had lower levels of many immune factors linked to clogged arteries, and less C-reactive protein, a biomarker of inflammation.

"Zinc may have a protective effect in atherosclerosis because of its anti-inflammatory properties," concluded the researchers in the *American Journal of Clinical Nutrition*.

How Much Zinc Is Best?

"The recommended daily intake of zinc is 12 to 15 mg a day, but in many people 55 and older the intake is no more than 6 to 8 mg," says Dr. Prasad. And studies on people in laboratory settings show that a mild deficiency of zinc—enough to harm the immune system and make you more vulnerable to infections—occurs after only 10 weeks of zinc intake at the low dose of 5 mg a day.

Dr. Prasad recommends that everyone aged 55 and older take 45 mg of zinc a day to prevent deficiency.

Caution: Zinc and copper act in tandem, and more than 50 mg daily of zinc daily may cause a copper deficiency, he says.

For optimal results: He recommends using one of two forms of the mineral...*zinc acetate* and *zinc gluconate*. More commonly used forms are problematic. Zinc oxide is not well-absorbed, he says. And zinc sulfate can cause stomach problems.

Ananda Prasad, MD, PhD, professor in the Division of Hematology/Oncology at the Wayne State University School of Medicine in Detroit.

Stopping Colds and Flu With Vitamin D

America has a nasty cold. Collectively, we cough, sniffle and sneeze our way through one billion colds a year, spending $1.5 billion for doctor's visits and $2 billion on non-prescription cough and cold treatments. Fortunately, few people die of a cold, even a severe one. But you can't say that about influenza, also known as the flu.

The influenza virus hospitalizes more than 200,000 Americans a year and kills 36,000, many of them over 65. And flu shots are no guarantee of protection. In a recent year, the shot was only 44% effective in stopping the flu.

Is there any way to make yourself less vulnerable to these two infections?

Yes, says a recent study in the medical journal *Plos One*. Make absolutely certain you have higher-than-normal blood levels of vitamin D.

Here's what you need to know about the study and its practical application...

The Cold/Flu Study

The study was led by James R. Sabetta, MD, at Yale University School of Medicine and the Section of Infectious Diseases at Greenwich Hospital in Greenwich, Connecticut. He and his colleagues observed the obvious: rates of "acute respiratory tract infections" (colds and flu) rise in the fall and winter. But why? Could the seasonal drop in blood levels of vitamin D—a hormonelike nutrient produced most abundantly in the body when the skin is exposed to the strong, direct sunlight of summer—explain the phenomena?

To find out, the researchers took monthly measurements of blood levels of vitamin D (25-hydroxyvitamin D) in 195 healthy adults. The measurements started the third week in September and continued for the next four to five months. At the same time, the study participants were asked to report any acute respiratory tract infections.

Results: Those who had blood levels lower than 38 ng/ml (nanograms per milliliter) had twice as many upper respiratory tract infections.

Among the 18 people in the study who consistently maintained blood levels of vitamin D above 38 ng/ml, 15 were completely free of upper respiratory tract infections—no colds, no flu. (Of those 18 folks, 13 were taking vitamin D supplements. More about that in a minute.)

And when the above-38 group did succumb to cold or flu, their illnesses were shorter. The number of days ill with acute respiratory tract infections in the above-38 group was five times lower than in the below-38 group.

Of the other 180 participants—all of them with blood vitamin D levels consistently below 38 ng/ml—81 developed colds and flu.

The study's statistical summary: the 38+ group had a two-fold decrease in the risk of developing a cold or flu.

Standout scientific evidence: The Yale researchers aren't the first to link vitamin D levels and the flu...

In recent research in the *American Journal of Clinical Nutrition*, Japanese doctors studied 334 children, half of whom took 1,200 international units (IU) of vitamin D daily. Eighteen of the children taking vitamin D developed the flu, compared with 31 children not taking the vitamin, a risk reduction of 58%.

And a study in the *Archives of Internal Medicine* looked at 19,000 adults and adolescents and found that those with the lowest blood levels of vitamin D were 40% more likely to have had a recent cold or flu, compared with those with the highest levels.

In another study, women taking 2,000 IU of vitamin D (to protect bones) had an average of nine episodes of colds and flu over three years of taking the supplement—compared with an average of 30 episodes in a group of women taking 200 IU of vitamin D.

But the Yale study was the first to methodically track vitamin D levels and colds/flu incidence during the cold/flu season. What did the Yale researchers have to say about their startling results?

Bottom line: "Maintenance of a 25-hydroxyvitamin D serum concentration of 38 ng/ml or higher should significantly reduce the incidence of acute viral respiratory infections and the burden of illness caused thereby, at least during the fall and winter." Easier said than done.

Increasing Vitamin D

A deficiency of vitamin D is incredibly common, says James Cannell, MD, president of the Vitamin D Council and coauthor of the paper "Epidemic Influenza and Vitamin D," published in the *Journal of Epidemiology and Health*. In fact, your risk of a deficiency of vitamin D is 50%—one out of every two Americans is likely to have blood levels below 20 ng/ml, he says.

In fact, Dr. Cannell is convinced that a low blood level of vitamin D is the reason people are vulnerable to cold and flu viruses. "Vitamin D dramatically increases the production of the body's own antimicrobial peptides," he says. "If you have sufficiently high blood levels of vitamin D, you'll have enough of those peptides to kill cold and flu viruses before they have a chance to penetrate the mucosal barrier." Here are Dr. Cannell's recommendations for making sure your blood levels of vitamin D stay high throughout the year.

●**Get a vitamin D blood test.** There's only one way to know for sure if your levels are high enough—get a blood test. But you don't have to go to a doctor to do it. The ZRT Laboratory (*www.zrtlab.com*, 866-600-1636) provides a reliable in-home vitamin D blood test, says Dr. Cannell. He recommends a test every six months.

●**Maintain blood levels of 50 to 80 ng/ ml.** While 38 ng/ml was generally protective in the Yale study, Dr. Cannell says research shows this higher level is necessary for vitamin D to be stored in muscles and fat and most effectively do its preventive work. And that's a lot of work. In fact, high levels of vitamin D have been linked to a reduction of death from any cause. (The nutrient has such a wide ranging effect, says Dr. Cannell, because it targets more than 2,000 genes—10% of the human genome.)

●**Take a vitamin D supplement.** Dr. Cannell recommends 5,000 IU a day. (To get that amount from D-fortified milk, you'd need to drink 50 glasses a day, he points out.) "Anyone who takes this amount regularly shouldn't get a cold or flu," he says. "If you do get one, it should be mild."

He also recommends taking vitamin D3 (*cholecalciferol*), not vitamin D2 (*ergocalciferol*), its synthetic analog. "Vitamin D3 is the compound your skin makes naturally when you go in the sun, and it's more potent and safer than vitamin D2."

And don't worry about an overdose, says Dr. Cannell. "There is not a single case in the medical literature of vitamin D toxicity while taking regular doses of 25,000 IU or less." The ideal vitamin D supplement includes co-factors like magnesium and zinc, says Dr. Cannell, and he has formulated his own brand. You can purchase Dr. Cannell's Advanced D from Purity Products (*www.purityproducts.com*, 800-256-6102).

●**Spend some no-sunblock time in the sun during the summer months.** He recommends near-daily exposure of as much of your body as possible (not just the face and hands) for 5 to 10 minutes, when the sun is highest in the sky (when your shadow is longer than you are). "You're not making much vitamin D when your shadow is shorter," he says.

James R. Sabetta, MD, Department of Medicine, Yale University School of Medicine, and practicing physician, infectious diseases, Greenwich Hospital in Greenwich, Connecticut.

James Cannell, MD, president of the Vitamin D Council and coauthor of the paper "Epidemic Influenza and Vitamin D," published in the *Journal of Epidemiology and Health.* www.vitamindcouncil.com.

Vitamin E Prevents COPD

We hear a lot about preventing heart disease, the number-one cause of death in America. And cancer, the number-two cause. And stroke, at number three.

But we rarely hear about preventing the seldom-discussed number-four cause of death in the US—*chronic obstructive pulmonary disease* (COPD), also known as emphysema and chronic bronchitis, which affects 16 million Americans and kills 122,000 yearly.

Now: Results from a new study provide a nutritional strategy that may help ward off COPD—take vitamin E.

E Is for Easier Breathing

Researchers from Cornell University and Harvard Medical School analyzed data from a seven-year study on nearly 40,000 women aged 45 and older who took either 600 international units (IU) of vitamin E or a placebo every other day.

Results: Those who took the nutrient had a 10% lower risk of developing COPD—even if they smoked, the main risk factor for the disease.

"As lung disease develops, damage occurs to sensitive tissues through several processes, including inflammation and damage from free radicals," says Anne Hermetet Agler, study researcher in the Division of Nutritional Sciences at Cornell University. "Vitamin E may protect the lung against such damage."

"Vitamin E is a powerful antioxidant, which makes it quite useful in counteracting oxidative damage in the lungs," agrees Robert J. Green, ND, a naturopathic physician and author of *Natural Therapies for Emphysema and COPD* (Healing Arts Press).

And Dr. Green says you may want to take vitamin E if you already have COPD.

"Take 400 IU three or four times daily," he advises. "Take it with 50 to 100 milligrams of vitamin C to enhance absorption. You may need higher doses for therapeutic benefit, but don't exceed 1,600 IU daily without your physician's recommendation and supervision."

Recent Findings

The earliest symptoms of COPD might be a chronic cough and airway-clogging mucus (sputum). Later, you may find yourself unexpectedly short of breath while carrying groceries, climbing stairs or going for a brisk walk. As the disease advances, respiratory difficulties can turn into disasters. Eventually, your best friend could be an oxygen tank.

Good news: Recent research shows there are natural ways to control these and other symptoms of COPD.

•**A more active lifestyle.** In a study reported at an international conference of the American Thoracic Society, researchers found that people with COPD who had a more active lifestyle—more moving around during the day—performed better on a six-minute walk test (the distance they were able to walk in six minutes).

Recommendation: "COPD patients who wish to improve their ability to perform daily tasks may be better served by increasing their normal daily activities, such as walking to the post office, working in the garden, or doing housekeeping, rather than performing intense exercise once in a while," says Chris Burtin, PT, a hospital-based physical therapist in Belgium and the study leader.

"Daily walking is one of the best exercise activities for a person with COPD," adds Dr. Green. "Walking will help build your circulation and increase your stamina, and it will help build activity tolerance. Start out by walking half a block or less. Every other day, you should increase your walking distance a little bit. After a few months, you could be walking up to a mile without gasping."

•**Tai chi.** Researchers at Harvard Medical School studied 10 people with COPD, dividing them into two groups.

Five people took a twice-weekly, one-hour class in tai chi (gentle, meditative exercises that use flowing, circular movements, and balance and breathing techniques). Five didn't.

After 12 weeks, those taking tai chi had improvements in breathing capacity, walking distance and depression compared with those who didn't take the classes.

Recommendation: "Tai chi may be a suitable exercise option for patients with COPD," wrote the Harvard researchers in the journal *Respiratory Care.*

Resource: To find an accredited tai chi teacher near you, visit the Web site *www.tai chichih.org,* and click on "find a teacher."

•**Singing.** "Despite optimal pharmacological therapy and pulmonary rehabilitation, patients with COPD continue to be breathless," noted a team of UK researchers in the journal *BMC Pulmonary Medicine.* "There is a need to develop additional strategies to alleviate symptoms. Learning to sing requires control of breathing and posture, and might have benefits that translate into daily life."

To test their theory, the researchers studied 28 people with COPD—half took twice-weekly singing classes and half didn't.

Results: After six weeks, those taking the classes had better physical functioning and less anxiety about breathlessness, compared with the non-singers.

"Singing classes can improve quality-of-life measures and anxiety, and are viewed as a very positive experience by patients with respiratory disease," concluded the researchers.

Resources: Ways to learn to sing include…

• *www.teachyourselfsinging.com,* a Web site that offers online singing lessons.

• *www.takelessons.com,* a Web site that connects you to singing teachers in any one of 2,800 cites across the US. Phone: 877-231-8505.

• *www.singingvoicelessons.com,* a Web site that offers the Singing Voice Lessons Series on CD, from voice coach Shelley Kristen.

• *www.easysinginglessons.com,* a Web site providing downloadable "Singing Is Easy" lessons.

• *Singing for the Stars: A Complete Program for Training Your Voice* (Alfred Publishing) by Seth Riggs, a book and 2-CD set. *Singing for Dummies* (for Dummies), a book by Pamela S. Phillips.

Anne Hermetet Agler, Division of Nutritional Sciences, Cornell University, Ithara, New York.

Chris Burtin, PT, MSc, a hospital-based physical therapist, Katholieke Universiteit Leuven, Belgium.

Robert J. Green, ND, naturopathic physician and author of *Natural Therapies for Emphysema and COPD* (Healing Arts Press).

Is Your Air-Conditioning Poisoning Your Home?

Mold and bacteria are probably spreading throughout your house right now.

If you have central air-conditioning or a forced-air heating, ventilation and air-conditioning (HVAC) system, inadequate air filtration could be allowing mold and bacteria inside your home. Fewer than 10% of residential forced-air systems have filters capable of preventing mold and bacteria growth.

Mold and bacteria contamination can trigger or exacerbate respiratory problems, including allergies and asthma. Certain molds even produce cancerous toxins.

Paying big money for high-end air-filtration devices does not necessarily solve this problem. Many expensive filtration products do little to improve air quality. *Here's what works and what doesn't work…*

Use a Better Filter

The cheapest, easiest way to improve your home's air quality is to improve the quality of the disposable filter you use in your forced-air system.

Most home owners use fiberglass panel filters that have a Minimum Efficiency Reporting Value (MERV) of just 3 or 4. To avoid mold or bacteria growth, instead use a "pleated" filter rated MERV 8 or higher.

Buying advice: MERV 8 filters are available at home-improvement stores, such as The Home Depot and Lowe's, and many hardware stores for between $5 and $10 apiece. Don't worry about the filter's brand—focus instead on its MERV rating, which usually is clearly marked on the package. Using the correct size is equally important—even the best filter will not improve air quality if air can get around it in your system's filter compartment or if the compartment does not close properly with the filter inside. Measure your system's filter compartment before buying.

Do not pay extra for expensive "electrostatic" filters for central air-conditioning. Manufacturers claim that these are washable and reusable, but in my experience, there is no way to clean them adequately.

Downside: Switching from a one-inch-deep MERV 3 to a one-inch-deep MERV 8 filter is likely to reduce your system's airflow by up to 10%, increasing your cooling and heating bills. (Deeper filters—two-inch, four-inch, six-inch—do not reduce the airflow as much but are too deep to fit most units.) Replacing filters every three months will minimize the energy consumption increase—dirty filters force heating and cooling systems to work even harder.

Keep the System Clean

If you have used filters rated lower than MERV 8 in the past, it is likely that mold and bacteria already are growing on your air conditioner's blower and coil unless you live in an arid region. Installing a filter with a higher MERV rating will not kill existing mold and bacteria, nor will it prevent their spores from spreading throughout your home—the air conditioner's blower and coil are located after the filter. The only reliable way to remove existing contamination is to hire a duct-cleaning service.

Contact the National Air Duct Cleaners Association (NADCA) to find a pro in your area (202-737-2926, *www.nadca.com*). The duct-cleaning sector is rife with scammers, but NADCA members usually are legitimate. Expect to spend around $1,000 to clean the ducts of an average-sized home of about 2,350 square feet. Any company that promises to clean ducts for significantly less is likely to either do a slipshod job or find excuses to pad your bill during the job. Ducts should be cleaned once every five years or so.

Before signing a contract, confirm that the duct cleaner will clean your air conditioner's blower and coil—some duct cleaners ignore these components and clean only the ducts.

Best and Worst Upgrades

If someone in your household has severe allergies or asthma, you might be tempted to invest in an air-filtration or purification system. *While some high-end products truly deliver cleaner air, others are a waste of money...*

• **MERV 10** or higher pleated filters do a wonderful job of trapping particulates and preventing mold and bacteria growth—but there's a catch. Filters with MERV ratings above 8 or so tend to be too deep to fit in the filter compartments of standard residential HVAC systems. Installing a larger filter holder is likely to cost $700 to $1,000.

MERV 10 replacement filters typically cost $40 to $60 each and last around six months.

Verdict: This is probably the most cost-effective high-end filtration option, even if you have to retrofit your system to accommodate the filter.

Whole-house air cleaners that accommodate high-MERV filters include: Aprilaire Models 2210/2310/2410/2250, which ship with a MERV 10 but have the option to upgrade to a MERV 13 (800-334-6011, *www.aprilaire.com*)...Honeywell F100 Whole-House Media Air Cleaner (877-271-8620, *http://YourHome.Honeywell.com/home*).

• **High-Efficiency Particulate Air (HEPA)** whole-house filters have impressive MERV ratings of 16 and up. Unfortunately, residential whole-house HEPA filters are "bypass filters," which means that they subject only a small percentage of the air that passes through the HVAC system to extreme filtration on each circulation. Bypass systems do a fine job of removing particulates from the air, but they do little to prevent the growth of mold and bacteria within the HVAC system, which is the greater threat to residential air quality.

Verdict: Not worth the cost (around $2,000 to $3,000) except, perhaps, for those with severe allergies to particulates, such as pollen and pet dander.

• **Electronic filters** attach an electrical charge to particles that pass through, then collect the charged particles on an oppositely charged metal plate. In theory, that should be effective. In practice, these systems must be cleaned at least once a month to remain effective. Few home owners do this, so their electronic filters soon become useless.

Verdict: Don't bother. Residential electronic filters often fail to function properly after a year.

• **Ultraviolet-light air purifiers** supposedly kill germs by irradiating the air that passes through the HVAC system. The technology works well in hospitals and other large industrial applications, but residential UV purifiers are so much less powerful that they are essentially worthless.

Verdict: A total waste of money.

●**A hot water–circulating heating system** reduces the odds of respiratory problems by perhaps 50%, compared with forced-air heating systems—even if central air-conditioning is still used a few months of the year. Unfortunately, making this change in an existing home could cost tens of thousands of dollars.

Verdict: Switching to a water-circulating heating system is worth considering if you are remodeling or building a home and a family member suffers from serious respiratory problems.

Portable Air Cleaners

These do an effective job of removing particulates, such as pollen, from the air, but they will not prevent mold and bacteria from growing inside your home's central-air system.

Buying advice: Choose a model with a "Clean Air Delivery Rate" (CADR) of at least 100. Avoid those with electronic filters regardless of their CADRs, however. Not only do electronic filters become useless if not cleaned frequently, they often produce ozone, a lung irritant, so they can create respiratory problems. Also, check portable air cleaners' decibel rating before buying—you don't want one much over 50 decibels. Noisy portable air filters are a common complaint.

Window Air Conditioners

Window air-conditioner units tend to use filters rated MERV 3 or lower.

Buying advice: A company called WEB Products makes a MERV 7 "Washable Electrostatic Filter" specifically for window air conditioners. It's the best filter on the market for window units—though you should dispose of these filters each cooling season rather than washing and reusing them (800-875-3212, *www.webproducts.com*, search for "WRAC," $6.99 each).

Helpful Test

To determine whether better air filters and a duct cleaning will help any respiratory problems you have, wear an N95 filter mask (available at home-improvement stores and drugstores for about $1 each) for a few days whenever you are inside your home. If the mask helps you breathe easier, improved air filtration is likely to help, too.

Jeffrey C. May, MA, founder and principal scientist of May Indoor Air Investigations LLC, an air-quality assessment company in Tyngsborough, Massachusetts. He is author of several books on indoor environments, including *Jeff May's Healthy Home Tips* and *My House Is Killing Me!* (both from The Johns Hopkins University Press). *www.mayindoorair.com.*

Fight Foodborne Illnesses and Keep Your Immune System Safe

They could be just about anywhere. In the egg carton at the supermarket. In the potato salad at the buffet restaurant. In the hamburger patty you just put on the grill.

"They" are the bacteria, viruses and parasites that cause food poisoning, or what experts call foodborne illness—the salmonella, E. coli, listeria, Norovirus, toxoplasma and dozens of other bugs that can make people very ill.

Latest finding: An estimated 48 million Americans become sick with a foodborne illness every year—with 128,000 hospitalizations and 3,000 deaths, according to a new report from the Centers for Disease Control and Prevention.

Most people with foodborne illness suffer from a sudden and unexplained bout of the "stomach flu" (gastroenteritis), with symptoms such as stomach pain and cramps, nausea, vomiting, diarrhea and fever—as germs blitz the digestive tract and the immune system fights back. (Children under five and adults over 65 are most often hospitalized or killed with foodborne illness.)

But all those illnesses and deaths could be prevented by new food safety legislation, says the Food and Drug Administration in a statement about the CDC study.

While you're waiting around for Congress to act (and that might be a long wait), you can take some preventive action of your own—at the market and in the kitchen.

The Antidote to Food Poisoning

"Personal food safety requires four basic actions," says Marion Nestle, PhD, professor of nutrition, food studies and public health at New York University and author of *Safe Food* (University of California Press). "Clean your hands and surfaces often. Separate foods to avoid cross-contamination. Cook to the proper temperature. Chill, with prompt refrigeration.

"Much of the meat and produce we buy in supermarkets is contaminated with pathogens that can cause food poisoning," adds Elizabeth Scott, PhD, codirector of the Simmons Center for Hygiene and Health in Home and Community at Simmons College in Boston and coauthor of *How to Prevent Food Poisoning* (Wiley). "But you can protect yourself by learning how to safely transport, store and prepare that food."

● **Clean.** "A golden rule of food safety is to keep high standards of kitchen hygiene," says Dr. Scott, who offers the following advice…

●Wash your hands. "Before handling food, after handling raw foods and between handling different foods—wash your hands. Ditto for after using the toilet, changing diapers, touching or blowing your nose, handling garbage, gardening and handling pets."

In a recent study, Dr. Scott and her colleagues videotaped people preparing foods in their homes and hand-washing before and after. The average time of a washing: five seconds. "People completely underestimate the time it takes for a thorough hand-washing," she says. That would be 20 seconds, about the time it takes to sing all of "Happy Birthday to You."

●Wash counters and contact surfaces (handles, faucets, switches, knobs, etc). After any contact with raw food, use an antibacterial kitchen cleaner (when buying, check the label to make sure that it is registered by the Environmental Protection Agency, which assures its effectiveness for food surfaces), along with a disposable paper towel.

●Wash kitchen equipment and utensils. After each use, wash in the dishwasher or wash with hot soapy water. Air dry, or dry with a clean towel or a paper towel.

●Wash cutting boards. After contact with raw food, wipe down with antibacterial cleanser, and then wash in the dishwasher or kitchen sink.

●Wash sponges. After contact with raw food, wash in the dishwasher or launder. Replace regularly. "Sponges and cloths are ideal breeding grounds for bacteria, and many studies have shown them to be the most contaminated items in the kitchen, even harboring salmonella," says Dr. Scott. "Regularly put them in the laundry or through a dishwasher cycle."

●Wash vegetables. "That includes prepackaged salads," says Dr. Scott. "Labels may say 'Triple-washed and Ready to Eat.' But the product still needs rinsing because manufacturers re-use the water that supposedly cleans and decontaminates these foods."

Best: Before preparation, fill the sink with water and soak these and other vegetables for a few minutes.

● **Chill.** "The first step in preventing food poisoning at home is to store foods properly to ensure they remain in good condition when you're ready to eat them," says Dr. Scott. "As soon as you bring groceries home, get frozen and chilled foods back into a freezer or a refrigerator as quickly as possible. Once these foods begin to thaw and warm, any germs that are present can multiply rapidly."

Warning: Those germs will not be killed by any subsequent chilling or freezing.

● **Separate.** "Even the juices from raw meat and fish can carry food poisoning germs and contaminate other foods," says Dr. Scott. "This process of germs being carried from raw foods to other foods is called cross-contamination. "It can happen when food poisoning germs get onto your hands or onto cutting boards, countertops, sponges, dishcloths, scrubbers and brushes."

What to do: "To minimize the risk of cross-contamination, keep the preparation of raw foods separate from that of other foods," says Dr. Scott. "If possible, complete the preparation of raw foods and then remove all items that have been in contact with raw foods, clean and sanitize the counters, and wash your hands before starting on the preparation of other foods.

"Also keep a cutting board for raw meat and another for vegetables and fruits."

What many people don't know: "Recent scientific data don't support the common notion that the use of wooden cutting boards is more likely than plastics to produce cross-contamination of foods," says Dr. Scott. "It was also found that wooden boards can be effectively sanitized by microwaving at high setting for four minutes—but plastic can't be effectively sanitized in the microwave."

●**Cook.** "Fortunately, cooking takes care of a lot of food safety problems," says Dr. Nestle. "Bacteria usually don't survive heat. Cooking hamburger until it is well done or throwing a bunch of spinach into a pot of boiling water for just one minute will kill nasty bugs like E. coli and salmonella."

Important: Buy and use a cooking thermometer, says Dr. Scott. (Half of American households have one, but only 3% use them to test hamburgers and other high-risk foods.) And there is only one important temperature to remember: 160°F. "This is the lowest temperature that reliably kills food-poisoning germs and destroys heat-sensitive toxins," she says.

Marion Nestle, PhD, professor of nutrition, food studies and public health at New York University and author of *Safe Food* (University of California Press).

Elizabeth Scott, PhD, codirector of the Simmons Center for Hygiene and Health in Home and Community at Simmons College in Boston and coauthor of *How to Prevent Food Poisoning: A Practical Guide to Safe Cooking, Eating, and Food Handling* (Wiley).

Natural Medicine Takes On the MRSA Superbug

There was a time, not long ago, when few people had heard of the dangerous bacterium known as *methicillin-resistant Staphylococcus aureus* (MRSA). That's because what once caused only rare, hospital-acquired staph infections now appears much more frequently...accounts for more than half of all hospital-acquired staph infections...and causes the majority of staph infections transmitted in community settings, such as at gyms and sports facilities. This "superbug," which can be transmitted by skin-to-skin contact or contact with shared sports equipment, got its name because it is increasingly resistant to the effects of *methicillin*, the first-line antibiotic treatment for staph infections. MRSA (pronounced "mersa") can affect all areas of the body but is typically a skin infection. If the bacteria penetrate the skin and spread throughout the body, the infection can become fatal.

Because MRSA is so prevalent and can withstand some antibiotics, natural alternatives are becoming increasingly important to treat these infections. Michael Traub, ND, a naturopathic physician in Kailua Kona, Hawaii, specializes in an integrative approach to dermatologic conditions. Here are Dr. Traub's natural remedies to treat MRSA.

First Steps

How do you know it's MRSA? You don't. A MRSA infection of the skin looks like a boil or a spider bite. It's important to see a physician to get a diagnosis, especially if the spot is very painful or looks different from other boils or bites you have had. (Due to the potential seriousness of the infection, patients should never treat this infection on their own.) The doctor will lance and drain the boil and send the drained pus to a lab to be cultured. The results of this culture are important because it helps the physician pinpoint the antibiotic to be prescribed if one is necessary.

While waiting for the test results (which generally take two days), Dr. Traub immediately begins treatment with *mupirocin* (Bactroban), a prescription topical antibiotic ointment that can be effective, although there is growing microbial resistance to it. For his patients who do not want to use a prescription medicine, he uses tea tree oil. In about half of the MRSA cases he treats, lancing the boil and applying either of these topical treatments (three times daily) clears up the infection. Within 48 hours, it becomes clear if the infection is responding to the treatment or not.

Topical Treatment with Essential Oils

It is helpful to know that many essential oils have been found to kill MRSA in both human and laboratory tests. While tea tree oil is Dr. Traub's favorite, there are others to choose from. The following essential oils, available at most health-food stores, are known to be effective. Note that because there are different strains of MRSA, you and your physician may find that one topical treatment is more effective than others. These oils can be applied directly to the infection with a cotton swab.

• **Tea tree oil.** This powerful antibacterial substance, derived from a tree native to Australia, is effective against all types of Staphylococcus aureus bacteria, including MRSA. In a randomized study published in *The Journal of Hospital Infection*, treatment with a cream containing 10% tea tree oil successfully cleared 41% of MRSA infections.

Brand to try: Herb Pharm Tea Tree Oil (800-348-4372, *www.herb-pharm.com*).

• **Garlic oil** (available in oil, cream and spray form). Long known for its antibacterial effects, garlic has dozens of infection-fighting compounds and has been found effective against MRSA in human trials as well as test tube studies.

Brand to try: Nature's Way Garlic Oil (alcohol free) (800-962-8873, *www.natures way.com* for a store locator).

• **Oregano oil.** A study in Great Britain found that very small amounts of an oil extract of Himalayan oregano (which is not commercially available) outperformed 18 other antibacterial compounds in killing MRSA.

Brand to try: Herb Pharm's Oregano Spirits (800-348-4372, *www.herb-pharm.com*).

Also effective against MRSA: Lemongrass oil, lemon oil, cinnamon oil and white thyme oil. While Dr. Traub finds oils most effective, other holistic physicians also use colloidal silver to treat MRSA.

Next Steps

Physicians base their treatment decisions on the health of the patient and the extent of the infection. If a topical treatment doesn't lead to noticeable improvement within 48 hours, Dr. Traub often prescribes an oral form of garlic or oregano in addition to continuing with the topical treatment.

First choice: Garlic. A product such as Allimed (800-827-7656, *www.allimed.us*) contains allicin, a compound found in garlic that has antibiotic properties. Oregano is available in capsule form. Both the oral and topical treatments should be continued for another 48 hours. If the oral treatment (in combination with the topical treatment) does not heal the infection, Dr. Traub prescribes an oral pharmaceutical antiobiotic.

If at any point the infection gets worse or spreads (and is red, swollen or tender), then oral pharmaceutical antibiotics are prescribed based on the results of the lab test. (MRSA is resistant to some antibiotics, such as methicillin and amoxicillin, but not to all antibiotics.)

Mark A. Stengler, NMD, naturopathic medical doctor in private practice, Encinitas, California, and author of the *Bottom Line/Natural Healing* newsletter. *www.drstengler.com*.

Michael Taub, ND, naturopathic physician in private practice in Kailua Kona, Hawaii. He is author of *Dermatological Diagnosis and Natural Therapeutics*.

Chapter 15

SKIN CONDITIONS

Curry Cream Erases Wrinkles

The spice turmeric is a kitchen staple in India, found in just about every dish that crosses the table, including curries—and it's one of nature's most powerful healers," says Bharat Aggarwal, PhD, professor of experimental therapeutics at MD Anderson Cancer Center in Houston and author of *Healing Spices* (Sterling).

"Turmeric owes it preventive and curative skills to curcumin, its active ingredient," he continues. "Curcumin is a compound so diverse and powerfully rich in antioxidant and anti-inflammatory actions that it has been shown to protect and improve the health of virtually every organ in the body."

And that includes the body's biggest organ—your skin.

New finding: In studies presented at the annual meeting of the American Academy of Dermatology (AAD), a turmeric-based moisturizing cream reduced fine lines, wrinkles and age spots.

Anti-Wrinkles, Anti-Spots

"For the first time, we've shown clinically relevant anti-aging benefits from a turmeric extract," says Cheri Swanson, PhD, the leader of the two studies.

●**Smoothing fine lines.** In the first study, 89 women, aged 40 to 60, applied a turmeric-containing skin cream to one side of their face twice daily, and a placebo cream to the other side.

Results: Dermatologists evaluated photographs of the women's faces at the beginning of the study and after eight weeks of using turmeric—and found the turmeric cream was "significantly better at reducing the appearance of fine lines and wrinkles" than the placebo cream.

●**Erasing age spots.** In a similar study, 105 women aged 25 to 55 used the skin cream or the placebo cream for eight weeks. But this time they were evaluated for age spots, or what dermatologists call *hyperpigmentation*.

Results: The turmeric-based cream reduced the appearance of age spots by 15%. "Even a 10% change is very noticeable," says Dr. Swanson.

●**Confirming the mechanism of action.** In another study, Dr. Swanson and her colleagues found that a turmeric extract activated 11 different "antioxidant genes" and deactivated genes involved in the production of oxidizing free radicals. They also found the extract was anti-inflammatory. "Antioxidant and anti-inflammatory properties of turmeric" were confirmed, the scientists told dermatologists at the AAD meeting.

Product: The colorless, odorless "Turmeric Complex" used in the studies is contained in several Doctors Dermatological Formula (DDF) products from Procter & Gamble. *They include…*

●**DDF Advanced Firming Cream**

●**DDF Advanced Eye Firming Concentrate**

●**DDF Advanced Micro-Exfoliation Cleanser**

●**DDF Restoring Night Serum**

You can find DDF products on the Web at *www.ddfskincare.com* and other online stores, and at beauty and skin-care retailers such as Sephora.

Wrinkle-Reducing Turmeric Mask

If you don't want to spend money on over-the-counter skin-care products, you can make your own turmeric-containing, wrinkle-reducing facial mask, says Dr. Aggarwal.

"My wife and many other Indian women use such a facial mask to keep the face smooth, radiant and free of wrinkles and blemishes," he says.

To make the mask, Indian women use sesame oil made in India, but any odorless oil, such as vegetable or canola, will do. "To use sesame, you must get the sesame oil found in Indian markets, as the sesame oil generally found in supermarkets has a strong smell and is expensive," says Dr. Aggarwal.

"This formula should last for several uses, and feels fresh and clean as a spa facial—at a fraction of the cost!" he says.

Turmeric Facial Mask

Ingredients…

½ cup garbanzo (chickpea) flour
1½ tablespoons turmeric
Odorless cooking oil
Water

Instructions…

1. Mix the flour and turmeric in a container with a tight-fitting lid. Store container in a dry place.

2. To make the mask, mix about 1 tablespoon of the flour mixture in a small dish with about 5 drops of oil. Add enough water to make a paste. It should be the consistency of cake batter.

3. Pull your hair back or cover it with a towel. Using your fingertips, spread the mixture on your face and neck, making sure to stay clear of the eyes. Let the mixture stay on your face until it dries, about 15 minutes. Wash it off in the shower.

Bharat Aggarwal, PhD, professor of cancer research, biochemistry, immunology and experimental therapeutics, director of the Cytokine Research Laboratory, MD Anderson Cancer Center, Houston, Texas, and author of *Healing Spices: How to Use 50 Everyday and Exotic Spices to Boost Health and Beat Disease* (Sterling).

Cheri Swanson, PhD, senior scientist, Procter & Gamble, Cincinnati, Ohio.

Don't Let Stress Age Your Skin

You know how important it is to control stress to feel better. But did you know that the outward signs of aging—lines, wrinkles, dull skin, dark circles under the eyes—are not necessarily the inevitable results of time but often the signs of emotional wear and tear? If allowed to progress, "stress aging" can add three…or seven…or even more years to your appearance.

The desire to look younger has fueled a multibillion-dollar industry that includes Botox and collagen injections, face-lifts and cosmetics too various to count.

Good news: Simple, no-cost solutions, which rival these expensive products and invasive procedures, can improve the look of aging skin.

Stress Takes Its Toll

The body's response to stress has an impact on virtually every organ. We all know about its effect on the heart and arteries, the digestive tract and the brain. But the skin is also an organ—and it is exquisitely sensitive to stress.

Our skin, which is richly supplied with nerves and blood vessels, marshals its own immune system. Stress causes this network to release *epinephrine* (also known as adrenaline), the fight-or-flight hormone that tightens blood vessels, depriving the skin of robust circulation and causing a pale, patchy complexion.

The bigger damage-causer, however, is *cortisol*, the hormone released when stress levels are kicked up a notch. Cortisol takes a toll on elastin and collagen, fibers that give body and texture to the skin and fill it out with a layer of connective tissue just beneath the surface.

Collagen, which makes up 90% of skin tissue, is in a state of constant renewal…until stress steps in. Cortisol drastically slows the turnover, tipping the balance away from the formation of new collagen. The skin literally grows thinner, less elastic and less able to repair itself. Wrinkles at any age are the direct result of weakened, diminished collagen and elastin.

Fortunately, fighting the effects of stress is very much within your control. *Here's how…*

Get Better Sleep

We know that getting enough sleep is crucial to our health, but many people don't realize that not getting enough sleep has a direct impact on our ability to handle stress. During sleep, growth hormone, which stimulates cell growth and renewal, is secreted, while cortisol levels dwindle.

Without adequate sleep, facial blood circulation diminishes, leaving skin pale and washed out. Sleeping long and deeply enough to rest your body completely can knock years off your appearance.

When it comes to sleep, individual needs differ. Let your body guide you…if you don't awaken refreshed, you need more sleep. All too often, people who claim they can get by on five or six hours of sleep are fooling themselves. Seven to eight hours is the average goal.

Stress can also cause sleep troubles. *If stress keeps you up at night, try the following…*

●**Drink valerian tea or chamomile tea one hour before bedtime.** These teas help many people relax enough to ease into a regular sleep rhythm. Also make sure you're following good sleep habits (such as not watching TV and not using the computer at least 30 minutes before bedtime).

If you need even more help, consider trying a sedating antihistamine (such as Benadryl) 30 minutes before retiring.

Note: Antihistamine use for this purpose should be considered a short-term solution (no more than three days).

●**Eat a well-chosen bedtime snack.** Combine complex carbohydrates (such as a whole-wheat cracker) and protein (a piece of low-fat cheese)—that combination helps ease the body into sleep. Calcium promotes production of *melatonin*, a natural sleep hormone. This is why if you take calcium supplements, it's best to take them at night.

If you still have trouble sleeping, go to the National Sleep Foundation Web site, *www.sleepfoundation.org*, for more advice.

Take "La-la-laaah" Breaks

You can modify something you do every minute of every day—breathe—to combat stress and improve your appearance. Practice abdominal breathing—letting the muscles of your torso relax so that as air fills your lungs and expands your chest, your belly pushes out. Take a five-minute break and practice this type of breathing—in the morning and the busy part of the afternoon, sitting quietly with your feet on the floor and hands in your lap. You'll break the cycle of escalating stress.

Here are two simple, helpful breathing exercises…

●**Inhale slowly through your nose for a count of five and let it all out through your mouth.** As the exhalation ends, silently repeat, "la-la-la-la-laaah" to extend it, fully releasing the air from your lungs. Repeat five times.

●**Breathe in and out through your nose,** counting to three on the in-breath and three on the out-breath, followed by a three-beat pause. Repeat five times. Try increasing the count to four or five, depending on what's comfortable.

Once you've built breathing breaks into your routine, you'll be able to use them whenever you need to relax.

The Ideal Exercise Regimen

Since exercise reduces the effects of stress for about 24 hours, it's wise to build plenty of physical activity into your daily schedule. It improves circulation, nourishing cells and removing waste. The beta-endorphins released by exercise counteract the effects of cortisol.

Helpful: Several 10- to 20-minute bouts of activity over the course of the day are the equivalent of a sustained workout. An ideal exercise program includes aerobic work (such as brisk walking, biking and swimming)…strength training (with weights)…and stretching. Any combination of activities will do as long as you enjoy them and stick with them. If you've been sedentary, talk to your doctor first. You'll want to start at a low level and increase slowly.

Amy Wechsler, MD, one of eight doctors in the US who is board-certified in both dermatology and psychiatry. She has a private practice in New York City and is the author of *The Mind-Beauty Connection: 9 Days to Reverse Stress Aging and Reveal More Youthful, Beautiful Skin* (Free Press). *www.dramywechsler.com.*

How to Stop a Scar From Forming

Accidents often leave a mark. To prevent a scar from forming after a minor injury to your skin…

Clean the wound immediately with hydrogen peroxide or warm water and gentle soap, such as Dove or Cetaphil. Apply an over-the-counter antibiotic ointment, such as Polysporin or Bacitracin, to prevent infection and keep the wound moist. Use a bandage or sterile gauze to keep dirt out and prevent a scab from forming—new cells grow in from the sides of a wound toward the middle, and a scab slows them. If the wound is deep or on your face, see a dermatologist or plastic surgeon. If a wound heals with a raised scar, laser treatment to flatten the scar is most effective within the first two to three months.

Neal Schultz, MD, assistant clinical professor at Mount Sinai School of Medicine, and cosmetic dermatologist in private practice, Park Avenue Skin Care, both in New York City.

Natural Ways to Soothe A Dry, Itchy Scalp

Are you scratching your head and wondering what's causing those icky flakes? It could be that your commercial hair-care products contain chemicals that are too harsh. *Take a natural approach…*

●**Try homemade herbal scalp treatments.** Prepare one of the following (ingredients are sold at health-food stores and online), pour into a spray bottle and store in the refrigerator. Once or more per week, wet your hair and then apply four to eight ounces, massaging it into your scalp for several minutes. Wait 15 minutes, then shampoo.

Options for all hair types…

●**For flare-ups.** Tea tree oil. In a small bowl, combine eight ounces of water with 40 drops of tea tree oil (a natural antifungal and antiseptic).

• **Preventative.** Burdock root and nettle. In a saucepan, mix one tablespoon of dried or three tablespoons of fresh, finely chopped burdock root (which supports oil glands and hair follicles) with two cups of water. Bring to a boil, reduce heat, cover, and simmer 30 minutes. Remove from heat. Stir in one tablespoon of dried or three tablespoons of fresh, chopped nettle, an anti-inflammatory. (With fresh nettle, wear rubber gloves to avoid getting stung.) Let sit, covered, for 15 minutes. Strain through cheesecloth, cool.

• **Buy gentle products.** Choose shampoos, conditioners and styling products free of harsh or potentially toxic ingredients. Avoid *sodium lauryl sulfate* (a strong detergent), various *parabens* (preservatives) and *cocomide DEA* (a foaming agent).

Recommended: Products from Aubrey Organics (800-282-7394, *www.aubrey-organics. com*) or Giovanni Cosmetics (*www.giovanni cosmetics.com*).

• **Use henna instead of hair dyes** (which contain chemicals that can irritate the scalp). Made from a flowering plant, henna provides a reddish tint that blends with your natural color and lasts up to six weeks. Henna is best for brown or black hair (it can be used on blond or gray hair but may turn light hair too orange).

To intensify color: Instead of mixing powdered henna with water, mix it with brewed coffee for a richer brown tint…with red wine for auburn highlights…or with beet juice to tone down henna's orange cast.

• **Nourish your scalp from the inside out.** Take a daily probiotic supplement that contains live *bifidobacterium* and *lactobacillus* to help balance the beneficial bacteria in your digestive tract.

Good brands: Enzymatic Therapy Pearls IC (800-783-2286, *www.enzymatictherapy. com*) and Sedona Labs i-Flora Multi-Probiotic (888-816-8804, *www.sedonalabs.com*).

Crystal Renée Stelzer, an herbalist and adjunct faculty member in the Department of Botanical Medicine at Bastyr University in Kenmore, Washington. She teaches classes in herbal medicine making, nutrition and plant identification in the wild.

You Don't Need a Drug to Cure Hives

Hives, which are not contagious, can be caused by skin contact with allergens, such as those found in plants, pets, latex or insect stings. Eating certain foods, such as shellfish, eggs, peanuts, wheat and dairy products, or consuming food dyes or other food additives also can cause hives. Hypersensitivity to certain drugs is another cause—the most common triggers include penicillin and penicillin-related antibiotics, aspirin and other nonsteroidal anti-inflammatory drugs (NSAIDs). In short, chances are good you will suffer hives (technically known as *urticaria*) at some point—roughly one of every five Americans experiences it during his/her lifetime—and the condition may occur even if you've never had a reaction to a particular substance before.

The over-the-counter antihistamine *diphenhydramine* (Benadryl) helps reduce the inflammation and itch associated with hives but is rarely 100% effective and has a long list of potential side effects. These include dizziness, drowsiness, nervousness and sleeplessness. In addition, diphenhydramine should not be taken by people with certain health problems, such as ulcers, an enlarged prostate, sleep apnea, asthma, difficulty urinating or glaucoma, without consulting a doctor. *If you have hives and would prefer to use a safe and effective natural treatment, consider…*

• **Homeopathic remedies.** Try the one that best matches your symptoms. Arsenicum album—when skin burns as well as itches, and the sufferer is restless and anxious…sulfur—when itching is worse with heat, such as in bed or in a bath or direct sun…Urtica urens—when itching skin appears blotchy and also stings and feels scalded.

Typical dose: Two pellets of a 30C potency of one remedy, three times daily for up to five days.

• **Aloe vera gel.** To soothe the itching, apply chilled pure aloe vera gel (available in stores that sell botanical medicines) directly to your skin up to five times daily. Also, take oatmeal baths as often as desired.

What to do: Put one cup of raw rolled oats in a cotton sock, slide the open end over a faucet and tie the sock to the faucet so that bath water flows through the oats into the tub. Soak for 20 to 30 minutes. Keep the temperature moderate (about 100°F is best). Hot water can worsen itching.

• **Drink a lot of fluids (64 ounces daily),** get plenty of rest and take brisk walks (several times a day) to speed healing and reduce inflammation. Once the cause of your hives has been identified and is avoided, urticaria generally clears up in seven to 10 days.

Hives are not dangerous, but repeat exposure to the cause can lead to an ever-worsening reaction. If you have difficulty swallowing or shortness of breath with hives, seek immediate medical care.

Jamison Starbuck, ND, naturopathic physician in family practice and a guest lecturer at the University of Montana, both in Missoula. She is a contributing editor to The Alternative Advisor: The Complete Guide to Natural Therapies and Alternative Treatments *(Time Life).*

Freckle Faders

Should you be concerned if your face and back have more freckles every year? And is there a safe way to make them fade?

If you like your freckles, there's no need to worry. Freckles are harmless pockets of the skin pigment *melanin* that become prominent on sun-exposed areas of the body. Abundant freckling does not mean that you will develop skin cancer, but it does suggest that your skin is sun-sensitive and your risk for skin cancer may be elevated. Use sunscreen, wear a wide-brimmed hat and limit exposure to midday sun to help prevent existing freckles from darkening, keep new freckles from developing and reduce your skin cancer risk. If any freckle or other spot looks strange—lumpy, scaly, reddish, unusually large—see your dermatologist.

Don't even think of rubbing lemon juice on freckles in an attempt to lighten them.

This old folk "remedy" can make skin blister or break out in a rash when you're in the sun. Instead, try an over-the-counter fade cream, such as Ambi or Porcelana, with 2% hydroquinone...or a prescription 4% hydroquinone cream. These work by blocking the synthesis of new melanin (not by bleaching existing spots)—so it may take several months of daily use for old melanin to migrate out through the natural process of exfoliation.

For faster and more thorough results, see your dermatologist for laser therapy. It works by using specific wavelengths of light to break down the melanin, which is then expelled from the surface and also carried away by your body's lymphatic system. Most people experience mild discomfort from the laser procedure, so your doctor may use a numbing cream on your skin before starting. Usually one session eliminates or substantially reduces existing freckles (though future sun exposure may create new ones). A session typically costs $500 to $1,500, depending on the size of the area treated, and generally is not covered by medical insurance.

Jessie S. Cheung, MD, associate director of cosmetic dermatology and assistant professor of dermatology, Langone Medical Center, New York University, New York City.

Is Your Sunscreen Dangerous? New Rules And What You Can Do

Protecting your skin from sun damage is a year-round concern. But many widely available sunscreens contain potentially dangerous (possibly cancerous) ingredients, provide inadequate protection and are often portrayed by their marketers as being far more beneficial than they actually are.

According to a recent report by the Environmental Working Group (EWG), an organization that works to protect public health and the environment, the list of offenders includes leading sunscreen brands that are readily displayed in your local drugstore and even some products designed just for babies.

Close on the heels of this report are guidelines issued by the FDA for the labeling of sunscreen products.

The EWG (*www.ewg.org*) issued its fifth annual guide to the best and worst sunscreens in May 2011. After reviewing standard industry, government and academic data sources and analyzing hundreds of sunscreen ingredient listings, the nonprofit watchdog recommended only 1 in 5 out of more than 600 beach and sport sunscreen products (an improvement over last year, when only 1 in 12 products made the cut).

In June 2011, the FDA issued new regulations on sunscreen labeling. These regulations should take effect by summer 2012, although the FDA expects to see labels change for the better sooner.

The New Rules

According to FDA.gov, only sunscreens that pass the FDA's test for protection against both ultraviolet A (UVA) and ultraviolet B (UVB) rays can carry the label "Broad Spectrum."

"After reviewing the latest science, the FDA determined that sufficient data are available to establish a standard broad spectrum test procedure that measures UVA radiation protection in relation to the amount of UVB radiation protection. This designation will give consumers better information on which sunscreen products offer the greatest protection from both UVA and UVB exposure that can lead to an increased risk of skin cancer," states the FDA.

Also per the regulations, manufacturers can no longer label sunscreens as "waterproof" or "sweatproof" or identify their products as "sunblocks," since, according to the FDA, these claims overstate effectiveness. Only Broad Spectrum sunscreens with an SPF value of 15 or higher can claim to reduce the risk of skin cancer and early skin aging—those between 2 and 14 can only claim to help prevent sunburn.

Sunscreens also cannot claim to provide sun protection for more than two hours without submitting sufficient data and obtaining FDA approval. And water resistance claims on the front label must indicate whether the sunscreen remains effective for 40 minutes or 80 minutes while swimming or sweating, based on standard testing. Sunscreens that are not water resistant must include a direction instructing consumers to use a water-resistant sunscreen if swimming or sweating.

All sunscreens must also include standard "Drug Facts" information on the back and/or side of container.

Dangerous Ingredients

None of the recommended products in EWG's 2011 sunscreen guide include chemicals that EWG considers harmful, such as *oxybenzone*, which is linked with hormone disruption and cell damage, and *retinyl palminate*, a vitamin A compound that has photo-carcinogenic properties that may speed up cancer formation.

What to buy: EWG research analyst Nneka Leiba urges that consumers read ingredient labels and avoid any sunscreen containing oxybenzone and retinyl palminate, especially lotions for children. The organization recommends using broad-spectrum sunscreens that derive their protective properties not from chemicals that penetrate the skin, but from the metals titanium or zinc, which stay on the surface of the skin, do their job to protect you and can be washed off entirely. EWG also recommends that people avoid sunscreen sprays, since the chemicals they contain can be easily inhaled.

What's Next...and What You Can Do Now

Although the new FDA rules are a step in the right direction, the industry has a way to go. Sunscreen makers are still not required to test for SPF protection or to truthfully limit SPF claims...but the FDA is working on it. Along with the specific regulations stated above, the FDA issued a "proposed rule." If finalized, the proposed rule would limit the maximum SPF value on sunscreen labels to "50+" because, according to the FDA, "there is no sufficient data to show that products with SPF values higher than 50 provide greater protection for users than products with SPF values of 50."

According to Leiba, the high SPF levels (such as "SPF 100") touted on many sunscreen labels are a big concern at EWG. Products with numbers that are double or triple the standard figures of 15 or 30 seem to provide twice as much protection, allowing extra sun time...but this is not the case. According to the American Cancer Society, higher SPF rates only impart a percentage point or two more protection (SPF 15 sunscreens filter out about 93% of UVB rays, while SPF 30 sunscreens filter out about 97%, SPF 50 sunscreens about 98%). Also, the SPF rating applies to UVB rays only. A higher number does not mean extra protection against cancer-causing UVA rays.

What to do to protect yourself: Apply safe sunscreen* in lavish amounts. Studies show that most consumers use only one-quarter to two-thirds of the amount needed to reach a product's SPF rating. Sunscreen should be applied early (30 minutes before sun exposure) to allow its protective capabilities to work...and often, typically every two hours or more if swimming or exercising.

There's no consensus on an optimal SPF: The American Cancer Society recommends that you use a sunscreen with an SPF of at least 15...while the American Academy of Dermatology says 30. And since the "proposed rule" confirms that the FDA concurs high sunscreen ratings are inherently misleading, consumers should think twice before paying more for any SPF rating above 50.

*For EWG's list of best (and worst) sunscreens and more information on sunscreen safety, visit *http://breakingnews. ewg.org/2011sunscreen/.*

Nneka Leiba, MPH, research analyst, Environmental Working Group (*www.ewg.org*), Washington, DC.

US Food and Drug Administration. "Questions and Answers: FDA announces new requirements for over-the-counter (OTC) sunscreen products marketed in the U.S." *http://www. fda.gov/Drugs/ResourcesForYou/Consumers/BuyingUsing MedicineSafely/UnderstandingOver-the-CounterMedicines/ ucm258468.htm.*

The American Cancer Society. "Skin Cancer Prevention and Early Detection." *http://www.cancer.org/Cancer/SkinCancer-Melanoma/MoreInformation/SkinCancerPreventionandEar lyDetection/skin-cancer-prevention-and-early-detection-u-v-protection.*

The Salad Cure for Sun-Damaged Skin

What are the hottest ingredients in skin care that can help protect you from the ravages of the sun, such as wrinkles and sags...and even skin-cancer?

Tomatoes, carrots and broccoli.

What you may not know: According to recent scientific studies, what you put in your body—the foods you eat—may be just as important for youthful, healthy skin as any skin-care ingredients that you put on your body.

"High-quality nutrition provides all the raw materials necessary for both structure and functioning of skin—and a steady stream of optimal nutrients goes a long way in supporting healthy skin over the course of a lifetime," says Alan C. Logan, ND, a naturopathic doctor and author of *Your Skin, Younger* (Cumberland House).

Newest Research

"A diet rich in a variety of colorful vegetables and fruits can put the brakes on the skin's aging process," says Dr. Logan. *The latest studies show he's right...*

• **Tomatoes.** Researchers from the University of Manchester in England studied 17 women aged 21 to 47, dividing them into two groups—one group ate a "scientific snack" of about two ounces of tomato paste with olive oil every day, while the other group just consumed olive oil. At the beginning of the study and after three months, a small section of skin on the women's buttocks was exposed to a dose of skin-aging ultraviolet (UV) radiation (the same type of radiation from the sun), to see how much UV light it took to produce damaging redness.

Results: After eating tomato paste every day for three months, it took 28% longer for the UV radiation to produce redness. There was no difference in the women who just ate the olive oil.

And those who ate the tomato paste also had lower levels of skin damage and healthier skin when they were exposed to UV light. Specifically, they had...

• **Less damage to fibrillin-1,** a protein that helps form elastin, the fiber that maintains the elasticity of skin (so that it doesn't sag).

• **Less buildup of matrix metalloproteinase,** enzymes that damage collagen, protein fibers that help maintain the firmness and youth of skin (so that it doesn't wrinkle).

• **More procollagen,** the molecule that forms collagen.

• **Less DNA damage in skin cells.**

In short, they had less of what dermatologists call *photoaging*—damage from the sun's UV radiation.

"Tomato paste provides protection against acute and potentially longer-term aspects of photoaging," concluded the researchers in the *British Journal of Dermatology.*

Why it works: Tomatoes contain the carotenoid lycopene, an antioxidant and pigment that has UV-protecting properties, says Dr. Logan. "Lycopene is abundant in tomato products, and also in apricots, pink grapefruit, guava and watermelon. If you decide to incorporate lycopene in your diet, consider eating tomatoes or taking a tomato-extract supplement."

Example of a tomato-extract supplement: Lyc-O-Mato, from LycoRed (*www.lycored.com*).

• **Carrots, sweet potatoes, romaine lettuce, spinach and kale.** Beta-carotene is another carotenoid, found abundantly in carrots, sweet potatoes, winter squash, romaine lettuce, spinach, kale, dandelion greens, collard greens and turnip greens.

And like lycopene, it can protect skin.

The study: Korean researchers in the Department of Dermatology at Seoul National University studied the skin of 30 women aged 50 and over, who took beta-carotene for three months.

"Beta-carotene improved facial wrinkles and elasticity significantly," reported the researchers in the medical journal *Dermatol-*

ogy. The women also had four times more procollagen.

"Thirty milligrams (mg) per day of beta-carotene supplementation is demonstrated to prevent and repair photoaging," they concluded.

You can get 30 mg of beta-carotene in about five servings of red, orange or dark green vegetables.

• **Broccoli sprouts.** Researchers in the School of Medicine at Johns Hopkins University conducted an experiment with two groups of hairless mice, feeding one group an extract from broccoli sprouts, and then exposing both groups to 17 weeks of UV radiation.

Results: The broccoli-eating mice developed 25% less skin cancer, and the tumors they developed were 70% smaller. The results were reported in *Photochemical & Photobiological Sciences.*

Why it works: Broccoli sprouts are the richest dietary source of *sulforaphane glucosinolate* (SGS), containing 50 times more than mature broccoli—and SGS is the precursor to *sulphoraphane*, a powerful anti-cancer compound.

See page 92 for complete instructions on growing broccoli sprouts.

• **Berries and nuts.** *Ellagic acid* is an antioxidant found in blackberries, raspberries, strawberries and cranberries, and also in walnuts, pecans and in pomegranates.

The study: Korean researchers conducted studies with human skin cells and experimental animals, and found that ellagic acid could reduce the breakdown of collagen...reduce inflammation from UV exposure...and help prevent the formation of wrinkles and age-related skin thickening.

"Dietary interventions with berries rich in ellagic acid may be a promising treatment strategy for interrupting skin wrinkling and inflammation associated with chronic UV exposure," concluded the researchers in the journal *Experimental Dermatology.*

And in another animal study, researchers from the Department of Dermatology at the University of Wisconsin found that a pomegranate fruit extract rich in ellagic acid reduced seven different biomarkers of skin cancer.

The extract "affords substantial protection from the adverse effects of UVB radiation," wrote the researchers in the journal *Photochemistry and Photobiology.*

• **The Mediterranean diet.** All the foods just discussed are found in abundance in the Mediterranean diet, which is rich in vegetables, fruits and nuts. And an Israeli researcher thinks the Mediterranean diet is very good for your skin.

"Foods such as colorful fruits and vegetables—as well as olive oil, fish and yogurt—fight the oxidizing effect of the sun," says Niva Shapira, PhD, RD, of the Stanley Steyer School of Health Professions at Tel Aviv University, in the journal *Nutrition Reviews.* "The presence of these foods in the traditional Greek-style Mediterranean diet may have contributed to the low rates of melanoma in the Mediterranean region, despite high levels of solar radiation."

To help prove her point, Dr. Shapira conducted a study, dividing participants into two groups—for two weeks, one group drank an antioxidant-rich fruit beverage supplemented with the antioxidants vitamin C, vitamin E and selenium, and one group didn't drink the beverage. During the two weeks, both groups had four to six hours of sun exposure a day.

At the end of two weeks, those drinking the antioxidant-rich beverage had no increase in blood levels of *malondialdehyde* (MDA), a biomarker of skin-damaging oxidation—while those not drinking the beverage had a 50% increase.

She also cites a study that links the following features of the Mediterranean diet to lower risk for skin cancer…

• **Weekly consumption of fish** (omega-3 fatty acids in fish protect the skin)

• **Daily drinking of tea** (both black and green tea are rich in antioxidants)

• **High intakes of vegetables** (particularly carrots, broccoli and other cruciferous vegetables, and leafy green vegetables)

• **High intakes of fruit**

• **High intakes of carotenoids** (such as found in tomatoes).

"If you provide the body with sufficient and relevant antioxidants, you can reduce damage from sun exposure," she concludes.

Bottom line: "The health of your skin starts with what you eat," says Julia Hunter, MD, a holistic dermatologist and medical director of Skin Fitness Plus in Beverly Hills, California. "Food is your medicine—along with external sun protection, it's a crucial way to prevent the aging of skin, and to rejuvenate skin that has aged. And the more anti-inflammatory antioxidants in your diet, the better."

Alan C. Logan, ND, naturopathic doctor and author of *Your Skin, Younger* and *The Clear Skin Diet* (Cumberland House). His scientific articles have appeared in *Archives of Dermatology*, the *International Journal of Dermatology*, the *Journal of the American Academy of Dermatology* and the *British Journal of Dermatology. www.drlogan.com.*

Niva Shapira, PhD, RD, School of Health Professions, Tel Aviv University.

Julia Hunter, MD, holistic dermatologist and medical director of Skin Fitness Plus in Beverly Hills, California. *www.skinfitnessplus.com.*

Quick Cure for Sunburn Pain

To ease the pain of sunburn, take the homeopathic preparation Cantharis. Use a 30C potency four to six times daily for two days. This remedy helps to prevent or reduce blistering and burn pain. Cantharis is safe for everyone. In addition, you can apply a gel of 90% to 99% aloe. Both are available at health-food stores.

Mark A. Stengler, NMD, licensed naturopathic medical doctor in private practice, Encinitas, California, author of the *Bottom Line/Natural Healing* newsletter. *www.drstengler.com.*

A Contrarian View on Tanning Beds

The World Health Organization (WHO) recently announced that it has elevated sun beds, used for tanning by tens of millions of people in the US alone, to its highest cancer risk category—at the same level as mustard gas and arsenic. According to Andrew Rubman, ND, we shouldn't be so quick to condemn.

In recent years, public health experts concerned about the rising incidence of skin cancer have issued blanket warnings about the dangers of tanning by both natural and artificial means. However, along with many other naturopathic practitioners, Dr. Rubman believes that the WHO and the mainstream medical community have gone overboard in their admonitions. Yes, it's true that excessive exposure to ultraviolet UVA and UVB rays can cause skin cancer, but moderate exposure to sun or other light is not harmful and actually facilitates good health by enabling your body to manufacture a key nutrient— vitamin D.

Nice Tan

For most people, spending 10 to 20 minutes outdoors each day will provide all the vitamin D you need. Natural sunlight is best, confirms Dr. Rubman, noting that we are genetically "primed" to use it for vitamin D synthesis. But when sunshine is scarce—for example, if you live in the northern US during cold and gray winter months—you can replace what you're missing by visiting a tanning salon from time to time, he says. Keep in mind, however, that tanning beds deliver a more intense and concentrated dose of ultraviolet radiation, which poses a greater threat of skin cancer.

How Much Is Too Much?

The degree to which you can safely bask in the sun or on a sun bed is determined by factors such as your ethnicity, skin type and pigmentation, whether you freckle easily or have a lot of moles, cumulative sun exposure, medical history and general vulnerability to sunburn or skin cancer. Put simply, the darker your skin, the more natural protection you possess against the dangers of UV radiation and the longer you can safely spend on the beach or in the tanning booth. Dr. Rubman says there is no consensus among experts as to how much time is considered "safe." He advises erring on the side of caution, taking into account your individual risk factors and consulting with your doctor to set your own standards.

Not All Salons Are the Same

The next step is to locate a reputable tanning salon. While requirements vary from state to state and even within states, most license such facilities to ensure that staff is properly trained…that the equipment complies with FDA standards for radiation-emitting products (including that it carries appropriate warning labels and specific information for safe use)…that the facilities are sanitary… and that they have a list of medications with side effects associated with exposure to sunlight or tanning.

Inquire whether the tanning beds are properly sterilized between uses and be skeptical if you notice that the facility is less than sparkling clean. UVB rays are the triggers for vitamin D manufacture, but since they're also more likely to burn skin than UVA radiation, many tanning beds contain bulbs that emit primarily UVA rays. Not only will this not facilitate the health benefit of vitamin D, since UVA rays have longer wavelengths and penetrate deeper into skin, you may unknowingly damage deeper layers of skin and raise cancer risk—without even getting a sunburn that would alert you to the danger.

Additional safety tips include…

● **Visit a tanning salon no more than once a week.**

● **Limit your exposure.** As a rule of thumb, spend about half as much time on a tanning bed as you would spend in the sun. Since 10 to 20 minutes is sufficient for vitamin D synthesis, determine your tanning-bed time from there—if you typically go outdoors for 15 minutes to stoke your vitamin D levels, tan for 7½ minutes.

• **Position the "cover" so that it is about six inches from your body.**

• **Wear UV-protective eyewear** (opaque black plastic cups that completely cover the eyes, letting no light in). Make sure that these fit securely and are not cracked or broken.

• **Make sure that trained staff is on duty at all times to ensure that there is no malfunction of the timer,** so you don't inadvertently stay under the lights longer than is safe.

Be especially careful if you have any of the known risk factors for skin cancer. For such people, the risk of using tanning beds may outweigh the potential benefits. Dr. Rubman also warns young people to use sun beds with extreme caution, if at all, since overexposure to UV radiation in your teens and 20s increases the risk of life-threatening melanoma later on. For most healthy adults, a careful approach to tanning can help you maintain a good biochemical balance of vitamin D and all the health benefits that come with that.

Andrew Rubman, ND, medical director, Southbury Clinic for Traditional Medicines, Southbury, Connecticut. *www. naturopath.org.*

STRESS, INSOMNIA & FATIGUE

Five Science-Proven Ways to Ease Stress

" It is estimated that up to 75% of all visits to physicians are from people with a stress-related problem," says Edward Charlesworth, PhD, a clinical psychologist, director of Willibrook Psychological Associates in Houston, Texas, and author of *Stress Management: A Comprehensive Guide to Wellness* (Ballantine Books).

Want to reduce stress and feel better? Scientists in the US and around the globe spent a lot of time recently discovering how to ease tension and stress. *Some of their top findings...*

Eat a Handful of Walnuts

Eating a diet rich in walnuts and walnut oil helps the body cope with stress, reports a team of researchers from Pennsylvania State University in the *American Journal of Clinical Nutrition*. The researchers fed 22 healthy adults three different diets, with each dietary phase lasting six weeks. In one phase, the participants ate a handful of walnuts a day (9 walnuts) and a tablespoon of walnut oil (as a salad dressing or baked into a muffin).

The walnut diet was the only one that lowered blood pressure responses to psychological or physical stress (making a speech or immersing a foot in cold water)—probably because the omega-3 fatty acids in the walnuts helped relax arteries.

"This is an important finding, because we can't avoid all of the stressors in our daily lives," says Sheila G. West, PhD, a study author and associate professor of biobehavioral health and nutritional sciences at Pennsylvania State University.

What to do: Eat one serving of walnuts in place of another snack, says Dr. West. Use a tablespoon of walnut oil in a salad dressing as a replacement for another oil.

Relax Your Muscles

Researchers in Germany found that people in a telephone call center (a very stressful job) who practiced the stress reduction technique of progressive relaxation for 20 minutes over lunch breaks had less "post-lunchtime and afternoon strain" than people who made "small talk" with coworkers over lunch. The results were in the *Journal of Occupational Health Psychology*.

What to do: "Progressive relaxation is an excellent starting point for stress management," says Dr. Charlesworth. "It increases general bodily awareness and the recognition of specific muscles where tension is troublesome." *His basic instructions…*

1. Wearing loose, comfortable clothing, recline on a sofa, lie on a bed or sit in a comfortable chair in a quiet room with dim lights. Separately tense your individual muscle groups (head, neck, shoulders, arms and hands, chest, back, abdomen, hips, legs and feet).

Examples: For your head, wrinkle your forehead, squint your eyes tightly, open your mouth wide, push your tongue against the roof of your mouth, and clench your jaw tightly. For your back, arch your back.

2. Hold the tension about five seconds in each group.

3. Release the tension slowly, and at the same time silently say, "Relax and let go."

4. Inhale a deep breath.

5. As you breathe slowly out, silently say, "Relax and let go."

For best results: Practice the technique for 20 minutes every day. After one month, you'll be able to do what Dr. Charlesworth calls "cued relaxation"—whenever you're feeling uptight, just take a deep breath, and as you breathe out think, "Relax and let go."

"You'll immediately feel a wave of relaxation all over your body," he says.

Visualize Success

If you're bashful, sensitive to criticism, have difficulty trusting people, have difficulty talking in groups or have low self-confidence—you're likely to experience what psychologists call "social stress," says Dr. Charlesworth.

And in a recent study by researchers at UCLA, people with the highest levels of so-cial stress (while making a speech in front of a "panel" of people in white lab coats who exhibited obvious facial and bodily signals of social rejection) also had the highest blood levels of two inflammatory biochemicals linked to heart disease, cancer, depression, asthma, rheumatoid arthritis and other chronic health problems—once again showing the link between stress and ill health. The study appeared in the *Proceedings of the National Academy of Sciences*.

What to do: "If we imagine taking control over stressors while feeling calm and relaxed, we can conquer them when we need to," says Dr. Charlesworth. He recommends first practicing progressive muscle relaxation to become "as completely relaxed as possible," and then, with eyes closed…

"See yourself very much in control, confident and the master of your social stressor—for example, talking in front of a group or with a person of the opposite sex. Visualize yourself very successfully meeting the situation head-on and coping successfully with your social stress. Continue to rehearse being calm and in control, seeing yourself face to face with your 'social stressor' for thirty seconds.

"If you frequently practice using your imagination to rehearse acting in a skillful and relaxed manner in the face of your social stressors, not only will you become less anxious—you'll build up your confidence and your ability to handle the situation."

Take a Probiotic

A team of French and Canadian researchers gave a supplement of probiotics (friendly digestive bacteria) or a placebo to 55 people who reported a high level of daily stress. After one month, those taking the probiotics had fewer physical and psychological symptoms of stress (less anxiety, depression, anger and irritability, and fatigue) and a greater ability to cope with the stress of everyday life. And in an earlier study of 75 people under stress, the supplement reduced GI-related symptoms of stress, such as abdominal pain and nausea.

The probiotics replace bad bacteria in the gut, decreasing inflammation, which in turn affects the central nervous system (an estimated 70% of nerve fibers in the body are in the digestive tract), changing levels of emotion-controlling neurotransmitters in the brain, explain the researchers in the *British Journal of Nutrition.*

"Probiotics could represent an innovative, effective and natural solution to cope with stressful situations," says Guy Rousseau, PhD, a professor in the Department of Pharmacology at the University of Montreal in Canada.

What to do: The probiotic supplement used in the study was Probio'Stick, from Istitut Rosell Lallemand in Canada, a good-tasting, stick-shaped supplement that instantly dissolves in your mouth. The dose was 1.5 grams daily (one stick). You can order the product at the Web site *www.aviva.ca* or call 866-947-6789.

Indulge Yourself

In a study on animals, researchers at the University of Cincinnati found that pleasurable activity—in this case, good-tasting food and more sex—reduces stress by inhibiting anxiety responses in the brain.

"Even small amounts of pleasurable foods can reduce the effects of stress," and the effects continue for seven days, suggesting a long-term benefit, says Yvonne Ulrich-Lai, PhD, a research assistant professor at the University of Cincinnati Academic Health Center.

What to do: "Many of my patients with stress-related illnesses take care of everyone else in the world, but don't know how to take care of themselves," says David Clark, MD, a clinical assistant professor emeritus at Oregon Health and Science University in Portland, and author of *They Can't Find Anything Wrong!— 7 Keys to Understanding, Treating, and Healing Stress Illness* (Sentient Publications).

"I ask them to learn 'self-indulgent recreation skills'—to take some time to focus purely on their own needs and pleasures, for regular periods of healthy self-indulgence."

Smart idea: "To find a self-indulgent recreation, I tell my patients to think of something that would give them the same level of joy as finger-painting does a four-year-old—who doesn't care about how many paintings per hour she's producing, or the quality of work, but just knows she's having a blast. It could be bird-watching or bicycling or going to the movies—anything you do purely for the fun of it, and not with any other goal."

Edward Charlesworth, PhD, clinical psychologist, director of Willowbrook Psychological Associates in Houston, Texas, and author of *Stress Management: A Comprehensive Guide to Wellness* (Ballantine Books).

David Clark, MD, clinical assistant professor emeritus, Oregon Health and Science University, and author of *They Can't Find Anything Wrong!—7 Keys to Understanding, Treating, and Healing Stress Illness* (Sentient Publications). *www.stressillness.com.*

Guy Rousseau, PhD, professor, Department of Pharmacology, University of Montreal, Canada.

Yvonne Ulrich-Lai, PhD, research assistant professor, University of Cincinnati Academic Health Center.

Sheila G. West, PhD, associate professor of biobehavioral health and nutritional sciences, Pennsylvania State University.

The Best Stress-Fighting Foods

Powerhouse foods, such as salmon (with its heart-protective omega-3s) and spinach (with its cancer-fighting flavonoids), win lots of praise for their ability to help fight diseases.

Few people realize, however, that these foods—and some others—also help reduce and protect against the harmful effects that ongoing stress can have on the body, be it from a chronic illness or a hectic work schedule. By consuming a variety of foods that work synergistically, you can help prevent many of the negative effects of stress.

Powerful stress-fighting foods…

● **Black-eyed peas.** These are an excellent source of folate, a B vitamin crucial to fighting stress.

Advice: Try to eat one-half cup daily of black-eyed peas (or other folate-rich legumes, such as chickpeas, red beans, black beans or lentils).

Also good: Try one ounce of sunflower seeds (toasted kernels) or one-half cup to one cup of cooked broccoli daily.

● **Mangoes.** Antioxidants, such as vitamin C, help repair the damage that occurs to our cells when we are under stress. Oranges are one option, but mangoes may be an even better choice because they not only contain vitamin C but also disease-fighting carotenoids, including beta-carotene and vitamin E.

Advice: Enjoy mango at least once a week when in season. Because frozen fruit is picked at the height of the season and promptly frozen, it is a great substitute if fresh fruit is not available. Mango can be cubed and eaten alone or tossed in a mixed fruit salad. Use frozen mango in smoothies or chopped mango in salsa.

If you don't like mangoes (or you are allergic): Try other vitamin C sources, such as kiwi (two small fruits daily)…or cranberry, orange, blueberry, pomegranate or grape juice (six to eight ounces of 100% juice daily).

● **Nuts.** Almonds, pistachios and walnuts are rich in vitamin E, another antioxidant that helps curb stress-induced cell damage.

Advice: Eat a handful (one ounce) of almonds, pistachios or walnuts daily or every other day. Be sure to keep the portions small—nuts are relatively high in calories. If you have high blood pressure, choose nuts that are unsalted or low in sodium.

If you don't like nuts (or you are allergic): Try avocado. One or two thin slices daily (or one-quarter cup cubed) has the same beneficial fats found in nuts plus potassium, a mineral that has been shown to help lower elevated blood pressure.

● **Sweet potatoes.** These creamy, almost dessertlike root vegetables are brimming with antioxidant carotenoids, such as beta-carotene. In addition, sweet potatoes provide vitamin C, potassium and an appreciable amount of fiber (five to six grams for a medium potato), which contributes to the widely recommended 25- to 30-gram-per-day goal.

If you don't like sweet potatoes (or you are allergic): Eat carrots (one-half cup daily)…cantaloupe (one-quarter cup daily)…apricots (three to five dried or one fresh daily)…or acorn squash (one-half squash daily).

● **Yogurt or kefir.** Stress can lead to elevated levels of the stress hormone cortisol, which, in turn, wears down the immune system. Although it's not widely known, a significant amount of immune system activity takes place in the gastrointestinal tract.

When a person is under chronic stress, he/she is more susceptible to infections and, as a result, may take an antibiotic. These drugs destroy not only the harmful bacteria that are making you sick, but also the "good" bacteria in your gut.

By consuming yogurt or kefir (a tangy, yogurtlike drink), you can replace those healthful bacteria, which are key to maintaining a vital immune system.

Advice: Add one serving a day (a single-serving container of yogurt or a cup of kefir) to your diet. Choose a yogurt or kefir product that says "live and active cultures" on the label—and be sure that it contains the following strains of healthful bacteria—*Lactobacillus casei*…and/or *Lactobacillus acidophilus*. If you're taking an antibiotic, look for *S. boulardii* or *Lactobacillus GG*—these strains are most effective in people who take these medications.

Good news: Many people who are lactose-intolerant are able to consume yogurt and/or kefir. Start with only one-quarter cup of yogurt or kefir once or twice a week and slowly increase the amount as your body adjusts. Naturally fermented foods, such as sauerkraut, also contain healthful bacteria—try one-half cup serving daily.

Susan Mitchell, PhD, RD, a registered dietitian based in Winter Park, Florida. She has coauthored three books, including *Fat Is Not Your Fate* (Simon & Schuster), and hosts a nutrition and health podcast on WDBO.com.

The Safe, Natural Insomnia Solution

A good night's sleep...there's nothing more restorative—or elusive...for the 64% of Americans who report regularly having trouble sleeping. A disconcertingly high percentage of the sleepless (nearly 20%) solve the problem by taking sleeping pills. But sleeping pills can be dangerous and addictive, physically and/or emotionally—and swallowing a pill when you want to go to sleep doesn't address the root cause of the problem. What, exactly, is keeping you up at night?

Slow Down...

According to Rubin Naiman, PhD, a psychologist and clinical assistant professor of medicine at the University of Arizona's Center for Integrative Medicine, most of our sleep problems have to do not with our bodies, per se, but with our habits. The modern American lifestyle—replete with highly refined foods and caffeine-laden beverages, excessive exposure to artificial light in the evening, and "adrenaline-producing" nighttime activities, such as working until bedtime, watching TV or surfing the Web—leaves us overstimulated in the evening just when our bodies are designed to slow down...and, importantly, to literally cool down as well.

Studies show that a cooler core body temperature—and warmer hands and feet—make you sleepy. "Cooling the body allows the mind and the heart to get quiet," says Dr. Naiman. He believes that this cooling process contributes to the release of melatonin, the hormone that helps to regulate the body's circadian rhythm of sleeping and waking.

Deep Green Sleep

Dr. Naiman has developed an integrative approach to sleep that defines healthy sleep as an interaction between a person and his/her sleep environment. He calls this approach Deep Green Sleep. "My goal was to explore all of the subtleties in a person's life that may be disrupting sleep. This takes into account your physiology, emotions, personal experiences, sleeping and waking patterns and your attitudes about sleep and the sleeping environment." This approach is unique because it values "the subjective and personal experience of sleep," he says—in contrast with conventional sleep treatment, which tends to rely on "computer printouts of sleep studies—otherwise known as 'treating the chart.'"

It's important to realize that lifestyle habits and attitudes are hard to change, so Dr. Naiman cautions that it often can take weeks, even months, to achieve his Deep Green Sleep. The good news is that the results are lasting and may even enhance your waking life.

Here are his suggestions on how you can ease into the night...

● **Live a healthful waking life.** "The secret of a good night's sleep is a good day's waking," says Dr. Naiman. This includes getting regular exercise (but not within three hours of bedtime) and eating a balanced, nutritious diet.

● **Cool down in the evening.** It's important to help your mind and body cool down, starting several hours before bedtime, by doing the following...

●Avoid foods and drinks that sharply spike energy, such as highly refined carbohydrates and anything with caffeine, at least eight hours before bedtime.

●Limit alcohol in the evening—it interferes with sleep by suppressing melatonin. It also interferes with dreaming and disrupts circadian rhythms.

●Avoid nighttime screen-based activities within an hour of bedtime. You may think that watching TV or surfing the Web are relaxing things to do, but in reality these activities are highly stimulating. They engage your brain and expose you to relatively bright light with a strong blue wavelength that "mimics daylight and suppresses melatonin," says Dr. Naiman.

- **Create a sound sleeping environment.** It is also important that where you sleep be stimulation-free and conducive to rest.

In your bedroom:

- Be sure that you have a comfortable mattress, pillow and bedding. It's amazing how many people fail to address this basic need—often because their mattress has become worn out slowly, over time, and they haven't noticed.

- Remove anything unessential from your bedside table that may tempt you to stay awake, such as the TV remove control or stimulating books.

- When you are ready to call it a night, turn everything off—radio, TV and, of course, the light.

- Keep the room cool (68°F or lower).

- **Let go of waking.** Each day, allow your mind and body to surrender to sleep by engaging in quieting and relaxing activities starting about an hour before bedtime, such as…

- Gentle yoga

- Meditation

- Rhythmic breathing

- Reading poetry or other nonstimulating material

- Journaling

- Taking a hot bath.

Sex seems to help most people relax and can facilitate sleep, in part because climaxing triggers a powerful relaxation response, Dr. Naiman says.

- **Consider supplementing with melatonin.** If sleep is still elusive after trying these Deep Green Sleep tips, Dr. Naiman often suggests a melatonin supplement. Dr. Naiman believes that this is better than sleeping pills since melatonin is "the body's own natural chemical messenger of night." "Melatonin does not directly cause sleep, but triggers a cascade of events that result in natural sleep and dreams," he says, adding that it is nonaddictive, inexpensive and generally safe. Not all doctors agree however, so it is important to check with your doctor first.

If you're interested in learning more about Dr. Naiman's Deep Green Sleep program, you can visit his Web site (*www.thesleepadvisor.com*) and take a free quiz that helps identify your particular sleep challenges. But, since it is computer-based, make sure you do it several hours before bedtime!

Rubin Naiman, PhD, psychologist specializing in sleep and dream medicine and clinical assistant professor of medicine at the University of Arizona's Center for Integrative Medicine. He is author of the book *Healing Night* (Syren).

Nap for Health

If you're like most Americans, you probably consider napping an indulgence.

What you may not realize: Napping is widely known to sharpen mental fitness (including memory), and it also confers significant overall health benefits.

Important finding: When researchers from the Harvard School of Public Health and the University of Athens Medical School recently followed about 23,000 healthy Greek adults (average age 53), they found that study participants who napped at least 30 minutes three times a week or more were 37% less likely to die from heart disease and stroke over a six-year period.

How to get the greatest health benefits from napping…

It's Time to Nap!

Humans are biologically programmed to nap. Our bodies experience a slight drop in physiological processes such as body temperature, blood pressure and the secretion of digestive juices (at around 2 pm for people who awaken at 8 am)—similar to the larger dips that occur at night. These drops signal the body that it's time to sleep.

There's strong scientific evidence showing that people who nap are more alert, make better decisions, score significantly higher on creativity and memory tests and have better motor function after napping compared with people who don't nap.

Surprising fact: Despite the popular notion that lunch makes people sleepy due to the digestion process, research shows that it's actually the body's temperature drop that is responsible. This temperature drop occurs whether or not you eat lunch.

Why napping provides so many benefits: Napping just 20 minutes is enough time for restorative processes that occur during sleep to take place.

The Right—and Wrong— Way to Nap

Here are my five secrets for getting the most from your naps—and some common mistakes to avoid...

Secret 1: Make a 20-minute nap part of your daily routine, like exercising and brushing your teeth.

Common mistake: Squeezing in a nap whenever you can.

Recommendation: Take a nap at the same time every day (even if you don't feel sleepy) so that your body adjusts to falling asleep then. Because most Americans have trained themselves to not nap, the instinct needs to be relearned.

The ideal time to take a nap from a biorhythm standpoint is six hours after awakening for the day.

Example: If you usually wake up at 7 am, your best napping time will be around 1 pm.

Of course, your exact nap time may depend on your daily activities. Just don't nap within three hours of your bedtime.

Secret 2: Choose a comfortable, quiet place where you won't be disturbed.

Common mistake: Napping in your living area at home or in an office at work. Even if you're not disturbed by noise or other interruptions, you will still feel the emotional tug of your daily activities.

Recommendation: Go to a place unrelated to daytime tasks, such as your bedroom, an empty conference room, a park or your car

with the seat reclined and the window slightly cracked so that you get some fresh air.

Also, try earplugs if you have trouble drifting off to sleep. Or consider using a white-noise machine to block out distracting sounds.

New option: The Apple iPhone White Noise App is very effective at blocking out noise.

Secret 3: Cover yourself with a light blanket or jacket, if possible. This will make you more comfortable because your body temperature is lower than usual while napping.

Common mistake: Many people think that they need to be in a darkened room to nap. This may not be true. Research being conducted at the University of California, San Diego's sleep laboratory has found no effect from different levels of light on a person's ability to nap.

Possible reason: Since napping appears to be programmed into us, we may have evolved to fall asleep for brief periods during daylight without a need for melatonin, the sleep hormone that the body produces only in darkness.

Secret 4: Set an alarm to go off after 20 minutes. Use whatever is most convenient— an alarm on your watch or cell phone, for example. The Nap App on the Apple iPod functions as an alarm that awakens nappers with a tone or vibration.

Using an alarm will prevent you from napping too long. It also allows you to relax, because you won't have to worry about the clock.

Interesting fact: Even when nappers thought they were awake throughout their nap times, researchers' anecdotal observations have shown that the nappers usually did dip into light sleep, which can help with alertness and motor performance.

Common mistake: Napping for more than 30 minutes. These longer naps take you from light "Stage 2" sleep into deeper "Stage 3" and "Stage 4" sleep, which are harder to wake up from and will leave you groggy.

Recommendation: If you would like to take a longer nap, make sure that it lasts for 60 to 90 minutes. That's long enough to move through the deeper sleep stages and return to lighter Stage 2 and rapid-eye movement (REM) sleep—also known as "dreaming sleep."

This type of longer nap has the added benefit of stimulating the brain regions that integrate newly learned information into your long-term memory.

New finding: In a recent study conducted at the University of California, Berkeley, 39 healthy adults were given a rigorous learning exercise at noon. Half of them then took a 90-minute nap at 2 p.m., while the other half didn't. When doing new exercises at 6 p.m., the group that had napped did significantly better than those who did not nap.

Secret 5: Go back to sleep for five minutes if you feel groggy from over-napping. If you're groggy, this means that you have moved into the deeper stages of sleep. Going back to sleep for five minutes will allow you to move further out of those sleep stages.

If you find that you're groggy after a 20-minute nap: Shorten your nap to 10 minutes to avoid progressing into deeper sleep.

When Napping May Mean Trouble

Even though the bulk of research has found that napping is a healthful practice, one widely publicized study found the opposite—specifically, that older women who take excessive daily naps are more likely to die.

The study subjects (age 69 and older) who died napped the longest (more than three hours daily). They were 44% more likely to die from any cause and 58% more likely to die from cardiovascular causes than those who did not report taking naps.

The details of the research results suggest that the study participants had underlying sleep disorders, such as obstructive sleep apnea (temporary cessation of breathing during sleep) or an illness such as depression or heart disease.

Key fact not widely reported: The same study found that women who napped three hours or less per week had no increased mortality.

In addition, those who slept nine to 10 hours per 24-hour period (overnight sleep plus naps) were at greater risk of dying than those who slept eight to nine hours total in the same time period. Researchers are unsure whether these findings would also apply to men.

Advice: If you're sleeping excessively at night, consult a sleep doctor, who will place you on a strict sleep schedule that will not include napping.

To find a sleep clinic near you that is accredited by the American Academy of Sleep Medicine, go to *www.sleepcenters.org.*

Sara Mednick, PhD, assistant professor of psychiatry at the University of California, San Diego. In addition to authoring numerous published studies on napping, she is coauthor of *Take a Nap! Change Your Life* (Workman) and the recipient of a National Institute of Mental Health Mentored Research Career Scientist Award. *www.saramednick.com.*

Pick the Perfect Pillow

Lots of people think that mattresses are more important than pillows when it comes to getting a good night's sleep. But that's a mistake. If you have occasional or frequent body aches, pillows are just as important as mattresses—or even more so.

Neck Pain

If you randomly X-rayed 100 people over age 55, 70% to 80% would have arthritis of the neck.

If you have neck pain, don't sleep on your stomach. This position twists the neck. Instead, sleep on your side while hugging a second pillow. This offers the comforting sensation of something against your stomach but is far better for your neck.

My advice: If you have arthritis of the neck or neck pain due to another condition (such as muscle strain or injury) and find that it's comfortable to sleep on your side, choose a pillow that is just thick enough to fill the space between your downside ear and neck and the mattress.

Good choice: The Molded Natural Rubber Pillow (queen or standard size), available at 888-562-8873, *www.greenfeet.com.*

To determine the proper pillow thickness for you: When lying on your side with your head on the pillow, your head should be parallel to the mattress. Ask someone to see whether your nose is aligned with the middle of your chest.  If your nose is higher than your chest, you need a thinner pillow…if it's lower, you need a thicker pillow.

Before buying a pillow: At the store, compress the pillow with your head by lying down on it or lean your head on the pillow up against the store wall.

Smart idea: Call around before shopping to find stores that allow for pillow returns.

If you have neck pain and typically sleep on your back, choose a pillow that just fills the gap between your neck and the mattress. A pillow that is too thick will push your neck forward, placing stress on the muscles in the back of the neck.

Good choices: Fluffable down, such as the Superior Goose-Down Pillow (soft) by Eddie Bauer (standard to king size), available at 800-426-8020, *www.eddiebauer.com.*

Or try an easily shapable buckwheat pillow, such as those from Buckwheat Co., which can also be heated in the microwave before bed, *www.buckwheattherapy.com.*

Low Back Pain

For years, low back pain sufferers were advised to sleep on their backs on very firm mattresses or even on the floor. We now know that these people should choose whatever sleeping position feels best—except on the stomach, which can increase the forward curve of the lower back and jam the spinal joints.

My advice: If you have back pain and like to sleep on your back, slip a pillow under your knees. This flattens your lower back against the mattress, discouraging the muscle spasms that can occur if the low back is arched. The pillow can be made of any material as long as it's about three to four inches thick.

Good choice: The Duro-Med Elevating Leg Rest, available at Amazon.com.

If you're a side sleeper, you may straighten your bottom leg and bend your upper leg in front of you to avoid the discomfort of your knees rubbing together. But this position twists your body from the waist, placing strain on your lower back.

My advice: Place a pillow or a rolled-up towel between your knees to keep your top leg parallel with the bed.

Good choice: The Back Buddy Knee Pillow, available at Amazon.com.

If you tend to switch back and forth in your sleep between your side and back, try a dual pillow, such as Therapeutica's Sleeping Pillow (average to large size), 800-348-5729, *www.therapeuticainc.com.* It is designed to offer correct support and stability whether you're sleeping on your back or side.

Rounded Shoulders

Most people's shoulders are rounded to some degree—due, for example, to spinal arthritis or prolonged computer usage. If you typically sleep on your side, your top shoulder may sag forward, exacerbating poor posture.

My advice: Try a boomerang-shaped pillow that supports your head and neck while curving down the front of your torso to provide shoulder support.

Good choice: The Dr. Mary Side Sleeper Pillow, available at The Pillow Bar, 214-232-9881, *www.thepillowbar.com.*

Bill Lauretti, DC, associate professor of chiropractic clinical sciences at the New York Chiropractic College in Seneca Falls, New York. He is author of numerous journal articles and textbook chapters on neck and back pain.

Illustration by Shawn Banner

7 Surprising Ways to Boost Your Energy

As many as one of every five American adults has fatigue that is severe enough to interfere with daily activities.

Problem: Most of these people take the wrong steps when trying to regain their energy. For example, drinking popular "energy" drinks, which contain substantial amounts of caffeine, merely masks fatigue by stimulating the nervous system for only a few hours.

Solution: Try safe natural strategies that help produce sustained energy.

Important: If you suffer from fatigue that interferes with your ability to complete your daily activities, see a doctor to rule out an undiagnosed condition—such as anemia, heart disease or hypothyroidism (underactive thyroid). If your doctor finds no underlying cause, try the remedies below for several days. If you still feel fatigued, consider seeking additional medical guidance.

What you need to know about overcoming fatigue…

Your Body's Energy Source

Your body's real energy source is a molecule called *adenosine triphosphate* (ATP), which is constantly being produced by the thousands of mitochondria (tiny energy factories) in each of your body's cells.

An important way to truly boost your energy is to properly nourish these ATP-producing powerhouses, while also reducing your body's level of stress chemicals—one of the biggest energy drains in modern life.

For More "Get Up and Go"

For starters, try well-known strategies, such as getting enough sleep, eating healthfully, exercising regularly and lowering stress. Then supplement these strategies with the following steps—any one of them may give you an immediate boost. *After seven days, you'll likely begin to feel an even greater, more sustained level of energy…*

1. Switch from coffee to green tea. Most people enjoy a caffeinated beverage, such as coffee, in the morning for a quick energy boost. However, this approach can be counterproductive. Coffee, which contains an average of 120 milligrams (mg) of caffeine per cup, hypes up your nervous system tem-porarily, which can lead to an energy slump within hours.

For this reason, people who typically drink coffee or another highly caffeinated beverage in the morning should consider switching to green tea. In addition to having less caffeine (just 10 mg to 30 mg per cup), green tea also contains theanine, a calming amino acid that moderates caffeine's nervous system–stimulating effect for a gentle, steady boost.

Helpful: If you suffer withdrawal symptoms, such as headaches, when giving up coffee, cut consumption of your usual morning drink in half and substitute green tea for each cup given up. Within a short time, you'll be off coffee altogether.

If you find green tea to be bitter, try flavored green teas, such as peppermint or peach. Ultimately, it's best to limit consumption of any caffeinated drink to two cups daily.

Also important: Stay hydrated. Without proper hydration, the body cannot supply nutrients to its energy-producing cells.

To avoid a mid-afternoon slump: Drink five to six cups of fluids (preferably water, juice, herbal tea or decaffeinated coffee) before 3 pm—this ensures that you're hydrated during what are hours of peak activity for most people.

2. Eliminate wheat from your diet. About 1% of Americans have celiac disease (a condition that leads to digestive problems when gluten, a protein found in wheat, barley and rye, is consumed). However, there's a far more common condition, known as wheat intolerance, which causes myriad symptoms when wheat—but not barley or rye—is consumed. About half of my patients have wheat intolerance by age 40, often leading to fatigue, and also to headache, indigestion and joint pain.

Likely reason: Modern wheat, which was one of the earliest foods to be grown in hybrid forms, contains newer proteins thought to trigger inflammatory responses with repeated exposure. Brown rice, quinoa and amaranth make great substitutes.

3. Take ayurvedic ashwaganda daily. Available in supplement form, this herb is an adaptogen that increases energy by reducing the effects of stress.

Ashwaganda stimulates energy production while calming the nervous system…helps the body more efficiently metabolize the stress hormone cortisol…and strengthens the immune system.

Good product: The "sensoril" variety of ashwaganda, such as that from Jarrow Formulas (310-204-6936, *www.jarrow.com*)… and Natural Factors Nutritional Products, Inc. (800-322-8704, *www.naturalfactors.com*).

Typical dose: 250 mg, twice daily. Consult your doctor before taking this or any other herbal remedy.

4. Take a sauna. Research suggests that saunas (steam or dry) have the potential to eliminate toxins from your body, including mercury, dioxin and PCBs—all commonly found in our environment and can wreak havoc on one's energy production system.

However, check with your doctor first—saunas are not recommended for some people, including those with heart disease, pregnant women or individuals taking certain medications, such as those prescribed for high blood pressure or depression.

5. Undergo a relaxation-oriented acupuncture session. While most people associate acupuncture with its well-known ability to decrease pain and help heal inflamed tissue, it's also great for reducing stress and boosting energy.

One 20-minute treatment is often enough to help balance the nervous system and neurotransmitters (such as endorphins and serotonin) and enhance energy levels for up to two days. To find an acupuncturist, contact the American Association of Acupuncture and Oriental Medicine (866-455-7999, *www.aaaomonline.org*).

6. Do an "energy ball" exercise several times daily. This two-minute, beginner-level exercise is derived from the ancient Chinese system of energy movement known as Qi gong. Similar to other martial arts derivatives, such as tai chi, Qi gong connects energy circuits through mind, muscle and breath control.

What to do: Stand with your knees slightly bent, your buttocks tucked under and arms at your sides. While taking slow, deep abdominal breaths, allow your arms to slowly float up, shoulder-width apart, while your palms roll inward then face you (as if holding a giant ball of energy). Bend your arms as if bringing the ball closer to you, then rotate your wrists so that your palms face outward.

"Push" the ball away from you until your arms are straight while stepping forward onto your left foot. Let your arms float apart to form the top of a "T," then bring your arms gently down to your sides as you move your left foot back to its starting position.

Finally, "lift" the ball overhead and let it go, then let your arms float back down to your sides, palms facing inward. Repeat, stepping forward with your right foot.

7. Use a fatigue-fighting stress reducer each day. The following products are great for calming the nervous system so that less energy is wasted during the day. Each is available at health-food stores.

●**Bach Rescue Remedy (an extract that contains 38 flower essences)**—use as directed on the label.

●**L-theanine amino acid**—take 500 mg capsules, twice daily.

●**Lavender essential oil**—massage into the skin or use as aroma therapy.

Try one of these stress reducers and see how it works for you. As with all supplements and herbal remedies, first check with your doctor.

Woodson Merrell, MD, chairman, Department of Integrative Medicine at Beth Israel Medical Center, Manhattan campus of Albert Einstein College of Medicine, and assistant clinical professor of medicine at the Columbia University College of Physicians and Surgeons, both in New York City. He is coauthor of Power Up—Unleash Your Natural Energy, Revitalize Your Health, and Feel 10 Years Younger *(Free Press)* www.woodsonmerrell.com.

Beets Beat Fatigue

In 2009, scientists at the University of Exeter in England conducted a six-day experiment—with results they described as "remarkable" (a word rarely used in the understated world of scientific research).

The study: They divided eight men into two groups. Every day for three days, four men drank two cups of beetroot juice. (Beetroot juice is juice from the beets themselves, not from beet greens.) The other four drank a look-alike, taste-alike placebo juice.

Over the next three days, the eight men engaged in several short bouts of exercise on a stationary bike, at two levels of intensity...

1. Moderate intensity (similar to brisk walking)

2. Strenuous intensity, exercising to total exhaustion, when they couldn't exercise anymore.

Results: During the moderate exercise, the men who drank beetroot juice used 19% less oxygen than the men who didn't drink the juice—in other words, they needed less energy to accomplish the same amount of exercise.

During the strenuous exercise, the men who drank beetroot juice exercised 16% longer until total exhaustion than the men who didn't drink the juice—in other words, they had a lot more energy.

Beetroot juice can boost energy levels—a nifty finding, for sure. But what was so "remarkable" about it?

"The oxygen cost of exercise is a fundamental tenet of human physiology," says Andrew Jones, PhD, a professor in the Department of Sports and Health Sciences at the University of Exeter and a study researcher. "It is highly consistent in humans, and it is virtually unchanged by all other interventions, including long-term endurance training. Therefore, we were very surprised when we saw these remarkable reductions in the oxygen cost of exercise after drinking beetroot juice."

Bottom line: Drinking beetroot juice accomplished what no other training method,

Foods High on the Nitric Oxide Index

Kale
Swiss chard
Arugula
Spinach
Chicory
Wild radish
Bok choy
Beet
Chinese cabbage
Beetroot juice
Lettuce
Cabbage
Mustard greens
Cauliflower
Parsley
Kohlrabi
Carrot
Broccoli

drug, food or supplement has ever accomplished—it allowed the body to use less oxygen during exercise!

And this remarkable result is remarkable even if you're not an exerciser—because maybe you're one of the millions of Americans who would be able to function more energetically if only your muscles demanded less oxygen. For example...

• **If you're over 50,** you have the "significantly reduced lung capacity" of aging, says Dr. Jones—and could benefit from muscles that used less oxygen.

• **If you have heart disease,** your heart muscle probably receives less oxygen—if it needed less, it wouldn't suffer as much "metabolic stress," says Dr. Jones.

• **If you have diabetes**—which can narrow arteries, reducing blood flow to the heart—you'd also benefit if your heart required less oxygen.

• **If you have chronic obstructive pulmonary disease** (also called emphysema and chronic bronchitis), with frequent breathlessness, you could have a higher activity level if your body demanded less oxygen.

In short, supplementing the diet with beetroot juice can reduce the "oxygen cost" of daily activities and could "enhance functional capacity and the quality of life" for all the above-mentioned groups, says Dr. Jones—and that includes tens of millions of Americans.

Problem: Who wants to drink beetroot juice every day? You'd have to either juice fresh beets (a lot of work) or shop for it (a lot of money—a sixteen-ounce bottle of beetroot juice is a specialty item costing about $5).

Solution: A new study from the same team of UK researchers shows that a specific nutritional compound in the beetroot juice is behind its remarkable oxygen-sparing, energy-boosting effects—a compound that's available in a wide range of vegetables and a new dietary supplement.

The Power of Nitrate

In the first study, the UK researchers theorized that the active ingredient in beetroot juice was nitrate—the men drinking beetroot juice had a 49% increase in blood levels of this nutritional compound, which is found abundantly in beets and in leafy green vegetables.

In the body, nitrate turns into nitric oxide (NO).

NO is a signaling molecule, explains Nathan Bryan, PhD, assistant professor in the School of Medicine at the University of Texas Health Science Center and coauthor of *The Nitric Oxide (NO) Solution* (Neogenis). It signals the body to oxygenate muscles. (It also signals the lining of the arteries to relax, lowering blood pressure.)

In the new study, the UK researchers gave nine people either regular beetroot juice, rich in nitrate, or beetroot juice with the nitrate filtered out. Once again, the study participants exercised after drinking the two types of juice.

Results: The beetroot juice with nitrate reduced oxygen requirements and increased time-to-exhaustion—just as in the first study. The beetroot juice without nitrate didn't have those effects.

"A high-nitrate diet may be beneficial for health and performance," Dr. Jones says. "It also has the potential to improve the cardiovascular health of healthy people and of people with high blood pressure."

Boosting Nitrate

"I think the primary take-home message from my research is to eat a diet that contains lots of high-nitrate foods, such as beets and spinach," says Dr. Jones.

One of the best ways to increase nitrate in the diet is with nitrate-rich, NO-creating vegetables, agrees Dr. Bryan.

To guide people to the foods highest in NO-creating nitrate, Dr. Bryan created the Nitric Oxide Index (see page 300). It assigns an overall value based on several factors, including the food's total amount of NO-creating nitrate, and its total amount of antioxidants, which help preserve NO so the body can use it.

Also try: Dr. Bryan has formulated a special beetroot-containing, NO-boosting supplement called NEO40 Daily. It also contains hawthorne (a nitrate-rich herb) and two amino acids (*L-arginine* and *L-citrulline*) that help generate NO in the body. The supplement is dissolved in the mouth rather than swallowed, making use of a recently discovered saliva-based NO-creating mechanism.

In a clinical study conducted at the University of Texas, NEO40 doubled blood levels of a biomarker for increased NO—and 50% of the people taking the supplement said they felt more energetic.

Resource: You can order NEO40 Daily at *www.neogenis.com* or call 888-898-5872.

Follow the dosage recommendations on the label.

Andrew Jones, research group leader and professor in the Department of Sports and Health Sciences at the University of Exeter, UK.

Nathan Bryan, PhD, assistant professor in the School of Medicine at the University of Texas Health Science Center and coauthor of *The Nitric Oxide (NO) Solution* (Neogenis). *www.neogenis.com*.

The Real Reason You're Tired—Worn-Out Adrenals

Few medical doctors recognize and treat adrenal fatigue, so millions of people feel exhausted…constantly. This is unfortunate…because once adrenal fatigue is diagnosed, it can be treated and resolved, with patients feeling better in just a few months' time.

Running on Empty

Under normal circumstances, the adrenals (small walnut-sized glands that sit on top of the kidneys) produce numerous hormones—adrenaline and others—that impact bodily functions including blood pressure, heart rate and metabolism, liver function and immunity. They also produce two crucial stress hormones—DHEA and cortisol—that balance the body's response to stressful influences, including blood sugar fluctuations. According to Mark Stengler, NMD, living with stress—whether mental, physical or emotional—for an extended period results in a situation where the need for a constant supply of these two hormones outstrips the adrenals' capability to produce. This deficiency dulls cognitive function, energy levels and defenses against stress. It also slows the immune response and with it the ability to fight off infections and even possibly cancer.

Do You Have Adrenal Fatigue?

Fatigue is just one adrenal fatigue symptom. If you are chronically tired and have any of the following, you may want to consider asking your doctor for a blood or saliva (Dr. Stengler's preference) test to determine whether you have adrenal fatigue…

- **Morning fatigue**
- **Mood swings**
- **Light-headedness after standing up**
- **Decreased sex drive**
- **Inability to focus**
- **Memory problems**
- **Body aches, including pain in the lower back**
- **Craving for salt and/or sugar**
- **Slower recovery from illness than is usual for you.**

Given the mainstream resistance to recognizing adrenal fatigue, Dr. Stengler suggests that those with symptoms seek out naturopathic physicians.

Fixing Your Fatigue

Once adrenal fatigue is diagnosed, treatment is multi-pronged, including a combination of nutrients and lifestyle changes:

- **Stress reduction.** Not surprisingly, your first task is to review what's causing all the stress in your life so that you can determine what changes need to be made to reduce it.

- **Get more sleep.** You need plenty of high-quality, restorative sleep—Dr. Stengler says to aim for eight to 10 hours every night, and he also advises taking daily naps. For those who have trouble falling asleep or who find themselves awakening in the night, he often prescribes 0.5 milligrams (mg) to 3 mg of melatonin, the "sleep" hormone, or 100 mg of the amino acid 5-HTP an hour before bedtime to help the body prepare for sleep. Ask your doctor which you should take.

- **Adjust your diet.** Dr. Stengler points out that people with adrenal fatigue often have blood sugar swings and cravings for sweets, so it's very important to have breakfast every day and to eat small, healthy snacks between meals. He advises eating plenty of whole-grain foods and protein, including almonds, walnuts and macadamia nuts, and avoiding processed foods and simple sugars, including refined grains, fruit juices and, of course, sugary sodas. Also stay away from caffeinated beverages and alcohol. And if you have low blood pressure, which often results from adrenal fatigue and further contributes to fatigue, do be sure you are getting enough salt, which helps maintain blood volume and proper circulation. However, don't go overboard—2,400 mg per day of sodium from all sources is usually about right.

● **Exercise—in moderation.** While exercise helps regulate stress hormones, too much will exhaust adrenal fatigue patients further, says Dr. Stengler. He advises his patients to start by walking 15 minutes a day, adding time as symptoms improve until reaching 45 minutes per day, but again, keeping it to a moderately intense level. Reduce the amount of exercise if afterward you find yourself feeling more tired rather than less—the goal is to increase overall energy.

Supplements

To help speed recovery, Dr. Stengler often prescribes the following nutritional supplements...

● **Vitamin B5**—(pantothenic acid) is especially important for stress-hormone production...he often prescribes 500 mg of B5, three times a day. A good multivitamin (or B-complex) will supply enough of the other B vitamins needed, says Dr. Stengler.

● **Vitamin C**—typically 1,000 mg to 2,000 mg twice daily is prescribed, but reduce this dose if loose stools develop.

● **Adrenal glandular extract (AGE)**—made from cow, pig or sheep adrenals, AGE contains growth factors that promote cell healing and also has nutrients to support gland function and repair. Take one to two tablets daily without food, and reduce the dosage if you become jittery or have trouble sleeping.

● **Ashwagandha**—this herb, popular in Ayurvedic medicine, helps normalize adrenal functioning. A brand Dr. Stengler often dispenses is Jarrow Sensoril Ashwagandha... typically one to two capsules are taken daily on an empty stomach.

● **Rhodiola rosea**—most often, he directs his patients to take 500 mg twice a day away from food...he uses a standardized formula of 3% to 5% rosavins, such as Paradise Herbs' Dual Action Rhodiola.

Note: Those with bipolar disorder should not use this product, since it can increase brain levels of serotonin, a chemical that affects mood.

Dr. Stengler says he sometimes uses hormone therapy consisting of DHEA, cortisol or other hormones and supplements to treat severe adrenal fatigue, but he notes that such measures require the supervision of a physician who is well practiced in the therapy.

Effective adrenal fatigue treatment ends up being an intensive self-care regimen in which you ratchet back the unreasonable demands you've been making on your mind and body. Fortunately, given time to recover, the adrenals are able to regain their strength...and with it, your natural energy will return.

Mark A. Stengler, NMD, licensed naturopathic medical doctor in private practice, Encinitas, California, and author of the *Bottom Line/Natural Healing* newsletter.

The One-Supplement Secret to Over-60 Strength

As you age, you inevitably become weaker. You lose muscle mass. You lose strength. And activity fatigues you faster.

But one nutritional supplement can increase muscle mass and strength...and increase your resistance to fatigue, says Eric Rawson, PhD, in the Department of Exercise Science at Bloomsburg University in Pennsylvania.

It's the amino acid creatine, a natural component of muscle—and if you start taking it, you might start creatin' a whole new you.

The Creatine Advantage

Scientists have studied a lot of nutritional supplements in the hopes that one or more of them could reverse age-related declines in strength, says Dr. Rawson. They've looked at antioxidants, polyphenols and omega-3 fatty acids—and "the results of these studies are not as encouraging as had been expected."

But studies on creatine have been very encouraging, says Dr. Rawson, who reviewed all the research on creatine, strength and aging in a recent issue of the scientific journal *Amino Acids. For example...*

• **More muscle.** Seven men aged 65 to 82 took either 5 grams of creatine or a placebo—and after only five days the men taking creatine had a two-pound increase in muscle mass, reported Canadian researchers.

• **More power.** Noting that "muscle power and strength decrease with age, leading to reduced independence and increased health risk from falls," researchers in the Department of Health and Physical Education at the University of Hawaii gave creatine or a placebo to thirty women, aged 58 to 71. After one week, the women taking creatine were a lot stronger—able to perform two weight-lifting exercises (bench press and leg press) with heavier weights and to walk faster.

The same team of researchers conducted a study on older men (aged 59 to 72) with similar results—after seven days, the men taking creatine had more strength and power.

"Creatine supplementation may be a useful therapeutic strategy for older adults to attenuate loss in muscle strength and performance of functional living tasks," concluded the researchers in the journal *Medicine & Science in Sports & Exercise.*

• **Less fatigue.** Researchers in the Department of Health and Exercise Science at the University of Oklahoma studied 15 men and women with an average age of 75 to see if supplementing the diet for two weeks with creatine could increase the amount of time it took for exercise to fatigue their muscles. Creatine decreased time to fatigue by 16%, they reported in the *Journal of Nutrition, Health & Aging.*

• **More overall strength.** In a study of 39 men and women over 65 years old, taking a creatine supplement during six months of muscle training improved "all measurements of strength" compared with people who

muscle trained but didn't take creatine, reported a team of Canadian researchers in the journal *PLoS One.*

Why Not Meat?

"Meat is the primary source of dietary creatine," says Dr. Rawson. So why not eat more meat for more creatine?

Meat, he says, "is expensive, might increase the risk for several diseases that are more common in older people, such as heart disease and cancer, and might present chewing problems for those with dentures."

That's why, he says, many people actually decrease their intake of meat as they age—decreasing their intake of creatine. And why a creatine supplement is your best bet for a regular, muscle-building intake of the nutrient.

Healthful strategy: "A number of studies support beneficial effects of creatine supplementation on fatigue resistance, strength, performance of activities of daily living, and muscle mass in older adults," observes Dr. Rawson. "When battling age-related declines in muscle strength and muscle mass, it appears that creatine supplementation and physical activity are the two most successful interventions."

Creatine supplementation also has an "excellent safety profile" in older people, he says. And, he adds, creatine supplements are inexpensive.

Suggested intake: In a recent study, a daily dose of 2.3 grams (2,3000 mg) a day for six weeks improved "muscle function" and "fatigue resistance," reported Dr. Rawson in the medical journal *Nutrition.*

Consult with a knowledgeable health-care professional before taking creatine, he advises.

Creatine supplements are widely available, both online and in retail stores where supplements are sold.

Eric Rawson, PhD, associate professor of exercise science, Department of Exercise Science at Bloomsburg University in Pennsylvania.

Chapter 17

WOMEN'S HEALTH

The Latest on Soy for Menopause: It's Safe— And It Works!

Soy contains *isoflavones*, a type of *phytoestrogen*—a plant compound that functions in the body like a very low dose of estrogen.

For years, many health scientists have recommended soy supplements (such as the isoflavone *genistein*), soy powder and soy foods as a natural treatment for the symptoms of menopause—a gentler, drug-free version of estrogen-replacement therapy (ERT).

But other experts have cautioned against the long-term use of soy, saying that—like ERT—it might increase the risk of breast and uterine cancer.

And some experts also warn that soy isoflavones might adversely affect the thyroid gland, blocking the action of *thyroid peroxidase*, a compound key to the production of thyroid hormone.

Latest development: Recent research shows soy does *not* increase the risk of cancer or harm a healthy thyroid gland—and that it's just as effective as ERT in easing some of the symptoms of menopause, such as hot flashes.

No Cancer Risk

Researchers in the Department of Nutrition at the University of California, Davis, gave either a soy supplement or a placebo to 403 postmenopausal women. After two years, there was no difference in the rates of breast or uterine cancer between the two groups.

Daily supplementation for two years with soy isoflavones has minimal risk in menopausal women, concluded the researchers in the *American Journal of Clinical Nutrition.*

Another important development: Research shows that rather than increasing the risk of breast cancer, soy may lower it.

Breast cancer survivors with the highest intake of soy protein had a 32% lower risk of breast cancer recurrence, reported researchers from Vanderbilt University Medical Center in the *Journal of the American Medical Association*.

And in a study reported at a conference held by the American Association for Cancer Research, researchers from the University of Buffalo found that women with the highest intake of soy isoflavones had a 30% lower risk of Stage 1 breast cancer, compared with women with the lowest intake.

"There is a wealth of scientific data indicating that soy consumption is not linked to an increased risk for breast and uterine cancer," says Mark Messina, PhD, adjunct associate professor in the Department of Nutrition at Loma Linda University in California and president of Nutrition Matters, Inc., a nutritional consulting company.

Soy and Your Thyroid Gland

"Genistein [the strongest soy isoflavone] positively affects postmenopausal symptoms," but "questions about its long-term safety on the thyroid gland still remain," wrote a team of Italian researchers in the *Journal of Clinical Endocrinology and Metabolism*.

To help answer those questions, they studied 389 postmenopausal women, giving them 54 milligrams (mg) of genistein daily and measuring 11 indicators of thyroid function after one, two and three years of genistein intake. They saw no difference in any of the thyroid measurements.

"Genistein intake does not significantly increase the risk of clinical or subclinical hypothyroidism at the dose of 54 mg daily," they concluded.

(*Subclinical hypothyroidism* means that your blood tests show low thyroid function but you don't have symptoms. *Clinical hypothyroidism* means a blood test is positive for low thyroid levels and you have symptoms, such as dry skin and hair, fatigue, weight gain, and feeling cold all the time.)

"This excellent study—which follows 14 earlier clinical studies with similar results—seals the deal for healthy people about soy and thyroid," says Dr. Messina. "Isoflavones

do not adversely affect thyroid function in people with normal thyroids."

However: "The jury is still out on whether or not isoflavones pose a risk to people who *already* have subclinical or clinical hypothyroidism," he says.

Easing Menopause Symptoms

Italian researchers conducted a four-month study with 60 postmenopausal women, giving them either 90 mg of isoflavones, hormone therapy (HT) or a placebo. The isoflavones were just as effective as HT in reducing hot flashes and vaginal dryness.

"Dietary soy supplementation may constitute an effective alternative therapy for... symptoms of menopause," concluded the researchers in the medical journal *Maturitas*.

"I recently presented a scientific paper that reviewed 19 studies on isoflavone supplements (such as genistein) and hot flashes—and there is absolutely no question that genistein works to ease this menopausal symptom," says Dr. Messina.

However: New research also shows there are many ways soy probably doesn't work to protect postmenopausal health, he says.

Putting more soy isoflavones in your diet probably won't...

- Strengthen bones
- Balance blood sugar, protecting you from prediabetes and diabetes
- Lower your body fat.

Studies do show a modest reduction in total cholesterol and blood pressure from soy intake, says Dr. Messina.

Increasing Soy Intake

"I don't see any scientific basis for differentiating the health effect of soy isoflavones from foods and soy isoflavones from supplements, because they are processed the same way in the body," says Dr. Messina.

However, he recommends soy foods as the first choice, because they deliver a natural, balanced intake of isoflavones.

- **Eating more soy.** "I would suggest eating two servings of soy food a day, which would deliver approximately 50 mg of isoflavones," he says. "Getting two servings a day isn't difficult, considering all the soy foods on the market.

"You can have soy milk with cereal, snack on soy nuts or eat edamame—green soybeans harvested in the pod—as a vegetable. The choices are virtually endless."

"There are many ways to add soy to your diet," agrees Nancy Chapman, RD, executive director of the Soyfoods Association of North America. *Her additional recommendations…*

- Stir-fry tofu and add it to vegetable dishes. (For the best flavor and texture, Chapman recommends the "firm" or "extra-firm" variety.)

- Try a meatless meal, substituting soy burgers for hamburgers or soy dogs for hot dogs. Use soy-substitute crumbles instead of meat in recipes. "There's a nearly limitless variety of soy substitutes for meat," says Chapman, "including soy patties, links and deli slices."

- Try soy cheese.

- **Choosing a soy supplement.** "The ideal supplement contains all three isoflavones—genistein, *daidzein* and *glycitein*—with genistein as the leading ingredient," says Dr. Messina.

Helpful: One way to guarantee you're getting that combination is to look for a "Novasoy" logo (a small green leaf) on the supplement label, says Dr. Messina. "It indicates the product contains a mixture of isoflavones standardized for genistein."

Recommended intake: 50 mg of total isoflavones daily, with at least 15 to 20 mg from genistein, says Dr. Messina.

Mark Messina, PhD, adjunct associate professor in the Department of Nutrition, School of Public Health, Loma Linda University, president of Nutrition Matters, Inc., a nutrition consulting company, and executive director of the Soy Nutrition Institute.

Nancy Chapman, RD, executive director of the Soyfoods Association of North America.

Acupuncture for Menstrual Pain

Here's a Jeopardy-style quiz in the "Women's Health" category, delivered in the form of an answer, for you to guess the question:

Answer: 14

Question: How many scientific studies were conducted in the past year showing that acupuncture can help relieve menstrual cramps?

It's not surprising that so many researchers are trying to find an effective treatment for menstrual cramps and pain (*dysmenorrhea*)—the problem afflicts an estimated 50% of women during their periods, and some have pain so intense they can't participate in everyday activities such as work or school.

To deal with the pain, most women take a painkiller…or apply a heating pad…or if the problem is debilitating, they take prescription birth control pills, which lighten, regulate or end periods, thereby easing or ending period-caused pain.

But drugs can have unwanted side effects, some of them very serious. (For example, birth control pills have been linked to cardiovascular disease and to uterine cancer.) And heating pads provide only temporary (and homebound) relief.

Acupuncture to the Rescue

Acupuncture is a main modality of Traditional Chinese Medicine, or TCM. It employs tiny needles that are inserted painlessly into specific points that TCM practitioners say can balance and enhance *chi*, an invisible energy or life force that flows through the body along channels called *meridians*. (The names of the meridians in English reflect the organs they intersect, such as the Liver Meridian and the Kidney Meridian.)

And acupuncture treatments are an excellent option, for short- and long-term relief, because they can not only ease the current pain but also possibly banish menstrual pain for good, says Kathleen Albertson, LAc, PhD, an acupuncturist, herbalist and holistic nutrition-ist in private practice in Irvine, California, and author of *Acupuncture and Chinese Herbal Medicine for Women's Health* (CreateSpace).

Pinpoint Pain Relief

Two of those 14 studies about acupuncture and menstrual pain analyzed other recent (and earlier) studies—with very positive findings.

●**More effective than drugs or herbs.** Korean researchers reviewed 27 studies on acupuncture and menstrual cramps, involv-ing nearly 3,000 women. They found that acupuncture was more effective than pain-relieving drugs or herbal medicine in treating menstrual pain. The results were in *BJOG: An International Journal of Obstetrics & Gynecology.*

Australian researchers conducted a similar analysis, reviewing 10 studies on acupunc-ture and menstrual pain involving 944 wom-en. *They found acupuncture was…*

●**9 times more effective than a placebo**

●**70% more effective than Tylenol or NSAIDs (nonsteroidal anti-inflammatory drugs, such as Advil and Midol)**

●**134% more effective than Chinese herbs.**

"Acupuncture may reduce period pain," concluded the researchers in *Cochrane Da-tabase of Systematic Reviews.*

●**Acupressure works, too.** Researchers studied 194 women with menstrual pain, teaching half of them how to do *acupres-sure*—applying firm, steady finger pressure to an acupuncture point. After four menstrual cycles of using acupressure, the women had a lot less menstrual pain than women not us-ing the technique, reported the researchers in the *International Journal of Gynecology & Obstetrics.*

The Acupuncture Advantage

Practitioners of TCM think most menstrual cramping and pain is caused by a condition called "blood stasis," says Dr. Albertson.

"The blood is stuck rather than moving, and the points used to treat the problem open up meridians that move the blood, regulating menstruation." Other commonly used points help relieve pain, she says.

For professional care: If you want to use acupuncture to treat menstrual pain, you have several different options, says Dr. Albertson.

●**Right before the period.** You can have one to three treatments one week before your period starts, which allows the "period to come freely and easily without pain," she says.

●**During the period.** A treatment dur-ing the period "moves the blood and stops bleeding, if it's heavy," she says.

●**Between periods.** One or more treat-ments between periods also tone the body, and may particularly help women who have vaginal discharge and bloating and are over-weight, all of which are signs of "dampness" in TCM.

Cycle by cycle treatments may completely resolve the problem in four to six months (but may take up to a year if the pain is severe).

For self-care: Concentrate on two acu-pressure points, says Dr. Albertson.

1. The "Liver 3" point in the furrow be-tween the big toe and second toe.

2. The "Large Intestine 4" point on the web between the thumb and index finger.

Work clockwise—left foot to right foot, and right hand to left hand. Press each point with your tip of your thumb, using a clock-wise, rubbing action, for about three minutes on each point.

Treat these points two to three times a day, starting one week before the onset of the painful period. You can continue the acupressure during days 1, 2 and 3 of the period itself, says Dr. Albertson.

"Some women will respond to light pres-sure, and some to medium or heavier pres-sure," says Dr. Albertson. "Find out what works best for you."

●**Try herbs, too.** Although TCM practi-tioners customize herbal formulas for each patient, there are also standardized, over-the-counter formulas that may help, says Dr. Albertson. *They include…*

For the week before the period: Tao Hong Si Wu Tang (Four Substances with Safflower and Peach Seed). "This is a blood-regulating formula for women with premenstrual cramping, who may also have shorter menstrual cycles with heavy bleeding and sharp, fixed pain," says Dr. Albertson.

For premenstrual syndrome (PMS): Xiao Yao Wan (Free and Easy Wanderer). "This is a harmonizing formula used for menstrual irregularity, bloating, irritability and insomnia," says Dr. Albertson. The main herb in the formula is Chai hu, or bupleurum, which is nicknamed "Chinese Prozac."

Dr. Albertson also recommends drinking cinnamon tea—a warming herb—if your symptoms include not only painful periods, but also dark, small blood clots in your menstrual blood and a feeling of coldness, which indicates that cold may have "invaded" the Kidney Meridian and that you need warming.

Also helpful: Dr. Albertson recommends several nutritional supplements for menstrual problems, including…

• **Fish oil (1,500 milligrams [mg] two times daily of EPA/DHA)**

• **Magnesium (up to 600 mg per day during menstruation)**

• **Vitamin B-6 (up to 300 mg per day during menstruation)**

• **Vitamin E (400 to 600 international units for five days prior to menstruation).**

Kathleen Albertson, LAc, PhD, acupuncturist, herbalist and holistic nutritionist in private practice in Irvine, California, and author of *Acupuncture and Chinese Herbal Medicine for Women's Health: Bridging the Gap Between Western and Eastern Medicine* (CreateSpace). *www.orange countyacupuncture.com.*

Stop Running To the Bathroom

U p to two million Americans have interstitial cystitis (IC), also known as painful bladder syndrome. Those with a severe form of the disease urinate up to 60 times a day.

Even though many people assume that this chronic form of nonbacterial bladder inflammation affects only women, research shows that 10% of sufferers are men. Unfortunately, the average person with IC has symptoms for five years and sees up to five doctors before a correct diagnosis is made.

Surprising development: Researchers are now discovering that some of the symptoms of IC may originate in the colon—that is, nerve impulses from an irritated colon (perhaps due to the consumption of certain foods, such as citrus fruits or spicy dishes) may "accidentally" stimulate nerves that carry impulses to the bladder.

A Painful Cycle

Besides an urgent and/or frequent need to urinate, IC causes pelvic pain. Women also may have discomfort in the area between the vagina and anus…in men, between the scrotum and the anus.

One current theory: Research now suggests that IC is caused by an abnormality in the *urothelium*, the thin layer of cells that makes up the bladder's inner lining. A breakdown in this lining allows irritating substances to penetrate the bladder.

Up to 40% of IC patients have recurrent urinary tract infections. This is consistent with the hypothesis that urothelium damage is to blame—infections can damage the bladder's protective lining. Some researchers also speculate that IC is a form of auto-immune disorder, in which the body's immune response attacks tissues in the bladder.

Getting the Right Diagnosis

If you urinate more than eight times a day… get up repeatedly (more than two times) at night to urinate…and/or have pelvic or bladder discomfort, see your primary health-care provider. He/she may refer you to a urologist or urogynecologist specializing in IC. These symptoms are not normal—regardless of your age.

Red flag: People with IC tend to void small amounts (usually less than four ounces) at a time, which leads to more frequent urination.

IC symptoms can be similar to those caused by such conditions as a urinary tract infection, kidney stones or even bladder cancer, so you may require...

• **Urinalysis to rule out a urinary tract infection.**

• **Potassium sensitivity test.** A potassium solution and plain water are placed in the bladder at different times via a catheter. If you have IC, you will have more urinary urgency and pain with the potassium solution. Those without IC won't notice a difference.

• **Cystoscopy.** A doctor examines the bladder and urethra with a drinking-straw–sized tube with lenses and a light. This helps rule out bladder cancer. A bladder biopsy also may be performed to test for bladder cancer.

• **Computed tomography (CT) scan to rule out kidney stones.**

How to Help Yourself

Up to 91% of IC patients suffer worse, or more frequent, symptoms when they eat certain foods. These foods may irritate the bladder or irritate nerves that send impulses to both the colon and bladder. Nerves for both organs originate in the same region of the spinal cord.

This may be why 30 to 40% of those with irritable bowel syndrome (a chronic condition marked by abdominal pain with constipation and/or diarrhea) also suffer from IC. Effective strategies...

• **Avoid the "4 Cs"—caffeine (including chocolate)...carbonated drinks...citrus fruits...and vitamin C–rich foods.** They frequently trigger flare-ups in patients with IC. Most patients also need to avoid spicy or acidic foods (such as tomatoes, lemon juice and vinegar), as well as alcohol.

• **Sip water every five minutes when you're awake.** Some people cut back on water to reduce urinary frequency. This doesn't work.

What Is Interstitial Cystitis?

Interstitial cystitis (IC) occurs when the wall of the bladder becomes chronically inflamed for unknown reasons. The condition typically causes an urgent and/or frequent need to urinate and pressure or pain in the bladder and pelvic area.

Drinking less water makes urine more concentrated and increases discomfort. Always carry a water bottle and drink often. Most people with IC need to drink about two quarts daily to dilute urine so that the bladder can process a constant, steady amount of urine.

• **Work with a pelvic-floor physiologist.** This health-care professional can teach gentle stretching and strengthening of the pelvic-floor muscles to reduce urinary urgency and discomfort.

• **Practice bladder training.** This technique involves timed urination—going to the bathroom according to the clock, not the urge. Intervals typically start at 30 minutes and gradually lengthen.

• **Reduce stress with guided imagery.** Anything that helps you relax—yoga, Pilates, taking a walk, etc.—can help control IC. When you relax, it lowers stress hormones, which reduces pain.

Kristene Whitmore, MD, professor of urology and obstetrics-gynecology, and chair of urology and female pelvic medicine and reconstructive surgery at Drexel University College of Medicine in Philadelphia. She is founder and medical director of the Pelvic and Sexual Health Institute, also in Philadelphia.

So You Think You Have A Yeast Infection?

When itching, burning and vaginal discharge make their unwelcome appearance, many women assume that they have a yeast infection—an overgrowth of the candida fungus that often is a normal part of the vaginal environment. To end the outbreak, they use a nonprescription anti-yeast medication, such as *miconazole* (Monistat).

Problem: More often than not, yeast is not to blame. In a recent study, 153 women thought they had yeast infections—but in 74% of cases, tests revealed that symptoms actually had a different cause.

This is just one of many common misunderstandings about vaginal infections, a group of conditions collectively called *vaginitis*. Each misunderstanding can lead to misdiagnosis, ineffective treatment and unnecessary suffering. *Here's what you need to know to protect yourself...*

The Leading Culprit

● **Bacterial vaginosis (BV).** The most common kind of vaginitis, this accounts for 40% to 45% of cases. It is an overgrowth of anaerobic bacteria, a type that doesn't need oxygen. BV develops when (for reasons that are unclear) the vagina's pH changes from a healthy acidic level of 3.8 to 4.2 to a less acidic, more alkaline level of above 4.5. This allows anaerobic bacteria to thrive.

Symptoms: Thin gray discharge...fishy odor...itching...burning during urination.

Diagnosis: If you suspect BV, see your doctor if you've never had the symptoms before (to ensure an accurate diagnosis) or if recurrent BV occurs more than twice a year (to confirm the diagnosis and discuss prevention strategies). To diagnose BV, the doctor performs a physical exam...does a pH test...prepares a wet mount (a sample of vaginal discharge to examine under a microscope)...and conducts a whiff test by adding a chemical solution to the wet mount that, in the case of BV, releases fishy-smelling proteins.

Treatment: Typically a prescription antibiotic, such as *metronidazole* (Flagyl), is used orally for seven days or in topical gel form for five days—or longer for recurrent BV.

Soothing: Twice daily, soak for 10 minutes in a sitz bath of lukewarm water mixed with four tablespoons of baking soda.

Prevention Strategies...

● **Launder panties, towels and other articles that come in contact with your genital area using dye-free and fragrance-free detergent, such as All Free Clear.** If you use a stain remover on these articles, soak and rinse them afterward in clear water, then machine-wash. Skip fabric softener and dryer sheets.

● **Wear white 100%-cotton panties and thigh-high nylons, not panty hose.**

● **Use nonperfumed soaps, body washes and lotions.**

Good brands: Basis, Dove Hypoallergenic, Neutrogena, Pears. Never use bubble bath, bath salts or scented bath oils.

● **Use white, unscented toilet paper.** Avoid adult or baby wipes.

● **Do not douche or use feminine hygiene spray.**

● **Avoid deodorized sanitary products.** Use a tampon only when your flow is heavy enough to soak it within four hours—otherwise, use a pad.

● **To keep the groin area dry, apply moisture-absorbing Gold Bond Powder or Zeasorb powder (not talcum powder) daily...and change your panties if they become damp.** Panty liners can keep moisture trapped in—so wear them only on days when menstrual flow is light, not daily.

The Fungi

● **Yeast infections.** These account for 20% to 25% of vaginitis cases. Up to 95% of yeast infections are *candida albicans*...the rest are *candida glabrata, candida parapsilosis* or another strain. *Factors that increase susceptibility to yeast...*

● **Weakened immune system** (for instance, from stress, high-dose steroids or chemotherapy).

•**Antibiotics**, which disturb the normal balance of vaginal flora.

•**Elevated blood sugar** due to diabetes or a diet high in potatoes, sugar and/or refined carbohydrates.

Symptoms: Thick, white, cottage-cheese-like vaginal discharge…itching…redness.

Diagnosis: Unlike bacterial infections, yeast infections do not raise vaginal pH—but a normal pH result on an over-the-counter test (such as Vagisil Screening Kit) does not confirm that you have yeast rather than something else. So if you suspect a first yeast infection or if bouts recur more than twice yearly, see your doctor for a yeast culture, physical exam, pH test and wet mount.

Treatment: A doctor-diagnosed first yeast infection or flare-ups that occur twice per year or less can be treated with nonprescription antifungal medication. But for frequently recurring infections, it is better to take a stronger prescription antifungal, such as *fluconazole* (Diflucan), for one to three days. If symptoms persist, ask your doctor about doing a yeast culture to identify and tailor treatment to the species. Do not try to treat yeast with "natural" douches, such as tea tree oil—vaginal tissues are easily irritated.

Prevention: Follow the BV guidelines above—they also guard against yeast—and reduce dietary sugar.

The STD

•**Trichomoniasis ("trich").** Responsible for 15 to 20% of vaginitis cases, trichomoniasis is the only sexually transmitted form of vaginitis—you can't "catch" BV or yeast from a sexual partner. Trich is caused by a parasitic *protozoan* (single-celled organism) that burrows under the vagina's mucous lining.

Symptoms: Heavy, yellow-green discharge and intense itching.

Diagnosis: Again, you should have a physical exam, pH test and wet mount. Trich is the diagnosis with a pH greater than 4.5, the presence of large numbers of inflammatory white blood cells and microscopic detection of the pear-shaped protozoa. If you have trich, your risk for other sexually transmitted diseases rises—so get screened for chlamydia and gonorrhea, too.

Treatment: A one-day course of *metronidazole* eradicates trich. Your sex partner also needs antibiotics so he doesn't reinfect you.

The Menopausal Misery

•**Atrophic vaginitis.** Vaginal tissues are very sensitive to declining estrogen—so this type of vaginitis is common, affecting an estimated 10 to 40% of postmenopausal women to some degree.

Signs/symptoms: Vaginal dryness, itching and burning…smelly yellow discharge…painful intercourse.

Diagnosis: A physical exam reveals dry, thin vaginal and vulvar tissues. When diagnosing atrophic vaginitis, your doctor should rule out other problems that cause similar symptoms, such as *lichen planus* (a skin disorder that involves vulvar tissue degeneration).

Treatment: Vaginal estrogen rings or tablets are very effective. However, they are not appropriate for women with migraines or a history of, or increased risk for, breast cancer or cardiovascular disease.

Natural alternative: Twice daily and also before intercourse, gently rub a dab of vegetable oil (such as olive oil) or solid vegetable shortening onto the vulvar tissues and inside the vagina. Within six weeks of starting this regimen, women who have suffered for years with atrophic vaginitis and painful intercourse often get complete relief.

Cherie A. LeFevre, MD, associate professor of gynecology and director of the Vulvar and Vaginal Disorders Specialty Center at St. Louis University School of Medicine.

The Perfect Dose of Cranberry to Beat UTIs

One out of three women will experience a urinary tract infection (UTI) sometime in her life…up to 30% of those women will have a second UTI…and two-thirds of those women will have several each year.

Important: If you think you have a UTI (also called a bladder infection)—with symptoms such as urgent, frequent and burning urination; cloudy (and maybe bloody) urine and, in severe cases, back and groin pain and/or fever—visit your doctor, who will determine if you have the infection. If you do, you'll probably receive a prescription for antibiotics that kill E. coli, the bladder-infecting bacteria. In many cases, that's that—infection defeated, once and for all.

But if you're one of the millions of women with recurrent UTIs, one of the best strategies for preventing them is including cranberry in your daily diet, either by drinking cranberry juice or taking a cranberry supplement.

Latest development: Research shows exactly how cranberry prevents UTIs...and exactly how much cranberry you need in juice or a supplement to keep recurrent UTIs at bay.

How Cranberry Works

The active compounds in cranberry are *proanthocyanidins* (PACs)—also found in grapes, apples, pomegranates, chocolate, green tea and other foods—and they're so good for you some nutritional experts call them "super." When it comes to beating bacteria, the PACs in cranberry products are truly superheroes.

That's because they have a unique, nearly unbreakable type of molecular bond that links PAC parts called *catechins*. And those heavy-duty bonds also block E. coli bacteria as they try to attach sticky, hairlike appendages called *fimbriae* to cell receptors on the inner wall of the bladder—after which the bacteria start to multiply and spew toxins, the microscopic ruckus you experience as a UTI. With cranberry on the scene, the bacteria can't attach and bob harmlessly in the urine, which washes them out of the bladder.

New study: Scientists dipped E. coli bacteria into five solutions of bladder cells that contained progressively higher concentrations of cranberry in cranberry juice cocktail

(0%, 2.5%, 5%, 10% and 27%). Then they used an atomic-force microscope to measure the ability of the bacteria to attach their fimbriae to the cells.

The stronger the cranberry juice cocktail, the weaker the attachment—with the 27% mixture weakening it 12 times more than the 0%.

"It's incredible that the mechanism of how cranberry works to prevent UTIs has now been shown on the molecular level," says Amy Howell, PhD, an associate research scientist at the Marucci Center for Blueberry and Cranberry Research at Rutgers University in New Jersey.

Another important development: This study points to another way you can use cranberry to deal with a UTI, she says.

"The study showed that when E. coli start to attach to the bladder wall, the attachment is somewhat looser," says Dr. Howell.

"If you begin drinking cranberry at that point, you weaken the attachment even more, so a natural flow of urine can knock the bacteria off the bladder cells.

"That means if you start drinking cranberry juice as soon as you start feeling the symptoms of a UTI—in the first 12 hours of an infection—you may be able to ward off the infection."

Best Dose and Supplements

Led by Dr. Howell, a team of researchers studied the clinically proven dose of 36 milligrams (mg) of PACs a day. They gave 32 women either 36 or 72 mg a day in a cranberry supplement and then tested the "bacterial anti-adhesion activity" in their urine.

"There was a little more activity at 72 milligrams, but not enough to justify an increase in dosage," says Dr. Howell.

Recommended intake: 36 milligrams of PAC daily.

"You want to take the minimum supplemental amount to get the job done, because that's the amount you're likely to take day after day—and 36 milligrams is that amount."

The minimum amount is also maximally safe. "You can get too much of a good thing," says Dr. Howell. "For example, you'd never take three times the recommended dosage of an antibiotic because you know that would be overdoing it. Similarly, a functional food such as cranberry is very active in the body, affecting genetic pathways and enzymes—and you don't want to overwhelm the body with too much of that activity."

Trap: But you do want an adequate level of activity, and many cranberry supplements don't contain 36 mg of PACs—even when their labels say they do.

"Seventy-five percent of the cranberry supplements on the market are junk," says Dr. Howell. "Many companies don't know the right dosage of PACs or whether the PACs they're using actually have biological activity.

"Some products don't include any PACs, and their labels have meaningless phrases such as '400 mg of cranberry solids,' which could be nothing but fiber."

In one case, Dr. Powell tested a supplement with a label claiming that one tablespoon of the product equaled eight glasses of cranberry juice. She found no cranberry in the supplement. In fact, it contained nothing but sugar!

Good brands: Dr. Howell and her colleagues developed a new test to measure the PAC level and biological activity of cranberry supplements. *As of this writing, three products have made the grade...*

• **Ellura (one 36-mg capsule per day).** You can order the product online at *www. myellura.com* or call 877-421-7160.

• **CraLief, from Nutramax Laboratories (one 36-mg capsule per day).** You can order the product online at *www.nutramaxstore. com* (888-886-6442) or *www.drugstore.com* (800-378-4786).

• **TheraCran, from Theralogix (two capsules per day).** You can order the product online at *http://www.theralogix.com* or call 800-449-4447.

Cranberry Juice

Dr. Howell and a team of researchers tested the bacteria-beating power of cranberry juice cocktail (CJC)—and found that 8 to 10 ounces a day of juice effectively lowered the "adhesion forces" of bacteria in urine. The results were in the *Journal of Medicinal Food*.

"Cranberry juice cocktail contains 27% cranberry juice, and that's plenty of cranberry to do the job," says Dr. Howell.

For optimal results: Make sure any cranberry juice you purchase in the supermarket contains at least 27% real cranberry juice. "Some juices have very little cranberry, even when they say 'cranberry' on the label," she says.

And don't worry about CJC delivering huge amounts of sugar. It contains the same amount of carbohydrate as apple juice, and less carbohydrate than grape juice, says Dr. Howell. If you want, choose a low-calorie, low-sugar version, which is just as effective as regular-calorie CJC.

There's no therapeutic reason to choose 100% cranberry juice, she adds. "It's very bitter for daily use and may cause digestive problems."

Amy Howell, PhD, associate research scientist, Marucci Center for Blueberry and Cranberry Research, Rutgers University, New Jersey.

Do You Have Dense Breasts and Not Know It?

About 30% of women have dense or extremely dense breasts—meaning breasts that contain more glandular or connective tissue than fatty tissue—and most of them don't realize it. *Why breast density matters...*

• **Breast cancer risk is higher in dense-breasted women.** In fact, a recent study found that breast cancer is about four times more common in women with extremely dense breasts than in women with very low-density breasts.

●**It is harder to screen for cancer in dense breasts** because mammogram X-rays do not see through dense tissue as well as they do fat tissue. Radiologist Rachel Brem, MD, director of the Breast Imaging and Interventional Center at the George Washington University Medical Center, says, "Cancerous tissue and dense areas both appear white on a mammogram, so identifying cancer is like trying to pick out a particular cloud in a cloud-filled sky."

Comparison: Overall, only about 15% of breast cancers are undetectable on a mammogram…but in dense breasts, about one-third of cancers are undetectable.

What's Your Density?

Breast density cannot be determined by touch. It must be assessed visually, with a mammogram or other imaging test. To find out how dense your breasts are, ask the radiologist the next time you have a mammogram. Or ask your primary care doctor, who receives written reports on your mammogram results.

Radiologists rate density on a scale of one to four. A rating of one means the breast contains less than 25% dense tissue…two indicates 25% to 49% dense tissue…three indicates 50% to 74% dense tissue, the range within which breasts are termed "dense"… four means 75% or more dense tissue, also called "extremely dense" breasts.

It is common for density to decrease at menopause. A recent Mayo Clinic study suggests that women whose density does decrease have a 28% reduction in breast cancer risk.

But: Density may increase after menopause if a woman uses hormone therapy or loses a significant amount of weight.

Screening Tests You Need

You can't do anything to decrease breast density other than to not use hormone therapy—but you can decrease the risk of having cancer go undetected. *If you have dense breasts, Dr. Brem recommends…*

●**Get an annual mammogram starting at age 40**—and be sure the test is done using the newer digital technology, which provides more accurate results. Digital mammograms are significantly better at revealing cancer in dense breasts than traditional analog technology because they produce images on a computer screen that can be enhanced and magnified for closer viewing. "More than 70% of all mammograms in the US are now done on digital machines, but facilities that do a smaller volume of mammography may not have upgraded yet," Dr. Brem points out. Your doctor can refer you to a radiology facility that provides digital mammograms.

●**Ideally, get your digital mammogram done at a facility that has computer-aided detection (CAD) software.** Now widely available, CAD uses a computer to analyze mammogram results and highlight any abnormal areas, alerting the radiologist to check those areas closely. CAD increases mammography's cancer-detection ability by about 20%—even in women with dense breasts.

●**If you have dense breasts and no other risk factors, you do not need to have an annual breast MRI,** Dr. Brem says. But you might want to ask your doctor about getting an annual ultrasound along with your mammogram. "Ultrasound and mammography look at very different characteristics of the breasts and provide different information," Dr. Brem explains. At present, ultrasound is mainly used in women with unusually dense breast tissue to help determine whether a questionable image on a mammogram is a noncancerous, liquid-filled cyst or a solid mass that might be a cancerous tumor. However, some doctors do recommend routine annual ultrasounds for dense-breasted patients even when there are no other risk factors.

On the horizon: An ongoing study is evaluating 22,000 women using automated whole-breast ultrasound (ABUS). Standard 2D ultrasound uses a handheld transducer that scans the breast section by section, in a piecemeal fashion…whereas ABUS creates 3D images using an automated transducer that consistently and quickly scans the entire breast so no areas are inadvertently missed.

Study goal: To determine whether routine screening with ABUS plus mammography is more accurate than mammography alone in detecting cancer in dense-breasted women. "ABUS is an exciting technology—and so far, this approach has definitely detected more cancers than mammography alone," Dr. Brem says.

To join the clinical trial: Visit *www.so moinsightstudy.org* for more information.

Rachel Brem, MD, professor of radiology and director of the Breast Imaging and Interventional Center at the George Washington University Medical Center in Washington, DC.

Should You Quit Taking Calcium to Protect Your Heart?

D id you toss your calcium pills in the trash after a recent study concluded that calcium supplementation could increase heart attack risk? What about osteoporosis? There's no need for panic. Here's what that widely publicized study really showed…and what women should do with the information.

As reported in the journal *BMJ*, investigators analyzed data from 11 clinical trials in which nearly 12,000 patients—mostly women age 70 or older—were randomly assigned to receive calcium supplements or placebos for an average of nearly four years.

The shocker: People who took 500 milligrams (mg) or more of calcium daily were about 30% more likely to have a heart attack than those who did not take calcium.

Many physicians were surprised by these findings, as other research (detailed below) suggests that calcium generally has a neutral or even protective effect on the heart. Still, this study raises the possibility that calcium supplements should not be used as widely as they are now.

The concern: In recent years, researchers have discovered that *vascular calcifi-cation* (calcium buildup in atherosclerotic plaques in the arteries) is a risk factor for heart attacks…and it may be that overzealous consumption of calcium can contribute to vascular calcification or even to the development of atherosclerosis itself. *But before you panic, consider the following…*

The *BMJ* study's results do not necessarily apply to dietary calcium. Indeed, a high intake of calcium from foods, including calcium-rich low-fat dairy products, has been associated with lower risks for various heart attack risk factors, including diabetes…high blood pressure…and metabolic syndrome, a cluster of symptoms that includes abdominal obesity, high triglycerides, high blood pressure, high blood sugar and low HDL (good) cholesterol.

Why might dietary calcium have more favorable effects than supplemental calcium? Because dietary calcium may interact with other nutrients in food to yield health benefits…and because calcium from food may be absorbed into the bloodstream more slowly than calcium from supplements, thus reducing the likelihood of high blood calcium levels.

The *BMJ* study findings do not necessarily apply to calcium supplements taken in combination with vitamin D. The *BMJ* study focused on calcium supplements taken alone, without vitamin D. However, many calcium supplements sold in the US also contain vitamin D. Available research suggests that the same heart risks are not found with such combination supplements because vitamin D regulates calcium metabolism, the mechanism by which the body maintains appropriate calcium levels.

Example: The Women's Health Initiative—in which about 36,000 postmenopausal women were randomly assigned to take either placebos or 1,000 mg of calcium plus 400 international units (IU) of vitamin D per day—did not find an increased risk for either vascular calcification or heart attack.

According to the *BMJ* study, calcium supplementation did not increase heart attack risk in people whose dietary calcium intakes were less than about 800 mg per day. This bolsters the idea that excess calcium might be responsible for the *BMJ* study results. It may be especially true for older people who have decreased kidney function.

What Women Should Do

This study has a clear take-home message. For bone health, you should get the currently recommended amount of calcium each day, taking into account both your dietary and supplemental calcium sources—but avoid ingesting more than this amount. Many experts recommend 1,000 mg of calcium per day up to age 50 and 1,200 mg per day thereafter...as well as about 800 international units per day of vitamin D from food and/or supplements.

Bottom line: If you get this much calcium from food alone, skip the supplements. If you do not get sufficient calcium from your diet, make up the difference by supplementing (and take care to get enough vitamin D, too).

To estimate the amount of calcium in your diet, check the calcium content of specific foods on the USDA Web page at *www.ars. usda.gov/services/docs.htm?docid=18877*...on the National Institutes of Health Web page at *http://ods.od.nih.gov/factsheets/calcium*...and/ or on food labels.

Rich Dietary Sources Of Calcium Include...

Yogurt, plain, low-fat: 415 mg per cup.

Sardines, canned with bones: 325 mg per three-ounce serving.

Milk, low-fat: 305 mg per cup.

Cheddar cheese: 204 mg per ounce.

Salmon, canned with bones: 181 mg per three-ounce serving.

Collard greens: 178 mg per ½ cup chopped and cooked.

Figs: 155 mg for five figs.

Cottage cheese (1% milk fat): 138 mg per cup.

Unless you consume a lot of dairy products, you are unlikely to get too much calcium from food alone.

But: It is easy to get too much supplemental calcium—so check labels not only on your calcium tablets but also on your multivitamins, calcium-plus-vitamin-D supplements and any calcium-containing medications that you may be taking.

JoAnn E. Manson, MD, DrPH, professor of medicine and women's health at Harvard Medical School and chief of the division of preventive medicine at Brigham and Women's Hospital, both in Boston. She is one of the lead investigators for two highly influential studies on women's health—the Harvard Nurses' Health Study and the Women's Health Initiative. Dr. Manson is author, with Shari Bassuk, ScD, of *Hot Flashes, Hormones & Your Health* (McGraw-Hill).

The Mother Nature Makeover

The Mother Nature Makeover is a makeover of a very different kind. You don't buy a new dress and new shoes. There's no new hairdo, manicure or pedicure. You don't learn a new way to apply makeup. And there's no facelift or Botox.

The Mother Nature Makeover can change you in a way that women in modern society are rarely changed—you learn to accept yourself for exactly how you look, right now!

The Body Image Dilemma

If you're like most women, you have a negative body image—the sense that your body, as it is, isn't beautiful or that you're too heavy.

"Our society has an ideal of the 'super thin' woman and doesn't accept a wide variety of body types," says Kari Hennigan, PhD, program director at the Sanctuary Psychiatric Center in Santa Barbara, California. "We don't support women to love and accept how their body actually looks. Instead, our society teaches women that if you find the perfect diet, and you work hard enough, and you're good and strong-willed, you can be skinny and beautiful.

"That is such a trap, because for the most part there is only so much change that is going to occur with your body, no matter what you do. But instead of teaching self-acceptance—instead of a focus on being present in the body, and using it to experience pleasure—we focus on ways that women can control and contort their bodies into something they were never meant to be.

"Women end up feeling like they're coming up short, no matter how hard they try, which often leads to feelings of worthlessness and despair, and eventually to depression."

Time Well Spent

The great outdoors can change the way you experience your body…and how you feel and think about it.

"Spending time in nature may be one way to reduce the negative impact of these social and cultural ideals," says Dr. Hennigan, who conducted a study of 12 women aged 24 to 55, interviewing them at length about their experience of spending time in nature.

What she learned from these women was no surprise. Previous research in the new field of "ecopsychology" has shown that time in nature can help a woman reevaluate and reformulate her own norms for the female body and can challenge the social ideal of extreme thinness.

"I expected that women who spent time in nature would find the experience had a positive impact on their body image," she says. Which is exactly what her study confirmed.

There are three main reasons why time in nature can help heal a negative body image, she says.

• **Distance from cultural ideals.** "If you're continually worrying about how you look in those pants, and what people are thinking about the way your hair looks, and otherwise self-monitoring your appearance, there's not a lot of room for healing of negative body image," she says.

"That's why I think it's really important for a woman to have a space in her life where she can ask herself questions such as, 'What is beauty to me?' And I think that nature in its vast diversity is the perfect setting to ask that question—an opportunity to question the internalized messages of the culture, and to come to new conclusions about the truth of one's experience and beliefs.

"Women seem to leave behind the judgmental attitudes toward themselves and others when they immerse themselves in nature," says Dr. Hennigan.

Example: "I remember feeling happy, glowing, earthy and natural—alive and confident," one study participant said, after a wilderness trip. "I remember feeling I was radiating and I felt beautiful. I felt very attractive, regardless of how I looked in the mirror."

• **Embodied experience.** "I've come to believe that negative body image can only be healed from an embodied place, rather than from an intellectualized or mental place," says Dr. Hennigan.

"Being embodied means being really present in one's body, and being tuned in to all your senses, rather than being caught up in the mind and worried how you look and what other people think about how you look.

"Once you can drop down into your body and into that felt experience, you can tap into your own strengths. You can see yourself not only for your appearance, but for the functionality of your body, for what you're capable of doing, and for the pleasure you're able to experience through your body.

"And it's much easier for women to have embodied experiences in nature because there's so much sensory stimulation, and you become interested in what's happening around you."

Example: "When I'm out in nature, I feel stronger, strengthened and grounded," one woman told Dr. Hennigan.

• **Connection to nature.** "As women spend more time in nature, their sense of the interconnectedness between self and nature increases, and this facilitates self-acceptance and positive body image," she says.

Example: "With nature, body image doesn't matter," another study participant told Dr. Hennigan. "It doesn't matter how big your body is or how small. Your body is a part of nature, and that's really all that matters."

Nature as Therapy

To use and maximize the therapeutic power of time spent in nature, Dr. Hennigan recommends *place-bonding*.

"This is one of the easiest and most accessible ways to use nature to heal negative body image," she says.

"Choose one spot—your backyard or a local park or your favorite trail—that is accessible and that you can visit every day."

And spend at least 30 minutes a day in that place, just paying attention to the sights and sounds and how you feel there.

"Observe the animals, the details of the terrain and changes in yourself. By taking time out for embodied experience, you will gradually develop a deep connection to that specific place and a deeper connection to yourself.

"I've seen many clients develop greater compassion for themselves and greater self-acceptance through the observation of the natural world, and its beauty and diversity," she says. "Such a client is able to see that bodies are very diverse, and to see her own body as beautiful, even if it doesn't look anything like the cultural ideal."

Kari Hennigan, PhD, program director at the Sanctuary Psychiatric Center in Santa Barbara, California, and author of the article "Therapeutic Potential of Time in Nature: Implications for Body Image in Women," which appeared in a recent issue of the journal *Ecopsychology*.

The Truth About Sexual Desire in Women— Best Simple Ways to Increase Libido

Ever since an FDA advisory panel rejected the approval of a so-called "female Viagra" last year—the drug was deemed no more effective at increasing libido than a placebo—there's been a lot of debate on the female libido.

Key issue: If a woman's desire for sex is low, is that necessarily a "dysfunction" that should be treated? *What women—and their partners—need to know...*

Is There a Problem?

According to Leah Millheiser, MD, director of the Female Sexual Medicine Program at Stanford University School of Medicine, when it comes to libido, medical experts agree that there is no "normal" or "abnormal." Doctors diagnose a libido dysfunction only when there is a recurrent or persistent problem with libido that causes personal distress to the woman.

Therefore, if a woman has no sexual desire but is undisturbed by this fact, then no dysfunction exists. Alternatively, if a woman wants to have sex twice a week but is distressed because she used to want it more often than that, then the decrease in libido is a dysfunction for her.

To diagnose low libido: A woman needs to answer just one basic question—do *you* think you have a problem with your level of sexual desire?

Note: When a man and woman's desire don't match, it's called "desire mismatch," which is not truly a sexual dysfunction, though the partners may benefit from sex therapy.

Causes of Low Libido

Not all doctors ask about their patients' sexual health, so any woman who experiences chronic or recurrent low libido should tell her gynecologist and/or primary care physician. *Most common causes...*

●**Health problems.** Some chronic diseases, such as diabetes and atherosclerosis (clogged arteries), can decrease blood flow—including that feeding the sex organs. Without proper blood flow, sex can feel uncomfortable, and orgasm may be impossible—both of which may negatively impact a woman's libido. And because sexual desire starts in the brain, doctors shouldn't ignore the possibility that low desire could be a side effect of a brain injury from, say, a fall, car wreck or stroke.

• **Medication use.** The side effects of many drugs may include a change in sexual desire and/or difficulty reaching orgasm.

Common culprits: Antidepressant drugs known as *selective serotonin reuptake inhibitors* (SSRIs), such as *fluoxetine* (Prozac) and *sertraline* (Zoloft)…and cholesterol-lowering statin medications, such as *atorvastatin* (Lipitor) and *simvastatin* (Zocor).

• **Psychosocial factors.** If a woman is in a relationship that is physically, emotionally or verbally abusive, her sexual desire can diminish. Past physical or sexual abuse can also lower libido. Any woman experiencing abuse should work with her doctor to create a plan to improve the relationship or leave it. Those experiencing current or past abuse may also benefit from therapy.

• **Partner's health issues.** If a woman with low libido has a partner who has a sexual dysfunction—such as low sex drive, erectile dysfunction or inability to orgasm—both partners can drag each other's desire down even further. Therefore, both people should be evaluated by a sex therapist.*

• **Hormone levels.** The primary male hormone (testosterone), which is also present in females, plays a crucial role in women's libido. Postmenopausal women, in particular, have decreased testosterone, which lowers libido and makes it more difficult to have an orgasm. Premenopausal women may experience lowered testosterone levels if they take birth control pills.

While it might seem that taking testosterone would be an easy fix for libido, research has been mixed. Some studies have shown a benefit, while others have shown no or only slight improvement in sexual desire. Because the potential side effects (such as excessive body hair and acne) are serious, women taking testosterone need to be carefully monitored with blood tests every three to six months.

• **Stress.** For many women, a low libido starts with a stress-filled life, according to

Barbara Bartlik, MD, psychiatrist and sex therapist in New York City. She describes a typical patient as "very upset, working too many hours, feeling that she has little control over her life and burning the candle at both ends." Living under such intense stress can also cause a woman's testosterone levels to sink, leading to biological changes as well as emotional distress.

What You Can Do

It's important to work with your doctor to rule out underlying physical problems that may be leading to your low libido. *In the meantime, simple therapies may help…*

• **Identify what flips your sexual switch to "on."** For instance, reminisce about falling in love with your partner…dance at a party or wedding…flirt…whatever helps wake up that "loving feeling." Discuss your feelings and desires with your mate.

• **Take care of yourself.** Engage in activities just for you, ones that make you feel good—yoga, spa treatments, nights out with friends. Watch what you eat. Junk foods deplete energy and add to stress.

• **Reduce vaginal dryness.** Vaginal moisturizers—which are different from lubricants in that they are used two to three times a week, not just before sex—add moisture barriers in the vagina. This helps provide a layer of protection and comfort so that sex is not painful—a common complaint among women who experience vaginal dryness.

Recommended: KY Silk-E or Replens.** Follow label instructions.

Important: You must use such vaginal moisturizers for at least two months before judging results.

• **Masturbate.** Yes, this simple action can be a powerful libido booster for women—partly because it turns out that sexual desire really is a "use it or lose it" function.

• **Use lubricants.** Sexual lubricants help make sex more comfortable—painful sex is a common cause of low libido.

---

*To find a sex therapist or MD in your area who specializes in treating sexual dysfunction, consult the International Society for the Study of Women's Sexual Health, *www.isswsh.org.*

**All the products mentioned in this section can be purchased from *www.drugstore.com*, which ships its orders in a plain box labeled only with the company name.

Recommended: Pjur Eros Bodyglide, which is a silicone-based, glycerin-free product. This combination offers several advantages, including a reduced risk for yeast infections or vaginal inflammation, compared with products that contain glycerin.

●**Increase stimulation before and/or during sex.** When testosterone drops, some women need more stimulation to become aroused and to have an orgasm. The best method is to use a vibrator for clitoral stimulation. Dr. Millheiser's patients report that the best vibrator is the Hitachi Magic Wand—it provides a very strong vibration.

Helpful: Using an over-the-counter botanical oil with a vibrator has been shown in studies to increase a woman's ability to have an orgasm.

Recommended: Zestra Essential Arousal Oils.

●**Exercise.** We know that exercise elevates mood, improves blood circulation and general health, and helps enhance body image. All of these factors can improve sex drive.

Recommended: Any aerobic exercise, but especially walking and dancing because they are low-impact, low-stress exercise and can be fun to do. Aim to get out and walk (or dance) every day for at least 20 minutes.

Leah Millheiser, MD, clinical assistant professor in the Department of Obstetrics and Gynecology and director of the Female Sexual Medicine Program at Stanford University School of Medicine in Stanford, California.

Barbara Bartlik, MD, psychiatrist and sex therapist in New York City.

Maximum Heart Rates for Women Are Wrong! (Your Workout Just Got Easier)

There are two fitness formulas that most people think are as accurate as 2+2=4.

●**Maximum heart rate is the highest heart rate you can safely achieve.**

The formula to calculate it: 220 minus age.

●**Target heart rate is the heart rate during exercise that works to keep you fit.**

The formula to calculate it: 65 to 85% of your maximum heart rate.

Example: A 60-year-old has a maximum heart rate of 160 (220 minus age) and a target heart rate of 104 (75% of maximum) to 136 (85% of maximum).

For women, there's just one problem with the maximum heart rate formula. It's wrong.

New study: The unisex formula for maximum heart rate produces a number that is *too high* for women, perhaps leading women to unnecessarily tough workouts that discourage them from exercising, says cardiologist Martha Gulati, MD, director of Preventive Cardiology and Women's Cardiovascular Health at Ohio State University, and author of *Saving Women's Hearts* (Wiley).

New Formula for Women's Hearts

Dr. Gulati conducted a 16-year study on the heart health of 5,437 women, aged 35 to 93, which involved regular treadmill stress tests during which the women exercised as hard as they could.

Analyzing results from her study, she found that the correct formula to figure out an accurate maximum heart rate for women is slightly different than the existing formula.

The new formula: 206 minus 88% of a woman's age.

Example: A 60-year-old woman would have a maximum heart rate of 153 (not 160). Her target heart rate of 65 to 85% of maximum would be 100 to 130 (not 104 to 136).

"I'd seen enough women patients who couldn't achieve their target heart rate that I didn't believe the general formula could be correct for women—and it wasn't," says Dr. Gulati, who published her results in the medical journal *Circulation*.

Unfortunately, the inaccurate formula is programmed into just about every heart monitor and exercise machine.

What to do: If you're already comfortably achieving your target heart rate with the old formula, don't worry, says Dr. Gulati.

"Just keep doing what you're already doing."

But if you start an exercise program and can't achieve your target heart rate using the old formula, don't think you're a fitness failure—use the new formula.

What's most important, however, is not whether or not you meet your target heart rate during exercise, says Dr. Gulati—it's whether or not you exercise regularly.

"Physical activity and physical fitness is essential for maintaining the health of your heart and your overall health," she says.

In fact, an earlier study she conducted showed that fit women were three times less likely to die from any cause compared with women who weren't fit.

The Best Fitness Measurement

The measurement Dr. Gulati used in that study to determine physical fitness wasn't maximum heart rate or target heart rate.

It was a measurement called metabolic equivalents (METs), or the amount of oxygen required for any physical activity.

If you're able to perform an exercise at a certain level of METs, you're physically fit for your age, she says.

Here are her calculations for "age-predicted fitness level" of METs, and examples of activity that are at or near that level:

- **30 years old, 11 METs** (jumping rope)

- **40, 9.5** (singles tennis)
- **50, 8.2** (rowing)
- **60, 7** (jogging at 5 miles per hour)
- **70, 5.6** (walking briskly)
- **80, 4.3** (leisurely biking, at less than 10 miles per hour)

If you can't do the type of exercise for your age that indicates you're fit, your first goal should be to become active, says Dr. Gulati.

Your second goal should be to get as fit as possible and try to achieve your age-predicted fitness level for some duration of your workout. (She points out that most exercise machines in gyms display METs.)

She sums up her guidelines for women's fitness with these five rules:

Rule #1: Just be active—doing something is better than doing nothing.

Rule #2: Make changes gradually, not abruptly, to avoid injury.

Rule #3: Before you start any exercise program, discuss with your doctor if it is safe to do so.

Rule #4: Do activities you enjoy…dancing, gardening or taking the dog for a walk. Have fun!

Rule #5: Remember that more is better. So move, move, move!

Martha Gulati, MD, associate professor of medicine in the Division of Cardiology, the Sarah Ross Soter Chair in Women's Cardiovascular Health and the Section Director for Preventive Cardiology and Women's Cardiovascular Health, Ohio State University and author of *Saving Women's Hearts* (Wiley).

NATURAL HEALING MODALITIES

HEALTHY DIET

Good and Easy...Eating the Mediterranean Way

There is abundant scientific evidence on the health benefits of the so-called Mediterranean diet, which promotes the traditional eating habits of long-lived people in such countries as Greece and Italy.

Landmark research: Among the most compelling evidence is one long-term European study of healthy men and women ages 70 to 90.

It found that following the Mediterranean diet as part of an overall healthful lifestyle, including regular exercise, was associated with a more than 50% lower rate of death from all causes over a decade. Numerous studies have associated this type of eating with reduced risk for heart disease, cancer, cognitive decline, diabetes and obesity.

But many Americans are reluctant to try the Mediterranean diet for fear that it will be difficult or costly to follow because it emphasizes such foods as omega-3–rich fish, vegetables and nuts.

Surprising findings: Mediterranean eating does not increase food costs, according to a recent study—and this style of eating need not be complicated.

Wendy Kohatsu, MD, an assistant clinical professor of family medicine at the University of California, San Francisco, and a chef who conducts cooking demonstrations for patients and doctors, explains the best ways to incorporate Mediterranean eating into your daily diet...

Easy Ways to Get Started

To effectively tap into the Mediterranean diet's powerful health benefits, it's important to know exactly which foods should be eaten—and in what quantities.

Start by getting four to five daily servings of whole grains (one serving equals one-half cup of cooked quinoa, brown rice or whole-wheat pasta, for example, or one slice of whole-wheat bread) and two to three daily servings of low- or nonfat dairy products (such as yogurt, cottage cheese or milk), which are an important source of bone-protecting calcium. *In addition, be sure to consume...*

● **Oily fish.** This high-quality protein contains abundant omega-3 fatty acids, which help fight the inflammation that plays a role in cardiovascular disease, Alzheimer's disease and asthma.

Best choices: Follow the acronym SMASH —salmon (wild)...mackerel (Spanish, not king, which tends to have higher levels of mercury)...anchovies...sardines...and herring.

How much: Three ounces (the size of a deck of cards), twice a week.

Chef's secret: Drain canned sardines (the large size), grill briefly, sprinkle with fresh lemon juice and chopped parsley.

Beware: Some fish—such as shark, swordfish, golden bass (tilefish), king mackerel and albacore tuna—can be high in mercury. Avoid these. If you eat tuna, choose the "light" version, which contains less mercury than albacore tuna does.

If you don't like fish: Take a fish oil supplement (1,000 milligrams [mg] daily). Choose a brand that guarantees that no lead or mercury is present.

Dr. Kohatsu's favorite brands: Carlson's and Nordic Naturals.

Vegetarians can get omega-3s from flaxseed, walnuts and other nonfish sources. However, nonfish food sources of omega-3s are largely in the form of alpha-linolenic acid (ALA), which is not as potent as the more biologically powerful fatty acids found in fish. Algae-derived docosahexaenoic acid (DHA) capsules contain the omega-3s found in fish. The recommended dose of DHA capsules is 1,000 mg daily.

What most people don't know: A small but important study shows that eating oily fish with beans, such as lentils and chickpeas (also known as garbanzo beans), improves absorption of the iron found in beans.

●**Olive oil.** Olive oil contains about 77% healthful monounsaturated fats. Olive oil is also high in sterols, plant extracts that help reduce LDL "bad" cholesterol and increase HDL "good" cholesterol.

Best choice: Look for extra-virgin (or "first-press") olive oil. ("Extra virgin" means that the oil is derived from the first pressing of the olives.)

How much: Use olive oil as your primary fat—in salad dressings, marinades and sautées. To minimize your total daily intake of fat, do not exceed 18 grams (g) to 20 g of saturated fat and 0 g of trans fat from all food sources.

Chef's secret: If you dislike the "grassy" taste of some extra-virgin olive oils, look for Spanish and Moroccan versions, which tend to be more mellow. One good choice is olive oil made from the arbequina olive, which has a buttery taste.

What most people don't know: Nutrients in extra-virgin olive oil may offer some pain-relieving qualities over the long term.

●**Nuts.** Like extra-virgin olive oil, nuts are high in healthful monounsaturated fats.

In fact, a recent Spanish study found that a Mediterranean diet that included walnuts significantly lowered risk for heart disease.

What kinds: Besides walnuts, best choices include almonds and peanuts. Choose plain raw nuts—not salted or honey-roasted.

How much: One-quarter cup daily.

Beware: A quarter cup of nuts contains about 200 calories. Eat only a small handful daily—for example, about 23 almonds or 35 peanuts. If you're allergic to nuts, try pumpkin, sunflower or sesame seeds instead.

Chef's secret: Store nuts in your freezer to prevent them from going rancid.

●**Fruits and vegetables.** Many of the most healthful vegetables—including those of the brassica family, such as cabbage, kale, broccoli and cauliflower—originated in the Mediterranean area.

What kinds: Choose brightly colored fruit, such as citrus and berries, and vegetables, such as spinach, watercress, beets, carrots and broccoli.

How much: Five to nine servings daily. (A serving is one-half cup of cooked vegetables, one cup of leafy greens, one medium orange or one-half cup of berries.)

Contrary to popular belief, frozen vegetables, which are often far less costly than fresh produce, are just as nutritious—if not more so because they're frozen at their peak level of freshness and don't spoil in the freezer.

Chef's secret: Cooking tomatoes in olive oil concentrates the tomatoes' levels of *lycopene*, a powerful antioxidant that has been associated with a decreased risk for prostate, lung and stomach cancers.

Wendy Kohatsu, MD, assistant clinical professor of family medicine at the University of California, San Francisco, and director of the Integrative Medicine Fellowship at the Santa Rosa Family Medicine Residency Program in Santa Rosa, California. Dr. Kohatsu is also a graduate of the Oregon Culinary Institute.

The Healthiest Fish To Eat

Many of us are in a quandary when it comes to fish. Fish is a great dietary source of omega-3 fatty acids, which are needed by the body to maintain heart health, reduce inflammation and prevent mental decline. But fish often has high levels of toxins—particularly mercury and *polychlorinated biphenyls* (PCBs)—that pose health risks to people of all ages.

Individuals concerned about eating the most healthful fish should follow guidelines from the Environmental Defense Fund (EDF) (*www.edf.org*), a nonprofit environmental protection organization. The EDF provides information on the types of fish that are safe to consume based on the latest mercury and PCB data.

Below are some types of fish with low levels of contaminants that the EDF says can safely be eaten as a regular part of your diet—and which, according to the EDF, have the highest amounts of omega-3 fatty acids.

*A **word about canned fish:*** Canned foods, including canned anchovies, sardines, salmon and tuna, have been found to contain *bisphenol-A* (BPA), an estrogen-like compound that has been linked to health problems, including cancer. It leaches into the fish from the cans' lining—so choose fresh fish, whenever possible, including fresh sardines from the fish market or sold online.

You also can look for fish sold in pouches, which are BPA-free. Or select fish in glass jars (anchovies) or BPA-free cans, which is sold by companies such as Vital Choice (*www.vitalchoice.com*) and EcoFish (*www.ecofish.com*). For details on the safety of other fish species, go to *www.edf.org* and search for "Health Alerts—Seafood Selector."

Mark A. Stengler, NMD, naturopathic medical doctor in private practice, Encinitas, California, and author of the *Bottom Line/Natural Healing* newsletter. *www.drstengler.com.*

Safe and Healthy Fish

Type of fish	Amount of omega-3 per serving (serving equals 100 grams or 3.5 ounces)
Atlantic mackerel (the only type of mackerel that's healthful)	2,450 mg
Sardines (fresh)	1,900 mg
Sablefish/black cod	1,660 mg
Anchovies	1,480 mg
Wild Alaskan salmon	1,400 mg
Rainbow trout (farmed)	986 mg
Oysters (farmed)	680 mg

Do You Get Enough Omega-3s?

Most people don't. Now there's a way to find out. The HS-Omega 3 Index (800-949-0632, *www.omegaquant.com*) is a blood test that measures your total level of omega-3 fatty acids, including a breakdown of EPA and DHA, the main components of fish oil. It also provides a complete fatty acid profile, indicating levels of saturated fatty acids, trans-fatty acids and others.

The test can be ordered and used by your physician, or you can order your own test kit made just for consumers. The cost is $199.95 per test.

How it works: You collect a drop of blood from your finger, dry it on a collection card and return it to the manufacturer, who analyzes your results and sends them to you.

According to William Harris, PhD, founder of the HS-Omega-3 Index test, most Americans have an HS-Omega-3 Index of about 4%, and the desired level is 8%. If your omega-3 levels are low, speak to a naturopathic physician about increasing your intake and then test your levels again in about four months.

Mark A. Stengler, NMD, naturopathic medical doctor in private practice, Encinitas, California, and author of the *Bottom Line/Natural Healing* newsletter. *www.drstengler.com.*

Fabulous Fruits You Really Ought to Try

Eating a wider variety of fruits is a good idea, according to nutrition expert Steven V. Joyal, MD, vice president of scientific and medical affairs for Life Extension Foundation, a Fort Lauderdale-based research organization.

Reason: Different fruits provide different nutrients, each of which has its own set of beneficial effects on the body. What's more, taste buds that are treated to a variety of healthful fruits are less likely to get bored ("Not another apple! We want candy!")—so it's easier to resist cravings for nonnutritious foods.

Health-food stores, farmers' markets and larger supermarkets carry a wide selection of fruits. *Dr. Joyal recommends trying these especially nutritious, yet underappreciated, items…*

- **Carambola,** also called star fruit, is rich in vitamin A, which promotes eye health…vitamin C, to help support a healthy immune system…and potassium for cardiac function. Buy it green and let it ripen at room temperature until the ridges darken. Some varieties (such as the Arkin carambola) have a very sweet pineapple-orangey flavor…others (such as Golden Star) are more tart. Slice carambola crosswise (no need to peel it first) to make pretty star shapes that are perfect for fruit salad, avocado salad or Asian stir-fry.

- **Cherimoya** looks like a hand grenade. Ripen it at room temperature until it is slightly soft, then peel it and discard the skin and seeds. The creamy white flesh inside, which tastes like a mango-pineapple-strawberry mix, can be scooped out or sliced and eaten raw or baked into a pie…or mashed to a custard texture and added to whole-grain waffle batter. The cherimoya contains niacin, which maintains "good" HDL cholesterol…lots of the antioxidant vitamin C…and iron for red blood cell production.

- **Guava** provides protein for tissue repair…fiber for digestion…and calcium and phosphorus for bones. The guava may be green or maroon on the outside and white, pink or reddish inside. It is ready to eat when slightly soft and fragrant…expect a grainy texture and pear-kiwi-strawberry hybrid flavor. Eat a guava out of your hand as you would an apple…slice and salt it as you would a tomato…dice it into salads…or boil it to make jam.

- **Pomegranate** provides powerful antioxidants, promotes blood vessel relaxation and may ease symptoms of inflammation from arthritis. Round and red on the outside, the pomegranate is filled with hundreds of crimson, gel-covered seeds called arils. Remove the crown and the bottom with a knife, then score the sides of the hard outer peel from top to bottom. Place the fruit in a bowl of cold water and pry it apart. Pluck out the fleshy arils, letting them sink to the bottom of the bowl…discard the peel and internal white membranes…drain the seeds. To eat, suck off the sweet-tart gel and either swallow or spit out the soft inner seeds. For juice, put the gel-covered seeds in a blender and blend well, then strain to remove the remnants of the pulverized inner seeds, if desired.

- **Ugli fruit** looks like a lopsided grapefruit with baggy skin and tastes like a sweet-and-sour cross between a tangerine and a grapefruit. Packed with vitamin C and fiber, its segments can be eaten alone or added to salads (try it with fresh spinach leaves and shrimp). Juice it to add tang to marinades, sauces and salad dressings…or mix the juice with warm rum and honey for a hot toddy.

Steven V. Joyal, MD, vice president of scientific and medical affairs for Life Extension Foundation, a nonprofit organization based in Fort Lauderdale, Florida, that supports research related to the prevention of degenerative diseases. www.lef.org.

Is Butter Better?

For many years, butter was replaced by margarine on the menus of health-conscious consumers. But like many dietary taboos, that's beginning to change. A little butter is better than the fake stuff, says Andrew L. Rubman, ND. Butter is a natural food that supports good health, while margarine is a processed product chemically fashioned from refined polyunsaturated oils. This doesn't mean you can now drench your vegetables in pools of butter or slather it on your toast with abandon. But unless you have health challenges such as a serious digestive or metabolic disorder, Dr. Rubman says to go ahead and use the real thing (in moderation).

Butter with Benefits

Butter consists of butterfat and trace amounts of milk proteins and water. Butterfat is *butyric acid*, which is basically the same substance that mothers produce to nourish their babies, Dr. Rubman explains.

Butter's beneficial components include....

●**Antioxidants.** Beta-carotene, selenium and other antioxidants shield the body from free-radical damage.

●**Butyric acid.** This short-chain fatty acid supports colon health.

●**Conjugated linoleic acids.** CLAs fight cancer, build muscle and boost immunity.

●**Iodine.** Butter is rich in iodine, which is essential to thyroid health.

●**Lauric acid.** A medium-chain fatty acid, lauric acid encourages the body's immune system to fend off yeast and other infections.

●**Lecithin.** This phospholipid protects cells from oxidation and may contribute to cholesterol metabolism.

●**Vitamin A.** Butter contains the readily absorbable form of vitamin A, which is a must for eye and endocrine health.

●**Vitamin D.** This vitamin helps your body absorb calcium to maintain strong bones and plays a role in reducing your risk for chronic diseases such as osteoporosis, heart disease, and colon and other cancers.

●**Vitamin E.** Anti-inflammatory vitamin E speeds wound healing, promotes skin health, enhances immunity and may protect against a host of illnesses, including diabetes, heart disease and Alzheimer's.

●**Vitamin K.** Proper blood clotting and bone health are among the benefits offered by fat-soluble vitamin K.

But What About the Fat?

The biggest rap against butter is its high fat content. Butter bashers argue that saturated fat and cholesterol in butter contribute to heart disease, but Dr. Rubman disagrees—and the research bears him out. In a study published in *The Lancet*, scientists point out that countries with the highest saturated fat consumption have lower cardiac mortality rates than countries that consume the least fat. For example, the French enjoy three times more saturated fat than the Azerbaijanis, but have one-eighth the rate of heart disease deaths. The Finns eat half as much fat as the French, but the death rate from heart disease is three times greater in Finland. In research from the UK, 2,000 men with heart disease who cut back on saturated fat for two years had no fewer heart attacks than men who did not cut back.

Saturated fat and cholesterol have been falsely demonized by manufacturers of cholesterol-lowering statin drugs, observes Dr. Rubman, noting that since butter is typically used in small amounts, this can be a good place to get the fat your body needs, not only for optimal health but for life itself. Every cell in your body contains saturated fat and cholesterol, which contribute to proper digestive function, growth and other essential processes. According to Dr. Rubman, for best health, most people should follow a diet that contains approximately 15 to 30% fat, including some saturated fats. How much saturated fat depends on factors such as caloric expenditure and digestive efficiency—the more calories you burn, the more saturated fat you can appropriately consume.

Go with Organic

You are best off with organic butter made from the milk of grass-fed cows, Dr. Rubman notes—since conventional butters often contain dangerous pesticides, antibiotics and added growth hormones. The Pesticide Action Network North America ranked non-organic butter as one of the top 10 foods most contaminated with *persistent organic pollutants* (POPs), toxic chemicals linked with breast cancer, immune system suppression, nervous system disorders, reproductive damage, hormone disruption and more.

Besides containing toxins, non organic butter also is less nutritious than organic butter...less creamy...and less tasty. Is there any reason to buy any butter that's not organic? Well, organic butter is more expensive than conventional butter—but the difference in a household's overall budget is truly small, especially now that national grocery chains, such as Whole Foods and Trader Joe's, are offering their own organic store brands.

Andrew L. Rubman, ND, founder and director, Southbury Clinic for Traditional Medicines, Southbury, Connecticut. www.southbury.com.

The Newest "Healthiest" Food: Black Rice

Black rice is anything but new. But new research shows that it contains more antioxidants and valuable plant compounds than blueberries. In fact, in ancient China it was known as "Forbidden Rice" because peasants were forbidden from eating it since it was so rare.

Black rice is similar to brown rice in that both are whole grains, meaning that they are unprocessed—after the rice hull (the inedible tough outer shell) is removed, these darker colors of rice both have a nutrient-rich layer of bran on their surface. This is what makes them more wholesome than highly processed white rice, from which virtually all nutrients have been removed.

Zhimin Xu, PhD, associate professor in the department of food science at Louisiana State University Agricultural Center in Baton Rouge, says that the basis for saying that black rice is "healthier" than blueberries is that it is richer in the health-promoting anthocyanin antioxidants than blueberries, and

Ten Top Antioxidant Foods

1. Red beans
2. Wild blueberries
3. Red kidney beans
4. Pinto beans
5. Cultivated blueberries
6. Cranberries
7. Artichokes
8. Blackberries
9. Prunes
10. Raspberries

Source: US Department of Agriculture

has less sugar and more fiber. The colorful anthocyanins that give the "black" layer of bran its rich color are the same types of pigments that make blueberries blue...raspberries red...and grapes purple.

Dr. Xu adds that the antioxidants in black rice also have the benefit of being both water- and fat-soluble. "Vegetables and fruits, like blueberries, are rich in the water-soluble antioxidants (vitamin C), while other cereal brans contain predominantly fat-soluble antioxidants (such as vitamin E)." What makes black rice exceptional is that it contains a rich mix of both classes of antioxidants.

Where to Buy It

You may not be able to find black rice in your supermarket, but you can easily find it in specialty stores, including health-food stores and Asian groceries, as well as at markets such as Whole Foods. Black rice costs about the same as brown rice—perhaps slightly more. One good brand is Lundberg Family Farms (*www.lundberg.com*), which uses "eco-friendly" farming to grow their "Black Japonica" rice and comes with a tempting stir-fry recipe on the package.

In Asian cooking, black rice often is mixed with white to create a pleasing visual presentation. You could mix it with brown just as easily.

Zhimin Xu, PhD, associate professor, department of food science at Louisiana State University Agricultural Center, Baton Rouge.

NUTRITIONAL SUPPLEMENTS

Vitamins and Minerals: What's Good for You... What's Not

When it comes to vitamins, don't fall into the trap of thinking "the more the better." Gone are the days when everyone was advised to take a multivitamin, says Leo Galland, MD, an internist and founder of PillAdvised (*http://pillad vised.com*), an online resource for information about medications and supplements. It's better to get nutrients from dietary sources as much as possible—and it's now clear that some of the ingredients in these pills may be unnecessary or even harmful.

Here, Dr. Galland evaluates the most commonly used vitamins and mineral supplements. Are any of them dangerous...and do you really need them?

•**Folic acid** is a synthetic "previtamin" that the body converts into the vitamin folate. It's important for the health of the brain, nervous system and immune system...for normal cell growth and normal fetal development...and for the prevention of cancer. Though folate is found naturally in some foods (including liver, green leafy vegetables and citrus fruits), most people don't get enough of it in their diets.

The dilemma: We need folate, but taking supplements made of the synthetic form (folic acid), even in doses as low as 400 micrograms (mcg), which is the amount prescribed by OB-GYNs during pregnancy, has been linked to several types of cancer. Too much folic acid can mask symptoms of vitamin B-12 deficiency and can even lead to permanent nerve damage if the B-12 deficiency is not corrected. Also, certain common drugs—including nonsteroidal anti-inflammatory drugs (NSAIDs) and some medications for inflammatory bowel disease—can interfere with the body's ability to convert folic acid to folate.

Dr. Galland's advice: Far better than folic acid is to take 500 mcg a day of *L-methylfolate*, a form of folate that circulates in the blood and is therefore more physiologically accessible. This is most particularly important for adults over age 50.

•**Vitamin A** deficiency, which can cause impaired immunity, night blindness, susceptibility to infection and rough, dry skin, is quite common. The body creates vitamin A from beta-carotene (found in orange and red vegetables and fruits, liver and whole milk), but some people don't get enough from their diets. In other folks, a vitamin A deficiency is caused by their inability to properly absorb vitamin A or to convert it from beta-carotene.

The dilemma: Vitamin A supplements have the potential to cause a host of problems, including headaches, bone loss, yellow or orange skin, rash, loss of eyebrows and liver disease. Also, supplementing with beta-carotene can increase the risk for lung and colon cancer in people who are or were heavy smokers.

Dr. Galland's advice: If you have any clinical signs of vitamin A deficiency (listed above) and think you could benefit from a beta-carotene supplement, look for one formulated with other carotenoids (often called "mixed carotenoids" on product labels). Or, if your blood test shows that you have a low vitamin A level, your doctor may prescribe a form of the vitamin called *retinol,* which also circumvents these problems.

•**Vitamin D** is all over the news these days. This vitamin helps strengthen the immune system and prevent cancer and ensures that the body properly absorbs calcium, while a deficiency of vitamin D is linked to a variety of health problems, including certain autoimmune disorders (such as type 2 diabetes), chronic metabolic and systemic diseases, and an increased risk for multiple sclerosis. Our bodies manufacture vitamin D when the skin is exposed to sunlight—which is problematic for individuals living in the northern hemisphere, since sunlight is in short supply.

Another problem: Aging reduces the skin's ability to produce vitamin D from sunlight. For these reasons, most Americans need supplemental vitamin D.

The dilemma: Excessive vitamin D supplementation brings its own list of problems, some quite serious—including kidney damage and leaching of calcium from bones into soft tissue. Plus, vitamin D supplements may cause problems for people with diabetes (talk to your doctor) and should not be taken by people with high calcium levels, kidney stones or sarcoidosis, a disease where scar tissue is deposited in multiple sites throughout the body.

Dr. Galland's advice: Do not take vitamin D in doses higher than 2,000 international units (IU) per day without your doctor's approval. Take vitamin D-3, the form that's absorbed best, after your largest meal of the day.

• **Vitamin E** was once a wildly popular supplement, thought to have many potential benefits, including prevention of heart disease and cancer. While those claims have been called into question, research does show that vitamin E can help reduce risk for recurrent strokes in people with diabetes.

The dilemma: Most people get only a minimal benefit from vitamin E supplementation, while excessive amounts or the wrong type of vitamin E has the potential to do some serious damage. Studies show that vitamin E supplements can increase the risk for heart failure in people with heart disease, mainly by depleting the body of coenzyme Q10, which is needed for proper coordination of the pumping mechanism.

Dr. Galland's advice: If you wish to take supplemental vitamin E, choose the natural form of a "mixed tocopherol" product (labeled "d"—not "dl") that contains alpha, beta, gamma and delta tocopherols—this is closer to what you'd find in food. No one should take vitamin E doses exceeding 100 IU per day (unless under the advice of a physician), and vitamin E should not be taken at all by anyone who takes statin drugs. Research has demonstrated that statins inactivate the antioxidant effects of vitamin E and that vitamin

E may interfere with the therapeutic effect of statins, so people who take both may end up getting the benefit of neither.

Here's what Dr. Galland says people need to know about mineral supplements…

• **Calcium.** You've been hearing lots about this mineral in the news lately. While it may help prevent colon cancer and improve bone health, it may also increase the risk for heart attack or prostate cancer. This danger is due to the way calcium interacts with vitamin D. If your calcium consumption is high but your vitamin D level is low, calcium can render the vitamin D in your body less active. That, in turn, increases heart and cancer risk. Meanwhile, the lack of vitamin D also means that your bones, heart and other tissues absorb less calcium, which increases the risk for heart attack and kidney stones.

The research: An analysis of 11 studies published in *BMJ* found that women taking high doses of calcium (averaging 1,000 milligrams [mg] a day) without vitamin D, and also getting about 800 mg/day of dietary calcium in their diets, had an increased risk for heart attacks. Another study, the Harvard Health Professionals Follow-Up Study, involving 48,000 men with no history of cancer (other than nonmelanoma skin cancer), found that high calcium intake from supplements or food was associated with an increased risk for highly invasive prostate cancer.

Dr. Galland's advice: Most people should limit calcium supplementation to 500 mg a day, to be taken with 1,000 IU of vitamin D after dinner. He advises aiming to get another 500 mg daily from food (for instance, one ounce of cheddar cheese has 204 mg of calcium) but adds that if you have a history of kidney stones, speak first to your doctor regarding how much calcium in any form you should consume.

• **Selenium.** This powerful antioxidant may decrease the risk for heart attacks and cancers of the stomach, lung, colon and prostate…but don't take it if you've had skin cancer or are at especially high risk for it due to personal or family history.

The danger: Some studies have found that selenium supplements increase the risk for skin cancer, while others suggest an elevated risk for type 2 diabetes.

Dr. Galland's advice: If you are not at high risk for skin cancer but are at risk for prostate, colon or breast cancer, take 50 mcg to 200 mcg of selenium a day.

•**Magnesium.** Magnesium has a calming effect on the nervous system and helps with stress-related conditions. It also boosts calcium absorption. Magnesium supplements have many benefits, with studies showing that they may prevent some of the complications of diabetes, improve breathing and airflow in adults with asthma, and reduce blood pressure in people with hypertension.

Potential problems: In some people, magnesium has a laxative effect and can cause diarrhea. This is a particular danger for people with digestive disorders such as IBS or Crohn's disease. What's more, if your kidneys aren't working well enough to excrete the magnesium your body doesn't need, high blood levels can develop, leading to slowed heart rate, reduced blood pressure, slowed breathing and even coma and death.

Dr. Galland's advice: Twenty-six million Americans have chronic kidney disease and millions more are at increased risk, so do not take magnesium supplements unless you have first had a serum creatinine blood test (typically done during a normal physical), which indicates how well your kidneys are functioning. If your blood tests show that you would benefit from magnesium supplementation or your doctor advises it to address particular symptoms such as muscle spasms or tension, palpitations, difficulty falling asleep or anxiety, Dr. Galland says to start slowly, with 100 mg a day, and then work up to 400 mg/day if needed—but stop if you find that the supplements cause diarrhea.

•**Zinc.** A zinc deficiency can affect immune function, tissue repair and brain function. According to Dr. Galland, people who have problems resisting infection or whose cuts and wounds heal too slowly could have a zinc deficiency. Zinc is also known to improve mood and helps antidepressant medications work better. Zinc can be particularly helpful for elderly people—or for anyone—who will be undergoing surgery.

Caution: Zinc in excess of 40 mg/day may cause a deficiency of copper, which can cause unusual anemia and neurological problems. Zinc can also cause nausea in some people.

Dr. Galland's advice: Take zinc (15 mg to 40 mg/day) only if your doctor prescribes it based on a blood test.

•**Copper.** This mineral is taken primarily in multimineral supplements but sometimes on its own by people taking zinc supplements (to prevent a copper deficiency).

The dangers: Copper can be very toxic, especially to the nervous system. High levels can cause neurological effects such as insomnia, depression, anxiety or liver or kidney damage, and some experts believe high levels may increase the risk for Alzheimer's disease. Because copper spurs the growth of new blood vessels, it's not recommended for anyone with cancer.

Dr. Galland's advice: Sources for dietary copper include chocolate, nuts, seafood, mushrooms and legumes. The usual dose for those who need supplemental copper is 0.5 mg a day, but people with low blood levels of copper (unusual but sometimes the case in patients with chronic disease) may need much more, 2 mg to 4 mg/day. If you take a copper supplement, it is important to have your serum copper level checked annually, as copper is absorbed more rapidly from a supplement than from food.

•**Iron.** Iron deficiency can cause anemia, fatigue and impaired cognitive function, so iron supplements have been standard fare for those who need them for many years.

Problems: Iron supplements are potentially toxic. Since the body eliminates iron slowly (except in bleeding episodes), it can accumulate in the liver, where it can cause cirrhosis… in the heart, causing heart failure…or in the pancreas, causing diabetes. When iron levels are too high, the toxicity can also generate free radicals that can contribute to cancer risk.

How to Buy Safe Supplements

Whatever supplement you take, be very particular. Dietary supplements are not required to be standardized in the US, so an herb from one company may be completely different in quality and potency from what is ostensibly the same herb from another company. In addition, manufacturers are not required to list the country of origin of ingredients—so a botanical medicine "made in the USA" may contain herbs from another country. While plenty of high-quality herbs are imported, others are farmed under conditions we'd consider unacceptable, such as using toxic pesticides or grown in soil contaminated with lead or mercury.

Steps to Take

● Work with a doctor who is trained in evaluating the products. For instance, naturopathic physicians are well-schooled in how to identify quality natural-product manufacturers.

● Look for supplements with a USP stamp on their labels. The US Pharmacopeia (USP) is an independent organization dedicated to quality control that tests products and visits sites of companies that join their program. Dietary-supplement manufacturers are not required by law to follow USP standards, but some do so voluntarily.

● Single-ingredient products can be a safer choice. Other than multivitamins, the supplements with more ingredients have a greater likelihood that they'll contain contaminants or have harmful side effects.

● Look for evidence of supplements' safety and effectiveness from objective, third-party sources. For example, visit reputable Web sites such as *http://nccam.nih.gov/health/supplements* and *www.consumerlab.com*.

● Start taking only one new supplement at a time. This allows you to know what might be causing any side effects such as a rash, diarrhea, constipation or insomnia.

● Avoid weight-loss, erectile dysfunction and athletic-performance supplements unless recommended by your doctor or trained practitioner.

● Report any suspected adverse effects from a supplement to the FDA—this is especially important given that, at present, such reporting is the best mechanism we have to get dangerous products off the market. File a report at *www.fda.gov/safety/medwatch/howtoreport/ucm053074.htm*.

● Talk to your doctor. Make sure he/she is aware of and up-to-date on all supplements you take, and discuss dosage, possible interactions and other safety issues.

Pieter A. Cohen, MD, associate residency director, Cambridge Health Alliance, Somerville, Massachusetts, and instructor, Harvard Medical School, Boston, Massachusetts.

Dr. Galland's advice: Most adult men and postmenopausal women don't need iron supplements—they should be taken only if the level of blood ferritin is found to be low, and then only long enough to bring it up to the desired level. Dr. Galland notes that this is true even among premenopausal women. The usual dose for those who need iron is 20 mg to 30 mg a day.

Read Labels and Get Rid of What You Don't Need

In summary, Dr. Galland says that mineral supplements aren't for everyone. In fact, he says, "a lot of people shouldn't be taking them individually," adding that for a few vulnerable individuals even the amounts found in typical multivitamins can prove dangerous. He stresses that mineral supplementation must be tailored to individual needs, emphasizing the importance of taking minerals only under the supervision of a doctor trained in their use.

And one final tip: Noting that many people take supplements that are in combination pills or capsules, Dr. Galland points out that it's possible you aren't even aware of what minerals you are taking. He urges readers to look closely at the label of any supplements they take to be sure they're getting only what they need and aren't ingesting anything that could prove harmful.

Be Careful About Taking Vitamins

Vitamins should not be taken indiscriminately, cautions Dr. Galland. All the vitamins listed above are frequent components in multivitamins in amounts that can be problematic for some people, so it is vitally important to read labels carefully even for seemingly safe multivitamins. Don't take a multivitamin if it contains ingredients that you don't need, and stop taking individual vitamins if you are getting sufficient quantities of them in your multivitamin. And remember, these are all reasons why it is so important to have an expert in nutritional medicine on your health-care team.

Leo Galland, MD, internist, author and internationally recognized leader in integrated medicine, based in New York City. For more information about supplements and drugs and free access to Dr. Galland's Web application, visit http://www.pilladvised.com.

The Rise of Vitamin "T"—The Amazing Healing Properties of Tocotrienols

Several years ago, food scientist Barrie Tan, PhD, was on a trip to South America investigating plant pigments when he stumbled across a colorful, lipstick-red plant—and couldn't take his eyes off it. Dr. Tan knew that the annatto plant (*Bixa orellana*) was phototropic, meaning that it moved and turned its blossoms toward the sun. Usually plants with blossoms this color don't follow the sun—if they did, they would be harmed by overexposure to UV rays. What was in this plant that protected it?

Dr. Tan discovered that the plant's protector was *tocotrienols*, one of two main groups of compounds that constitute vitamin E. It was the first time a plant had been found to be a source of pure tocotrienols. Dr. Tan found that the tocotrienols in the annatto plant (the purest form ever found) consisted of 90% delta-tocotrienol and 10% gamma-tocotrienol. And they helped to prevent cardiovascular disease, cancer and certain eye diseases.

Tocopherols, the other main compound that constitutes vitamin E, do not provide these same benefits.

Even today, most vitamin E supplements are made mainly of tocopherols. Alpha-tocopherol is most often used, and most vitamin E research before Dr. Tan's discovery had focused on this subtype.

The Tail Tells the Story

Both types of vitamin E neutralize disease-causing free radicals, but the key functional difference between tocopherols and tocotrienols lies in their "tails." Tocopherol molecules have longer, stiffer tails that anchor them in place in the body's cell membranes, while tocotrienol molecules have shorter, more flexible tails that enable them to move around the cell to more effectively neutralize free radicals. It is estimated that tocotrienols are 50 times more potent than tocopherols.

How to Benefit

How tocotrienols can help you…

•**Cardiovascular disease protection.** Tocotrienols seem to protect cardiovascular health by…

•**Lowering LDL cholesterol and triglycerides.** Tocotrienols inhibit the same LDL (bad) cholesterol–producing enzyme that is targeted by statin drugs but without statins' side effects, such as fatigue and muscle pain. In one study, people with high cholesterol took 25 milligrams (mg), 50 mg, 100 mg or 200 mg daily of tocotrienols in combination with a heart-healthy diet. The researchers found that 100 mg daily provided optimal benefit, since it lowered LDL cholesterol levels by 25% and triglycerides (blood fats) by 12%. It also raised HDL (good) cholesterol slightly in some studies. More than 100 mg provided no additional benefit.

•**Preventing atherosclerosis.** This effect stems from the inhibitory effect of tocotrienols on molecules that help plaque adhere to artery walls. In a landmark study at Elmhurst Medical Center in Queens, New York, 50 people with atherosclerosis of the carotid arteries, a major risk factor for stroke, were given 240 mg daily of tocotrienols (along with 60 mg of alpha-tocopherols).

Result: 88% showed either stabilization or regression of arterial plaque, while only 8% in the placebo group had stabilized or improved amounts of plaque. About 60% in the placebo group had plaque buildup during the study. (Alpha-tocopherols on their own do not reduce atherosclerosis.) Tocotrienols also have been found to reduce the formation of blood clots that can lead to heart attack and stroke.

•**Anticancer activity.** Tocotrienols appear to fight cancer in several ways. They neutralize vascular endothelial growth factor (VEGF), the chemical that stimulates development of new blood vessels needed for tumor growth—an effect known as anti-angiogenesis. Tocotrienols also interfere with the processes that tumor cells use to multiply. Clinical trials are currently under way to study the safety of delta-tocotrienol for treating breast and pancreatic cancers. Because preliminary studies are promising and there is no toxicity related to tocotrienols, it seems that cancer patients may benefit when taking 300 mg daily of tocotrienols.

•**Eye health.** Tocotrienols' anti-VEGF effects appear to inhibit the sight-damaging growth of blood vessels associated with macular degeneration and diabetes-related retinopathy (damage to the retina).

Dose: 50 mg to 100 mg daily.

For these conditions, a concentrated form of vitamin E is best—namely, a supplement made of "pure" annatto-derived tocotrienols consisting of 90% delta- and 10% gamma-tocotrienols.

Brands to try: A.C. Grace Unique E Tocotrienols, 125 mg (800-833-4368, *www.ac grace.com*)…Doctor's Best Tocotrienols, 50 mg (800-333-6977, *www.drbvitamins.com*, for a store locator)…and Nutricology Delta-Fraction Tocotrienols, 50 mg and 125 mg (800-545-9960, *www.nutricology.com*).

If You Are Healthy

Tocotrienols are found in small amounts in foods such as coconut and wheat germ—but not enough to provide the benefit of supplements. People who are healthy (and don't have one of the conditions described above) would benefit by taking a multivitamin or a full-spectrum vitamin E product that contains a blend of tocopherols and tocotrienols (5 mg is a good amount), which is still the best choice for disease prevention.

If you are healthy but have elevated cholesterol, try taking 50 mg to 100 mg of tocotrienols daily in addition to your multivitamin.

Caution: Tocotrienols inhibit blood clotting, so people on blood thinners should consult their doctors before taking them.

Mark A. Stengler, NMD, naturopathic medical doctor in private practice, Encinitas, California, and author of the *Bottom Line/Natural Healing* newsletter. *www.drstengler.com.*

Fish Oil—How to Choose Wisely

Fish oil capsules are among the most popular nutritional supplements—and for good reason. Their key ingredients, the omega-3 fatty acids *eicosapentaenoic acid* (EPA) and *docosahexaenoic acid* (DHA), have been linked to health benefits including reduced risk for heart attack and stroke as well as macular degeneration and other retinal diseases. The omega-3s in fish oil also have been shown to fight arthritis because of their anti-inflammatory effect…and even may help protect against the development of certain types of cancer, such as prostate, colorectal and breast cancer. Fish oil also seems to help depression and other psychiatric disorders.

But with so many fish oil products on the market, it's not always easy to find the highest-quality products at good prices.*

*If you take a daily aspirin or some other blood thinner, such as *warfarin* (Coumadin) or *clopidogrel* (Plavix), check with your doctor before taking fish oil supplements—they can have a blood-thinning effect. If you take blood pressure–lowering medication, be aware that fish oil may further lower blood pressure.

Choosing a Supplement

ConsumerLab.com, an independent evaluator of health and nutrition products, selected and tested 24 of the most popular brands of fish oil and krill oil (from tiny, shrimp-like crustaceans). Fifteen other brands of fish oil were voluntarily submitted by their manufacturers for testing, including one with omega-3s from algal oil, derived from algae. *What was found...*

• **EPA and DHA concentrations that varied greatly from brand to brand.** With fish oil supplements, what's important isn't the total amount of fish oil but the EPA and DHA content within that oil. Most health benefits require consuming a combination of EPA and DHA that totals at least 500 mg daily.

Beware: Not all fish oil product labels list EPA and DHA content.

• **EPA and DHA amounts as advertised were found in nearly all products tested,** but three had less than their claimed amounts.

• **Safe levels of contaminants.** No detectable mercury was found in any products. And while the dangerous chemicals known as *polychlorinated biphenyls* (PCBs) are now ubiquitous in fish products, the capsules tested contained only trace levels, well below what's considered safe for humans and lower than what's generally found in fish.

• **Not all products were fresh.** Three of the products tested contained rancid fish oil, which will increase the likelihood of fishy burps or aftertaste.

Advice: Always check the product's expiration date to make sure you won't pass it before finishing that batch...tightly reseal the container after each use to minimize air exposure...and refrigerate fish oil capsules to be on the safe side. Liquid fish oil, which is poured from a bottle rather than contained in capsules, must be refrigerated.

• **A huge cost variation, with prices ranging from six cents to 90 cents per 500 mg of EPA and DHA.** (Remember, it's the cost per amount of EPA/DHA—not the cost per capsule or ounce—that counts with fish oil.) Krill oil and algal oil products were even more expensive, costing around 35 cents for just 120 mg of EPA and DHA. Some people prefer krill oil because it is bound to phospholipids that may increase the bioavailability of omega-3s in the body. Algal oil offers an effective vegetarian source of EPA/DHA for people who want to avoid fish products and also is considered "burpless."

Recommendations

Given the factors noted above, three products stood out in recent evaluations...

• **Best value for softgel fish oil**—Swanson EFAs Super EPA (300 mg EPA and 200 mg DHA per softgel). At six cents (not including shipping costs) per 500 mg total of EPA and DHA, this product offered the best value of all standard softgel fish oil capsules that were tested. This product is available at 800-824-4491, *www.swansonvitamins.com.*

• **Good value for enteric-coated fish oil**—Nature Made Odorless Fish Oil, at about 10 cents per pill, was one of the top values among enteric-coated softgels. It is available at many retailers. The label claims 360 mg per pill of omega-3 fatty acids (of which 311 mg are EPA and DHA, according to ConsumerLab.com's testing). With enteric-coated capsules, which dissolve in the intestine rather than the stomach, there is usually less fishy aftertaste.

• **Highly concentrated fish oil**—VitalOils1750 (250 mg EPA and 750 mg DHA per enteric-coated softgel) was among the most concentrated products to pass ConsumerLab.com's testing. The product is available at 877-342-3721, *www.vitaloils1750.com.*

Concentrated fish oil products are convenient for people who want high doses of EPA and DHA without swallowing several capsules at a time.

Tod Cooperman, MD, president and founder of ConsumerLab.com, a White Plains, New York–based company that conducts independent testing of health, wellness and nutrition products. He is editor of ConsumerLab.com, a subscription-based Web site ($29.95/yr.), and the book *Health, Harm or Rip-off: What's Really in Your Vitamins & Supplements* (Bottom Line Books).

Exciting New Health Benefits of CoQ10

Until recently, the dietary supplement coenzyme Q10 (CoQ10) was recommended primarily for people who wanted to avoid the side effects of cholesterol-lowering statin drugs, including muscle pain and weakness.

Now: Researchers are discovering that CoQ10 may confer a variety of other health benefits that are unrelated to statin use.

Peter H. Langsjoen, MD, one of the world's foremost CoQ10 researchers,* provides insight into the latest developments in this research.

What Is CoQ10?

CoQ10 is a vitamin-like substance that plays a key role in the production of energy in every cell in the body. Discovered in 1957, the substance is naturally present in such foods as organ meats (including cow's liver and kidney), and, in smaller amounts, in beef, sardines, mackerel and peanuts. Because CoQ10 appeared to be everywhere in the body—or "ubiquitous"—it was fittingly dubbed *ubiquinone*.

Without adequate levels of CoQ10, the body's organs and systems, including the immune system and nervous system, will not function optimally.

Unexpected Health Benefits

Increasing scientific evidence now offers support for the use of CoQ10 supplements to help treat...

● **Heart disease.** CoQ10 is involved in creating 90% of cellular energy in the heart.

Research has shown that people with heart failure (inadequate pumping action of the heart) have lower blood levels of CoQ10, on average, than people without heart failure—and the lower the CoQ10 level, the worse the problem.

*Dr. Langsjoen has no financial interest in any company that manufactures or sells CoQ10 supplements.

Recent research published in the journal *Biofactors* showed that the ejection fraction (the amount of blood pumped with each heartbeat) in heart failure patients who took CoQ10 supplements rose from an average of 22% to an average of 39% after six to 12 months.

Important: Because statin medications deplete the body's supply of CoQ10, ask your doctor about adding CoQ10 supplements (to help protect the heart and counteract statin-related side effects) to your regimen if you take one of these drugs.

● **High blood pressure.** CoQ10 can also help improve high blood pressure (hypertension). Studies have shown that about half of people using one or more drugs for high blood pressure can stop taking at least some of their medications after taking CoQ10 supplements for about five months.

● **Cholesterol.** CoQ10 also acts as a powerful antioxidant. It is transported in the blood (along with cholesterol and other fat-soluble nutrients) and helps protect cholesterol from damaging oxidation, which plays a role in atherosclerosis (fatty buildup in the arteries).

● **Fatigue.** Because CoQ10 is part of the body's energy-producing processes, it is particularly valuable in reducing fatigue—even among people with severe fatigue, including that caused by such conditions as chronic fatigue syndrome.

● **Migraines.** In one study, 32 people who took CoQ10 supplements for three months had only half their usual number of migraines.

● **Neurological disorders.** Some of the most promising recent research involves the ability of CoQ10 to slow the progression of degenerative neurological disorders, including Parkinson's disease, Alzheimer's disease and Huntington's disease (a genetic disorder).

How to Use CoQ10 Safely

People who eat organ meats at least once or twice weekly usually have healthy CoQ10 levels. But other adults can improve their blood levels of CoQ10 by taking supplements. Work with your doctor to find an optimal dose.

For best absorption, do not take more than 180 milligrams (mg) at one time. CoQ10 is fat-soluble (dissolves in fat), so it is best to take the supplement with meals that contain at least a little bit of fat (any type).

In some people, CoQ10 may cause temporary side effects, such as nausea and other gastrointestinal disorders…dizziness…insomnia…or headache. However, these side effects are rare. If you experience side effects, try a different CoQ10 formulation.

Caution: One case study suggested that CoQ10 may act like vitamin K, lessening the blood-thinning effect of *warfarin* (Coumadin). But a controlled trial subsequently found no such effects.

Nevertheless, people taking warfarin or any other blood-thinning medication should consult a doctor before taking a CoQ10 supplement. After a few weeks of taking CoQ10, anyone who uses a blood thinner should have his/her prothrombin time (a measure of clotting ability) checked.

Also important: Because CoQ10 may cause your blood pressure and/or blood sugar (glucose) level to gradually improve, your doctor may want to adjust the dosage of any medications you may be taking to control elevations of either.

Finding the Best Product

One reliable producer of CoQ10 is the Japanese company Kaneka, which sells CoQ10 in the US under many different brand names, including Healthy Origins (888-228-6650, *www.healthyorigins.com*) and Jarrow Formulas, available through ProVitaminas (800-510-6444, *www.provitaminas.com*). Kaneka uses a yeast fermentation process with 99.9% pure natural CoQ10.

In addition to CoQ10 supplements, you may see products labeled "ubiquinol." Ubiquinol is a more bioavailable (absorbable)—and more expensive—form of CoQ10. However, if you take CoQ10, your body will naturally convert it to ubiquinol. While most healthy adults readily absorb CoQ10, patients with advanced heart failure absorb ubiquinol about four times better than CoQ10.

If you purchase ubiquinol (not CoQ10), test it for freshness (in case it has deteriorated during storage or shipping).

What to do: Cut one capsule in half, and look at the color of the contents. Cream colored is good—orange or brown means that the product has become oxidized.

Whichever form you choose, shop around —a month's supply of a high-quality supplement can cost $20 to about $60.

Peter H. Langsjoen, MD, cardiologist in private practice in Tyler, Texas, who specializes in noninvasive treatment. *www.icqa.org.*

Whey Protein: Not Just For Bodybuilders

We know that food sources of protein are good for us. But what about protein powders? There's soy powder (good for people who have a milk intolerance) and egg protein powder (good for those allergic to soy and/or dairy). What about whey protein powder? Is whey good? Who can benefit?

A popular nutritional supplement for bodybuilders, whey protein is often overlooked by people who want to boost their protein intake, including older adults who have a difficult time consuming enough dietary protein…athletes who want to build lean muscle mass…people who want to lose weight…and those who are underweight and need to consume extra calories in order to reach a healthy weight.

What's so good about whey protein: Whey is one of two proteins that come from milk (the other is casein)—and it is the liquid remaining after milk has been curdled to make cheese. Whey protein contains all the amino acids that the body needs to synthesize protein. It has the highest bioavailability of any protein (eggs are second), meaning that it is the most efficiently digested, absorbed and utilized in the body.

Compared with other protein sources, whey has a high concentration of branched-chain amino acids (BCAAs)—*leucine, isoleucine* and *valine*—amino acids that are vital for tissue growth and repair. Whey protein, which also is rich in the sulfur-containing amino acids *cysteine* and *methionine*, can enhance immune function as well.

How to use whey: Look for whey powder (whey tablets contain very little protein). As a meal replacement, mix 20 grams (g) to 25 g with water or low-fat milk. Nonsweetened almond milk is a good choice because it is lactose-free and low in sugar. For those who are underweight and need to gain, use 25 g daily in addition to meals. People allergic to dairy should avoid whey. Those with lactose intolerance can select a pure whey protein isolate, a concentrated form that has less lactose.

Caution: If you have liver or kidney disease and need to monitor your protein intake, speak to your physician before adding any extra protein to your diet.

Look for a product that is low in sugar—5 g or less per serving.

Brand to try: Whey Factors by Natural Factors (available online at *www.iherb.com*).

Mark A. Stengler, NMD, naturopathic medical doctor in private practice, Encinitas, California, and author of the *Bottom Line/Natural Healing* newsletter. *www.drstengler.com*.

EXERCISE AND MOVEMENT

Use Yoga to Treat Asthma, Insomnia and More

Yoga has long been known to reduce stress while also boosting strength, flexibility and overall well-being.

Now: More and more scientific studies are showing that yoga helps treat specific medical conditions ranging from high blood pressure to asthma. Unfortunately, many people never

---

Yoga Safety 101

If you have a chronic medical condition, check with your doctor before beginning a yoga program, and consider consulting a qualified yoga teacher for a customized "prescription" of yoga poses.*

Caution: While doing yoga, don't hold your breath! That may raise your blood pressure. If you have high blood pressure, any eye condition where increased pressure should be avoided or neck injuries, forgo postures in which your head is inverted, such as headstands—these poses can significantly increase blood flow to the brain, increasing your risk for a stroke or other cardiac event.

*To find a qualified yoga therapist, consult the International Association of Yoga Therapists, 928-541-0004, *www.iayt.org*.

---

even try yoga because they assume that it's too difficult or unconventional.

What you should know…

Yoga for Everyone

Yoga is easy to do at home and requires a minimal investment in special equipment. It is best performed in your bare feet (so your feet won't slide) while wearing comfortable clothing. Many people perform yoga on a bare floor or clean carpeting, but a yoga mat keeps your feet even more secure (available in some sports-equipment stores and from online retailers such as *www.yogadirect.com*, 800-331-8233…and *www.jadeyoga.com*, 888-784-7237).

For the introductory postures below: Hold for at least five "slow breaths" (close your mouth and breathe in through your nose for a few seconds as your lower belly rises…exhale slowly for about six seconds). Each pose can be repeated two to three times at each session (one to three per week).

For High Blood Pressure

A single 10-minute session of "slow breathing" can result in a temporary lowering of both systolic (top number) and diastolic (bottom number) blood pressure. How much depends on such factors as diet, stress level and genetics.

Recommendation: Do Face Up Dog Posture and Face Down Dog Posture followed by Child's Pose.

What to do: For **Face Up Dog**, start by lying facedown on the floor with your feet (tops flat on floor) in line with your hips. Place your arms at the sides of your chest and hands directly under your shoulders. While keeping your knees on the floor, push into your arms straightening them, roll your shoulders back, arch your back slightly and keep your neck aligned with your spine. Hold for five breaths. Then exhale into **Face Down Dog** (by turning your feet so that your heels are flat on the ground, and pushing up and back into an upside-down V). For **Child's Pose**, kneel with your feet folded under flat and extend your arms straight in front of your head, palms flat on your mat. Touch your forehead to the ground if possible.

Asthma

In a recent study of 20 people with asthma, those who took two one-hour yoga classes plus a half-hour home class weekly for 10 weeks reported reduced symptoms.

Recommendation: Do the **Extended Side Angle Posture.** It increases lung capacity by stretching and activating the intercostal muscles between each rib, which expand when you inhale and contract when you exhale.

What to do: From a standing position at the top of your mat, inhale and step back with the right foot, taking your feet wide apart, about four to five feet. Turn your left foot out and your right foot in about 45°, and raise your arms parallel to the floor. Exhale while bending your left knee directly over your ankle as

you rest your left forearm on your left thigh. Reach your right hand out over your head and ear. Keep your head in alignment with the spine and your abdomen pulled in. Look up and take five breaths. Inhale, and come up out of the posture. Reverse your feet and arms and exhale down to the other side, repeating the stretch.

Insomnia and Anxiety

Yoga is excellent for insomnia and anxiety—breathing slowly and deeply through your nose slows your brain waves and calms the nervous system.

Recommendation: Try the **Warrior I Posture.**

What to do: From a standing position, inhale and step your left foot out in front of you three to four feet. Turn the back heel inward about 45° toward the midline of your body, the outside edge of the foot flat on the floor. Use a wall or back of a chair to help with balance if necessary. Bend your left knee directly over your left ankle. Keep the belly pulled in and inhale deeply.

Exhale, raise your arms overhead as high as you can, touching your palms over your head if possible. Take five breaths. Repeat with the opposite leg in front.

Low-Back Pain

In a recent study, people with chronic low-back pain who practiced yoga (two 90-minute sessions weekly for six months) reported less pain and disability than those receiving conventional treatment, such as medication and surgery.

Recommendation: Do the **Locust Posture.**

What to do: Lie on your stomach with your legs and feet together, arms back at your sides, face-down and chin on the floor. Inhale, then exhale while raising your head, shoulders and legs into the air. Press your hands into the floor for balance.

Beryl Bender Birch, founder of The Hard & The Soft Yoga Institute and the nonprofit Give Back Yoga Foundation, *www.GiveBackYoga.org*, both based in East Hampton, New York. She is the author of *Power Yoga* (Simon & Schuster), *Beyond Power Yoga* (Fireside) and *Boomer Yoga* (Sellers).

Water Workout: A Fun Way to Get Fit

Swimming lap after lap, day after day, can turn a healthful exercise into a mundane routine. But there are other ways to benefit from a water workout…and have fun too.

Mary E. Sanders, PhD, associate professor of health education at the University of Nevada School of Medicine and author of *YMCA Water Fitness for Health,* points out water training's advantages over land-based exercise…

• **Because water is denser than air,** working out in the water efficiently and effectively tones muscles and raises heart rate—all at the same time during a single exercise.

• **Maintaining your position while water currents push and pull against your body** works the "core" muscles of the abdomen and back, strengthening them—which helps improve posture and reduces the risk for back problems.

• **A water workout reduces stress on the joints and bones of the lower body.** Its gravity-defying effect minimizes the risk of falling (and cushions a fall if it does occur), making exercise safer and more comfortable for people with arthritis, osteoporosis or balance problems.*

• **The pressure of the water stimulates blood circulation**—making water training

*Important: Check with your doctor before beginning any new exercise program to make sure that it is appropriate for you. Water training may not be recommended if you recently had surgery or have a skin condition, such as psoriasis. If you are anxious about being in the water, meet with a water fitness instructor to learn personal safety skills and gain confidence.

especially beneficial for people who have peripheral arterial disease or swelling in the legs.

How to Get Started

Water fitness classes are offered at many YMCAs, community centers and fitness clubs. Dr. Sanders says, "A good, comprehensive class typically lasts 45 to 90 minutes and includes a warm-up, cardio workout, muscle conditioning, stretches, balance exercises and a cool-down."

If you want to experiment with some water exercises before committing to a class, or if you prefer to work out at your own convenience, Dr. Sanders suggests trying the moves below, repeating each for three to six minutes.

Helpful: Do these moves while standing in water that comes up at least as high as your navel but no higher than your nipples, choosing the depth in which you can move with greatest control. Ideally, for comfort and safety, water temperature should be 84°F to 86°F.

Optional: Water shoes provide traction so that you can move more quickly, and webbed gloves intensify your workout by increasing resistance (both are available at sporting-goods stores).

• **Jumping Jacks**—to build muscular endurance and raise heart rate. Start by standing with feet together and arms down at your sides (hands should be underwater). Jump and spread your legs, landing with your feet about 20 to 30 inches apart…at the same time raise your arms, elbows slightly bent and palms facing down, until your hands reach the surface of the water. Then jump again, bringing legs together and arms down to return to the starting position.

Additional challenge: As you jump, travel across the pool forward, backward and then sideways.

• **Stand on a noodle**—to improve balance. Push a Styrofoam tube or "noodle" to the bottom of the pool and stand with your left foot in the center of the tube. Keeping right leg straight, bend left leg and slowly lift left knee as high as you can…hold for 30 seconds…return to starting position. Repeat, this time raising right knee. Continue alternating sides, moving arms gently at the surface to maintain balance.

Additional challenge: Do the exercise while lifting arms above the water and/or keeping eyes closed.

• **Spiderman**—to build core strength and raise heart rate. To start, face the pool wall and stand about an arm's length away. Moving arms back and forth as if treading water, raise your legs and "run" up the pool wall from bottom to top, then run down again and return to standing. Repeat, keeping abdomen pulled in throughout.

Additional challenge: Increase your speed.

Mary E. Sanders, PhD, associate professor of health education at the University of Nevada School of Medicine in Reno and author of *YMCA Water Fitness for Health* (Human Kinetics).

MIND/BODY HEALING

Ready, Set, Meditate

Meditation has many benefits—but for many, creating the right frame of mind is easier said than done.

Solution: Proper preparation. Neuropsychologist Rick Hanson, PhD, a meditation teacher and author of *Buddha's Brain: The Practical Neuroscience of Happiness, Love & Wisdom*, says, "A few simple steps, when taken at the beginning of your meditative sessions, lay the neurological foundation for a better practice." *To prepare yourself to meditate, get into a comfortable position and spend about a minute on each of the following steps...*

• **Silently say to yourself, "My mind is calming and settling."** This marks your intention to meditate and activates the executive systems in the prefrontal cortex of your brain, thereby directing other systems in the brain toward the goal you've set—in this instance, calming the mind.

• **Take a few deep breaths** with long exhalations of about 10 seconds each, either through your nose or mouth. This activates the parasympathetic part of the autonomic nervous system—the part that controls "rest and digest" body functions without conscious effort—thus helping to relax and steady your mind. Slow exhalations also tone down the sympathetic part of the autonomic nervous system that triggers the fight-or-flight response, Dr. Hanson says, further calming your body and mind.

• **Remind yourself that you are safe.** "We have evolved to be vigilant and nervous. That helped keep our ancestors alive but also makes it harder to bring attention inward," Dr. Hanson explains. To counter that, meditate in surroundings or situations that help you feel protected and secure, such as in your home or with other people who are meditating. Then focus for a few moments on that feeling of safety...on the resources inside you and around you...or on a memory of being with someone who cares about you.

• **Activate positive emotions.** Think about something that makes you feel good, such as a mountain retreat or beloved pet. Or give a half smile—the facial expression activates associated feelings of well-being in your neural networks. "Encouraging even mildly positive feelings brings more peacefulness by dialing down the stress response from the sympathetic nervous system," Dr. Hanson says. This also activates the neurotransmitters *norepinephrine* and *dopamine,* which help you stay alert and focused on your meditation so you don't get distracted by worries or other thoughts.

• **Now you are ready to meditate.** For the most beneficial experience, consider these words from Dr. Hanson: "Our brains are like Velcro for negative experiences but Teflon for positive ones. This evolved to help our ancestors remember and react to threatening events." To counteract that, take a moment from time to time throughout your session to really enjoy the good feelings of your meditation.

Rick Hanson, PhD, neuropsychologist and meditation teacher, is founder of the Wellspring Institute for Neuroscience and Contemplative Wisdom in San Rafael, California. He is author of the best-selling *Buddha's Brain: The Practical Neuroscience of Happiness, Love & Wisdom* (New Harbinger). His work has been featured on the BBC and NPR.

Visualize Your Way To Healing

People often are surprised to find out that they can use their imaginations to heal. Whether you're coping with a debilitating disease…chronic aches and pains…or seasonal allergies, visualization, a form of guided imagery in which you use your imagination to gain a greater understanding of yourself, has been proven to help relieve symptoms. David E. Bresler, PhD, a pioneer in the field of guided imagery techniques advises on how you can use visualization to feel better…

Use Your Mind to Ease Your Symptoms…

We don't know exactly why imagery works, but studies have shown that guided imagery can help patients ease the symptoms of many chronic conditions (such as arthritis and fibromyalgia) and psychological problems (such as depression and anxiety).

Best: Practice visualization for five to 20 minutes once or twice a day. There is no harm in doing it as frequently as you like. *Follow these steps…*

1. Quiet your breathing. Sitting comfortably in a quiet place, begin to slow down your breathing. Let it become more regular…deeper…quieter. Quieting yourself will enable you to focus your mind's power on any symptoms you are experiencing.

2. Release tension. Imagine a ball of energy that starts in your lower abdomen and rises to your forehead as you inhale. As you exhale, the imaginary ball goes down your spine and your legs and then into the ground. As this "energy sponge" travels around your body, it absorbs and drains away any tension, tightness, pain or discomfort as you breathe.

3. Bring to mind any symptom that is present. Allow an image to form in your mind's eye that represents or symbolizes a symptom (pain, palpitations) or condition (diabetes, cancer, arthritis). Someone with allergies might imagine them as pollen, red or yellow lights, creatures, energy fields, smells or tastes. Examine the image and notice what part seems to be most uncomfortable.

4. Imagine that your body can heal the symptom. Create an inner healing movie in your mind's eye by imagining that your body is using all of its resources to heal what is most uncomfortable.

Example: A woman with peripheral neuropathy viewed the pain as "fire ants chewing on the nerve." With the help of guided imagery, she learned to focus on her breathing and to imagine that, with each breath, the nerve could release its own natural "insecticide," causing the ants to become smaller and fewer in number. This helped to significantly reduce the intensity of her pain.

5. Create an inner adviser. You can base this image on a mentor or teacher who, in the past, provided you with wise advice, encouragement and guidance. You might ask the adviser, "What can I do to speed up healing?" or, "Am I doing anything that is getting in the way of healing?" You might discover that your body needs more sleep or a change in diet, for example. And with your adviser's help and support, you will be more likely to try it—and succeed.

Work with a Practitioner

Many patients benefit from following instructions on guided imagery CDs or audiotapes, which can be purchased online. You also can work with a certified guided imagery professional. To find one in your area, contact the Academy for Guided Imagery (800-726-2070, *www.acadgi.com*).

David Bresler, PhD, LAc, president and cofounder of the Academy for Guided Imagery and executive director of the Bresler Center in Los Angeles. He is the author of *Free Yourself from Pain* (Awareness Press).

Mark A. Stengler, NMD, naturopathic medical doctor in private practice, Encinitas, California, and author of the *Bottom Line/Natural Healing* newsletter. *www.drstengler.com*.

HERBS AND ESSENTIAL OILS

Your Natural Healing First-Aid Kit

It's always a good idea to keep a few natural remedies on hand to treat common injuries and conditions. (Doses for adults and children are the same except where noted.) *Put together your own natural healing first-aid kit with the following...*

What you need: Aloe vera gel.

For: Minor burns, skin rashes, sunburn.

How to use: Apply a gel that is 90% or more pure aloe three to four times daily.

What you need: Bach Rescue Remedy.

For: Feelings of anxiety.

How to use: Take four drops in a glass of water four times daily.

What you need: Calendula.

For: Healing scrapes and cuts.

How to use: Apply a salve over the injury two to three times daily until wound has healed.

What you need: Colloidal silver (For children, use half the dose. Not recommended for women who are pregnant or breast-feeding.)

For: Sore throat.

How to use: Ingest one teaspoon four times daily, up to seven days.

For: Pinkeye.

How to use: Put two drops in one-half ounce saline solution, and wash eye three times daily for seven days.

For: Ear infection.

How to use: Place two drops in affected ear three times daily for seven days.

What you need: Gingerroot capsule or tincture (For children, use half the dose.)

For: Digestive upset, such as diarrhea, gas or bloating or stomach and menstrual cramps.

How to use: Take 300 milligrams of the capsule form, or 20 drops of the tincture, every waking hour until symptoms improve.

What you need: Homeopathic Arnica.

For: Pain and swelling of minor injuries and bruises.

How to use: Take two 30C pellets four times daily for two days. Topical arnica also is an option.

What you need: Homeopathic Arsenicum album.

For: Vomiting and diarrhea due to food poisoning or flu.

How to use: Take two 30C pellets four times daily for one day.

What you need: Homeopathic Oscillococcinum.

For: First symptoms of cold or flu.

How to use: Take on first day of a cold or flu. Follow label instructions.

What you need: Homeopathic Rhus Toxicodendron.

For: Muscle pain and stiffness caused by overexertion.

How to use: Take two 30C pellets four times daily for up to two days.

Mark A. Stengler, NMD, naturopathic medical doctor in private practice, Encinitas, California, and author of *Bottom Line/Natural Healing* newsletter. *www.drstengler.com.*

Top Natural Inflammation Fighters

More and more is being learned about the harmful effects of chronic inflammation—and its connection to everything from arthritis and diabetes to heart disease and cancer. Yet, most people don't have an effective strategy for fighting it.

What you can do: In addition to making appropriate lifestyle changes, consider taking one or more herbal remedies that have shown significant anti-inflammatory properties in clinical trials. These herbs have been used for centuries as natural remedies.

Curcumin/Turmeric

Curcumin, a powerful antioxidant, is one of the most active biological agents in the herb turmeric, which is used as an ingredient in curries and mustard. For general inflammation prevention, it helps to eat foods containing curry, as well as yellow mustard—which, unlike Dijon mustard, is rich in turmeric.

Anti-inflammatory benefits: Turmeric is thought to inhibit *eicosanoids*, signaling molecules that play a key role in the inflammatory response. In one controlled study of 18 people with rheumatoid arthritis, those taking 1,200 milligrams (mg) of curcumin daily for two weeks found it to be just as effective as 300 mg daily of the nonsteroidal anti-inflammatory drug (NSAID) *phenylbutazone* (Butazolidin) in reducing joint swelling.

Other studies have found that curcumin supplements reduce levels of C-reactive protein (CRP), a general inflammation marker linked to arthritis and cardiovascular disease.

Cancer-fighting benefits: Curcumin also has been shown to kill cancer cells in laboratory studies. Phase II clinical trials are currently under way to study its benefits for colorectal cancer. In addition, researchers are investigating curcumin's role in possibly preventing pancreatic cancer and multiple myeloma.

Recommended products: Meriva-SR, available at NEEDS (800-634-1380, *www.needs. com*)…or Curamin, which also contains the anti-inflammatory herb boswellia, described later, manufactured by EuroPharma (866-598-5487, *www.curamin.com*).

Zyflamend Herbal Combination

Zyflamend is a popular herbal anti-inflammatory product that contains extracts of turmeric, ginger and rosemary (which has antioxidant and anti-inflammatory properties). Among the other herbs found in Zyflamend are holy basil (used in India's traditional Ayurvedic medicine for its immune-boosting and anti-inflammatory properties) and the Chinese herb *polygonum cuspidatum* (a rich source of resveratrol, the powerful antioxidant that also is found in grapes).

Anti-inflammatory benefits: Zyflamend lowers the body's general inflammatory response.

Cancer-fighting benefits: Zyflamend has been studied as a therapy for a type of prostate inflammation called *high-grade prostatic intra-epithelial neoplasia* (HGPIN), which is associated with precancerous changes in prostate cells. Zyflamend may be able to return these precancerous cells back to their normal state. Zyflamend may inhibit the proliferation of human prostate cancer cells, as well.

To purchase Zyflamend: Go to the Web site of the manufacturer, New Chapter, Inc. (*www.newchapter.com*), or call 800-543-7279.

Rose Hip

An extract of a certain type of rose hip called Rosa canina is especially high in the anti-inflammatory chemical *glycoside of mono and diglycerol*.

Anti-inflammatory benefits: Clinical trials have shown rose hip extract to benefit osteoarthritis of the knee, hip, wrist and neck. Another trial of rheumatoid arthritis sufferers showed significant improvement in their pain, movement and quality of life after six months of treatment with rose hip extract.

Recommended product: Swanson Ultra Danish Rose Hips i-flex (dried powder of a special type of rose hip), available from Swanson Health Products (800-824-4491, *www.swansonvitamins.com*).

Boswellia

Boswellia extract is another herb used in traditional Ayurvedic medicine. Its active ingredient is boswellic acid.

Anti-inflammatory benefits: Boswellia inhibits production of inflammation-promoting chemical agents without the gastrointestinal side effects of steroid drugs and NSAIDs.

Recommended products: Nature's Way Boswellia Standardized, available at Nature's Way (800-962-8873, *www.naturesway.com*) …or Curamin (described earlier).

Important: You may need to experiment to find which supplement (or supplement combination) works best for your condition. Take the supplements described in this article as directed on the product labels. Consult

Try it! Aromas That Heal

There are several ways to benefit from aroma-therapy…

• **Inhalation therapy.** Add three to six drops of an essential oil to a large bowl of steaming water. Position your head over the bowl—and a towel over the bowl and your head to trap the steam. Take deep breaths for five to 10 minutes. (Don't get too close to the hot steam.)

• **Massage therapy.** For topical applications, most essential oils must be diluted (that's because they are very concentrated and can harm the skin) by mixing one ounce of a "carrier" oil, such as almond, olive, grapeseed or sesame oil, with 10 to 20 drops of an essential oil. Or combine the essential oil with an unscented moisturizing lotion.

• **Warm bath.** Add six to 10 drops of an essential oil to a warm bath. Essential oils are available at health-food stores and online.

Typical cost: Starting at $6 for 0.5 ounce. You can purchase oils from Aura Cacia, whose parent company is Frontier Natural Products Co-Op (800-437-3301, *www.auracacia.com*), and The Essential Oil Company (800-729-5912, *www.essentialoil.com*).

Which Oils to Use

Condition	Essential Oil	Method
Arthritis	Cypress, Eucalyptus, Hyssop, Lavender, Rosemary	•Massage into sore joint •Warm bath
Bronchitis	Cedarwood, Hyssop, Lavender, Peppermint, Pine, Rosemary, Sandalwood	•Massage into the chest •Inhalation therapy
Hypertension	Bergamot, Chamomile, Lavender, Lemon, Rose, Ylang-ylang	•Massage into back, chest and shoulders •Warm bath
Indigestion	Chamomile, Geranium, Rose, Rosemary	•Warm bath
Migraine	Chamomile, Eucalyptus, Lavender, Lemon, Marjoram, Rosemary, Peppermint	•Massage into temples •Inhalation therapy
Stomachache	Peppermint	•Massage into abdomen

your doctor first if you take medication—some herbs may interact with it.

Mark Blumenthal, founder and executive director of the American Botanical Council (ABC), a nonprofit educational organization dedicated to the responsible use of herbs and medicinal plants, *www.herbalgram.org*. He is editor and publisher of the ABC's journal, *HerbalGram*, and senior editor of several books, including *The ABC Clinical Guide to Herb*s (American Botanical Council).

Scents to Boost Mood, Sex Life and More

Scents have subtle yet powerful effects on emotions. Here's how to use your sense of smell to manage your moods…and other people's, too!

• **Feel younger with pink grapefruit.** To make others perceive you as youthful (so you feel that way, too), apply a grapefruit-scented or other citrusy body lotion or spray right after your shower.

Avoid: Lavender, which makes you seem granny-ish.

• **Feel more secure with baby powder.** Keep a small bottle or resealable plastic bag of baby powder in your purse or briefcase. Before heading into a challenging situation (a job interview), open the container slightly and take a small whiff. Don't inhale too deeply—you may sneeze!

• **Combat claustrophobia with evergreens.** Keep a small vial of evergreen essential oil in your pocket or purse. When in a cramped space (an elevator, a crowd), hold the vial near your nose and inhale two or three times. Repeat every 10 minutes as needed.

•**Assuage anger with cucumber.** Hold a sliced cucumber one-half inch from your face and level with your lips...inhale deeply, continuing for several minutes. To reduce road rage, use a cucumber-melon air freshener in the car.

Avoid: Barbecuing or roasting meat when you're angry—the scent stirs up fiery feelings that heighten aggression.

•**Rev up a man's libido with pumpkin pie or black licorice.** Bake a pumpkin pie for maximum effect...or use a reed diffuser (a stick that wicks the aroma from a bottle of scented oil).

On a date: Nibble on black licorice.

Noteworthy: Perfume is only 3% effective at arousing a man's romantic feelings...versus 40% for pumpkin pie and 13% for licorice.

Alan Hirsch, MD, founder and neurological director of the Smell & Taste Treatment and Research Foundation and an assistant professor in the departments of neurology and psychiatry at Rush-Presbyterian-St. Luke's Medical Center, both in Chicago. He is the author of *Sensa Weight-Loss Program* (Hilton). *www.smellandtaste.org.*

HANDS-ON HEALING

Prescription Massage

Rx: Massage, once weekly. Don't you wish your doctor would hand you that prescription?

It could happen—increasingly, doctors are ordering patient massages via prescriptions to treat medical conditions, especially for orthopedic problems. Your health insurance might even cover the cost...but don't be fooled into thinking you're off to a day at the spa, because this kind of massage is truly a "treatment."

According to Herbert Levin, LMT, MMP, founder of Medical Massage Practitioners of America, what's unique about medical massage is that the therapist works only on the injured area as specified by a doctor's prescription. If your doctor has diagnosed a problem with, say, your left shoulder, you can expect the therapist to focus solely on that problem. Massage treatments can help migraine headaches and orthopedic injuries, and some people find them beneficial for a variety of other maladies, too, including fibromyalgia, temporomandibular joint disorder (TMJ), osteoarthritis and other conditions.

What to Expect

At the start of your first session, you can expect that your medical massage therapist will begin by assessing your muscle and joint function—strength, range of motion, degree of pain, etc. Dr. Levin explains that this is done by applying active, passive and resistive forces to your muscles to determine which ones aren't functioning right—then the same tests are repeated after each treatment to check its effectiveness. How much pressure is used during massage will vary depending on your condition and what feels comfortable to you, and often therapists include stretching as part of the treatment, too.

Types of Massage

These three techniques are the most widely used, Dr. Levin says...

•**Neuromuscular massage.** This involves applying pressure to a specific body part to release tension.

•**Trigger point massage.** This technique targets spasms that reduce blood flow into other parts of the muscle, causing pain—which gets even more painful when the spasm pressures nearby nerves.

•**Myofascial release.** This technique is used to stretch and release tension in the myofascia (the soft connective tissue that surrounds all muscles), which can become constricted and sometimes inflamed because of trauma, overuse, inactivity, poor posture, chronic stress and inflammatory agents (including chemotherapy drugs).

Note: If you have cancer, it is critical to first seek approval for any kind of massage from your oncologist, because there are concerns that manipulation near a tumor may spread the disease.

Want to Give It a Try?

If you and your doctor agree that medical massage might help a condition you have, ask him or her for some recommendations to good therapists in your area. Costs vary according to region but typically run about $60 per massage. Insurance covers some massages, depending on your condition and your carrier. To locate a qualified therapist, visit the Web site of the American Massage Therapy Association, *www.amtamassage. org*, and click on "find a massage therapist."

Herbert Levin, LMT, MMP, founder of Medical Massage Practitioners of America (MMPA), Fort Lauderdale, Florida.

Heal Yourself with Self-Massage

Most forms of massage are administered by a massage therapist. But do-it-yourself massage can help ease a variety of health problems ranging from pain due to arthritis and headaches to digestive complaints, fatigue, insomnia and urinary frequency.

One highly effective system of self-massage is included in traditional Chinese medicine (TCM). According to TCM, when a person is unwell or injured, or when one of his/her organ systems, such as the digestive tract, is not functioning optimally, small areas of soreness called trigger points appear on the body.

There can be anywhere from three to 10 trigger points for each ailment. Trigger points are located at problem areas and at "reflexes," points that are a distance away from problem areas and connected through the nervous system. Massaging trigger points can be highly effective at easing symptoms.

In addition to targeting trigger points, massage causes us to relax, which helps the endocrine glands produce body-healing hormones and allows more oxygen to be delivered to the body as blood vessels expand. Massage also enhances the lymphatic system, which helps remove waste products from our bodies while fortifying the immune system.

Self-massage can work for prevention, too. For example, kneading the toes and tops of the feet may prevent an oncoming headache.

Although the hands, feet, ears and abdomen are associated with specific ailments, it's wise to self-massage all of these parts of the body from time to time to search for any tender spots. This is your body's signal that you should focus on those areas.

Fully massaging your hands, feet, ears or abdomen is considered a "session" and takes about 10 minutes. People in generally good health should aim for one session a day. Those with a more serious health problem, such as cancer, diabetes or heart disease, can (with a doctor's OK) try it twice daily. *How to practice self-massage…*

Hands

In TCM, tender spots around the edges of your palm, closer to the fingers than the heel of the hand, are generally associated with problems in your upper body, including your heart, lungs or throat. Tenderness toward the heel of the hand usually signals a problem in the lower body, such as the hips, legs or pelvis.

What to do: With your left hand palm up, start at the upper-left corner of your palm and rub across with your right thumb, applying pressure at numerous points. Start with light pressure and gradually use more force. While using the right thumb in the palm of the left hand massage the back side of the left hand with the fingers of the right hand. Squeeze your left hand with firm (but not painful) pressure. If you find areas of soreness, hold firmly for 10 seconds, then release. Repeat the self-massage five times. Massage each finger from palm to nail, then work on the other hand.

Success story: Richard, a 72-year-old golfer who had arthritis in his hands, not only eased his arthritis pain but also reduced his urinary frequency after practicing self-massage on his hands.

Feet

The toes and tops of the feet are associated with the upper body (head, eyes, neck and shoulders), according to TCM. The middle part of the foot is linked to the torso (kidneys and stomach), while the heels and bottoms of the feet correspond to the lower body (bladder and small and large intestines).

What to do: While holding your foot with your opposite hand, apply pressure and move the thumb of the other hand along the entire bottom of the foot. Start by moving across the top of the foot, including the toes, down toward the middle of the foot and then back to the bottom of the foot (usually the primary focus). Note areas of tenderness, and return to them a second or third time. Repeat on the other foot. If it's easier for you, place a golf ball or rolling pin on the floor and roll your foot over it to access any tender spots on the bottom of your foot.

Success story: Sandy, a 56-year-old woman who had migraines, discovered through trial and error that her areas of soreness were located in the middle of the foot between the first and second toes. By doing foot massage for four to five minutes per foot twice daily, Sandy reduced the frequency and severity of her migraines. Such results typically last a few days.

Ears

In TCM, the earlobes are related to the upper body (head and sinuses, for example), while the tops of the ears are linked to the lower body (low back, hips, legs and feet).

What to do: Use moderate pressure and work over the entire ear, both the inner part (against the skull) and the outer part (along the edges) using a kneading motion between the thumbs and forefingers. It's fine to work on both ears simultaneously.

Success story: Eileen, a 60-year-old piano teacher with urinary urgency, discovered that massaging the tops of her ears helped reduce the bladder spasms that made her urinate. In TCM, the upper-inner rim of the ear corresponds to the bladder.

Abdomen

The abdomen is primarily associated with gastrointestinal functions (such as digestion and bowel movements), according to TCM.

What to do: While sitting or lying down, place one hand on top of the other and move them in a circular clockwise motion around the abdominal area. Start below the breastbone, moving the hands to the top-left edge of the rib cage, down to the left corner of the pelvis and across the pubic bone. Then move the hands to the right corner of the pelvis, up to the top-right edge of the rib cage and back to below the breastbone.

Success story: Margie, a 65-year-old woman who had severe left hip pain, discovered a painful area on the left side of her abdomen near the ribs. Regularly massaging this and other points around the abdomen has decreased the intensity of her distant hip pain. She has remained pain-free for several years.

Illustrations by Shawn Banner.

Roger Jahnke, OMD, doctor of Oriental medicine and director of the Institute of Integral Qigong and Tai Chi in Santa Barbara, California, *www.iiqtc.org.* He is author of *The Healer Within* (HarperOne) and *The Healing Promise of Qi* (McGraw-Hill).

You Can Conquer Nagging Pain Once And for All

Can you imagine living well into your 90s and being able to eliminate virtually all of the aches and pains that you may develop from time to time?

Ninety-seven-year-old Bonnie Prudden, a longtime physical fitness advocate, stays pain free—even though she has arthritis that led to two hip replacements—by using a form of myotherapy ("myo" is Greek for muscle) that she developed more than 30 years ago.

Now: Tens of thousands of patients have successfully used this special form of myotherapy, which is designed to relieve "trigger points" (highly irritable spots in muscles) that develop throughout life due to a number of causes, such as falls, strains or disease.

By applying pressure to these sensitive areas and then slowly releasing it, it's possible to relax muscles that have gone into painful spasms, often in response to physical and/or emotional stress.

A simple process: Ask a partner (a spouse or friend, for example) to locate painful trigger points by applying his/her fingertips to parts of your body experiencing discomfort—or consult a practitioner trained in myotherapy.*

If you're working with a partner, let him know when a particular spot for each body area described in this article is tender.

Pressure should be applied for seven seconds (the optimal time determined by Prudden's research to release muscle tension) each time that your partner locates such a spot.

On a scale of one to 10, the pressure should be kept in the five- to seven-point range—uncomfortable but not intolerable.

The relaxed muscles are then gently stretched to help prevent new spasms.

If you prefer to treat yourself: Use a "bodo," a wooden dowel attached to a handle, and a lightweight, metal "shepherd's crook" to locate trigger points and apply pressure. Both tools are available at 800-221-4634, *www.bonnieprudden.com*, for $8 and $30.95, respectively.

For areas that are easy to reach, use the bodo to locate trigger points and then apply

*To find a practitioner of Bonnie Prudden's myotherapy techniques, go to *www.bonnieprudden.com* or call 800-221-4634. If you are unable to find a practitioner near you, call local massage therapists and ask whether they are familiar with the techniques.

pressure to erase them. For spots that are difficult to reach, use the shepherd's crook to find and apply pressure to trigger points.

As an alternative to the specially designed tools, you can use your fingers, knuckles or elbows on areas of the body that can be reached easily. Common types of pain that can be relieved by this method...**

Shoulder Pain

Finding the trigger point: Lie face down while your partner uses his elbow to gently apply pressure to trigger points that can hide along the top of the shoulders and in the upper back. If you are very small or slender, your partner can use his fingers instead of his elbow.

Place one of your arms across your back at the waist while your partner slides his fingers under your shoulder blade to search for and apply pressure to additional trigger points. Repeat the process on the opposite side.

While still lying face down, bend your elbows and rest your forehead on the backs of your hands. With his hands overlapped, your partner can gently move all 10 of his fingers along the top of the shoulder to locate additional trigger points.

Pain-erasing stretch: The "shrug" is a sequence of shoulder exercises performed four times after myotherapy and whenever shoulder tension builds.

From a standing or sitting position, round your back by dropping your head forward while bringing the backs of your arms together as close as possible in front of your body. Extend both arms back (with your thumbs leading) behind your body while tipping your head back and looking toward the ceiling.

Next, with both arms at your sides, raise your shoulders up to your earlobes, then press your shoulders down hard.

**Check with your doctor before trying this therapy if you have a chronic medical condition or have suffered a recent injury.

Low-Back Pain

Finding the trigger point: Lie face down while your partner stands to your right and reaches across your body to place his elbow on your buttocks in the area where the left back pocket would appear on a pair of pants. For seven seconds, your partner should slowly apply pressure to each trigger point—not straight down but angled back toward himself.

Repeat on the other side. If the pressure causes slight discomfort, your partner has found the right spot. If not, your partner should move his elbow slightly and try the steps again. Two to three trigger points can typically be found on each buttock.

Pain-erasing stretch: Lie on your left side on a flat surface (such as a bed, table or the floor). Bend your right knee and pull it as close to your chest as possible.

Next, extend your right leg, keeping it aligned with the left leg and about eight inches above it.

Finally, lower the raised leg onto the resting one and relax for three seconds. Perform these steps four times on each leg.

Hip Pain

Finding the trigger point: The trigger points for hip pain are often found in the gluteus medius, the muscle that runs along either side of the pelvis.

Lie on your side with your knees slightly bent. Using one elbow, your partner should scan for trigger points along the gluteus medius (in the hip area, roughly between the waist and the bottom seam of your underpants) and apply pressure straight down at each sensitive spot for seven seconds.

The same process should be repeated on the opposite side of your body.

Pain-erasing stretch: Lie on your left side on a table with your right leg hanging off the side and positioned forward. Your partner should place one hand on top of your waist and the other hand on the knee of the dangling right leg.

This knee should be gently pressed down eight times. The stretch should be repeated on the opposite side.

Bonnie Prudden helped create the President's Council on Youth Fitness in 1956 and has been one of the country's leading authorities on exercise therapy for more than five decades. Based in Tucson, Arizona, she is author of 18 books, including *Pain Erasure* (M. Evans).

DETOXIFICATION

The Healing Power of Detoxification

Studies show that the vast majority of us harbor traces or metabolites of *polychlorinated biphenyls* (PCBs), dioxins, bisphenol A, heavy metals and other hazardous substances in our bodies. This toxic load contributes to a wide range of maladies ranging from "mere" confusion and fatigue to diabetes, lupus and cancer.

It's easy to feel overwhelmed and powerless knowing that we're all soaking up dangerous chemicals...but there is hope. Most people can achieve real health benefits by incorporating detoxification into their health routines, says Walter J. Crinnion, ND, chair of the environmental medicine department at the Southwest College of Naturopathic Medicine & Health Sciences in Scottsdale, Arizona, and author of *Clean, Green & Lean*, a book about getting healthy and slim by cleaning up your diet. Dr. Crinnion's suggestions for how to clean up your system aren't extreme—you'll barely notice you're making an effort, but you will eventually notice how much better you feel.

Contaminated at Birth

Toxic exposure begins in the womb and worsens over time as chemicals accumulate in your body. A recent study detected 232 chemicals foreign to the human body in the umbilical cord blood of 10 newborn babies from the US! The Environmental Protection Agency and World Health Organization report that about

85,000 different chemicals are currently registered for use in manufacturing and 800 new ones are introduced each year, many of which have little or no data on toxicity.

According to Dr. Crinnion, toxic chemicals can attack three primary body systems...

●**Your immune system.** By weakening your body's defenses, toxic chemicals contribute to allergies, asthma, autoimmune diseases such as lupus and rheumatoid arthritis, chronic viral or fungal infections, chemical sensitivity, cancers, etc.

●**Your nervous system.** Chemicals can affect mental function, leading to fatigue, confusion, poor concentration, memory disturbances, mood swings, anxiety, depression, headaches, nerve pain, balance problems, tremors, muscle weakness and more—even, potentially, Parkinson's disease.

●**Your endocrine system.** Damage to the hormonal system can potentially cause early puberty and reproductive difficulties, ongoing hormonal problems, diabetes, obesity and cancers, such as liver cancer and leukemia.

Purge Your Body of Toxins

To stimulate excretion of toxins, Dr. Crinnion recommends...

●**Drink three cups of unsweetened organic green tea daily**—it's rich in antioxidant polyphenols, which help flush the toxins from your body.

●**Eat organic brown rice several times a week**—its fiber helps move toxins out in your stool. If you don't like brown rice, take a rice bran fiber supplement.

●**Include more chlorophyll in your diet.** Known as "nature's cleanser," chlorophyll neutralizes destructive chemical pollutants and prevents the build-up of toxins. Good food sources include green, leafy vegetables...seaweed...and green drinks such as wheat grass juice "shots" available at health-food stores. Another option: Blue-green algae supplements such as spirulina and chlorella, also available at health-food stores.

●**The less sugar you eat, the better.** It suppresses your immune system and your liver's ability to purge toxins.

●**Sweat it out.** With your doctor's okay, take a sauna (about 135°F) several times a week to release toxins in your sweat. Enhance your ability to detoxify by using a loofah to remove dead skin cells and unclog pores.

Reduce Your Chemical Exposures

To assure good health, Dr. Crinnion advises also committing yourself to reducing your exposure to toxins. Some of these are strategies that you're familiar with, but they're definitely worth a reminder...while others may surprise you...

●**Don't wear your outside shoes indoors.** Along with the dirt and dust from outdoors comes residue from diesel auto exhaust, lead, pesticides and other toxins.

●**For floors, choose wood, tile and stone,** which are less likely to harbor and generate toxins than carpets.

●**Keep your house clean,** minimizing dust-collecting knickknacks so environmental toxins don't have the chance to accumulate.

●**Filter, filter, filter.** Filters should be changed every six weeks in homes with a central forced-air heating/cooling system. If you have a different type, consider installing a portable air-filter system. Filter your tap water, too.

●**Minimize use of products that contain harmful chemicals.** Buy unscented, eco-friendly cleaners and laundry detergents. Drink and serve food from glass containers—many plastic ones are made with toxic chemicals that can leach into your food.

Don't Eat Toxins

●**Organic fruits, vegetables and meats contain the fewest toxins.** It's especially important to buy organic apples, bell peppers, blueberries, celery, cherries, imported grapes, kale, collard greens, nectarines, peaches, potatoes, spinach and strawberries, as these in nonorganic form are most likely to be drenched in pesticides.

• **Generally less toxic produce** (meaning it's not as important to buy organic) includes asparagus, avocado, cabbage, cantaloupe, eggplant, grapefruit, honeydew melon, kiwi, mango, onions, pineapple, sweet corn, peas, sweet potato and watermelon.

• **Be picky about fish.** Farmed fish can contain significant levels of toxic PCBs, chemicals that can wreak havoc with your health, so eat only wild salmon and other varieties. (This rules out most of what's sold in restaurants and supermarkets.) Avoid fish with a high mercury content, including swordfish, shark, tuna and orange roughy—check *http://www.ewg.org/safefishlist* to see what's safe to eat and what's not.

• **Buy organic butter.** Nonorganic butter can be high in PCBs!

By minimizing exposure to toxins and supporting your body's innate healing processes, you can gradually take control of toxins and restore your health. In just weeks, expect increased energy, less brain fog and fewer allergy symptoms such as congestion. Over time, if you keep up the good work, it will only get better.

Do You Need a Detox Expert?

Dr. Crinnion suggests everyone should follow the above strategies—but if, after giving this detox lifestyle a try for two months, you still find that you are experiencing problems such as allergies, brain fog or fatigue, consult a physician who is knowledgeable about environmental toxins. You can find a list of physicians who have studied with Dr. Crinnion at his Web site, *http://www.crinnionmedical. com/referral.php*. A trained and experienced doctor will help you identify and eliminate toxic exposures and cleanse harmful chemicals from your body with a personalized program that may include diet, supplements (e.g., magnesium, vitamin B-6, selenium and glutathione), hydrotherapy and other strategies.

Walter J. Crinnion, ND, professor of naturopathic medicine and chair of the environmental medicine department, Southwest College of Naturopathic Medicine & Health Sciences, Scottsdale, Arizona. He is author of *Clean, Green & Lean* (Wiley). More information is available at *www.crinnionmedical.com*.

Detoxification for Ex-Smokers

Smoking is an extremely difficult habit to break. If you have recently stopped smoking, congratulations.

What you might not know: Anyone who has stopped smoking (whether recently or within the past year) needs to detoxify. Detoxification helps to improve liver function and get rid of some of the toxins, such as cadmium and arsenic, that have built up in the body. All ex-smokers can try the following detoxification program, which involves taking all of the supplements below for four weeks. To further help detoxification of the lymphatic system, have a weekly massage or a dry or wet sauna, which is safe for everyone except pregnant women, children, frail elderly people and people with diabetes, heart or circulation problems. All of the supplements below are safe for everyone…

• **Milk thistle.** This herb has been used for centuries for liver disorders and liver cleansing. Studies show that it enhances detoxification. Take 250 milligrams (mg) of a product standardized to contain 70 to 85% silymarin twice daily 30 minutes before meals.

• **Psyllium husks.** These husks of the seeds of an east Asian plant provide fiber and promote detoxification by regulating bowel movements and expelling toxins. While you may know psyllium husk as the main ingredient in Metamucil, it also is available on its own in powder or capsule form. Take 5 grams (one teaspoon) of powder twice daily mixed into eight ounces of water.

• **Pneumotrophin PMG.** This propriety blend, made by a company called Standard Process (800-558-8740, *www.standardprocess.com*), contains nutrients that support healthy lung tissue. Take one tablet three times daily before meals.

• **Omega-3 fatty acids.** To reduce lung inflammation, take either krill oil (1,000 mg daily) or a daily fish oil supplement with a combined 1,000 mg of *eicosapentaenoic acid* (EPA) and *docosahexaenoic acid* (DHA).

Choose the omega-3 fatty acid that is easiest for you to take. Some people prefer krill oil because it is less likely to cause fishy burps or aftertaste.

• **Multivitamin.** Everyone should take a multivitamin as the basis of his/her supplement regimen. This helps to ensure that your body gets crucial nutrients.

Mark A. Stengler, NMD, naturopathic medical doctor in private practice, Encinitas, California, and author of the *Bottom Line/Natural Healing* newsletter. *www.drstengler.com.*

BREAKTHROUGH THERAPIES

The Awesome Healing Power of "Blended" Medicine

The practices of conventional and so-called complementary medicine used to inhabit separate worlds.

Now: With more and more Americans embracing elements from both worlds, an increasing number of physicians are prescribing a combination of conventional and complementary treatments—an approach known as "blended" medicine.

Blended treatments that you should know about…

High Cholesterol

Every year, about 1 million Americans have a heart attack, and nearly half a million die from heart disease—in part, because of uncontrolled high cholesterol.

Conventional approach: The use of cholesterol-lowering statin drugs, such as *pravastatin* (Pravachol) and *atorvastatin* (Lipitor). People who take these drugs and modify their diets can sometimes reduce their risk for a heart attack by 25 to 50%.

Drawbacks: Statins, particularly at high doses, can cause severe muscle pain and other side effects in up to 30% of patients. Also, statins have little effect on triglycerides, another type of blood fat that's linked to heart disease.

Blended approach: By using plant stanols and sterols (modified plant extracts found in a number of "functional" foods, including butter substitutes such as Benecol and Promise activ Light), people with mildly elevated cholesterol often can control their cholesterol levels.

Those with higher cholesterol levels can combine one of the butter substitutes described above with a statin drug for better results than from either treatment alone. In some cases, the medication dosage can be reduced, which lowers the risk for drug side effects.

For example, people who eat the equivalent of three pats of one of these butter substitutes daily can achieve reductions of 10 to 20% in LDL "bad" cholesterol—in addition to the reductions achieved with medications.

Helpful: Many people with high cholesterol also have elevated triglycerides—fish oil (1,000 mg to 3,000 mg daily from a supplement) reduces triglycerides by up to 50% in some patients.*

Remember: When striving to reduce cholesterol levels, start by exercising regularly and following a healthful diet, such as the Mediterranean diet.

Back Pain

Four out of five Americans suffer from back pain (due to injury, back strain or a herniated disk, for example) at some time in their lives.

Conventional approach: A combination of short-term rest, mild exercise (such as stretching) and nonsteroidal anti-inflammatory drugs (NSAIDs), such as ibuprofen (Motrin). Less often, surgery is required for conditions such as a herniated disk.

Drawbacks: Conventional treatments are only modestly successful for most patients.

Blended approach: Acupuncture—combined with the use of other medical treatments, including physical therapy and pain

*Consult your physician before trying any of the dietary supplements described in this article.

medications. Patients who have six to eight acupuncture treatments, usually given once or twice a week, often have long-lasting relief—although some require monthly "tune-ups" to stay pain-free.

The National Institutes of Health has concluded that acupuncture is often effective for low-back pain.

Good news: Many insurance companies cover the cost of acupuncture as a treatment for back pain.

Also helpful: An herb known as devil's claw is very popular in Europe for low-back pain. More than a dozen reputable studies show that it's effective—and it's less likely than ibuprofen or other drugs to cause side effects, including gastrointestinal upset. Follow the label directions.

To relieve osteoarthritis: Consider trying devil's claw alone or in conjunction with a regimen that includes heat and cold therapy… exercise…glucosamine and chondroitin supplements (typical dose: 1,500 mg of glucosamine and 1,200 mg of chondroitin daily)…and over-the-counter anti-inflammatory medication.

When buying devil's claw, look for a product that is standardized to contain 50 mg to 100 mg of *harpagoside* (the active anti-inflammatory ingredient). Check the product label for dosage instructions.

Anxiety Disorders

One of the most common psychiatric problems in the US, anxiety disorders can lead to a variety of symptoms, including heart palpitations and a persistent fear and worry in situations that would not feel threatening to most people. Only a minority of patients ever seek treatment—and those who do often have limited success.

Conventional approach: In addition to counseling, some patients may be advised to take a *benzodiazepine* tranquilizer, such as diazepam (Valium) or *lorazepam* (Ativan). Or they might be given a prescription for an antidepressant, a beta-blocker or another drug to help relieve anxiety.

Drawbacks: Many psychiatric drugs cause side effects, including unwanted seda-

tion, weight gain or problems with libido and sexual function. Some anxiety medications can be addictive.

Blended approach: Meditation—with or without drug therapy—has a strong record of success in treating anxiety. Studies show that people who meditate for 20 minutes at least once a day experience less anxiety (and less depression).

All forms of meditation seem to be effective. One of the easiest involves breathing exercises, in which patients take a series of deep breaths, hold them briefly and then slowly exhale.

What to do: Inhale through the nose for a count of four…hold your breath for a count of seven…then exhale through the mouth for a count of eight.

Important: People who meditate for longer periods—and more often—tend to experience less anxiety overall than those who do it for less time.

Also helpful: Kava, an herbal supplement. Some studies show that it's about as effective as benzodiazepines for anxiety. Follow the dosage instructions on the label.

Important: The FDA issued a warning in 2002 that kava had been linked to liver damage. Although it can be effective for many patients with anxiety disorders, kava should be used only under a doctor's supervision.

Fatigue

Often due to stress or poor sleep habits, fatigue also can be caused by underlying health problems.

Conventional approach: Patients who experience severe and frequent fatigue should get a complete medical workup (your doctor will recommend specific tests) because it can be caused by literally hundreds of disorders.

Drawbacks: Unless your doctor can identify a specific underlying cause for fatigue, the treatment options are limited. People usually are advised to exercise more and get sufficient sleep—but that doesn't work for everyone.

Blended approach: Ginseng, an herb that has traditionally been used by athletes to improve stamina, seems to help many patients with fatigue.

Look for the American form of ginseng with at least 5% ginsenosides (the active chemical ingredient). Follow the dosage directions on the label.

Brent A. Bauer, MD, director of the Complementary and Integrative Medicine Program and a physician in the Department of Internal Medicine at the Mayo Clinic in Rochester, Minnesota. He is medical editor of the *Mayo Clinic Book of Alternative Medicine* (Time).

Balneotherapy: The Benefits of Bathing

Lots of people take a hot bath to unwind and help release muscle tension. But few people take advantage of the other health benefits provided by bathing. Also known as "balneotherapy," therapeutic bathing has long been used with many forms of water—for example, hot springs, cold pools, tap or pond water. But mineral springs are among the most well-known for their healing powers. In the 1800s, bathing in mineral springs—also known as "taking the waters"—was fashionable, and mineral water was even bottled and sold as a medicinal beverage. Scientific evidence proving that mineral spring therapy is helpful is limited. But scientists seem to agree that balneotherapy is not harmful, and there's no question that it feels good.

You can create your own mineral spring soak at home using a simple, inexpensive substance—Epsom salts. In fact, Epsom salts (a four-pound container is available at most drugstores and supermarkets for less than $4) are a mainstay of home treatment for patients suffering from insomnia, arthritis, fibromyalgia, flu, back strain, acute sprains, itchy dermatitis, sunburn and shingles.

Epsom salts contain magnesium sulfate. Magnesium is, of course, essential to human health (particularly heart and muscle function) and acts as a muscle relaxant. Because magnesium is often depleted in the processing of foods, magnesium deficiency is common—it's estimated to affect more than half of Americans—and can contribute to fatigue, muscle spasm, weakness, irritability, insomnia, high blood pressure, sugar cravings and anxiety. Magnesium-rich foods, such as nuts, whole grains and blackstrap molasses…and magnesium supplements (*typical dose:* 300 milligrams daily) are your best options to keep your magnesium levels adequate. But soaking in a hot tub of Epsom salt water also provides some magnesium via absorption through the skin.

To create your own healing bath: Add two cups of Epsom salts to a tub of comfortably hot water, and soak for 20 minutes. At the end of your soak, moisten a washcloth with cool water and rub it all over your arms, legs and trunk for 30 seconds—to prevent chilling and promote blood circulation. Towel off and then relax by lying down for at least 30 minutes. To complete the healing environment of your mineral soak, use low lights and/or candles, drink several ounces of cool water throughout the bath and ask family members to not disturb you.

As described above, Epsom salt soaking is very safe. However, people with high blood pressure or arterial disease should avoid hot mineral soaks—the high temperature of the water can aggravate these conditions. For this reason, pregnant women should consult a doctor before trying a hot mineral bath.

Jamison Starbuck, ND, naturopathic physician in family practice in Missoula, Montana. She is contributing editor to *The Alternative Advisor: The Complete Guide to Natural Therapies and Alternative Treatments* (Time Life).

NATURAL HEALTH PROFESSIONALS

Dental Detectives: Holistic Dentistry for Whole-Body Health

Dentists have always been considered health professionals, but some take the concept further than others. As a growing body of medical research affirms the strong connection between poor oral health and chronic disease, including cancer, diabetes and heart disease, some dentists now dedicate their practices to improving and protecting overall health, not just what happens in your mouth. Mark A. Breiner, DDS, founder of the Breiner Whole-Body Health Centre in Trumbull, Connecticut, and author of *Whole-Body Dentistry*, explains how holistic dentists work in an entirely different paradigm.

Dr. Breiner likens standard dentistry to carpentry, calling it "a restorative profession, taking care of cavities and making crowns." The holistic approach looks at how the state of your mouth affects and reflects everything about your health. "Everything I do is with that in mind," he says. He asks patients to fill out extensive health forms and then spends a half-hour or so going over those at the first appointment, discussing their health in general. "I am playing detective, working to learn how their health may have been impacted by current or past dentistry that, with an additional stressor, has caused their health to take a turn for the worse."

What's Different?

Dr. Breiner offers some examples of how the two approaches differ…

●**Gum check.** Conventional dentists check for periodontal (gum) disease, associated with heart disease and stroke, by evaluating how red patients' gums are and if they are bleeding…whereas even if gums seem healthy on examination, in Dr. Breiner's office they investigate further by taking a plaque sample from under the gums, which is viewed under a microscope to determine whether there are destructive microbes and/or parasites.

● **Heavy metals.** Perhaps the most controversial difference relates to the material used for fillings. The American Dental Association continues to support use of mercury-containing amalgam fillings, which some conventional dentists still use. But how can it be, asks Dr. Breiner, that mercury is considered toxic everywhere in the world but not in the mouth? He points out that after removing amalgam fillings from the mouth, the law requires him to treat them as toxic waste.

Beyond the obvious concerns about the toxicity of mercury that is in your mouth, Dr.

Breiner says there are other potential health problems, too. He explains that placing dissimilar metals (mercury fillings contain 50% mercury and 50% copper, tin, zinc and silver) in a salt solution (such as saliva) creates a battery-like electrical current. If a nearby tooth then gets a gold filling, the current gets even stronger. "Every tooth is on an acupuncture meridian, so these currents can interfere with the meridian's energy flow," says Dr. Breiner.

Beware: Only have your mercury fillings removed by a professional who is experienced and knowledgeable in this area. He/she must know how to evaluate if your health can tolerate such removal. Unfortunately, Dr. Breiner says, he has seen too many people who are now very sick because they had their mercury removed by a practitioner ignorant on this topic.

●**Energy meridians.** Dr. Breiner uses EAV (Electro-Acupuncture according to Voll) to test the energy of acupuncture meridians, emphasizing that this technique uses no needles. "Think of it as an energy stress test of the acupuncture points," he says. According to Dr. Breiner, "Each tooth energetically relates to a specific organ, vertebrae and/or muscle. Since this is a two-way street, with teeth affecting other parts of the body and vice versa, a root canal may be unnecessarily performed due to a problem elsewhere in the body." EAV helps in this discovery, he believes.

● **Tooth extractions.** Most dental anesthetics contain *epinephrine,* which reduces bleeding, and dentists often advise use of ice to minimize swelling. (Dr. Breiner uses an epinephrine-free alternative.) Both of these practices, however, slow blood flow and increase the likelihood of a *cavitation* (a hole in the bone where a tooth has been extracted and never properly healed). Such cavitations are potential reservoirs for toxins and can cause facial pain and *trigeminal neuralgia* (inflammation of the primary nerve going to the face). Dr. Breiner uses both X-rays and EAV to locate areas on their way to becoming cavitations and to determine if they're likely to become problematic.

Some holistic dentists also believe that all teeth with root canals should be removed because they are breeding grounds for toxicity. Dr. Breiner does not find that to be the case, however. He says numerous factors determine whether a root canal is the cause of other problems, including the health of the associated meridian and the health of the patient.

Forecast: More Holistic Dentistry

Saying that "it is not enough to be a molar mechanic any more," Dr. Breiner believes more dentists are moving in the direction of holistic dentistry—and that a more informed public will be the catalyst that eventually transforms the dental profession. In the meantime, he reminds people that what is good for the heart is good for the mouth including coenzyme Q10, magnesium, vitamin C and other antioxidants—preferably from food and supplements that are whole-food derived.

If you are interested in finding a holistic dentist, you can contact the International Academy of Biological Dentistry and Medicine, *www.iabdm.org*.

Mark A. Breiner, DDS, founder of the Breiner Whole-Body Health Centre, Trumbull, Connecticut, and author of *Whole-Body Dentistry* (Quantum Health Press).

Are Naturopathic Physicians Good for Primary Care?

Have you tried lately to find a primary care provider (PCP) who takes new patients and also takes a real interest in you? If so, good luck. PCPs—the doctors we used to refer to as "general practitioners" or "family doctors"—are in short supply, and it's getting worse. The result? Longer waits for appointments, and once you get into the exam room, you're likely to face a harried, preoccupied doctor who can't spare more than a few minutes for you.

A Solution

One solution is to choose a naturopathic physician (ND) as your PCP.

Some critics point out that NDs don't have the same knowledge and experience as medical doctors...and, actually, that's quite true, says California naturopathic doctor Mark Stengler—because NDs are very specifically trained in primary care. An aspiring ND (or NMD—naturopathic medical doctor—a similar designation) attends a four- or five-year graduate-level naturopathic school with a science curriculum similar to that of a conventional medical school. In addition to the standard medical school courses, naturopathic doctors have training in less invasive (and incidentally, less expensive) health strategies, such as dietary changes, nutritional supplementation, botanical medicine, homeopathy, acupuncture and counseling.

What to Expect

If you choose to visit an ND, you can expect your first exam and consultation to last 60 to 90 minutes (yes, with the doctor), with subsequent visits taking about a half hour each. This gives you and your ND time to explore the many factors that shape your health. This may involve a lengthy discussion of your medical history (and that of your family, since genetics is a key to health)...what you eat...your past and present daily habits...and the overall quality of your life. Recommendations might include a plan to adopt more healthful habits...prescription of natural remedies (and, in certain cases, drugs)...administration of therapies such as homeopathy or acupuncture...and, if appropriate, a referral to a medical specialist—including an MD if that's what you need.

According to Lise Alschuler, ND, past president of the American Association of Naturopathic Physicians (AANP), people should look for specific qualifications when choosing an ND. First and foremost, she says, it's important to check credentials very carefully. Dr. Alschuler cautions against seeking naturopathic medical care from anyone who

357

has certification from what she calls "diploma mills" (schools that provide degrees via correspondence rather than based on classroom and lab work and practical experience). Your ND should have graduated from a four-year school accredited by the Council on Naturopathic Medical Education (*www. cnme.org*) and, once you've verified that, Dr. Alschuler suggests scheduling a meeting or a telephone conversation to interview the doctor, asking for information about the following topics…

● **Education and training,** including information about his/her schooling, residency, specialty society memberships, etc.

● **Licensing or certification.** You can take a look at the list below to see what the current state of affairs is where you live, since states vary in terms of what they require of NDs and what they allow them to do.

● **Training and experience in treating your particular medical condition(s).**

● **Partnerships and/or associations with other health professionals,** including medical doctors. You want to hear that the doctor is open to the concept of collaborative care and has a history of working well with MDs.

● **Costs**—especially whether or not services are covered by your health insurance.

Note: While many NDs do not accept insurance, don't let this hold you back from seeing if this type of care can help lower your medical costs in the long run.

State of the States

Some states license NDs, and some do not—and the latter situation is the more complicated one, since this actually means that there are more restrictions on what these doctors can do. If you live in a state with no licensing, you can certainly seek care from local NDs, but there are limitations on their abilities to prescribe medical tests, make formal diagnoses, perform medical procedures and, of course, prescribe drugs. An option might be to consider choosing an ND from a licensing state—a neighboring one if it is close enough

to travel to, or even a distant one if the doctor is accustomed to working by phone with patients from afar and collaborating with local MDs for necessary lab tests and so forth.

There's variance, too, among states that license NDs—you can check with your state's health department to learn the specifics. *Just to get you started, here's a list of states with current or pending licensure for NDs.…*

States that currently license NDs: Alaska, Arizona, California, Connecticut, District of Columbia, Hawaii, Idaho, Kansas, Maine, Minnesota, Montana, New Hampshire, North Dakota, Oregon, Utah, Vermont and Washington, as well as Puerto Rico and US Virgin Islands.

States with pending legislation for licensure of NDs: Colorado, Illinois, Iowa, Massachusetts, New York, North Carolina, Pennsylvania and Wisconsin.

To find names of qualified, credentialed NDs, check the Web site of the American Association of Naturopathic Physicians at *www.naturopathic.org.*

Lise Alschuler, ND, past president, AANP, vice president, quality and education, Emerson Ecologics, Bedford, New Hampshire. *www.emersonecologics.com.*

Mark A. Stengler, NMD, naturopathic medical doctor in private practice, Encinitas, California, and author of the *Bottom Line/Natural Healing* newsletter. *www.drstengler.com.*

How to Find a Good Holistic Doctor In Your Area

Finding a holistic doctor is easier than ever, but finding a good one is a different matter.

Alternative and complementary medicine have become big business, and many conventionally trained physicians have jumped on the bandwagon. While some of these doctors are quite good, many others have only the most basic knowledge of alternative and natural therapies—not nearly enough to treat people with chronic illnesses.

Example: A prominent hospital in the San Diego area has what they call an "integrative center," but several of its practitioners dispense little more than multivitamins and coenzyme Q10 supplements.

Getting Started

Searching professional associations can be a good place to start because they specify which treatment modalities a particular provider offers.

Example: If you want a doctor who does nutritional therapies, homeopathy, or oxygen therapies, these membership directories will often tell you…

●**American Association of Naturopathic Physicians,** 866-538-2267 or *www.naturo pathic.org.*

●**International College of Integrative Medicine,** 419-358-0273 or *www.icimed.com.*

●**American College for Advancement in Medicine,** 800-532-3688 or *www.acamnet.org.*

The downside is that directories don't necessarily tell you whether the doctor is any good. Membership in an association doesn't guarantee a great practitioner—only that he or she has met certain standards and pays annual dues.

What Helps

The best way to find a good holistic doctor is to talk to people who see one regularly. A great place to get recommendations is your local health-food store. Ask your fellow customers and store workers about their experiences. After you've spoken to five or ten people, you'll start hearing the same one or two doctor's names that are the ones you should call.

Once you're at the doctor's office, you can gauge how good he or she is by asking the following magic question, "What are the root causes of my condition, and how shall we address them?" Mediocre holistic doctors will look at your symptoms and prescribe their remedies (just like conventional physicians who prescribe drugs). Superior practitioners look for the root cause of your condition to achieve true healing.

How to Choose an Acupuncturist

Make sure the acupuncturist you choose has graduated from an accredited school and has at least two years' experience. You can find practitioners by contacting the American Association of Acupuncture and Oriental Medicine (866-455-7999, *www.aaaomonline.org*). Confirm a practitioner's certification through the National Certification Commission for Acupuncture and Oriental Medicine (904-598-1005, *www.nccaom.org*).

Be wary of conventional physicians who practice acupuncture. MDs are not required to complete the same three-or-four-year program as licensed acupuncturists. Many MDs by law have done nothing more than take a few weekend courses to learn 10 or 15 pressure points, instead of hundreds. The best way to find a good acupuncturist is through recommendation from another patient.

Mark A. Stengler, NMD, naturopathic medical doctor in private practice, Encinitas, California, and author of the *Bottom Line/Natural Healing* newsletter. *www.drstengler.com.*

INDEX

Index

ABOUT THE AUTHOR

Bill Gottlieb is a health educator and author of seven books, including *Alternative Cures* (Ballantine), *Speed Healing* (Bottom Line Books), *Breakthroughs in Drug-Free Healing* (Bottom Line Books) and *The Natural Fat-Loss Pharmacy* (Broadway). His articles on health and healing have appeared in *Bottom Line Personal, Bottom Line Health, Reader's Digest, Prevention, Men's Health, Self* and many other national publications. He is the former editor-in-chief of Rodale Books and Prevention Magazine Books. He lives in northern California.